Business Improvement Districts

Research, Theories, and Controversies

PUBLIC ADMINISTRATION AND PUBLIC POLICY

A Comprehensive Publication Program

EDITOR-IN-CHIEF

EVAN M. BERMAN

Huey McElveen Distinguished Professor
Louisiana State University
Public Administration Institute
Baton Rouge, Louisiana

Founding Editor

JACK RABIN

Professor of Public Administration and Public Policy
The Pennsylvania State University—Harrisburg
School of Public Affairs
Middletown, Pennsylvania

Available Electronically

Principles and Practices of Public Administration, edited by Jack Rabin, Robert F. Munzenrider, and Sherrie M. Bartell

PublicADMINISTRATION*netBASE*

Business Improvement Districts

Research, Theories, and Controversies

Edited by

Göktuğ Morçöl
The Pennsylvania State University–Harrisburg
Middletown, Pennsylvania, U.S.A.

Lorlene Hoyt
Massachusetts Institute of Technology
Cambridge, Massachusetts, U.S.A.

Jack W. Meek
University of La Verne
La Verne, California, U.S.A.

Ulf Zimmermann
Kennesaw State University
Kennesaw, Georgia, U.S.A.

CRC Press
Taylor & Francis Group
Boca Raton   London   New York

CRC Press is an imprint of the
Taylor & Francis Group, an **informa** business

Auerbach Publications
Taylor & Francis Group
6000 Broken Sound Parkway NW, Suite 300
Boca Raton, FL 33487-2742

Library of Congress Cataloging-in-Publication Data

Business improvement districts : research, theories, and controversies / [edited by] Göktug Morçöl ... [et al.].
    p. cm. -- (Public administration and public policy ; 145)
    Includes bibliographical references and index.
    ISBN 978-1-4200-4576-5 (alk. paper)
    1. Industrial districts. 2. Enterprise zones. I. Morçöl, Göktug.

HD1393.5.B864 2008
338.9--dc22   2008009062

Visit the Taylor & Francis Web site at
http://www.taylorandfrancis.com

and the Auerbach Web site at
http://www.auerbach-publications.com

Dedication

To the memory of Jack Rabin,

our colleague and the founding executive editor of the
book series in which this book is published

Contents

PART II: BIDS IN THE UNITED STATES

PART III: BIDS IN CANADA, BRITAIN, AND IRELAND

Preface

As the significance of business improvement districts (BIDs) has grown in recent years in the governance of urban and metropolitan areas, not only in North America but also in a variety of European, Asian, and African countries, academic interest in them followed. BIDs are self-assessment districts that are initiated and governed by property or business owners and authorized by state or local governments to operate in designated urban and suburban geographic areas. In the relatively short history of the academic literature on BIDs, they have been interpreted in a variety of ways and analyzed through different theoretical lenses. To some, they are yet another example of the privatization of the delivery of public services. To others, they are hopeful examples of self-governance by communities of business owners, promising examples of public–private partnerships, and/or local governments' tools to revitalize decaying urban cores.

The growth in the numbers and functions of BIDs has naturally increased the number of professionals (planners, analysts, managers) who specialize in BID operations and work for these entities. There is also a growing interest in BIDs in the academic community. In the United States and Canada, where BIDs are most active, the public is also becoming increasingly aware of the existence of BIDs and the controversies that surround them. This growing interest in BIDs among professionals and academics as well as the general public is the reason we have collected the papers that are included in this volume.

This book is the first collection of scholarly works on BIDs. The only two predecessors of this book—Lawrence Houstoun's *Business Improvement Districts* (2nd ed., Washington, D.C.: Urban Land Institute, 2003) and David Feehan's edited volume *Making Business Districts Work* (Binghamton, NY: Haworth Press, 2006)—laid the groundwork for this. They chronicled the histories of BIDs in North America and elsewhere, summarized the experiences of early BID professionals, and provided the growing number of professionals with guidance and practical advice in establishing and running BIDs. As the editors of this volume, our aim is to bring together the highest-quality theoretical, legal, and empirical studies on BIDs in a volume that would be useful not only for BID professionals, but also for academic researchers and university professors who conduct research or teach in urban planning, urban politics, local economic development, and local government law. The book will also benefit policymakers who function in state, regional, provincial, and local governments.

Academic research on BIDs has gained momentum since the early 1990s. We selected leading articles on the subject that had been published in scholarly journals and invited their authors to revise and submit these to be included in the book. The majority of these authors accepted our invitations; others opted to write original manuscripts for this volume.

Seven of the chapters in the book were originally published as peer-reviewed articles in a special issue of the *International Journal of Public Administration* (IJPA) (vol. 29, nos. 1–3, 2006). These are the chapters by Göktuğ Morçöl and Ulf Zimmermann (two chapters), Jonathan Justice and Robert Goldsmith, Göktuğ Morçöl and Patricia Patrick, Gina Caruso and Rachel Weber, Lorlene Hoyt, and Jack Meek and Paul Hubler. Seven other chapters in the book are revised versions of peer-reviewed articles that were published in journals other than IJPA. These are the chapters by Susan Baer (a synthesis of two earlier publications), Brian Hochleutner, Martin Blackwell, Jill Simone Gross, Susanna Schaller and Gabriella Modan, Tony Hernandez and Ken Jones, and Alan Reeve. Four chapters have been written originally for the book: those by James Wolf, Robert Stokes, Lorlene Hoyt and Devika Gopal-Agge, and John Ratcliffe and Brenda Ryan.

No book can come into existence without the coordinated hard work and dedication of multiple individuals. This is true particularly for edited volumes. This book could not have happened without the vision and insights of the former executive editor of the Public Administration and Public Policy book series of Taylor & Francis, the late Jack Rabin. We dedicate this book to his memory.

We also express our gratitude to the publishers of the journals in which a majority of the chapters of this volume first appeared, for permitting revised versions of the original papers to be published in this book. The names of these journals are cited in the chapters that were published originally in them. We also thank the authors of the chapters. Without their collaboration, dedication, and responsiveness, this book could not have come into being.

Last, but decidedly not least, we acknowledge the contributions of the professionals at Taylor & Francis. Their guidance from the beginning of this project, through the editorial process, and on to its production has substantially contributed to the quality of this book.

Göktuğ Morçöl
Lorlene Hoyt
Jack W. Meek
Ulf Zimmermann

The Editors

Göktuğ Morçöl is an associate professor of public policy and administration at the Pennsylvania State University at Harrisburg. His research interests are business improvement districts, complexity theory applications in public policy and governance, particularly metropolitan governance, and the methodology of public policy research. He is a coeditor of *New Sciences for Public Administration and Policy* (2000), the author of *A New Mind for Policy Analysis* (2002), and the editor of *Handbook of Decision Making* (2007). His works have appeared in *Administrative Theory & Praxis, International Journal of Public Administration, Politics and Policy, Policy Sciences, Emergence: Complexity and Organization*, and others.

Lorlene Hoyt, Ph.D., is an assistant professor in the Department of Urban Studies and Planning at the Massachusetts Institute of Technology. Her core interests include downtown revitalization, community economic development, and spatial information technologies. Dr. Hoyt's research in these areas has been published in academic journals such as *Environment and Planning B: Planning and Design, Journal of Planning Education and Research, Economic Affairs, International Journal of Public Administration, Geography Compass, Cityscape*, and *Journal of Urban Technology*. Since 1998, she has served as general partner of Urban Revitalizers, a women- and minority-owned real estate and urban planning consultancy with offices in Boston and Philadelphia.

Jack W. Meek, Ph.D., is professor of public administration at the College of Business and Public Management at the University of La Verne, La Verne, California. Professor Meek teaches courses in research methods, policy analysis, and collaborative public management. His research focuses on metropolitan governance, including the emergence of administrative connections and relationships in local government, regional collaboration and partnerships, policy networks, and citizen engagement. Professor Meek has published articles for various encyclopedias, chapters for several books, and articles in academic journals, including the *International Journal of Public Administration, Public Administration Quarterly, Journal of Public Administration Education, Administrative Theory and Practice,*

Public Productivity and Management Review, Public Administration Review, and *Emergence: Complexity and Organization*. He serves on the editorial board of the *International Journal of Organizational Theory and Behavior* and is an international advisor to *Social Agenda*.

Ulf Zimmermann, Ph.D., has taught at Carleton College, Northfield, MN, and the University of Houston and served as a research affiliate at the U.S. Department of Housing and Urban Development, where he coauthored a White House Briefing Report, *The Condition of Central Cities*, and coedited a special issue of the journal *The Urban Interest* on targeting to urban areas. He has also published articles and book chapters on sprawl in Atlanta, politics in Imperial Weimar, and pre- and post-Wall Berlin, as well as on bureaucracy and democracy in America and public administration education. He currently teaches in the Master of Public Administration (MPA) program at Kennesaw State University, Kennesaw, GA.

Contributors

Susan E. Baer is an associate professor of public administration in the School of Public Affairs at San Diego State University. Her recent work has explored community development, urban governance, and needle exchange program policy, among others.

Martin Blackwell is course leader for the masters in real estate development at the University of Westminster, London. He is property research coordinator for the School of Architecture and the Built Environment. Mr. Blackwell is CEO of a real estate and regeneration consultancy practice. He has both research and practical experience of a number of regeneration and redevelopment proposals in the UK. He holds a first class honours degree in Urban Estate Surveying from Nottingham Trent University and a Masters in advanced commercial property law from Northumbria University. Mr. Blackwell is the co-author of *The Businessman's Guide to Rating* (Jutland Press) and author of *Property and the PFI/PPP: A Practical Guide* (Estates Gazette). He is a Fellow of the Royal Institution of Chartered Surveyors; his research interests cover real estate development, redevelopment, regeneration, valuation and taxation.

Gina Caruso is an assistant commissioner with the Development Support Services Division in the City of Chicago Department of Planning and Development. She oversees special district and tax incentive programs as well as business retention and attraction initiatives. Her current policy emphasis has focused on maturing the Special Service Area program and serving as the Enterprise Zone Administrator. Prior to working with the City, Ms. Caruso consulted to economic development organizations on Special Service Areas and urban planning issues. She is a member of the American Institute of Certified Planners, received her undergraduate degree from Cornell College and her master's degree in Urban Planning and Policy from the University of Illinois at Chicago.

Robert S. Goldsmith is a partner in the law firm of Greenbaum, Rowe, Smith & Davis LLP in its Real Estate Department, where he chairs the Redevelopment

Practice Group. Mr. Goldsmith concentrates his practice in downtown redevelopment and revitalization. He has counseled and consulted with both developers and municipalities for numerous redevelopment projects throughout the state and over 30 special improvement districts. Mr. Goldsmith was special counsel to Morristown for the Headquarters Plaza Project from 1978 to 1990. He has served as counsel to the Morristown Parking Authority since 1983 and has been involved in numerous redevelopment projects in that capacity. He has served as special counsel to the City of Long Branch, Borough of Princeton, Town of Westfield, City of North Wildwood and City of Millville for redevelopment projects. Mr. Goldsmith has also been involved in redevelopment and revitalization projects in Woodbridge, Rahway, South Amboy, Jersey City, Morristown, South Bound Brook, Matawan, Wildwood, Stanhope, Netcong, Phillipsburg, Trenton, Aberdeen and East Brunswick. Mr. Goldsmith has developed and currently teaches a redevelopment law course at Rutgers Law School, Newark. He frequently lectures on downtown redevelopment and revitalization issues. He is past president of Downtown New Jersey, a board member of New Jersey Future and a member of the New Jersey Committee of the Regional Plan Association.

Devika Gopal-Agge is an associate with Partnership Solutions, a London-based consultancy specializing in the implementation and development of business improvement districts that led the first BID pilot program in London. With research interests in public-private partnerships and commercial revitalization, she recently co-authored a paper on the debates about the BID model in Geography Compass. She earned a Master of Economics degree from Bombay University and a Master in City Planning degree from the Massachusetts Institute of Technology, where her thesis explored the impact of BIDs on downtown retail.

Jill Simone Gross, Ph.D., is an associate professor of political science in the Department of Urban Affairs and Planning, Hunter College, City University of New York. Her recent research has explored urban governance, digital development, tourism, business improvement districts, and political participation in the inner cities of New York, London, Paris, Copenhagen, and Toronto. She teaches courses on applied urban research, comparative urban development, comparative urban politics, and popular participation in urban development. In addition to teaching at both the graduate and undergraduate levels at Hunter, she has also taught in the CUNY Honors College, and at Barnard College, Columbia University, New York University, Brooklyn College and Queens College. She is the co-editor of *Governing Cities in a Global Era: Urban Innovation, Competition, and Democratic Reform* (Palgrave MacMillan, 2007) and one of the North American editors for the Journal *Environment and Planning C: Government and Policy*. Her work has appeared in *Economic Development Quarterly* and *New Political Science*, among others places.

Tony Hernandez, Ph.D., is the Eaton Chair in Retailing and director of the Centre for the Study of Commercial Activity (CSCA). The CSCA is a non-profit research unit based at Ryerson University in Toronto that studies private-sector economic activities that deal directly with consumers. The centre is supported by over 60 public and private sector organizations. Dr. Hernandez is an active researcher in the area of business geomatics, with his research interests including retail location planning, urban change, segmentation, decision support, spatial analysis and data visualization. As an associate professor in the Department of Geography, he teaches undergraduate and graduate courses in retail location, geodemography, and market segmentation. In addition to his research and teaching commitments, he has provided consulting advice in the area of retail network planning for firms in Canada, the US, and Europe.

Brian R. Hochleutner is an attorney in the Los Angeles office of Munger, Tolles & Olson LLP. He joined the firm in January 2004, and his practice is focused on real estate and land use law. Mr. Hochleutner received his undergraduate degree from Yale University in 1995. Before pursuing a career in law, Mr. Hochleutner spent several years working in New York City government, where he was the Chief of Staff for Capital Projects and Senior Advisor to New York City Parks Commissioner Henry J. Stern. Mr. Hochleutner attended New York University School of Law, where he was a John Norton Pomeroy Scholar, a Florence Allen Scholar, winner of the Anne Petluck Poses Memorial Prize, and a Gold Fellow in Housing & Urban Renewal. During law school, Mr. Hochleutner was also elected to the Order of the Coif, served as a Special Assistant District Attorney in the Manhattan District Attorney's Office, and was an Articles Editor for the New *York University Law Review* and a Student Managing Editor for *The Authority*, a quarterly digest of public housing and development law. He graduated *magna cum laude* in 2002. After law school, Mr. Hochleutner served as a law clerk to the Honorable Dennis Jacobs of the United States Court of Appeals for the Second Circuit.

Paul Hubler is Community Relations Project Manager for the Alameda Corridor-East Construction Authority, a public authority charged with building transportation infrastructure improvements along rail corridors in the Los Angeles region. He formerly served as Deputy Chief of Staff to a Congressman representing a Los Angeles area district, working on transportation, environmental and campaign finance reform legislation on Capitol Hill. Before working in public affairs, he was the managing editor of a community newspaper in Burbank, California. Paul holds a Master's in Public Administration degree, which he earned in May 2004 from the University of La Verne in Southern California. His research interests include special districts, transportation and environmental issues.

Ken Jones, Ph.D., is the Dean of the Ted Rogers School of Management at Ryerson University—Canada's largest undergraduate business school. Dr. Jones has earned an international reputation for his expertise in retail research and business geomatics. He founded the Centre for the Study of Commercial Development, a world-renowned not-for-profit research centre at Ryerson University that provides information and analysis to Canada's commercial and retail industries. Dr. Jones holds an M.A. and Ph.D. from York University and has authored three books that have examined the contemporary retail environment in Canada: *Specialty Retailing in the Inner City*; *Location, Location, Location*; and *The Retail Environment*. His works have discussed issues associated with retail site selection methodologies, market area analyses, retail corporate concentration, e-commerce, and future trends associated with Canadian retailing. In addition to his activities as a researcher, Dr. Jones has been a consultant to numerous retail chains, financial institutions, and shopping centre developers on aspects of store network planning, sales forecasting, market area evaluation, and site evaluation.

Jonathan B. Justice is an assistant professor in the School of Urban Affairs & Public Policy at the University of Delaware. His public-sector professional experience has included work in local economic and community development, capital facilities planning, and budgeting and financial management. His current teaching, research, and service activities are focused on public budgeting and finance, local economic development, public-sector accountability and decision making, and the management capacity of local governments in Delaware. His work has appeared in *Administration & Society*, the *American Review of Public Administration*, the *International Journal of Public Administration*, *Public Budgeting & Finance*, *Public Performance & Management Review*, and other publications.

Greg Lloyd is Professor of Planning in the Department of Civic Design at the University of Liverpool. Prior to this he was based at the University of Dundee and University of Aberdeen. He is a land economist and a land use planner. He has served as an adviser to the Scottish Affairs Committee in Westminster and currently sits on the Scottish Executive's National Planning Framework Advisory Group. His research interests include the modernisation of land use planning practice, the effectiveness of strategic spatial planning, the new thinking around the relations between regulations, new contractualism and land and property development. He has published widely and is on the editorial boards of *Town Planning Review, Journal of Property Research*, and *International Planning Studies*. His interest in business improvement districts is drawn from an international study of alternative fiscal arrangements for regeneration and planning funded by the Economic and Social Research Council.

Gabriella Modan is an associate professor of sociolinguistics in the Department of English at the Ohio State University. Her research examines the role that language plays in constructions of place identity, with a particular focus on the politics of ethnicity and gentrification. She is the author of *Turf Wars: Discourse, Diversity, and the Politics of Place* (Blackwell, 2007).

Patricia A. Patrick is an associate professor of accounting at Shippensburg University, Pennsylvania. Patricia's research interests include government accounting, forensic accounting, and administrative ethics. A certified public accountant and certified fraud examiner, shes has published in the *International Journal of Public Administration,* the *Journal of Ethnicity in Criminal Justice,* the *Journal of Criminal Justice, Security Journal, Security Management,* and the *International Academy of Business Disciplines.*

Deborah Peel is a lecturer in the Department of Civic Design at the University of Liverpool. Her research interests span the modernisation of planning practices and the associated implications for skills, knowledge and learning. She has developed a particular research expertise around development management, the role of spatial planning in public policy, the implementation and management of change, and marine spatial planning. She has worked in local government, the private sector and in higher education in both Scotland and England. Her interest in Town Centre Management and business improvement districts stems from researching contemporary attempts to address new state-market dynamics in regeneration and the implications for legislation, governance, public diplomacy and community relations. She retains strong links with planning practitioners and serves on the Planning Summer School Council. She is a member of the Royal Town Planning Institute and Higher Education Academy. She is joint editor of *Transactions* and sits on the editorial board of the *Journal of Education and the Built Environment.*

John Ratcliffe, is a professor and director of the Faculty of the Built Environment at Dublin Institute of Technology. He is also the chairman of the Futures Academy at Dublin Institute of Technology and secretary-general of the World Futures Studies Federation.

Alan Reeve, Ph.D., is a reader at Oxford Brookes University, Oxford, England. He leads the Masters in Urban Design programme at Oxford Brookes; he is also director of the Townscape and Heritage Research Unit, which carries out research into issues of townscape quality in heritage settings. He led the Diploma in Town Centre Management course by Distance Learning, again at Brookes University, for several years. As well as teaching and research interests in Town Centre Management, he has also written on urban design theory, and is currently writing a book on the subject of "anxiety" and aesthetics in urban design culture. He has degrees in English, Architecture and Urban Design.

Brenda Ryan is a research officer in The Futures Academy at Dublin Institute of Technology. She is a past student of University College Cork, graduating with a degree in Earth Science. She continued her studies in Dublin Institute of Technology, graduating with a first class honours MSc in Sustainable Development. In her work as researcher with The Futures Academy, she has been involved in the pan-European LUDA network (Large Urban Distressed Areas) as part of the Key Action 4 "City of Tomorrow and Cultural Heritage" of the programme "Energy, Environment and Sustainable Development." Her other works include a study on the application of sustainability principles in public private partnerships, in conjunction with consultancy groups in the UK and Corenet, the global CSR forum. Most recently, she has been collaborating with Dublin business associations in assessing the progress towards the introduction and formation of business improvement districts in Ireland.

Susanna Schaller is the senior planner at the Municipal Art Society in New York City. She earned her Ph.D. from the Department of City and Regional Planning at Cornell University. Her research examines the implications of business improvement districts as strategies to revitalize ethnically and economically diverse urban neighborhoods. In her professional practice, she has focused on urban economic development, neighborhood revitalization and small business development as well as microfinance.

Robert J. Stokes, Ph.D., is an assistant professor at Drexel University in Philadelphia PA. His recent research includes a project to assess the impacts of business improvement districts on crime and community development outcomes in Los Angeles, CA. Another current research project involves measuring the health impacts of a land use and mass transit implementation in Charlotte, NC. He has been published in the *Journal of Crime and Delinquency, Urban Affairs Review, Urban Studies, Economic Development Quarterly,* the *Security Journal,* and *Health and Place.*

Rachel Weber is an associate professor in the Urban Planning and Policy Program at the University of Illinois at Chicago, where she teaches courses and conducts research in the fields of economic development and real estate finance. Much of her recent work has focused on the design and effectiveness of property-tax based incentives for urban development. Recent publications on this topic have appeared in *Urban Affairs Review, The Journal of the American Planning Association, Regional Science and Urban Economics, Housing Policy Debate,* and *Urban Studies.* Her book *Swords into Dow Shares: Governing the Decline of the Military Industrial Complex* (2000) examined the role of financial markets in the defense drawdown of the early 1990s. In addition to her academic research agenda, Dr. Weber has served as a consultant to local governments and community-based organizations on issues related to public financial incentives and neighborhood revitalization. She received her undergraduate degree from Brown University and her master's degree and doctorate in City and Regional Planning from Cornell University.

James F. Wolf is a member of the faculty of the School of Public and International Affairs' Center for Public Administration and Policy at Virginia Tech. His resent research has focused on regional governance at both the metropolitan and sub-municipal levels. This research has included an examination of the roles metropolitan planning organizations and voluntary regional councils play in regional governance. At the same time, he has examined the role of business improvement districts in local and regional governance.

Chapter 1

Business Improvement Districts: Research, Theories, and Controversies

Göktuğ Morçöl, Lorlene Hoyt, Jack W. Meek, and Ulf Zimmermann

Contents

The Role and Significance of BIDs

Business improvement districts (BIDs) are self-assessment districts that are initiated and governed by property or business owners and authorized by governments to operate in designated urban and suburban geographic areas. The term *BID* is used for both the designated area that receives special services and the organization that governs and provides services to the area.* It is estimated that there are somewhere between 800 and 1,200 BIDs in the United States and Canada as of the writing of this chapter; they are particularly popular in large metropolitan areas, such as Toronto, Los Angeles, New York City, and Philadelphia (Houstoun, 2003; Mitchell, 1999; Ross and Levine, 2001). Great Britain, Ireland, South Africa, New Zealand, Japan, Serbia, Albania, and Jamaica have adopted the principles and organizational forms of BIDs or BID-like entities since the early 1980s; in Germany, Austria, and Holland, BID-enabling legislation is being considered (Hoyt, 2003; see also the chapter by Hoyt in this volume).

The functions of BIDs have expanded over time as states in the United States have adopted new laws and BID managers have imported new strategies through global networks. They operate in a wide range of areas, from service provision to businesses in their respective areas (e.g., consumer marketing and economic development assistance) to policy advocacy, provision of traditional local government services (e.g., trash collection, tree trimming, managing and maintaining parking systems, providing safety and security, and capital improvements in downtowns and other areas), strategic land-use planning for neighborhoods, public space regulation, and even establishing and running community courts.†

There is a growing interest in BIDs in the general publics of the countries in which they exist and among the scholars of public administration and policy, urban/metropolitan economic development, urban planning, and geography. The growing interest in BIDs among the general publics is evidenced in the number of articles published in local and national magazines and newspapers. An electronic search conducted by one of the authors of this chapter on the newspaper articles published on the Center City District in Philadelphia between 1993 and 2005 generated 426 results, for example. The Center City District is one of the biggest and oldest BIDs in the United States, and therefore a high-level of interest in its workings is expected. Similarly, the big BIDs in New York City (e.g., Grand Central Station, Times Square) made the headlines of the *New York Times* and other papers for the controversies they created in local economic development and governance. Not all of the more than 1,000 BIDs in North America garner the same level of

---

* This dual usage of the term can be seen in the chapters of this book as well. Whether the authors refer to the area or the organization will be clear in the context of the discussion.
† See the chapters in this volume for listings of different services provided or functions fulfilled by BIDs and the different taxonomies used for them, particularly the chapters by Morçöl and Zimmermann ("Metropolitan Governance…"), Gopal-Agge and Hoyt, and Hernandez and Jones.

public interest, but the increased media coverage of BIDs in recent years indicates an increased level of public awareness.

The growth in the number and functions of BIDs naturally increased the number of professionals (planners, analysts, managers) who specialize in BID operations and work for these entities. BID professionals formed networks of communication and organized in regional, statewide, and national/international organizations. Besides the informal networks of the managers and board members of BIDs (for an example in Georgia, see Chapter 15 by Morçöl and Zimmermann in this volume), there are statewide organizations, e.g., the Pennsylvania Downtown Center, and an international organization, the International Downtown Association. These professionals have generated quite an extensive literature to share their experiences with BIDs (e.g., Ashworth, 2003; Colley and Bloetscher, 1999; Cybriwsky, 1999; Hogg et al., 2003; Houstoun, 1994, 1997, 1998, 2002, 2003; Jones et al., 2003; Lavery, 1995; Levy, 2001; Rogowsky and Gross, 1998; Segal, 1998a, 1998b).

In the literature, BIDs are praised for their innovativeness in problem solving and efficiency in service delivery and criticized for ignoring the needs and voices of residential property owners (Ross and Levine, 2001, p. 245), creating social segregation in cities (Lavery, 1995), creating problems for equal representation of citizens, and not being accountable to elected governments or people (Briffault, 1999). These and other concerns regarding BIDs have attracted the interests of academic researchers, particularly beginning in the early 1990s. An increasing number of scholars in urban affairs, public policy, public administration, and law have conducted research on BIDs and published their empirical findings and theoretical arguments (e.g., Baer and Feiock, 2005; Baer and Marando, 2001; Barr, 1997; Blackwell, 2005; Briffault, 1993, 1997, 1999; Davies, 1997; Foster, 1997; Gardonick, 2000; Gross, 2005; Hernandez and Jones, 2005; Hochleutner, 2003; Hoyt, 2001, 2005; Hudson, 1996; Kennedy, 1996; Lloyd et al., 2003; Mallett, 1993; Mitchell, 2001a, 2001b; Morçöl, 2006; Schaller and Modan, 2005; Symes and Steel, 2003).

This book includes, among many others, chapters written by some of the above-cited researchers and theorists. It includes chapters on the findings of empirical studies and theoretical and legal discussions on BIDs and BID-like entities in the United States, Canada, Great Britain, and Ireland. The authors address a wide variety of issues, such as the implications of BIDs for democracy (e.g., representation of the residents in the districts, weighted voting schemes they use, their impacts on different groups in metropolitan areas, accountability of BIDs to local governments and their publics), the effectiveness of BIDs in reaching their goals, and evaluating their performances.

A major challenge in studying BIDs academically is to conceptualize their nature and functions. A part of the problem is the names used for BIDs. BIDs are called by a variety of names in different countries and different states of the United States: "business improvement areas" in Canada, "city improvement districts" in South Africa; in the U.S., "community improvement districts" in Georgia, "community benefit districts" in Maryland, "special improvement districts" in New Jersey, and "special service areas" in Illinois (Hoyt, 2003; see also the chapters in this volume). There are also what we call "BID-like entities." The primary example of such entities is the "town center management associations" (TCMs) in Great Britain, where the central government recently decided to enable BIDs that are modeled after those in the United States (see the chapters by Blackwell, Reeve, and Lloyd and Peel in this volume). Whereas BIDs are generally defined as self-governed self-assessment organizations of local business (or property) owners, TCMs are typically voluntary collaborations between local governments and local businesses.

A more important conceptual issue in studying BIDs is the blurring of the theoretical line between the public and private realms, which has important theoretical and practical implications. As discussed in various chapters of this book, BIDs are conceptualized as private governments (Baer), public–private partnerships (Meek and Hubler), tools of public policy (Justice and Goldsmith), and actors in governance networks (Morçöl and Zimmermann, both chapters, and Morçöl and Patrick).

In short, the BID phenomenon is highly complex. As Reeve observes in his chapter in this volume, the study of such a complex phenomenon requires multidisciplinary perspectives and a wide range of research methods. The contributors to this book look at BIDs from the perspectives of public administration and policy, economic development, urban politics and policy, and policy transfer and diffusion. They also use different theoretical perspectives in their analyses and interpretations of BIDs, from rational (public) choice to social constructionism and structural/historical theories of power.

Theoretical Perspectives and Issues

The observers of BIDs are either enthusiastic or skeptical about them. The proponents of BIDs praise them as a nonbureaucratic and private-sector-driven (hence effective and efficient) methods of delivering services. The critics see them as undemocratic organizations that are unaccountable to the general public, particularly to those who are not business or property owners. The reader will see these arguments and variations on them in the chapters of this book. The differences in opinion on BIDs reflect, for the most part, different theoretical perspectives, primarily the dichotomous difference between rational choice theories and social constructionism/critical political economy.

Rational choice theories (public choice, institutional rational choice, polycentrism, and others) make the fundamental assumption that individuals are actors in economic and social life who make rational (utility maximizing) decisions, which in the end benefit all those who are involved. In the theoretical framework of rational choice, individual preferences are universal and predetermined. The general normative preference of rational choice theorists is for less external (governmental) intervention in the decisions of individuals, and therefore for smaller governmental units that are "closer" to decision makers. BIDs fit this definition of smaller and closer units. Social constructionists and critical theorists, although highly diverse in their interpretations, make the common assumption that the forms and patterns of individual preferences or behaviors are not universal, but are culturally and historically determined. Social constructionist researchers aim to understand those conditions, and many of them (particularly critical theorists) also critique such conditions with the aim of transforming them. They favor political acts and governmental interventions that would help transform social conditions, particularly the conditions of the disadvantaged groups in society (the poor, homeless, and others). That is why they are more likely to be critical of BIDs, which are created and governed by business and property owners and tend to take away some governmental powers from popularly elected and democratically accountable local governments. The reader will see these different perspectives and variations on them in the chapters of this book.

The polycentric perspective Baer advocates in her chapter favors private governments such as BIDs. Polycentrism contrasts the perspective of metropolitan reformers who favor monocentric metropolitan governments. Polycentrism argues that it is better, in general, to have many decision-making centers and fragmented authority in metropolitan areas, than only one big government (Gargantua, as the theorists of polycentrism call it). Baer stresses that private governments exist in a mixed system where they sometimes compete with traditional local governments and other times provide supplementary services. Although, she points out, no a priori judgment can be made that a polycentric system is better than a monocentric one, the former is in general more beneficial in meeting service preferences of more homogenous populations (e.g., business owners in a downtown area). In this perspective, BIDs and similar entities in particular can be beneficial because these self-governed and self-financing units can meet the needs of their smaller and more homogenous constituencies.

Gross's analyses of the BIDs in New York City point to the importance of the context (the kind of a community in which the BID is located) in understanding whether and to what extent this self-governing and self-financing is beneficial to constituencies. She accepts the notion that BIDs offer power to local communities, but, she argues, "they do not offer equal power to all interests." Gross compares the BIDs in the high-income and low-income neighborhoods in New York City and concludes that, whereas "BIDs in high-income neighborhoods face fewer socio-economic problems, have fewer stakeholders, and greater resources that enable increased investment in the physical infrastructure of the area," those in "low-income communities are faced with a wider range of needs, a wider range of stakeholders and limited resources (revenue and expertise) to respond." More specifically, she notes, low-income neighborhood BIDs face more difficulties in governance because they have more diverse constituencies (more ethnically diverse and larger numbers of small retail business and property owners) and less financial and human capital to apply to service provision.

Stokes reports in his chapter that the city of San Diego, California, has set up a mechanism to address the issues of lack of financial and human capital available for the smaller BIDs in poorer neighborhoods. San Diego's small BIDs are supported by a range of financial sources, including public funds, and an intermediary non-profit organization, called the BID Council, which assists them in the formation and administration of their program goals.

Schaller and Modan examine the problems of a neighborhood BID in Washington, D.C., not from a political economy perspective, but from a social constructionist one. They argue that the BID concept is rooted in public choice theory, which "reduces individuals to their functions as simple consumers of both privately and publicly provided goods and services." The primary concern of BID advocates is to reinvigorate the urban economy by marketing the strengths of the city (pedestrian-friendly sidewalks, heterogeneous architectural environments, and bustling streets). In doing so, they "reinvent the urban landscape as a sanitized economic space." This is problematic because, according to Schaller and Modan, it obscures the social processes in which public spaces are negotiated and built. People living in BIDs hold different views of what constitutes acceptable use of streets, parks, and building stoops; not all these views are shaped by economic interests. In the end, the authors argue, BIDs exacerbate tensions over the use of spaces and, in many cases, restrict freedom of expression and force some disadvantaged populations out by increasing property values and rents.

Lloyd and Peel also use a social constructionist perspective to examine the town center management practices in Britain and the transition to the BID system. In their view, both the TCM practices and BIDs should be interpreted in terms of the following: "the plurality of interrelations and interactions in the public domain are continuously negotiated and renegotiated, and are differentiated across time and locale." In their analysis of this context, Lloyd and Peel make the observation that TCM practices and BIDs are used "to address a complex of governance and resource issues associated with the broader objectives of attaining urban sustainability" and a "countervailing pressure to addressing the negative impacts of suburban sprawl and out-migration." The authors further argue that TCM practices and BIDs represent a broader social transformation that has been taking place in the recent decades: a deliberate rearticulation of state-market-civil relations and a "new contractualism" with respect to public service provision in defined jurisdictions.

No matter what theoretical perspective they come from, BID theorists and researchers agree that BIDs problematize the traditional notions of public and private and governmental and nongovernmental. BIDs are seen as occupying a space between the public and private realms. The terms *private governments*, *quasi-governmental entities*, and *public–private partnerships* are used to signify this in-between place. The reader will encounter these usages in the chapters of this book.

According to Meek and Hubler, the BIDs in California are public–private partnerships. As we mentioned before, Baer sees BIDs and similar entities as private governments. Stokes does not label them, but points to the special position of BIDs in public–private relations; they "afford the creation of public benefits through privately funded services and planning activities." Caruso and Weber observe that BIDs are a mechanism that occupies a middle ground between voluntary participation in membership organizations, such as chambers of commerce, and involuntary property taxes imposed on everybody.

In their chapter, Justice and Goldsmith recognize the in-between position of BIDs (they operate in a "twilight zone," according to the authors) and argue that BIDs, at least the ones in New Jersey, can best be understood as "genuine public-private partnerships." BIDs "serve simultaneously as *policy tools* through which state and local governments seek to advance general public interests and as self-help entities to further the more particular interests of local business communities" [emphasis added]. In Justice and Goldsmith's view,

> As business people became personally involved in local improvement planning and implementation, as active providers and producers, rather than merely consumers of place, they came increasingly to identify their private interests with the general public interest in public space and other local public goods. In this sense, BIDs can be understood as being not just private governments, but also instruments of public policy.

In Chapters 2 and 13, Morçöl and Zimmermann and Morçöl and Patrick observe that BIDs should be seen not as tools of service delivery (or policy tools), but as increasingly influential participants in public policymaking. With their explicit or implicit authorities to prepare and implement land-use plans and their participation in creating and operating community courts, BIDs have become like general-purpose governments. BIDs, they argue, challenge the sovereignty of governments in urban/metropolitan areas and force us to rethink the traditional distinctions between the public and private realms.

History of BIDs

One issue that looms large in the background of the discussions in the chapters of this book is, why BIDs? What were the (economic, political, and historical) conditions that created them, or enabled their creation? Did BIDs emerge in response to the economic hardships cities suffered as a result of the suburbanization process? Did the sharp declines in the aid from federal (central) governments to cities, particularly in the 1980s, force local business and government leaders to create BIDs as an alternative funding mechanism? Are BIDs products of a conservative worldview that favors less governmental role in service delivery? How much of a part did the traditions and cultures of societies (e.g., the self-help and privatist traditions of the United States)* play in their creations? A related question is, are BIDs a North American phenomenon? (They originated in Canada and the United States and are most pervasive in these two countries.) But then why and how have they spread to countries like Britain and Ireland? The authors of the chapters answer these and other related questions from their perspectives.

It is well known that the largest numbers of BIDs exist in the United States and Canada: at least 400 in the United States as of 1999 (Mitchell, 1999) and at least 300 in Canada as of 2007 (see Hernandez and Jones, in this volume). It is also known that the first BID was created in Canada.

In her chapter, Hoyt retells the story of the creation of the first BID in Toronto in 1969—the Bloor-Jane-Runnymede Improvement Area.† Hoyt also notes that the first BID in the United States was the New Orleans Downtown Development District, which was established in 1975. After these first BIDs, it took another decade before the creation of BIDs gained momentum; most of the U.S. BIDs that existed in 1999 had been created in the 1990s (Mitchell, 1999, p. 17).

Obvious questions are, why are BIDs most popular in the United States and Canada, and why were they created in this particular period? The authors contributing to this volume attempt to answer these questions. The most common explanation offered in this book and other sources (e.g., Houstoun, 2003) is that BIDs were a response to the combined effects of the economic decline in urban centers and the decreased funds from the federal government to the cities in the United States, particularly in the 1980s. Although this explanation doubtless has some validity, there may be more to the story.

In their chapter, Justice and Goldsmith point out that BIDs are extensions of the two concepts used in local government and service delivery in the United States: special assessments and special districts. These concepts, they argue, reflect a broader tradition in U.S. local government: "blending public and private interests in creating entities to further local collective action." Morçöl and Zimmermann's analysis in Chapter 2 agrees with Justice and Goldsmith's. They argue that BIDs are rooted in the long *privatist* tradition of urban governance and politics in the United States. Morçöl and Zimmermann cite the urban history literature that reminds us that "in the colonial period American cities were founded as commercial enterprises, and that business interests played large roles in their governance," and that "from early times on there has been an established tradition of private governance, often with public resources."

---

* See the Morçöl and Zimmermann chapter (Chapter 2) in this volume for a discussion of this.
† In Canada BIDs are officially known as "business improvement areas." It is also noteworthy that there were laws that enabled the creation of BIDs in the United States earlier than 1969, for example, Pennsylvania's Business Improvement Districts Law of 1967 (see the Morçöl and Patrick chapter in this volume), but the first BID that was actually created as a separate entity was the Bloor-Jane-Runnymede Improvement Area.

Morçöl and Zimmermann also trace the history of suburbanization, which began in the 19th century and accelerated particularly after World War II in the United States. This process drained urban cores of their populations, and thus their tax bases over time. In the 1970s, the problems of cities reached a crisis level; their need for the support of the federal government increased. The policies of the Reagan administration in the 1980s actually decreased federal financial support to cities. BIDs were a response to the need for financial support for declining urban cores, and the long-standing privatist tradition enabled the business leaders in American cities to create them.

This narrative of the process in the United States does not answer the question, were there a similar privatist tradition and a parallel process in Canada? Future studies may help answer this question. A related question is, why and how did the BID idea spread to Britain, Ireland, and other countries? One answer to this question can be found in Hoyt's policy transfer explanation (see her chapter in this volume). According to Hoyt, the BID is a relatively new urban revitalization model that policy entrepreneurs have deliberately transferred, both intra- and internationally.

One nagging problem in policy transfers (or policy learning) is the incompatibility of the social and historical contexts of the source and target jurisdictions. Because of the differences in the contexts, the policies that the target jurisdiction adopts may be quite different from the ones in the source. Also, for policy transfers to happen, there must be some compatibility between the contexts of the source and target jurisdictions. The town center management practices in Britain are a case in point.

In the 1980s, when the town center management movement developed, there were economic and political conditions in Britain that were somewhat similar to those in the United States. The policies of the Thatcher government were similar to those of the Reagan administration. Lloyd and Peel argue in their chapter that both TCM and BID models draw from neoliberal traditions of political economy thinking. And Reeve argues in his chapter, "the growth of TCMs must be understood in a context of the disempowering of local government, both administratively and fiscally, in the Thatcher years," which was quite similar to the process in the Reagan years in the United States. And yet, Reeve points out, the TCM practices were also different from BIDs, because of the greater separation of the two cultures of the private and public sectors in the United Kingdom compared with the United States.

The transition from the TCM model to the BID model in the United Kingdom also reflects the contextual differences between the United States and the United Kingdom. Blackwell points out that the framework of BIDs in the latter is notably different from the one in the former. In the United Kingdom, BIDs are financed by the supplementary taxation of the business owners, rather than property owners, for example. But the current BID model in the United Kingdom is, arguably, closer to the BID model in the United States than its predecessor, the TCM model. Lloyd and Peel see the shift from the relatively voluntary and differentiated arrangements in the TCM practices to the mandatory levies used in the BID model as a significant one. They observe that the BID model builds on the TCM model and addresses the "free-rider weaknesses" in the latter.

The recent history of the passing of the BID legislation in Ireland, which is recounted by Ratcliffe and Ryan in their chapter, shows that similar economic and political conditions instigated the process there. Ratcliffe and Ryan point out that the ever-greater demand on the services provided by the local authority and the dwindling national budgets created frustration in many Irish towns and cities. BIDs are expected to address the issue of financing local services and deliver a new era of urban revitalization. The Irish experience also confirms Hoyt's point that policy entrepreneurs deliberately transfer the BID model. Ratcliffe and Ryan report that the business leaders in Ireland studied the U.S. BIDs and pioneered the adoption of the BID model for their country, and the national government supported it.

Democracy and BIDs

The unusual position of BIDs between the private and public domains, together with their increasing numbers and powers, raised concerns among the general public and academics about their role in a democratic society. One of the most common criticisms of BIDs is the weighted voting schemes many use in the elections of their board members. In states such as New York and Georgia (see Chapter 10 by Gross and Chapter 15 by Morçöl and Zimmermann in this volume), owners of larger properties have more votes in the elections. Because BIDs are considered a form of "special-purpose governments" (Foster, 1997, pp. 7–22), the one person–one vote principle that is required for general-purpose governments can be waived, according to some legal scholars. In his extensive legal analysis of BIDs, Briffault (1999) criticizes the exceptions granted to BIDs: as they become more like general-purpose governments, with their expanded functions and authorities, they should be subjected to the same legal principles, he argues. But Briffault's suggestion may run counter to the inner logic of establishing BIDs. In Chapter 15 in this volume, Morçöl and Zimmermann point to the contradiction between the democratic principle of one person–one vote and the nature of BIDs: "Equal voting rights for all property owners would undermine the creation of BIDs. Without the incentive of having more say in their operations, owners of large properties would not be willing to join BIDs, much less to put in the great effort to establish them." This potential tension between the respective logics of democracy and BIDs needs to be investigated further in future studies.

Another controversial principle regarding the election and composition of BID boards is the exclusion of residents (Briffault, 1999; Ross and Levine, 2001, p. 281). Different states in the United States deal with the issue of resident representation on the boards in different ways. In New York, residents can be represented on the boards, but in Georgia they cannot (see Chapter 15). In Pennsylvania, the state laws do not address the issue of the representation of residents directly, and the practice is mixed: they are represented on the boards of some BIDs, but not on others (see Morçöl and Patrick in this volume). It seems that the resident representation issue will continue to be debated in the legal and political realms.

BIDs have also been criticized for their redistributional effects. Pack (1992) is concerned that BIDs may be pushing crime out of their areas and into other neighborhoods. She is also concerned that BIDs may deprive other neighborhoods of vigorous businesses by attracting such businesses into their areas. Morçöl and Patrick report in their chapter that the BID representatives they interviewed agreed with Pack's observations, but they did not see anything wrong with ridding their areas of criminals and thought that attracting vigorous businesses was a natural outcome of a competitive economy. A broader issue is whether BIDs have the power to redistribute power and wealth on a larger scale than merely redistributing crime or attracting businesses. Justice and Goldman argue in their chapter that BIDs do not have any "greater potential as instruments for redistributing power and wealth to business elites than do a variety of longer standing forms of redevelopment partnerships, routine 'privatism,' growth machines, and urban governing regimes." In fact, they argue, by "facilitating the enhancement of shared places, they can serve to further public purposes in the course of advancing private interests."

One of the biggest concerns about BIDs is whether they can be held accountable for their decisions and actions. As we mentioned earlier in this chapter, and the chapters in this volume highlight repeatedly, BIDs have played increasingly important roles in and made significant contributions (or done damage) to the lives of larger publics in metropolitan areas. So should they be held accountable? If yes, to whom and how? Several BID scholars—authors of some of the chapters in this volume and others—expressed their concerns about BID accountability, and some offered conceptual frameworks to assess BID accountability.

In his chapter, Reeve notes that there are concerns about TCMs in Britain, particularly because they are driven by commercial values and acquiring powers without being held accountable to democratically elected bodies. Caruso and Weber observe in their chapter that "taxpayers and local government often have little control over how BIDs spend mandated tax revenues," and note that the ability of BIDs to pursue a "private agenda" with "public funds" has raised suspicions about their lack of accountability. Morçöl and Zimmermann's findings in Georgia confirm Caruso and Weber's point that taxpayers or local governments may not have control over BIDs (see Chapter 15). They note that the BIDs in this state have no obligation to report their activities to local governments. Schaller and Modan point to the problem that, once established, "the BID board of directors becomes insulated from public accountability, for board members cannot be voted out of office." Therefore, they argue, "BIDs are deliberately removed from public democratic channels of accountability."

In the chapters by Justice and Goldman and by Hochleutner, the authors disagree with the critics and skeptics of BIDs; they argue that BIDs can be held sufficiently accountable by the laws that enabled their creations. Justice and Goldman argue that BIDs can in both theory and practice be held accountable by the local governments that created them in the first place. They point out that BIDs are "created under the authority of and subject to the laws of the sovereign states, generally cannot employ coercive authority, or even collect the revenues they need to operate, except on the sufferance of the general-purpose municipalities, which created and can dissolve them."

Hochleutner's chapter is exclusively on BID accountability. In his discussion, he makes the points that accountability is difficult to define precisely and that it is not an all-or-nothing concept. Given this ambiguity and relativity in the definition of accountability, he argues, "BID accountability concerns are diminished by both the relatively small size of BIDs, which limits the number of BID stakeholders, and the limited scope of BID power." He reasons:

> Because the discretion of BID officials is constrained ex ante by limitations on BID power, the need for ex post accountability is diminished.... BIDs are created to serve a public purpose—improving business and enhancing the condition of commercial areas—that is chosen by elected legislatures, not by BID officials or any particular group of BID stakeholders. BID officials are empowered ex ante by specific limited grants of authority found in state statutes and local ordinances that restrict BID power to improving the quantity and quality of commercial activity within the district. These powers are further curtailed by limitations imposed as part of management contracts between those who run the BID and local officials. The officials who grant BIDs their limited power to promote local business and economic development can also, as per Dillon's rule, take that power away. Even within the limited sphere of business improvement, BIDs are not sovereigns. In sum, less BID power means BID officials make fewer choices about fewer things; this means that BID officials need not be as accountable as more traditional public officials.

Morçöl and Zimmermann (Chapter 2) offer a different perspective. They point out that the legal powers of local governments over BID boards are limited, at least in some states like Pennsylvania and Georgia. For instance, as Morçöl and Patrick report in their chapter, in Pennsylvania at least some of the BIDs are created as municipal authorities, a status that curtails the power of local governments over them. An authority is not considered the creature or agent of the municipality; it is an independent agent of the state. Morçöl and Zimmermann (Chapter 15) make the point that the fact that BIDs are subject to Dillon's rule does not necessarily reflect the actual situation with their accountability, because "according to Dillon's rule, counties and cities are creatures of the state, and the state technically has the authority to create and dissolve all local governments." But that rarely happens. As Morçöl and Zimmermann argue, "the legal façade may disguise, to an extent, the real power relations in and around BIDs." For instance, the power of local governments to appoint board members in some states (e.g., Pennsylvania) may be considered a mechanism of accountability, but Morçöl and Patrick note that the BID leaders they interviewed reported that in Pennsylvania business leaders make the selections and the mayor and city council merely rubber-stamp the nominations. In Georgia, Morçöl and Zimmermann (Chapter 15) note that BIDs only voluntarily share their information with local governments (they are not legally required) and their reports are simply ignored by government officials.

The discussions in the chapters of this book present a complex picture of BID accountability. It is not merely a legal issue, nor is it only a bureaucratic and procedural issue. Morçöl and Patrick observe in their chapter that bureaucratic models of accountability are not easily applicable to BIDs. They offer Koppell's (2000) multidimensional model of accountability as a better way to conceptualize it. Koppel defines accountability on five dimensions: controllability, liability, responsibility, transparency, and responsiveness. Morçöl and Patrick argue that among these five dimensions, the most realistically applicable one is responsiveness, which can be assessed by measuring their performances in reaching their set goals and the satisfaction of their property owners. This approach, however, addresses only the accountability of BIDs to their property owners and excludes the two other groups that BIDs should be held accountable to, according to Briffault (1999): residents of the BID and residents of the municipality. Perhaps, because of the very nature of BIDs, it would be difficult to hold them accountable to all those groups whose lives they affect directly or indirectly.

Effectiveness of BIDs

Assessing the effectiveness of BIDs is important for holding them accountable to their constituents and general publics. Though the very nature of BIDs makes it difficult to hold them accountable to all groups whose lives they affect directly or indirectly, many scholars have argued the need to assess their effectiveness on a regular basis.

In their chapter, Meek and Hubler report their findings on how the five Los Angeles area BIDs they studied evaluate their effectiveness and share the information with their property owners and local governments. It is not easy to determine what and how to measure when evaluating the effectiveness of BIDs. Caruso and Weber offer a comprehensive model that can be used in evaluating BID effectiveness.

They identify the outputs, outcomes, and indicators that should be used to evaluate BIDs in reaching six principal objectives: real estate development, business development, convenience, distinctive identity, aesthetically pleasing environment, and safety. They also note that the performance measures they propose should be geared toward the interests and demands of different stakeholders.

Chapters of the Book

The chapters of the book are divided into three parts: chapters on theoretical and legal issues, chapters on BIDs in the United States, and chapters on BIDs outside the United States. The chapters in Part I assess BIDs in general terms and from different theoretical perspectives. This does not mean that these chapters do not have any empirical content or that the chapters in the other two parts of the book lack theory. The chapters in Part I are more general and more theoretical in their discussions, however. The other chapters in the book are divided into two parts on the basis of the national boundaries in which they exist. The chapters on the BIDs in the United States are separated from the others because there has been more research on the former, which is reflected in the larger number of chapters in Part II. The chapters in Part III are on the town center management applications and BIDs in the United Kingdom and the BIDs in Canada and Ireland.

Part I: Theoretical and Legal Issues

The chapters in this part of the book discuss BIDs from different theoretical perspectives: a political-economic and historical perspective, polycentrism (rational choice), a policy transfer perspective, an economic development perspective, and a legal perspective. At issue are some fundamental questions about BIDs: What were the conditions that helped create BIDs? Are they a North American phenomenon, or does the BID model have universal applicability? (How) Do they contribute to urban revitalization? Are they good for democracy?

In Chapter 2, Morçöl and Zimmermann argue that, because of their growing number and the increasingly significant roles they play in providing services in metropolitan areas and in influencing public policymaking in these areas, BIDs must be viewed as a significant element in the newly emerging network governance paradigm, which goes beyond the traditional public administration conception of the public sector populated and operated predominantly by public employees. BIDs harken back, beyond this Progressivist conception, to the United States' foundational privatism and the corporate origins of American governments. Until the Progressive movement turned urban services into what came to be known as public services, many urban services were provided privately. Following the privatization movement that began in the late 1970s and has been accelerating ever since, BIDs have arisen as a new form of private government. BIDs were initially single- or limited-purpose districts. As they expanded their menus of services, often including even land-use planning, and approached a general-purpose government status, BIDs have begun to raise issues of representation and accountability. This has become a challenge to the conventional view of politics and public administration in the urban/metropolitan arena and calls for a new view. The authors contend that the best way to capture the role of BIDs in the metropolitan governance process is network governance theory, which takes into account not only the many and varied local governments but also the numerous nonprofit as well as for-profit organizations that actually participate in this process.

Susan E. Baer points out that community benefit districts (CBDs), entities similar to BIDs, constitute a form of private governments and offers an assessment from a polycentric theoretical perspective. Instead of viewing CBDs as detracting from successful metropolitan governance—for which metropolitan reformers have long proposed single, centralized metropolitanwide governments—she portrays them as positive elements of the polycentric governance of metropolitan areas. These smaller autonomous units have the benefit of bringing decision making to the most local level possible, avoiding the Madisonian dilemma of minorities oppressed and rendered voiceless by large majorities. Moreover, these small governments do not, as is sometimes claimed, deprive the majority, the rest of the metropolitan area, of benefits, because the interests that the small district wishes to represent and promote must be negotiated with that majority in the form of local and state governments. She illustrates her points in an analysis of the Charles Village Community Benefit District in Baltimore, Maryland.

Greg Lloyd and Deborah Peel critically examine the ideological basis and context of the introduction of BIDs in Britain, but their assessment has implications beyond Britain. They argue that both TCMs and BIDs offer important insights into the evolving dynamics of state-market-civil relations. The authors differentiate TCM and BIDs in three ways. First, they contend that BIDs represent a step-change in urban economic policy and urban revitalization practice because they institutionalize the more informal and localized partnership arrangements put in place through TCM. Second, they point out that BIDs are presented as a mechanism to address a complex of environmental, economic, social, and resource issues associated with the broader objectives of attaining urban sustainability. Finally, they claim that BIDs represent a new contractualism of state-market-civil relations because they are subject to a formal ballot, legitimated through specific legislative and financial provisions.

Brian R. Hochleutner assesses BIDs from a legal perspective. He reminds us that because BIDs are often managed by private entities controlled principally by local property or business owners, critics from many fields have charged that BIDs are undemocratic and insufficiently accountable. He argues that BIDs are actually both democratic and accountable, at least to the BID's most likely stakeholders and to the extent that those stakeholders are likely to be affected by the BID's activities. The typically small size of a BID and its fairly limited purpose work to limit accountability concerns generally, and these also work with other aspects of the BID model (such as substantial oversight by local government officials and the BID's own corporate governance mechanisms) to ensure that BIDs are not only particularly responsive to the interests of local property and business owners, but also sufficiently accountable to the interests of local residents. Hochleutner contends that the BID model, in fact, provides a way of governing sublocal commercial districts and downtown areas that is fairer and more accountable to those actually governed than any obvious alternative.

In her chapter, Lorlene Hoyt examines BIDs from a policy transfer and learning perspective and argues that the BID is a model of urban revitalization that policy entrepreneurs—such as property owners, business owners, local governments, public agencies, elected officials, private consultancy firms, international organizations, and researchers—have deliberately transferred, both intra- and internationally. This chapter details how and why the BID model was first instigated, where it was subsequently transferred, and where it is currently emerging. It also identifies BID policy entrepreneurs, discusses their motivations, and explains the circumstances under which they occasionally experience failure. To illustrate how entrepreneurs apply new policies in contexts with divergent historical, political, and socioeconomic conditions, the author contrasts operational BIDs in the United States to those in the Republic of South Africa. In the end, Hoyt suggests, policy entrepreneurs devise reliable methods of prospective policy evaluation, especially with regard to acquiring accurate information, assessing differences in setting, and predicting policy application.

Devika Gopal-Agge and Lorlene Hoyt's chapter complements Hoyt's by providing a framework to analyze the roles of BIDs in urban revitalization. The authors argue that BIDs with a retail-focused strategy are capable of contributing to downtown revitalization. To assist in making their case, they develop a tier-structure diagram that they use to examine numerous BID organizations in the United States and Canada. They find that most BIDs undertake tier I and tier II activities for the purpose of creating and promoting clean, secure, and attractive downtown environments, and that such enhancements play a direct role in increasing footfall while indirectly promoting retail. In contrast, these BIDs vary with respect to proactive retail promotion (tier II) and monitoring and feedback activities (tier III), despite the belief that both functions are essential for ensuring long-term and holistic growth. The authors close the chapter by offering a set of recommendations for improving the relationship between BID and retail-related activities.

Part II: BIDs in the United States

The nine chapters of Part II cover what researchers have learned about BIDs in two states (New Jersey and Pennsylvania) and six cities (New York, San Diego, Atlanta,

Chicago, Washington, and Los Angeles) of the United States, and one chapter examines the BID–local government relations in cities located across the country. This part of the book is organized into two general areas: the first group of chapters explores the functions and nature of BIDs, and the second group highlights specific problem areas that arise with the implementation of BIDs. The chapters in Part II present empirical studies that cover a wide range of issues and uses of a broad array of research strategies and methodologies, including an ethnographic and discourse-based approach, statistical inference, case study analysis, secondary data analysis, case law, focus groups, surveys, and interviews.

The first six chapters of this section seek to assess the identity, functions, and nature of BIDs and how they work with local governments. Jonathan B. Justice and Robert S. Goldsmith argue that the multidimensional nature of BIDs constitutes a form of public–private partnership that can serve as an instrument of both public policy and self-help collectives simultaneously. Consequently, BIDs can advance general public interests and serve more particular interests. The authors substantiate this characterization by using data from case law, case studies of local practices, and a statewide survey of the special improvement districts (SIDs) in New Jersey. The authors conclude that, given the legal foundation and spread of SID practices, future research into a number of areas is warranted, including democratic performance, service performance, economic outcomes, and how current statutory design competes with other legal contexts.

The theme of public–private partnership is also taken up in the chapter by Jack W. Meek and Paul Hubler. This chapter presents an assessment of the nature and functioning of BIDs within the Los Angeles metropolitan area. The increasing numbers and influence of BIDs in metropolitan areas have governance implications, including accountability to local governments, the significance of BID budgetary capacity on service design, the demands for joint responsibility through partnership, the potential of expanding special district influence, and the contextual nature of BID design. The authors characterize BIDs as a form of complementary governance and substantiate this by describing the strong partnerships between BIDs and local governments and governmental oversight over BIDs.

Meek and Hubler emphasize budgetary capacity as a differentiating characteristic among BIDs. This is the main theme in Jill Simone Gross's chapter as well. She examines 41 New York City BIDs to address differences in form, function, and operating practices. Her findings suggest that the functions of the BIDs in New York City can be distinguished by size, particularly the size of their budgets: small BIDs attend to the physical maintenance needs of their jurisdictions, medium-sized BIDs concentrate on marketing and promotional activities, and large BIDs engage in capital improvement activities in addition to maintenance and promotion. Gross also addresses the factors that contribute to explaining BID behaviors, such as community resource capacity.

Resource capacity and the beneficial role BIDs can play in the extended metropolitan community is the focus of Robert J. Stokes's chapter. He points out that

BIDs offer an innovation to the problem of urban commercial decline and addresses a key policy question: How can cities use BIDs to assist their small business base? Stokes answers this question with the case of a citywide BID program in San Diego, California. Stokes outlines the use of 18 BIDs within the context of economic planning in San Diego that have been made more prominent due to California's limitations on local taxation as well as recent fiscal challenges. San Diego's unique approach is highlighted by the 1989 creation of an umbrella organization, the BID Council (BIDC), to provide various management support services that are not possible for the smaller decentralized special districts. The BIDC assists in coordinating internal as well as external (federal) funds for the strategic concerns of BIDs and extends funds and services to micro business districts in San Diego or districts that reside outside the existing BID jurisdictions. In this manner, Stokes notes, the BIDC represents an example of how special districts can be utilized to assist small businesses with funding and services.

The chapter by James F. Wolf reports the results of a survey of 12 BIDs across the country on the topic of the common strategies and approaches BIDs used to work with local governments. The survey results reveal that BIDs' relationships with local governments vary in the extent that they have adversarial or cooperative relationships. Longer-established BIDs and those with more expansive programs tend to opt for cooperative working relationships, and most BIDs in the survey do maintain cooperative arrangements with city governments. BIDs' working arrangements include "joined at the hip" approaches, contract-based strategies, and agreement on separate parallel responsibilities without contracts. BID representatives reported that staff-to-staff relationships between city and BID organizations are essential for goal achievement. The chapter reports on additional dimensions of this BID–city government relationship, including accountability, daily working relationships, as well as specific kinds of program areas that require interaction between BIDs and city governments.

In Pennsylvania, BIDs were legally enabled early, and this state's laws now support a wide variety of them. Göktuğ Morçöl and Patricia A. Patrick review the evolution of the BID laws in Pennsylvania and examine the processes of BID creation, continuation, and dissolution; the proliferation of their functions and powers; their revenue sources; and their accountability to local governments and general publics. Their findings suggest that multiple theoretical explanations are needed to understand BIDs, because they are simultaneously mechanisms of privatized public service delivery and policy implementation and active participants in metropolitan governance.

The next three chapters in this part of the book provide assessments of BIDs and identify a number of concerns and shortcomings, specifically in the areas of performance, accountability, and the encroachment on public space. Gina Caruso and Rachel Weber explore the central and critical question regarding Chicago's BIDs (known as special service areas [SSAs] in Illinois): Are they an effective means of providing additional services and amenities to relevant stakeholders? Through a survey analysis and case studies of 14 Chicago SSAs, the authors report that these entities do not systematically evaluate their performances. Yet, part of the promise of BIDs rests in understanding and measuring their performance. Having highlighted the complex nature of BID performance evaluation, the authors offer a typology of indicators that are most appropriate and discuss ways to institutionalize their use.

The accountability concern raised in the performance-based assessment is taken up by Göktuğ Morçöl and Ulf Zimmermann in Chapter 15. The authors observe that in metropolitan Atlanta, unlike most other metropolitan areas, BIDs (known as community improvement districts [CIDs] in Georgia) arose first in response to an excess of success in suburban commercial nodes that required large-scale capital investments and transportation improvements. This unusual foundation of CIDs in metro Atlanta and their constitutionally established status as autonomous local governments in Georgia make this state a particularly important case to study. In the business-friendly political environment of the state, the autonomous legal status of CIDs and their ability to leverage public money create accountability challenges for local governments and general publics, the authors argue.

The final chapter in this part of the book is by Susanna Schaller and Gabriella Modan. The authors offer an examination of the conflicting views about public space and citizenship that are heightened by the consideration of instituting a neighborhood business improvement district (NBID) in an economically and ethnically diverse neighborhood in Washington, D.C. Their analysis illuminates how local power relations and inequalities can become inscribed in urban planning projects like NBIDs. They found that NBIDs exacerbated tensions over public space, especially in economically and ethnically mixed neighborhoods, each with differing levels of public decision-making access and divergent views of public space. Based on a community mapping project and use of the community neighborhood's e-mail list, the authors illustrate that notions of "appropriate" uses of public space are conditioned by class and ethnic relations. The value of this kind of deliberation may lead to a rejection of the use of BIDs as a meaningful financial and public enhancement instrument. The authors conclude that city officials, planners, and community development practitioners considering NBIDs or similar special assessment districts need to integrate community members' views at every stage of the planning process and avoid the suppression of human experiences in public life, and to develop contextually rich and reflective innovative solutions to urban life, as opposed to simply joining the trend to apply the BID model to urban neighborhoods.

Part III: BIDs in Canada, Britain, and Ireland

In this part of the book the authors chronicle the emergence of BIDs and BID-like organizations in Canada, Britain, and Ireland and discuss legal, theoretical, and practical issues surrounding them. These chapters demonstrate that BIDs are spreading around the world, and that there are some commonalities in their applications in different national contexts. Canada has a long history of BIDs; in fact, the first BID in the world was created there. Britain has been experimenting with the town center management model since the 1980s, and recently the U.K. government adopted the BID model. Ireland is another recent adopter of the BID model.

Tony Hernandez and Ken Jones chronicle the structural changes experienced by Canada's downtowns over the past three decades. In particular, they document the rapid growth of large-format retailers in a variety of suburban shopping malls and retail parks, describing the challenges that result for retailers located in the downtown. The authors also examine the evolving role of BIDs (known as business improvement areas [BIAs] in the Canadian context) in promoting downtown vitality to cope with such changes. Through a careful case study analysis of Toronto's Downtown Younge BIA, the authors observe the manner in which BIDs evolve from basic operational and tactical tasks to more strategic tasks. They advocate the need for tracking and comparing BID performance to suburban retail activity using spatial data. These metrics, they argue, will assist BIDs in assessing their market potential and competitive environment and encourage the development of shared strategies between BIDs in similar circumstances.

In his chapter, Alan Reeve presents the reader with a history of town center management in the British context, explaining the values, transfer, and application of TCMs throughout Britain. The author also discusses the differences between the TCM model and the BID model, as well as the role of the Association of Town Center Management (ATCM) as the professional body that provides appropriate skills training for the job and officially represents TCM managers. He provides an overview of the literature and research in the area of TCMs. Reeve identifies a number of themes that deserve attention, but have been overlooked or somewhat underexplored. Having framed TCM as an important and promising profession, Reeve closes the chapter by proposing a framework for future research.

Martin Blackwell describes the BID model as it has been applied and adapted in England. One of the significant, and possibly problematic, differences is that in these English BIDs the additional taxation, which is typically levied to sustain BID authorities and support the services they provide, is levied not on the property owners, but on the current occupants of the property. This creates a tension between owners and occupants, between short- and long-term benefits, that will warrant further study. The taxation system is also complicated by the fact that there is a central, nationally determined list of taxable properties as well as, in each case, a local list of these, and it may occur that a property that is only on the central list nonetheless gets taxed if the property moves from the central list to the local list, though it has not been able to vote on the creation of the BID, and hence represents taxation without representation. Then, too, the number of categories, taxation levels, and exemptions for various types of properties render the successful defining and creating of BIDs complicated at best. Many of these practices could benefit from streamlining the policies and, perhaps most importantly, permitting those policies to be made much more at the actual level of the BID (rather than the state/national, which is the source of much of the distortion), the author suggests.

In their chapter, John Ratcliffe and Brenda Ryan examine the emergence of the BID model in Dublin, Ireland. The authors identify the Dublin City Business Association—a professional association representing the interests of property owners, retailers, and transport organizations—as the policy agency most responsible for importing the BID model. This chapter also provides an account of the national government's progress in drafting and implementing BID enabling legislation as well as the long-term plan for transferring the BID model to other parts of urban and rural Ireland. In describing the historical, political, and socioeconomic context in which Ireland's BID advocates operate, and reviewing the issues and controversies associated with importing the BID model to Ireland, this chapter demonstrates how prospective policy evaluation operates on the ground.

References

Ashworth, S. 2003. Business improvement districts: The impact of their introduction on retailers and leisure operators. *Journal of Retail and Leisure Property* 3:150–156.

Baer, S. E., and Feiock, R. C. 2005. Private governments in urban areas: Political contracting and collective action. *American Review of Public Administration* 35:42–56.

Baer, S. E., and Marando, V. L. 2001. The subdistricting of cities: Applying the polycentric model. *Urban Affairs Review* 36:721–733.

Barr, H. 1997. More like Disneyland: State action, 42 U.S.C. 1 1983, and business improvement districts. *Columbia Human Rights Law Review* 28:393–412.

Blackwell, M. 2005. A consideration of the UK government's proposals for business improvement districts in England: Issues and uncertainties. *Property Management* 23:194–203.

Briffault, R. 1993. Who rules at home? One person/one vote and local governments. *University of Chicago Law Review* 99:339–368.

Briffault, R. 1997. Symposium: The law of economics and federalism: The rise of sublocal structures in urban governance. *Minnesota Law Review* 82:503–550.

Briffault, R. 1999. A government for our time: Business improvement districts and urban governance. *Columbia Law Review* 99:365–402.

Colley, S., and Bloetscher, F. 1999. Betting on BIDs. *American City and County* 114:21–27.

Cybriwsky, R. 1999. Changing patterns of urban public space: Observations and assessments from the Tokyo and New York metropolitan areas. *Cities* 16:223–231.

Davies, M. S. 1997. Business improvement districts. *Journal of Urban and Contemporary Law* 52:187–223.

Foster, K. A. 1997. *The political economy of special-purpose government.* Washington, DC: Georgetown University Press.

Gardonick, D. R. 2000. What's the BID deal? Can the Grand Central Business Improvement District serve a special limited purpose? *University of Pennsylvania Law Review* 148:1733–1785.

Gross, J. S. 2005. Business improvement districts in New York City's low-income and high-income neighborhoods. *Economic Development Quarterly* 19:174–189.

Hernandez, T., and Jones, K. 2005. Downtowns in transition: Emerging business improvement area strategies. *International Journal of Retail and Distribution Management* 33:789–805.

Hochleutner, B. R. 2003. BIDs fare well: The democratic accountability of business improvement districts. *New York University Law Review* 78:374–395.

Hogg, S., Medway, D., and Warnaby, G. 2003. Business improvement districts: An opportunity for SME retailing. *International Journal of Retail and Distribution Management* 31:466–469.

Houstoun, L. O., Jr. 1994. Betting on BIDs. *Urban Land*, June, pp. 13–18.

Houstoun, L. O., Jr. 1997. Are BIDs working? *Urban Land*, January, pp. 32–36.

Houstoun, L. O., Jr. 1998. Smart money: New directions for business improvement districts. *Planning* 64:12–16.

Houstoun, L. O., Jr. 2002. BIDs at home and abroad. *Urban Land*, January, pp. 42–47.

Houstoun, L. O., Jr. 2003. *BIDs: Business improvement districts*. 2nd ed. Washington, DC: The Urban Land Institute in cooperation with the International Downtown Association.

Hoyt, L. 2001. Business improvement districts: Untold stories and substantiated impacts. Ph.D. dissertation, University of Pennsylvania. *Dissertation Abstracts International* 62:3961–4221.

Hoyt, L. 2003. *The business improvement district: An internationally diffused approach to revitalization*, 1–65. Washington, DC: International Downtown Association. http://www.cima.de/freedocs/projekte/BID%20Studie%20MIT%20Juni%202003.pdf (accessed July 25, 2007).

Hoyt, L. 2005. Do business improvement district organizations make a difference? Crime in and around commercial areas in Philadelphia. *Journal of Planning Education and Research* 25:185–203.

Hudson, K. 1996. Special district governments: Examining the questions of control. *American City and County*, September, pp. 54–71.

Jones, P., Hillier, D., and Comfort, D. 2003. Business improvement districts in town and city centers in the UK. *Management Research News* 26:50–59.

Kennedy, D. J. 1996. Restraining the power of business improvement districts: The case of the Grand Central Partnership. *Yale Law and Policy Review* 15:283–299.

Koppell, J. G. S. 2000. *The politics of quasi-government: Hybrid organizations and the dynamics of bureaucratic control*. Cambridge, UK: Cambridge University Press.

Lavery, K. 1995. Privatization by the back door: The rise of private government in the USA. *Public Money and Management* 15:49–54.

Levy, P. R. 2001. Paying for the public life. *Economic Development Quarterly* 15:124–128.

Lloyd, M. G., McCarthy, J., McGreal, S., and Berry, J. 2003. Business improvement districts, planning and urban regeneration. *International Planning Studies* 8:295–321.

Mallett, W. J. 1993. Private government formation in the DC metropolitan area. *Growth and Change* 24:385–416.

Mitchell, J. 1999. *Business improvement districts and innovative service delivery*. Grant report. Arlington, VA: PricewaterhouseCoopers Endowment for the Business of Government.

Mitchell, J. 2001a. Business improvement districts and the management of innovation. *American Review of Public Administration* 31:201–217.

Mitchell, J. 2001b. Business improvement districts and the new revitalization of downtown. *Economic Development Quarterly* 15:115–123.

Morçöl, G., ed. 2006. Special issue on business improvement districts. *International Journal of Public Administration* 29:1–243.

Pack, J. R. 1992. BIDs, DIDs, SIDs, SADs: Private governments in urban America. *Brookings Review* 10(4), 18–22.

Reeve, A. 2004. Town centre management: Developing a research agenda in an emerging field. *Urban Design International* 9:133–150.

Rogowsky, E. T., and Gross, J. S. 1998. To BID or not to BID? Economic development in New York City. *Metropolitan* 4:7–8.

Ross, B. H., and Levine, M. A. 2001. *Urban Politics; Power in metropolitan America.* 6th ed. Itasca, IL: F. E. Peacock Publishers.

Schaller, S., and Modan, G. 2005. Contesting public space and citizenship: Implications for neighborhood business improvement districts. *Journal of Planning Education and Research* 24:394–407.

Segal, M. B. 1998a. A new generation of downtown management organizations. *Urban Land*, April, pp. 86–89.

Segal, M. B. 1998b. BID districts revitalize New York neighborhoods. *American City and County*, May, pp. 46–47.

Symes, M., and Steel, M. 2003. Lessons form America: The role of business improvement districts as an agent of urban regeneration. *Town Planning Review* 74:301–313.

THEORETICAL AND LEGAL ISSUES AND PERSPECTIVES

I

Chapter 2

Metropolitan Governance and Business Improvement Districts*

Göktuğ Morçöl and Ulf Zimmermann

Contents

* This chapter is a revised version of Morçöl and Zimmermann (2006). We acknowledge the contributions and comments by Patricia Patrick, Paul Hubler, and Beverly Cigler on the original.

Business Improvement Districts as Part of the New Public Administration Problem

Although business improvement districts (BIDs), self-assessment districts formed by property or business owners, are a relatively recent phenomenon, their numbers have increased sharply in the past two decades, and they are playing increasingly important roles in the economic (re-)development of business districts in central cities and economic activity centers in suburbs (Houstoun, 2003). They deliver public services and influence the making and implementation of public policy in their areas. They receive and use public funds, or influence the use of such funds, in policy implementation.

With the broadening scope of their activities and their influences in public policy and administration, BIDs are becoming part of what Salamon (2002) terms the public administration problem. He sees a fundamental revolution taking place in the way government works and contends that this requires fundamental changes in our thinking about government. In the emerging third-party govern-ment system, public authority is shared with an array of nonprofit and private organizations. Public authority has been shared with private actors in U.S. history before, but the past few decades have witnessed an expansion of the scope of the public authority shared. Salamon proposes that we should expand the scope of the public administration problem from one that focuses mainly on public agencies to one that includes all the for-profit and nonprofit organizations that are involved in public policymaking and service delivery. He argues that this expansion of scope requires a new theoretical perspective, a new paradigm, what he calls the new governance paradigm.

In this chapter we argue that BIDs constitute a particularly apt exemplar of the expanding scope of the public administration problem, which forces us to rethink the distinctions drawn between the public and private realms and the traditional definitions of accountability. BIDs blur the line between the public and the private so much that they are termed "quasi-governmental entities" (Ross and Levine, 2001, p. 244), "private governments" (Lavery, 1995), and the "parallel state" (Mallett, 1993). We also argue that although the particular quasi-governmental configura-tions BIDs represent are unique and recent, they are rooted in the long *privatist* tradition of urban governance and politics in the United States (Warner, 1987). We will briefly highlight the history of privatism in American cities and discuss the specific challenges the BID phenomenon poses to public administration theory, particularly to the theory of metropolitan governance.

Definitions and Characteristics of BIDs

As the other chapters in this volume demonstrate, the BID phenomenon is quite complex and still evolving. In the literature the term *BID* is used sometimes in reference to specified districts where special funding mechanisms are used and special services are delivered, and sometimes to an organization that delivers such services in such districts.* Segal's and Hoyt's definitions are examples of these different usages of the term. Segal defines BIDs as "benefit districts" with geographic boundaries in which property owners use assessments to finance services that range from district maintenance to security, consumer marketing, business recruitment and retention, regulatory advocacy and enforcement, parking and transportation management, urban design, social services, visioning, and capital improvements (cited in Houstoun, 2003, pp. 3–8). Hoyt (2003) defines BIDs as "publicly sanctioned, yet privately directed organizations that supplement public services to improve shared, geographically defined, outdoor public spaces."

BIDs operate in different legal frameworks in the various states of the United States and in other countries (see the other chapters in this volume for descriptions of these frameworks). Different names are used across the United States (e.g., downtown improvement districts and neighborhood improvement districts in Pennsylvania, community improvement districts in Georgia, community benefit districts in Maryland, self-help business improvement districts in Alabama, and self-supported municipal improvement districts in Iowa) and other countries (e.g., business improvement areas in Canada and city improvement districts in South Africa) (Hoyt, 2003; also see the other chapters in this volume).

There have been some attempts to distinguish BIDs from similar entities. Hoyt (2003) makes a distinction between BIDs and BID-like organizations on the basis that the former uses self-assessment as its primary funding mechanism, whereas the latter relies on sources like voluntary donations and funding from governments. In her international survey of BIDs and BID-like entities, Hoyt found that there were BIDs in the United States, Canada, New Zealand, and South Africa. She also found that BID-like entities existed in Japan, Belgium, Germany, Holland, and the United Kingdom.† The distinction Hoyt makes has some validity, but it does not account for the variations within each category and possible overlaps

---

* Our usage of the term in this chapter follows this tradition of dual usages of the term. In the context we use the term, *BID* may refer to a district or an organization.

† For extensive discussions of the BID-like town center management schemes in the United Kingdom, see the chapters by Lloyd and Peel and by Reeve in this volume.

between them. The research reported in the Morçöl and Patrick chapter in this volume shows, for example, that there are BIDs in Pennsylvania that operate solely on voluntary contributions (i.e., they are BID-like) but act very much like the ones that use self-assessment as their primary source of funding (i.e., they are BIDs). Chapter 15 in this volume shows that some BIDs in Georgia use (or "leverage") government funds at rates that are much larger than their self-assessments (i.e., self-assessments are not their primary source of funding).

Although it is difficult to define BIDs in a common way with which everybody would agree and to distinguish them from similar entities, for our purposes in this chapter, we offer the following: BIDs are publicly sanctioned special districts and the organizations that provide a wide range of services to these districts and most commonly rely on self-assessments as a major revenue source.

The public sanctioning of BIDs and the self-assessment approach they adopted have their roots in the ideas that shaped special-purpose governments in the United States.* Foster (1997, pp. 7–22) defines two forms of special-purpose governments: taxing districts (special-benefit districts or special-assessment districts) and public authorities. Taxing districts are formed by groups of citizens who tax themselves and use the money for specific district projects. They are created by state and local governments, with enabling laws and ordinances. These districts are governed by elected boards, which enjoy substantial autonomy from their parent governments. Public authorities, on the other hand, are government corporations without taxing powers; they collect user fees, issue bonds, and raise money through grants. They are governed by boards appointed by officials of their parent government (city, county, or state). Though appointed, their boards also enjoy substantial autonomy from their parent governments (cf. the Port Authority of New York and New Jersey).

BIDs display the characteristics of both taxing districts and public authorities. Most BIDs are self-taxing districts that are enabled by state legislation and legally established by cities and counties. In most states, BIDs are governed by boards whose members are elected by district property owners, but there are also states (such as Pennsylvania) in which BIDs are created as municipal authorities with appointed boards. In this latter case, the enabling legislation ensures that large majorities of boards are composed of representatives of local property owners and allows a token representation by local governments. Legally, BID boards are under the oversight authority of state and local governments. The extent of the oversight authority and the mechanism of its implementation vary from one state to another, as the empirical studies presented in other chapters in this volume show, but governments rarely, if ever, use their oversight authorities (see particularly the chapters

---

* We acknowledge that the BID is not an exclusively American phenomenon and that the first BID was not even created in the United States (it was created in Canada, as the chapter by Gopal-Agge and Hoyt in this volume discusses). Our focus in this chapter is on the BIDs in the United States. Where the idea of public sanctioning of self-assessment originated and how it spread to other countries are beyond the scope of our discussions here.

by Morçöl and Patrick and by Morçöl and Zimmermann). Both types of BIDs (with boards elected and appointed) have multiple sources of revenue: they are authorized by law to assess property owners within their districts as well as to issue bonds and to receive grants from federal and state governments.

BIDs pose unique challenges to the theory and practice of metropolitan governance with their increasing numbers, the autonomy of their governing boards, their legal and political powers to generate revenues through a variety of sources, and the increasing numbers of services they deliver and public functions they fulfill. We will address these challenges in the following sections.

Explanations of BIDs

BIDs are an evolving phenomenon. The first BID was created in Toronto, Canada, in 1970 (Houstoun, 2003, p. 68). The first assessment-financed BID in the United States was the Downtown Development District in New Orleans, which was authorized by the Louisiana state legislature in 1974 (p. 19). Their numbers have increased and their geographic spread has expanded in North America and elsewhere since the 1970s; the increase in their numbers accelerated in the 1980s and 1990s (Hoyt, 2003; Lavery, 1995). As of the late 1990s, there were 800 to 1,200 BIDs in Canada and the United States, according to some estimates (Houstoun, 2003, p. 2; Ross and Levine, 2001, p. 244). They are most popular in large metropolitan areas, particularly in New York City, Los Angeles, Philadelphia, Boston, Baltimore, Milwaukee, San Diego, and San Francisco (Ross and Levine, p. 244). The first American BIDs were created with the aim of revitalizing depressed downtown areas. Downtown BIDs are still being created for this purpose, but BIDs are not a solely downtown phenomenon anymore. In states with high rates of population growth and suburbanization, such as Georgia, there are as many suburban BIDs as there are downtown, or urban, BIDs (see the other Morçöl and Zimmermann chapter in this volume).

Why did the BID creation accelerate in the 1980s? One possible answer is that BIDs were among the responses to the economic conditions and public policy changes in this decade. Briffault (1999) and others see BIDs as institutionalized forms of public–private partnerships that emerged in the economic environment of the 1980s, particularly in response to the Reagan administration's privatization policies and abandonment of urban areas. Backed by the public choice arguments that some public services could be delivered more efficiently by private organizations, and that public sector ownership was unnecessary in many areas of service delivery, policymakers in the United States and other countries (Britain, Brazil, Turkey, Argentina, and others) launched large-scale privatization policies in the 1980s. Following this logic, the U.S. federal government cut subsidies to city governments. The ensuing budget shortfalls in city governments forced them to abandon or cut some services and search for alternative methods of delivery. With their capacity to generate extra money for services, BIDs emerged as an alternative.

The explanations of BIDs in terms of the declines in city government revenues have some validity. But for a better understanding of the existence of BIDs, we need to look further back in history and deeper into the political economy of urban areas. As Mallett (1993) points out, the structural changes that took place in the metropolitan areas in the United States in the 20th century created the conditions for BIDs to emerge. He reminds us that the process of suburbanization, which began in the 19th century and accelerated particularly after World War II, drained urban cores of their populations and thus their tax bases. Warner (1987, pp. 178–190) illustrates this process in his case study of Philadelphia. He notes that downtown Philadelphia began losing its resident population in the late 19th and early 20th centuries. During this time period, residential neighborhoods were replaced by blocks of office buildings for large corporations and small businesses (lawyers, accountants, architects, etc.), department stores, theaters, and restaurants. The downtown became the functioning center and symbol of an industrial economy. After World War II, a second wave of transformation swept through the downtown: large corporations and other businesses began moving their offices to the periphery of urban areas. Mainly mass shopping and entertainment businesses (department stores, theaters, movie houses, and their complementary stores and restaurants) were left behind. The remaining businesses gradually lost their revenues, as the migration of residents and other businesses to the suburbs continued in the following decades.

The inability of the cities to stop the sharp declines in their revenues (most prominently illustrated by the 1975 New York City fiscal crisis), combined with the above-mentioned abandonment of cities by the Reagan administration in the 1980s, created the need for alternative sources of revenue. BIDs were an answer to this need.

The structural changes in metropolitan areas and the fiscal crises in cities in the 1980s created the conditions for BIDs, but they do not explain fully the complex phenomenon of BIDs. They do not explain, for example, the emergence of suburban BIDs (see the other Morçöl and Zimmermann chapter in this volume). We argue that what set BIDs into motion were the enlightened self-interest of business owners and their traditionally powerful roles in urban political economy (Lavery, 1995).

Economic Growth and Business Coalitions in Urban Areas

Monti's (1999, p. 245) observation that "American towns and cities were founded as commercial enterprises" is key to understanding the history of business influences on city government in the United States. It is commonly recognized that commercial interests have always influenced urban politics and governance, but researchers differ on the extent of this influence. Lynd and Lynd's (1929, 1937) and Hunter's (1953, 1980) empirical studies in the earlier decades of the 20th century showed that business elites dominated urban politics and even ran cities directly. Dahl (1961) and Polsby (1963) countered these "elitist" theories by highlighting the heterogeneities of the top decision makers in cities and the consequent diffusion of power in them.

But Molotch's (1976) *growth machine* theory and Stone's (1989) *urban regime* theory offer better explanations of the roles of business interests in urban politics and governance. These theories acknowledge both the economic factors and the intentional and organized involvement of business leaders in shaping the landscape and governance of urban/metropolitan areas. Molotch emphasizes that American localities have always desired economic growth and that this desire unified local economic and political elites, regardless of their differences on other issues. Particularly those who have the most to gain or lose from land-use decisions (local businessmen, locally oriented financial institutions, lawyers, syndicators, realtors) forge what he calls "growth machine coalitions." These coalitions, sometimes joined by others, directly or indirectly influence local governments' decisions to further their cause of economic growth. Stone (1989) also underscores the roles of political coalitions; he defines urban regimes as "the informal arrangements by which public bodies and private interests function together to be able to make and carry out governing decisions" (p. 6).*

Both Molotch and Stone acknowledge the role of macroeconomic factors, such as the increasingly global and mobile nature of capital, in shaping urban landscapes, but they also emphasize the proactive and organized role downtown business elites play in trying to attract global mobile capital to their cities. In their conceptualizations, business leaders act as agents and forge the institutions that maintain their leadership statuses. In some cases, organized business elites and their coalitions recognize the increased political powers of others and cede parts of their own power to them (e.g., the electoral majority African Americans gaining power in the city of Atlanta in the early 1970s). Such conscious political acts create a variety of growth machine coalitions, or urban regimes, but in all these variations what remains the same is the common desire to grow the economy of the city. This essential desire, we would add, is the engine that powers the political and economic system within which BIDs are created and sustained.

Monti (1999, p. 260) notes that pro-growth coalitions consist not only of downtown business interests and political constituencies in central cities, but also of business interests in suburban areas. He also notes that these growth coalitions have been supported and nurtured by the federal government through its subsidies and grant programs. Monti's insights help us understand two important aspects of the

---

* The differences between Molotch's and Stone's conceptualizations are important for a general theory of urban politics, but they are not significant for our purposes here.

BID phenomenon. First, the growth coalitions that extend to suburbia constitute the political and economic bases of BIDs in suburbia as well as those in downtowns. Suburban business leaders actively organize others to form BIDs to promote and sustain growth in their areas (see the other Morçöl and Zimmermann chapter in this volume). Second, the federal government's grants and subsidies play significant roles in the creation and maintenance of BIDs (again, see the other Morçöl and Zimmermann chapter).

Privatism and BIDs

The activism of business leaders in forging and leading growth machine coalitions, or urban regimes, has its roots in the long-standing tradition of *privatism* in urban America. In his case study of Philadelphia, Warner (1987) reminds us that the city was founded and run for a long time by private interests (businessmen and their associations); from the beginning, its citizens accepted the notion that the city was a place for private interests to compete and prosper. Privatism was a total worldview that subsumed the belief systems about all aspects of life, according to Warner. Privatism justified an individual's search for wealth and affirmed it as a search for happiness and personal independence. Privatism also meant that communities should be unions of wealth-seeking individuals. Political communities were meant to keep peace among their members so that they would have opportunities to prosper. In Warner's own words:

> The tradition of privatism has always meant that the cities of the United States depended for their wages, employment, and general prosperity upon the aggregate successes and failures of thousands of individual enterprises, not upon community action. It has also meant that the physical forms of American cities, their lots, houses, factories, and streets have been the outcome of a real estate market of profit seeking builders, land speculators, and large investors. Finally, the tradition of privatism has meant that the local politics of American cities have depended for their actors, and for a good deal of their subject matter, on the changing focus of men's private economic activities. (p. 4)

Privatism did not mean, however, that wealth-seeking individuals would be selfish or ignorant of others' needs. In fact, the dominant ideology of the colonial and revolutionary eras and the early American Republic fostered a public-regarding attitude. In Monti's (1999) words, "Fueled by the promise of prosperity and a belief in order, colonists built their new world around a kind of commercial communalism that wedded the principle of corporate responsibility to the practice of sharing risks with one's fellow townsfolk" (pp. 245–246). He also notes that the commercial leaders of these eras "embraced piety, believed in sharing, and demanded public accountability when assessing everyone's contribution to the community" (p. 248). According to Monti, "commercial communalism" was different from "government communalism," which emerged later, in the late 19th and early 20th centuries. Government communalism involves assisting larger numbers of citizens through official (governmental) activities.

Today's BIDs are surely the products of the economic and political conditions of our times, which are in turn the products of the structural changes that took place in urban areas during the 20th century. But they are also enabled by the underlying American privatist, or commercial communalist, beliefs: cities exist to create opportunities for individual wealth accumulation and business leaders are best qualified to devise (or advise) policies toward that end; as leaders, they should also be responsible for the well-being of their communities.

The privatist worldview has had its ups and downs in American history. Monti (1999) notes that for a long time during the 18th and 19th centuries "urban elites and business leaders could rightly claim to be stewards of the city in which they lived and worked" (p. 205). They withdrew from the public realm and urban politics during the late 19th and early 20th centuries. This was the period of Progressivism, an era in which public goods or public interests were defined separately from private goods and private (business) interests. The withdrawal of business interests from the direct governance of cities and the conceptual de-linking of public interests from private interests have complex histories and explanations, which are beyond the scope of this chapter. We should emphasize, however, that the withdrawal and de-linking did not end the influence of business interests in urban politics, but externalized it. As we mentioned earlier, urban theorists showed that the influence of business interests continued in forms that were external to governmental (public) institutions. Such influences needed justification in the public discourse; they were not accepted automatically. In that sense, the privatist worldview was in decline. It resurfaced in the 1980s, making it acceptable once again that business leaders would conduct the public's business. The privatization and public choice discourse of the Reagan era and later years made BIDs acceptable and fashionable.

Reinvestment in Urban Cores and BIDs

The emergence of BIDs did not sideline governments. Governments continued to make investments in building (or rebuilding) the infrastructure and making large-scale capital investments and improvements in urban areas. Judd (2003) notes that, parallel to the structural changes in urban areas, and in response to the abandonment of downtowns by corporations and retail businesses, the largest portion of capital investments has been in the tourism and entertainment sector. He observes: "In an attempt to rebuild the urban core, older U.S. cities have tended to construct a standardized set of facilities such as sports stadiums, convention centers, festival malls, performing arts centers, and other cultural facilities" (p. xii). To make all this construction possible, governments have solicited private sector financing and management. They also became more accepting of private business involvement in the delivery of public services. The confluence of these factors (investments in the entertainment and tourism sector, attempts to attract private money for capital investments, and acceptance of private businesses in public service delivery) created the conditions for public–private partnerships such as BIDs.

According to Judd (2003, p. 20), three new discourses justified the emergence and development of public–private partnerships. The first of these was built around the argument that the state cannot mobilize the resources necessary to meet the mounting infrastructure demands of urban society, which thus necessitates attracting domestic and international equity capital for private investment in public works. The second discourse was about the organization and constitution of government to accommodate new debt structures, create relationships with the capital markets, and regulate public–private infrastructure agreements. A third discourse justified the "privatization" of essential pubic infrastructure—a whole host of transfers of public works to the private sector through such arrangements as concessions, contracting out, and private management and control.

The capital investments in tourism and entertainment facilities did not solve all the problems; they were not sufficient to attract tourists or suburbanites to downtowns. These facilities had to be safe and aesthetically pleasing to attract them. Judd (2003) points out that cities attempted to create safe enclaves in downtowns and provided intensive policing and surveillance in and around them. But city budgets were often not sufficient for the upkeep and safety of downtowns (p. 7). Meeting these needs required BIDs. Local business owners agreed to tax themselves and use the extra money for safety and cleanliness, which they thought would bring in more customers. Consequently, as Monti (1999, p. 13) notes, the popularity of BIDs increased dramatically in the closing years of the 20th century.

Monti (1999) rightly observes that BIDs are a continuation of the commercial communalist (privatist) tradition in American cities:

> There is nothing new about businessmen dunning each other so that they can improve the areas where their shops are located. This has been going on for more than 200 years in the United States. Local store-owners initiated subscription campaigns to add sidewalks, put in sewer lines, or to pave the roads in front of their places of business long before local officials began taxing citizens for the privilege of extending these improvements to many other parts of the city. These additions were seen as benefiting the whole town or city, even if they only went to a small part of the municipality at first. (pp. 13–14)

BIDs are new, however, in the sense that the legal forms in which they are created are not like their predecessors. Although there is no common legal form for the BIDs in the United States, some commonalities can be observed (for the commonalities and differences among the states, see the chapters in this volume). BIDs display the characteristics of special-benefit districts, as well as those of public authorities, as we mentioned earlier. More important, they are becoming less like special-purpose entities and more like general-purpose governments, as they take on larger and more governmental powers and deliver a broader range of services. They are also gradually gaining more legal and de facto autonomy from the local governments that created them.

Legal and Theoretical Issues Concerning BIDs

The literature on BIDs is not extensive, but a few legally and theoretically important questions have been raised. In all these questions, the underlying issue is whether they are public or private organizations. The ambiguity in their status has led to designations such as quasi-governmental entities, private governments, and the parallel state, as noted. We will address the sources of this ambiguity in more depth in this section.

The ambiguity is partly caused by the variations in the legal statuses granted to BIDs in different states. In many states, the governing boards of BIDs are incorporated as nonprofit organizations, but in others they are incorporated as public authorities or constitutionally sanctioned governmental entities. In New York, the state with the largest number of BIDs, some of which are among the oldest and wealthiest in the nation, the governing boards of BIDs (district management authorities) are incorporated as nonprofits (The State of New York, 1989). In neighboring Pennsylvania, another state with some of the oldest and biggest BIDs, the early 1967 and 1980 acts required BIDs to incorporate as public authorities; the 1998 and 2000 acts granted them the option of incorporating as nonprofits (see the Morçöl and Patrick chapter in this volume). In the District of Columbia, the laws require that the governing body of a BID be a nonprofit corporation (Wolf, 2006). In California, BIDs are designated as public–private partnerships: either the local government that created a BID (county or city) or, more typically, a private nonprofit is designated as the service provider or agent responsible for implementing the improvements identified in the BID plan (see the Meek and Hubler chapter in this volume). The community improvement districts (CIDs) in Georgia are constitutionally sanctioned governments. The Georgia state constitution grants CIDs an array of governmental responsibilities and allows them to function as local governments (see the other Morçöl and Zimmermann chapter in this volume).

This variation in their legal statuses is not the only source of the ambiguity about their public or private nature. There are other and theoretically more important issues: their relations with the (other) organizations of private businesses and with (other) local governments and state governments, the gradual expansion of their functions and services, and the sources of their finances.

BIDs and (Other) Business Organizations

BIDs are first and foremost organizations of businesses. Many BIDs have close relations with local business associations and chambers of commerce. The BID creation process is initiated in many cases by the leaders of the local business association or chamber of commerce. These business organizations support BIDs financially, at least in their first years of existence, provide them with staff support, and house their offices. Many leaders of business associations also serve on the boards of BIDs.

There are many examples of the close relations between business associations, chambers of commerce, and private development corporations on the one hand and BIDs on the other. The Atlanta Downtown Improvement District was created in 1995 by the leaders of the Central Atlanta Progress, which has been the organization of the "downtown business elite" since its first incarnation as the Central Atlanta Improvement Association in 1941.* Other BIDs in Georgia have similar relations with business associations or chambers of commerce (see the other Morçöl and Zimmermann chapter in this volume). In Philadelphia, the website of the Center City District (CCD) notes that it was founded in 1990 by the leadership of the Central Philadelphia Development Corporation (CPDC), a membership organization of businesses (established in 1956); the two entities are so close to each other that in 1997 they entered an agreement to merge their managements (Center City District, n.d. a.). The Frankford Special Services District (FSSD) in Philadelphia was formed in 1996 by the Frankford Community Development Corporation (FCDC), which had been created in 1993 by the two local business associations and Frankford Group Ministry, with the support of a grant from the Pew Charitable Trust; FCDC and FSSD share their offices and their managements are indistinguishable (S. Folks, director of economic development of FCDC and de facto director of FSSD, personal interview, June 22, 2004).

These examples of close relations between voluntary business organizations and BIDs inevitably bring up the possibility that the latter are not much more than legal shells for already organized business interests. The BID phenomenon is more complex than this characterization, however. First, business (or property) owners in districts are not homogeneous, which complicates the BID-business owner relations. Second, legally, BIDs are created by local governments. In many cases local governments take active parts in, at least strongly support, the creation of BIDs.

Representation of and Accountability to Property Owners

BIDs are criticized for potential violations of the democratic rights of a variety of groups in metropolitan areas, including residents and their own members

---

* See Stone (1989) for a history of the Central Atlanta Progress and the Central Atlanta Improvement Association.

(Briffault, 1999; Ross and Levine, 2001, p. 245).* The problems of BID-resident relations stem from the fact that BIDs are typically created by and for commercial and industrial property and business owners. Commercial and industrial property and business owners are the ones who are taxed and served in districts. Typically, representatives of these owners constitute majorities on BID boards. The statuses of residents (homeowners and tenants) in BIDs differ from one state to another, but they are always problematic.

In Georgia, residents are not taxed, nor are they allowed to serve on boards. However, the community improvement district directors in Georgia report that they make efforts to informally include residents, particularly in strategic planning decisions (personal interviews, various dates). In the District of Columbia residents are not taxed, but they may be represented on boards (Wolf, 2006). The situation in Pennsylvania is more complicated. According to the 1996 amendments to the Business Improvement District Acts of 1967 (Business Improvement Districts Act of 1996), BIDs are supposed to be created only in commercial areas, but if they do include residences in their areas, they will tax homeowners (although they try to avoid including them in their district maps in the first place) and they may be represented on boards through appointments by local governments (see the Morçöl and Patrick chapter in this volume).

In Georgia, the board members of community improvement districts are elected by property owners. This may seem to be democratic, but in these elections voting is weighted in proportion to the amount of property owned (see the other Morçöl and Zimmermann chapter in this volume). The weighted voting schemes used in BID board elections have been criticized for violating the one person–one vote principle (Briffault, 1999).

The controversy over the weighted voting schemes highlights a contradiction inherent in the BID phenomenon. On the one hand, as Briffault points out, they are undemocratic. On the other hand, if weighted voting schemes are not used, that will diminish the incentive for large property owners to join, much less to initiate, BIDs. This lack of incentive may make it more difficult to form BIDs. The situation in Georgia illustrates the point. In Georgia the state constitution requires, for the formation of a BID, the approval of the owners of properties whose total market value constitutes at least 75 percent of the total value of all the properties in the proposed district. A logical consequence of this is that the initiators and founders of BIDs in Georgia aim to gain the support of large property owners first to make sure that they can meet the 75 percent requirement (see the other Morçöl and Zimmermann chapter in this volume). The weighted voting scheme used in this state gives an incentive to large property owners to join: they know that they will have more power in the running of its operations. The one property owner–one vote principle, though democratic, would diminish the chances of forming BIDs in this state.

---

* See the Hochleutner chapter in this volume for the view that because of the limited discretion they are given and the limited sizes of their areas, the accountability of BIDs is not much of a problem.

BID and (Other) Government Relations

The laws governing BID creation and termination give local governments some authority over BIDs, but the laws are only part of the story. First, there are legal limitations to local governments' power over BID boards. Second, the legal façade may disguise, to an extent, the real power relations in and around BIDs.

Legally, BIDs are enabled by state governments and created by local governments, and they can be terminated by local governments. The authority of local governments over the creation and termination of BIDs may seem absolute, but actually it is limited by state enabling laws. In no state, as far as we know, can local governments create BIDs against the will of a majority of property or business owners (majorities are defined differently by different states, but all of them establish threshold percentages). On the other hand, in some states (e.g., Georgia, Pennsylvania, and California) local governments have the authority to reject the creation of BIDs, even if majorities of property and business owners approve of their creation. The District of Columbia is unique in that once the legal threshold is met by local property owners, the local government cannot block the creation of a BID. Once a statement to create a BID is signed by owners of 51 percent of the property in the district (for some BIDs, also 51 percent of tenants), the mayor certifies that the process has been followed; if the mayor does not do it within a certain time, the BID application is automatically approved, according to the law (Wolf, 2006).

Typically, states set term limits for the existence of BIDs. Their continuation must be approved at the end of their terms by property owners and the local government that created them. There is a sunset provision for BIDs in Washington, D.C.: they have to be renewed after 25 years. In Pennsylvania, the BIDs that are created as public authorities must be renewed every 5 years, but the recent laws authorize them to renew for longer periods (up to 20 years). In Georgia, CIDs in some counties are terminated after their six-year initial term unless they are reapproved by property owners and the county; in others they continue to exist after the end of their six-year terms unless majorities of property owners file petitions for termination.

These examples of local government authority over the creation and termination of BIDs shed light only on a part of the story. The empirical studies we and our colleagues conducted in Georgia, Pennsylvania, and the District of Columbia show that local governments rarely, if ever, attempt to use their authority over BIDs (see the chapters by Morçöl and Zimmermann and by Morçöl and Patrick in this volume; also see Wolf, 2006). Legally, counties and cities can create and terminate BIDs under certain conditions. But we did not find any cases of local governments terminating a BID against the will of local businesses.*

---

* A major case of BID termination in Pennsylvania happened in 2002. The Allentown Downtown District Authority, the first operational BID of the state, was terminated with the approval of both the property owners and the newly elected mayor.

The legal authority of local governments over BIDs diminishes after their creation. State laws do have some provisions about the accountability of BID boards to local and state governments. These provisions vary across states. Whatever the powers granted to local governments by state laws, in practice, local governments do not have much say in the operations of BIDs. Briffault (1999) points out that though they have a legal obligation to do so, it is not clear that governments hold BID boards accountable. Our inquiries as well as those of our colleagues reveal that Briffault's concern is justified: BIDs are more autonomous in their operations than laws may indicate; local and state governments rarely exercise their legal authority over them.

The legal accountability of BIDs to state and local governments varies among states. In the District of Columbia, BIDs only have to submit a review every five years indicating how they have met their objectives and what they will be doing in the future. In Georgia, newly incorporated community improvement districts file with the secretary of state's office and the Department of Community Affairs. After these initial filings, they are not obligated to report to any state or county agency until they request renewal. Those community improvement districts that are renewed automatically unless there is a request from property owners not to do so are not obligated to report at all. However, the executive directors we interviewed reported that they do report to local and state governments to maintain good relations with them.

In Pennsylvania, under the 1980 act, BIDs are incorporated as municipal authorities. As such, the members of their boards are appointed by the legislative bodies of local governments, which, on paper, gives local governments significant power over BIDs. But once created, municipal authorities are not considered legally agents or representatives of local governments; they are independent entities (Governor's Center for Local Government Services, 2002). In other words, the state law allows BIDs and other authorities to operate independently. Furthermore, our interviewees reported that the "appointments" of board members are not much more than simple rubber stamping of the nominees of the local, and powerful, business leaders by city councils. The 1998 and 2000 acts went one step further. Under these acts, the boards of directors of the neighborhood improvement district management associations are to be elected by property owners, not appointed by local governments. Interestingly, however, some of the BID directors we interviewed expressed reluctance to switch to the more autonomous status that is allowed by the 1998 and 2000 acts, citing that under the old law they get their nominees approved by city councils without a problem anyway.

Expanding Functions of BIDs

The first BIDs were created to address the safety and cleanliness problems in their designated areas. The functions of today's BIDs are much more encompassing. They provide a larger number of services, and the kinds of services they provide have changed the nature of BIDs. Their original service functions (safety and cleanliness) qualified

BIDs as single-purpose governmental entities; with their multiple and still expanding functions today, BIDs have become more like general-purpose governments.

The literature cites the following as BID functions and services (Briffault, 1999; Mitchell, 2001a, 2001b):

1. Consumer marketing (festivals, events, self-promotion, maps, newsletters)
2. Economic development (tax abatements and loans to new businesses)
3. Policy advocacy (promoting public policies, lobbying)
4. Maintenance (trash collection, litter removal, washing sidewalks, tree trimming, snow shoveling)
5. Parking and transportation (public parking systems, maintaining transit shelters)
6. Security (security guards, electronic security systems, cooperating with police)
7. Social services (aiding homeless, providing job training, youth services)
8. Capital improvements (street lighting, street furniture, trees, shrubbery)
9. Strategic planning (the design of public spaces)
10. Public space regulation (managing vendors, panhandlers, and vehicle loading)
11. Establishing and operating community courts

Not all these groups of functions and services are equal in significance. We propose a framework to better understand the nature and implications of the expanding BID functions and services. BID functions and services can be grouped into four hierarchical levels; the degree of publicness increases from the first to the fourth levels:

1. Business services (1 and 2 on the above list)
2. Policy advocacy (3 on the list)
3. Traditional public services (4 through 8 on the list)
4. Comprehensive governmental authority (9 through 11 on the list)*

Business services are the kind of services traditionally provided by merchant associations, such as marketing of downtowns or other business areas with promotional events (festivals, etc.) and offering economic incentives to relocate businesses or start new ones. These self-interested activities are considered to belong to the private realm and have been accepted as legitimate activities of private organizations. Policy advocacy (lobbying, influencing policy) by private groups and organizations is an attempt to shape the public domain; as such, it is accepted as a legitimate function in interest group politics in a democracy.

The line between the private and the public is blurred at the traditional public services level (level 3).† In the traditional framework of public administration,

---

* See the Hochleutner chapter in this volume for a commonly used conceptualization of BID activities. Also see the Gopal-Agge and Hoyt chapter in this volume for an alternative model of BID activities.

† These services are not necessarily traditional if we go further back to the foundation of American cities, as we did in the introduction of this chapter. They can be defined as traditional in the framework of the Wilsonian/Weberian public administration, which emerged during the Progressive Era in the United States (Frederickson and Smith, 2003).

services such as capital improvements, maintenance, parking and transportation, security, and social services are supposed to be provided by governments. BIDs' "intrusion" into these service areas shows the changing nature of the public service delivery system in the United States.

In our categorization, the fourth level (comprehensive governmental authority) includes strategic planning, regulating public spaces, and operating community courts. Strategic planning is becoming an increasingly common function of BIDs, particularly larger ones with more economic power and political clout (e.g., the Center City District in Philadelphia and the Cumberland Community Improvement District in Cobb County, Georgia). What is significant in this development is that, under the guise of strategic planning, BIDs are actually performing land-use planning. As is well known, in the United States land-use planning is designated as a prerogative of local governments (Platt, 2004).* Some state governments provide more detailed planning guidelines to their local governments and oversee their implementation more closely than others. In recent years state laws equipped BIDs with the power to develop strategic plans in their areas (e.g., the state-enabling laws in Georgia and the 1998 and 2000 laws in Pennsylvania, which include provisions about strategic planning authorities of BIDs). These laws do not grant BIDs the authority for land-use planning explicitly, but what BIDs actually do with the authority granted to them is indistinguishable from land-use planning in their designated areas. What we found in our empirical studies in Georgia and Pennsylvania is that local and state governments are more than happy to carry out the plans developed by BIDs or help them carry out the plans themselves.

BIDs use the strategic (land-use) planning authority at three levels. The first level is their streetscaping authority (8 on the list above). Streetscaping is one of the most commonly accepted functions of BIDs across the nation. This authority involves modifying public spaces for the benefit of the property owners. Arguably, this authority should belong to the public, but its use by BIDs is one of the least controversial, as our research shows.

The second area is de facto infrastructure planning BIDs use in some states, such as Georgia. Laws do not grant explicit authority to BIDs to do so, but we learned in our interviews that, particularly, the more powerful suburban and urban community improvement districts in Georgia prepare plans for major infrastructure improvements (e.g., highway and main street interchanges and transportation planning) that either become parts of larger plans or are implemented directly by local and state governments.

---

* This is a product of the Progressive Era reforms. The first zoning ordinance was passed in New York City in 1916; before that time, land-use decisions were left to the private sector. In the 1920s, public-land-use laws swept the country, especially in the wake of the final Supreme Court decision in *Euclid v. Amber*, 1926. (For a full discussion of this landmark case, see Platt [2004].) So, one can argue that with the new strategic planning authority given to BIDs, the private sector has merely been given back what it used to have.

Another comprehensive governmental authority BID use is public space regulation. Again, this is a de facto authority; laws do not allow BIDs to use such authority. In our interviews we found that some BIDs act as though they had the authority to regulate the use of sidewalks (e.g., the use of sidewalks by restaurant owners) and other public spaces (e.g., enforcing rules on panhandling). Although this is not legal, some governments seem to be more than happy to let BIDs use such authority or collaborate with them in regulating public space.

A practice that is less common among BIDs, but noteworthy because of its implications for the blurring of the line between the public and private realms, is the establishment and operation of community courts. Mainly the larger and older BIDs are involved in the creation of and providing operational support for community courts. The nature of the relations of BIDs with community courts is varied and evolving. The extent of BIDs' influences over the community courts in their neighborhoods is worth studying comprehensively in a separate study. Our limited investigation has yielded the following information.

Community courts are local courts that are set up to deal with quality-of-life crimes, such as minor drug possession, prostitution, shoplifting, and disorderly conduct; the judges of the courts deliver justice for such crimes and collaborate with the members of their communities in community service projects (Cabrera, 2001). According to the Center for Court Innovation (n.d.), there are over 30 community courts in operation in the United States as of 2007.

These courts are all modeled after the Midtown Community Court, which was established in Times Square, New York City, in 1993. The Times Square BID was instrumental in establishing this court. The BID contributed to the initial funding of the court, through an umbrella organization of businesses called the Fund for the city of New York; the city and federal government provided the remaining funds (Hoffman, 1993). The Atlanta Community Court, which was modeled after Midtown Community Court, was established in 2000, with the support of the city of Atlanta and Central Atlanta Progress—the organization of the downtown business elite in Atlanta, as we mentioned earlier (Atlanta Downtown Improvement District, n.d.). Central Atlanta Progress (CAP), we must note here, is organizationally intertwined with the Atlanta Downtown Improvement District (ADID), to the extent that their website is one and the same and their initiatives are displayed at the website as "CAP/ADID initiatives." The Atlanta Community Court is listed as a CAP/ADID initiative at the website.

The roles of the BIDs in the operations of community courts are not clearly stated in published documents, but it can be inferred from Cabrera's (2001) report that they can be quite influential over the courts. Cabrera points out that in general, community residents and business representatives choose the community service projects that community court judges administer and that community advisory boards review the operations of the courts and their results. BIDs are probably quite active on advisory boards and in selecting service projects.

The website of the Center City District in Philadelphia gives some indications of the level of these activities. The website lists the Philadelphia Community Court as one of its "programs and services" and cites the nature of its relationship with the court as a "partnership" (Center City District, n.d. b.). Among the other partners of the network of organizations that support the operations of the court are another BID (University City District), the city of Philadelphia, first judicial district, district attorney, and police department. The Center City District website also reports that the court sentences emphasize "restitution to the community by requiring that offenders perform community service," which includes working with the crews of the BIDs (Center City District and the University City District) to clean sidewalks, maintain landscape, and remove graffiti. It seems that in the case of Philadelphia the partnership of the BIDs with the court is quite a close one.

Our limited observations on BID–community court relations do not allow us to make specific theoretical generalizations. However, it would not be wrong to make the observation that BIDs are beginning to take part in using this comprehensive governmental authority.

Financing of BIDs

The main source of revenue for most BIDs is assessments levied on property and business owners in their areas. Self-assessment among businesses is, in fact, the main reason for the existence of BIDs. The assessment models for BIDs vary from one state to another, but typically assessments are calculated on the basis of the appraised values of properties. In California, property-based assessments in BIDs are calculated according to the square footage of properties (see the Meek and Hubler chapter in this volume). In Pennsylvania, the older laws allowed the assessment of noncommercial properties, while the new ones are designed to exclude them, as discussed earlier (see the Morçöl and Patrick chapter in this volume). These and other details of the similarities and differences among states and the potential equity problems they generate (see Briffault, 1999) are beyond the scope of this chapter. However, the revenue sources other than assessments, particularly the public monies BIDs leverage for their purposes, are of interest to us because they have important implications.

The other sources of BID revenues include voluntary tax-exempt donations by businesses, proceeds of bonds, and federal and state grants. Neither tax-exempt donations nor bonds are a distinguishing factor for BIDs. The extent of the federal and state grants BIDs receive and the manner in which they are used are quite important, however. Overall, less than 10 percent of BID funds come from government resources, according to Briffault (1999). But this is a questionable estimate; in our studies we found that with their organizational capabilities and connections with governments, BIDs can be very effective in attracting federal, state, and local government dollars to their areas. The community improvement districts in Georgia leverage substantial amounts of money from governments (grants, redirected public investments, etc.). It is reported that they attract public dollars at the rates of 6 to 10 dollars per dollar they assess from their property owners (see the other Mörçöl and Zimmermann chapter in this volume).

Not all the dollars they attract from governments are counted in the financial statements of community improvement districts. Grants they receive directly from federal and state governments are counted, obviously, but they attract much larger portions of the public money in the form of government expenditures in their areas, which, just as obviously, are not listed in financial statements. We are not familiar with a nationwide study focusing on this issue, but suspect that such a study could yield some theoretically significant results.

Conclusions

BIDs pose both legal and theoretical challenges. Legally they are unique; they stand at the intersection of the traditionally defined realms of the public and the private. As such, the BID phenomenon is an exemplar of the expansion of the public administration problem. BIDs are often called quasi-governmental entities, private governments, and the parallel state for a good reason. The ambiguity about their public or private nature, which is reflected in these labels, has its sources in the variations in the legal statutes of their governing bodies across states, their close relations with (other) business organizations, their legal relations with (other) governments, the expansion of their functions and services, and the expansion of their financial sources.

The BID phenomenon forces us to rethink our dichotomous conceptual foundation of public versus private on which traditional public administration was built. In the traditional conceptualization, the sovereign power in a democratic society should rest in governments because they represent the will of the people. This sovereign will is associated with the public interest and contrasted with private or group interests. Private and group interest must not conflict with the public interest, and this is ensured through procedural accountability (i.e., that individuals and groups follow preset procedures and public authorities check whether they did so).

The problem with this dichotomous conceptualization is that the line between the public and private realms is inevitably blurred in BIDs. As Donahue (1989, p. 39) points out, "publicness" and "privateness" are contingent and even artificial categories. In his extensive review of the literature, Goodsell (1990) concedes that there is no clear definition of the public interest and concludes that public interest is a social construct, or a value, that emerges in public discourse. However, he argues, it is not an artificial construct; it is a construct that is constitutive of social institutions. Public administration is an institution that is constituted by this construct, and public administration reinforces the value of the public interest.

Arguably, the social construct of the public interest still has a significant norma-tive value, but the emerging phenomenon of BIDs and similar organizations forces us to rethink the value of directly associating the public interest with the institution of public administration. As the 20th-century notion of public administration—which is associated with bureaucracy, hierarchy, accountability, and the supply of public goods and services (Frederickson and Smith, 2003, p. 207)—becomes increasingly untenable, a new conceptualization is needed. We do not propose a comprehensive alternative conceptualization in this chapter. However, we propose that two theoretical frames can help us develop a conceptualization: a theory of privatism and a network governance perspective.

The privatist tradition (Warner, 1987), or the commercial communalist tradi-tion (Monti, 1999), which emerged in the colonial and revolutionary eras in U.S. history, merged the self-interested behaviors of business people with public-regarding behaviors. Unquestionably, BIDs are motivated by the self-interests of business owners. They are motivated by concerns about the declines in economic activities and property values in their areas, and they create BIDs to reverse or stem these trends. This is not a narrowly defined individualistic self-interest, however. They form BIDs to promote the interests of their local business communities, because it has to be done communitywide to be effective.

In our interviews we found that the leaders of BIDs are concerned about the well-being of their communities, even their larger metropolitan communities. Most BID leaders hold regionalist perspectives. By their very nature, BIDs are focused on small areas of cities or suburbs. They compete with each other to attract busi-nesses, customers, and public dollars. BID leaders acknowledge these competitive conditions, but they also recognize that they need to work with local and state governments and other BIDs to promote their cities and metropolitan regions. BID leaders establish informal networks of information exchange and solidarity. The community improvement districts in metropolitan Atlanta hold informal meetings to discuss their common problems, for example. They even conduct joint projects. It is also common that the leaders of older BIDs help establish BIDs in other cities or other parts of the same metropolitan area. The Center City District in Philadelphia functions as a school for future BID leaders and as a clearinghouse of information for smaller BIDs, for example.

BID leaders also recognize the roles of local and state governments in promoting and maintaining the well-being of their local and larger communities. They have the business people's mindset: that services should and can be delivered efficiently, without going through cumbersome bureaucratic and political procedures. But this business mentality seems to be tempered by their recognition that local and state governments are serving important functions. They do appreciate that these governments have to balance the interests of different geographic areas and different social interests in their communities, and they recognize that BIDs could not sub-stitute for what these governments do for their communities.

As Molotch (1976) and Stone (1989) insightfully observe, business interests drive politics in cities and metropolitan areas, and their concern for economic growth is the engine of business leaders' political activities. Their leadership in urban and metropolitan politics is not automatic, however. The interests of individual businesses are not necessarily the same. It takes leadership and organizational skills to bring together the divergent interests of business and property owners. In many cases, BIDs are initiated directly by preexisting business associations or local chambers of commerce. In some cases, mayors or other local political leaders lead the creation of BIDs. These are powerful actors in their local communities. But the creation and maintenance processes take time, effort, and skills. Local business and political leaders take their time (typically it takes about two years to create a BID), exercise leadership to convince other business and property owners that a BID would be beneficial to them, and play politics (for example, they occasionally gerrymander the districts to exclude uncooperative property owners and thus to gain the majorities required by law for the establishment of a BID).

We think that network governance perspectives offer a better alternative to the hierarchical bureaucratic models of traditional public administration; they help us better understand the networked nature of relations among BIDs and between BIDs and (other) governments, and the role of the agency in the formation and operations of BIDs. As recent scholarship (Agranoff and McGuire, 2003; Frederickson, 1999; Kickert et al., 1997; O'Toole, 1997) documents, in recent decades the role of "sovereign authorities" has diminished and governance is practiced in networks. Governments have become less sovereign and mere actors in network governance. As the participation of nonprofit and for-profit organizations in governance has increased, the meaning of public has broadened. Public policies are increasingly made and implemented in networks and network constellations. Frederickson observes that the governance of metropolitan areas best illustrates these emerging governance networks.

Our observations confirm the network governance theorists' insights. BIDs challenge the sovereignty of governments in urban/metropolitan areas; they have become makers and implementers of public policies in collaboration with governments. As such, they have become part of the new and broadened public administration problem. Researchers and theorists of metropolitan governance will have to take BIDs and BID-like entities into account. We agree with O'Toole (1997), who argues that practicing public administrators will have to learn the new network realities and develop skills to deal with them, and Frederickson (1999), who suggests that the primary skills they will need are negotiation and diplomacy.

References

Agranoff, R., and McGuire, M. 2003. *Collaborative public management: New strategies for local governments.* Washington, DC: Georgetown University Press.

Atlanta Downtown Improvement District. n.d. Current CAP/ADID initiatives. http://www.centralatlantaprogress.org/CapAdidInitiatives.asp (accessed July 17, 2007).

Briffault, R. 1999. A government for our time? Business improvement districts and urban governance. *Columbia Law Review* 99:365–477.

Business Improvement Districts Act. 53 Penn. Stat. Ann. §§ 54-5401–5406 (1996).

Cabrera, G. 2001. Legislative analyst report: Community courts model and feasibility of implementation in San Francisco. http://www.sfgov.org/site/bdsupvrs_page.asp?id=4801 (accessed July 17, 2007).

Center City District. n.d. a. About us. http://www.centercityphila.org/aboutus/default.aspx#cpdc (accessed July 17, 2007).

Center City District. n.d. b. Programs and services. http://www.centercityphila.org/programs/community_court.aspx (accessed July 17, 2007).

Center for Court Innovation. n.d. Community court. http://www.courtinnovation.org/index.cfm?fuseaction=page.viewPage&pageID=570&documentTopicID=17 (accessed July 17, 2007).

Dahl, R. A. 1961. *Who governs? Democracy and power in the American city.* New Haven, CT: Yale University Press.

Donahue, J. D. 1989. *The privatization decision: Public ends, private means.* New York: Basic Books.

Foster, K. A. 1997. *The political economy of special-purpose government.* Washington, DC: Georgetown University Press.

Frederickson, H. G. 1999. The repositioning of American public administration. *PS: Political Science and Politics* 32:701–711.

Frederickson, H. G., and Smith, K. B. 2003. *The public administration theory primer.* Cambridge, MA: Westview.

Goodsell, C. T. 1990. Public administration and the public interest. In *Refounding public administration*, ed. G. Wamsley, R. N. Bacher, C. T. Goodsell, P. S. Kronenberg, J. A. Rohr, C. M. Stivers, O. F. White, and J. F. Wolf, 96–113. Newbury Park, CA: Sage.

Governor's Center for Local Government Services. 2002. *Municipal authorities in Pennsylvania.* Harrisburg: Department of Community and Economic Development.

Hoffman, J. 1993. A user-friendly experiment in justice. *New York Times*, October 1, p. B1.

Houstoun, L. O., Jr. 2003. *Business improvement districts.* 2nd ed. Washington, DC: Urban Land Institute and International Downtown Association.

Hoyt, L. M. 2003. The business improvement district: An internationally diffused approach to revitalization. http://web.edu/course/11/11204/www/webportfolio/inquiry/IBP_WB_.pdf (accessed January 12, 2005).

Hunter, F. 1953. *Community power structure.* Garden City, NY: Anchor Books.

Hunter, F. 1980. *Community power succession: Atlanta's policymakers revisited.* Chapel Hill: University of North Carolina Press.

Judd, D. R., ed. 2003. *The infrastructure of play: Building the tourist city.* Armonk, NY: M. E. Sharpe.

Kickert, W. J. M., Klijn, E. H., and Koppenjan, J. F. 1997. *Managing complex networks: Strategies for the public sector.* Thousand Oaks, CA: Sage.

Lavery, K. 1995. Privatization by the back door: The rise of private government in the USA. *Public Money and Management* 15:49–53.

Lynd, R. S., and Lynd, H. M. 1929. *Middletown*. New York: Harcourt Brace.

Lynd, R. S., and Lynd, H. M. 1937. *Middletown in transition*. New York: Harcourt Brace.

Mallett, W. J. 1993. Private government formation in the D.C. metropolitan area. *Growth and Change* 24:385–416.

Mitchell, J. 2001a. Business improvement districts and the management of innovation. *American Review of Public Administration* 31:201–217.

Mitchell, J. 2001b. Business improvement districts and the "new" revitalization of downtown. *Economic Development Quarterly* 15:115–123.

Molotch, H. L. 1976. The city as a growth machine. *American Journal of Sociology* 82:309–31.

Monti, D. J., Jr. 1999. *The American city: A social and cultural history*. Malden, MA: Blackwell.

Morçöl, G., and Zimmermann, U. 2006. Metropolitan governance and business improvement districts. *International Journal of Public Administration* 29:5–29.

O'Toole, L. J. 1997. Treating networks seriously: Practical and research-based agendas in public administration. *Public Administration Review* 57:45–52.

Platt, R. H. 2004. *Land use and society: Geography, law, and public policy*. Revised ed. Washington, DC: Island Press.

Polsby, N. W. 1963. *Community power and political theory*. New Haven, CT: Yale University Press.

Ross, B. H., and Levine, M. A. 2001. *Urban politics: Power in metropolitan America*. 6th ed. Itasca, IL: F. E. Peacock Publishers.

Salamon, L. M. 2002. The new governance and the tools of public action: An introduction. In *The tools of government: A guide to the new governance*, ed. L. M. Salamon and O. V. Elliott, 1–47. New York: Oxford University Press.

The State of New York General Municipal Law. Article 19-A, Business Improvement Districts (1989).

Stone, C. N. 1989. *Regime politics: Governing Atlanta, 1946–1988*. Lawrence: University Press of Kansas.

Warner, S. B. 1987. *The private city: Philadelphia in three periods of its growth*. Revised ed. Philadelphia: University of Pennsylvania Press.

Wolf, J. F. 2006. Urban governance and business improvement districts: The Washington, DC BIDs. *International Journal of Public Administration* 29:53–75.

Chapter 3

Private Governments: A Polycentric Perspective[*]

Susan E. Baer

Contents

Private Governments and the Polycentric Model

The urban landscape is increasingly populated by new organizations created within the boundaries of existing cities or other local governments. Examples include familiar organizations such as homeowner associations and newer institutions such as community benefits districts (CBDs) and business improvement districts (BIDs).

---

[*] Parts of this chapter were originally published in Baer and Marando (2001) and Baer and Feiock (2005). The current version was adapted from the originals by permission from Sage Publications, Inc., and the authors.

These private or quasi-governmental organizations play an important, if little noticed, role in urban governance. The focus of this chapter is the CBD, a private governance organization whose property owners, both residential and commercial, pay property taxes in addition to what the city levies to receive supplemental services such as safety, sanitation, and economic development. Whereas BIDs traditionally have assessed or charged a fee only to commercial property owners, CBDs assess both residential and commercial property owners. As a result, I suggest that the CBD is a BID-like organization that might be considered a sister to the BID. Others, however, might suggest that the difference between the CBD and BID is so insignificant that the two concepts are equivalent. This essay examines the creation of the Charles Village Community Benefits District (CVCBD), a private governance organization in Baltimore, Maryland, from a polycentric perspective.

Although these various types of organizations such as CBDs and BIDs are not monolithic in institutional form, Helsley and Strange (1998) characterize them as private governments with a number of common features and view their formation as a kind of secession because members withdraw from the civic whole and limit their interactions to other group members. Private governments, also referred to as nested governments, share the following key features: First, they are formed by firms or households that are dissatisfied with the services provided by the public sector. In this sense, they are voluntary. Second, they provide additional services only to those who join the private government. In this sense, they are exclusive. Third, members continue to pay for and receive the services provided by the traditional public sector. In this sense, they are governments within governments, inherently supplementary in nature. Fourth, they pay for the services they provide with taxes and fees imposed on members, rather than with broad-based taxes imposed on firms and households that may not benefit from the services. In this sense they are self-financing. Fifth, private governments operate in a mixed system, where they must compete with the traditional public sector. In this sense, they are strategic (Helsley and Strange, 1998, p. 282).

This essay will examine polycentric issues affecting the creation of the CVCBD, including issues of boundary size, population size, income inequality, and population mobility. First, though, it will explore general issues involving polycentricity and private governments.

Private governments play a role in the central debate between metropolitan reformers and polycentrists. Traditionally, metropolitan reformers have considered the urban problem to be the large number of independent political jurisdictions located within a single metropolitan area. To reformers, this problem includes overlapping units of government, such as CBDs, that are said to confuse citizens. As a result, metropolitan reformers recommend that there should be only one local government. In effect, they advocate a monocentric or consolidated government (Ostrom, E., 1999, p. 146).

In fact, a truly monocentric metropolitan government does not exist. Opponents such as polycentrists call such a political system with a single dominant center for making decisions "Gargantua." Although a form of Gargantua might be appropriate for providing large-scale public services such as mass transit, it is not the most appropriate form of organization for the provision of all types of public services. For example, Gargantua might become insensitive to the daily demands that citizens make for public services in the area of policing or sanitation. Such bureaucratic unresponsiveness may produce cynicism and frustration on the part of citizens who are unable to find a point of access for solving public problems. Due to its failure in addressing local needs, blight in the community may result. The problem for Gargantua is to recognize the smaller political systems, such as CBDs, that may exist within its boundaries (Ostrom et al., 1961). CBDs as private governments serve as one component of a polycentric alternative to monocentric governments.

In contrast to Gargantua, the term *polycentric* connotes "many centers of decision-making which are formally independent of each other. In addition, whether these centers actually function independently, or instead constitute an interdependent system of relations, is an empirical question in particular cases" (Ostrom et al., 1961, p. 831). To the extent that the various political jurisdictions in a metropolitan area take each other into account in competitive relationships, enter into various contractual and cooperative undertakings, or have recourse to mediating mechanisms to resolve conflicts, they function in a coherent manner with consistent and predictable patterns of interacting behavior (Ostrom, 1994).

The concept of polycentrism suggests that a system of ordered relationships underlies the fragmentation of authority and overlapping jurisdictions that had frequently been labeled chaotic and the principal source of institutional failure in the government of metropolitan areas (Ostrom, V., 1999). Thus, for a polycentric system to exist and persist, a structure of ordered relationships would need to prevail, perhaps, under an illusion of chaos. No a priori judgment can be made that a polycentric system is better than a consolidated one. If a polycentric system can resolve conflict and maintain competition within certain boundaries, it can be a viable political arrangement.

Vincent Ostrom et al. (1961) argue that scholars should not label the complex patterns of organization in metropolitan areas as pathological. Parks and Oakerson (1999) contend that no single form of organization could be optimal for the provision and production of public goods and services in all metropolitan areas. A mix of different-sized governments is required, and polycentrism offers this mix.

Those in the reform movement argued on grounds of efficiency that many local jurisdictions be consolidated into a single unit of government for a particular metropolitan region. They contended that overlapping jurisdictions created a duplication of services, and they assumed that duplicating services was inefficient. Polycentrists challenged this presumption, arguing that such inferences need not hold if agencies are offering similar but differentiated services that affect diverse communities of interest. For example, private governments might offer safety services that are differentiated from what a city government offers as police services.

Michael Polanyi (1951) is thought to be the first person to use the term *polycentricity*. Polanyi distinguishes between two different kinds of social order: (1) deliberate or directed order and (2) spontaneous or polycentric order. In a deliberate or directed order, a superior directs subordinates. This type of order might be conceptualized as a unitary or monocentric order.

According to Polanyi, a polycentric order is "one where many elements are capable of making mutual adjustments for ordering their relationships with one another within a general system of rules where each element acts with independence of other elements" (Ostrom, V., 1999, p. 57). Individuals are the basic unit of analysis in a theory of polycentrism. Subject to the constraints inherent in the enforcement of decision rules, individual decision makers are free to pursue their own interests within this set of rules.

A key element in the design of a polycentric system is spontaneity. Spontaneity suggests self-generating or self-organizing patterns of organization within a polycentric system. To manifest spontaneity in the development of ordered relationships in a polycentric system, self-organizing patterns will need to occur at several different levels. First, one level applies to the conditions of entry and exit in a particular polycentric ordering. A second level applies to the enforcement of general rules of conduct. A third level concerns the formulation and revision of the basic rules of conduct. Rules can be changed to create appropriate responses.

Although polycentrists might be most associated with small units of government, the polycentric system involves many centers of decision making—small, large, and in between. Regardless, critics of polycentrism have attacked small units of government that they associate as being polycentric.

Critics of small local governments find these units to be undemocratic and discriminatory, and their critique may be extended to private governments. For example, McConnell (1966) takes Madison's argument favoring a large republic and utilizes it to show the downside of small governments. Namely, the smaller the society, the fewer diverse parties and interests likely composing it, and thus the greater probability that a majority will be found that can more easily be oppressive toward the minority. McConnell further asserts that the majority will be much more cohesive in a small community, and the chance of developing effective opposition to the dominant interest is much less in a small than in a large community.

The polycentric model of local governance, in contrast, helps to illustrate the advantages of small homogeneous units of government. Such units of government may, in fact, prove more beneficial in meeting service preferences than large diverse units. The creation of private governments formalizes service level differences among residents and businesses within cities (Briffault, 1997, 1999), and these differences may allow services to be tailored to best meet the needs of those within particular private governments.

In addition, the larger the government, the greater its mix of services, and the less voice an individual user will have in voicing demands for his preferred bundle of public goods and services. A government will be responsive to user preferences only as long as some governments are organized on a small scale capable of responding to neighborhood demands.

The CBD as a private government is also "nested." As the term implies, nested governance organizations are part of the intergovernmental system of sharing authority and delivering services (Hawkins et al., 1997). The extent to which higher-level governments regulate the creation and operation of such private governments varies by place and organizational form. Neighborhood residents typically cannot create a private government by themselves. A higher-level local or state government is necessary for creating the organization. In other words, neighborhood interests for creating private governments need to be negotiated with representatives of city or state interests (Thomas and Hawes, 1999). The creation of a nested governance organization is the result of a compact or officially sanctioned intergovernmental agreement involving not only the residents and businesses seeking to provide themselves a service, but also state and municipal governments as well (Briffault, 1997).

As previously stated, private governments provide supplemental public services. The definition of a public good is a good or service subject to joint use or consumption where exclusion is difficult or costly to attain. Governments may be viewed as collective consumption units. Governments might also be production units. A well-constituted collective consumption unit would include within its boundaries the beneficiaries who share a common interest in the joint good or service and would exclude those who do not benefit. The unit would be able to make operational decisions without requiring unanimity. It would also have authority to exercise sanctions. Because citizens are considered to be the best judges of their own interests, the preferred set of rules takes account of citizen–consumer interests. A collective consumption unit operates as the provider or arranger of a service, and a production unit operates as the producer or supplier of a service. Provision concerns arrangements for financing and using or consuming a public good, and production combines various factors or inputs to generate outputs. A production unit is able to aggregate technical factors of production to yield goods and services meeting the requirements of a particular government.

Six major options for obtaining public services exist. First, a collective consumption unit may supply a public good or service using its own production unit. Second, a collective consumption unit might contract with a private firm to supply a public good or service. Third, standards of service applicable to all residents of a community might be established and left to each household to decide what private firm should supply service to that household. Fourth, taxes may be collected, and then a voucher is made available to each household so that it can decide among different service producers. Fifth, a collective consumption unit might contract with a production unit that is organized by a different unit of government. Sixth, a collective consumption unit might produce some services within its own unit, and it might purchase other services from other jurisdictions and from private firms.

Applying Polycentrism to Inner City Communities

Two major components of the polycentric model are articulated in the classic articles by Tiebout (1956) and Ostrom et al. (1961). The two components are (1) that residents and businesses will locate to those local units that best meet their public goods preferences (Tiebout, 1956), and (2) that local government in metropolitan areas can be organized and reorganized to meet service preferences (Ostrom et al., 1961).

The first component of the polycentric model suggests that residents and businesses will maximize their public goods (tax and service) preferences by "voting with their feet." Thus, they locate or relocate to those local jurisdictions that best meet their public goods and services preferences (Stein, 1987). There is also evidence to support the contention that those who move do so in part because of services and taxes in the new jurisdiction (Teske et al., 1993). The model further posits that the greater the number of local governments in metropolitan areas, the more likely residents and businesses' public goods preferences will be realized.

A polycentric system is not a market, and a theory of polycentric organization is not a market model. However, polycentric systems might be organized to induce elements of market organization among public enterprises. These conditions can only exist if there is a rich structure of overlapping jurisdictions and fragmentation of authority (Ostrom, V., 1999). Ostrom et al. (1961) did not intend to offer a market model for the supply of public goods and services. However, variation in public service levels among different independent local government agencies within a larger metropolitan community may create a quasi-market choice for residents. In this sense, residents are able to pick the particular community within the metropolitan area that most closely approximates their public service needs. Public agencies might then be forced to compete over different levels of service in relation to taxes charged.

The second component of the model suggests that a decentralized governance system may provide services efficiently in response to a variety of demands. The explosion of suburban jurisdictions over the past four decades has been taken as evidence of the efficiency of these jurisdictions in meeting the public goods and services needs of many metropolitan residents and businesses (Stein, 1987; Dowling et al., 1994). This explosion also shows people's natural desire to have governing units tailored to their particular needs and preferences. However, rarely has the polycentric model been applied to explain intracity decentralization.

This chapter contends that the polycentric model has empirical application for explaining the creation and organization of private governments located within a city. The creation of private governments formalizes service level differences among residents and businesses within cities, because to receive supplemental services, property owners in private governments like CBDs and BIDs are taxed at higher rates than nondistrict property owners (Briffault, 1997, 1999). Also, while a large number of neighborhoods have lost population and businesses in part because they did not have adequate discretion or authority to meet property owner and renter service preferences, many city residents do not desire or cannot move to another neighborhood or jurisdiction. The polycentric model does not fully articulate this fact. Private government formation within cities is instead a response to residents and businesses staying in "place" for the purpose of obtaining particularized goods and services (Briffault, 1996). In other words, the creation of private governments within cities may be a feasible and effective option for obtaining public goods without these groups having to move to another jurisdiction. In effect, it is an exercise of "voice" rather than "exit" (Hirschman, 1970; Orbell and Uno, 1972; Parks and Oakerson, 1989; Williams, 1971).

Polycentrism in the Formation of the Charles Village Community Benefits District (CVCBD)

The Charles Village Community Benefits District (CVCBD), a private government, was initiated at the grassroots level by a neighborhood business in Baltimore. The district's genesis was triggered by a random and deadly act of violence in the city's South Charles Village community. Charles Village is located north of downtown and in the central part of Baltimore. According to a prominent member of the South Charles Village business community who made a strong contribution toward the formation of the CVCBD, the district's creation began on December 30, 1990, when two 15-year-old youths robbed and murdered an employee of the engineering and architectural firm Whitman, Requardt and Associates, LLP, in the firm's parking lot. The two teens then lingered in the neighborhood and attacked another person. After the murder, management at Whitman, Requardt and Associates questioned whether its 250-employee firm should exit, leaving South Charles Village and the city of Baltimore. It is natural for a company located in the inner city to consider whether to flee to a safer suburban location after one of its employees is murdered.

Rather than exit the community, the company instead decided to exercise voice to improve the safety of the area, and thus remain in Charles Village. In doing so, the firm's executives initiated the "political contracting process" required to create the CVCBD, and this process involved overcoming three problems of cooperation: coordination, division, and defection. The murder of the firm's employee was a random act of violence in that anyone who happened to encounter the two teens that day could have become their victim. The perception that everyone in the community was at risk of falling prey to violent offenders provided a common interest in collective action to increase safety and recognition of joint benefits from cooperation. Cooperative action by residents and businesses in the community also involved third parties, because support from both the city of Baltimore and the state of Maryland was necessary for the creation of the district.

Due to intense concern about crime in the area, supplemental safety services were emphasized at the time of the CVCBD's formation. However, from its inception, the CVCBD has always included all three supplemental services of safety, sanitation, and economic development. This is due to the fact that the district's founders believed that the perception of an orderly neighborhood enhances its safety, and they recognized that improvements in both sanitation and economic development contribute to a perception of order (personal communication, May 2004).* Thus, the founders felt that all three supplemental services would work together in a synergistic manner to increase the community's safety.

This study now examines a number of institutions (rules)† that were involved in the creation of the CVCBD. In fact, understanding these institutions proves key in analyzing private governments from a polycentric perspective. Polanyi (1951) emphasized the importance of rules in a polycentric system. He considers formulation, revision, and enforcement of general rules of conduct from a polycentric perspective. In contrast, Ostrom et al. (1961) neglected the issue of a general system of rules as providing a framework for ordering relationships in a polycentric system. In fact, they glossed over the essential relationship of rules to the structure of political systems. However, Ostrom later wrote, "Whether the governance of metropolitan areas can be organized as a polycentric system will depend upon whether various aspects of rule making and rule enforcing can be performed in polycentric structures" (Ostrom, V., 1999, p. 58).

Transaction resource theory blended with a study of institutions (rules) helps to explain how collective action problems including coordination, division, and defection were overcome to create the CVCBD as a private government in a polycentric system. Each of the three problems might be discussed as corresponding with a distinct phase in the contracting process in theory, although transaction resource theory recognizes that the problems may be intertwined (Heckathorn and Maser, 1987a). In practice, each type of problem may occur in any of the three contracting phases or in more than one phase.

In order for the CVCBD to form in a polycentric system, rules that overcome the coordination problem are required. The coordination problem may correspond to the *prephase* in the contracting process. To prevent a coordination problem, the expected outcome of the contract must satisfy *joint rationality*. In other words, no participant will initiate contracting with another unless he expects an opportunity for both to gain (Maser, 1998; Heckathorn and Maser, 1987b). If people do not know whether coordination will be feasible, they extend their endogenous resources on search costs. In addition, "the *risk of incoordination* creates a demand for rules to promote *stability and decisiveness* in governance" [italics in original]

---

* Because I want to keep all interviewee names confidential, I will not list any of them in the chapter.

† These two terms are used interchangeably in polycentricism and institutional rational choice in general.

(Maser, 1998, p. 541). Constitutional rules that generate stability and satisfy joint rationality guard against both rejecting outcomes that constituents jointly prefer and accepting outcomes constituents jointly dislike. A constitution can promote stability if its rules are clear and if the outcomes of political activity show predictability. Cooperation between parties occurs under contracts, because each party realizes that there is stability in the rules to solve controversies and enforce the contract. This stability decreases the ability for parties to change the rules, however.

In the case of CVCBD, a task force devised three institutional rules to help satisfy joint rationality and prevent coordination problems. These rules included the principle of fiscal equivalence—if everyone benefits, everyone pays for it; the rule that both residential and commercial property owners within the district would be required to pay an additional property tax in exchange for receiving supplemental services; and defining the scope of supplemental services—safety, sanitation, and economic development.

The task force agreed upon and crafted these institutional rules after careful deliberation and communication with residents and businesses. The task force included a 23-member steering committee whose representatives served as ambassadors to their area in disseminating positive information about the proposed benefits district. The group also sought the support of local churches, particularly the five main congregations in the area, because an estimated 3,000 families worshipped there (The 25th Street Task Force, 1993). The task force held open meetings for residents and businesses; it also held meetings with neighborhood groups to discuss and gain support for the proposed district.

Each of the three institutional rules responded to concerns about the allocation of costs and benefits, referred to by Maser (1998) as compensability. The fiscal equivalence rule ensured that all property owners in the district would have to pay a cost, a supplemental tax, to receive a benefit, supplemental services. Requiring that both residential and commercial property owners pay a supplemental tax was an obvious cost to these individuals, but it also enabled them to receive the benefits of supplemental services. As noted earlier, neighborhood residents and businesses were largely willing to cooperate jointly to receive these benefits, such as enhanced safety, due to their perception that the neighborhood was unsafe. In other words, crafting an institutional rule requiring fiscal equivalence helped to create the political buy-in needed to successfully form the district.

Institutional arrangements created to overcome potential coordination problems in the formation of the nested CVCBD included state enabling legislation as a requirement to form CBDs, a first Baltimore city ordinance required to form CBDs in Baltimore and this ordinance's rules, and a second Baltimore city ordinance required to enlarge the boundaries of the CVCBD. These higher-level rules defined the powers of the private government and the constraints on its exercise of power. Maryland statutes required that a community benefits district first receive state enabling legislation to tax property owners. Legally, the state's role was to pass legislation to enable community benefits districts to be established in communities in which the city gave its authorization. Moreover, with state enabling legislation, the Baltimore City Council needed to enact the necessary local ordinances for allowing a community to establish a district.

The first local ordinance creating the CVCBD also required a referendum in the proposed area as a prerequisite for benefits district adoption. Specifically, it required a super majority of 58 percent of property owners and renters in the district to support adoption of the private government and its additional taxes. The additional tax rate levied on both residential and commercial property owners to pay for CVCBD supplemental services is equivalent and is currently 12 cents per $100 of assessed valuation (personal communication, May 2004). The city ordinance authorizing the CVCBD also required a sunset clause that mandated that the private government would have to be reauthorized every four years. This sunset provision gave city officials an opportunity to abolish the private government if political conflict arose or if residential or commercial support diminished. In essence, the provision served as a city administration "escape hatch" and not a precedent for a permanent city commitment to benefits districts. The task force lobbied for the enactment of both state enabling legislation and this first city ordinance.

Considering equity, one finds that the CVCBD utilized the principle of fiscal equivalence—those that receive the benefit of a service pay the costs for that service. This principle allows for the development of an appropriate collective consumption unit. The beneficiaries exercise the dominant voice in determining the quantity and quality of the service. In addition, these beneficiaries can also be assigned substantial constitutional authority to establish and change the terms and conditions that apply to the future governance of the provision unit (Ostrom and Ostrom, 1994).

In addition, the initiation of the Baltimore CBD involved a struggle between two approaches to distributional equity in drawing the CBD's boundaries. The first approach, one advocated by traditional reformers, calls for private government consolidation followed by redistribution, while the second polycentric approach relies on larger overlapping provision units to provide intergovernmental aid and equalizing services to the smaller private government (Oakerson, 1999).

Under polycentrism, provision-side efficiency calls for CBD or BID boundaries to be large enough to include the affected group of people and, at the same time, to not be so large as to include groups of individuals with very heterogeneous preferences (Oakerson, 1999). In terms of production-side efficiency, one finds that private government residents desire and receive those labor-intensive public services exhibiting diseconomies of scale, such as safety, garbage collection, and neighborhood revitalization. And small production units supply these services most efficiently. In contrast, larger production units with economies of scale supply capital-intensive public goods most efficiently. This concept of production-side efficiency informs the discussion of private governments and helps to explore how efficiency is related to the size of local organization (Tullock, 1994). As a result, a mixed system that includes both smaller units like private governments and larger overlapping units may possibly increase service delivery efficiency. In other words, polycentrism recognizes that the diversity of life requires complex organizational arrangements that are neither exclusively Gargantua nor the land of Lilliputs (Ostrom and Parks, 1999).

It is important to note that polycentrism does not offer clear guidelines concerning the appropriate size of private governments other than general ones relating to provision- and production-side efficiency and equity. A second city ordinance required that the CVCBD's boundaries be enlarged from 30 to 100 blocks and its population size be increased from 3,000 to 14,000 residents. Although the originally proposed 30-block CBD was located in a lower-income area, the mayor, the city delegation to the general assembly, and several Baltimore City Council persons rather paradoxically expressed concern that by creating private governments the city would become balkanized with white middle-income neighborhoods becoming engaged in an elitist movement to obtain services that exclude lower-income neighborhoods. Several legislators were further concerned that such balkanized units aimed to promote lifestyle homogeneity through subtle forms of "gating." Perhaps they were concerned that future private governments might be located in white, affluent areas, thus creating balkanization by race and class. To safeguard against this, the city ordinance mandated that all private governments, including the originally proposed 30-block lower-income district, be relatively large in geographic scope and population and diverse economically and racially. Thus, the required, enlarged 100-block CVCBD was mixed-income rather than low-income in nature. State enabling legislation and both city ordinances were enacted.

This mandate, it should be noted, embodies and represents adoption of one of the two well-known strategies for promoting intercommunity distributional equity—that of traditional metropolitan reformers. In classic reformist style, it required enlarging the boundaries of the private government from 30 to 100 blocks to include a more heterogeneous community with respect to income and race. However, this mandate also meant that the provision unit would be less tailored or specialized, and thus less able to satisfy particularized constituent needs. It might also prove more conflictual due to including more heterogeneous populations. The proponents of this approach did not support the other strategy for achieving intercommunity equity, that embraced by polycentrist theory.

Expanding the private government from 30 to 100 blocks added to its political base and potential influence with city and state officials. But private government expansion also implies that city residents and businesses may not be allowed to do what suburbanites have long done and continue to do—create their own homogeneous governance formations—because of a city government's ideology. Allowing the private government to remain its original 30-block size is a polycentric alternative to expanding the area that the city council and administration did not permit.

Under this alternative, other smaller private governments, including low-income ones, may also be able to form and achieve equity with the help of intergovernmental equalizing aid or services from higher-level overlapping governments. City officials were aware of this alternative but instead selected the reformist option of consolidation followed by redistribution. The original smaller private government that includes 3,000 residents may also have been more efficient than the larger, more heterogeneous 14,000-resident private government. The smaller private government may have been better able to meet more homogeneous citizen preferences in its provision of labor-intensive public services, and it is less costly to meet homogeneous needs than heterogeneous ones, other things being equal. However, although the originally proposed smaller CVCBD might have proven more efficient than the current larger private government, this study finds that the larger district seems to be efficient enough, at least in terms of achieving reauthorization, reducing crime, and enhancing sanitation and economic development.

The city ordinance requiring larger CVCBD boundaries speaks to two characteristics addressed by transaction resource theory: population size and income inequality. Because city officials paradoxically feared that CBDs might balkanize the city of Baltimore by race and income, they mandated an ordinance that increased the geographic size of the originally proposed CVCBD that, as a result, increased its population size and racial heterogeneity and also created a private government that was mixed income in nature. According to transaction resource theory, increased population size and income inequality hinder contracting. Thus, requiring the second city ordinance as a method to prevent balkanization, public officials ended up creating a private government with attributes that might hinder the contracting process and might fail to get sufficient political buy-in from a more diverse group of constituents (Maser, 1998). However, without such an ordinance, city officials would not have supported the creation of the CVCBD, and the political contracting process would also have failed.

Another community characteristic that hinders contracting is population mobility. In the case of the CVCBD, this characteristic was central to the creation of the district. In a polycentric system, concerns existed that local businesses might relocate from the neighborhood if public safety did not improve, and that residents might also move if they were not satisfied with the services and safety in the neighborhood. These concerns motivated the task force to identify ways to improve conditions in the neighborhood. The result was the creation of the CVCBD. If Whitman, Requardt and Associates, along with other key area businesses and residents, had instead decided to exit the neighborhood, the contracting process needed to create the CVCBD might never have begun. Even if it had started, it would likely have failed.

The next problem of cooperation, the division problem, may arise in the contract's *negotiation phase*, the time when the decision of how to contract is made. In this phase, parties decide the terms of the contract and specify the manner in which the gains resulting from the contract and the burdens of enforcing it will be allocated (Heckathorn and Maser, 1987b). The division problem occurs if parties possess opposing preferences regarding how to allocate the benefits and costs of the contract. If this is the case, the parties negotiate concessions, and the expected outcome is called concession rationality. The goal is to achieve an equitable agreement, and mitigating inequitable divisions creates a demand for rules to promote responsiveness (Maser, 1998). Division problems can be eased through either a coalition or arbitrating third party that has the ability to allocate cooperation gains or is able to narrow the division range. However, an individual may inevitably refuse to accept a contract or constitution, because he or she finds it unfair due to requiring excessive concessions (Heckathorn and Maser, 1987a). In the case of the CVCBD, it appears that all of the institutional rules crafted to satisfy joint rationality, and thus overcome coordination problems, also specify benefits and costs. For example, the rules of fiscal equivalence, taxing both residential and commercial property owners, state enabling legislation requirement, and mandated city ordinances all effectively safeguarded against division problems.

The CVCBD's governance rules were also products of efforts to safeguard participants from threats to cooperation and to gain support for the referendum creating the district. The larger boundaries of the private government increased its heterogeneity, and increased heterogeneity hinders contracting as previously discussed. As a result, the founders formed a governing body for the CVCBD, a board of directors, with an elaborate system of representation in order for the diverse interests that are levied a supplemental tax to be represented and to address potential problems of cooperation.

The board meets monthly in a public meeting. At least two-thirds of the board must be composed of owners or representatives of property owners who are subject to the additional property tax. Under existing CVCBD bylaws, between 14 and 27 board members must govern the CVCBD. The board is composed of members representing all four major neighborhoods within the CVCBD and is designed to be responsive to the community. These four neighborhoods include Abell, Charles Village, Harwood, and Old Goucher.

Under current CVCBD bylaws, board members must include at least eight representatives elected by each of the four neighborhoods, representatives from three business associations located within the district, four at-large members elected by the community, two representatives from nonprofit and religious institutions located within the district, one member appointed by the mayor, at least two members of the Baltimore City Council appointed by the president of the city council, and four representatives from the neighborhood associations that border the CVCBD ("By-Laws of the Charles Village Community Benefits District Management Authority"). The representatives from neighboring areas are included in the system of representation because activities that the CVCBD undertakes are thought to impact these areas. Thus, those designing the board structure believed that representatives from the areas should be included, albeit as nonvoting members (personal communication, May 2004). The board structure also ensures functional representativeness.

In the *postphase*, each party decides to uphold or violate the contract and monitors the compliance of other parties. Defection, the third and most difficult contracting problem, occurs if one or both sides do not comply with the agreement. "Defectors enrich themselves at *greater* cost to the collectivity. They, so to speak, poison the common well from which they steal" [italics in original] (Heckathorn and Maser, 1987a, p. 159). This free riding manifests the troublesome nature of mutual trust and shows the necessity that contracts be efficient, enforceable, and hold people accountable to decrease defection and increase compliance. In order for a party to agree to a contract, its expected outcomes must satisfy *individual rationality* so that neither party is left worse off than the status quo (Heckathorn and Maser, 1987b; Maser, 1998). In public or private governments, defection can occur when leaders or constituents defect from the preferences of the community to pursue their own interests. The initial authorization process to create and make the district legitimate and the process for its reauthorization provide a powerful safeguard against defection.

During the initial authorization process to create the district, the contract could be rejected by individuals voting "no" in the referendum needed to create the district, legislators voting against state or city legislation creating CBDs, or the mayor opposing legislation to create CBDs. Many of the institutional rules discussed previously that mitigated coordination and division problems also safeguarded the new private government against defection problems and generated the political support necessary to create the district. For example, the rule of fiscal equivalence and the requirement that both residential and commercial property owners pay a supplemental tax both helped to win grassroots political support for the referendum.

In addition, the CVCBD's reauthorization process provides a safeguard against defection similar to a recall provision, but in this case it is the entire government that is recalled. In this process that occurs every four years, the city examines the private government's performance. The CVCBD has taken the following actions prior to or during the reauthorization process to win constituent and city council support. It has performed or sponsored surveys and interviews to assess constituent satisfaction prior to reauthorization (Hyde, 2002). In addition, the CVCBD holds community meetings to attempt to persuade constituents to support reauthorization (personal communication, May 2004). Also, the CVCBD has engaged in public relations that resulted in news articles, published an annual report, published a newsletter sent to a wide audience, and met regularly with legislators. "These activities kept people informed and made people feel they were getting something" (personal communication, May 2004).

In the formal reauthorization process, the City Planning Commission first makes a recommendation to the Baltimore City Council about reauthorization. Then, city council hears from neighborhood residents and business persons concerning their views of the private government. During the most recent reauthorization process, the Baltimore City Council went directly to the district's constituents by holding a public hearing in the Charles Village community (personal communication, May 2004). Individuals often stand in long lines to testify for or against the CVCBD's reauthorization (personal communication, May 2004). After hearing public testimony, the council makes its decision to either support or reject reauthorization.

Although some detractors currently exist (personal communication, May 2004), as they did during the CVCBD's creation, public testimony and the private government's actions and performance have thus far persuaded the council to support reauthorization. In the next step of the process, the council presents a bill to the mayor either supporting or opposing reauthorization, and the mayor makes the final decision. The CVCBD was most recently reauthorized in 2003.

As discussed, the nested CVCBD had to originate and exist under a number of institutions created or approved by the state of Maryland and Baltimore City government. As such, this CBD is less autonomous than some other BIDs.

It is not surprising that the seminal polycentric model as presented in the Tiebout (1956) and Ostrom et al. (1961) articles is largely silent on how intracity private governments are created. These articles served as theoretical models, not empirical research. And while the two articles had a profound impact on the study of metropolitan governance, the authors recognized the need for empirical inquiry into how local circumstances and conditions affected the provision of public goods and services. The CVCBD case illustrates that population homogeneity may not be politically feasible for creating a private government, even though population heterogeneity hinders political contracting. From a citywide perspective, allowing the creation of a private government may potentially lead to balkanization, and therefore separates the city by class and race. To minimize this possible outcome in the case of the CVCBD, city-community negotiations led to the private government being enlarged and made more economically and racially diverse, meeting a necessary objective of city and state officials. For example, the enlarged private government's residential population was 55 percent white and 45 percent African American in 1998.

In the end, an efficient metropolitan governance arrangement may be a mixed system that includes both larger overlapping provision units and smaller overlapping provision units. It is considered difficult for low-income communities to form and operate private governments. Traditional reformers argue that a larger provision unit will ensure that the wealthy pay for services of the poor. However, in large provision units, residents of poor neighborhoods may have even less voice about the type of services desired than they do in small provision units. Thus, large provision units do not serve as a panacea. All areas of a city, including low-income communities, may be able to form their own private governments if overlapping units of government give them intergovernmental aid as polycentrists desire.

If all areas of the city are able to form private governments, a CBD's benefits may outweigh its potential abuses. If city property owners and renters do not form CBDs, and therefore do not receive needed supplemental services, they may find themselves living and working in neighborhoods that are becoming more and more unstable. Or they may simply decide to exit the city for the suburbs. Alternatively, through voice, city property owners and renters may create CBDs and similar private governments such as BIDs that have the potential to help stabilize and prevent population decline and business closures in inner city neighborhoods, and these private governments may even attract new residents and businesses from outside the city. Because many inner cities continue to experience instability, population loss, and business closures, CBDs and similar private governments such as BIDs may serve as a structural policy option to aid in stemming these trends.

Conclusion

The debate between polycentrists and metropolitan reformers hinges on whether we should have many overlapping governments of varying sizes as polycentrists desire or one large consolidated government as reformers espouse, and this debate directly affects private governments. Metropolitan reformers argue that overlapping governments duplicate services, confuse citizens, and create a chaotic governance system. In contrast, polycentrists denounce reformers' call for consolidated government as equating Gargantua and argue that not all public goods and services should be provided on a large scale. Policing, for example, might be provided on a small scale, by a smaller government. Metropolitan reformers do not recognize that different public goods require different delivery mechanisms, and instead argue for a one-size-fits-all solution.

In addition, polycentrists contend that a polycentric system is not chaotic, although it might appear to be so. Instead, it allows for service differentiation where citizens are able to get different public services from different-sized governments. One of these governments that provides supplemental services, usually on a small scale, is a private government such as a CBD or BID. Private governments serve as a polycentric alternative that enables citizens to receive additional public services that are not provided by or are not provided effectively by the traditional public sector. These services are tailored to meet the desires of those property owners and renters located within the private government's boundaries.

The chapter discussed polycentrism in the formation of a private government in Baltimore, Maryland, called the Charles Village Community Benefits District (CVCBD). After a random act of violence in the community, area residents and businesses that decided to remain in the neighborhood and form this private government exercised voice rather than exit. An examination of institutions blended with transaction resource theory helps to explain how collective action problems, including coordination, division, and defection, were overcome to create the CVCBD as a private government. These problems were overcome through a political contracting process.

During the private government's formation, a key polycentric issue of controversy involved determining the CVCBD's boundaries. Using a reformist approach, city government officials required that the private government's boundaries be enlarged from 30 to 100 blocks and from 3,000 to 14,000 residents. A polycentric alternative would have allowed the CVCBD's boundaries to remain 30 blocks, and this choice would have kept the private government more homogeneous, thus allowing services to be tailored to meet residents' desires. The enlarged district was more heterogeneous, thus hindering its ability to provide services tailored to residents' demands. Due to increased heterogeneity, founders also needed to craft an elaborate set of governance rules for the private government.

The city ordinance requiring larger CVCBD boundaries speaks to population size and income inequality, two characteristics addressed by transaction resource theory. Because city officials feared that polycentric CBDs might balkanize the city of Baltimore by race and income, they mandated an ordinance that increased the geographic size of the originally proposed CVCBD that, as a result, increased its population size and racial heterogeneity. The ordinance also created a private government that was mixed income in nature. According to transaction resource theory, increased population size and income inequality hinder contracting. Thus, requiring the second city ordinance as a method to prevent balkanization, officials ended up creating a private government with attributes that might hinder the contracting process and might fail to get sufficient political buy-in from a more diverse group of constituents (Maser, 1998). However, without such an ordinance, city officials would not have supported the creation of the CVCBD, and the political contracting process needed to create this polycentric entity would also have failed.

Other institutions were created to ensure that problems of cooperation in the private government's formation were resolved. For example, a referendum with a super majority of both renters and property owners was required in order for the CVCBD to form. Also, fiscal equivalence was utilized, so that only those who paid for the services received them. In addition, a sunset clause required that the CVCBD be reauthorized every four years. These rules also helped to create the political buy-in needed for the CVCBD to form as a polycentric unit of government.

An effective governmental system requires units of varying size, according to the polycentric model. Private governments are one smaller unit among others in a polycentric system. If all areas of the city are able to form private governments, including low-income ones, these governments might aid in stemming blight and decline that many inner city neighborhoods face.

References

Baer, S. E., and Feiock, R. C. 2005. Private governments in urban areas: Political contracting and collective action. *American Review of Public Administration* 35:42–56.

Baer, S. E., and Marando, V. L. 2001. The subdistricting of cities: Applying the polycentric model. *Urban Affairs Review* 36:721–733.

Briffault, R. 1996. The local government boundary problem in metropolitan areas. *Stanford Law Review* 48:1115–1171.

Briffault, B. 1997. Symposium: The law of economics and federalism: The rise of sublocal structures in urban governance. *Minnesota Law Review* 82:503–550.

Briffault, R. 1999. A government for our time? Business improvement districts and urban governance. *Columbia Law Review* 99:365–477.

By-laws of the Charles Village Community Benefits District Management Authority. http://www.charlesvillage.org/media/pdf/by_laws.pdf (accessed July 19, 2007).

Dowling, K., John, P., and Biggs, S. 1994. Tiebout: A survey of empirical literature. *Urban Studies* 31:767–797.

Hawkins, B. W., Percy, S., and Montreal, S. 1997. Residential community associations and the American intergovernmental system. *Publius* 27:61–74.

Heckathorn, D. D., and Maser, S. M. 1987a. Bargaining and constitutional contracts. *American Journal of Political Science* 31:142–168.

Heckathorn, D. D., and Maser, S. M. 1987b. Bargaining and the sources of transaction costs: The case of government regulation. *Journal of Law Economics and Organization* 3:69–98.

Helsley, R. W., and Strange, W. C. 1998. Private government. *Journal of Public Economics* 69:281–304.

Hirschman, A. O. 1970. *Exit, voice, and loyalty: Responses to decline in firms, organizations, and states.* Cambridge, MA: Harvard University Press.

Hyde, C. 2002. Evaluation report: Charles Village community benefits district. Unpublished manuscript.

Maser, S. M. 1998. Constitutions as relational contracts: Explaining procedural safeguards in municipal charters. *Journal of Public Administration Research and Theory* 8:527–564.

McConnell, G. 1966. *Private power and American democracy.* New York: Alfred A. Knopf.

Oakerson, R. J. 1999. *Governing local public economies: Creating the civic metropolis.* Oakland, CA: ICS Press.

Orbell, J. M., and Uno, T. 1972. A theory of neighborhood problem solving: Political action vs. residential mobility. *American Political Science Review* 64:471–489.

Ostrom, E. 1999. Metropolitan reform: Propositions derived from two traditions. In *Polycentricity and local public economies: Readings from the workshop in political theory and policy analysis*, ed. M. D. McGinnis, 139–160. Ann Arbor, MI: University of Michigan Press.

Ostrom, E., and Parks, R. 1999. Neither Gargantua nor the Land of Lilliputs: Conjectures on mixed systems of metropolitan organization. In *Polycentricity and local public economies: Readings from the workshop in political theory and policy analysis*, ed. M. D. McGinnis, 284–305. Ann Arbor, MI: University of Michigan Press.

Ostrom, V., ed. 1994. *The meaning of federalism: Constituting a self-governing society.* San Francisco: ICS Press.

Ostrom, V. 1999. Polycentricity (part 1). In *Polycentricity and local public economies: Readings from the workshop in political theory and policy analysis*, ed. M. D. McGinnis, 52–74. Ann Arbor, MI: University of Michigan Press.

Ostrom, V., and Ostrom E. 1994. Public goods and public choices: The emergence of public economies and industry structures. In *The meaning of American federalism: Constituting a self-governing society*, ed. V. Ostrom, 163–197. San Francisco: ICS Press.

Ostrom, V., Tiebout, C. M., and Warren, R. 1961. The organization of government in metropolitan areas: A theoretical inquiry. *American Political Science Review* 55:831–842.

Parks, R. B., and Oakerson, R. J. 1989. Metropolitan organization and governance: A local public economy approach. *Urban Affairs Quarterly* 25:18–29.

Polanyi, M. 1951. *The logic of liberty: Reflections and rejoinders.* Chicago: University of Chicago Press.

Stein, R. M. 1987. Tiebout's sorting hypothesis. *Urban Affairs Quarterly* 1:140–160.

Teske, P., Schneider, M., Mintrom, M., and Best, S. 1993. Establishing the micro foundations of a macro theory: Information, movers, and the competitive local market for public goods. *American Political Science Review* 87:702–713.

Thomas, R. D., and Hawes, D. W. 1999. *Changing coalition politics in Houston: Municipal districts to tax increment reinvestment zones.* Paper presented at the Annual Meeting of the Urban Affairs Association, Louisville, KY.

Tiebout, C. M. 1956. A pure theory of local expenditures. *Journal of Political Economy* 64:416–424.

Tullock, G. 1994. *The new federalist.* Vancouver, CA: The Fraser Institute.

The 25th Street Task Force. 1993. 25th Street Task Force Community Benefits District Steering Committee Meeting Minutes. Hard copy. March 2.

Williams, O. 1971. *Metropolitan political analysis.* New York: The Free Press.

Chapter 4

From Town Center Management to the BID Model in Britain: Toward a New Contractualism?

Greg Lloyd and Deborah Peel

Contents

Introduction

The implications of transferring a concept such as a business improvement district (BID) into the British context have attracted considerable critical attention in terms of planning and governance (Hoyt, 2004; Ward, 2006; Peel and Lloyd, 2005). The purpose of this chapter is to critically examine the ideological basis and context for the introduction of BIDs in Britain by examining the preceding and parallel practices of town center management. Commonly referred to as TCM, this is a generic term that encompasses a wider range of diverse management practices and development strategies in town and city centers. The chapter seeks to contrast the nature of the interrelationships of the two approaches, and to explain the consequential receptivity to the BID model in British urban policy. Finally, this chapter seeks to demonstrate what may be described as the emergence of a new contractualism in local urban governance, urban revitalization, and economic development in the public domain in Britain.

Mitchell and Staeheli (2006) identify the public domain as a "marker of urbanity" (p. 152). Our starting point, then, is that the realm of public and private spaces in urban environments comprises a complex composite of private, public, and common property rights that together inform social actions (Blackmar, 2006). In light of this highly politicized property rights premium, it follows that there will be a plurality of private, corporate, developmental, and governance perspectives interpreting the appropriateness of TCM interventions. These seek to adapt to shifting social and economic compositions, to respond to evolving environmental and place-based considerations, and to shape governance actions in defined areas. Here, Smith and Low (2006) point to the layered concepts involved in varied discussions around public spaces, public spheres, and urban open space. In contrast, Mandanipour (2003) explores the interplay of individual and collective experience in the urban realm, and the need to find a sensitive equilibrium that accommodates the balance of public and private arenas of human well-being. The term *public domain* suggests that the social differentiation of town centers may be explained by the intricate balance of the private, public, and common property rights involved. In this context, the dynamics of the reallocation of property rights are held to lead to ever more intricate patterns and valuations of the public domain (Webster and Lai, 2003). The important point, however, is to recognize that this layering allows us to develop the argument that town centers represent increasingly competitive arenas that demand ever more sensitive and appropriate forms of governance, management, and regulation.

Following Massey (2005) we deploy a broad social constructionist perspective to examine how the plurality of interrelations and interactions in the public domain are continuously negotiated and renegotiated, and are differentiated across time and locale. This line of thinking underpins advances in urban design practice, for example, where traditional constructions of the nature of public space and what is understood by the concept of "publicness" are being reevaluated and challenged

(Hajer and Reijndorp, 2002). While such dimensions as the environmental quality, type of animation, sense of safety, and accessibility are important features of BIDs and TCM practices, our focus is the governance and mode of interagency working in the common realm.

As a distinct type of space, we argue that town centers, which are the commercial and service districts in urban areas, continue to assert a particular set of dynamics in terms of the pluralities of ownership, occupation, management, and development involved, which together inform the arrangements for regulation. In effect, their multifunctional nature tends to differentiate them from other physical forms where use and ownership, for example, are less complex, and where property rights are relatively more clearly defined (Needham, 2006). Such an analysis is confirmed by the increasing interest in public space management and attempts to understand the complexity of regulatory controls in urban areas (Magalhães and Carmona, 2006; Tiesdell and Slater, 2006). It is evident that regulatory frameworks have to be sensitive to the composite of uses, users, behaviors, activities, and social constructs that crisscross the commercial, public, private, and imagined spheres of the public domain.

It is this intrinsic complexity that serves to explain how and why the public domain represents a particular paradox in terms of devising appropriate spatial management and governance arrangements. Formal and informal rules, and legally and culturally defined norms and values, intersect and compete in such contested spaces (Webster and Lai, 2003). This is evident in the established literature around the locational patterns of urban land uses, and theories of urban structures and morphologies (Balchin et al., 1995). As Healey demonstrates, the relationships between the private and public sectors around land and property development in urban contexts are highly complex and layered, and drive to the core of the capacities of each in delivering intended outcomes (Healey, 1991). As particular models of urban intervention, then, TCM and BID initiatives operate in a particularly negotiated environment. Moreover, operational effectiveness will be mediated, in part, through the particular policy climate and the receptivity to policy ideas in practice in which TCM and BID initiatives are located.

In tracing the introduction of BIDs in Britain we focus on how the state and the market have attempted to resolve the paradox of the public domain over time. Drawing on Giddens' (1998) articulation of postwar political thinking in Britain, the evolution of political economy ideas may be characterized in terms of social democratic principles (1945–1979), neoliberal thinking (1979–1997), and the Third Way policy agenda that underpinned the election of (New) Labour in 1997, and which generally prevails to the present. These three broad ideological frames assert very particular sets of state-market-civil relations, and are helpful in informing a better understanding of how the specific paradox of the public domain in town and city centers has been addressed. As a traditional marketplace for the trading of goods and services, town and city centers in Britain are also the locus for the exchange of ideas, practices, and policy lessons. This particular construction of urban mercantilism presents an opportunity for exploring the conceptual and ideological bases of TCM and BIDs, and further, it frames their individual application in addressing governance, funding, public service delivery, and political decision making.

In the course of the narrative we follow Hambleton (1988) with respect to the different dimensions of public policy planning. These include the nature of the policy message associated with BIDs and TCM practices, the administrative arrangements put in place to orchestrate these particular public policy initiatives, the underlying perspectives and ideologies driving the associated social actions, the resources made available, and the power and political relations involved. Taken together, these dimensions inform a deeper understanding of the origins, cultures, and practices of TCM and BIDs in Britain. This conceptual approach accentuates the importance of public learning, which draws attention to government's recognition of specific policy problems and to their adaptive capacity in designing a more appropriate response (Hambleton, 1988). In effect, this approach highlights the importance of understanding the necessary transformation of institutional structures and mechanisms to address the practicalities of operational management. Further, applying this finer-grain understanding of public policy planning to TCM and BIDs complements the insights of Rose (1991) into policy transfer and international lesson drawing. It offers the potential for a longer-term perspective on policy and implementation because it alerts us to the continuous processes of communication, renegotiation, and bargaining that underpin the operation of policy innovations in practice (Hambleton, 1988).

The chapter first addresses some definitional and conceptual issues and traces the roots of BIDs through the maturation of TCM practices. This seeks to explain the heterogeneity of the approaches in an international context, and to examine whether BIDs represent a transformation in the governance of the town center public domain in Britain. We conclude with some remarks around the changing nature of public service delivery in defined urban spaces, and the rise of a new contractualism in public service governance, management, and delivery.

The Paradox of the Public Domain

In terms of a defined entity, the distinction between town and city centers in Britain has become sufficiently blurred in practice that the terms are used interchangeably (Woolley et al., 1996). The generic term *town center* has been used to refer to city, town, and suburban district centers, which at a variety of scales and governance levels provide a broad range of facilities and services and act as a focus for community and public transport activities (Department of the Environment, 1996). Following this logic, in this chapter we use the generic term *town center* to set the context to BIDs.

Cities are quintessentially complex. As Amin and Thrift (1995) observe, "Cities are places of work, consumption, circulation, play, creativity, excitement, boredom. They gather, mix, separate, conceal, display. They support unimaginably diverse social practices. They juxtapose nature, people, things, and the built environment in any number of ways" (p. 3). Moreover, geographical delimitations and administrative boundaries may be differentiated from relatively more personal associations (Nasar, 1998). From this perspective, individual sentiments and experiences can serve to connect communities and individual locales, and thereby provide a "sense of place" (Lynch, 1960, p. 19).

In planning and management terms, town centers are characterized by their mix of functions and activities, including acting as marketplaces, business centers, and offering services, and supporting meeting places, arts and cultural facilities, transport hubs, and residential areas (Department of the Environment, 1996). They have traditionally tended to act as the host for the principal public administration functions and buildings (Larkham, 2004). Moreover, the particular morphology of urban growth, change, and development roots individual towns and cities in very specific historical and cultural contexts and differentiates them in a number of ways, including scale, shape, architecture, ownership, mix of use, and governance (Hall, 1998). While town centers are conventionally the location of the principal business district and related commercial activities, the nature of their boundaries is fluid and constantly in transition. These dimensions appear to require an increasingly complex web of regulatory, licensing, surveillance, enforcement, and management techniques to mediate contemporary urban life (Roberts and Turner, 2005; Roberts et al., 2006). This may be explained by the arguments that the civic identity and polity dimensions of town centers have been increasingly eroded as a consequence of powerful processes of corporate, economic, and social relocation (Zukin, 1995). This may provoke a number of physical, institutional, and social responses as individual places seek to accommodate a variety of interests with different time horizons, loyalties, and policy expectations (Peel, 2003). Town centers are thus a cauldron of positive and negative qualities that require explanation.

The dynamic and volatile character of the town center sets the evolutionary context to specific urban management and development initiatives, such as TCM and BIDs. Three observations are relevant here. First, as a town or city expands, what may be described as the central business district may well become a smaller proportion of the urban area (Balchin and Kieve, 1985). It follows that the spatial qualities and physical attributes of what are held to be vibrant commercial spaces may then be undermined. Here, it has been argued that the principles of new urbanism* may offer positive benefits and legitimize the setting up of a BID in these contexts

---

* New urbanism is an expression of contemporary urban design that draws on traditional approaches to planning urban communities. It rejects established Anglo-Saxon dependencies on the motorcar and promotes accessibility on foot. It asserts a strong case for the positive use of public space in promoting community cohesion and sustainable development.

(Davies et al., 1999). Second, as city spaces reconfigure, this alters the parameters for collective action at the submunicipal level. It is relevant to identify debates pertaining to a rethinking of community in this context and to acknowledge the perceived rise of civil society (Friedmann, 1999). This line of reasoning highlights a number of concerns around the potentially exclusive nature of emerging spatial forms such as gated communities and BIDs (Steel and Symes, 2005). Third, there is an institutional dimension with respect to how such measures are implemented. Specifically, we draw attention to the body of critical literature and practice that relates to local partnership working, and which is then critical to appreciating contemporary urban agendas and forms of action (Bailey et al., 1995).

There is a cultural ingredient to this deeper understanding of the public domain and of contemporary urban policy action that serves to flesh out the broader civil dimension. Here Zukin (1995) asserted that cities are often criticized because they represent the "basest instincts of human society" (p. 1). In this vein, Hill (1994) elaborated a number of tensions and suggested that cities are synonymous with "unsettling changes in values and attitudes: dependency, changing family structures, … decline in civility and civic pride … moral and attitudinal deficiencies, alienation and anomie" (p. 2). The sense that cities have lost cohesion and coherence and therefore need to be reimagined and made liveable again represents a powerful strand of contemporary British political rhetoric around the need for a new vision of city living (Association of Town Center Management, 2000; Civic Trust Regeneration Unit, 1994; Department of the Environment, Transport and the Regions, 2000a, 2000b). Here, then, attempts are made to socially reconstruct the idea of the urban realm, as well as the associated rights and responsibilities that are held to relate to it.

The contemporary urban policy *zeitgeist* is captured in the exhortation made by the British government's Urban Task Force in its report advocating an "urban renaissance" (Urban Task Force, 1999). Here there are echoes of Mumford's (1963) important celebration of cities as the "crucible" of cultural, intellectual, political, and economic human endeavor and achievement. In more recent times, and recognizing the intrinsic value and resilient nature of cities, it has been explicitly asserted that the pessimistic approach that appeared to underpin a negative social construction of cities had to be challenged and urban policy realigned to optimize the inherent richness of urban life (Worpole and Greenhalgh, 1999). In short, the reformulation of British urban policy reflects various attempts at attaining a relatively more optimistic view of the nature and potential of British towns and cities, based on an acknowledgment that they involve a complex of economic, social, physical, cultural, and legal influences (Department of the Environment, 1994). This provides an intriguing context for rethinking urban social action because it would suggest the need for not only a fundamental public policy planning approach, and cultural change in mind-sets and behaviors, but also a fundamental reformulation of the central message. In particular, contemporary debates have drawn attention to the potential demise of public space and its loss through continuing waves of privatization (Jones et al., 2003; Steel and Symes, 2005). This sets a very specific context in which to consider the management and regulation of the public domain.

Managing and Regulating the Public Domain

Following Evans (1997), the existence of distinctive academic and professional views of town centers may variously frame the physical, economic, and institutional dimensions of town centers. Indeed, the cultural layering of professional identities, sectors, and political interpretations lies at the heart of understanding how different interests socially construct the successes and failures of human activities and development. In this chapter, we are concerned with how the multidisciplinary context of town centers configures—and reconfigures—the dominant regulatory frameworks to steer, secure, and sustain particular developmental paths in the public domain.

Various attempts have been put into place in Britain to better design, administer, and regulate the physical and community conditions appropriate to what are held to be liveable cities (Civic Trust Regeneration Unit, 1994; Tibbald, 1992). Particular attention has been paid to better countering the symptoms of uneven urban decline and dysfunctional growth and to addressing the perceived underperformance of different town and city centers (Department of the Environment, 1994; Grayson and Young, 1994; Urban Task Force, 1999). In this context, Evans (1997) traced how the formulation and implementation of public policy with respect to the administration and regulation of town and city centers has evolved. This analysis drew attention to the shifting priorities at the central and local government levels, changing market decisions and external corporate pressures, and wider public criticism of specific governance interventions that were held to be ineffective—both in maintaining the quality of local environments and in fostering economic development.

How town center success—or failure—has been socially constructed, measured, and evaluated has changed over time (Pal and Sanders, 1997). This evolution mirrors how the nature of town centers has been constructed. Since the 1980s, for instance, there has been a growing concern with the economic viability and social vitality of town and city centers (Department of the Environment, 1994). In more recent times, the perceived scale of the urban problem has been described in dramatic terms, such as instability, rupture, and conflict (Healey et al., 1995; Urban Task Force, 1999). Taken together, such dramatization of the crisis suggests that cities are located at the front line of economic restructuring, corporate relocation, and community change. Importantly, it is this catalog of perceived ills that has prompted a rediagnosis of a town center's overall well-being and alternative prescriptions to secure and restore the health of specific business and commercial areas (Peel, 2003).

In response to a perceived urban *malaise*, individual government and corporate interests have explored the potential of TCM schemes and BIDs. Both forms of urban management regime are "situated." They reflect particular political economy impulses and methodologies and are informed by particular cultures of working between the state and the market. In Britain, active corporate engagement in local governance has traditionally been relatively weak. Thus, TCM arrangements emerged from experiments to foster partnership working between local municipalities and retailers and to capitalize on shopping-center experience. The shift to partnership working through TCM was an explicit attempt at a given point in time to encourage and strengthen private engagement in local matters in response to central government policy. In contrast, the development of BIDs in North America reflected a relatively more established ethos of state-market relations in urban governance.

As we trace in more detail below, the evolution of TCM and BIDs in Britain involves defined modes of governance and institutional relations. These are informed principally and to a different extent by neoliberal traditions of political economy thinking. They represent very specific measures, which differ from the forms of urban development and management associated with the relatively more centrist and *dirigiste* interventions of the earlier postwar period (Cooke and Morgan, 1998). In advocating more flexible, responsive, and grounded ways of addressing local town center conditions, TCM practices and BIDs challenge an established culture of a strong centralized state, with an emphasis on "command and control" regulatory arrangements and expenditures. Part of the argument for individual TCM and BID initiatives is that they enable local differentiation in design and remit. They may therefore be understood as representing relatively more sensitive tools for effective urban action, and as having the capacity to respond to the specific differential contexts and contingencies of defined geographical, market, and institutional contexts.

Town Centers and Social Democracy

> The location of desperately needed new homes and industries, the dispersal of people and factories from overcrowded city centers were to be planned across the entire nation rather than left to the free market or the scrappy, voluntary efforts of local councils. (Schoon, 2001, p. 38)

This quotation captures the flavor of the land-use planning system and the rebuilding priorities put in place in the immediate postwar period in Britain. The prevailing social democratic political agenda of the time was dominated with a concern for urban reconstruction, and as a consequence, the priorities concentrated on the built environment dimensions of town and city centers and on generating the physical fabric necessary to support economic growth and nurture civic life (Rydin, 2003). At the same time, there was an emphasis on facilitating use of the motorcar, extending personal choice, and promoting greater accessibility into the town centers. In terms of economic mix, the importance of the town center was further underlined by the expansion and diversification of retailing in the urban areas, and a wider enthusiasm to accommodate the anticipated lifestyle and consumer expectations that were being supported by technological advances, social change, marketing, and advertising, together with a more general sense of economic well-being (Evans, 1997). During this period, town centers in Britain assumed considerably greater importance as civic and commercial spaces for community life in the wider urban agenda.

The incremental processes of decline that subsequently affected town centers stemmed from a complex array of factors. First, the growth in disposable household income and the share of turnover held by multiple retailers prompted decisions that challenged and changed the established hierarchy and locations of retail activities (Schiller, 1986). This created a new competitive context for town centers. Second, the broader processes of economic and corporate restructuring further undermined urban areas at large. Third, the emergence of the perceived inner cities crisis prompted specific government policy intervention to the relatively disadvantaged residential areas (Robson, 1988). Although caught up in the same processes of urban restructuring and contraction that accentuated the subsequent inner city crisis, commercial centers did not attract this level of specific public sector and political interest. Fourth, the governance of town centers during the social democratic period was conducted through arrangements that were principally sector specific in character. The ensuing demise of town centers may therefore be seen as a consequence of a passive management attitude by government. In the 1970s, for example, many town centers continued to deteriorate in terms of relative economic performance and viability, physical quality, and social vitality. Fifth, processes of decentralization effectively hollowed out the commercial core of some cities and weakened their fundamental economic ecologies. Significantly, this flight of economic activity mirrors the experience in Canada, which had initiated an early interest in the BID model.*

Town Centers and Neoliberalism

> This decade [the 1980s] has seen much of the practical machinery for the Conservatives' free-market economy put into place, and dramatic fluctuation in economic performance and expectations. Political aspirations and social priorities have shifted so far that what would have caused controversy in 1979 is taken for granted in 1989. (Nadin and Doak, 1991, p. 3)

---

* For brief histories of the BIDs in Canada, see the chapters by Gopal-Agge and Hoyt and by Hernandez and Jones in this volume.

In terms of governance, local authorities have traditionally been responsible for providing the regulatory and administrative framework for managing town centers. Yet, research findings from a range of sources during this next period contended that town center decline was a direct result of "institutional inertia and neglect" by local government (Department of the Environment, 1994). The perceived failure was also attributed to a professional legacy of departmentalism. Worpole (1992) contended that "the quality of local civic life had disappeared into the gaps between planning, housing, transport and leisure.... There was often no corporate policy, no 'mission statement,' no coherent set of policy objectives which informed local authority provision as a whole" (p. 98). The perceived fragmentation of services and committees and departmental thinking was clearly identified as problematic. Further, the potential for service overlap was accompanied by a possibility of service underprovision—as was experienced by many town centers. It was thus the joining up of the myriad services, agents, and departments with an interest in the town center that made the solution of a relatively more corporate approach through partnership working so attractive.

An important explanation in tracing the perceived decline of town centers is bound up with wider processes of change in the market and particularly the retail revolution of the mid-20th century, which Schiller (1986) graphically described as comprising three waves of retail decentralization. This witnessed the relocation tendencies of (1) the principal food convenience supermarkets, (2) the nonfood bulky goods warehouses, and (3) the specialist town center clothing and quality comparison shopping, which vacated the traditional urban areas in favor of what were seen as more appropriate and accessible out-of-town locations. Indeed, it was the rapid growth in new retail formats that led to increasing concerns about the health of the high street (Spridell, 1980). This medical metaphor has persisted, although whether the development of out-of-town facilities did or did not precipitate the "death of the high street" remains contested (Nuttall and Hornsby, 1995).

Nonetheless, research has continued to suggest that the shift in retail location was clearly perceived to have had a particularly acute impact on many town centers, and this may well have spurred local authorities into reassessing and recognizing the variety of threats to their individual town centers (British Property Federation, 1995; Wells, 1990). Indeed, an appreciation of the diverse processes of economic, retailing, and corporate restructuring, and interurban competition served to popularize the health-check approach to understanding the problems and potential of town centers (Department of the Environment, 1994; Peel, 2003; Tomalin, 1997). As a consequence, the heterogeneity of individual town centers in terms of property rights, physical form, and use, for example, increasingly became important considerations in public policy.

At this time, opportunities for learning were informed by private sector experience in the design, administration, and management of individual shopping centers. Indeed, the perceived operational success of these retail spaces clearly had comparative implications for the nature and quality of the town center experience and the growing dissatisfaction and perceived inferiority of the public domain (Spridell, 1980). Yet, the philosophy of the private shopping center turns on a space that is planned, designed, built, and managed with a specific purpose in mind (Beddington, 1991). This was informed by a number of factors, including the discharge of defined legal and contractual obligations; the management of public and landlord–tenant relations; the execution of management and administrative duties, such as staffing, accounting, maintenance, security, and insurance; and, ultimately, financial profit (Martin, 1982). Such privatized and delineated arrangements provide a stark contrast with town centers, which tend to have evolved more organically with relatively less clearly defined private property rights, a composite of blurred public and common property rights, and with particular metrics of success defined in terms of the public interest (Peel, 2003). Indeed, the commercial imperatives of privately managed space stand in sharp relief to the moral and political requirements of the state's obligations to the public realm and frame contemporary concerns about the privatization of public space (Reeve, 1996). An associated emphasis on sustaining spaces of consumption that can be variously marketed (Shields, 1992) forms part of the wider context for understanding TCM practice and, more recently, that of BIDs.

In light of these insights and comparative evidence from the perceived health of town centers in mainland Europe, Spridell (1980) suggested transferring techniques of shopping-center management from the private into the public sphere, and to centralize all service needs into a town management department covering everything from footpaths, drains, flower beds, car parks, and street lighting to rubbish collection and cleanliness. This, he contended, would provide a single point of information and control and avoid overlap. More importantly, in terms of style of governance, Spridell made the case for a more supportive and proactive approach by business and retailers to work in partnership with local authorities.

This cultural shift can be explained by the parallel interest in corporate responsibility. A government review of the impact of out-of-town shopping facilities on town centers, for example, highlighted the extent to which the out-of-town debate had "provoked a degree of collective response on behalf of interest groups, organisations and private sector businesses which is unprecedented in the history of planning and development" (Department of the Environment, 1992, para. 8.73). Indeed, the perceived need for an interagency response was also asserted by business with an acknowledgment that "no one group has a monopoly on the town center. No one group has a monopoly on solutions. No one group can deliver all the remedies for improvement" (Boots, 1996, p. 4). Thus, a strong case was made for understanding the different roles and cultures of those with a responsibility for, and an interest in, the effective management of the town center (Association of Town Center Management, 1994).

Arguments were marshalled to drive this approach forward. The neoliberal diagnostic was based on a view that local authorities were "fundamentally the wrong body to deliver the future of town centers," lacking funding, power, and experience and, above all, being associated with a "bad track record" (Roberts and Freedman, 1996, p. 51). This reflected a wider perspective that promoted the introduction of private sector cultures in public administration (Stoker, 1995). This analysis is important because it captured the emergent *zeitgeist* of liberal market thinking in Britain during this period. In short, far more than representing a pragmatic response to addressing a complex of town center ills, the very concept of TCM may be seen as reflecting the then prevailing criticisms of established state intervention, assertions of government failure, and preferred management styles around private sector operational models.

The emergence of a relatively more consensual approach by the protagonists within the town center witnessed an exhortation that landlords, investors, retailers, businesses, and local authorities work together to manage the public domain as a business (Warman, 1995). The underpinning mercantile philosophy, then, was quite clear. It was claimed, for example, that TCM was "not a bureaucratic function undertaken by some faceless committee. It is an entrepreneurial enterprise that needs people who can assess a situation and work in partnership to implement a planned response" (Association of Town Center Management, 1996, p. 8). In contrast to the relatively more passive management of town centers that had prevailed during the earlier social democratic period, this asserted the perceived need for a relatively more corporate and proactive management response. A more consensual form of governance was clearly asserted. The British Property Federation, for example, promulgated TCM as "a philosophy designed to bring focused active management to town centers to ensure that they meet the needs of their users (customers)" (British Property Federation, 1995, p. 4). Toward the end of the neoliberal period some 78 percent of local authorities had a form of TCM scheme (URBED, 1997). These varied in size, constituency, leadership, and format, and the interest continues to the present.

From its inception, there has been a strong focus on the commercial and retail element of TCM (Medway et al., 1999). Claims were made that the TCM model has the potential to encourage more people into the town; to maintain and enhance its trading potential; to facilitate the redevelopment, refurbishment, and enhancement of its environment; to promote a climate that encourages owners to maintain properties; and ultimately to better protect the potential investment value of the center and existing shopping streets in capital and rental terms (Wells, 1990). This comprehensive agenda resulted in what may be categorized as comprising janitorial responsibilities (such as the removal of fly posters and graffiti, street cleansing, and shop-front enhancement), physical or "hard" interventions (such as pedestrianization, street furniture, lighting, and public art), and promotional or "soft" interventions (such as those associated with the use of the local media, campaign and marketing strategies, and branding activities). A strong case for the TCM model was that it could create economies of scale in local business interests to better target a relatively more corporate response for individual centers; improve lines of communication around, say, the project management of basic infrastructure; act as a lever for securing regeneration funding; and, importantly, raise awareness of the needs of particular social groups (Peel, 2003).

Notwithstanding the positive rhetoric surrounding the TCM model, a perennial concern has been that of establishing sustainable funding arrangements. The inability to secure sufficient revenue funds has frequently been identified as problematic in the longer-term development of TCM schemes (Boots, 1994; Association of Town Center Management, 1998; Evans, 1997). Three observations are appropriate. First, there was a perceived dysfunctional relationship between the local taxation regime for business and the reciprocal services provided in many town centers (McGreal et al., 2002). The perceived shortfall became important in encouraging negative business attitudes toward local governance. Second, the apparent dominance by the retail sector in this context served to highlight the free-rider problem (Forsberg et al., 1999). This clearly weakened the representation of the groups involved in TCM. Third, as a consequence, the financial base for effecting TCM was rather narrow. Indeed, the number and diversity of interests who actually contributed to TCM was relatively limited (Medway et al., 1999). The various alternatives for encouraging new ways of bringing private finance and expertise into TCM were clearly a key issue by the mid to late 1990s. These features provide an important link to an emerging interest in BIDs.

Town Centers and the Third Way

Following Giddens (1998), the third way represents a synthesis of the earlier political ideologies, priorities, and practices. Together with an emphasis on social justice, a principal concern with enhancing the efficiency and effectiveness of governance arrangements and public sector working has continued to inform recent debates about public service provision and delivery. Over three terms of office, a Labour government has pursued a raft of policy initiatives concerned with promoting the urban agenda, notably through a commitment to delivering "well designed, compact and connected cities supporting a diverse range of uses—where people live, work and enjoy leisure time at close quarters" (Urban Task Force, 1999, p. 2). Within this context, town centers were specifically identified as a management priority. This extensive policy agenda prioritized the use of brownfield rather than greenfield sites; the introduction of new submunicipal governance mechanisms, such as urban regeneration companies and BIDs; and new fiscal measures, including the introduction of a local council tax on the owners of empty properties. Further, BIDs have to be understood against the government's main objectives for public service reform and the modernization of local government. This seeks to strengthen the link between local government and communities and to promote stronger local leadership and quality public services. Within this context there has been a concern with enhancing quality and creating more choice for the consumer (McCabe, 2006; Sullivan and Skelcher, 2002).

The emphasis on devising more appropriate forms of regulation has implications for established state-market relations (Allmendinger et al., 2003). Attention has been paid to streamlining existing regulatory structures to reduce the costs of administering regulation (Arculus Report, 2005; Hampton Report, 2004). There has been general and critical questioning of established conventional forms of regulation and management, and a concomitant reliance on promoting greater private sector engagement within public policy and local governance arrangements. This prompted attempts to reform the established local government finance system, particularly with respect to conventional urban policy and planning responses (Lloyd et al., 2003). As a consequence, town centers have assumed a higher or a more visible priority in policy and economic development agendas.

The new political economy awareness of the importance of town centers in the wider urban frame was driven by two imperatives. First, following Amin and Thrift (1995) there was a clear acknowledgment of the challenges and implications of globalization, and the growth of place competition in a global marketplace. This was of considerable significance for the responses of individual cities to defining and securing competitive advantage. Globalization precipitated a new emphasis by cities to promoting urban entrepreneurship and innovation in a number of institutional and policy arenas. This has involved visible strategies to put into place marketing measures and image enhancement, and high-profile, large-scale property-based initiatives. Critically, the reconfiguration of local governance arrangements has witnessed increased business management in the delivery of core public sector services and a reconsideration of the regulatory regimes prevailing in towns and cities (Borja and Castells, 1996).

Second, there was a concern with the perceived ineffectiveness of earlier regeneration interventions to address the complex of structural and spatial dimensions of that problem (Imrie and Thomas, 1999; Lawless, 1994). The established approaches based on regulation and area-based initiatives supported by public spending were being questioned in the context of a broader understanding of the severity of the challenge (Cochrane, 1999). This prompted a more imaginative search for policy innovation in urban regeneration (Lloyd et al., 2003). Attention turned to exploring alternative forms of local and regional governance (Adams et al., 1999; Evans and Bate, 2000; Urban Task Force, 1999). This included an interest in the potential role of fiscal incentives in securing intended regeneration and development outcomes (Fulford, 1998; Urban Task Force, 1999). Indeed, it was asserted that "the principal reasons for non-investment in urban regeneration include the perception of bureaucratic grant regimes, negative image of neighbouring environments, and lack of or low rates of capital appreciation and/or rental growth" (Adair et al., 2002, p. 2).

This suggests that the cultural attitudes underpinning established state-market relations persist. It is, perhaps, unsurprising that alternative fiscal models for securing urban regeneration were explored at this time to inform policy. An academic survey, for example, reviewed the tax relief model that had been deployed in Ireland to secure the refurbishment of inner city dereliction, as well as the tax incremental funding and BID models used in the United States (McGreal et al., 2002). These alternatives suggested that the use of tax-based incentives to supplement conventional planning and regulation could offer a means of addressing urban regeneration concerns in the British context. Nonetheless, it was asserted that any direct transferability of the BID model had to be sensitive to the very major differences in legal provisions, land ownership, taxation regimes, and cultures operating in the different U.S. and British contexts (McGreal et al., 2002).

In Britain, a BID is defined as "a flexible funding mechanism to improve and manage a clearly defined commercial area" (Association of London Government, 2005, p. 3). The BID model involves an additional and mandatory levy on all the defined rate payers within a precisely delineated area. Such an approach has been heralded as a step-change in public service delivery and taxation arrangements in the UK (Evans and Bate, 2000; Urban Task Force, 1999). Indeed, it has been identified as a practical example of how the private sector can invest in the regeneration of strategic urban areas (Adair et al., 2002). The potential of the BID concept in Britain is described as drawing on the established principles of partnership to rework public service provision and quality (Ward, 2006). Furthermore, advocates point to the growing international literature on BIDs (Hoyt, 2005; Travers and Weimar, 1996). Two parallel strands of action to introduce BIDs in Britain are evident.

First, arising out of a bottom-up concern with recalibrating established TCM practices, there has been an explicit interest in the broad principles of the BID approach at the local level. For example, the Central London Partnership—formed in 1995 as a public–private partnership of the eight central London local authorities, a number of public organizations, and private sector representatives with the objective of actively improving local areas—identified the BID model, in the late 1990s, as offering the potential to better harness the emerging collective business interest and to structure financial investment in defined locales. A Local Improvement Partnerships Task Force was established to examine the potential of BID-style partnerships (Central London Partnership, 2000). This led to the Circle Initiative, which was an early experimental form of the BID approach (Central London Partnership, 2001). This initiative involved five pilot BID areas, which were funded over five years through central government's Single Regeneration Budget and the London Development Agency. This focused on promoting the advancement of BIDs on a pan-London basis, disseminating best practice, and lobbying central government (Central London Partnership, 2006). Significantly, and in parallel, the Association of Town Center Management promoted a national BID pilot project that examined 23 localities in England and Wales over three years, together with 11 regional pilots in Northwest England.

Second, at central government level, statutory measures were put into effect to facilitate the formal introduction of BIDs in parallel with a consultation exercise on the preparation of draft guidance on BIDs (UK BIDs, 2003, 2004a, 2004b). Subsequently, legislation was passed, and the concept has transferred across Britain's devolved administrative arrangements (Mullen, 2006; Peel and

Lloyd, 2005). BIDs have now assumed a visible position in the national urban policy landscape.

The Paradox of the Public Domain: Policy Planning Reconsidered

In this chapter we have argued that the nature of the social and physical context and the changing political economy in Britain provide the canvas upon which urban measures and policy learning in central business districts must be understood. The evidence in rhetoric and practice would suggest that there has been an important shift in approach that has progressively witnessed a rethinking of governance around management and partnership, through the relatively more informal and voluntary medium of TCM, to a reforming of governance around the more formalized and contractualized concept and arrangements of BIDs. This evolving argument is consistent with Ward's (2006) reference to "policies in motion." In effect, the implementation of the BID model in Britain represents an evident transformation in policy practice. Here, BIDs may be explained as demonstrating an iterative and experiential approach to policy learning (Lloyd and Peel, 2006). In short, BIDs are presented as a way of addressing the funding and free-rider weaknesses identified in earlier urban management and governance arrangements, have built upon the established momentum of TCM, and further represent a relatively more active engagement by the business sector in the public realm.

Following Hambleton (1988), the policy message associated with the shift to BIDs in Britain is very evident. This is significant in terms of both its substantive content and the mode of communication with respect to the language used and its potential symbolic value in stimulating action. In practice, concerns around free riders and a lack of a sustainable funding stream provided a fertile environment in which the seed of the BID concept could be sown. In Inverness, for example, the interest in establishing a BID was prompted both by the earlier experience with TCM, which was inhibited by funding and free-rider limitations, and by the more strategic city-visioning process and outcomes in which the city sought to achieve its economic vision as a competitive place (Peel and Lloyd, 2005). In effect, a BID can be deployed directly to address the specific issues, which were perceived as having bedeviled TCM in practice.

A practical dimension concerning the implementation of the BID idea turns on the necessary administrative arrangements. Hambleton (1988) highlights the "mechanical difficulties of achieving communication and co-ordination between a multiplicity of agents" (p. 14). The important point is that the plurality of stakeholders in the town center context demands an important degree of network building so as to sustain the necessary involvement by business interests. The BID concept draws on the partnership experience and learning derived from practices in TCM. Further, it directly addresses the acknowledged deficits in that approach, particularly with respect to free riders. Here, the BID model would appear to offer relatively more formal and clear administrative arrangements for engaging those active participants. The constitutional form of BIDs seeks to secure a more regular enfranchisement of those interests in town centers than the relatively more organic arrangements of TCM. Given the statutory basis of a BID, the forms of communication will have to be more disciplined. It follows that the rules by which a BID will debate issues, reach decisions, and allocate resources will have to be open and transparent. More specifically, the precise remit and expectations for the type of action undertaken in each BID area will have to be articulated through individual service level agreements.

There has been a variety of responses by relevant actors to potential BID areas. This suggests the importance of stakeholder comprehension and cognition in informing the associated response to the idea (Hambleton, 1988). In practical terms, this reflects the understanding of what a BID can offer over and above the services achieved through TCM. A response to a proposed BID will be conditioned by prior experience, which may be positive or negative, and may apply to a number of circumstances. These may include participant interrelations, links to local governance, and the nature of the outcomes achieved. It is also the case that the BID idea is relatively new in Britain. On one hand, this novelty may cause problems for a critical understanding and appreciation of what it offers, particularly with respect to the financial aspects of BIDs. Here, the international transferability requires clarity and sensitive application. On the other hand, expectations may be raised unrealistically, which may serve to undermine the sustainability of the concept. Although initial enthusiasm may be sufficient for the introduction of a BID, its longer-term viability needs to be stewarded and nurtured.

Central to the concept of a BID is the levying of a marginal tax that is then hypothecated according to the constitutional processes of the local arrangement. This will reflect local circumstances and the priorities articulated through the BID governance arrangements. An acknowledged driver for the introduction of a TCM initiative was the perceived underprovision of local services. For the BID, this issue has not disappeared, and there will also likely be difficult questions around the disbursement of the marginal BID levy. This necessitates the need for robust governance arrangements of individual BIDs and transparency with respect to how the measures of success are defined, collected, interpreted, and disseminated.

The origins of TCM and BIDs in Britain, and their associated ideas and practices, would appear to confirm Hambleton's (1988) assertion of the primacy of the political process. Each measure has demonstrated a changing flux of state-market-civil relations, and a changing combination of different stakeholders seeking to address the problems of town centers. The BID model places the business interests in town centers on a more formal footing with respect to governance, funding, and the delivery of customized services. Thus, the shift from a relatively voluntary arrangement to what represents a new contractualism in submunicipal governance is significant in challenging the looser, more differentiated approaches to TCM. Yet, BIDs continue to operate in a public domain characterized by diversity and plurality.

Conclusions

The argument presented in this chapter is that TCM and BIDs offer important insights into the management of what constitutes the contemporary public domain and, further, are emblematic of the current evolution of public service management practices in Britain. In terms of wider international experience, the institutional framework further provides for an understanding of the evolving dynamics of state-market and civil relations that underlie and inform such collaborative approaches in the differentiated private–public spheres of central business districts. Three observations stand out in terms of understanding the evolving policy framework of town center management practices.

First, the concept of BIDs in Britain builds on, and continues to run in parallel with, an established tradition of TCM. Indeed, TCM developed organically since the early 1980s and gathered considerable momentum during the 1990s (Evans, 1997; Spridell, 1980). During this time TCM also gained central government backing and encouragement (Department of the Environment, 1996). The introduction of BIDs arguably represents a step-change in urban economic development policy and regeneration practice, because this approach is predicated on a redesign of the fiscal relations at the local level. Moreover, BIDs operate in defined areas within broader jurisdictions. The introduction of BIDs has effectively institutionalized what were the relatively more informal and localized partnership-working arrangements put in place through TCM schemes, although the latter similarly had their own spatial impacts.

In this way BIDs represent a shift toward a new contractualism of the relationships and service delivery standards involved at the submunicipal level. This step-change is supported by a concern with distilling and disseminating the wider learning from the implementation of BIDs in practice. As such, the contemporary enthusiasm for pilot projects and best-practice guidance forms part of an expanding interest in propagating evidence-based learning in government and business circles (Lloyd and Peel, 2006). Here, then, the evidence of efficiency and effectiveness in urban management is an important objective in broader societal attempts to instill a cultural change in governance arrangements and economic development initiatives around notions of corporate social responsibility.

Second, BIDs are currently positioned as a potential catalyst for the relatively more robust regeneration of service and commercial areas, and as a conduit for enhancing defined service delivery in specifically delineated areas (Scottish Executive, 2003). Indeed, the very choice of nomenclature is important in characterizing this initiative and distinguishing it from the wider family of measures (Hoyt, 2005).

It also alerts us to the particular impetus for this policy option. Significantly, the contemporary interest in BIDs arose from a wider concern with actively promoting an urban renaissance (Urban Task Force, 1999). There was also a parallel questioning of established public sector approaches to urban policy, service delivery, and, crucially, their financing and resourcing (McGreal et al., 2002). Notably, this line of reasoning involves a recasting of the established financial arrangements in urban areas (Lloyd et al., 2003). Importantly, then, BIDs, as part of a suite of potential policy scenarios, are presented as a mechanism to address a complex of governance and resource issues associated with the broader objectives of attaining urban sustainability. Indeed, this geographical focus on the urban core represents an important countervailing pressure to addressing the negative impacts of suburban sprawl and outmigration (Hoyt, 2005). Critically, BIDs are also influenced by contemporary attempts to better integrate and "join up" public service delivery as part of a wider commitment to modernize service provision and realign resource availability in submunicipal governance.

Finally, the themes of transparency and accountability in governance are fundamental dimensions of the contemporary drive to reinvigorate civic engagement and civil democracy, with a particular emphasis on redefining local leadership (Department of the Environment, Transport and the Regions, 2000a). From this perspective, it is important to note that in Britain, the arrangements for BIDs are subject to a formal ballot, would operate within defined local authority boundaries and in conformity with precise parameters articulated through service level agreements, and are to be legitimated through specific legislative and financial provisions. BIDs therefore represent a deliberate rearticulation of state-market-civil relations and a new contractualism with respect to public service provision in defined jurisdictions.

References

Adair, A., Berry, J., McGreal, A., and Quinn, A. 2002. *Factors affecting the level and form of private investment in regeneration.* Report to the Office of the Deputy Prime Minister. Belfast, UK: University of Ulster.

Adams, D., Disberry, A., Hutchinson, N., and Munjoma, T. 1999. *Do landowners constrain urban redevelopment?* Aberdeen, UK: University of Aberdeen.

Allmendinger, P., Tewdwr-Jones, M., and Morphet, J. 2003. Public scrutiny, standards and the planning system: Assessing professional values within a modernised local government. *Public Administration* 81:761–780.

Amin, A., and Thrift, N. 1995. Globalisation, institutional "thickness" and the local economy. In *Managing cities: The New Urban context,* ed. P. Healey, S. Cameron, S. Davoudi, S. Graham, and A. Mandanipour, 1–91. Chichester, UK: Wiley.

Arculus Report. 2005. *Better regulation Task Force Final Report, Department of Trade and Industry.* London: Author.

Association of London Government. 2005. *Local authority guide to business improvement districts.* London: Author.

Association of Town Center Management. 1994. *The effectiveness of TCM.* London: Donaldsons and Healey and Baker.

Association of Town Center Management. 1996. *Setting the scene, about town: Balancing the issues of town center management.* London: Author.

Association of Town Center Management. 1998. *Getting it right: A good practice guide to successful TCM initiatives.* London: Author.

Association of Town Center Management. 2000. *Liveability.* London: Author.

Bailey, N., Barker, A., and MacDonald, K. 1995. *Partnership agencies in British urban policy.* London: UCL Press.

Balchin, P. N., Bull, G. H., and Kieve, J. L. 1995. *Urban land economics and public policy.* 5th ed. Basingstoke, UK: Macmillan.

Balchin, P. N., and Kieve, J. L. 1985. *Urban land economics.* 3rd ed. Basingstoke, UK: Macmillan.

Beddington, N. 1991. *Shopping centres: Retail development, design and management.* London: Butterworth.

Blackmar, E. 2006. Appropriating "the Commons": The tragedy of property rights discourse. In *The politics of public space,* ed. S. Low, and N. Smith, 49–80. London: Routledge.

Boots. 1994. *Caring for our towns and cities: A definitive manual documenting the key issues which contribute to the vitality and viability of our town and city centers.* London: Civic Trust Regeneration Unit.

Boots. 1996. *TCM: How to get started, A "tool kit."* Nottingham: Author.

Borja, J., and Castells, M. 1996. *Local and global: Management of cities in the information age.* London: Earthscan.

British Property Federation. 1995. *TCM: A policy initiative.* London: Author.

Central London Partnership. 2000. *Study trip to New York. 27–30 June 2000. Summary Document.* London: Author.

Central London Partnership. 2001. *The circle initiative.* London: Author.

Central London Partnership. 2006. *Thirty nine steps to developing a business improvement district.* London: Author.

Civic Trust Regeneration Unit. 1994. *Liveable towns and cities.* Consultation document, prepared by the European Institute for Urban Affairs, Liverpool, UK. Liverpool: John Moores University.

Cochrane, A. 1999. Just another failed urban experiment? The legacy of the urban development corporations. In *British urban policy: An evaluation of the urban development corporations,* ed., R. Imrie and H. Thomas, 246–58. London: Sage.

Cooke, P., and Morgan, K. 1998. *The associational economy.* Oxford: Oxford University Press.

Davies, H. T. O., Nutley, S. M., and Smith, P. C. 1999. What works? The role of evidence in public sector policy and practice. *Public Money and Management,* January–March, pp. 3–5.

Department of the Environment. 1992. *The effects of major out of town retail development.* London: BDP Planning and the Oxford Institute of Retail Management; HMSO.

Department of the Environment. 1994. *Vital and viable town centers: Meeting the challenge.* London: HMSO.

Department of the Environment. 1996. *Planning policy guidance note 6: Town centers and retail developments*. London: HMSO.

Department of the Environment, Transport and the Regions. 2000a. *Our towns and cities: The future delivering an urban renaissance*. London: HMSO.

Department of the Environment, Transport and the Regions. 2000b. *The state of English cities*. London: HMSO.

Evans, R. 1997. *Regenerating town centers*. Manchester, UK: Manchester University Press.

Evans, B., and Bate, R. 2000. *A taxing question: The contribution of economic instruments to planning objectives*. London: Town and Country Planning Association.

Forsberg, H., Medway, D., and Warnaby, G. 1999. Town center management by co-operation. *Cities* 16:315–322.

Friedmann, J. 1999. The new political economy of planning: The rise of civil society. In *Cities for citizens*, ed. M. Douglass and J. Friedmann, 19–38. Chichester, UK: Wiley.

Fulford, C. 1998. *Urban housing capacity and the sustainable city: The costs of reclaiming derelict sites*. London: Town and Country Planning Association.

Giddens, A. 1998. *The third way: The renewal of social democracy*. Oxford: Policy Press.

Grayson, L., and Young, K. 1994. *Quality of life in cities: An overview and guide to the literature*. London: British Library in association with London Research Center.

Hajer, M., and Reijndorp, A. 2002. *In search of the new public domain*. Rotterdam: Netherlands Architecture Institute.

Hall, P. 1998. *Cities in civilization*. London: Phoenix Giant.

Hambleton, R. 1988. Policy planning reconsidered. *The Planner* 74(11):12–15.

Hampton Report. 2004. *Reducing administrative burdens: Effective inspection and enforcement*. London: HM Treasury.

Healey, P. 1991. Urban regeneration and the development industry. *Regional Studies* 25:97–108.

Healey, P., Cameron, S., Davoudi, S., Graham, S., and Mandanipour, A., eds. 1995. *Managing cities: The new urban context*. Chichester, UK: Wiley.

Hill, D. M. 1994. *Citizens and cities*. London: Simon & Schuster.

Hoyt, L. 2004. Collecting private funds for safer public spaces: An empirical examination of the business improvement district concept. *Environment and Planning B* 31:367–380.

Hoyt, L. 2005. Planning through compulsory commercial clubs: Business improvement districts. *Economic Affairs* 25:24–27.

Imrie, R., and Thomas, H. 1999. Assessing urban policy and the urban development corporations. In *British urban policy: An evaluation of the urban development corporations*, ed. R. Imrie and H. Thomas, 3–40. London: Sage.

Jones, P., Hillier, D., and Comfort, D. 2003. Business improvement districts in town and city centers in the UK. *Management Research News* 26:50–59.

Larkham, P. J. 2004. Rise of the "civic center" in English urban form and design. *Urban Design International* 9:3–15.

Lawless, P. 1994. Partnership in urban regeneration in the UK: The Sheffield Central Area Study. *Urban Studies* 31:1303–1324.

Lloyd, M. G., McCarthy, J., McGreal, S., and Berry, J. 2003. Business improvement districts, planning and urban regeneration. *International Planning Studies* 8:295–322.

Lloyd, M. G., and Peel, D. 2006. *The public realm, knowledge transfer and learning around business improvement districts*. Paper presented at Public Administration Committee Annual Conference, Durham, UK, September 4–6.

Lynch, K. 1960. *The image of the city*. Cambridge, MA: MIT Press.

Magalhães, C. D., and Carmona, M. 2006. Innovations in the management of public space: Reshaping and refocusing governance. *Planning Theory and Practice* 7:289–303.

Mandanipour, A. 2003. *Public and private spaces of the city*. London: Routledge.

Martin, P. G. 1982. *Shopping center management*. London: Spon Press.

Massey, D. 2005. *For space*. London: Sage.

McCabe, T. 2006, October 24. Business improvement districts. Press release. Minister for Finance and Public Service Reform, Scottish Parliament.

McGreal, S., Berry, J., Lloyd, M. G., and McCarthy, J. 2002. Tax-based mechanisms in urban regeneration: Dublin and Chicago models. *Urban Studies* 39:1819–1831.

Medway, D., Alexander, A., Bennison, D., and Warnaby, G. 1999. Retailers' financial support for town center management. *International Journal of Retail and Distribution Management* 27:246–255.

Mitchell, D., and Staeheli, L. A. 2006. Clean and safe? Property redevelopment, public space, and homelessness in downtown San Diego. In *The politics of public space*, ed. S. Low and N. Smith, 143–176. London: Routledge.

Mullen, F. 2006. *Planning etc. (Scotland) bill: Business improvement districts*. SPICe Briefing 06.14. Edinburgh: Scottish Parliament Information Center.

Mumford, L. 1963. *The city in history: Its origins, its transformations, and its prospects*. London: Secker and Warburg.

Nadin, V., and Doak, J. 1991. *Town planning responses to city change*. Aldershot, UK: Avebury.

Nasar, J. L. 1998. *The evaluative image of the city*. London: Sage Publications.

Needham, B. 2006. *Planning, law and economics: The rules we make for using land*. London: Routledge and the RTPI.

Nuttall, N., and Hornsby, M. 1995. High streets doomed report claims. The *Times*, November 1.

Pal, J., and Sanders, E. 1997. Measuring the effectiveness of town center management schemes: An exploratory framework. *International Journal of Retail and Distribution Management* 25:70–77.

Peel, D. 2003. Town center management: Multi-stakeholder evaluation—increasing the sensitivity of paradigm choice. *Planning Theory and Practice* 4:147–164.

Peel, D., and Lloyd, M. G. 2005. A case for business improvement districts in Scotland: Policy transfer in practice? *Planning, Practice and Research* 20:89–95.

Reeve, A. 1996. The private realm of the managed town center. *Urban Design International* 1:61–80.

Roberts, J., and Freedman, C. 1996. BCSC predicts town center strife. *Estates Gazette*, November 16, p. 51.

Roberts, M., and Turner, C. 2005. Conflicts of liveability in the 24-hour city: Learning from 48 hours in the life of London's Soho. *Journal of Urban Design* 10:171–193.

Roberts, M., Turner, C., Greenfield, S., and Osborn, G. 2006. A continental ambience? Lessons in managing alcohol related evening and night-time entertainment from four European capitals. *Urban Studies* 43:1105–1125.

Robson, B. 1988. *Those inner cities*. Oxford: Clarendon.

Rose, R. 1991. *Lesson-drawing in public policy: A guide to learning across time and space*. Chatham, NJ: Chatham House.

Rydin, Y. 2003. *Urban and environmental planning in the UK*. Hampshire, UK: Palgrave Macmillan.

Schiller, R. 1986. Retail decentralisation: The coming of the third wave. *The Planner* 72:13–15.

Schoon, N. 2001. *The chosen city*. London: Spon Press.

Scottish Executive. 2003. *Business improvement districts*. A consultation paper. Edinburgh: Author.

Shields, R. 1992. *Lifestyle shopping: The subject of consumption*. London: Routledge.

Smith, N., and Low, S. 2006. The imperative of public space. In *The politics of public space*, ed. S. Low and N. Smith, 1–16. London: Routledge.

Spridell, P. H. 1980. *Retailing: Town centers in the 1980s*. Reading, UK: Unit for Retail Planning Information.

Steel, M., and Symes, M. 2005. The privatisation of public space? The American experience of business improvement districts and their relationship to local governance. *Local Government Studies* 31:321–334.

Stoker, G. 1995. Regime theory and urban politics. In *Theories of urban politics*, ed. D. Judge, G. Stoker, and H. Wolman, 54–71. London: Sage.

Sullivan, H., and Skelcher, C. 2002. *Working across boundaries: Collaboration in public services*. Basingstoke, UK: Macmillan.

Tibbald, F. 1992. *Making people-friendly towns: Improving the public environment in towns and cities*. Harlow, UK: Longman.

Tiesdell, S., and Slater, A. M. 2006. Calling time: Managing activities in space and time in the evening/night-time economy. *Planning Theory and Practice* 7:137–157.

Tomalin, C. 1997. Town center health checks: Some developments from practice. *Planning Practice and Research* 1294:383–392.

Travers, T., and Weimar, J. 1996. *Business improvement districts: New York and London*. London: The Greater London Group, London School of Economics and Political Science.

UK BIDs. 2003. *Talking BIDs*, 1. Newsletter. London: Association of Town Center Management.

UK BIDs. 2004a. *Talking BIDs*, 2. Newsletter. London: Association of Town Center Management.

UK BIDs. 2004b. *Talking BIDs*, 3. Newsletter. London: Association of Town Center Management.

Urban Task Force. 1999. *Towards an urban renaissance*. Final report of the Urban Task Force Chaired by Lord Rogers of Riverside. London: Department of the Environment, Transport and the Regions.

URBED. 1997. *Town center partnerships: Their role, organisation and resources*. London: Author.

Ward, K. 2006. "Policies in motion," urban management and state restructuring: The trans-local expansion of business improvement districts. *International Journal of Urban and Regional Research* 30:54–75.

Warman, C. 1995. Who can sell the high street? *The Times*, August 23, p. 33.

Webster, C., and Lai, L. W.-C. 2003. *Property rights, planning and markets: Managing spontaneous cities*. Cheltenham, UK: Edward Elgar.

Wells, I. 1990. *TCM: A future for the high street?* Geographical Paper 109. Reading, UK: University of Reading.

Woolley, H., Dunn, J., and Rowley, G. 1996. *Breaking the downward spiral: Current and future responses of children to their town centers*. Sheffield, UK: University of Sheffield.

Worpole, K. 1992. *Towns for people*. Buckingham, UK: Open University Press.

Worpole, K., and Greenhalgh, L. 1999. *The richness of cities: Urban policy in a new landscape*. Final report. London: Comedia in association with Demos.

Zukin, S. 1995. *The culture of cities*. Oxford: Blackwell.

Chapter 5

BIDs Farewell:
The Democratic
Accountability of Business
Improvement Districts

Brian R. Hochleutner

Contents

Introduction

A new form of sublocal governmental body, the business improvement district (BID), is changing the way America governs its shopping districts, commercial areas, and downtowns. More than 40 states have statutes allowing for the formation of BIDs, and there are already more than a 1,000 throughout the United States (Mitchell, 1999). A BID is a territorial subdivision within a municipality in which property or business owners pay a district-specific tax to fund district-specific services (e.g., sanitation, policing, social services, infrastructure improvements, and marketing) that supplement the services already provided by local government (Briffault, 1999, pp. 368–369). The BID model of sublocal governance is a unique mixture of public and private: public funds generated by district-only taxes are channeled into the hands of private entities that manage district affairs (Briffault, 1999, p. 366).

State statutes, local ordinances, and individual district contracts take different approaches to even basic questions about BID formation, control, financing, and functions, but some generalizations can be made (Briffault, 1999, p. 366). BID formation is generally governed by statutes that require local government and property owners to approve the district; BIDs are usually managed by a public or private BID board that advises, or is advised by, local government officials; BIDs are financed primarily by assessments on local property; and BID activities tend to focus on the delivery of traditional municipal services, such as providing street and sidewalk maintenance and security in the district (Briffault, 1999, p. 366).

The BID model is popular largely because it works (Mac Donald, 1996, p. 29). More nimble than traditional city bureaucracies, BIDs have improved conditions within their borders, particularly in terms of increased business activity. According to their backers, BIDs are more effective and efficient than traditional models of local governance, and because of their success, BIDs have become *the* means for revitalizing America's downtowns (Vitullo-Martin, 1998, p. A14). Despite the praise, however, the *quid pro quo* implicit in the BID model—payment of additional taxes in exchange for extra services and (more critically) a degree of control by local property owners—has been attacked by critics and challenged in the courts (Briffault, 1999, p. 455).

The most serious legal challenge to the BID model's quid pro quo essentially was based on the charge that BIDs were so undemocratic as to be unconstitutional.

In *Kessler v. Grand Central District Management Association* (1998), residents of a Manhattan BID sued the BID's corporate management entity. The residents argued that the BID's method of electing BID board members (giving property owners majority control) violated the constitutional one person–one vote principle, a doctrine derived from the Equal Protection Clause that generally prohibits allowing nonresident property or business owners to vote in local elections. The U.S. Court of Appeals for the Second Circuit rejected the residents' claim, holding that BIDs are exempt from the one person–one vote doctrine because they exist for a special limited purpose, have a disproportionate impact on property owners, and have "no primary responsibilities or general powers typical of a [general purpose] governmental entity" (*Kessler*, 1998).

The *Kessler* (1998) litigation represents part of a lively debate about BIDs and the one person–one vote doctrine (see, for example, Barr, 1997; Briffault, 1999)—a debate that this chapter will not rehash. Instead, this chapter will focus on a related, but distinct, issue: the democratic accountability of BID officials and whether they are accountable to BID stakeholders in proportion to the extent to which those stakeholders are impacted by BID activities. The chapter is divided into three sections. The first section provides an overview of the BID model, describing how BIDs are formed and funded, what they do, and how they are governed. The second section examines who BID officials are accountable to and for, identifying three categories of stakeholders impacted by BID activities—property and business owners, BID residents, and city residents—and arguing that BID accountability should be measured in relation to these groups and the degree to which BID activities impact them. The third section looks at the BID model and how it makes BID officials accountable, arguing that BID officials are (properly) most accountable to property and business owners—who are most impacted by BID activities—but that the BID model also includes safeguards to ensure that the interests of BID and city residents are not disregarded.

Overview of the BID Model

Specific schemes for BID formation vary from jurisdiction to jurisdiction. The framework for BID formation is usually set out in a BID enabling statute enacted by the state legislature (Houstoun, 1997, pp. 24–25). The majority of these statutes establish a two-step process through which a BID's proponents must show local support: (1) district property or business owners must vote for formation, and (2) local elected officials must enact an ordinance that formally creates the BID and determines its powers and boundaries (Briffault, 1999, pp. 378–379). Typically, both of these steps involve numerous public hearings and other opportunities for community debate, helping to ensure the existence of significant local backing or at least the lack of significant opposition.

After a BID has been created, revenues normally are generated through a special assessment on district property (Mitchell, 1999, pp. 17–18). Assessments usually are collected along with other local property taxes by local government officials and are then remitted to the BID's governing body (Houstoun, 1997, p. 36). Some jurisdictions place a limit on BID assessments keyed to property taxes or assessed valuation of land. Even in jurisdictions without such limits, "assessments are effectively capped by the need to win the support of those who have to pay the assessments" (Briffault, 1999, p. 390), just as local property taxes are functionally capped by the desire of local politicians to get reelected.

The assessment imposed upon a particular property may be calculated according to many possible formulas, taking into account factors such as the property's size, frontage, assessed value, and use ("Cities within Cities," 1995, pp. 8–10). As one might expect, assessments range considerably. Assessment formulas generally are designed to impose the heaviest burden for financing a BID upon commercial property owners, the group that is likely to receive the most tangible benefit from increases in local business ("Managing the Micropolis," 1997). In fact, residential property owners often pay only nominal amounts, and nonprofit corporations and governmental entities rarely pay anything ("Cities within Cities," 1995, p. 9).

The funds raised through BID assessments generally are dedicated to BID activities. These activities vary significantly, even among BIDs in the same locality, and annual expenditures can range from a few thousand dollars to many millions per year (Mitchell, 1999, p. 17). Still, there are four types of core BID activities: (1) the provision of traditional municipal services to supplement the services provided by the local government (particularly sanitation and security), (2) the construction of capital improvements, (3) the marketing and promotion of district businesses, and (4) the provision of social welfare services (Mitchell, 1999, pp. 20–21).* In addition to these core activities, BIDs also often act as informal advocates for the interests of their members, using the BID's relationship with city hall to lobby for legislation, regulation, or other action (or inaction) favorable to the interests of the BID's constituents (Martin, 1995, p. B3). Just who these constituents are will be discussed in the next section.

Schemes of BID governance differ significantly from locality to locality, as well as from BID to BID within localities. Nonetheless, the management scheme for most BIDs includes some division of power between district property or business owners and officials elected by local residents (Briffault, 1999, p. 409). While a significant minority of BIDs are managed directly by governmental bodies or by public nonprofit partnerships, the majority are operated by nonprofit corporations under the supervision of local government (Mitchell, 1999, p. 17). In these BIDs, formal decision-making authority rests with the BID management corporation's board of directors, often known as the BID board. While most BID boards are

---

* See the Morçöl and Zimmermann (Chapter 2) and Gopal-Agge and Hoyt (Chapter 7) chapters in this volume for further discussion of the types of BID activities/functions.

appointed, many states provide for the election of board members (Briffault, 1999, p. 413). In these elections, there are often several different classes of voters (i.e., business or property owners, local residents, and nonresidents), but the groups responsible for funding the BID (whether property or business owners) generally are given weighted voting power so that those most directly burdened by BID assessments get the most say over BID governance (Briffault, 1999, p. 413).

The BID board usually appoints a BID manager or executive to oversee day-to-day operations. While a significant amount of day-to-day decision-making power is exercised by BID staff in general and by the BID manager or executive in particular, the board is officially the principal decision maker in a BID's management structure, just as a corporate board of directors is in a more conventional nonprofit company (Briffault, 1999, pp. 413–414). The responsiveness of the BID board to the BID's various stakeholders or constituents will be the focus of the third section of this chapter, but first those stakeholders are defined in the next section.

BID Accountability Defined: How Much and to Whom?

Accountability is difficult to define precisely (Behn, 2001). In the context of local government, it is related to responsiveness and concerns the degree to which officials must report to—and be punished or rewarded for their actions by—their constituents. Making public officials accountable to their constituents helps improve the chances that the officials will act in ways that benefit those constituents. There is, however, no agreed-upon standard by which to measure the accountability of BID officials (or any governmental officials for that matter), and different people would probably choose to hold BID officials accountable for different things (Behn, 2001, p. 10). This section examines the scope of the BID accountability problem and to whom BID officials should be accountable.

Scope of the BID Accountability Problem

Accountability is not an all-or-nothing concept, and BID accountability concerns are diminished by both the relatively small size of BIDs, which limits the number of BID stakeholders, and the limited scope of BID power. These characteristics work to protect the interests of all potential BID stakeholders and make it more difficult for BID officials to abuse public power (Behn, 2001, p. 6).

Because the discretion of BID officials is constrained ex ante by limitations on BID power, the need for ex post accountability is diminished (Wheatley, 1997, p. 63). BIDs are created to serve a public purpose—improving business and enhancing the condition of commercial areas—that is chosen by elected legislatures, not by BID officials or any particular group of BID stakeholders. BID officials are empowered ex ante by specific limited grants of authority found in state statutes and local ordinances that restrict BID power to improving the quantity and quality of commercial activity within the district. These powers are further curtailed by limitations imposed as part of management contracts between those who run the BID and local officials. The officials who grant BIDs their limited power to promote local business and economic development can also, as per Dillon's rule, take that power away. Even within the limited sphere of business improvement, BIDs are not sovereigns. In sum, less BID power means BID officials make fewer choices about fewer things; this means that BID officials need not be as accountable as more traditional public officials (*Kessler*, 1998).

To the extent that BIDs do exercise governmental power, their small size limits the number of the BID's constituents (again, ex ante) and makes it easier for those constituents to monitor BID activities, measure BID performance, and respond when BID officials act improperly. A BID's reduced stakeholder pool will likely mean less diverse stakeholder views about the choices that BID officials do make. In a larger, general-purpose government, it is often difficult to hold elected representatives accountable because voters can cast only one vote for only one candidate in a given election. Thus, a representative may take actions that deviate from stakeholder preferences on isolated occasions with relative impunity, knowing that it is unlikely that voters will punish her as long as she acts in concert with constituent preferences on most other occasions. Because BID officials exercise narrow power over relatively few stakeholders, their actions are more likely to be monitored, making it less likely that these officials will act contrary to their constituents' preferences. Thus, each stakeholder's inquiry is simplified because there are relatively few things to monitor, and a BID official's inquiry is simplified because the constituency is small and likely to be relatively homogeneous in its desire for enhanced district services.

Smaller BIDs with fewer stakeholders mean that each stakeholder also has a greater opportunity to participate in BID affairs personally, increasing the chance that she will be enriched by taking part in the democratic process. Active participation by constituents should facilitate accountability by increasing awareness of the BID officials (Houstoun, 1997, p. 103). In large, general-purpose governments, stakeholders rarely have an incentive or opportunity to become personally involved in government; similarly, officials generally have little incentive or opportunity to care about the kinds of uniquely local issues that tend to be the focus of BID activities (Briffault, 1997). The BID model involves a subdivision of local government into more local jurisdictional units, each of which creates opportunities for individual participation in governance. While a BID is not a full-fledged government and can hardly be called a comprehensive decentralization of government decision making, it does represent "a departure from the traditional centralized big city" (Briffault, 1997, p. 508).

Accountability concerns are also diminished insofar as small, decentralized units of local government promote competition between different neighborhoods and different public officials responsible for those neighborhoods (Wheatley, 1997, p. 63). It would not be efficient for residents, property owners, or business managers to "vote with their feet" every time a BID official does something they dislike, but the price of district real estate should reflect preferences for living in, working in, and owning land in the district (Tiebout, 1956, pp. 421–422).

While BIDs' small size and limited powers constrain BID officials and empower stakeholders to reduce accountability problems generally, these characteristics do not wholly solve such problems. BID critics continue to argue that BIDs represent an attempt by city governments to delegate responsibility for (and control over) public spaces to the private sector and that BIDs "have grown too powerful and too self-serving, and have assumed municipal duties without adequate oversight or accountability" (Gabriel, 1997, p. 19). In other words, the small size and limited scope of BIDs notwithstanding, concern that BID officials need to be held more accountable remains ("Managing the Micropolis," 1997, pp. 3–4).

To Whom Should BIDs Be Accountable?

Before it is possible to determine whether BID officials are sufficiently accountable, a basic question must be answered: accountable *to whom*? Answering this question will help define a BID's constituents and establish a set of expectations with which to evaluate BID accountability mechanisms. The identification of specific stakeholder groups is necessary because BID accountability cannot mean simultaneous and equal fidelity to everyone all the time. Every unhappy stakeholder does not equal an accountability failure, because a BID official's decision to do something that one or more stakeholders dislike might amount to nothing more than a case of democracy (or accountability) at work. Actions by BID officials, like those of more traditional public officials, produce winners and losers, even when the official does the right thing or acts in the relevant public's interest (Briffault, 1999, p. 457).

Accountability, Residency, and One Person–One Vote

Because BIDs are special-purpose governmental bodies dedicated to the improvement of a district's *business*, BIDs cannot be accountable solely to local residents. Normally, because the reapportionment revolution of the 1960s, local government officials are held accountable through an electoral system in which the only fully legitimate basis for political representation has been residential population and the one person–one vote rule (Briffault, 1993). This traditional accountability scheme is not constitutionally required for BIDs, lifting what would otherwise be inflexible restrictions on the groups to which BID officials could be made accountable.

One of the virtues of the one person–one vote rule, however, is its arithmetic simplicity (each person who resides in the relevant area gets an equal vote) and the ease with which it can be applied (Ely, 1980; *Wit v. Berman*, 2002). Once it is not required, determining to whom public officials should be accountable and designing a system that seems fair becomes quite difficult. The danger of perceived unfairness is amplified in the BID context: because BIDs are created for the single purpose of improving business, it is important for BID officials to be accountable to local business interests, or rather, to the *people* responsible for local businesses.

Once it is recognized that a governmental body dedicated to business improvement should be directly accountable to representatives of local business, the plain vanilla one person–one vote residency-only system proves to be an inefficient and arbitrary way of holding BID officials accountable. This is largely because of a BID's characteristic features, discussed above, of small size and limited scope. With small size comes increasingly arbitrary distinctions between residency and nonresidency—as a district gets smaller (BIDs as small as one block have been formed), the relationship between residency and interest in the outcome of a district election breaks down—and an increasing percentage of those impacted by the government are likely to be nonresidents. Further, the wholesale exclusion of all nonresidents from any election, while perhaps desirable in other contexts, is indefensible when the officials being elected have a mandate that is limited (by officials elected by residents) to improving business (*Kessler*, 1998). Obviously, local business leaders are better positioned to hold BID officials accountable for fulfilling this mandate than are residents. A purely residence-based voting or accountability system is desirable for larger, general-purpose governments and might be desirable for a small district not devoted to business improvement, but it makes little sense for a BID.

Accountability Unrestrained by Residency and One Person–One Vote

In the absence of a one person–one vote residents-only rule, the BID model, to be fair and legitimate, must be faithful to the principle that democracy requires government by "consent of the governed." Under this premise, to the extent that BIDs do actually govern, BID officials must be made accountable or responsive to (so as to govern at the implied consent of) those they govern. Put somewhat differently, to the extent that BID activities are governmental activities, and to the extent that BID activities affect a BID's stakeholders, BID officials should be made accountable to those stakeholders.

Including nonresidents in a BID accountability scheme, however, has created a problem: it is necessary to decide how to make BID officials accountable to both residents and nonresidents, and therefore how to compare apples (residents) to oranges (nonresidents). Implicit in the premise of "consent of the governed" is that the need for consent is relative to whether (and thus to what extent) a person is governed. While equal protection and fairness principles require that all residents be treated equally, they do not require that every resident be treated like every nonresident. Instead, principles of fairness suggest that BID officials be made most accountable or responsive to the stakeholder group with the most at stake, and less accountable or responsive to other groups. This approach—making the accountability of public officials to their constituents proportional to the interests those constituents have in governmental decision making—has also been defended on utilitarian grounds, in that it would tend to further the public's aggregated best interests (Downs, 1961).

Measuring who is affected by a BID's (or any government's) activities is not easy, and this accountability calculus becomes even more complicated once it is recognized that a failure to take action can have just as much effect as official action itself. Of course, if it were possible to measure the impact of BID activity (or inactivity) on every potential BID stakeholder, and if it were also possible to devise a voting system that gave each person impacted by BID actions (or inactions) a vote that was exactly proportional to the impact, it would be easy to make BID officials proportionately accountable to the various sets of stakeholders. Because this is impossible, the best that can be attempted is to make BID officials accountable to those stakeholders who are most likely to be impacted by BID activities, to the extent that these stakeholders can be readily identified.

Identifying Likely BID Stakeholders

Professor Richard Briffault, author of the most exhaustive legal analysis of BIDs to date, has suggested three primary groups on which to judge BID accountability: (1) the local property or business owners subject to BID assessments (owners), (2) residents of the BID (BID residents), and (3) residents of the municipality (city residents) (Briffault, 1999). Although this list is not exhaustive or perfect, it does provide a starting point for an inquiry into BID accountability for two reasons: first, as discussed below, these three groups include the vast majority of BID stakeholders, and second, as discussed above, this does not seek to take on the impossible task of analyzing BID accountability in relation to every possible BID stakeholder; rather, it seeks to examine whether BID officials are adequately accountable to a BID's most likely or important stakeholders.

For reasons that should be clear by now, a BID's likely impact on owners is obvious and easily measured in clear monetary terms (Houstoun, 1997, p. 103; *City of Seattle v. Rogers Clothing for Men, Inc.*, 1990). Owners pay for day-to-day BID activities by funding BID assessments, and a BID's power to assess is the most governmental or coercive of its powers because an owner cannot opt out of paying the assessment. While owners are burdened by BIDs, owners also benefit from BID activities: improvement in local business is likely to lead to increases in local property and business values.

The likelihood of BID activities impacting BID residents is also high, although the impacts on these residents are not easily measured in monetary terms (Garodnick, 2000, pp. 1763–1765). BID activities begin with the basic task of keeping the streets clean, and it is difficult to dispute that the lives of BID residents are likely to be impacted by cleaner streets (Houstoun, 1997, p. 105). BID residents are not, however, likely to be burdened in any real way by having to fund BID activities because (at least in most BIDs) residential properties are exempt from assessments. Because they are likely to be directly benefited, but unlikely to be directly burdened, the accountability concerns implicated by BID residents are significantly less than those implicated by owners.

Finally, BID activity certainly impacts many city residents, although the effects are again likely to be less direct or significant than those felt by owners. City residents, like BID residents but unlike owners, are not likely to be burdened by BID activities because they are not forced to pay assessments. The impact of BID activities on city residents differs largely in degree, rather than in kind, from the impact on BID residents. Neither group is likely to be directly burdened, but both are likely to include people that benefit from BID activity insofar as they spend a significant amount of time traversing the sidewalks of the BID. Obviously, as a group, city residents are somewhat less likely than BID residents to be impacted by BID activities; nevertheless, BIDs are often located in central business districts that serve as regional hubs for commercial activity, and thus it is likely that many city residents will be impacted by BID activities. There is overlap—every BID resident is also a city resident—but because every BID resident spends time living in the BID and many city residents live far away and may not visit the BID at all, city residents are (as a group) affected less by BID activities than BID residents.

Obviously, one could think of other groups that might be impacted by BID activities. Some of these groups are extremely difficult or impossible to define with any certainty, and most groups have interests that largely overlap with those of owners, BID residents, city residents, or some combination thereof (Houstoun, 1997, p. 106). Rather than engage in anything approaching a comprehensive review of the particular groups potentially affected by BIDs and examining how each can or cannot hold BID officials accountable, this chapter addresses the general question of BID accountability, acknowledging that local variations in stakeholders and BID structures will have to be examined more closely on a case-by-case basis. In any event, the inclusion of city residents as a group ensures that the interests of a broad range of stakeholders will be considered in the analysis of BID accountability.

Accountability Mechanisms and the BID Model

This section examines the ways in which BIDs and BID officials are made accountable to each of the three stakeholder groups identified in the previous section—owners, BID residents, and city residents (collectively "residents"). The first subsection here examines BID accountability to owners, a BID's most important stakeholder group. The second subsection examines BID accountability to BID residents and city residents. These two groups are examined together to avoid unnecessary repetition because their interests are similar and because the mechanisms through which

BIDs and BID officials are made accountable to these two groups of stakeholders are generally the same.

BID Accountability to Owners

BID Formation Procedures

Accountability to owners begins before a BID is created, and owners generally have the greatest voice in BID formation ("Managing the Micropolis," 1997, pp. 7–8). BIDs are born pursuant to a "district plan," which is drafted by a sponsoring organization to provide the basic blueprint for the BID. A district plan is akin to a BID's constitution, but it is also analogous to a corporation's charter, bylaws, and business plan (Manshel, 1995). Local property owners generally form the nucleus of the entrepreneurial group that drafts the plan, and most states allow for and anticipate that the basic framework of the BID, including specific boundaries, assessment rates, and the mix of services to be provided, will be determined preliminarily by owners (Houstoun, 1997, pp. 39–41).

In addition to their input into the district plan, owners also generally have the power to defeat BID formation: after development of the plan and before the local legislature can vote on BID formation, a sponsoring organization usually needs to demonstrate support from owners. BID statutes generally have strict notice requirements to ensure that owners are fully informed, and some states require that formation be approved by a supermajority of owners.

Owners are not always in agreement as to the need for a BID, and a BID proposal can prompt heated debates not only about whether a BID is needed, but also about the appropriate level of services to be provided and the assessment to be levied (Briffault, 1999, p. 384). For this reason, boundaries of the proposed BID are often drawn to include, to the extent possible, only those properties with similar interests and concerns.

In sum, BID formation procedures consist of a series of practical safeguards to ensure not only that owners support the idea of BID formation, but that they have input into the delineation of district boundaries and the determination of the level of services provided by the BID. While these safeguards do not ensure that there will be unanimity on any given issue, they are designed to encourage consensus building generally.

BID Corporate Governance and Oversight by Local Public Officials

In BIDs that are managed by private nonprofit corporations, once the BID is formed, BID officials are held accountable to owners through the corporate governance mechanisms of the BID, under which owners vote in periodic elections to select members of the BID board. Whether formally invested with power or labeled "advisory," BID boards can exercise considerable influence over all but the most trivial of decisions affecting BID governance. State law often guarantees owners a weighted or even controlling interest. For BIDs in which the BID board has been formally invested with power and where owners exercise exclusive or enhanced voting rights, BID governance is analogous to governance of a for-profit corporation, with owners likely to act very much like shareholders would—i.e., trying to maximize their profit.

The success of the various mechanisms of BID corporate governance in practice, of course, will depend on a variety of factors, many of them relating to the willingness of local officials to police the BID board's actions (Briffault, 1999, p. 460). There have been few examinations of the operation of BID corporate governance in practice. Several recent audits conducted by the New York City Comptroller's Office of a range of different BIDs in New York, however, suggest that BID boards, when supervised by local public officials, are accountable to owners. Of the three BID audits completed in 2002, two were overwhelmingly favorable: audits of the Lower Eastside and Columbus/Amsterdam BIDs showed that the BID boards had been governing in accordance with the wishes of local property and business owners. The third audit suggested a similar result had been achieved in the East Brooklyn Industrial Park BID, but only after an earlier audit had turned up problems and BID officials implemented reforms to improve corporate governance and to successfully address concerns voiced by BID owners. The inconclusiveness of any audits of particular BIDs notwithstanding, even BID critics have acknowledged the success of BIDs in responding to the needs of the local business community (Barr, 1997, p. 396).

Accountability to BID and City Residents

This subsection shows how BIDs are proportionally accountable to residents. While it addresses BID accountability to both BID residents and city residents and largely treats the two groups together (BID residents are, after all, also city residents), it does differentiate where appropriate.

BID Formation Procedures

While residents have less input than owners into the formation of a BID, the procedures governing BID formation do provide safeguards to residents' interests ("Cities within Cities," 1995, pp. 7–10). As opposed to property owners, residents—and even commercial tenants in BIDs financed by property taxes—usually have little or no direct formal role in the BID formation process. Still, residents can voice their concerns during the crucial consensus-building stage of BID formulation, which generally takes many months and involves extensive public outreach by the BID's sponsors. Both formal public hearings and informal outreach must take place to ensure a high level of support for the BID (or alternatively to provide notice to those opposed to BID formation), giving residents ample opportunity to voice their concerns. Due to their proximity if nothing else, BID residents are likely to have more input into these public hearings than city residents as a whole.

BID formation procedures also include a more formal safeguard to protect residents who want to fight, or influence, BID formation: even after extensive public review and the approval of local property owners or businesses, a BID plan cannot be implemented unless it is approved by the local elected legislative body. Thus, while the BID's plan is often initially drafted and in large part shaped by local business leaders, the final product must be approved by officials who are directly accountable to resident voters.

Once a BID is created, the involvement of local elected officials lessens but remains significant, as the intensive procedural safeguards associated with BID formation continue to act as a prerequisite to any significant change to the BID's structure (Briffault, 1999, pp. 458–461). After the intense public scrutiny associated with a BID's formation, a similar gauntlet must be run to alter the boundaries of an existing BID or to increase its capacity to issue debt. Action by the local legislature is also required before a BID can increase the maximum assessment imposed on BID properties.

BID Corporate Governance and Oversight by Local Public Officials

Typically, while BID boards are largely controlled by representatives of owners, seats are apportioned among various classes of stakeholders. The interests of residents are protected by these nonowner board members. BID corporate governance does not work in exactly the same way for BID residents and city residents; while the interests of both groups are typically safeguarded by the appointment of representatives of public officials to a BID board, BID residents generally have their own additional, nongovernmental representative on the board. While outnumbered by representatives of owners, the BID residents on the board are nonetheless able to represent their own interests to the BID's decision-making body. To the extent that the board respects these representatives' views, the board will be accountable and responsive to BID residents' interests. At least one commentator—a general counsel for several New York City BIDs—has stated that because BID board decisions "are almost always made by consensus, any one board member has leverage out of proportion to his or her one vote" (Manshel, 1995, p. 104).

The interests of both city residents and BID residents are also furthered by the presence of public officials on the BID board. These representatives, who often include both citywide officials and district-specific representatives, help to ensure that any interests unique to BID residents or city residents are considered. While outnumbered, the very presence of public officials (or their direct representatives) on BID boards helps to ensure that the interests of residents are protected;

because of their stature, elected officials may be given particular deference by other board members.

Further, representatives of owners on BID boards are unlikely to act in ways that are contrary to the interests of residents, for owners and residents frequently have common interests (Houstoun, 1997, p. 105). Because the qualities that make a neighborhood great for consumers, employees, employers, and visitors also tend to make a neighborhood a nice place to live, the self-interests of owners will only occasionally diverge from the interests of BID and city residents (Siegel, 1992, p. 37). Thus board members representing the owners might provide BID and city residents with a sort of virtual representation on BID boards, with the owners' representatives acting as proxies to represent the interests of residents.

The accountability or responsiveness of the BID board to residents depends somewhat (as it does for owners) on the degree to which local government officials supervise the board. Most BIDs have formal contracts with local government, and ongoing supervision by municipal government of the contract is another important means by which BIDs are held accountable to residents (Briffault, 1999, p. 456). Intensity of supervision in practice is not a certainty and may depend on the level of local confidence in the BID, but this supervision generally includes, for example, regular audits.

The results of one such audit, viewed in conjunction with the response of local elected officials to the auditor's findings, further support the view that BID corporate governance and local government oversight do make BID officials accountable to residents. In 1997, New York City's comptroller conducted an audit of the Grand Central Partnership BID (GCP), one of the most controversial BIDs in the country and the subject of the *Kessler* (1998) litigation. This audit found that the BID's internal controls "provided adequate accountability over funds" and that the BID had generally complied with applicable laws and regulations (*Kessler*, 1998, pp. 764–765). The GCP audit also identified several significant weaknesses in the BID board's supervision of the BID's president and employees, pointing in particular to the board's policy allowing for outside employment of BID employees and to its failure to review certain contracts. And while some aspects of the BID board's response were encouraging—the board agreed with many suggestions and immediately implemented new procedures to address some of the auditor's concerns—the BID took exception with other portions of the audit. More importantly, the source of many of the irregularities identified in the audit—the fact that the GCP's president, Daniel Biederman, and his top staff also ran two other large midtown BIDs, giving them abnormally outsized stature in relation to the GCP's board—remained (Mac Donald, 1996).

Ultimately, oversight by local public officials worked to eliminate this problem, in that the audit, combined with extensive press coverage of Biederman's power, led to a struggle between Biederman and New York City mayor Rudolph Giuliani for control of the GCP. Giuliani essentially held the BID hostage, using the mechanism of the BID's management contract to his advantage by refusing to renew the contract for another term—and withholding the assessments collected for the BID—until Biederman resigned ("This Was Not Rudy's Finest Hour," 1998, p. 70). After Biederman did step down as BID president, along with the BID's chairman, the remaining BID officials resigned rather than be ousted by the mayor's hand-picked replacement to run the GCP (Bagli, 1998, p. B5).

Although the local press was divided as to the propriety of Giuliani's actions, the episode illustrates how the BID model's various accountability mechanisms work together to make BID officials accountable. As the GCP grew more power-ful because of factors related less to the structure of the GCP alone than to its president's power over other BIDs, it was criticized; an audit that followed (and the *Kessler* 1998 litigation) identified problems; the BID itself resolved many but not all of these problems; and the problems that the BID did not resolve were corrected by local public officials. This shows not that BIDs are inherently unaccountable, but rather that local elected officials can and will take on even the most powerful of BID leaders, and the oversight of BIDs by local government serves to rein in BIDs when problems arise (DeNitto, 2001, p. 6).

Conclusion

BID critics charge that BIDs amount to an unsavory transfer of authority from politically accountable public officials to unaccountable private actors. This chapter has sought to demonstrate that BID officials are, in fact, politically accountable to the BIDs' relevant public. It defined BIDs' likely stakeholders and showed that because of the small size and narrow purpose of BIDs, these stakeholders are few and the BIDs' powers over them limited, reducing accountability concerns. It then examined the BID model's accountability mechanisms, including BID forma-tion, corporate governance procedures, and the oversight of local elected officials. It argued that these features work to make BID officials accountable to the BID's likeliest stakeholders in rough proportion to how much those stakeholders are impacted by BID activities.

BIDs exist because they help keep the streets cleaner, but over the long term, the success of BIDs will depend as much on BID accountability as on anything else. Clean streets or dirty, BIDs must continue to be responsive to the varied stakeholders of America's shopping districts, commercial areas, and downtowns.

References

Bagli, C. V. 1998. Business group fails to mollify Giuliani. *New York Times*, September 24, p. B5.

Barr, H. 1997. More like Disneyland: State action 42 U.S.C. § 1983, and business improve-ment districts in New York. *Columbia Human Rights Law Review* 28:393–430.

Behn, R. D. 2001. *Rethinking democratic accountability.* Washington, DC: The Brookings Institution.

Briffault, R. 1993. Who rules at home? One person/one vote and local governments. *University of Chicago Law Review* 60:339–424.

Briffault, B. 1997. The rise of sublocal structures in urban governance. *Minnesota Law Review* 82:503–550.

Briffault, R. 1999. A government for our time? Business improvement districts and urban governance. *Columbia Law Review* 99:365–478.

Cities within cities: Business improvement districts and the emergence of the micropolis. 1995. New York: Council of the City of New York.

City of Seattle v. Rogers Clothing for Men, Inc. 787 P.2d 39. Washington 1990.

DeNitto, E. 2001. Giuliani nods to BID leader. *Crain's New York Business,* June 4, p. 6.

Downs, A. 1961. In defense of majority voting. *Journal of Political Economy* 69:192–199.

Ely, J. H. 1980. *Democracy & distrust: A theory of judicial review.* Cambridge, MA: Harvard University Press.

Gabriel, F. 1997. As roles, powers expand, BIDs come under scrutiny. *Crain's New York Business,* September 1, p. 19.

Garodnick, D. R. 2000. What's the BID deal? Can the grand central business improvement district serve a special limited purpose? *University of Pennsylvania Law Review* 148:1733–1770.

Houstoun, L. O., Jr. 1997. *BIDs: Business improvement districts.* Washington, DC: Urban Land Institute.

Kessler v. Grand Central District Management Association. 158 F.3d 92. Second Circuit 1998.

Mac Donald, H. 1996. BIDs really work. *City Journal* 6:29–42.

Managing the micropolis: Proposals to strengthen BID performance and accountability. 1997. New York: Council of the City of New York.

Manshel, A. M. 1995. Business improvement district accountability. *Citylaw,* December 1, p. 102.

Martin, D. 1995. Veterans fighting for right to peddle in Midtown once again. *New York Times,* June 6, p. B3.

Mitchell, J. 1999. *Business improvement districts and innovative service delivery.* Grant report. New York: PricewaterhouseCoopers.

Siegel, F. 1992. Reclaiming our public spaces. *City Journal* 2:35–45.

This was not Rudy's finest hour. 1998. *New York Post,* December 6, p. 70.

Tiebout, C. M. 1956. A pure theory of local expenditures. *Journal of Political Economy* 64:416–424.

Vitullo-Martin, J. 1998. The private sector shows how to run a city. *Wall Street Journal,* May 20, p. A14.

Wheatley, C. 1997. Home-made sanctuaries. *Estate Gazette,* October 25, p. 63.

Wit v. Berman. 306 F.3d 1256. Second Circuit 2002.

Chapter 6

From North America to Africa: The BID Model and the Role of Policy Entrepreneurs

Lorlene Hoyt

Contents

Introduction

Property and business owners in urban areas around the globe are using state authority to create a new form of government to protect their interests. With the power to impose taxes and provide collective services, business improvement districts (BIDs) supplement publicly funded efforts to attract visitors and investors, enhance the pedestrian experience, and improve the city's ability to compete with regional office parks, shopping malls, and suburban living. The BID, as this chapter demonstrates, is a relatively new urban revitalization model that policy entrepreneurs have deliberately transferred, both intra- and internationally.

BID organizations implement compulsory funding mechanisms within geographically defined areas to achieve three principal goals: they aspire to make their areas delightful, safe, and clean. Under the rubric of delightful, BIDs seek to attract visitors, investors, and residents to commercial areas. Such campaigns range from aggressive marketing schemes to comprehensive streetscape improvement programs. For example, nearly all BID organizations craft a single identity for their jurisdiction and take on activities designed to reinforce a positive image or market niche. Self-promotion and public relations are typically manifested in the form of landscape improvements like the installation of plants and trees in public spaces, organizational logos, slogans, websites, newsletters, outdoor events like concerts and festivals, and colorful banners.

To promote safety, many BID organizations develop and implement crime prevention programs, including service arrangements with police and the provision of private security patrols (Hoyt, 2004). A variety of combinations exist. In Canada, the Downtown Winnipeg BID, Prince George Downtown BID, and the Bank Street Promenade BID supplement policing efforts with private security patrols, but the Downtown Oakville and Downtown Orillia BIDs rely solely on local police to address crime-related issues. The deployment of private security patrols is a popular crime deterrence method among BID proponents. BID security personnel, commonly known as ambassadors, carry cellular phones or two-way radios and function as the "eyes and ears" of the police; they also perform hospitality-related functions such as assisting visitors with directions (Hoyt, 2005a). They make arrangements with the police that range from informal requests for additional patrol cars to formal and ongoing commitments. For example, in Canada, the United States, and South Africa, some BID organizations—particularly those in large urban settings—establish police ministations within district boundaries, purchase their equipment, and cover their salaries. The Green Point City Improvement District in Cape Town pays the salaries for the South African Police (SAP) officers assigned to the area and purchases shared equipment such as cell phones, radios, bicycles, vehicles, and uniforms. BID safety programs may also include such services as monitoring public space with surveillance cameras, operating computerized crime mapping systems, and on-site crime prevention assistance for business owners. The Times Square BID in New York City, for example, relies heavily on closed-circuit television surveillance cameras for the purpose of crime prevention.

With regard to cleanliness, BIDs manage activities like mechanical and manual sweeping as well as high-pressured washing. Graffiti removal includes painting and scraping activities to remove tags, stickers, and bubble gum from buildings, signage, and telephone poles. The Center City BID in Philadelphia assumes responsibility for administering its own sanitation program, while others, like the Green Point and Oranjekloof BIDs in Cape Town, enter into a fee-for-service arrangement with private vendors.

What Is Policy Transfer?

Policy transfer is a widespread practice. For example, Americans borrowed the idea of a national income tax from the British (Waltman, 1980), and Europeans imported the concept of skyscrapers and cloverleaf intersections from the United States (Nasr and Volait, 2003, p. 94). The literature on policy transfer has substantially grown in the past decade (Dolowitz and Marsh, 2000; Wolman and Page, 2002; Mossberger and Wolman, 2003; James and Lodge, 2003). Policy transfer, also known as lesson drawing (Rose, 1993), policy borrowing (Cox, 1999), policy shopping (Freeman, 1999), policy band wagoning (Ikenberry, 1990), and systematically pinching ideas (Schneider and Ingram, 1988), is a term that describes the voluntary flow of ideas between individuals and is regarded as a type of policy learning because it involves the acquisition and utilization of knowledge about policies elsewhere (Dolowitz, 1997). Put simply, policy transfer attends to the way that policies and practices in one context are used to develop policies and practices in other settings (Dolowitz and Marsh, 2000, p. 5).

Individually, policy agents represent public, private, or public–private organizations and function as experts or "policy transfer entrepreneurs" (Dolowitz and Marsh,

1996) who advocate the spread of certain policies and information. Collectively, and within specialized domains, they create transnational information networks. For hundreds of years, urban policy entrepreneurs—architects, planners, and other experts—traveled to study other places, made contacts, attended lectures, and returned to their homelands to report what they had learned. For example, French planners visited the United States to study the New Deal projects and housing schemes (Nasr and Volait, 2003). In the early 1950s, the United States developed large shopping malls in suburban locations to accommodate automobile-oriented customers. Nations like Canada and Australia, which had ample space and affluence, quickly followed suit. More recently, British officials implemented the Urban Development Grant after the United Kingdom's Department of the Environment examined "potentially adoptable" policies for inner city revitalization in the United States, such as the Urban Development Action Grant (Wolman, 1992).

Much of the policy transfer literature focuses on domains such as labor (Knoke et al., 1996; Dolowitz, 1997; Martin, 2001), education (Mintrom and Vergari, 1998; John and Cole, 2000), and the environment (Hoberg, 1991; Daugbjerg, 1998; Smith, 2000; Stone, 2000; Montpetit, 2002); the urban revitalization policy transfer literature is scant. While this chapter does not seek to test or expand policy transfer theory, it does intend to make a modest contribution to the policy transfer literature through a description of the work done by urban revitalization policy entrepreneurs. Additionally, it contributes to the BID literature by identifying policy agents and their motivations, explaining why BID policy entrepreneurs sometimes experience failure, and describing the challenges of applying BID policy in new contexts.

A systematic examination of the BID model through a policy transfer lens is important, because the practice of policy transfer is on the rise (Dolowitz et al., 1999). It is also reasonable to believe that policy transfer within the urban revitalization domain is becoming more popular. Consider the following examples. Tax increment financing (TIF), an area-based tool for revitalization like the BID, originated in California in 1952 as a means to provide local matching funds for federal grants. By 2000, TIF enabling legislation was on the books in 48 states. Other development tools like community development corporations (CDCs) and main streets have recently multiplied in a similar fashion. The first CDC, the Bedford-Stuyvesant Renovation Corporation, was formed in 1966 with funding from the Model Cities Program. Today there are more than 3,600 CDCs nationwide, according to a 1998 study by the National Congress of Community Economic Development. Likewise, more than 1,700 downtown commercial districts in 39 states operate main streets programs that are sponsored by the National Trust for Historical Preservation.

The transfer of urban policy is an increasingly common practice because public sector involvement and support for revitalization efforts is diminishing. Thus, new coping mechanisms are necessary. Moreover, advancements in information and communication technologies, like the Internet, allow urban policy entrepreneurs to save time and resources in importing best practices from other cities. Such quick importations of practices are a cause for concern because some policy entrepreneurs adopt new concepts without critically analyzing the legislative, economic, political, and other differences between the exporting and importing contexts (Hambleton and Taylor, 1993). This hurried new policy importation may fail to solve the urban problems it was intended to resolve or may even aggravate them.

Research Questions

For the purposes of this chapter, the policy transfer literature provides a framework for examining the relationship between three important factors: urban revitalization policy (which in this case is the BID), the entrepreneurs who actively promote and deter policy adoption, and the setting where these policies are applied. In doing so, this study will answer a discrete set of research questions. The primary questions are: (1) Does the BID model represent an instance of transnational urban policy transfer? (2) If so, where did the model originate? (3) Why and where did the model transfer? This chapter demonstrates why certain entrepreneurs transferred the BID model from one country to the next and identifies the countries that have successfully adopted BID legislation and initiated fully operational BID organizations. It also answers such ancillary questions as: (4) How did the BID model transfer? (5) Which policy entrepreneurs aggressively promoted the BID model? (6) What motivated them to share information, and what are the most common mechanisms for sharing information? Despite the successful transfer of the BID model to a wide range of national contexts, there are contexts, like the city of Boston, where BID policy has encountered considerable resistance. This case provides valuable insights for BID advocates by addressing the question: (7) Under what conditions do policy entrepreneurs experience difficulty with importing ideas? Finally, a comparative analysis of the BID model shows how urban policy entrepreneurs apply new policies in contexts with divergent histories, political, and socioeconomic conditions.

Approach

The objective of this exploratory study is to document the transnational transfer and application of urban revitalization policy through an exhaustive examination of the BID model.

To accomplish this objective, I used a multimethod qualitative and quantitative research design, collecting data from a range of primary and secondary sources. Primary data collection involved the distribution of a five-page survey instrument and the execution of semistructured personal interviews with BID managers, public and private service providers, and government officials in cities throughout Australia,

Canada, Japan, European countries,* New Zealand, and South Africa. Secondary sources included BID enabling legislation, public hearing transcripts, scholarly papers, newspaper articles, trade magazines, and conference proceedings.

The survey instrument contained questions in open-ended and multiple-choice formats and was organized into five sections: the formation, structure and scope, purpose, performance evaluation, and evolution of BIDs (Appendix A). Some portions of the survey instrument were identical to the one designed by Mitchell (1999) to survey American BIDs. To begin with, I identified BID and other downtown management organizations by obtaining and compiling mailing lists from previous studies, the Internet, professional membership organizations, and national, state, and local governments. Next, I compiled a comprehensive list of 1,200 non-American downtown management organizations in countries around the globe: Australia (185), Canada (347), Japan (261), European countries (225), New Zealand (140), and South Africa (42). To increase the likelihood of participation, I modified the language in the survey instrument for each country. Minor changes included referring to BIDs as business improvement areas for Canada and city improvement districts for South Africa. Surveys sent to Japanese town management organizations were translated into Japanese. A research team comprised of five graduate students at the Massachusetts Institute of Technology (MIT) mailed envelopes—each containing a cover letter, survey, and postage-paid reply envelope—to the manager of each downtown management organization identified. Managers who did not return a completed survey received reminders in the form of letters, phone calls, and electronic mail messages. In the end, 398 non-American BID organizations returned their surveys (32 percent return rate).

The research team selected a group of BID directors from among the 398 who returned their surveys, contacted them on the telephone to describe the study, requested promotional documents such as newsletters and pamphlets, and scheduled personal interviews. From June 1999 to January 2003, I conducted a total of 72 interviews throughout Canada, the United States, and South Africa, which augment the survey data; 59 of the 72 were face-to-face interviews, 13 were telephone interviews, and the average interview was 90 minutes in length. Participants received a copy of the interview questions in advance, as shown in Appendix B. The face-to-face contacts not only aided an expeditious and in-depth investigation, but also facilitated the establishment of working relationships with BID managers. Interviews varied in style and length. Some were less than an hour in duration and took place over the telephone, some were several hours long and were held in the BID manager's office, and others spanned several days and included a tour of the BID areas.

In addition to the survey and personal interviews, this study relied on a review of BID enabling legislation, public hearing transcripts, scholarly papers, newspaper

---

* The countries included in this category are Austria, Belgium, Denmark, France, Germany, Holland, Norway, Portugal, Spain, Sweden, and the United Kingdom.

articles, trade magazines, conference proceedings, BID websites, newsletters, reports, and personal correspondence with BID directors and other officials. In the United States, public hearing transcripts for BID authorization, reauthorization, plan approval, and plan amendment are available to citizens upon request. Such hearings record the testimonies of BID advocates and opponents, providing valuable information about the policy transfer process. For this study, I conducted a comprehensive assessment of the transcripts recorded by the city of Philadelphia. These transcripts include nearly 1,000 pages of testimony, spanning a period of more than eight years. While public hearing transcripts for American BIDs are typically available to the public, considerable difficulties arise with respect to accessing internal BID reports, correspondence, and meetings. However, my relationship with Philadelphia's BID directors resulted in my having access to official reports, such as those submitted to the city of Philadelphia's Commerce Department, the Philadelphia police commissioner, and the transcripts of organizational meetings. Hence, this study incorporates observations made from August 1999 through July 2000 in such forums as the University City District's Public Safety meetings, the South Street BID's monthly meetings, the Center City District's roll call, and the Philadelphia police department's weekly Compstat meeting (Compstat is an approach to crime reduction and resource management that originated in New York City). In short, these observations supplemented the more traditional data sources and assisted me in developing a more intimate understanding of BID-related policies and activities.

Policy Success, Emergence, and Resistance

To facilitate a discussion on how BID policy is subject to transfer, this chapter builds on a study (Martin, 2001) that examined the rapid transfer of living wage ordinances in the United States and made a distinction between two stages: policy emergence and policy success. A policy is in the emergence stage before BID enabling legislation has been adopted, and when policy entrepreneurs are involved in importation-related tasks, including the study of BID policies in other places as well as activities such as proposing, drafting, and lobbying to implement BID legislation in their homeland. My investigation reveals that BID policy in at least seven countries—Japan, Austria, Germany, Lithuania, the Czech Republic, Poland, and Romania—is currently in this stage of transfer. In contrast, the transfer of BID policy is successful once BID enabling legislation is approved; therefore, the existence of functional BID organizations is evidence of policy success. At present, BID organizations exist in eight countries: Canada, the United States, New Zealand, South Africa, Serbia, Albania, Jamaica, and the United Kingdom. Because policy entrepreneurs sometimes fail, this chapter introduces a third stage of policy transfer: policy resistance. Policy resistance is a stage of policy transfer that is characterized by ongoing and considerable opposition to the importation of BID policy or the adoption of BID enabling legislation. The next section of this chapter details the origins of the BID model, its successful transfer and emergence in numerous nations, and the types of conditions that may prevent policy transfer.

BID Policy Success

The First BID in Canada

Where did the BID model originate? It was in Toronto, Canada. By the mid-1960s, the impacts of rapid suburbanization began to negatively affect retail sales and commercial growth rates throughout the city of Toronto. From the early 1920s through the mid-1960s, streetcars delivered visitors to the thriving commercial area now known as West Bloor Village, but the opening of several regional malls, including the Yorkdale Mall, along with the completion of the Bloor–Danforth subway line in 1967, detrimentally impacted this small commercial area located in the western corner of Toronto. Malls offered shoppers a climate-controlled environment with free parking and other amenities, and the shoppers that once rode streetcars on Bloor Avenue were directed underground (Hoyt, 2005c).

In 1963, Neil McLellan, a jewelry store owner and chairman of the Bloor-Jane-Runnymede Business Men's Association's Parking Committee, invited members of the city's planning board to discuss the possibility of a business district (Boytchuk, 1971; Grys, 1972). For several years, the Business Men's Association relied on voluntary contributions; however, as participation waned, disagreement among business owners intensified and the association's coffers diminished significantly. This development started a long dialogue between local representatives and businessmen, and spawned the formation of a committee. The committee included the representatives of the Business Men's Association, City of Toronto Planning Board, City Council, Department of Public Works, Parking Authority, City Surveyors Department, City Real Estate Department, City Legal Department, Department of Streets, Metro Roads and Traffic Department, Department of Parks and Recreation, Development Department, Toronto Transit Commission, Toronto Hydro Electric Commission, and Ontario Hydro. The committee explored the feasibility of forming a business district with a self-imposed tax on local property owners as a means to circumvent the free-rider problem and to make collective improvements that would protect their individual investments (Grys, 1972). After considerable research into the subject, the committee discovered that the formation of such a district required enabling legislation. With cooperation from the Department of the City Solicitor, the committee crafted the necessary legislation, which passed in the legislature on December 17, 1969 (Grys, 1972; A. Ling, personal interview, August 30, 2002). Six months after the province of Ontario passed section 379g of the Municipal Act, the Council of the Corporation of the City of Toronto passed bylaw 170-70 and the world's first BID, Bloor West Village (then known as the Bloor-Jane-Runnymede Improvement Area), became a legal reality.

With a modest budget, the voluntary management board designed the first BID program. The agenda focused on streetscape improvements and special events. In the first year they supervised the installation of more than 100 large planters, new benches, trash receptacles, banners, lighting, newspaper dispensers, and holiday decorations. They also worked with Ontario Hydro and Toronto Hydro Electric System to remove utility poles from the street and move services below grade (Grys, 1972). According to Alex Ling, businessman, property owner, and BID director for more than 30 years, these basic streetscape elements dramatically improved the pedestrian experience and attracted customers to the area.

Why and where did the BID model transfer? With the power to tax members, the BID model of Toronto represents a persistent, competitive, and flexible strategy to confront local dilemmas through the provision of additional public services. Hundreds of governments throughout the providence of Ontario have since allowed the authorization of BID organizations. Though the Canadian BID movement began in the 1960s and peaked in the 1980s, the BID model remains popular, as evidenced by the more recent establishment of the Downtown Yonge Street BID in Toronto and the Downtown Montreal Commercial Development Association in Montreal. One reason why the model transferred so rapidly throughout Canada is that Canadian governments encouraged the establishment of BIDs; in the 1970s, the province of Ontario made infrastructure grants only to BID organizations (A. Ling, personal interview, August 30, 2002).

BIDs in the United States

Despite my best efforts, I was unable to pinpoint exactly how the BID model migrated from Canada to the United States. There is, however, agreement among experts that the New Orleans Downtown Development District, established in 1975, was the nation's first BID (Houstoun, 1997, p. 15). Currently, BIDs exist in many large American cities, including New York, Los Angeles, San Diego, Houston, and Philadelphia. The Center City District (CCD) in Philadelphia has been frequently visited and studied by BID policy entrepreneurs from around the world and previous researchers. In my research I also conducted an in-depth examination of Philadelphia's BIDs in general and CCD in particular (Hoyt, 2001).

Throughout the first half of the 20th century, Philadelphia's population grew at an impressive rate. However, suburban shopping malls appeared in the 1950s, and the exodus of both central-city businesses and the white middle class to the urban periphery instigated a decline in population that continues today. Interested in making Philadelphia's central business district more competitive, the Central Philadelphia Development Corporation (CPDC), a not-for-profit membership organization supported by Philadelphia's business leaders that was formed in 1956, deliberately imported the BID model.

In 1985, the CPDC invited Richard Fleming, then president of the Downtown Denver Partnership—a nonprofit business organization that planned, managed, and developed downtown Denver and its BID—to attend a "special meeting of interested downtown parties" (Hoyt, 2001). Shortly after Dick Fleming's visit, the representatives of the CPDC, the Greater Philadelphia Chamber of Commerce, the Chestnut Street Association, and the Foundation for Architecture held a series of meetings to discuss the formation of a downtown management association for Philadelphia. For more than four years, Peter Wiley, then executive director of CPDC, had led the effort by researching BID organizations throughout the country. Working with an attorney, Wiley gained a detailed understanding of the state enabling statutes (P. Levy, personal interview, July 24, 2000). He also communicated with the managers of nearby BIDs in Allentown, Pennsylvania, and New York City. Philadelphia's business leaders then created a Downtown Management Task Force, allocating $50,000 to conduct a feasibility study, which later recommended the creation of a BID. By May 1988, Philadelphia police commissioner Kevin Tucker, an active proponent of community policing, and Mayor Wilson Goode publicly supported the formation of a BID for the central business district. In 1989, Ronald Rubin, president and CEO of the Rubin Company, agreed to take on the responsibility for advancing the BID model. As a well-respected and established real estate developer, he led the property and business owners in supporting the BID endeavor (P. Levy, personal interview, July 24, 2000). In 1990, Mayor Goode signed the bill into law, and by 1991, the Center City District (CCD) was operational.

The CCD served as a model for subsequently formed BIDs in Philadelphia because its programs were visible, it possessed considerable wherewithal, and it was managed by a group of highly dedicated, creative, and charismatic professionals. From 1992 to 1998, the CCD's executive director, Paul Levy, testified in support of the seven BID plans brought before the city council, because he hoped the entire city, not just its center, would become more competitive with the formation of these BIDs (P. Levy, personal interview, July 24, 2000).

BIDs in New Zealand

It is not entirely clear whether or how the BID model migrated from the United States to New Zealand. However, in an interview, Karen Remetis, the founder and chair of the National Main Street Trust in New Zealand, mentioned that the Main Street model had migrated from the United States to Australia, and from Australia to New Zealand. The mall developments in New Zealand began in the 1960s, and its towns and cities—like their counterparts in Canada and America—were negatively impacted by suburbanization. In the early 1990s, council planners throughout the country imported the Main Street model from the United States, and at least 30 of the more than 150 main streets have implemented a separate rate, or self-funding mechanism, which qualifies them as BIDs. Remetis noted that while the term *BID* is not used in New Zealand, town center organizations have borrowed ideas like uniformed ambassadors from the American BID model.

BIDs in South Africa

The BID model is relatively new to South Africa and was imported directly from the United States by a small group of actors in Johannesburg. The first BID enabling legislation passed in South Africa in 1999. Johannesburg, the economic hub of South Africa for more than a century, began to decline in the 1970s. Much like North American cities, the development of suburban shopping centers and office parks attracted people to the urban periphery. This trend continued throughout the 1980s, and by the early 1990s, disinvestment in the urban core resulted in higher vacancies, increased crime, and considerable physical decline (Bremner, 2000; Tomlinson, 1999). In November 1991, property owners, developers, and businesses organized the Strategic Initiative Workshop. With more than 200 private and public sector participants, the two-day workshop resulted in a mandate to form a trilateral partnership among business owners, community members, and the then city council (N. Fraser, personal interview, January 6, 2003). Financed entirely by the private sector and charged with transforming Johannesburg into "an attractive, clean, safe and vibrant city," the Central Johannesburg Partnership (CJP) Ltd. was established in August 1992. With an interest in investigating international urban renewal practices, Executive Director Neil Fraser visited several American cities in 1993. The same year, the CJP implemented a pilot BID, the Central Improvement District. However, without the requisite enabling legislation, the BID represented a voluntary effort to reduce crime in a 12-block area of the downtown.

The first democratic elections that were held at the end of 1995 in South Africa resulted in the formation of legitimate local governments in the country, and the newly elected urban authorities quickly expressed an interest in combating decline and marketing the city as a world city (Bremner, 2000). Simultaneously, the Johannesburg Inner City Development Forum (JICDF) emerged, representing a partnership between the private and public sectors, including senior planners in Gauteng government and the local authority as well as several Johannesburg city councilors. In 1996, 21 JICDF representatives attended the First World Congress on Town and City Center Management in Coventry, England. Subsequently, the conference attendees toured cities in the United States such as Atlanta, Baltimore, Washington, Philadelphia, and New York City. After this on-site inspection of best practices, the JICDF conducted a visioning exercise to adopt a shared image for the city of Johannesburg (Bremner, 2000, p. 189; Tomlinson, 1999). During the exercise, the JICDF representatives worked with the International Downtown Association and noted that there were significant commonalities between the central city of Johannesburg and those of Pittsburgh and Detroit: increased vacancies and crime, decreased property values, and physical decay (Tomlinson, 1999).

At the October 1996 Vusani Amadolobha Conference, the Gauteng provincial government in South Africa carefully examined the BID model. The CJP, in collaboration with the Provincial Department of Development Planning and local government, drafted the *Gauteng City Improvement Districts Bill*, which the Gauteng provincial legislature passed in 1999. Partnerships for Urban Renewal, established in 1999 by Neil Fraser to handle urban renewal strategies for areas beyond the Johannesburg city limits, successfully established South Africa's first BID in the city of Pretoria. Today, there are dozens of BID organizations operating in communities throughout the country, including the ones in Johannesburg, Midrand, and Pretoria.

The BID model quickly migrated from the Gauteng Province to South Africa's peninsula. In the late 1990s, Cape Town property owners and city management raised concerns regarding urban decay in the central business district and researched a variety of international models for urban revitalization in Denver, Seattle, New York, Washington, D.C., and Coventry. As a result, the Cape Town Partnership (CTP) formed and the Cape Town City Council enacted a municipal bylaw authorizing the creation of BIDs. Tygerberg and South Peninsula municipal administrations soon replicated this bylaw, save minor modifications (T. Veley, personal interview, January 13, 2003).

BIDs in Other Countries

BID organizations also exist in Serbia, Albania, the United Kingdom, and Jamaica. According to Steven Rosenburg, chief of party for the Serbia Local Government Reform Program, there are four functioning BID organizations in Serbia. In his capacity as general counsel of New York City's Office for Economic Development, Rosenburg facilitated the implementation of more than 40 BIDs throughout the city. He said in an interview that with his assistance the U.S. Agency for International Development (USAID) deliberately imported the concept to Serbia (to the cities of Krusevac, Nis, Valjevo, and Zrenjanin) and Albania (to Durres) since 2000 for the purpose of improving local government performance, including financial management and citizen participation. In 2002, business leaders from Serbia visited New York City and examined a dozen of its BIDs. One Serbian business leader was so fond of the trash receptacles in Lincoln Square that he noted and later implemented the design. Generally speaking, the BID organizations in Serbia focus on capital improvements—such as lighting, façade enhancements, benches, and banners—as well as marketing and sanitation services.

Similarly, USAID assisted with the development of the BID legislation for Jamaica. In 1995, the Downtown Kingston Management BID was established to handle problems such as crime, grime, and illegal street vendors.

After extensive research and considerable debate among the founders, the first British BID, the Kingston-upon-Thames, began operations on January 1, 2005. England's central government began a deliberate investigation into the adoption of the BID model in 1992 by studying organizations in the United States, and several public sector bodies and national businesses provided the funding and support for a pilot BID project a decade later. The British government looked at the experience in the United States with BIDs and decided to change the legislation, so that the American model could be imported and implemented in the United Kingdom (Symes and Steel, 2003; Lloyd et al., 2003; Hoyt and Gopal-Agge, 2007). Ultimately, the Association of Town Center Management (ATCM), the entity entrusted with administering the pilot project, selected 23 sites for the implementations in cities such as Birmingham and Bristol, Coventry and Manchester, Liverpool, Lincoln, and London. For a successful policy transfer, researchers compared and contrasted the economic, political, and social contexts of the United Kingdom and United States and carefully considered the potential spatial repercussions of policy application (Symes and Steel, 2003; Lloyd et al., 2003).

BID Policy Emergence

Policy entrepreneurs in countries around the globe continue to advocate for the transfer of BID policy. Throughout the course of my investigation, I discovered that although BID organizations do not yet exist in Japan, Austria, Germany, Lithuania, the Czech Republic, Poland, and Romania, enabling legislation is under consideration in these countries. For example, the Japanese government is investigating the BID enabling legislation enacted in other countries and the Tokyo metropolitan government is testing the feasibility of a BID. In 1999, the Japanese government passed legislation allowing the creation of town management organizations (TMOs) to assist with the revitalization of central business districts in Japan (Levy, 2001). To establish a TMO, local governments must submit an application describing proposed development plans to the prefecture as well as the central government. If their plan is approved, the municipality receives financial assistance and the authority to appoint a TMO to oversee the implementation of the plan. In principle, TMOs do not impose compulsory assessments on property owners, and therefore do not qualify as BIDs according to the definition used for this study. But there is a pilot BID in Japan: the Shiodome-chiku Machizukuri Kyogikai TMO, a nonprofit corporation, established in January 2003, makes use of mandatory assessments and oversees security and maintenance services for the area.

BID Policy Resistance

To gain a deeper understanding of policy transfer, it is critical to identify the reasons why a policy fails to transfer from one place to another, yet the literature contains little information on the subject of resistance. To date, work in this area has been limited to the importance of special-interest groups (Damro and Mendez, 2003) and the strategies of resistance employed by recipient actors (Bache and Taylor, 2003). Although BIDs appear to proliferate around the world, there are a few contexts where they have encountered considerable resistance. I address the question: Under what conditions do BID policy entrepreneurs experience difficulty with importing ideas?

Property and business owners are sometimes unable to establish BIDs in cities, even though the enabling legislation exists, for the following reasons: they find themselves without the leadership necessary to formulate a collective vision for the area; they lack the financial wherewithal necessary to operate a BID; or they face opposition from a significant proportion of the local property and business owners. Sudden shifts in political leadership may also prevent policy implementation. In 2000, the then Mayor of Rio de Janeiro, Luis Paulo Conde, hired an independent consulting firm to assess the feasibility of creating several BIDs in the city. After studying the BIDs in New York, Philadelphia, and Denver, the consultants planned to build a pilot BID. Although city bylaws allowing the establishment of BIDs were drafted, a new mayor was elected, and the BID model permanently moved to the back burner.

The resistance to the formation of BIDs in the city of Boston was not merely a result of the change in political leadership. Here, a faulty state law, union opposition, and a contentious legislative environment led to the failure of policy entrepreneurs to complete the policy transfer. Despite nearly a decade of consensus among the mayor, city council, and property owners, the Downtown Crossing BID has yet to be realized. Experts blame the state law that authorizes the establishment of BIDs, which was passed in 1994. The law contains an opt-out provision whereby property owners have the right to decline participation within 30 days of the organization of the BID. Then Governor William Weld added the provision because of his public position against new taxes and his concern that BID revenues would upset the state cap on property tax levies. It is important to note that the opt-out caveat, albeit contradictory to the fundamental purpose of a BID, has not prevented the establishment of such organizations in other parts of the state, like Hyannis and Springfield. Downtown Crossing BID proponents refused to adopt the opt-out approach, because a large number of the properties in Downtown Crossing were owned by individuals and companies abroad that would be difficult to contact. Instead, they decided to pursue a mandatory BID in the form of a home-rule petition. This approach required approval by the Boston City Council as well as the legislature. In 1998, after some wrangling between the Boston Redevelopment Authority and the city's chief financial officer over whether BID levies would subordinate to city taxes in a foreclosure, Mayor Thomas Menino filed the home-rule petition and the city council approved it. However, the opposing groups—the Massachusetts AFL-CIO, the Boston Police Patrolmen's Association, and a handful of locally elected officials—cited excessive pay, conflicts of interest, and other problems with the BIDs in New York City and expressed concern that such entities privatize jobs by replacing police officers with private security guards. At the time of the writing of this chapter, the opposition persists. In 2003, the staff of the legislature's Local Affairs Committee completed a study that further criticized the BID proposal for favoring the interests of larger property owners, failing to require sufficient government supervision, and extending the right to tax to a corporation. The bill remains on hold as of the time of the writing of this chapter.

Findings from Surveys and Interviews

Results from the mail surveys and personal interviews I conducted on the transfer of BIDs across several national contexts show that a wide range of policy entrepreneurs, including, but not limited to, property owners, business owners, local governments, public agencies, nongovernmental organizations (NGOs), elected officials, private consultancy firms, international organizations, and researchers, are responsible for the intra- and international transfer of the BID model. They also provide evidence that the BID policy network is an open system whereby relationships rely on such principles as trust, respect, and reciprocity. Within this system and through a variety of communicative mechanisms, BID policy entrepreneurs deliberately and effectively maintain a network for sharing information, ideas, and resources within and beyond their national boundaries. They are motivated to share information because they recognize the advantages of urban policy transfer, especially the benefits associated with membership in a policy network such as the opportunity to benefit from the exchange of information. As demonstrated earlier, internationally focused entities like the International Downtown Association, Association of Town Center Management, and United States Agency for International Development fostered information exchange by providing centralized forums for parties with similar interests, thus allowing participants to form alliances and reduce transaction costs. The majority of BID policy entrepreneurs are formal members of at least one of these professional organizations, and they share information within the network by attending conferences, participating in study tours, and distributing written materials such as journal articles, professional magazines, and newspapers. Larger organizations also research on other BID programs, receive technical assistance from government agencies and private consultants, and collect information via telephone, electronic mail, and the Internet. Furthermore, interviews with BID managers indicate that these entrepreneurs regularly engage in prospective policy evaluation, but favor informal methods, such as advice and anecdotes from experts, and are less likely to employ more formal methods of prospective policy evaluation, like modeling and microsimulation.

In my study, I borrowed a set of guidelines that had been developed for policymakers (Mossberger and Wolman, 2003). Within a framework referred to as prospective policy evaluation, these guidelines highlight the issues that deserve consideration prior to policy adoption. I used them as a framework for interpreting the data that I gathered on how BID policy is transferred and applied in Canada, the United States, South Africa, and beyond. According to this framework, there are several conditions that local entrepreneurs should evaluate before they attempt to borrow ideas from other places: adequacy and accuracy of information, similarity of problems and differences in setting, policy performance, and policy application.

Responsible prospective policy evaluation requires access to ample and accurate information. According to data collected through the mail surveys and personal interviews, BID policy entrepreneurs consider a wide range of information before they support enabling legislation or implement BID organizations. Is the information that they need readily available? It seems so. As demonstrated earlier, Philadelphia's policy agents began their investigation into the model by inviting a national expert to speak on the subject of BIDs and later researched New York's enabling legislation. In contrast, policy entrepreneurs in South Africa started collecting information by conducting on-site visits and studying international practices in a handful of American and British cities. These two cases exemplify the experience of most BID policy entrepreneurs: new agents may readily enter the policy network and quickly gain access to a host of information without difficulty.

Is the information accurate? Although the majority of managers believe that information sharing is useful, it is important to point out that with respect to policy transfer, the BID model is problematic because it mandates self-promotion. Said another way, BID organizations with highly visible programs are not necessarily effective in creating delightful, safe, and clean environments; such a reputation may be, in part, the result of an impressive marketing scheme that is merely evidence that a BID manager is doing his or her job (Hoyt, 2005a). Therefore, importers are rightfully skeptical, and the BID policy entrepreneurs that I interviewed expressed some frustration with the task of borrowing ideas from organizations, especially when it was difficult to distinguish between objective and subjective accounts of success. They noted that self-evaluations, in particular, should be carefully scrutinized. Most interviewees agreed that seminars and conferences are useful mechanisms for sharing information and learning from peers. However, several mentioned that presentations of the BID model as a panacea for urban ills are superficial and raise suspicion.

Such activities beg the question: Why do urban policy entrepreneurs still advocate the transfer of the BID model? Although some researchers have raised concern about unfettered policy promotion, commenting that the role of the International Downtown Association is to sell advice and information about BIDs (Symes and Steel, 2003), my experience leads me to believe that policy entrepreneurs such as Fleming, Fraser, Houstoun, Levy, Ling, McLellan, and Rosenburg actively promote the model for the purpose of building a coalition of support that will justify their beliefs and publicize their redevelopment activities. Like Levy, who provided testimony in support of multiple BIDs throughout Philadelphia, and Rosenburg, who transported the BID model from New York City to Eastern Europe, McLellan initially advanced the movement by giving a presentation of the new model to a seminar of the Canadian Association of Renewal Officials in Toronto in 1971, and even continued to travel "across the province and the country preaching the BID gospel" during his retirement (A. Ling, personal interview, August 30, 2002).

Within this framework, prospective policy evaluation should also include an analysis of the similarity of problems and goals between the exporting and importing countries. Thus, a vital question for importers is: How similar is the problem in the originating country? In my research, I learned from BID managers, business leaders, and local officials that in each instance of successful BID policy transfer, key businesses and residents migrated from the central city due to the introduction of the automobile, suburban shopping mall, and modern office park—the driving forces for BID policy adoption. In short, the BID model initially materialized in response to suburbanization, and this condition remains the primary incentive for its proliferation.

The causes of suburbanization as well as the contemporary social and political characteristics of a city vary across countries, however. Therefore, it is essential that policy entrepreneurs not only consider the similarity of problems, but also understand the differences in setting. They should ask: How does the originator's policy setting compare to the recipient's? As previously described, the JICDF's visioning exercise entrepreneurs quickly drew parallels between cities like Pittsburgh and Johannesburg. Seemingly, their problems had common root causes; however, there were also a host of differences worthy of serious consideration. Historically, Johannesburg had no corporate commitment to the central city, leadership was nonexistent, and the mayor lacked the power necessary to rally public attention around the issues facing the central city (Tomlinson, 1999). Moreover, Johannesburg's experience with crime and order deviated significantly from the American experience. During the Apartheid, the South African Police (SAP) represented a force of oppression; presently, they are very few in numbers. Although the Metropolitan Police Force was established in the late 1990s, its focus is on traffic and council bylaw enforcement (N. Fraser, personal interview, January 6, 2003), so Johannesburg has extraordinarily low levels of public security services. Finally, the socioeconomic problems facing Johannesburg are vastly different than those faced by American cities. For example, Johannesburg has a very high unemployment rate (30 percent) and consequent chronic problems of informal traders, homeless people living on the streets, drug use, and violent crime.

According to the guidelines set forth by Mossberger and Wolman (2003), entrepreneurs should systematically evaluate prospective policies in the originating country prior to adoption. Put simply, entrepreneurs should refrain from borrowing ideas unless they have proof that they are successful elsewhere. Most BID policy entrepreneurs collect information by actively seeking out expert opinions, collecting promotional literature on BIDs, and conducting on-site visits to observe operational BIDs prior to borrowing ideas. Most are satisfied with these subjective accounts of success, and few systematically scrutinize the model or require evidence of effectiveness.

This is likely the case because most BIDs are not required to monitor performance and those that are usually self-monitored.* Additionally, it is important for entrepreneurs to engage in a systematic comparison of multiple urban revitalization policies prior to BID adoption because a detailed analysis of divergent policies leads to a deeper understanding of the historical, political, and socioeconomic conditions that they must confront, and such an approach improves the likelihood of designing an appropriate response to the problems at hand. Though few entrepreneurs have approached the adoption of BID policy methodically in the past, late adopters—such as the property owners and local officials in Cape Town as well as England's central government—practice rather creative and cautious techniques (Hoyt, 2005b). For example, the CTP methodically assessed and effectively blended revitalization models from a variety of contexts, including the United States (Denver, Seattle, Washington, D.C., and New York), Ireland (Dublin), England (Liverpool, Manchester, and Coventry), the Netherlands, Australia (Adelaide), and Brazil. England, as mentioned previously, launched a pilot project that involved the institutionalization of fewer than two dozen BIDs instead of wholeheartedly embracing the model.

Finally, prospective policy evaluation includes a critical consideration of the policy's application in a foreign context. As illustrated earlier, the BID model has three principal aims: delight, safety, and cleanliness. To achieve these goals, most BIDs support a combination of activities, including consumer marketing, capital improvements, policy advocacy, maintenance, security, economic development, transportation, and social services. To better understand the way the BID policy is applied in different national contexts, the survey instrument that I distributed asked managers to describe their level of involvement ("very involved," "somewhat involved," or "not at all involved") with each of these services. Results show that the services that Canadian and American BIDs provide are quite similar. For example, the majority of Canadian and American BID organizations are "very involved" in consumer marketing (Hoyt, 2005c; Mitchell, 1999). Furthermore, at least half of the Canadian and American BIDs surveyed indicated a high level of involvement with capital improvements as well as activities relating to policy advocacy, like lobbying government on behalf of business interests. Interestingly, security is more central to BID programs in South Africa, with 100 percent of the respondents stating that their organization is "very involved" with the provision of security services, compared to 28 percent of the American BIDs and 27 percent of the Canadian BIDs.

The BID model is flexible and responds to the historically, politically, and socioeconomically divergent contexts that Johannesburg and Cape Town present. For example, BID policy entrepreneurs in Johannesburg—a landlocked, Afro-centric, business-oriented city—had serious problems with violent crime and could not rely on publicly funded police departments for support. In Philadelphia's Center City District, security ambassadors attend the daily, military-style roll-call briefings held

---

* See the Caruso and Weber chapter in this volume for a discussion of the criteria of assessing BID effectiveness.

by the police on a daily basis. In Johannesburg, security ambassadors also attend such roll calls, but South African and Metropolitan Police do not participate. Instead, the BID assumes responsibility for protecting citizens and saturates the BID designated area with security ambassadors who utilize the right of citizen arrest when necessary. Under this right, they have the ability to apprehend, hold, and charge anyone engaging in illegal activity. Few security ambassadors are armed. Cape Town also faced grave crime problems that threatened the economic fate of this coastal, Euro-centric, tourist-oriented city with endless oceanfront property and scenic beauty. The political climate in Cape Town, however, was more conducive to supporting a positive relationship between the CTP and the police. Unlike the CJP, whose attempt to make use of public services was stopped by the police in Johannesburg, the CTP was able to negotiate contract services from the SAP in the form of community patrol officers (CPOs). With an annual budget of approximately $1.5 million, the Cape Town Central City BID's primary focus is crime prevention. In 2002, the comprehensive security program included 45 CPOs, who have the power to arrest criminal suspects, 32 security personnel from the city, 2 security managers, 160 security personnel working in shifts, 5 patrol cars, 10 horse-mounted patrols, 50 parking marshals, a 72-camera surveillance network, and a 24-hour operations and control center. It is worth mentioning that the CPOs fall under the SAP and the BID has little control over their training or activities.

Conclusion

Through a synthesis of data collected over a five-year period, this chapter demonstrates that the BID is a model of urban revitalization that policy entrepreneurs—such as property owners, business owners, local governments, public agencies, NGOs, elected officials, private consultancy firms, international organizations, and researchers—deliberately transferred within and across national contexts. Although the model that originated in Toronto, Canada, quickly spread to the United States, New Zealand, South Africa, Serbia, Albania, Jamaica, and the United Kingdom, BID policy entrepreneurs periodically experience resistance. Advocates in the city of Boston, for example, have worked for more than a decade to create a BID organization but have failed due to union opposition and an unfriendly legislative environment. Despite a handful of defeats, however, the BID movement is thriving.

In closing, entrepreneurs with an interest in establishing BID organizations in Asia and Eastern Europe should devise reliable methods of prospective policy evaluation. They should especially acquire accurate information, assess differences in setting, and predict problems in the application of the policy. Because the International Downtown Association currently functions as a central repository for information about BIDs for policy entrepreneurs around the globe, it would be appropriate for it to take the lead on devising such methods. Other internationally focused organizations such as the ATCM and USAID are reasonable alternatives.

References

Bache, I., and Taylor, A. 2003. The politics of policy resistance: Reconstructing higher education in Kosovo. *Journal of Public Policy* 23:279–300.

Boytchuk, W. 1971. Looking ahead. *Bloor West Villager* 5:1–2.

Bremner, L. 2000. Reinventing the Johannesburg inner city. *Cities* 17:185–193.

Cox, R. 1999. *Policy borrowing and welfare reform.* Paper presented at Global Trajectories Conference, European University Institute, Florence, Italy.

Damro, C., and Mendez, P. L. 2003. Emissions trading at Kyoto: From EU resistance to union innovation. *Environmental Politics* 12:71–94.

Daugbjerg, C. 1998. Linking policy networks and environmental policies: Nitrate policy making in Denmark and Sweden, 1970–1995. *Public Administration* 76:275–294.

Dolowitz, D. 1997. British employment policy in the 1980s: Learning from the American experience. *Governance* 10:23–42.

Dolowitz, D., Greenwold, S., and Marsh, D. 1999. Policy transfer: Something old, something new, something borrowed, but why red, white and blue? *Parliamentary Affairs* 2:719–731.

Dolowitz, D., and Marsh, D. 1996. Who learns from whom: A review of the policy transfer literature. *Political Studies* 44:343–357.

Dolowitz, D., and Marsh, D. 2000. Learning from abroad: The role of policy transfer in contemporary policy making. *Governance* 13:5–24.

Freeman, R. 1999. *Policy transfer in the health sector*, 1–25. European Forum Conference, European University Institute, Florence, Italy.

Grys, B. 1972. Anniversary. *Bloor West Villager* 5:7.

Hambleton, R., and Taylor, M. 1993. Transatlantic policy transfer. In *People in cities: A transatlantic policy exchange*, ed. R. Hambleton and M. Taylor, 1–28. Bristol, UK: School of Advanced Urban Studies.

Hoberg, G. 1991. Sleeping with an elephant: The American influence on Canadian environmental regulation. *Journal of Public Policy* 11:107–132.

Houstoun, L. 1997. *Business improvement districts*. Washington, DC: Urban Land Institute.

Hoyt, L. 2001. Business improvement districts: Untold stories and substantiated impacts. Ph.D. dissertation, University of Pennsylvania. *Dissertation Abstracts International* 62:3961–4221.

Hoyt, L. 2004. Collecting private funds for safer public spaces: An empirical examination of the business improvement district concept. *Environment and Planning B: Planning and Design* 31:367–380.

Hoyt, L. 2005a. Do business improvement district organizations make a difference? Crime in and around commercial areas in Philadelphia. *Journal of Planning Education and Research* 25:185–203.

Hoyt, L. 2005b. Planning through compulsory commercial clubs: Business improvement districts. *Economic Affairs* 25:24–27.

Hoyt, L. 2005c. The business improvement district: An internationally diffused approach to revitalization. In *International Downtown Association*, 1–65. Washington, DC: International Downtown Association.

Hoyt, L., and Gopal-Agge, D. 2007. The business improvement district model: A balanced review of contemporary debates. *Geography Compass* 1:946–958.

Ikenberry, G. J. 1990. The international spread of privatization policies: Inducements, learning and policy band wagoning. In *The political economy of public sector reform and privatization*, ed. E. Suleiman and J. Waterbury, 88–108. Boulder, CO: Westview Press.

James, O., and Lodge, M. 2003. The limitations of "policy transfer" and "lesson drawing" for public policy research. *Political Studies Review* 1:179–193.

John, P., and Cole, A. 2000. When do institutions, policy sectors, and cities matter? *Comparative Political Studies* 33:248–268.

Knoke, D., Pappi, F. U., Broadbent, J., and Yutaka, T. 1996. *Comparing policy networks.* Cambridge, UK: Cambridge University Press.

Levy, P. R. 2001. Paying for the public life. *Economic Development Quarterly* 15:124–131.

Lloyd, M., McCarthy, J., McGreal, S., and Berry, J. 2003. Business improvement districts: Planning and urban regeneration. *International Planning Studies* 8:295–321.

Martin, I. 2001. Dawn of the living wage: The diffusion of a redistributive municipal policy. *Urban Affairs Review* 36:470–496.

Mintrom, M., and Vergari, S. 1998. Policy networks and innovation diffusion: The case of state education reforms. *Journal of Politics* 60(1), 126–148.

Mitchell, J. 1999. *Business improvement districts and innovative service delivery.* New York: The PricewaterhouseCoopers Endowment for the Business of Government.

Montpetit, É. 2002. Policy networks, federal arrangements, and the development of environmental regulations: A comparison of the Canadian and American agricultural sectors. *Governance* 15:1–20.

Mossberger, K., and Wolman, H. 2003. Policy transfer as a form of prospective policy evaluation: Challenges and recommendations. *Public Administration Review* 63:428–440.

Nasr, J., and Volait, M. 2003. *Urbanism—Imported or exported? Native aspirations and foreign plans.* Hoboken, NJ: Wiley Academy Press.

Rose, R. 1993. *Lesson drawing in public policy: A guide to learning across time and space.* Chatham, NJ: Chatham House.

Schneider, A., and Ingram, H. 1998. Systematically "pinching" ideas: A comparative approach to policy design. *Journal of Public Policy* 8:61–80.

Smith, A. 2000. Policy networks and advocacy coalitions. *Environment and Planning C: Government and Policy* 18:95–114.

Stone, D. 2000. *Policy transfer: An overview of the debates.* Conference on the diffusion of environmental policy innovations, Environment Working Group of the German Political Science Association, Berlin.

Symes, M., and Steel, M. 2003. Lessons from America: The role of business improvement districts as an agent of urban regeneration. *Town Planning Review* 74:301–313.

Tomlinson, R. 1999. From exclusion to inclusion: Rethinking Johannesburg's central city. *Environment and Planning A* 31:1665–1678.

Waltman, J. 1980. *Copying other nation's policies: Two American case studies.* Cambridge, MA: Schenkman Publishing Company.

Wolman, H., and Page, E. 2002. Policy transfer among local governments: An information theory approach. *Governance* 1:477–501.

Wolman, H. 1992. Understanding cross-national policy transfers: The case of Britain and the United States. *Governance* 5:27–45.

Appendix A:
Survey Instrument

Formation

1. In your own words, briefly describe the impetus or need for planning the organization.
2. In what year did the planning phase begin?
3. In what year was your organization legally established? When did it begin operations?
4. Which best describes the group(s) responsible for forming the organization?
   (a) Business owners
   (b) Property owners
   (c) Elected officials
   (d) Government agencies
   (e) Residents
   (f) Medical institutions
   (g) Educational institutions
   (h) Other _____
5. Did they experience opposition? If so, from which group? (Same set of choices as above)

Structure and Scope

1. Which of the following best characterizes your organization?
   (a) Government agency
   (b) Nonprofit organization
   (c) Combination of government and nonprofit
   (d) Private agency
   (e) Public and private agency
2. Currently, your organization has how many full-time employees? Part-time employees?

3. How many members are on your governing board?
4. How many properties are located in the BID? How many city blocks does your organization cover?
5. Approximately, what is the current annual budget (in American dollars)?
6. Which of the following are sources of funding for your organization?
   (a) Special tax assessment on property and/or business
   (b) Voluntary donations or in-kind contributions
   (c) Subsidies or grants from federal/state/central/local government
   (d) Subsides or grants from foundations
   (e) Bonds (public or private)
   (f) City general tax revenues
   (g) Sale of goods and/or services
   (h) User fees
   (i) Other _____

Purpose

1. Briefly describe the organization's central mission.
2. To what extent is your organization involved in providing each of the following services?
   (a) Capital improvements
   (b) Consumer marketing
   (c) Economic development
   (d) Maintenance
   (e) Parking and transportation
   (f) Policy advocacy
   (g) Public space regulation
   (h) Security
   (i) Social services
   (j) Other _____

Performance Evaluation

1. Has your organization established standards of performance from which to evaluate its outcomes?
2. Is an agency or organization other than your own responsible for performance evaluation?
3. If so, which of the following has been used as a measure of organizational performance during the past year?
   (a) Crime rates
   (b) Retail sales
   (c) Number of jobs created

(d) Pedestrian counts
(e) Occupancy rates
(f) Customer surveys
(g) Number of businesses
(h) Other _____
4. If you circled "crime rates," which type of crime has been a problem during the past year?
   (a) Homicide
   (b) Rape
   (c) Robbery
   (d) Assault
   (e) Theft
   (f) Vandalism/graffiti
   (g) Prostitution
   (h) Panhandling/loitering
   (i) Other _____
5. Which of the following has been used as a method to deter or decrease criminal activity?
   (a) Paid security patrols
   (b) Volunteer security patrols
   (c) Police patrols
   (d) Closed-circuit television/surveillance cameras
   (e) Computerized crime mapping
   (f) Notification of property/business owners
   (g) Increased number of visitors/outdoor events
   (h) Sealing vacant buildings, rapid graffiti removal, etc.

Evolution

1. Which phrase best describes how your organization has changed its physical jurisdiction since implementation?
   (a) Increased drastically
   (b) Increased slightly
   (c) No change
   (d) Decreased slightly
   (e) Decreased drastically
   (f) Other _____
2. Which of the following describe how the number of full-time employees has changed since implementation?
   (a) Increased drastically
   (b) Increased slightly
   (c) No change

(d) Decreased slightly

(e) Decreased drastically

(f) Other _____

3. Approximately, what was your organization's first annual budget (in American dollars)?

4. In your own words, briefly describe how the organization's central mission has changed since implementation.

Appendix B: Personal Interview Questions

Policy Formulation (Policy Emergence)

1. Why was there interest in adopting the BID model? Who initiated the effort? Was anyone else influential?
2. Could you describe the process of how the policy was developed?
3. Did anyone oppose this proposal? Who? If so, why?
4. How long did it take to pass the legislation (from the first efforts at drafting legislation until it was enacted)?
5. Did any of the information you looked at raise any possible problems with the BID idea?
6. Did your city do any cost-benefit analysis or other policy analysis while the proposal was being developed or while legislation was pending? If so, was it favorable or critical of the proposal?
7. What information did you actually consider when developing the proposal? How was that useful?
8. Was there any particular program or legislation that you used as a model?
9. If so, did you make any adaptations? What were they and why did you make them?
10. Were there any organizations outside state government who took an interest in the regulations?
11. What influence did they have?
12. What information did you have about BIDs at the time? Who did you get this information from?

Policy Application (Policy Success)

1. Where did the monies come from to plan/organize/set up the BID?
2. How did the group negotiate the size and shape of the BID?
3. Was there a planning committee/interim board members?
4. How did the BID select an executive director?
5. How did the group mold an identity/on what assets did they focus?
6. What is the mission? What are the key goals?
7. How did the group negotiate the provision of services?
8. Which services does the BID provide?
9. Who provides and manages these services?
10. What are the BID's principal funding sources? What is the annual budget?
11. With which organizations does the BID collaborate? For what purpose?
12. Did the BID negotiate/document baseline services with local government?

Chapter 7

The BID Model in Canada and the United States: The Retail-Revitalization Nexus

Devika Gopal-Agge and Lorlene Hoyt

Contents

Introduction

Downtowns were once the regional hubs of commerce, culture, and shopping (Miles et al., 2000; Comedia, 1991). However, several economic, functional, political, and technological forces have challenged this position. The post-Fordist era saw an enormous flight of population and retail to the suburbs, which, unlike downtowns, were not plagued with problems like pollution, congestion, and crime (Ford, 1994; Burayidi, 2001). Transport infrastructure expansion programs and the Federal Home Ownership subsidy program in the United States only served to facilitate this outward move. As the wealthier families migrated away from the urban core, downtowns lost their standing as centers of civic activities and social functions (Loukaitou-Sideris and Banerjee, 1998). The outmigration of department and specialty stores soon followed (Evans, 1997; Kalman, 1985). This trend of economic and social disinvestment gradually affected the physical form of downtowns as the once vibrant streets were replaced with boarded-up shops and graffiti-covered building façades.

Though the deterioration of the retail structure was more pronounced in the United States, city center retailing in Canada also experienced considerable loss of revenue and clientele to the suburban shopping mall (Filion et al., 2004; Kalman, 1985; TD Economics, 2002; Hoyt, 2005c, 2006). From 1948 to 1954, overall retail sales were booming, but the share of downtown retailing fell by one-quarter in 13 of the largest metropolitan areas of the United States (Frieden and Sagalyn, 1989). In Toronto, core retail sales as a percentage of metropolitan Toronto declined from 43 percent in 1951 to 23 percent by 1966 (Gad and Matthew, 2000). This threat to the retailing structure in downtowns became more pervasive in the mid-1970s with the growth of catalog shopping, big discounters, category killers, and big-box retailers (Eade, 1999; Gruidl and Kline, 1992; Milder, 1997). The past decade of Internet retailing has only added to this decline (Jones, 2000; Miles et al., 2000).

In response, city governments in North America have partnered with the private sector to undertake several types of pro-business, urban renewal projects to reverse this trend of decline and decay (Burayidi, 2001; Cook, 1980). Most of these projects were combined with financial incentives to attract retail investment in the downtown (Gratz and Mintz, 1998). Walzer and Kline (2001) show that the five most popular economic development tools used by city governments in the United States between 1993 and 1998 were tax increment financing districts, business expansion and regulation programs, property tax abatement, low-cost municipal loans, and business assistance programs (Burayidi, 2001). However, most of these tools have been criticized because they failed to involve a range of stakeholders or formulate an integrated vision for the downtown (Jacobs, 1961; Abrams, 1965; Hannigan, 1998; Frieden and Sagalyn, 1989; Teaford, 1990).

In this study we argue that the BID model is not only able to address the aforementioned challenges, but also capable of promoting a holistic retail strategy for downtowns. We examine the role of the BID model by answering the following question: How do BID activities affect the retail economy of downtowns? This chapter is divided into four sections. First, we discuss the importance of retail vis-à-vis activity in downtowns. The second section presents a tier diagram to position and measure BID activities. The third applies the three levels of the tier diagram by examining each through the lens of six case studies. The aim is to provide a synoptic and macroscopic explanation of retail-oriented BID practices in both Canada and the United States. Drawing on these findings, we close the chapter by offering a set of recommendations for improving the relationship between BID and retail-related activities.

BIDs and Downtown Retail

A review of the urban planning literature shows that there is no standard definition for the terms downtown, retail, and BID. For the purpose of this investigation, downtown is a commercial hub within the city that may or may not be the central business district (Urban Land Institute, 1980). Therefore, problems associated with central business districts are treated as analogous to problems with downtowns. In contrast, the definition of retail is a challenge because of its dynamic nature. The early-19th-century retail structure, which was largely identified by its geographical location, has evolved into a complex industry that varies by country, region, age of retail stock, land-use controls, and consumer characteristics (Jones and Simmons, 1990). In short, this study defines retail as the business activity of selling goods or services to the final consumer. Lastly, BIDs are publicly sanctioned and privately directed organizations that pay for services to improve shared, geographically defined, outdoor public spaces; they also subscribe to a self-help doctrine whereby a compulsory self-taxing mechanism generates multiyear revenue.* Typical services include such activities as consumer marketing, maintenance, security, capital improvements, and economic development (Hoyt, 2005b).

In exploring the relationship between retail and downtown revitalization, the argument presented here is that retail and downtown economies are agglomeration economies (Christaller, 1933; Losch, 1939). Downtowns, with their various social and cultural assets, promote tourist-based consumer spending. Economic theory suggests that spending within the marketplace is a function of the population that can be attracted to the market (McClure, 2001, p. 224). Accordingly, tourist spending provides potential short-term revenues for retailers. At the same time, the presence of a strong retail offer is important for attracting consumers to the downtown (British Council of Shopping Centers, 2002). In the long term, interaction of the commercial and consumer environments creates brand and place equity, which supports sustainable economic development while promoting an environment complementary to the downtown's export economy. Though it is impossible to show causality between integrated long-term urban management and growth in rental values for the retail

---

* In Canada, BIDs are officially called business improvement areas (BIAs). In this chapter we use the term BIAs interchangeably with BIDs when referring to the Canadian BIDs.

Table 7.1   Range of stakeholders and expectations

Stakeholder	Expectation
Property owners (producers)	Short-term high rent and long-term place equity
Retailers (producers)	Short-term profit maximization and long-term brand equity
Consumers (users)	Retail and entertainment destination that has a "buzz"
Government (intermediaries)	Long-term sustainable development, increase in tax base

Source: Adapted from Gopal (2003).

sector, most academics and practitioners support the argument that promoting retail complements the downtown economy and plays an important role in revitalizing it (Briffault, 1999; Carley et al., 2001; Cuomo, 1999; Distributive Trades Economic Development Committee, 1988; Evans, 1997; Fleissing, 1984).

While downtown retail seems to provide an optimal way to revitalize downtowns, stakeholders often have divergent perceptions of the problems and potential solutions (Evans, 1997). For example, users see downtowns as dirty, unsafe, and inconvenient for shopping (Hoyt, 2004, 2005a); developers see them as congested places that may not give a high return for investment; and retailers are concerned with profit maximization and brand equity. Moreover, these stakeholders also have different expectations, as summarized in Table 7.1.

Though the aims of the stakeholders are seemingly divergent, their motivations are interdependent and can be unified through a retail-led solution. The findings of the International Downtown Association (IDA) Retail Panel (2006) suggest that there is a growing recognition among the divergent stakeholders that "retail is the glue that holds downtown together as a community" (p. 4). Intermediaries, such as local governments, are satisfied when they get occupiers who contribute to the tax base and users who promote downtown's tourist economy. The interests of property owners are fulfilled when they attract occupiers such as retailers, who pay rent in the short term and contribute to place equity* in the long term. Retailer interests are satisfied when they secure profits in the short term and brand equity† in the long term. In sum, all interests are met through a retail-led focus, while the combined presence of both users and occupiers ensures long-term sustainability of the downtown. However, unlike the centralized management system of shopping malls that directs the collective interests of retailers and customers, there is often no organization apart from BIDs that delivers an integrated vision for downtown revitalization by providing a common forum to enable stakeholder dialogue.

---

* Place equity is defined as the added value a location brings to the occupiers beyond the functional benefits provided.

† Brand equity is defined as the added value a brand name identity brings to a product or service that, if properly managed, creates influence and generates value.

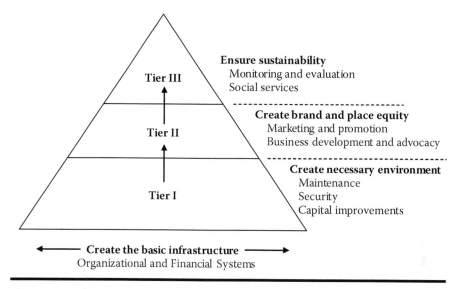

Figure 7.1 Three-tier structure depicting the BID model.

Positioning and Comparing BID Activities

Some BIDs have been functioning for more than three decades in North America. Yet, each municipality has adapted the model to suit its own specific needs. The diagram shown in Figure 7.1 depicts a tier structure to aid in visualizing the BID model (Gopal, 2003). According to this diagram, BIDs must carry out activities across all three tiers to promote a sustainable revitalization strategy in the long term. However, depending on the condition of the downtown, BID budget, and degree of participation from the local government, BIDs may directly commence with activities from tier II or III.

According to this diagram, the organizational and financial system provides the basic infrastructure essential for undertaking activities across all tiers. Tier I represents activities required to change both the physical environment and the negative perception of the downtown. Tier II activities are central to promoting and improving the retail offer of downtowns in the long term. The trends observed in the cases (discussed in detail in the following section) suggest that as BID activity matures, budgetary allocation for tier I activities such as maintenance and capital improvements may decrease relative to allocations made in the BID's early years, while allocations for tier II activities such as marketing and promotion usually increase.

Because developing sophisticated monitoring systems takes time and resources, which usually evolve only after BID activity has matured, these activities have been placed in the third level. In short, tier I and tier II activities promote all aspects of the downtown, and tier III activities ensure long-term sustainability of BID activities.

The tier diagram presents an idealistic way for BIDs to evolve their strategy. However, BID activity essentially complements and augments public sector intervention. As the efficiency of public sector intervention varies across downtowns, BIDs may undertake activities in more than one tier at a time if they have the financial and human resources available to support such an effort. The important thing is that in the long term, BID intervention should encompass activities across all tiers.

Application of the Tier Diagram

To understand BID practices in Canada and the United States, we applied the tier diagram to six case studies—three in each country. The BIDs selected for study in the United States are Times Square Alliance, Center City District, and Downtown Alliance. In Canada we selected Bloor-Yorkville, Downtown Vancouver, and Downtown Yonge.

The BIDs we selected as case studies are located in large cities, have operated for at least four years with annual budgets that exceed $200,000, and explicitly declare retail a strategic focus. The minimum requirement of four years of operation was chosen because it would ensure a sufficient timeline to study changes and challenges faced since the organization's inception. These cases were first studied in 2002–2003 (Gopal, 2003), and follow-up work was done in 2005–2006.

The analysis begins with an overview of the organizational and financial system that forms the basic infrastructure in the model. This is followed by a general discussion of the activities associated with each tier.

Organizational and Financial Systems

The organizational and financial systems create the foundation that underlies the success of the BID model. This foundation creates the support required to build a common management forum, which can bring different stakeholders together as a team to promote a common vision and strategy for the downtown. Table 7.2 profiles the organizational and financial details of the six BIDs.

Tier I Activities

Tier I activities involve the provision of basic services that change both the physical ambience and negative perception of the downtown and create the environment necessary to undertake activities associated with the other two tiers. Downtowns, unlike shopping malls, have no provision for enforcing maintenance and security requirements. To overcome this problem and enhance consumer experience, BIDs focus on administering maintenance and security programs. Similar to a shopping

Table 7.2 Organizational profiles

Name, location, and year established	Organization type and budget by expense (2004–2005)	Physical size	Financial structure	Identity	Performance measures
Times Square Alliance, New York, 1992	Nonprofit $10,487,500 (Times Square Alliance, 2005)	21 blocks[a]	0.3% of the assessed value of commercial buildings	Icon of entertainment, culture, and urban life	Customer surveys, pedestrian counts, and records of programs
Center City District, Philadelphia, 1990	Quasi-governmental $13,548,700	120 blocks	Assessed value $10 to $400,000 and other sources	Clean, safe and attractive destination to live, work, and visit, where retail, particularly restaurants and outdoor cafes, are important to help animate streetscape and public environment	Customer surveys, number of jobs created, occupancy rates and crime rates, and pedestrian counts
Downtown Alliance, New York, 1995	Nonprofit $17,784,296	40 blocks[a]	Special tax assessment on commercial space and other sources	Primarily a business district, where retailers are an important component	Customer surveys, pedestrian counts, and number of businesses
Bloor-Yorkville, Toronto, 1986	Nonprofit $1,155,562 (CAD$1,304,415)	27 blocks	Special tax assessment, subsidies and grants	Toronto's premiere shopping, dining, and tourist district with the ultimate fusion of historic charm and modern seduction	Records of programs

continued

Table 7.2 (continued)   Organizational profiles

Name, location, and year established	Organization type and budget by expense (2004–2005)	Physical size	Financial structure	Identity	Performance measures
Downtown Vancouver, Vancouver, 1990	Quasi-governmental $2,001,212[b] (CAD$2,258,997)	90 blocks	32 cents per $1,000 of assessed property value	A vibrant, healthy, and diverse place to live, work, shop, and visit	Public and member surveys, other surveys, and program records
Downtown Yonge, Toronto, 2001	Nonprofit $1,495,046.10[b] (CAD$1,687,630)	25 blocks	Special tax assessment, subsidies, and grants	Rebrand area as Toronto's premiere shopping, business, and entertainment destination	Customer surveys, surveys by other agencies, number of retail sales, occupancy rates, and crime rates

Source: Adapted from Gopal (2003).

[a] Divided total block land area of the BID by an approximated area of a city block (around 160,000 square feet, or 800 × 200).

[b] CAD = 0.885885 USD (live mid-market rates as of July 31, 2006, Universal Time Coordinate (UTC), where mid-market rates are derived from mid-point between the buy and sell rates of large-value transactions in the global currency markets).

Table 7.3 Principal BID activities for FY 2005 (by percent of budget allocated)

BID	Marketing	Security	Maintenance	Capital improvements
Times Square Alliance	12%	31%	21%	1%
Center City District	13%	21%	33%	10%
Downtown Alliance	26%	14%	15%	21%
Bloor-Yorkville	20%	0%	50%	20%
Downtown Vancouver	17%[a]	48%	Security and maintenance percentage is combined	N/A
Downtown Yonge	21%	16%	23%	39%

Source: Adapted from Gopal (2003).
Note: N/A = not available.
[a] Combines allocation for marketing and communication (11.8%) with communications (5.53%).

mall's common area maintenance program, these activities are intended to alter both the reality and perception of downtowns as "unkempt" and "unsafe" places (Segal, 2002). The need for such programs has been aptly stated by businesses in the Downtown Vancouver BID: "If the basic problems deterring people from coming downtown are addressed, business is quite capable of selling and promoting itself" (Downtown Vancouver BIA, 2002a, p. 4). Accordingly, the management of Downtown Vancouver has maintained a budget allocation close to 50 percent for clean and safe programs. Like Downtown Vancouver, most of the BIDs surveyed allocate a very high percentage of their budget to tier I activities, as shown in Table 7.3.

Table 7.3 shows that most BIDs in our study place a high importance on tier I activities (security, maintenance, and capital improvements) as these constitute half or more of the total budget (Times Square Alliance, 53 percent; Center City District, 64 percent; Downtown Alliance, 50 percent; Bloor-Yorkville, 70 percent; Downtown Vancouver, 48 percent; Downtown Yonge, 78 percent). Although the percentage allocated is high, it varies across BIDs and is determined by both need and the arrangement that the BID has with the local government for provision of these services (Gopal, 2003). This allocation may even decrease as the local context improves. As shown in Table 7.4, the percentage of the Times Square Alliance's total budget allocated for tier I activities decreased steadily and considerably over time.

Tier II Activities

The academic literature suggests that one of the most important ingredients of a successful commercial area is the presence of a "good retail mix," which is defined

Table 7.4 Tier I budget allocation, Times Square Alliance

Activity	1996	1997	1998	1999	2000
Public safety	31%	29%	28%	23%	17%
Sanitation	23%	22%	20%	16%	12%
Capital improvements	6%	3%	3%	1%	2%

Source: Gopal (2003).

as a retail offer that caters to every section of the population (British Council of Shopping Centers, 2002). Tier II activities are most important for achieving this goal. The retail focus of these activities provides an effective way of reconciling the divergent goals of retailers and property owners as it promotes both brand and place equity. However, while creating the right retail mix is desirable, it is often a difficult process because unlike a shopping mall, the downtown does not represent a cultivated retail environment. Though most downtowns started from such a position, their subsequent decline resulted in erosion of their retail diversity. Given this backdrop, it is hardly a surprise to learn that almost all of the BIDs in our study have undertaken development strategies to enhance the scope of retail offerings in their district. The only variation that we discovered was in the focus of the strategy and the BID's level of involvement.

To understand these differences, we have broadly classified BID business development strategies as proactive or passive recruitment strategies, following Milder's (1997) nomenclature. A BID is said to pursue a passive recruitment strategy when it does not try to either identify or directly attract prospective tenants and involves itself with research activities such as a market study. On the other hand, a BID is the proponent of a proactive strategy when it actively recruits retailers for the downtown. Such efforts include acting upon the market study to identify current and potential customers, informing stakeholders of the factors affecting their viability, and establishing actionable business recruitment programs (Cloar et al., 2002). Table 7.5 compares the type and focus of strategies for the six study BIDs.

As shown in Table 7.5, while most BIDs follow proactive strategies, often each BID has a different focus that is driven primarily by its mission. For example, Downtown Alliance focuses on marketing the area as a premier destination for retail and business activities, whereas the unique selling proposition for the Times Square Alliance is entertainment. Downtown Yonge, a relatively new BID, has managed to achieve considerable success in improving the business environment by making it more conducive to attracting quality retail and entertainment options into the district through proactive efforts like tourism designation, physical improvements, and marketing efforts. On the other hand, Center City District can support a passive strategy, as active efforts to augment and support comprehensive renewal in center city are being carried out by the Central Philadelphia Development Corporation, a private nonprofit corporation closely supported by the BID.

Table 7.5 Comparison of business development strategies

BID	Strategy type	Strategy focus
Times Square Alliance	Proactive	Entertainment-focused strategy that actively solicits businesses in that area
Downtown Alliance	Proactive	Targeted business and retail development
Center City District	Passive	Research reports providing key statistics about the center city to assist businesses in making decisions
Bloor-Yorkville	Passive to proactive	From publishing a development guide to undertaking Bloor-Street transformation project
Downtown Vancouver	Proactive	Targeted development of safe and vibrant downtown
Downtown Yonge	Proactive	Active measures such as getting area designated for tourism, which allows retailers to open on statuary holidays

Source: Adapted from Gopal (2003).

In the following section, we detail the evolution and impact of these strategies for a few of these BIDs.

Times Square Alliance's entertainment-focused strategy effectively changed the retail mix from one composed of mainly adult-use establishments and dollar stores into an entertainment and shopping destination. In the early 1970s, the 42nd Street area in Times Square was saturated with adult-use bookstores and establishments, secondary-level retail stores, and street crime. In the early 1980s, city and state officials united to create the 42nd Street Development Project administered by the New York Empire State Development Corporation, which established a 13-acre renewal site covering two city blocks along 42nd Street between Broadway and Eighth Avenue (About the New 42nd Street, n.d.). The project's plan was to restore and adapt the historic theaters for cultural and entertainment uses. In April 1990, the state succeeded in taking ownership of two-thirds of the project site, including six of the nine theaters. Shortly after the BID began operations in 1992, the 42nd Street Development Project cleared key sites on West 42nd Street. Although government initiated the development process, an organization like the Times Square Alliance was necessary to effectively manage the reinvestment process. This BID was successful in reducing adult-use establishments (from 47 in 1994 to 17 by 1998) as well as integrating the remaining establishments into the retail and residential fabric of the area (Sagalyn, 2001). The strategy focused on making the area an entertainment destination by attracting entertainment and dining providers into the area and enabled the BID to not only change the retail mix of the nighttime economy, but also create an identity that was distinct from the downtown business district.

The Times Square Alliance is an inspiring model for Downtown Yonge, a BID with a similar history and set of struggles. Yonge Street, once the premier street in downtown Toronto, fell into a state of disrepair by the late 1970s. The high-end shops and quality retailers had been replaced by secondary retail, adult-use establishments, vacant storefronts, street violence, drug dealing, and pan handling (Yonge Street Business and Resident Association, 1999, p. 3). In 1993, the owners of the Eaton Center, one of the largest and most successful retail establishments in the area, partnered with a group of concerned property owners to initiate a dialogue for the purpose of revitalizing the area. This resulted in the formation of the Yonge Street Business and Resident Association who, together with the city of Toronto, initiated the Yonge Street Regeneration Program. A recently published report describes how deep-rooted the problems were and that the range of necessary and fundamental changes could not have been achieved without "public intervention, in partnership with the private sector" (Yonge Street Business and Resident Association, 1999, p. 4). Accordingly, the Yonge-Dundas Regeneration Project was developed to improve the physical appearance of the area, create a sense of place, and attract new entertainment and retail by creating an urban entertainment center with a large megaplex cinema.

Marketing was considered critical to simulate interest in the project's marketplace area, and Times Square served as the main model in terms of creating a strong "branding" concept as well as for generating publicity. Although the project was successful in achieving most of its goals, funding constraints limited its success. Accordingly, the report recommended the formation of a business improvement area that would be able to carry forward the momentum of change more effectively (Yonge Street Business and Resident Association, 1999). In lieu of this recommendation, the city approved formation of the Downtown Yonge Business Improvement Association in 2001. The main focus in the first year of operation was security, maintenance, and capital improvements. In addition to these tier I activities, the BID worked with Eaton Center, one of the largest and most successful retail establishments in the area, to change a large concrete wall that occupied nearly an entire block into a more attractive and pedestrian-friendly façade. This marked the beginning of a series of interventions to attract investment, move out the adult-use establishments and dollar and convenience stores, and rebrand the area (Robinson, 2006a). It is worth noting that one of the major victories for the BID was designating Yonge Street as Toronto's first official tourist area; among other things, the ordinance enables retailers to remain open on statuary holidays. According to the BID's analysis of the market, 86 percent of respondents indicated that shopping was the main reason they spent time in the downtown and 77 percent of respondents said that they would recommend Downtown Yonge as a great place for retail shopping; only 17 percent said that they would recommend Bloor-Yorkville or other areas (Downtown Yonge BIA, 2005, pp. 3–6). These results are important because Bloor-Yorkville area is widely known as Toronto's premier shopping area. It would be interesting, at a later date, to explore whether the retail offer of Downtown Yonge effectively provides direct competition or if the high-end nature of Bloor-Yorkville is less appealing to the larger market of consumers.

Downtown Alliance faced a unique challenge after the terrorist attacks on New York's World Trade Center buildings in 2001. These attacks triggered outmigration and market volatility that played an instrumental role in the BID into pursuing proactive area promotion strategies. A survey of Lower Manhattan commercial tenants suggested 25 percent of the companies did not intend to renew their leases or planned to leave New York City altogether, and 50 percent of the companies that leased additional space after September 11 had leased space outside New York State (Downtown Alliance, 2003, p. 3). Given an investment climate where "office space is too available and visitors too few," the BID undertook proactive business development activities that offered innovative grants, loans, and financial services to both businesses and the large residential population in Battery Park City (International Downtown Association, 2002, p. 3). Along with Seedco, a national community development intermediary, Downtown Alliance created a $30 million grant-and-loan program to aid small retailers and businesses immediately at or near ground zero. It partnered with the Lower Manhattan Development Corporation and the government to create a number of grants and loan programs for small businesses in the affected areas. The BID also expanded its publicity efforts by coordinating a $7.5 million "River to River" festival to attract visitors and provide support to workers and residents. With more than 500 public events, the festival was the largest outdoor festival in New York City's history. The success of these initiatives is evident. After 9/11, only 9 of the 50 largest commercial tenants in and around the World Trade Center remained. However, a year later more than half of them had returned or made plans to return. By the end of 2005, the vacancy rate was down to 10.6 percent, the lowest since September 11, 2001 (Downtown Alliance, 2005, p. 4).

Finally, we examine the case of Bloor-Yorkville that has changed from a passive to proactive business development strategy. With more than 700 shops, the Bloor-Yorkville area has been compared to Fifth Avenue in New York and Rodeo Drive in Los Angeles (Bloor-Yorkville BIA, 2006a). It is also home to a number of luxury condominiums, housing some of the wealthiest residents of Toronto. However, the BID is faced with the challenge of managing the significant differences between the two principal retail streets—Bloor and Yorkville. Bloor Street is best known for its shopping and features retail chains such as Gucci, Prada, and Tiffany and Company. Also, the nearby vicinity of the street is home to several five-star hotels and multistory office complexes. In contrast, Yorkville Street is characterized by turn-of-the-century Victorian homes that have since been transformed into a variety of "mom and pop" businesses. The first few years of this decade have seen tremendous construction in this area that have "eroded the identity of the region" (J. Robinson, personal interview, March 17, 2003). Initially, the BID adopted a passive response by publishing a set of urban design guidelines that would lend some uniformity to various ongoing construction projects. However, given the lukewarm success of this strategy and increasing competition from other commercial areas such as Downtown Yonge, the BID has transitioned to a more proactive strategy. At the time of the writing of this chapter, the BID is actively involved with the Bloor-Street transformation project. According to the Bloor-Yorkville website, the project will transform Bloor Street into a more pedestrian-friendly area and will enable it to rebrand itself as "one of the most daring and exciting streets in the world!" (Bloor-Yorkville BIA, 2006b).

Tier III Activities

Thus far we have demonstrated that BIDs intend to provide a well-managed and marketed environment that creates "both the revenue and political will to keep commercial streets clean, safe and economically vibrant" (Segal, 2002, p. 2). Moreover, their approach employs the geographic, economic, social, and cultural resources of the area to create brand and place equity for the downtown. The focus on enhancing local attributes helps establish and preserve a distinct identity that differentiates the downtown from other retail and commercial locations both within and outside the city limits. Next, we provide evidence to support our claim that tier III monitoring and evaluation activities are essential to sustaining the retail efforts made through tier I and tier II activities. The City Center District has been chosen because it pioneered some of the activities of crime prevention and security in the United States; Downtown Vancouver has been selected because of its innovative monitoring program; and Downtown Yonge's security initiative highlights the importance of monitoring to realign the focus of ongoing initiatives.

In general, BID security activities are similar, though the crime and safety monitoring systems vary considerably across organizations. In the case of the Center City District, customer surveys, data in geographically referenced format, and advanced statistical tracking systems all help monitor the effectiveness of security and other BID initiatives. These systems have helped the BID drastically reduce the incidence and perception of crime in Philadelphia's downtown for more than a decade. For example, statistics from the police substation showed that between 2001 and 2005, major crime in the BID area has decreased 14.5 percent (Center City District, 2005). In the same period, theft from autos in the BID area decreased 30.5 percent (N. Goldenberg, personal communication, July 17, 2006). Along with security initiatives, the BID conducts periodic surveys to monitor consumer awareness and perception of these programs (Gopal, 2006a). Relying on such an extensive monitoring and feedback system, the BID continually fine-tunes its security measures. The effectiveness of this strategy is readily apparent. Since the BID's inception in 1990, serious crime has been cut in half and petty crimes have been reduced by more than two-thirds (Center City District and Central Philadelphia Development Corporation, 2006, p. 36).

Downtown Vancouver implemented several endeavors to monitor the effectiveness of their security initiatives. One such program is the "mystery shopper program," a scheme employed by retail franchises and theme parks. As a part of this program, BID members pose as ordinary citizens, approach BID street ambassadors for assistance, and report their findings. This program has been very successful, as it allows the BID to collect "concrete, quantified, unbiased data about services rendered; it monitors consistency of consumer relations; and it creates an awareness on the part of employees that their actions count and can have a serious impact on growth and success of business" (Downtown Vancouver BIA, 2002b, p. 2). Additionally, the BID commissions an external market research firm to conduct an annual public survey of the residents of Great Vancouver and a member survey to solicit opinions into the effectiveness of the BID's current programs and gain insights for future interventions (Downtown Vancouver BIA, 2005, 2006).

Finally, we use the Downtown Yonge case to show how monitoring helped the BID correct an oversight in its security initiative. In 2002, the Downtown Yonge BIA hired police officers to reduce criminal activity and improve public perception of safety because the city and police refused to increase police patrols in the district (Robinson, 2006b). An independent survey commissioned by the BID in 2003 showed that though crime had reduced, there was little or no change in the perception of safety among the BID members. In fact, very few of the members surveyed were aware that such a program was under way (Plum, 2003). As a result, the BID used these findings to launch an extensive campaign to improve awareness and realign its strategy. Having realized the importance of monitoring early on, this BID has been proactive in its efforts to create an effective monitoring and feedback system. To develop new strategies and improve the effectiveness of its ongoing programs, it has commissioned pro-bono studies from Ryerson University's Center for the Study of Commercial Activity and the Criminology Department of Carleton University (Gopal, 2006b).

Our findings suggest that while tier I and tier II activities create the environment necessary for retail and businesses to flourish, performance monitoring plays an important role in aligning strategy to the myriad needs in the continually evolving downtown.

Conclusions and Recommendations

Downtowns are distinctive because of their central locations and sociocultural and historic importance. However, the expansion of the physical boundaries of cities, rise of new transit technologies, and development of different retail forms have fueled alternative markets that have challenged the centrality of this position. The urban regeneration programs in the past have relied on strategies such as mixed-use zoning and pedestrian-oriented planning to revitalize the commercial core. However, these infrastructure-based efforts have had limited success, as they did not involve the key stakeholders. Moreover, they lacked a comprehensive and long-term vision. Our findings suggest that the BID model with a retail-led strategy addresses the concerns of multiple stakeholders and creates a consumer-oriented commercial environment that augments footfall and spending.

In this study we used a tier diagram to understand the role of BID activities in promoting the retail economy of the downtown. Our findings show that the goal of most BIDs is to create "destination retailing"—an area that attracts expenditures from outside the region to provide additional revenues to the key stakeholders, namely, the businesses and the government. BIDs promote destination retailing by promoting retail, dining, and entertainment. The higher financial return and higher growth opportunities promoted by this strategy enable them to sustain and attract new consumers, thus ensuring long-term sustainability. Interestingly, many urban regeneration projects have strived to meet this goal, but were later criticized for being able to create an inventory of retail space but being unable to change the underlying economics that create consumer demand. BIDs' retail-focused approach incorporates elements of both demand- and supply-side economics to effectively address the concerns and interests of the divergent stakeholders. Part of the success can be attributed to their centralized management strategy, distinctive organizational system, and innovative delivery style. These factors, when combined with strong marketing strategies and proactive interventions to leverage the local resources, help ensure the right retail mix. Moreover, they create brand and place equity that attracts footfall and spending and serves as the area's unique selling proposition.

However, there is great variation in the way BIDs implement retail and business development strategy and performance monitoring mechanisms. These variations could undermine the sustainability of this approach. Based on our analysis, we offer some suggestions to inform existing BID practices:

1. Create a targeted retail and business development strategy. As discussed earlier, a targeted retail and business development strategy (tier II activities) is essential for promoting sustainable retail and commercial development. A passive recruitment strategy is advisable only if the local government or another local agency is proactive and the BID is working in close conjunction with that agency to ensure pursuit of a common goal and prevent counterproductive activities.

2. Construct a rigorous performance measurement structure. Performance evaluation (tier III activity) is essential to understanding the utility of ongoing programs and mapping the direction of future interventions. Though most BIDs conduct consumer surveys, very few have adopted rigorous measure-

ment techniques or made an attempt to standardize data collection processes (Mitchell, 1999).*

3. Secure alternative sources of funding. Currently, the BID model relies on the buy-in of property owners and businesses within the area to finance its activities. Alternative sources of funding allow BIDs the flexibility to expand operations as well as sustain ongoing programs during economic downswings. Some BIDs, like the Center City District, engage in fee-for-service maintenance and security contracts with smaller, nearby BIDs.

4. Encourage regional coordination. In an era when mobility is increasing and consumerism has made most downtowns indistinguishable from one another, attracting consumer dollars requires a regional strategy. The advantage of this approach is that it links the downtown to other destinations while giving the BID access to a wider set of resources. However, this strategy may raise concern from assessment payers, who are principally interested in promoting their district. To mitigate such concerns, the BID should expand its scope only after it has become well established in the area.

In conclusion, the findings of this study suggest that BIDs have been successful in improving the commercial environment of the downtown and in enhancing the shopping experience for consumers. Their participatory style of operation stimulates local structures and networks while promoting the character and identity of a place. However, the level of success is varied, as most BIDs do not undertake activities from all tiers of the diagram that we have constructed. This may undermine the sustainability of their approach and, in some instances, lead to a business mix that fails to adequately support the downtown's retail economy. Our recommendations, therefore, should be deployed as necessary to direct BID delivery style.

References

About the New 42nd Street. n.d. History of the block. In About the new 42nd Street. http://www.new42.org/about_history.cfm (accessed May 10, 2006).

Abrams, C. 1965. *The city is the frontier*. New York: Harper & Row.

Downtown Alliance. 2003. The downtown report. http://www.downtownny.com/about/default.aspx?sid=192 (accessed April 9, 2003).

Downtown Alliance. 2005. Downtown Alliance annual report 2005. http://www.downtownny.com/about/default.aspx?sid=192 (accessed May 14, 2006).

Bloor-Yorkville BIA. 2006a, May 20. About us. http://www.bloor-yorkville.com/07abus.html (accessed May 23, 2006).

Bloor-Yorkville BIA. 2006b, May 20. Bloor Street Project. http://www.bloor-yorkville.com/09bloor.html (accessed May 23, 2006).

---

* For an extensive discussion of measuring the performances of BIDs, see the Caruso and Weber chapter in this volume.

Briffault, R. 1999. A government for our time? Business improvement districts and urban governance. *Columbia Law Review* 99(2), 365–477.

British Council of Shopping Centers. 2002. *Managing the retail-led development of the future*. London: The Henley Centre.

Burayidi, M., ed. 2001. *Downtowns: Revitalizing the centers of small urban communities*. New York: Routledge.

Carley, M., Kirk, K., and McIntosh, S. 2001. *Retailing, sustainability and neighbourhood regeneration*. York, England: Joseph Rowntree Foundation.

Center City District. 2005. 2005–2009 CCD plan and budget. http://www.centercityphila. org/docs/plan2005.pdf (accessed July 29, 2006).

Center City District and Central Philadelphia Development Corporation. 2006. State of center city 2006. http://www.centercityphila.org/docs/socc2006.pdf (accessed July 12, 2006).

Christaller, W. 1993. *Central places in southern Germany*. Englewood Cliffs, NJ: Prentice Hall.

Cloar, J., Stabler, E., and DeVito, A. P. 2002. *Centralized retail management*. Washington, DC: Urban Land Institute.

Comedia. 1991. *Out of hours: A study of economic, social, and cultural life in twelve town centres in the UK*. London: Comedia in association with Colouste Gulbenkian Foundation.

Cook, R. S. 1980. *Zoning for downtown urban design*. Lexington, MA: Lexington Books.

Cuomo, A. 1999. *New markets: The untapped retail buying power in America's inner cities*. Washington, DC: Department of Housing and Urban Development.

Distributive Trades Economic Development Committee. 1988. *The future of the high street*. London: National Economic Development Office.

Downtown Vancouver BIA. 2002a. Annual report: 2001–2002. http://www.downtown-vancouver.net/files/PDF/publications/annual_7_9_02.pdf (accessed July 29, 2006).

Downtown Vancouver BIA. 2002b, August 16. Customer focus for ambassadors. http://www.downtownvancouver.net/files/PDF/media/media_release_ _customer_focus_for_ambassadors.pdf (accessed July 29, 2006).

Downtown Vancouver BIA. 2005. Three year strategic plan: 2004–2007. http://www.downtownvancouver.net/files/PDF/dvbia.strat.plan04.pdf (accessed June 20, 2006).

Downtown Vancouver BIA. 2006. Annual report: 2005–2006. http://www.downtown-vancouver.net/files/PDF/DVBIA_Annual_Report_06.pdf (accessed July 29, 2006).

Downtown Yonge BIA. 2005, August 29. *Downtown Yonge BIA market analysis: Final report on 2005 telephone survey*. Toronto, Ontario, Canada: Author.

Eade, C. 1999. Wonder Wal. *Property Week*, November 5, pp. 34–36.

Evans, R. 1997. *Regenerating town centres*. Manchester, NY: Manchester University Press.

Filion, P., Hoernig, H., Bunting, T., and Sands, G. 2004. The successful few: Healthy downtowns of small metropolitan regions. *Journal of the American Planning Association* 70:328–343.

Fleissing, W. B. 1984. The Yerba Buena center. In *The city as stage*, ed. K. W. Green. Washington, DC: Partners for Livable Places.

Ford, L. R. 1994. *Cities and buildings: Skyscrapers, skid row, and suburbs*. Baltimore: John Hopkins University Press.

Frieden, B. J., and Sagalyn, L. B. 1989. *Downtown, Inc.: How America rebuilds cities.* Cambridge, MA: MIT Press.

Gad, G., and Matthew, M. 2000. Central and suburban downtowns. In *Canadian cities in transition*, ed. T. Bunting and P. Filion, 248–273. New York: Oxford University Press.

Gopal, D. 2003. Promoting retail to revitalize downtown: An examination of the business improvement district idea. Unpublished master's thesis, Department of Urban Studies and Planning, Massachusetts Institute of Technology, Cambridge, MA.

Gopal, D. 2006a. Center City District questionnaire. Unpublished questionnaire.

Gopal, D. 2006b. Downtown Yonge BIA questionnaire. Unpublished questionnaire.

Gratz, R. B., and Mintz, N. 1998. *Cities back from the edge: New life for downtown.* New York: John Wiley & Sons.

Gruidl, J., and Kline, S. 1992. The impact of large discount stores on retail sales in Illinois communities. *Rural Research Report*, Vol. 3, No. 2. Macomb, IL: Western Illinois University.

Hannigan, J. 1998. *Fantasy city.* London: Routledge.

Hoyt, L. 2004. Collecting private funds for safer public spaces: An empirical examination of the business improvement district concept. *Environment and Planning B: Planning and Design* 31:367–80.

Hoyt, L. 2005a. Do business improvement district organizations make a difference? Crime in and around commercial areas in Philadelphia. *Journal of Planning Education and Research* 25:185–203.

Hoyt, L. 2005b. Planning through compulsory commercial clubs: Business improvement districts. *Economic Affairs* 25:24–27.

Hoyt, L. 2005c. The business improvement district: An internationally diffused approach to revitalization. Washington, DC: International Downtown Association.

Hoyt, L. 2006. Importing ideas: The transnational transfer of urban revitalization. *International Journal of Public Administration* 29:221–243.

IDA Retail Panel. 2006. The future of retail in downtown. *Downtown News Briefs* 8:3–8.

International Downtown Association. 2002. Welcome to Boston! *Downtown News Briefs*, August, pp. 3–6.

Jacobs, J. 1961. *The death and life of great American cities.* New York: Random House.

Jones, K. 2000. Dynamics of the Canadian retail environment. In *Canadian cities in transition*, ed. T. Bunting and P. Filion, 404–422. New York: Oxford University Press.

Jones, K., and Simmons, J. 1990. *The retail environment.* New York: Routledge.

Kalman, H. 1985. Crisis on main street. In *Reviving main street*, ed. D. Holdsworth, 3–54. Toronto, Ontario, Canada: University of Toronto Press in association with Heritage Canada Foundation.

Losch, A. 1939. *The economics of location.* New Haven, CT: Yale University Press.

Loukaitou-Sideris, A., and Banerjee, T. 1998. *Urban design downtown: Poetics and politics of form.* Berkeley, CA: University of California Press.

McClure, K. 2001. Managing the growth of retail space. In *Downtowns: Revitalizing the centers of small urban communities*, ed. M. A. Burayidi, 223–48. New York: Routledge.

Milder, N. D. 1997. Niche strategies for downtown revitalization. New York: Downtown Research and Development Center.

Miles, M. E., Berens, G., and Weiss, M. A. 2000. Real estate development: Principles and process. Washington, DC: Urban Land Institute.

Mitchell, J. 1999. Business improvement districts and innovative service delivery. New York: The Pricewaterhouse Coopers Endowment for the Business of Government.

Plum, L. 2003. Responding to crime: Evaluation of the police patrol in the Downtown Yonge Street BIA. Unpublished study, Ryerson University, Toronto, Ontario, Canada.

Robinson, J. 2006a. Downtown Yonge: Key and new initiatives. Unpublished manuscript.

Robinson, J. 2006b. New police officers welcomed downtown. CNW Group Ltd. http://www.newswire.ca/en/releases/archive/May2006/16/c6615.html (accessed May 16, 2006).

Sagalyn, L. B. 2001. *Times Square roulette—Remaking the city icon.* Cambridge, MA: MIT Press.

Segal, M. B. 2002. ABCs for creating BIDs. Washington, DC: International Downtown Association.

TD Economics. 2002. A choice between investing in Canada's cities or disinvesting in Canada's future. TD Bank Financial Group Special Economics Report. http://www.td.com/economics/special/db_cities0402.pdf (accessed July 11, 2002).

Teaford, J. 1990. *The rough road to renaissance: Urban revitalization in America, 1940–1985.* Baltimore: John Hopkins University.

Times Square Alliance. 2005. Annual report 2005. http://timessquarenyc.org/about_us/indicator_reports.html (accessed May 14, 2006).

Urban Land Institute. 1980. *Downtown development handbook.* Washington, DC: Author.

Walzer, N., and Kline, S. 2001. An evaluation of approaches to downtown economic revitalization. In *Downtowns: Revitalizing the centers of small urban communities,* ed. M. A. Burayidi, 249–274. New York: Routledge.

Yonge Street Business and Resident Association. 1999. Yonge Street regeneration program: Final report of program director. Toronto, Canada: Yonge Street Business and Resident Association.

BIDS IN THE UNITED STATES

Chapter 8

Private Governments or Public Policy Tools? The Law and Public Policy of New Jersey's Special Improvement Districts*

Jonathan B. Justice and Robert S. Goldsmith

Contents

* An earlier version of this chapter was published as Justice and Goldsmith (2006).

Introduction

Business improvement districts (BIDs) are increasingly numerous and familiar worldwide. Their numbers have been increasing steadily since the early 1970s, in North America, where they originated, and elsewhere. In the United States alone more than 400 BIDs were documented in 1999, and the creation of BIDs has continued apace since then, spreading around the world to nearly every continent (Hoyt, 2003; Mitchell, 1999; Ratcliffe and Flanagan, 2004). In the United States, BIDs are now largely familiar, even taken for granted by commercial revitalization professionals and business people, while residents and visitors in the downtowns and neighborhoods of many large cities and hundreds of small towns experience BID-provided amenities and services. A conservative estimate would place the annual expenditures of U.S. BIDs at over $100 million, based on our calculations using data reported by Mitchell (1999).

Even as they have become familiar and widely accepted, however, BIDs remain the subject of controversies concerning the appropriate natures and relationships of public and private institutions and interests. BIDs are often described by their proponents and critics as *private governments*—organizations that "in varying degrees and in ways circumscribed by the ultimate coercive sanctions of public governments...exercise power over both members and non-members, often in vital areas of individual and social concern" (Lakoff and Rich, 1973, p. 1). Some observers enthusiastically endorse BIDs and similar special-district forms as a responsive, nonbureaucratic, and private-sector-led approach to reinventing the provision of local public services (Baer and Marando, 2001; Levy, 2001b; Mac Donald, 1996; Walker, 2003). Others see in BIDs all that is alarming in the hollowing out of general-purpose local governments at the turn of the century (Gallagher, 1995; Krohe, 1992; Mallett, 1995; Stark, 1998; Zukin, 1995) or reserve judgment (Pack, 1992). Are BIDs private governments created to serve new demands for services that result from social and spatial restructuring (see Mallett, 1993; Ward, 2006), or can they be better understood as *policy tools*—instruments employed by states and general-purpose local governments to mobilize a variety of tangible and intangible resources to advance public purposes (Salamon, 2002)?

In this chapter we use data from case law, case studies of local practices in four downtowns, and a statewide survey of New Jersey's special improvement districts (SIDs)* conducted by Downtown New Jersey (DNJ) in 2000–2001 and argue that New Jersey's BIDs can best be understood as genuine public–private *partnerships*† in that they serve simultaneously as policy tools through which state and local governments seek to advance general public interests and as self-help entities to further the more particular interests of local business communities. They take advantage of the complementarity of private and public interests in commercial revitalization. Business people's desires for greater business activity and property values are presumed to be advanced through enhancements to public space, and in turn to lead to improved government revenues and community access to goods and services, employment gains, and other amenities. Relevant New Jersey law facilitates this partnership by granting reasonable discretion to municipalities and their business sector partners in the formulation and pursuit of business district revitalization strategies.

We begin by reviewing briefly some of the literature about BIDs, taking note of various portrayals of the relationship of, and actual or apparent tensions between, private and public interests in the management of business districts. Next, we highlight selected provisions of New Jersey's enabling statute and present an overview of BIDs in New Jersey. Then, we discuss relevant case law that resolved questions concerning legislative intent and the balance of competing interests, costs, and benefits associated with BIDs in New Jersey. This is followed by a summary of case study research that examined the interplay of interests from the perspective of individual stakeholders in four New Jersey BIDs. BIDs in New Jersey are public–private partnerships that give significant, in many respects definitive, formal and practical authority to the local governments concerned. In this respect they are more genuine instruments of public policy than most other models of urban partnership. However,

---

* New Jersey's statute uses the terminology *special improvement district* (SID), but practitioners in New Jersey tend to use that state-specific terminology interchangeably with the more generic term *business improvement district* (BID). In this chapter we will usually use SIDs to refer to specific districts and legal provisions within New Jersey, and BIDs to refer to districts elsewhere and as a generic term for the category of districts that includes SIDs.

† By "partnerships" we mean cooperative arrangements of varying degrees of formality that "further the common interests of the partners beyond what is likely to be produced by the existing system or by each working independently" (Lichfield, 1998, p. 110). A preferred model of partnership is characterized by "mutual respect, equal participation in decision making, mutual accountability and transparency" between entities that cooperate to advance mutual interests but remain distinct and autonomous (Brinckerhoff, 2002, pp. 325–326). For present purposes, we draw a distinction between this mutual, balanced form of partnership and the "unequal partnerships" through which publicly assisted private redevelopment efforts have sometimes allocated costs and risks to one partner and benefits to another (Squires, 1989).

we cannot confidently generalize from our examples to the entire universe of BIDs in the United States or elsewhere. Nor does the current state of evaluation research make possible confident assertions about whether New Jersey's approach represents a normatively more desirable model than other states'. We conclude by identifying some directions for continuing research into the democratic as well as service performance of BIDs, based on our findings and the limitations of our research.

BIDs in the Eyes of the Beholders

In their legal form, BIDs combine elements of two more traditional entities: special assessments and special district governments (for a good, concise discussion, see Houstoun, 1997). Like special assessments, they raise revenue to fund local improvements that benefit spatially specific segments of the public from those specifically benefited segments. This in principle fosters efficiency and equity through *fiscal equivalence* (identified as a requisite for allocative efficiency by Olson, 1969, and described as a form of equity by Ostrom et al., 1993). Unlike traditional approaches to special assessments, they are used to fund recurring activities, not just one-time capital improvements such as roads, sidewalks, or sewers. They thus share with special districts the characteristic of being operating entities with narrow scopes of action.

In the United States, BIDs are typically created by municipal designation, pursuant to the authority granted by state-level enabling statutes. Specific provisions vary from state to state and among municipalities, but generally some evidence of property owners' and business operators' active interest or at least acquiescence is a political, if not legal, prerequisite for the formation and continuation of BIDs. Within the specified boundaries of a BID, special assessments are levied and the proceeds used to provide capital improvements and ongoing services designed to benefit the properties and businesses within the district. Ad valorem assessments on real property are the most common source of finance, although many states, including New Jersey, allow for a variety of bases for property assessments and the imposition of business license fees as sources of BID revenue. The services provided are almost always explicitly supplemental to general municipal services, and generally run the gamut of place management activities and physical improvements associated with the economic restructuring, organization, design, and promotional elements of a commercial revitalization effort.* In big cities particularly, BIDs have frequently focused on reducing visitor-deterring perceptions of urban "crime and grime" (Traub, 1996). The archetypal although not universal (there are significant differences in the specific provisions of enabling statutes, even among the states in the United States) approach to BID governance is that the planning and management of BID-provided services is overseen by an incorporated entity governed by the payers of the assessment, typically the district's property owners, business operators, or both.

---

* For a description of the four points of the Main Street approach to commercial revitalization, refer to the website of the National Main Street Center (National Trust for Historic Preservation, 2002).

It is this combination of governance by private commercial actors with the compulsory special-assessment-based financing arrangement that is generally regarded as the cause of BIDs' presumed distinctive effectiveness in selecting and accomplishing revitalization goals. Compulsory finance prevents the free-riding behavior that would otherwise result in undersupply of the collective good of business district improvements. Self-governance has proved a useful organizational principle for collective action in experimental settings, as well as in the management of actual common resources (Ostrom, 1990; Ostrom et al., 1994; Ostrom and Walker, 1997), and revitalization practitioners tend to believe that business leadership makes BIDs more responsive to the needs of commercial districts than other forms of organization would be. This combination of coercion and business leadership is also the basis for the private government designation, and prompts both the most enthusiastic endorsements, such as Mac Donald's (1996), and the most alarmed criticisms of the BID approach, such as Krohe's (1992) and Gallagher's (1995). Is the form of partnership between local governments and business interests that distinguishes BIDs from other approaches to organizing and financing commercial revitalization efforts too private, too public, or just right? Unsurprisingly, strong opinions exist on all sides, while the most careful analytical and evidence-based reports tend to be the most moderate in their concerns and claims.

Advocacy, Alarm, and Analysis

For advocates, key aspects of the BID approach to organizing commercial district revitalization include BIDs' operational leadership by business stakeholders, their narrowness of purpose, and their potential as a way to generate resources for BIDs in light of the fiscal stress experienced by general-purpose municipalities in the United States since the 1960s. Different observers and analysts of the BID approach vary, however, in their emphases on and understandings of these elements.

Emphasizing the role of businesses in organizing and managing BIDs, some advocates, such as journalist Heather Mac Donald (1996) or property owner Peter Malkin (as quoted by Traub, 1996), suggest that BIDs make it possible for the forward-thinking and efficient private sector to compensate for the failings of intellectually, financially, and organizationally bankrupt local governments. Others suggest that BIDs are a valuable tool that local governments seeking to revitalize business districts can use to mobilize resources in the face of severe fiscal constraints (Alexander, 2003; Bradley, 1995; Colley, 1999). Practitioners involved in helping to create and manage BIDs tend to portray the arrangement as representing a partnership for the mutual advantage of local governments and business people, although they may emphasize the role of business participation as ensuring that decisions are viewed by business people as legitimate, incorporate "business sense," and allow BIDs to move "at the speed of business."

For those alarmed by BIDs, the leading role they afford for business interests leads to the potential privatization and commodification of public space, especially through the use of abusive practices to exclude from urban commercial areas or other highly valued parts of cities the poor or other "undesirable" people and activities that might inconvenience shoppers and office workers (Gallagher, 1995; Krohe, 1992; Lofland, 2002; Mallett, 1994; Zukin, 1995). Municipal officials with no direct experience of BIDs are often fearful that a BID, once created, will run amok, spending recklessly and bringing fiscal and political hardships to all concerned. From another perspective, some business people view BIDs with suspicion, seeing them as instruments by which local governments will extract additional revenue from them without providing commensurate benefits.

There is still relatively little systematic evidence of BID's *actual* effects in terms of costs and benefits and the distribution thereof, but Pack (1992) offers a good summary of some of the potential costs and benefits of BIDs. Potential virtues of BIDs include increased property values and the assurance of fiscal equivalence in allocations of costs and benefits. Potential pitfalls include possible uncompensated costs to businesses, the diversion of city services and attention either toward or away from the district, possible externalities such as the displacement of crime to or businesses from adjoining areas, and the potential for the loss of a larger sense of community.

The potential for the creation of a partnership in local policy formulation as well as in operational decisions and administration is another significant aspect of BIDs. For some BID advocates, their role in influencing or even directly formulating local development policies can be seen as unambiguously beneficial (Levy, 2001a, 2001b), whereas for other observers it is a cause for caution in adopting the U.S. BID model elsewhere (Alexander, 2003). The director of Philadelphia's Center City District BID argues that "in addition to providing services, BIDs are clearly exercising a vital leadership role in their communities, articulating strategic alternatives, forging coalitions for change, and successfully implementing entrepreneurial solutions to chronic urban problems" (Levy, 2001b, p. 130). As examples of this beneficial policy role for BIDs, he cites the work of the Alliance for Downtown New York in directing tax abatements to stimulate residential redevelopment of older office buildings and his own BID's involvement in improving city social welfare programs and advising city government on strategic directions for downtown, both directly and in its capacity of providing staffing to a business advocacy organization (Levy, 2001a, 2001b).*

---

* An anonymous reviewer for an earlier version of this chapter pointed out that an alternative arrangement employed in such places as Atlanta, Denver, Seattle, St. Louis, Houston, and Raleigh is for BID stakeholders to work through companion membership organizations to address policy issues, while keeping the BID organizations themselves nominally focused on day-to-day service and management activities such as security and sanitation. This practice is also found in the United Kingdom, where town center management companies often retain strategic and policy-oriented roles in partnerships for downtown (re-)development, while creating BIDs to focus on delivering supplemental services to specific subdistricts within city centers (Justice et al., 2006). It remains an open question whether this is a substantively meaningful or merely formal distinction.

In the New Jersey context, practitioners observe that "merchants don't vote," because it is common for commercial property owners and business operators not to be residents of the municipalities in which their business interests are located. One advantage attributed to BIDs by proponents is that they provide the organizational and financial resources needed to counterbalance businesses' lack of influence over the operating environment for their businesses, as a number of New Jersey business people, local officials, and revitalization consultants pointed out in interviews conducted in 2002 and 2003. BIDs, these respondents asserted, were a valuable tool to help businesses respond to the electoral pressures on municipalities, which otherwise tend to foster neglect of investment in their business districts for the long run, in favor of short-term residential preferences. In the view of some critics, however, this enhancement of business influence is more worrisome or even downright undemocratic (Gallagher, 1995; Why RiverCenter Should be Abolished, 1999).

BIDs in New Jersey

Special improvement districts (SIDs) are enabled by New Jersey's highly flexible statute, which was adopted in 1984 as an extensive amendment to earlier legislation that had enabled the creation of a special-assessment district to finance the construction of a pedestrian mall in the state capital, Trenton (District Management Act, 1999). The first SID was created in 1985, in the township of Cranford, and the number of SIDs in the state grew exponentially thereafter, with more than 50 SIDs documented by 2001 (Justice, 2003) and nearly 80 by mid-2006 according to a guesstimate by the trade association Downtown New Jersey (B. Lippman, personal communication, September 5, 2006). By 2001, the latest date for which extensive descriptive data is available, New Jersey's SIDs in many ways were a microcosm of U.S. BIDs, in their range of sizes, governance structures, and services provided (see Table 8.1).

The provisions of the New Jersey statute make it possible to create SIDs that hew closely to the typical normative model of the BID, as well as forms that are quite different from that model. The statute empowers the state's municipalities* to employ "the broadest possible discretion" in creating SIDs and designating and empowering district management corporations (DMCs) to receive the special-assessment funds in order to plan and provide services and improvements for the districts. Districts are defined by listing the property tax block and lot identification numbers of each parcel included in a district. While the statute does require certain findings as part of the local governing body's rationale for creating a SID, there is no requirement that there be a formal referendum vote or petition in favor of designation (a positive stakeholder-approval test) or that municipalities drop SID proposals in the face of a certain

---

* New Jersey's 566 incorporated municipalities collectively encompass the total land area of the state.

Table 8.1 Comparison of selected New Jersey SID and U.S. BID population characteristics

	New Jersey SIDs, 2000–2001	U.S. BIDs, 1999
Survey responses/total population	33/52 (63%)	264/404 (65%)
Average BID size in blocks	20 blocks	20 blocks
Median number of businesses in BID	250	Not reported
Median number of property owners	153	Not reported
Annual budget, minimum	$45,000	$8,000
Annual budget, median	$214,000	$200,000
Annual budget, maximum	$3,972,074	$15,000,000
BIDs providing marketing services	94%	94%
BIDs providing maintenance services	85%	85%
BIDs providing public security (New Jersey) or public space regulation (United States)	36%	79%
Smallest governing board	7 members	3 members
Median governing board size	15 members	15 members
Largest governing board	30 members	51 members

Source: Data for U.S. BIDs in 1999 is from a census and mail survey conducted and reported by Mitchell (1999). Data for New Jersey SIDs in 2000–2001 is from a mail survey designed and administered by Downtown New Jersey, Inc. (DNJ), for which the results were compiled by one of the authors.

number of objections (a negative approval test). A SID can thus—in legal principle, if not in usual political practice—be designated or dissolved entirely at the discretion of the municipality.* In practice, SIDs in New Jersey, like BIDs elsewhere, tend to be designated at least in consultation with and most often with the active involvement of or upon the initiative of interested property owners and business people.†

DMCs may be entities incorporated under New Jersey's nonprofit corporation law or "created by municipal ordinance." While the archetypal, self-governing form of DMC is prevalent in New Jersey, the statute also permits DMCs to take the form of

---

* This reliance on a discretion approval test rather than the more usual petition test, and without recourse in the form of an objection or remonstrance, makes the New Jersey statute somewhat atypical in the United States, as we discuss in the concluding section of this chapter.

† The case of Gloucester City's downtown SID illustrates this point. The municipal governing body designated a SID and DMC in August 2001. A group of business people who opposed the SID sought election to the DMC's board in 2002 and won enough seats to adopt a zero budget for the subsequent fiscal period. The city for a time contemplated designating another DMC, but in the end acquiesced in this effective dissolution of the SID rather than compel the operation of a SID in the face of vocal and determined opposition. This is to our knowledge the only SID created in New Jersey to date that is not still in operation.

municipal commissions or nonprofit corporations governed by municipally appointed boards. Of 36 New Jersey DMCs surveyed for governance characteristics in 2002 and 2003 by one of the authors, two-thirds were self-governing nonprofit corporations—15 were membership corporations with elected boards of trustees, and 9 were corporations governed by self-perpetuating boards. The other 12 DMCs included five nonprofits with boards controlled by municipal appointees, four municipal commissions, and three nonprofits with mixed forms of corporate governance. The statute does require that, regardless of the form of the DMC, at least one member of every DMC board must be a member of the municipality's governing body.

Municipalities may grant DMCs any or all of 17 enumerated powers encompassing a fairly broad range of place management, revitalization, and redevelopment activities (see Table 8.2). In designating districts, municipalities may also by ordinance adopt façade design standards for building façades within the districts, and the statute permits them to delegate to DMCs the authority to review and approve or deny applications for façade alterations. At least one municipality (Somerville) has delegated such responsibility to a subcommittee of its municipal-commission-form DMC. The statute also permits municipalities to delegate to DMCs the letting and supervising of contracts for work on streets or other municipal property, subject to design approval by the municipal engineer.

DMCs may fund services and improvements from a variety of sources, including contract revenue, loans, and grants, in addition to special assessments on properties within the designated district. The statute mandates a two-stage procedure for levying special assessments on properties within SIDs. First, the DMC's proposed budget for a fiscal year must be approved by the municipal governing body at an advertised public hearing, which provides opportunity for interested parties to present any objections they may have to the proposed budget. A governing body may adopt amendments to the budget proposed by a DMC, without additional hearings if the amendments are sufficiently small, or subject to an additional hearing requirement for more significant amendments. Then, the resulting special-assessment roll must be prepared by the municipal assessor and approved by the governing body at an advertised public hearing. The statute stipulates that the share of a SID's property assessments borne by each property must be reasonably proportionate to benefits received by that property (this will be further discussed below). In addition to or in lieu of property assessments, SID services and improvements may also be funded through the imposition of special license fees based on "floor area of licensable business space, or sales volume, or some other reasonable basis or combination of bases." After the end of each fiscal year, DMCs are required to submit audit reports and annual reports of their activities to the municipality and to the state's Division of Local Government Services.

Of the 31 DMCs responding to the relevant question in the 2001 DNJ survey, all used special assessments on real property as sources of funds, and one used a combination of property-based assessments and business license fees. Assessments and fees accounted for 76 percent of total DMC revenue, on average, ranging from

Table 8.2   New Jersey DMC powers

Section 40:56–83 empowers municipalities to confer certain powers, selected from a list of 17, on DMCs by ordinance.

b. The district management corporation shall have all powers necessary and requisite to effectuate its purposes, including, but not limited to, the power to:

(1) Adopt bylaws...;

(2) Employ such persons as may be required, and fix and pay their compensation from funds available to the corporation;

(3) Apply for, accept, administer and comply with the requirements respecting an appropriation of funds or a gift, grant or donation of property or money;

(4) Make and execute agreements...including contracts with any person, firm, corporation, governmental agency or other entity;

(5) Administer and manage its own funds and accounts and pay its own obligations;

(6) Borrow money from private lenders...and from governmental entities...;

(7) Fund the improvement of the exterior appearance of properties in the district through grants or loans;

(8) Fund the rehabilitation of properties in the district;

(9) Accept, purchase, rehabilitate, sell, lease or manage property in the district;

(10) Enforce the conditions of any loan, grant, sales or lease made by the corporation;

(11) Provide security, sanitation and other services to the district, supplemental to those provided normally by the municipality;

(12) Undertake improvements...including, but not limited to, litter cleanup and control, landscaping, parking areas and facilities, recreational and rest areas and facilities, and those improvements generally permitted for pedestrian malls...pursuant to pertinent regulations of the governing body;

(13) Publicize the district and the businesses included within the district boundaries;

(14) Recruit new businesses to fill vacancies in, and to balance the business mix of, the district;

(15) Organize special events in the district;

(16) Provide special parking arrangements for the district;

(17) Provide temporary decorative lighting in the district.

Section 40:56–86 additionally provides that municipalities may by ordinance delegate to DMCs the contracting of work on streets or other public property, with plans and specifications subject to municipal approval.

as little as 22 percent to as much as 100 percent. Of the 31 DMCs, 16 reported using ad valorem property assessments, with 2 of the 16 assessing different rates for properties in different parts of the SID. Assessments were levied as a fraction of the applicable general tax rates in 11 SIDs, with one of this group imposing differential charges by location. Two SIDs' assessments were based on the street frontage of district properties, and another's on floor area. One SID levied varying property assessment rates for different categories of commercial property. Most SIDs excluded residential properties from their district designations or charged them only nominal annual assessment fees.

Morristown, New Jersey, Case Law Facts and Findings

Challenges to New Jersey SIDs, brought over the years by a number of assessment payers, have tested the validity of the special-assessment financing for SIDs, the use of property values as the basis for allocating assessment shares, the use of different rates of assessment for different properties within a SID, and the exclusion or exemption of residential properties from assessment. The challenge brought against the Morristown, New Jersey, SID in 1994 and subsequently carried to the New Jersey Supreme Court by two affected property owners raised all of these issues. The New Jersey Supreme Court's 1999 ruling in this case established securely that legislative intent granted broad discretion to municipalities to pursue general public policy ends related to business district revitalization through the SID mechanism, and that this grant of discretion was compatible with the state constitution (*2nd Roc-Jersey Assocs. v. Town of Morristown*, 1999).

Facts and Lower Court Rulings

The Morristown SID was created by local ordinance in December 1993. Morristown had been experiencing a gradual decline of its downtown for a number of years, and the catalyst for action was the 1993 closing of the downtown Macy's store. The ordinance was fairly typical of New Jersey SID ordinances, following closely the patterns of the ordinances of the approximately two dozen New Jersey SIDs that preceded it. A number of local property owners and business operators were active in organizing the SID effort, including the property manager for the Headquarters Plaza office complex across the street from the defunct Macy's. The ordinance provided for special assessments to be levied against commercial properties within the district in proportion to their assessed valuation (AV) for general property tax purposes (i.e., ad valorem), with residential properties and the residential portions of mixed-use properties exempted. Morristown Partners, Inc. (MPI) was designated as the DMC.

In response to the unpublished *Gonzalez v. Borough of Freehold* (1994) ruling by the Appellate Division of the New Jersey Superior Court (more details below),

Morristown amended its SID ordinance in October 1994 to exclude from the defined district, rather than exempt from the assessment, residential properties and the residential portions of mixed-use properties by altering the list of block and lot numbers that defined the district. The first special-assessment roll was approved by the town council at a public hearing on October 18, 1994, and bills were then mailed out to affected property owners. The several entities owning Headquarters Plaza (collectively referred to below as Roc-Jersey) filed their complaint on December 12, alleging that they had not been provided adequate notice,* and challenging the legality of the town's SID ordinance on the basis of its exclusion of residential properties, its reliance on AV for apportioning assessments, and its provision for assessing office buildings at the same rate as retail properties within the same sub-area of the SID. The trial judge dismissed the contentions of inadequate notice and stipulated that the central legal issues to be addressed were whether the local SID ordinance, as amended, violated the U.S. Constitution, the New Jersey Constitution, or the SID enabling statute.

The practical issues mainly turned around the basic fairness and property rights issues of whether adequate and proportionate benefits were being provided to justify the assessments. Because there were no proportionate benefits, the plaintiffs asserted, the assessments constituted a taking in contravention of the Fifth Amendment to the U.S. Constitution. Plaintiffs also asserted that the assessments were actually taxes, and that therefore the exemption of residential properties violated the uniformity clause of the New Jersey Constitution. In January, after an initial hearing, the judge ordered the town and MPI to produce a report concerning the fairness of the proposed assessment formula and whether the nonresidential portions of mixed-use properties should be assessed. Roc-Jersey also commissioned an expert report (Burchell-Listokin and Associates, 1995). After reviewing the reports and arguments, the judge ruled in favor of the town and MPI.

In accordance with the recommendations of the town's and MPI's expert reports, the assessment formula was subsequently adjusted by assessing commercial properties in a portion of the business district separated from the central portion by Interstate Route 287 at 75 percent of the rate charged to commercial properties in the main portion. The exemption of residential properties and the reliance on AV as the basis for determining assessment shares remained, however. Some mixed-use properties within the SID were also assigned assessment ratios based on their balance of commercial versus residential use. The logic underlying the updated

---

* The explanation for this apparent contradiction—the owners of the property claiming not to have received notice of the creation of a SID in the establishment of which their property manager played a leading role—appears to have been a lack of communication between the on-site property manager and the initiator of the lawsuit. Not all of the owners of Headquarters Plaza were involved in actively overseeing regular operations at the complex during the period when the on-site property manager was helping to organize the SID, and one key owner apparently was startled to receive the initial assessment bill.

formulae was that the location of a commercial property within one subarea of the district or the other was likely to be a significant enough distinction in terms of benefits enjoyed to serve as an appropriate basis for differential assessment rates, but that the precise nature of the commercial use (retail or office) within the same subarea was not.

The state's Appellate Division upheld the trial court's ruling, adding only some commentary concerning the core issues of local improvements' costs and benefits, based on the fundamental benefit principle underlying special assessments in general (economists might describe this as a form of fiscal equivalence). Benefits, the court noted, are anticipated to accrue from, but are not the same as, the (cost-creating) improvements themselves. The SID statute requires SIDs' costs to be apportioned in the same shares as benefits, and usually (but not always) the assessments should not exceed the costs. Although the highly complex assessment method described by the plaintiffs' expert report, based on techniques used to calculate the impact fees charged to land developers in many jurisdictions, might be theoretically more desirable, in practice the reliance on AV was good enough. Oral arguments before the Supreme Court were heard on September 28, 1998.

Issues Presented to the Supreme Court

The central issue, in the judgment of the New Jersey Supreme Court, was whether Morristown's SID ordinance (and so, by extension, dozens of nearly identical SID ordinances throughout the state) was constitutional. This issue turned primarily on the question of whether the SID charges are special assessments or taxes. The ruling, upholding the legality of the Morristown SID and its assessment formula, addressed (and dismissed) three central constitutional arguments, an issue of statutory interpretation, and a question of the validity of retroactive application of a curative statutory amendment.

First, the plaintiffs alleged that the charges imposed to fund the SID were taxes. Therefore, by assessing additional taxes against only a selection of the properties within the overall municipal jurisdiction, the SID violated the uniformity clause of the state constitution. The current provision was adopted by the 1947 New Jersey constitutional convention, largely in response to a long-standing history of what was deemed to be unfair preferential treatment granted to the properties of railroad companies. It stipulates that,

> Property shall be assessed for taxation under general laws and by uniform rules. All real property assessed and taxed locally or by the state... shall be assessed according to the same standard of value...and...shall be taxed at the general tax rate of the taxing district in which the property is situated.

Second, if SID charges are taxes, then the exclusion of residential properties further violates the state constitutional provision that authorizes only general- or special-purpose exemptions from taxation: "Exemption from taxation may be granted only by general laws."

Third, the plaintiffs asserted that if the assessment were a special assessment rather than a general tax, the use of AV as a means for apportioning costs was insufficiently precise and accurate as an indicator of benefits received. Traditional special assessments used a comparison of the values of individual properties before and after the (one-time) improvements as the basis for determining benefit shares. The expert report commissioned by the plaintiffs indicated that an optimal means for apportioning SID assessments would use methodologies similar to those used to apportion development impact fees. Thus, "the methodology used by Morristown results in an assessment that is not proportional with the benefit conferred," according to the plaintiffs, and therefore the assessments were takings without just compensation, in violation of the New Jersey Constitution and the Fifth Amendment to the U.S. Constitution.

Fourth, based on the unpublished (and therefore persuasive but not binding precedent) *Gonzalez* ruling, plaintiffs claimed that the exemption of residential properties violated the statutory provision at section 66(b) that a SID is "an area in which a special assessment on property [interpreted as meaning *all* property] shall be imposed." The *Gonzalez* ruling also turned on the language of section 68(b)(2), which made the anticipation of benefits for "businesses, employees, residents and consumers" a necessary finding in support of a SID ordinance.

Fifth, although the state legislature amended section 66(b) of the statute in May 1995, in response to *Gonzalez*, so as to clarify that the exemption of residential properties was explicitly permitted, that amendment postdated the Morristown ordinance and so did not apply to it.

Holdings and Reasoning

On the first issue, the court found that established precedent in New Jersey (*McNally v. Township of Teaneck*, 1977) confirmed that special assessments are not taxes subject to the uniformity clause. So the question is whether the SID charges are taxes or special assessments in this particular case. The traditional definition of a special assessment is that it supports local improvements, is a one-time charge, and is related to a direct benefit that is special and local. Further, the benefit must be certain rather than speculative, although it can take place in the future. Citing precedents from other states, as well as the *Fanelli v. City of Trenton* (1994) SID case from New Jersey, however, the court determined that this definition had evolved and become more flexible. A special assessment now was more flexibly defined as one that "is used to provide a combination of services and improvements that are intended and designed to benefit particular properties and demonstrably enhance the value and/or the use or function of the properties that are subject to the special assessment." The charges imposed by the Morristown SID were special assessments by this updated definition, rather than taxes.

Additionally, the court found that there were numerous precedents for using AV, which is readily available and easily applied, as the basis for apportioning special assessments. The issue of administrative feasibility renders impractical the use of methods that seek to be highly exact in determining the precise property-by-property benefit from a SID, which by its nature provides many benefits that are general and indirect in nature. Because SIDs' improvements are recurrent, as distinct from the one-time nature of traditional special-assessment-financed improvements, most means of apportioning benefit shares would be approximate, very cumbersome to compute, or both. AV takes into account locational, economic, and physical characteristics of properties, which would constitute bases for the apportionment of costs and benefits of this type of improvement anyway (Burchell-Listokin and Associates, 1995, p. 25), and there are already in place established procedures by which property owners can challenge what they believe to be inaccurate AV determinations. The annual review by the municipal governing body in public hearings of the SID's budget and assessment rolls provides a further assurance of transparency and fairness.

As to the constitutionality of exempting residential properties, the special assessments at issue here are not taxes. But, even if they were, the distinction made by exempting residential property is based on broad classifications of property use and zoning characteristics, rather than distinctions based on characteristics of the owner, or among different sectors of business activity. Therefore, the court found, "The SID legislation meets the exacting classification standards that are applicable to real property taxes" (*2nd Roc-Jersey Assocs. v. Town of Morristown*, 1999, p. 600). Exemptions upheld for historic properties are a similar example. As in *Fanelli*, the burden of proof here is on the plaintiff, and the municipal action is subject to minimum scrutiny, because "the SID ordinance is an economic regulation not affecting a suspect class" (p. 600).

With respect to the taking issue, the court concluded that as a matter of public policy, New Jersey, like many other states, seeks to address the problems of urban decay and suburbanization. SIDs are self-help and quasi-public attempts to do what municipal governments alone have been unable to do. All of the expert reports, including the plaintiffs', "furnish an evidentiary basis for the conclusion that SIDs offer benefits to commercial property" (p. 604). The court concluded on this point that "the SID provides sufficiently identifiable benefits to the subject properties and...that the special assessments are measured reasonably and fairly in proportion to the benefits conferred" (p. 604). This reflects "legislative purpose and intent and public policy" (p. 602). Therefore, the assessments do not constitute a taking.

On the question of the statutory permissibility of excluding residential properties from the list of properties defining the SID, the Supreme Court agreed with the Appellate Division that the May 1995 statutory amendment was clearly intended "to remedy what the Legislature perceived as a misapplication of the law" in *Gonzalez v. Borough of Freehold* (1994). Generally, laws may be considered retroactively applicable rather than prospectively only, which is the normal case, under three circumstances, one of which is "where the legislation is ameliorative or curative" (p. 604). Therefore, "the 1995 amendment qualifies under the curative exception for retroactive application" (p. 605).

Discussion

In New Jersey, as elsewhere, state courts have upheld the BID form as a reasonable extension of both the special assessment and special district concepts. This reflects a U.S. tradition in local government law of blending public and private interests in creating entities to further local collective action (Briffault, 1999). The principle of fiscal equivalence inherent in special-assessment finance is important enough to justify or even dictate nonuniformity of assessment, even within a district, such as the exclusion or exemption of residential properties or the differential assessment of commercial properties of different types in different parts of a district. In light of the practical challenges of calculating precisely the benefits to individual properties of continuing-service improvements, as opposed to more traditional capital improvements, however, BIDs and their parent municipalities are granted significant leeway in making reasonable allocations of costs among beneficiaries.

In New Jersey specifically, this further reflects the court's judgment that legislative intent and the state constitution both support the exercise of considerable discretion by municipalities in this area. The court concluded that the legislature saw this as a matter of public policy responding to the need to preserve downtowns in the face of ongoing sprawl and the competition between traditional business districts and single-owner shopping centers and office parks. SIDs in this light are a necessary and appropriate means for organizing collective action that is expected to yield substantial private benefits for the owners and occupants of commercial properties in business districts in the course of pursuing public policies of downtown renewal. That is, notwithstanding the emphasis by many of the most vocal proponents and opponents of BIDs on the *private* sector leadership of BID management entities as a defining characteristic of the approach, New Jersey's legislature and courts view SIDs as fundamental means for the advancement of *public* policies by state and local governments.

Four Cases of Collective Action

The arguments considered in the Morristown litigation involved the effects of a municipality's exercise of discretion pursuant to a state grant of authority. While the Morristown SID was held by the court to have been an appropriate and appropriately applied instrument of state and local public policy, its proximate origins were in the private initiative of concerned property owners and business operators. We now turn to a summary of relevant aspects of four 2002–2003 case studies of New Jersey SIDs reported in greater detail elsewhere (Justice, 2003), which help to illustrate the interplay and evolution of stakeholders' interests and actions in practice in the course of mobilizing material and cooperative resources for revitalization. Taken together, these cases indicate that New Jersey's SIDs might well be described as instruments of mutual exploitation by business people and local governments, with the latter presumably seeking to advance their residents' interests as well as their own "institutional self interest" (Sbragia, 1983), and self-exploitation by business people seeking to advance their private interests.

The analytic framework used for the case studies modeled business district revitalization as a collective action problem involving individual and organizational actors from the public and private sectors. Case study methodology and data sources (Yin, 2003) were used to investigate and compare the effectiveness of the four SIDs as means for mobilizing resources for the joint provision and production of viable business districts. Data—archival records, documents, 55 confidential semistructured interviews, and direct observations—was collected throughout 2002. Case-level sample selection was intentional and followed a quasi-experimental logic, seeking to focus on governance-related variables while controlling for a range of confounding factors. Accordingly, all four of the selected SIDs encompassed the downtown business districts of municipalities in the New York City metropolitan area, each was relatively close to the median size and budget of New Jersey SIDs (see Tables 8.1, 8.3, and 8.4), and the governance structures of the DMCs in the cases included two variants on self-governing membership corporations (Freehold and Red Bank), one municipal commission (Somerville), and one nonprofit with a municipally appointed board (Union Township). In all four cases, the "merchants don't vote" truism was largely accurate: relatively few of each SID's business operators and property owners currently lived in the municipalities, although many were former residents.* In each of the Freehold and Red Bank cases, however, one key leader of the initial effort to create a SID was a borough council member as well as a downtown business operator, while in Somerville local officials included at least one owner of a business located adjacent to the area designated for the SID.

Freehold Center Partnership, Freehold, New Jersey

Freehold's DMC, the Freehold Center Partnership (FCP), was organized by local business people in 1991 shortly before the Borough of Freehold designated its SID. In interviews in 2002, founders of the DMC indicated that they sought to organize

---

* Interestingly, in the case of Red Bank, a number of the DMC activists began moving into the borough in the late 1990s and early 2000s, from surrounding communities.

Table 8.3 Summary comparison of four New Jersey SIDs, selected characteristics

	Freehold	Somerville	Red Bank	Union Township
Date created	September 1991	June 1988	September 1991	June 1993
Date operational	July 1992	July 1988	September 1991	August 1993
Organizational form	Membership-controlled 501(c)(4)	Municipal commission	Membership corporation, 501(c)(3)	Governing body-appointed board, 501(c)(3)
Businesses in SID[a]	260	350	550	260
Total DMC budget, 2002	$249,300	$236,672	$435,800	$157,000
Assessment-funded share of budget, 2002	$164,300	$236,672	$400,000	$143,000
Assessment per business, 2002[b]	$619	$676	$727	$550
Assessment per property, 2002	$1,020	$1,679	$1,739	$1,444
Assessment per $100 of property value, 2002	$0.239	$0.269	$0.268	$0.254
Ratio of assessment to total general local property tax, 2000	8.7%	8.7%	13.2%	11%

Source: Justice (2003).

[a] Statewide average SID size was 341 businesses, median 250, in 2000–2001 (n = 28).

[b] Statewide assessment/businesses ratios ranged from $185 to $2,313 and averaged $678.

Table 8.4 Actual expenditures for four SIDs in 2001

	Freehold July 2001–June 2002	Red Bank January–December 2001	Somerville January–December 2001	Union Township January–December 2001
Marketing and promotion	$106,609	$67,853	$15,507	$53,193
Design and maintenance	18,904	53,046	126,773	35,088
Debt service		159,916	155,215	
Business development	31,173	2,013	242	
Staffing and organization	101,927	193,550	66,860	69,018
Total expenditures	$258,613	$476,378	$364,598[a]	$157,299

Source: Justice (2003).

[a] Expenditures for Somerville include an average of $100,000 per year in matching grants for façade improvement projects, funded by a grant from Somerset County and not presented by the DMC in its budget as reported in Table 8.3. For 2001, these county-funded façade grants totaled $111,890 and are included in the design and maintenance category of expenditures.

the SID as a way to maintain and continue the revitalization efforts begun by the borough at the instigation of local business operators and residents. As of 2002, the bylaws provided for a board with 13 voting members, 10 of them (4 property owners, 4 business operators, and 2 residents) elected by the membership (comprising all SID property owners automatically and all borough residents and SID business operators who elect to register for membership). Three other voting members were appointed by the borough and county governments (Freehold Borough is the seat of Monmouth County, and the county government has been extensively involved in the downtown revitalization efforts). Six nonvoting board members represented a range of local institutions, including major employers outside the SID and the regional chamber of commerce.

The FCP operates a revitalization program that emphasizes marketing and promotion of the central business district as a destination for dining, strolling, and shopping, with more than 20 activities and events per year organized by the volunteer-led marketing and restaurant committees of the DMC. These activities are largely self-supporting: of the $106,609 spent on marketing and promotion in the fiscal year beginning in 2001, $93,089 came from sponsorships and advertising sales rather than from assessment funds. Streetscape and parking improvements have been funded over the years by the borough and county governments, as have a variety of sanitation and maintenance services. FCP funds the purchase and installation of banners, planters, street cleaning equipment and services, improvements for tree wells, and other visual improvements. Volunteer labor is used to maintain plantings. A program of design assistance, small matching grants, and discounted loans from local lenders is meant to encourage attractive façade improvements. The SID has also produced a design manual and a guide to local permitting procedures, and provides related technical assistance to new and existing businesses.

The board and its several committees were active in formulating and executing the SID's improvement activities, and in mobilizing volunteers to help with special events and streetscape maintenance activities. For most of the SID's history, participants reported, the private and public representatives on the board maintained active communication, and the borough and DMC worked effectively in a balanced partnership to pursue shared goals. At the same time, private and public sector participants in the SID also reported some measure of contemporaneous discontent: some business people felt that the borough was insufficiently responsive to their needs, while some public representatives suggested that the business people sometimes forgot that the borough government's primary responsibility is to its residents. The research did not uncover evidence of significant concern by residents that the business district received an excessive share of public resources or attention. Critics of the SID within the local business community expressed their strongest objections not to the ad valorem special assessments, but to what they believed was the DMC leadership's unreasonable neglect of the aggrieved business people's suggestions for revitalization strategy. The DMC was described by participants and outsiders alike as primarily a business-led organization.

Somerville, New Jersey, District Management Corporation

The Borough of Somerville District Management Corporation (SDMC) is a municipal commission, created by the ordinance designating the Somerville SID in 1988. Like Freehold, Somerville is a county seat and was a significant regional retail and services center until the 1970s. Interviewees reported that a formerly cohesive local business community succumbed to infighting and disorganization in the 1960s, and local electoral politics were reported to be similarly combative. The borough government's desire in the 1980s to pursue physical improvements in the downtown business district without imposing the costs of the improvement on residential taxpayers was a central impetus to the designation of the SID, they reported (also see Herszenhorn, 1997). SDMC's board comprised nine voting members and a nonvoting (but influential) borough council liaison, all of whom were appointed by the council. The choice of the municipal-commission form appeared to reflect both the mimetic adoption of ordinance language from nearby Cranford, New Jersey (the state's first SID, designated in 1985), and the government-driven origins of the SID.

Somerville's program activities have been constrained by the need to dedicate about three-fifths of annual assessment revenue toward servicing the debt incurred for streetscape reconstruction (see Tables 8.3 and 8.4). Remaining funds have been devoted largely to general organizational expenses, maintenance of plantings in tree wells, sidewalk sweeping, and cooperation with the voluntary Somerville Business and Professional Association (SBPA). SDMC and SBPA share an executive director and have heavily overlapping memberships and boards, and participants describe the relationship between the two entities as beneficially "incestuous." SBPA organizes a variety of place-marketing and promotional activities and special events, funded through program revenues and member contributions. SDMC also administers a county government–funded program of matching grants for façade improvements, which typically allocates $100,000 per year to three to five projects and is promoted by the county government as a model for the county's other downtown organizations to emulate.

The SDMC was chaired in 2002 by a resident of the borough who did not own property or work within the SID boundaries. The majority of the board's members were business operators and property owners, and the actual decision-making process both observably and reportedly balanced the concerns and priorities of the municipality and of the private business stakeholders quite well. The only standing committee of the SDMC was its Architectural Review Board (ARB), created by the SID ordinance to review proposed façade construction and alteration projects within the SID. Most active participants in the DMC as well as outsiders tended to describe the DMC as a creature of municipal government. As in Freehold, there was no evidence of strong concern among residents about misdirection of resources to favor business interests, and business sector discontent was oriented more to strategy selection and implementation than to the fact or amount of the special assessment.

RiverCenter, Red Bank, New Jersey

The special improvement district of Red Bank, New Jersey, Inc. (Red Bank RiverCenter), the DMC for Red Bank's SID, was initially incorporated by the members of an ad hoc advisory committee of local officials and business people who recommended the creation of a SID in 1991. The committee was appointed by the borough council as a business-led parking advisory group chaired by a council member who was also a downtown business operator, but quickly arrived at the recommendation for a more comprehensive revitalization strategy to be pursued through the SID mechanism. Early RiverCenter activists noted the compulsory finance as a particularly attractive feature, which allowed them to focus on revitalization activities rather than fund-raising. Corporate governance is nominally the responsibility of a board comprising 22 members elected by SID property owners, 5 public representatives appointed by the borough government, and 3 representatives of local institutions located outside the SID boundaries. In practice, however, most significant organizational decisions are made by an authoritative executive committee, which ranges from 5 to 13 members and generally includes the mayor or borough administrator.

RiverCenter has systematically pursued coordinated promotional and economic restructuring efforts, targeting the very-high-income residents of surrounding communities and recruiting businesses to serve them. Events and promotions include a jazz festival and street performers. The DMC spent $45,000 on advertising and $12,000 on promotional activities in 2001, offset by $53,000 in related program revenues. As in Somerville, a major share of the district's assessment revenue is used to service the debt incurred for streetscape improvements, although in this instance the capital improvements extend through only a portion of the SID. A modest premium in assessment rates has been adopted for properties within the subarea of the SID in which the improvements were made. Sidewalk cleaning, holiday decorations, seasonal plantings, and other maintenance and visual improvements are funded through a combination of individual contributions and SID funds.

RiverCenter's board and committees have been very active and draw in significant numbers of local business people and residents for volunteer work. Positions as board members and committee chairs are used as incentives to encourage local stakeholders to contribute time and energy to the work of the organization. In interviews, RiverCenter board members emphasized the business-led nature of the DMC, and clearly believed they enjoyed a great deal of organizational autonomy. One SID property owner and RiverCenter activist even described the process of gradually socializing a skeptical borough official through repeated cooperative interactions, explaining, "He is now one of us, in the sense that he's been exposed to it enough…now he's sold." Outside Red Bank, however, it was reported that Red Bank's mayor effectively controlled the SID organization through force of personality and the shrewd deployment of official municipal authority.

Union Township, New Jersey, District Management Corporation

Union Township's "Union Center" SID encompasses the traditional central retail district of a suburban municipality, which also encompasses a number of large highway-oriented strip shopping centers on its fringe, as well as several other modest concentrations of commercial activity. The SID designation followed the recommendations of the township's chamber of commerce, which responded to a reportedly sudden and dramatic increase in the district's vacancy rate for commercial properties around 1993. The nonprofit DMC is governed by a board of nine trustees appointed by the township's governing body. Three SID property owners or employees of SID property owners, three proprietors or employees of SID business establishments, and two township residents without business interests in the SID are appointed to staggered three-year terms, and one member of the township committee (usually the mayor) is appointed annually. The DMC in 2002 had no active standing committees.

With the smallest budget among the four cases, Union Center minimizes administrative costs by sharing its two staff people with the township's economic development department. Major design-related activities include the purchase of sidewalk maintenance and cleaning services, holiday decorations, and decorative banners. Major capital streetscape improvements were funded by the township, which shares many of the maintenance and decoration costs with the SID as well. A program of matching grants for façade and signage improvements operated from 1995 through 2000, using funds from the federal community development block grant program. The DMC staff works actively to recruit suitable new businesses to the district, and to provide a range of technical assistance to new and existing businesses. Promotional activities include a number of special events, regular advertising of the district as a whole, and subsidized group advertisements keyed to seasonal sales and promotional events.

The DMC's business activists expressed considerable commitment to serving the interests of other business stakeholders, although the DMC's strategies and activities were largely driven by the staff. In interviews, local stakeholders portrayed the governing core of the organization as comprising an effective regime of township elected officials and staff, in a coalition with two particularly influential and economically significant business people in the finance and real estate sectors. As in the other cases, business stakeholders' expressions of discontent appeared to center more on SID strategy and implementation than on the monetary cost of the assessments. One central participant in the revitalization also reported that there was some concern among the township's elected officials and residents over the revitalization effort's apparent success in increasing the draw of shoppers from adjoining lower-income inner-ring suburban communities.

Private Government and Public Policy

On balance, the evidence from these cases tends to support the assertion that "business improvement districts don't fit our ordinary categories" of public and private (Walker, 2003). While New Jersey's SIDs in the eyes of the courts represent an incremental adaptation of the more familiar forms of special-assessment districts, and fit within a tradition of using incorporated forms to serve the purposes of specific publics (Briffault, 1999), in practice they tend to operate in the "twilight zone" (Collins, 1998) between the public (government) and private (for-profit business) sectors.

All four SIDs, regardless of the organizational forms of their DMCs, explicitly provided governing roles for representatives of SID business actors, local governments, and the larger jurisdiction's residents. In all cases, nominal governing control of DMC boards was in the hands of the business operators and property owners who were the direct payers of the special assessments. Evidence from meeting minutes, interviews, and observations indicated that borough residents other than SID business stakeholders were particularly influential in Somerville, and to some degree in Freehold as well, so that there was no obvious correspondence between the extent of resident involvement in decision making and the nominal forms of SID governance among the four cases. The initiative for SID formation in each of the four cases was taken either by the municipality (Somerville and Union) or jointly by the municipality and business people and with key individuals having a foot in both sectors (Freehold and Red Bank).

Business, government, and resident participants in DMC governance interviewed in all four cases described their beliefs that they had persuaded representatives of other sectors to become more sympathetic to their concerns at the same time as they described having acquired better understandings of those other sectors themselves. Simultaneously, their remarks indicated that the cooperation achieved through the SIDs was not so great as to eliminate all disagreements between public and private sectors. Municipalities had come through participation in SID planning and governance to be more helpful in many respects to business, but local officials in confidential interviews consistently highlighted the importance of attending to the needs of residents first. The stability of membership of most of the SIDs' core governing groups had the form of regime governance, but the limits of regime governance through the SIDs were apparent in the constraints on those regimes' abilities to influence public policies and resource allocations.

The cases also provide a gray-shaded perspective on the fears of exclusionary privatization of public space raised by some BID critics. In only one case among the four (Freehold) was fear of lower-income people or people of color by upper- and middle-income consumers explicitly identified as a concern by business people or other stakeholders interviewed. Their response to this problem, through the SID mechanism, was described by one participant as essentially a strategy of visual distraction.

> We used to have…a problem with perception. Freehold was thought to be…a dangerous place to go.…So I think we've overcome a lot of that, and we try to continue to work at that. And you do that through presentation, you know: presenting the town in a nice way, just like you would present your home, where you live, or your car. You keep it clean. That's what we try to do.

In fact, based on observations in Freehold and Somerville, pedestrians appeared to represent a broad range of races and income levels. The selection of businesses in both districts was quite broad as well, with expensive restaurants and sidewalk cafés sitting next to immigrant groceries, thrift stores, and the offices of bail bondsmen. In Union Center, the SID actually worked actively to increase the number of lower-income shoppers it drew, although improving higher-income residents' perceptions of cleanliness and safety was also an important priority.

Ironically, the only one of the cases in which concerns were raised about exclusion was the only one in which the anxieties of higher-income groups were never cited as having been a concern in the revitalization effort. The Red Bank SID had by 2002 come to be such a desirable location for businesses targeting very high-income consumers that, through the workings of the commercial real estate market, there was very little left that would attract lower-income residents and visitors. Concern among residents about having lost their downtown to the rich residents of surrounding McMansion developments was real, but was not the result of the kind of intentional exclusion feared by some BID opponents. Indeed, business participants in the revitalization effort tended to assert in interviews that their efforts were targeted at the areas in which their profit motives complemented residents' interests in having an attractive and vital central business district. They were evidently quite sincerely taken aback by some residents' vocal expressions of opposition to their activities and the presumed consequences of those activities.

The Red Bank and Freehold cases additionally offered evidence that the relationships fostered by nominally business-governed SIDs tended to generate a form of what might be described as "spatial capital" (Blau, 2000). While the SIDs served as vehicles for the advancement of businesses' self-interest, the interactions and active work of improving business districts through volunteer governance and labor led participants to form new or deeper attachments to place. This led to efforts by business interests in both places to contribute directly to the general welfare of the larger municipalities, through playground and park construction, involvement in local public schools, and other activities. Participants expressed loyalty to place and to other participants using language such as "camaraderie," "spirit," "community," or "hometown" (this last even among some who had never been residents of the towns in which their businesses were located) to describe their feelings and identifications.

Private Governments as Public Policy Tools

Are BIDs then private governments that threaten to undermine democratic control of municipal governments and public space and contribute to increasing social inequality as some pessimists fear (Garodnick, 2000; Krohe, 1992; Mallett, 1995)? Are they heroic private sector organizations rescuing cities and their public spaces in ways that their ineffective public governments cannot or will not (Mac Donald, 1996)? Or are they instead one more among the "tools of government" (Salamon, 2002) as the reasoning of the New Jersey Supreme Court in the Roc-Jersey case suggested? Another answer might be "None of the above, and all of the above." New Jersey's SIDs, like BIDs elsewhere, certainly qualify as private governments under the broad definition offered by Lakoff and Rich (1973), insofar as they have limited purposes and clienteles, are subordinate to public governments, and engage in activities that have consequences for nonmembers as well as members. But Lakoff and Rich's definition does not imply that such entities are necessarily good or bad for larger public interests; the details of context and implementation matter. (Indeed, professional associations and universities are among Lakoff and Rich's examples of private governments.)

With the proliferation of special-purpose governments and quasi-governmental entities in the United States and other parts of the world, it can plausibly be asserted that "what constitutes the public sector…is a contestable matter" (Ostrom, 1989, p. xv). Some respected scholars of public administration have in recent years argued that the legitimacy of administration and the reconciliation of efficiency and democracy can best be served by focusing on collective interests and the full range of instruments of collective action rather than on government organizations themselves as the central units of analysis for public policy and administration (Denhardt, 2000; Kirlin, 1996). Mallett's (1993) emphasis on BIDs as representing instruments of collective action developed to serve emergent group demands not satisfied by existing governments is not unlike some accounts of the formation of municipal corporations in the 19th and early 20th centuries (Karcher, 1998; Sbragia, 1996). Perhaps their path going forward will follow a similar pattern as well, resulting in their becoming more explicitly subject to control by superordinate governments as courts and other actors grow concerned with their public consequences.

From a collective action perspective, BIDs—at least as they have been implemented in New Jersey to date—appear to represent instances in which a subset of stakeholders—business operators and property owners—jointly provide some of the collective goods and services that lead to the creation and maintenance of public space and place, in addition to those provided by municipal governments. In terms of the logic of collective action (Olson, 1971), the analysis might be as follows. In the absence of a BID (or other compulsory finance mechanism), business stakeholders are subject to free riding in their efforts to provide the collective good of the public space that enables them to realize the greatest profit from their immobilized capital investments (Cox, 1993; Mallett, 1994). Once the BID exists, those stakeholders are able to marshal the resources necessary to provide that collective good, which residents, employees, and visitors then enjoy as a positive externality. There is no altruism involved—business people seek to maximize profits, and the amenities of public space and place are merely instrumental or incidental to that profit maximization—but the gains to this subset of stakeholders are perceived by them to be great enough to motivate them to provide public goods enjoyed for free by others (for a critical perspective on this phenomenon, see Lofland, 2002). Thus, even a sharp critic of BIDs might note the irony that the apparent privatization of place management can foster the creation of public space, as demonstrated by the reclamation of Bryant Park in midtown Manhattan through BID-funded services that helped attract the general public and deter the petty crime and drug dealing that had once prevailed (Zukin, 1995). But these New Jersey cases also suggested a corollary effect: as business people became personally involved in local improvement planning and implementation, as active providers and producers, rather than merely consumers of place, they came increasingly to identify their private interests with the general public interest in public space and other local public goods.

In this sense, BIDs can be understood as being not just private governments, but also instruments of public policy. In the eyes of the New Jersey Supreme Court and state legislature, the state's SID statute and local implementations of SIDs are means to promote the general welfare of municipalities by exploiting the profit motivations of their (mostly nonresident) business people. From a collective action perspective, New Jersey's SIDs are institutional arrangements that facilitate the necessarily joint provision and production of the local public good of *place*, with statutory stipulations that promote reasonable fiscal equivalence without unduly constraining the ability of municipalities and business communities jointly to devise the institutional arrangements that most suit their particular and shared interests. This in turn is presumed to enhance business districts' levels of business investment, employment, property values, and property and sales tax revenues as well as the availability of goods and services for community residents.

Limitations and Caveats

Some cautions regarding the limitations of our analysis and conclusions are in order, however. First, the extension of the BID model to primarily residential rather than commercial areas and improvements in the form of "community benefits districts" (Baer and Marando, 2001) may be somewhat more troublesome. Part of what makes New Jersey's SIDs (and BIDs in general) as a model of municipal subdistricting relatively benign is that business districts by their nature serve private interests best when they attract people. This minimizes exclusionary tendencies and means that BIDs in advancing private commercial interests tend to create public space and other amenities as positive externalities. And, of course, given the truism that merchants do not vote, the doubling of narrow influence is avoided. Residential associations, on the other hand, might be more likely to generate active exclusion of people deemed undesirable, negative rather than positive externalities, and effective secession by the wealthy.

Negative Externalities

Second, these case studies did not measure the actual economic and regulatory effects of the specific SIDs studied, and so they cannot address directly the potential for a range of negative externalities and other undesirable consequences potentially associated even with visitor-attracting BIDs. This includes a range of possible undesirable effects for businesses in BIDs, for residents of BIDs or areas near them, for users of public space, and for residents and businesses in other communities.

Possible consequences for businesses in BIDs include potential imbalances of BID costs and benefits, especially given the inevitable lack of precise knowledge of causality, costs, and benefits associated with BIDs. There is also the possibility that business tenants will be forced out of the district as a result of a BID's success in achieving increases in business activity, and therefore property values and rents, or in altering the demographic composition of a district's customer base. In fact, there may be some evidence that this has occurred in Red Bank, although it would be difficult definitively to attribute causality to the SID rather than to the workings of a capitalist property market responding to secular changes in the overall economy and in the demographics of the local trade area.

Commercial gentrification, whether occasioned by a BID or other causes, can also have implications for residents, as we have seen in the Red Bank case. Effects on residents can include the loss of particular businesses, goods, and services; the experienced loss of a sense of ownership of a business district; and the inconveniences, such as congestion, associated with busy commercial districts. These potential negative consequences of BIDs, of course, presume that their decision makers set out to achieve commercial gentrification and succeed in doing so.* Residents might also find themselves disadvantaged to the extent that BIDs succeed in overcoming the "merchants don't vote" balance of power over municipal government. At least one New Jersey BID consultant was explicit about his belief that a key purpose of SIDs in New Jersey's suburban towns is to create urban governing regimes, to "restore business dignity."

BIDs' success in regulating and marketing public space may also have consequences for residents and businesses of other areas. To the extent retail trade is drawn to one district, it may be drawn away from another, to the detriment of property owners and business operators in the losing area(s). Nonresident visitors to

---

* In at least one of the cases examined here, not even the first half of that presumption appears to be valid. To the extent the Union Center SID succeeds in drawing additional lower-income shoppers, that might also be viewed as a negative consequence by community residents.

a district may also be discouraged, not necessarily by the direct operation of BIDs' "security" services, but because the creation of environmental characteristics that enable an urban business district to attract higher-income suburbanites might as a by-product result in an environment experienced as unwelcoming by others.

Limited Generalizability

Finally, although New Jersey's SIDs overall are typical in many respects of the range of BID implementations in the United States in terms of size and budget, there are two ways in which the cases examined here may not be fully representative of BIDs in the United States. First, the SIDs examined here were intentionally selected to be comparable to one another in many dimensions and so encompassed a fairly narrow range of applications. They are all in relatively high-income areas in northern New Jersey, they are all in relatively small jurisdictions that are not central metropolitan cities, and in each case there was a degree of governmental involvement in the initial organizing efforts that may have been greater than is typical of U.S. BIDs in general. There is some reason to believe that larger "corporate" BIDs serving larger numbers of larger businesses in the central business districts of major cities may differ from these cases of "Main Street" BIDs in their institutional characteristics and effects (see Rogowsky and Gross, 2000, for an explanation of this typology). None of the SIDs examined here, for instance, employed or contracted for the uniformed greeters, ambassadors, or security personnel common to corporate BIDs, and none of them had a budget large enough to permit complete professionalization of its management decisions and operations. More professionalized BIDs, independently of the nature of their service programs, may well be less likely to promote the spatial capital discernable among active participants in BID governance and activities.

Second, these cases of SIDs in New Jersey were Main Street BIDs that all were populated predominantly by locally based, mom-and-pop businesses. Businesses with a strictly local scope may be more locally dependent (Cox, 1993), as are property owners. Business districts dominated by chain stores may have a business constituency less attached to a particular place. Further, in at least two of these cases there were a significant number of business operators who also owned the properties in which their businesses were located, which may also have contributed to a greater commitment to a specific place as well as to more cohesive relationships among business operators and property owners. Certainly the ranks of SID activists in all four cases included large proportions of property owners, including property-owning business operators.

Finally, as we have described here, SIDs in New Jersey are all creatures of an enabling statute and case law environment that explicitly reserves discretion and authority mainly to conventional general-purpose municipalities empowered by the state government. Anonymous reviewers of an earlier version of this chapter suggested that this sets New Jersey apart from most other states. Although we have not completed a comprehensive review of all the BID statutes in all the states,* there is some support for this assertion. At least 18 states and the District of Columbia provide for the creation of BIDs only in response to an affirmative petition by property owners, business operators, or both, of which four additionally make provisions for (disconfirmation) by means of referenda or remonstrance petitions. Of the (at least) 21 states that allow for local governments to take the initiative for designating BIDs, 6, including New Jersey, provide solely for discretionary designation without provision for remonstrance petitions, 6 provide only for municipal initiative but also provide for referenda or remonstrance, and 11 allow for BID creation by property owners' petition or by local government discretion, with 7 of these 11 including remonstrance provisions. Thus, a plurality of these 40 BID statutes appear to intend (and a majority to allow) that property and business owners—or organizations representing their interests—assume a leading role in BID formation, as does the legislation recently adopted for England and Wales (for more information concerning BIDs in the UK, see the chapters by Blackwell and by Lloyd and Peel in this volume). This is consistent with, if not strong evidence for, Mallett's (1993) private government thesis.

Even so, many of the characteristics of New Jersey's SIDs that help to bring about the complementarity of private government and larger public interests are precisely those that are generic to the form. They are created under the authority of and subject to the laws of the sovereign states, generally cannot employ coercive authority, or even collect the revenues they need to operate, except on the sufferance of the general-purpose municipalities which created and can dissolve them, and can both in theory and in practice be held accountable by officials of those municipalities.† Subject to a variety of disclosure and procedural requirements as they are, BIDs at worst have no greater potential as instruments for redistributing power and wealth to business elites than do a variety of longer-standing forms of redevelopment partnerships (Squires, 1989), routine "privatism" (Barnekov and Rich, 1989; Warner, 1968), growth machines (Logan and Molotch, 1987), and urban governing regimes (Stoker, 1995; Stone, 1989), in spite of (or perhaps in part because of) being more explicitly oriented to serving business interests specifically

---

* See Morçöl and Patrick's chapter in this volume for an illustration of why a complete survey is a challenging task. Pennsylvania, the subject of their chapter, is not the only state with multiple BID statutes; states use a variety of names to describe BIDs, and the provisions in those statutes covering BID creation and governance can be very complex. Even a preliminary review indicates that states vary widely both in their specific provisions and in the category of entities or local improvements/services that served implicitly or explicitly as precedents. We thank Eric Finkelstein, a summer associate at Grenbaum Rowe, Davis and Himmel, for his efforts in summarizing selected provisions of 40 U.S. BID statutes during July and August 2006.

† The reorganization of New York City's large, and by all accounts politically powerful and highly successful, Grand Central Partnership under pressure from Mayor Rudolph Giuliani in the late 1990s illustrated this in practice (see Bagli, 1998; Pristin, 1998, 1999).

than are those more familiar institutions of urban governance. In fact, BIDs' distinctive—and actively sought—visibility may tend to render them somewhat less useful as engines of appropriation. And at best, by facilitating the enhancement of shared places, they can serve to further public purposes in the course of advancing private interests.

Directions for Continuing Research

The limitations of this research, like the relative dearth to date of large-scale evaluation research on the economic effects of BIDs, indicate some directions for continuing research into the governance and effects of BIDs, not only in the United States, but in the other countries to which they have spread, often patterned explicitly on the U.S. model.* One set of questions, of course, has to do simply with economic outcomes: whether BIDs do in fact cause increases in economic activity within their territories, and if so, whether that comes at the expense of diminished economic activity in competing commercial areas. At present, it is unclear whether and when adequate data will be available to draw firm conclusions on either of these accounts, although there has been some work by researchers at New York University examining the effect of BIDs on property values in New York City (Ellen et al., 2006).

Data might be more feasibly obtained, however, for numerous questions raised by this and other contributions to this volume, about BIDs' service performance and outputs, their consequences for public space and its users, and their governance and "democratic performance" (Skelcher, 2006). Data on service outputs and performance measures is spotty to date, but performance measurement is increasingly a matter of interest in the United States (see Caruso and Weber in this volume) and abroad. For instance, BIDs in the U.K. have been fairly systematic in designing performance measures, and may generate a wealth of output measures over the next few years. Comparisons to non-BID models of town center management (TCM) there may become feasible, because some of the TCM organizations also collect performance data (for more on TCM, see Reeve in this volume). Similarly, hypothesized external economies may be difficult to measure and tie definitively to BIDs as causes, but it may be more feasible to identify alterations in municipal service efforts associated with BID activities (such as the diversion of police attention in Times Square observed by Vindevogel [2005]).

---

* Or on what is portrayed as the U.S. model. The variety of statutes in the BID suggest that there is not anything that could be presented as a model beyond the frequent, albeit not universal, combination of special-district, special-assessment, and self-governing features. For an account of how narrowly policy designers in the U.K. interpreted the American experience of BIDs, see Ward's (2006) claim that they used midtown Manhattan as a proxy for the entire United States. (We would note, however, that many of the features of the U.K.'s BIDs law are not found in New York's, but can be found in other states' laws. See Blackwell's and Lloyd and Peel's chapters in this volume.)

Although corporate BIDs were not a majority of U.S. BIDs at the time of Mitchell's (1999) survey, they are prevalent in the major central business districts that by their nature influence particularly large numbers of people. One line of inquiry should be to examine their service performance and the democratic performance in comparison to smaller Main Street or community BIDs: Are they really qualitatively different, and if so, is it their money, their autonomy, their different production technology, or all or none of those characteristics that makes them so? Is there support for our hypothesis that the visitor-seeking character of business districts makes them less likely than residential special-benefit districts to practice successful exclusions and effective enclosure of public space? The nascent proliferation of community benefits districts may provide opportunities for comparison.

More examination of alternative statutory provisions and the effects of BIDs operating with different legal frameworks is also warranted. Returning to the question we posed at the outset, how and to what extent does statutory design influence the behavior and consequences of BIDs? We concluded that New Jersey's SIDs can be seen as policy tools as much as, if not more than, private governments, and that they appear relatively benign by comparison with other familiar partnership models for urban redevelopment. Is this the result of New Jersey's distinctive statutory design, or of other elements? Do similar legal designs generate similar results in other social, economic, and legal contexts? Or might we see less benign results from the same design in other places or at other times? Will BIDs, like municipal corporations before them, eventually be deemed sufficiently threatening to individual and minority-group rights and liberties that they will be subjected to a 21st-century equivalent of Dillon's rule? In view of the continuing diffusion of BIDs and similar institutional arrangements in the United States and elsewhere (Baer and Marando, 2001; Hoyt, 2003; Mallett, 1995), a better understanding of the implications of their diverse institutional characteristics could usefully be employed in designing arrangements for the future. The BID phenomenon, because of its international diffusion as well as its huge range of variations in the United States alone, presents abundant opportunities for comparative analysis of institutional design features and their consequences for governance.

References

2nd Roc-Jersey Assocs. v. Town of Morristown. 158 N.J. 581 (1999).

Alexander, A. 2003. Business improvement districts: Progress toward implementation in the UK. *European Retail Digest*, March, 13–15.

Baer, S. E., and Marando, V. L. 2001. The subdistricting of cities: Applying the polycentric model. *Urban Affairs Review* 36:721–733.

Bagli, C. V. 1998. Business group fails to mollify Giuliani. *New York Times*, September 24, p. B5.

Barnekov, T. K., and Rich, D. 1989. Privatism and the limits of local economic development policy. *Urban Affairs Quarterly* 25:212–238.

Blau, J. R. 2000. Relational wealth in the commons: Local spaces of work and residence in a global economy. In *Relational wealth: The advantages of stability in a changing economy*, ed. C. R. Leana and D. M. Rousseau, 217–32. New York: Oxford University Press.

Bradley, R. 1995. Downtown renewal: The role of business improvement districts. *PM: Public Management* 77:9–13.

Briffault, R. 1999. A government for our time? Business improvement districts and urban governance. *Columbia Law Review* 99:365–477.

Brinckerhoff, J. M. 2002. Global public policy, partnership, and the case for the world commission on dams. *Public Administration Review* 62:324–336.

Burchell-Listokin and Associates. 1995. *Assignment of costs in special improvement districts (SIDs) according to proportionate benefits received: Issues and procedures.* Expert report for plaintiffs in 2nd-Roc Jersey case. Green Brook, NJ.

Colley, S. 1999. Betting on BIDs. *American City and County* 114:21–31.

Collins, S.-O. 1998. In the twilight zone: A survey of public-private partnerships in Sweden. *Public Productivity and Management Review* 21:272–283.

Cox, K. 1993. The concept of local economic development policy: Some fundamental questions. In *Community economic development: Policy development in the US and UK*, ed. D. Fasenfest, 45–64. New York: St. Martin's Press in association with the Policy Studies Organization.

Denhardt, R. B. 2000. *Theories of public organization.* 3rd ed. Fort Worth, TX: Harcourt Brace College.

District Management Act. N.J. Stat. Ann. §§ 40:56-65-89 (1999).

Ellen, I. G., Schwartz, A. E., and Voicu, I. 2006. The impact of business improvement districts on property values: Evidence from New York City. Unpublished manuscript.

Fanelli v. City of Trenton. 135 N.J. 582 (1994).

Gallagher, T. 1995. Trespasser on Main St. (you!). *The Nation* 261:787–790.

Garodnick, D. R. 2000. What's the BID deal? Can the Grand Central BID serve a special limited purpose? *University of Pennsylvania Law Review* 148:1733–1770.

Gonzalez v. Borough of Freehold. No. A-3476-92T2 (N.J. App. Div. June 30, 1994).

Herszenhorn, D. M. 1997. Rediscovering the heart of town; personal touch draws shoppers, bringing fading business centers back to life. *New York Times*, December 22, p. B1.

Houstoun, L. O., Jr. 1997. *BIDs: Business improvement districts.* Washington, DC: ULI—The Urban Land Institute in cooperation with the International Downtown Association.

Hoyt, L. 2003. *The business improvement district: An internationally diffused approach to revitalization.* http://web.mit.edu/course/11/11.204/www/webportfolio/inquiry/IBP_WEB_.pdf (accessed January 6, 2005).

Justice, J. B. 2003. Business improvement districts, reasoning, and results: Collective action and downtown revitalization. *Dissertation Abstracts International* 64:3064.

Justice, J. B., and Goldsmith, R. S. 2006. Private governments or public policy tools? The law and public policy of New Jersey's special improvement districts. *International Journal of Public Administration* 29:107–136.

Justice, J. B., Skelcher, C., and Mathur, N. 2006. BID partnerships, polycentrism, and problems of governance. Paper presented at the annual meeting of the Urban Affairs Association, Montreal, QC.

Karcher, A. J. 1998. *New Jersey's multiple municipal madness.* New Brunswick, NJ: Rutgers University Press.

Kirlin, J. J. 1996. The big questions of public administration in a democracy. *Public Administration Review* 56:416–424.

Krohe, J., Jr. 1992. Why reform government? Replace it. *Across the Board* 29:40–45.

Lakoff, S. A., and Rich, D. 1973. Introduction. In *Private government: Introductory readings,* ed. S. A. Lakoff and D. Rich, 1–6. Glenview, IL: Scott, Foresman and Company.

Levy, P. R. 2001a. Making downtowns competitive. *Planning* 70:16–19.

Levy, P. R. 2001b. Paying for the public life. *Economic Development Quarterly* 15:124–131.

Lichfield, D. 1998. Measuring the success of partnership endeavors. In *Public-private partnerships for local economic development,* ed. N. Walzer and B. D. Jacobs, 97–119. Westport, CT: Praeger.

Lofland, L. H. 2002. *Commodification of public space.* A LeFrak lectureship monograph. College Park: University of Maryland, Urban Studies and Planning Program Publications.

Logan, J. R., and Molotch, H. L. 1987. *Urban fortunes: The political economy of place.* Berkeley: University of California Press.

Mac Donald, H. 1996. BIDs really work. *City Journal* 6:29–42.

Mallett, W. J. 1993. Private government formation in the DC metropolitan area. *Growth and Change* 24:385–415.

Mallett, W. J. 1994. Managing the postindustrial city: Business improvement districts in the United States. *Area* 26:276–287.

Mallett, W. J. 1995. Privatizing the metropolis: The emergence of public-private government in the Washington D.C. metropolitan area. Unpublished Ph.D. dissertation, Cornell University, Ithaca, NY.

McNally v. Township of Teaneck. 75 N.J. 33 (1977).

Mitchell, J. 1999. *Business improvement districts and innovative service delivery.* Grant report. Arlington, VA: PricewaterhouseCoopers Endowment for the Business of Government.

National Trust for Historic Preservation. 2002. *National Main Street Center.* http://www.nationaltrust.org/main_street (accessed January 25, 2003).

Olson, M. 1969. The principle of "fiscal equivalence": The division of responsibilities among different levels of government. *American Economic Review* 59:479–487.

Olson, M. 1971. *The logic of collective action: Public goods and the theory of groups.* Cambridge, MA: Harvard University Press.

Ostrom, E. 1990. *Governing the commons: The evolution of institutions for collective action.* Cambridge: Cambridge University Press.

Ostrom, E., Gardner, R., and Walker, J. 1994. *Rules, games, and common-pool resources.* Ann Arbor: University of Michigan Press.

Ostrom, E., Schroeder, L., and Wynne, S. 1993. *Institutional incentives and sustainable development: Infrastructure policies in perspective.* Boulder, CO: Westview Press.

Ostrom, E., and Walker, J. 1997. Neither markets nor hierarchies: Linking transformation processes in collective action arenas. In *Perspectives on public choice: A handbook,* ed. D. C. Mueller, 35–72. Cambridge: Cambridge University Press.

Ostrom, V. 1989. *The intellectual crisis in American public administration.* 2nd ed. Tuscaloosa: University of Alabama Press.

Pack, J. R. 1992. BIDs, DIDs, SIDs, SADs: Private governments in urban America. *Brookings Review* 10:18–21.

Pristin, T. 1998. After Guiliani foes quit, business group drops plan to reorganize. *New York Times*, December 24, p. B7.

Pristin, T. 1999. Finance commissioner to head Grand Central business group. *New York Times*, January 21, p. B7.

Ratcliffe, J., and Flanagan, S. 2004. Enhancing the vitality and viability of town and city centres: The concept of the business improvement district in the context of tourism enterprise. *Property Management* 22:377–395.

Rogowsky, E. T., and Gross, J. S. 2000. Business improvement districts (BIDs) and economic development in New York City. In *Managing capital resources for central city revitalization*, ed. F. W. Wagner, T. E. Joder, and A. J. Mumphrey, Jr., 81–115. New York: Garland.

Salamon, L. M., ed. 2002. *The tools of government: A guide to the new governance*. New York: Oxford University Press.

Sbragia, A. M. 1983. Politics, local government, and the municipal bond market. In *The municipal money chase: The politics of local government finance*, ed. A. M. Sbragia, 67–111. Boulder, CO: Westview Press.

Sbragia, A. M. 1996. *Debt wish: Entrepreneurial cities, U.S. federalism, and economic development*. Pittsburgh, PA: University of Pittsburgh Press.

Skelcher, C. 2006. Does democracy matter? A transatlantic research design on democratic performance and special purpose governments. Unpublished manuscript.

Squires, G. D., ed. 1989. *Unequal partnerships: The political economy of urban redevelopment in postwar America*. New Brunswick, NJ: Rutgers University Press.

Stark, A. 1998. America, the gated? *Wilson Quarterly* 22:58–79.

Stoker, G. 1995. Regime theory and urban politics. In *Theories of urban politics*, ed. D. Judge, G. Stoker, and H. Wolman, 54–71. London: Sage Publications.

Stone, C. N. 1989. *Regime politics: Governing Atlanta, 1946–1988*. Lawrence: University Press of Kansas.

Traub, J. 1996. Can associations of businesses be true community builders? *The Responsive Community* 6:29–38.

Vindevogel, F. 2005. Private security and urban crime mitigation: A bid for BIDs. *Criminal Justice* 5:233–255.

Walker, J. 2003. Beyond public and private: Business improvement districts don't fit our ordinary categories. *Reason* 35:16–17.

Ward, K. 2006. 'Policies in motion,' urban management and state restructuring: The translocal expansion of business improvement districts. *International Journal of Urban and Regional Research* 30:54–75.

Warner, S. B. 1968. *The private city: Philadelphia in three periods of its growth*. Philadelphia: University of Pennsylvania Press.

Why RiverCenter should be abolished. 1999. *triCity News*, June 24, pp. 6, 7.

Yin, R. K. 2003. *Case study research: Design and methods*. 3rd ed. Thousand Oaks, CA: Sage Publications.

Zukin, S. 1995. *The cultures of cities*. Cambridge, MA: Blackwell Publishers.

Chapter 9

Business Improvement Districts in the Los Angeles Metropolitan Area: Implications for Local Governance*

Jack W. Meek and Paul Hubler

Contents

---

* This chapter is a revised version of a previously published work: Meek and Hubler (2006).

The Emergence of BIDs in the Los Angeles Metropolitan Area

Among the more fascinating developments in the Los Angeles metropolitan area in the past decade are the growth in numbers, influence, and official powers of business improvement districts (BIDs). Although the concept of special-assessment districts that pay for shared public facilities is rooted in collective action strategies to meet infrastructure needs, modern BIDs providing for promotional services and special facilities to improve the vitality of commercial areas first appeared in the mid-1960s. State laws authorizing BIDs often evolved from earlier laws allowing authorities to finance new public facilities, such as water, levee, and sewer systems, by levying assessments on the properties benefiting from the new facilities (Houstoun, 2003). Such was the case in California with the enactment of the Parking and Business Improvement Area Law of 1965, which expanded on earlier legislation that provided for assessment financing of public improvements such as street lighting by permitting assessments to be used for service provision as well as capital improvements.

BIDs are authorized to levy business license or property assessments for the purpose of improving a business area, typically through marketing efforts and "clean and safe" programs using contracted maintenance and private security teams. What makes BIDs of real importance to public administrators is their rapid rise in popularity as localities seek to spin off particularized or "boutique" service functions, their role in the revitalization strategy for moribund commercial areas, and their evolution into professionally run organizations that exhibit public and private characteristics. These unique characteristics make them worthy of attention in the years to come.

California's BID growth scene has mirrored a national trend, yet may also be due to particular developments and circumstances. Following a taxpayer revolt in the late 1970s, Californians set stringent limits on property tax increases. This, coupled with the power of the state to withhold local funds to balance the state budget during tough fiscal times, has forced local governments to focus on core service provision and seek alternative revenue streams to support services. One result has been growth in the number of BIDs, which offer relatively safeguarded revenue streams. California leads the nation in creating BIDs, with 73 BIDs formed by 1999 compared to 404 BIDs nationwide (Houstoun, 2003). (According to the International Downtown Association, more than 1,200 BIDs have been formed in the United States and Canada since the early 1970s.) The city of Los Angeles is home to more that 23 BIDs with some 20 additional BIDs requesting city council approval (City of Los Angeles, 2002). BIDs have emerged as a key tool for local businesses, property owners, and officials in Southern California seeking to revitalize aging downtowns and commercial areas.

The Los Angeles area BIDs studied here offer many of the functions typically provided by localities, ranging from business-promotion activities—such as consumer marketing—to providing security patrols and street cleaning squads (so-called clean and safe teams). Rather than duplicate city services, BIDs attract support from business and property owners assessed by offering a higher level of services concentrated on a defined business area. These two qualities (focused service and consistent funding) provide insight into current public administration practice. In interviews with directors of BIDs and with city officials in the Los Angeles area, a clear consensus is that BIDs provide services more effectively and efficiently than their host government jurisdictions, in most cases delivering more intensive services and, in some cases, inheriting the delivery of municipal services. It appears clear that BIDs do deliver added value. Certainly, BIDs and their host jurisdictions share an interest in delivering added value, with cities often legally bound to continue the pre-BID level of service to the business district.*

What follows is a report on five BIDs in the Los Angeles area, each created to meet unique needs of the business community and representing distinct sizes,

---

* Sources of this information and the information in the following section are the interviews conducted by the authors in 2003–2004.

origins, and relationships to the authorizing municipality. The chapter first reviews the legal foundation of BIDs under the California law, which establishes the authority by which they can function and the accountability framework from which they must operate. The chapter then reviews the five BID case studies conducted by the authors. Finally, the chapter summarizes the central findings of the case studies and poses questions for future examination.

Legal Framework of Business Improvement Districts in California

Most BIDs in California are formed by property or business owners seeking a heightened level of services financed by the imposition of an assessment on commercial or industrial property within a defined geographic area, typically a main street, downtown area, commercial strip, or industrial area. (Occasionally, as we have found, a municipality may play a co-instigating role with local business leaders in forming a BID.) Among the key benefits of a BID is that it energizes the private stakeholders to cooperatively organize in pursuit of a higher level of service to benefit a particular area. While organizations and groupings of merchants for mutual benefit are common, it is uncommon for property owners to be organized for mutual benefit. California's BID laws give merchants and property owners the vehicle to organize for mutual benefit.

BIDs typically must be approved by ordinance or resolution of local government in order for the business license or property tax assessment to be levied. Local governments derive authority to approve BIDs through state general enabling legislation, which sets forth requirements for governance, accountability, and financing of the BIDs.

BIDs are enabled through three sections of the California Streets and Highways Code: the Parking and Business Improvement Area Law (1965), the Parking and Business Improvement Law (1989), and the Property and Business Improvement District Law (1994). Table 9.1 lists the general characteristics of BIDs created under each of the three sections of law, starting with the earliest iteration of the law in 1965 and leading up to the 1994 law.

As can be noted in Table 9.1, the revenue base of BIDs was expanded in 1994 to include property tax assessments. According to BID experts, assessments on real property generate far greater revenues and collections are far simpler to administer than business license taxes. Property and business license fee BIDs are both portrayed by proponents as self-help mechanisms for providing higher levels of services for a particular area. In 2004, localities were statutorily authorized to issue BID revenue bonds, with a vastly increased potential for funding large-scale capital improvements.

Municipalities are also authorized to form alpha BIDs with special rules concerning governance. Under these rules, BID passage rates and fiscal sources are

Table 9.1 California BID enabling legislation

Name	Creation/special functions	Governance	Fiscal
Parking and Business Improvement Area Law of 1965	Authorizes cities to create parking and business improvement areas for the purpose of acquiring, constructing, or maintaining parking structures and to promote retail trade activities in the area. Establishment is subject to city council hearing and protest vote by a majority of business owners paying the tax.	City council has sole discretion as to use of revenues but may appoint an advisory committee.	Business license tax; tax assessment based on benefit.
Parking and Business Improvement Law of 1989	Authorizes cities and counties to establish parking and business improvement areas for the same purposes as above and, in addition, to pay for benches, street lighting, parks, fountains, and other business area capital improvements. Establishment is subject to petition, city council hearing, and protest vote by majority of business owners paying the tax.	City council has sole discretion as to use of revenues and is required to appoint an advisory committee to recommend expenditures.	Business license tax; tax assessment based on benefit.
Property and Business Improvement District Law of 1994	Authorizes cities and counties to establish property and business improvement districts to promote and support retail trade activities and capital improvements in the area in accordance with a management district plan. Establishment is pursuant to petition, hearing, and protest vote by majority of property owners paying the tax. Law expressly permits charter cities to adopt ordinances providing for different procedures for levying assessments for so-called alpha BIDs.	A private nonprofit entity, "owner's association," may be under contract to the city to implement the management district plan. The city council may approve annual financial reports filed by the owner's association. Owner's associations are private entities but are required to comply with state open meetings and public records laws.	Property or business license assessment. Assessment based on measured benefit. Residential and agricultural properties are exempt. City council may permit issuance of bonds based on property tax or business license assessments, not to exceed 30 years.

subject to city ordinance rather than state law. As noted in the chart above, the 1994 state law explicitly recognizes the independent authority of the charter cities to create alpha BIDs. The authors have found that charter cities typically do not stray far from state law practice in creating these alpha BIDs, other than to set a petition threshold lower than that required by state law. In the example in the city of Los Angeles, the city BID conforms to state law requirements with two key exceptions: the passage threshold is lowered from 50 percent of property owners to 30 percent, and the BID life span is lengthened from 5 years to 10 years. The authors are aware of only two cities in California that have passed ordinances creating alpha BIDs, the Chinatown BID in Los Angeles and a BID in Oakland. In both cases, these BIDs are located in economically depressed areas and city officials have sought to overcome perceived property owner and merchant apathy by lowering the petition threshold.

As noted in Table 9.1, current state law enables three types of BIDs in California: merchant-based business license BIDs, property-tax-based BIDs, and municipally created BIDs, already discussed above. These three types vary primarily by whether the assessment is levied against the merchant or the property owner, but also by the life span of the BID and by petition thresholds for initiation of the BID, characteristics that are outlined below.

Merchant-based BIDs may be initiated upon city council, county, or business owner request. Under legislative provisions that took effect in 2004, a petition of support from those business owners representing more than 50 percent of the assessment fulfills the constitutionally required weighted ballot vote. Assessments are levied on business owners, which may include landlords, with the assessment collected by the city. Merchant-based BIDs renew annually unless opposed by those paying more than 50 percent of the assessment, and can thus have indefinite life spans.

Property-based BIDs are initiated only upon property owner petition signed by property owners who will pay more than 50 percent of the assessments to be levied. (However, if there is a single property owner who will pay more than 40 percent of the total assessment, that assessment is not counted in determining whether the 50 percent benchmark is met.) Upon receipt of the petition, the city council may adopt a resolution expressing its intention to form a district. California law then requires a ballot vote in which more than 50 percent of the ballots received, weighted by assessment, are in support of the district. Unless rejected by the protest vote, the city council may adopt a resolution levying the assessment for a period of 5 years for new districts, and 10 years for renewed districts. Assessments are levied on property owners and collected by the county, through the property tax bill.

The petition and vote threshold requirements are important due process checks due to the mandatory nature of the BID assessment. As noted above, the boundaries and plan for the BID are initiated as a result of a petition of property owners in the cases of the property-based BID or merchants in the case of the merchant-based BID.

BIDs are generally managed by a private nonprofit corporation with oversight from an elected or appointed board of directors and a financial reporting requirement to the authorizing city council or county board of supervisors. At smaller BIDs, the city staff may assume the management role. State law requires the nonprofit corporation to provide an annual report to the city council to report on revenue received, expenditures made, and budgets for the upcoming year.

State law does require the assessment formula to be fair, balanced, and commensurate with benefits received. The law explicitly notes that assessments are not taxes and instead are fees based on benefit received. Nonprofits and owner-occupied residential properties are exempted from assessment. Municipalities typically pay assessments or in-lieu fees, while school districts may be exempted. Although not required to pay assessments, in some cases, state and federal agencies have voluntarily agreed to pay under "good neighbor" policies.

A feature of California BIDs that is perhaps unique to the state is that as a practical matter, property-based BID assessments cannot be based on a percentage of the assessed valuation of property. This is because of the great variance in assessed valuations that resulted from the tax reform initiative, Proposition 13, which imposes stringent limits on valuation increases unless a property changes ownership. Instead, property-based BIDs typically use a more complicated assessment based on lot and building square footage, shopping street frontage, and proximity to areas more intensely served by the BID.

California BIDs operate as public–private partnerships with various ranges of autonomy vis-à-vis the public authority, which is further discussed in the "Research Questions and Methods" section below. The primary role of the authorizing public entity, either a municipality or a county, is to exercise its authority to levy the assessment on behalf of the BID community. Either the city itself or, more typically, an owner's association or private nonprofit is designated as the service provider or agent responsible for implementing the improvements identified in the BID plan. By law, an owner's association must be a private nonprofit entity, either existing or newly formed, and expressly may not be considered a public entity. However, state law recognizes the challenge in ensuring public accountability by a private nonprofit that is the recipient of assessment revenues, as BID owner's associations are required to comply with the state open public meetings and public records acts applicable to local public entities. Unlike in Georgia and some other states, BIDs in California are not associated with transportation management associations, and transportation improvements are not among the primary purposes of California's BIDs (see Chapter 15 in this volume). The primary objectives of BIDs are to increase security, maintenance, and marketing of business areas, although they may undertake an essentially unlimited range of improvements and activities as identified in each individual BID plan.

In general, BIDs focus on achieving security and maintenance goals and relatively limited capital improvements within their jurisdictional areas, although they may seek to take on large-scale improvements with the enactment of a new law permitting BIDs to issue revenue bonds. In the California Streets and Highway Code, the Property and Business Improvement District Law, Section 36610 (1994), defines improvements as the

acquisition, construction, installation, or maintenance of any tangible property with an estimated useful life of five years or more including, but not limited to, the following:

Parking facilities.
Benches, booths, kiosks, display cases, pedestrian shelters and signs.
Trash receptacles and public restrooms.
Lighting and heating facilities.
Decorations.
Parks.
Fountains.
Planting areas.
Closing, opening, widening, or narrowing of existing streets.
Facilities or equipment, or both, to enhance security of persons and property within the area.
Ramps, sidewalks, plazas, and pedestrian malls.
Rehabilitation and removal of existing structures.

According to the California Streets and Highway Code, the Property and Business Improvement District Law, Section 36613 (1994), BID activities include but are not limited to:

Promotion of public events which benefit businesses or real property in the district.
Furnishing of music in any public place within the district.
Promotion of tourism within the district.
Marketing and economic development, including retail retention and recruitment.
Providing security, sanitation, graffiti removal, street and sidewalk cleaning, and other municipal services supplemental to those normally provided by the municipality.
Activities which benefit businesses and real property located in the district.

As noted above, the California legislature and governor enacted legislation that took effect in 2004 permitting BIDs to begin issuing bonds to finance public works and to levy assessments against business owners or real property to pay off the bonds. According to a staff analysis (Assembly Committee on Local Government, 2003),

Assembly Bill 944 also abolished the requirement of a weighted vote following the submission of a petition signed by business owners who would pay 50 percent or more of the total assessment. The legislation declared that the petition serves as the equivalent to the constitutionally required weighted vote ballot process, with property owners given votes based on the total assessment to be paid. Property owner BIDs would still be required to hold the weighted ballot vote. The bill was introduced with the intent of enabling the financing of a sports arena as the linchpin in the redevelopment of Sacramento's downtown rail yards (Assembly Committee on Local Government, 2003).

Research Questions and Methods

To better understand the functioning of BIDs in general, and those in the Los Angeles metropolitan area in particular, the authors collaborated with Göktuğ Morçöl, Jim Wolf, and Ulf Zimmermann as a research team.* This research team reviewed existing research on BIDs and developed fundamental questions that would focus the data gathering and analysis of BIDs. The design of the research team's instrument focused on the central concerns in the literature with regard to BIDs. These concerns included the following four areas of inquiry:

■ Why and how are BIDs established?
■ Where and how do BIDs work (location, revenues, membership, management, services)?
■ How are BIDs held accountable? How are they evaluated?
■ Are BIDs effective?

The research team felt that to get a fuller grasp of the functioning of BIDs, it would be necessary to rely on an in-depth case study approach to data gathering to develop a stronger contextual understanding of the establishment, operation, and effectiveness of BIDs. The research team also agreed to conduct open-ended interviews with both BID leaders and BID government liaisons so as to contrast the views on BID operations from the perspectives of both government and business, the two central players in the partnership.

For the research presented in this chapter, the authors hoped to select from a variety of BIDs, large and small, urban and suburban, from different cities, to retain the possibility of identifying differences in the approach that cities in the Los Angeles metropolitan area demonstrated in working with BIDs. Our selection process began with the city of Los Angeles, and a listing of BIDs in the city and

---

* For the reports of the research conducted by the other team members in Georgia and Pennsylvania, see the chapters by Morçöl and Zimmermann (Chapters 2 and 15) and Morçöl and Patrick in this volume and Wolf (2006).

interviews with leaders of the Department of Community Redevelopment. In our interviews we decided to select one of the original BIDs in Los Angeles, the Fashion District. From interviews at the Fashion District, we relied on references and contacts in other major cities in the region, and explored contacts with BID leaders and their city counterparts. Our approach led to the selection of five very different BIDs with a geographic spread within the region (see Table 9.2). We chose to examine current operating BIDs to see how they were functioning and how they were held accountable for their operations, and if there were significant issues related to their operations. Some BIDs have been dismantled in the past years, and these may be useful to examine in future research, but they were not selected for this examination due to our criteria that the BID had to be a current functioning operation.

Los Angeles: The Fashion District BID

Why and How Was the BID Established?

The Los Angeles Fashion District Business Improvement District was established in 1994 following a two-year organizing drive initiated by two prominent Fashion District property owners. Fashion District was the first BID in the city of Los Angeles and was initiated in an effort to revitalize the area formerly known by the less glamorous appellation of the Garment District. Formed as a demonstration merchant-based BID, the BID was subsequently authorized on January 1, 1995, as a property-based BID following the enactment of enabling state legislation.

Where and How Does the BID Work?

The BID was reauthorized in 2003 for five years to encompass a 90-block area. With each reauthorization vote, the BID has grown from the original 12-block demonstration area. The BID enjoys annual revenues of approximately $2.9 million, with assessments constituting the main source of revenue. There are 580 property owners assessed on approximately 1,118 parcels. The BID is governed by a 12-member board of directors and managed by a private nonprofit organization with seven staff members and another 60 contract employees providing clean and safe services. Other services provided include job training and marketing activities. More than 72 percent of the BID budget is dedicated to clean and safe programs.

How Is the BID Held Accountable? How Is It Evaluated?

The Fashion District BID provides regular reports of revenues and expenditures to the Los Angeles City Council. The BID evaluates its own performance by tracking

Table 9.2 Los Angeles metropolitan area case studies

City/BID	(BID year)/PBID year formed/affirmed Owners, parcels (blocks) BID size (assessment)	Services provided	Governance and accountability	Evaluation and effectiveness
Los Angeles— Fashion District	(1994)/1995/1998/2003 580 owners, 1,118 parcels (90 blocks) $2.9 million 2003 vote: 76%	72% clean and safe Job training Marketing	15-member board with no city representatives BID provides regular reports BID evaluates own goals	Intense and exclusive focus Increase in property values Increase in business owners (200)
Long Beach— Pine Avenue	(1973)/1999/2003 MBID: 1,100 owners PBID: 255 owners, 650 parcels (90 blocks) MBID: $450K PBID: $1 million (25% from assessed city property plus $100K–$145K a year in parking revenues) 2003 vote: 75%	68% clean and safe Marketing Special projects Advocacy/ administration	12-member board with two city representatives Annual management plan Monthly and annual reports	Responsive Focused service
Pasadena— Old Town	(1989)/2000 160 owners, 228 parcels (21 blocks) $1.1 million (50% from assessed city property)	66% clean and safe Advocacy Marketing	23-member board with three city representatives Annual plan, annual reports City liaison coordination	Focused service Provide voice for district

Table 9.2 (continued)   Los Angeles metropolitan area case studies

City/BID	(BID year)/PBID year formed/affirmed Owners, parcels (blocks) BID size (assessment)	Services provided	Governance and accountability	Evaluation and effectiveness
Burbank— Media City Center Mall	(1994)/2003 133 owners, 289 parcels (30 blocks) $750K 2003 vote: 82%	15% clean and safe Street signage, holiday décor, paseo upgrades Marketing and promotion	9-member board appointed by city council with two city representatives Annual financial reports City employee acts as BID executive director	Performance benchmarks established Engaged owners as stakeholders
Monrovia— Myrtle Avenue	(1965) 210 business license holders $40K (assessment), $20K (pass-through) Vote: No protest vote to date	No clean and safe funding Promotions Marketing	5-member advisory board appointed by city council City employee acts as BID executive director City-approved budget	Annual reports Increased property value

crime and trash counts through the clean and safe program, pedestrian counts, increases in property valuation, and decreases in vacancy rates.

Is the BID Effective?

The Fashion District BID can be more effective than the city at delivering services because of its intense and exclusive focus on a relatively small downtown area. According to BID CEO Kent Smith, property values in the assessed area have soared by 20 to 50 percent over the last five years and the BID area has added 200 businesses in the last two years. The BID strives to replace lower-wage garment manufacturing jobs with higher-wage jobs in creative fashion design.

Downtown Long Beach: The Pine Avenue BID

Why and How Was the BID Established?

Downtown Long Beach was first established as a merchant-based BID in 1973. Following an 18-month organizational effort, the property-based BID was established in 1999 for a period of five years in an effort to revitalize the downtown area. The property-based BID was recently reauthorized for a period of ten years. The merchant-based BID is authorized under state highways code and renews in perpetuity unless contested by a majority of those assessed. The property-based BID was established by business leaders in response to two external influences: (1) the announcement by the city of Long Beach that it would cease subsidizing higher levels of service for the downtown area, and (2) the enactment of state legislation permitting property-based BIDs.

Where and How Does the BID Work?

Long Beach has two BIDs focused in a similar downtown geographic area. The merchant-based BID encompasses a 175-block area; the property-based BID was initially authorized for a 75-block area in 1999, which increased to 90 blocks commencing on January 1, 2004. Because of the overlay, it is possible for businesses to be assessed twice: first as merchants through an assessment on their city business licenses, and second as tenants through a pass-through of the property assessment from their landlords. The merchant-based BID raises approximately $450,000 to $500,000 per year through assessments levied on business licenses of some 1,100 to 1,200 businesses. The property assessments generate another $1 million annually, with 355 property owners paying assessments on 650 parcels. Assessments constitute 90 percent of the income, with the city passing through the remaining 10 percent in the form of parking meter revenues. The city has also awarded the property-based BID a grant of $30,000 a year to fund the position of an economic development specialist.

"Operation Clean and Safe" accounts for 68 percent of BID expenditures. In addition, the BID is focusing greater efforts on homeless services and is one of two Los Angeles–area BIDs selected by the International Downtown Association for a federally funded case study of homeless services. The BID is managed by a private nonprofit organization, the Downtown Long Beach Associates, with five staff members and one contract controller.

How Is the BID Held Accountable? How Is It Evaluated?

The Downtown Long Beach Associates manages both the property-based BID and the merchant-based BID and is governed by a 12-member board. The board is comprised of five property owners, five merchants, one representative of the city of Long Beach, and one representative of the Long Beach Redevelopment Agency. BID board members are elected by the membership, with votes weighted by assessment and with the city, which owns some 24 percent of the property assessed, agreeing to abstain from voting.

The BID produces an annual management plan, as well as monthly and annual financial reports that are submitted for approval by the Long Beach City Council. The BID surveys customer satisfaction, counts visitors, and, for economic development measures, quantifies the number of businesses retained and the square footage of new leases generated. The BID also measures the volume of trash picked up and the square footage of sidewalks cleaned by the clean teams.

Is the BID Effective?

BIDs require a mutual awareness of shared problems and a contribution in the form of an assessment from their members. They tend to be more effective because they are more responsive, more focused on a smaller geographic area, and can implement their programs using their own resources rather than competing with other programs.

Pasadena: "Old Town" BID

Why and How Was the BID Established?

The Old Pasadena Business Improvement District, a property-based BID, was established in 2000, replacing a merchant-based BID that was started in 1989. It took approximately three years to organize the BID after the Old Pasadena Management Association was incorporated as a 501(c)(6) corporation in the fall of 1997. The leaders of the Old Pasadena Management Association felt that the city was providing an unsatisfactory level of services to the revitalizing of the downtown area. Sidewalks were described as filthy and police response times were thought of as poor. In addition, it was felt that merchant-based BIDs spent an inordinate amount of time enforcing revenue collection, whereas a property-based BID could collect revenue through a more reliable mechanism, the property tax bill.

Two key downtown property owners and a city redevelopment agency staff member assigned as a liaison to the downtown area initiated the property-based BID. The city staffer was attending International Downtown Association conferences and was bringing back information regarding the advantages of property-based BIDs.

Where and How Does the BID Work?

The boundaries of the property-based BID follow the contours of an existing area of city-installed parking meters for the designated downtown area. The area encompasses 21 blocks. The property-based BID has annual revenues of approximately $1.1 million, with the city of Pasadena providing approximately 50 percent of the annual budget. The city, which owns two parks and several parking structures within the boundaries of the BID, pays a flat assessment of $545,000. In addition, the Pasadena City Council voted in December 2003 on a proposal to transfer the management of the parking structures in the downtown area from the city to the BID, with a resulting 10 percent, or $110,000, increase in the BID budget, permitting the hiring by the PBID management company of a full-time dedicated marketing and communications specialist.

There are 160 property owners assessed on 228 parcels. The BID is managed by a private nonprofit organization, the Old Pasadena Management District, with three full-time members on staff, with one part-time temporary employee and one outside contract events organizer. Clean and safe operations account for 66 percent of expenditures.

How Is the BID Held Accountable? How Is It Evaluated?

A 23-member board, comprised of 16 property owners, retailers, or merchants and 3 representatives of the city of Pasadena, including a Pasadena police department lieutenant and one representative of the Castle Green residential complex, governs the BID. A governance committee recommends a slate of candidates for the board. Current board members, and not the general membership of the BID, select new members to the board. Thus, the board membership has remained very stable with little change in membership from year to year.

The BID provides annual financial reports to the city, which are audited by the city finance director. The BID also produces an annual management plan that is submitted to the city council for approval. In addition, the city tracks sales tax revenues generated by businesses within the BIDs.

Is the BID Effective?

Both city and BID leadership in Pasadena felt that BIDs could be more effective at delivering selected services than a city because they can be more innovative and are not hobbled by red tape. In addition, city and BID leadership in Pasadena agreed that BIDs give a voice to the business district in city matters that affect the BID. In Pasadena, BIDs are viewed not only as effective problem solvers, but also as a new platform or mechanism in the articulation of demands for city services. Pasadena and BID leadership interviewed also felt that BIDs have the ability to adopt the efficiency strategies of a private sector firm. For instance, the BID is not required to award contracts to the lowest responsible bidder as a city would be required to do. Instead, the BID can award the contract to the bidder that will provide the best service for security and maintenance. However, upon assumption of the management of the city parking structures, the Pasadena BID is complying with city bid requirements in awarding contracts to manage the garages.

Burbank: The Media City Center Mall BID

Why and How Was the BID Established?

The Downtown Burbank BID, with its focus on the Media City Center Mall, was established on July 22, 2003, following an 18-month organizational process. The Downtown Burbank Property and Business Improvement District was formed to replace the Burbank Village Business Improvement District, a merchant-based BID, which was formed on July 22, 1994. City and chamber of commerce officials considered the existing Burbank Village Business Improvement District, which assessed business owners rather than property owners and had an annual budget of approximately $70,000, but found that the improvement district failed to revitalize the downtown area. The city and business community have been seeking to revitalize the downtown area for the past decade. In addition, the city had experienced difficulty in collecting assessments under the merchant-based BID. Under the new property-based BID (PBID), the county collects assessments through the long-established property tax process.

The impetus for the creation of the property-based BID came from city officials, although the proposal had the support of the key downtown business leaders. The city hired a consultant to devise a property-based management district plan. The city council brought in a downtown manager from the Park and Recreation Department to organize and operate the BID. A majority of the downtown manager's time is expected to be devoted to the operation of the BID.

Where and How Does the BID Work?

The boundaries of the BID generally follow those of the already established downtown redevelopment project as well as those of Burbank's downtown. The only gerrymander appears to have been to include the downtown Metrolink/bus station in the BID boundary to better coordinate marketing of transportation alternatives.

The BID is anticipated to have annual revenues of $750,000 with assessments constituting 100 percent of revenues. One hundred thirty-three property owners on 289 parcels pay assessments. The BID is organized as a nonprofit corporation and is managed by a full-time Burbank Redevelopment Agency employee with the assistance of the consultant who helped establish the BID.

The BID will focus on providing better street signage, holiday décor, paseo upgrades, and marketing and promotional activities at a cost of approximately $500,000 a year. In addition, the budget contemplates expending $110,000 a year for maintenance and security.

How Is the BID Held Accountable? How Is It Evaluated?

The BID will provide annual financial reports to the city council. A nine-member board of directors appointed by the city council governs the BID. The city council has reserved the right to amend or modify the composition of the board of directors without amending the management district plan.

The board has established performance benchmarks and the performance goal of the downtown manager is to accomplish those services, signage, and events noted in the budget in the management plan.

Is the BID Effective?

According to city staff, the BID will be more responsive to downtown merchants and property owners as they request services because the BID has more leeway in accomplishing goals and fewer "bureaucratic hoops" to negotiate than would city staff. In addition, the PBID will offer property owners and merchants a greater feeling of ownership or sense of being stakeholders in the downtown area.

Monrovia and Myrtle Avenue BID

Why and How Was the BID Established?

This merchant-based BID was established in 1965, most likely by a merchants' association, at a time when Monrovia was a city in decline, with rising crime and a declining local economy. The BID was created among businesses on and along Myrtle Avenue in downtown Monrovia with the intent of revitalizing the city's traditional Main Street downtown. Founded in 1887, Monrovia is one of the older cities in Los Angeles County.

Where and How Does the BID Work?

The BID boundaries generally follow those of the long-established downtown area. The BID has annual revenues of $60,500, with assessments bringing in some $40,000 and the city passing through approximately $20,000 a year in filming permit fees for the downtown area. There are 210 business license holders assessed within the BID boundaries. City staff operates the BID, with the former assistant city manager serving as executive director, assisted by the city's downtown manager. The management of a weekly downtown street festival, which is not sponsored by the BID but which plays a role in attracting shoppers to the area, is contracted out to a private contractor. Most of the BID budget is spent on promotions and marketing for the downtown area. None of the budget is spent on clean and safe operations, which are provided by the city.

How Is the BID Held Accountable? How Is It Evaluated?

The BID provides an annual report of revenues and expenditures to the city council, which approves its budget. The BID does not conduct evaluations of its performance.

The Monrovia Old Town Advisory Board governs the BID, which is an official city commission whose five members are appointed by the mayor. Members serve staggered two-year terms and are charged with developing a budget.

Is the BID Effective?

City staff believe the efforts of the BID and those of the redevelopment agency have been instrumental in revitalizing and increasing property values in the downtown area. Essentially, the BID is indistinguishable from the city because it is organized and operated by city staff.

Implications of Research Findings

A summary of findings related to the case studies examined in this research is provided in Table 9.2. To summarize the general trend of BIDs in the Los Angeles metropolitan area: (1) There are 23 BIDs in the city of Los Angeles alone, with some 20 additional BIDs requesting city council approval, and there are numerous additional BIDs in Southern California; (2) each of the BIDs has a range of participants, and all have governing boards; (3) the BIDs are 501(c)(3) authorizations; (4) BIDs are able to be constructed because of state law; (5) BIDs are self-taxing and, in some cases, have city pass-through support; (6) BID boards are self-managed, held accountable for activities, and most have city representatives on the board.

In addition to the descriptive findings listed in Table 9.2, we offer five additional implications with regard to our research on these five Southern California BIDs.

1. *Context matters.* The source of the creation of the business improvement district matters. Business owners driven by a united business group initiated the formation of each of the five BIDs examined in this research. Two BID formations had significant city involvement along with a united business group. This may be a telling point for some cities in that active redevelopment agencies may be more aggressive partners in supplementing their roles in larger capital investments. Where there was significant city influence, there remains a deep city connection in terms of board membership. Regardless of city involvement, in each case there is an identifiable history of working together as well as a geographic sense of identity.

2. *Budget size matters.* The size of budget matters with regard to scope of operations and potential for influence. In almost all cases, the BID began as a merchant-based BID and evolved into a property-based BID. It was reported in the interviews conducted that the property-based approach allowed for two outcomes to emerge: increased financing for district services and increased commitment from property owners. All those interviewed indicated that the move to have property owners assessed led to a more engaged commitment on the part of the owners and in all cases enough budget to actually carry out significant services ranging from security, safety, and cleanliness to marketing and promotion. With a clear geographical representation, a common vision, and a dedicated staff, BIDs are taken seriously by cities, as they are a voice to be heard in city chambers with regard to matters within their districts. It is also clear that the city often advises owners to work with the BID leadership on various district matters that concern the owner rather than seeking individual assistance from the city.

3. *Spillover to expanded BID services matters.* Spillover effects of BID successes are feasible. As operations become successful, one can conceive that there will be spillover to other areas of the city. For example, the Pasadena BID was granted authority by the city council to take over parking management in the district from the current contracting source managed by the city in January 2004. Approval was granted after the city and the BID approved the terms of the agreement. As another example, the Los Angeles and Long Beach BID leadership will be working on homeless issues in a cross-national study sponsored by HUD with IDA. Homelessness issues have been a priority and source of controversy for BIDs. For instance, the Fashion District BID and three other downtown Los Angeles BIDs were sued and settled over treatment of the homeless and mentally ill, as noted by one of our interviewees and reported locally in a business journal (Bronstad, 2002).

   One can conjecture that a number of areas would be attractive to allocate to special districts in the hope of securing consistent service funding and focusing on specific functions in a geographic area. There may be a number of consequences to this strategy. First, there are labor costs issues: As BIDs take over city functions, do the operations of these reduce labor costs (to the disadvantage of some groups), or are there increases or decreases in overall employment? Second, there are evolutionary concerns: As BIDs evolve, is there a "nondemocratic effect" or an outcome effect that resembles private government? It is evident that BIDs have a political prowess potential: BIDs can unduly influence the political system. BIDs are certainly "voices" that are heard in city hall, and these voices are often welcomed because they represent a consensus among a significant representation of citizens and business interests. While alignment issues within the district may be of little concern, it is unclear what happens when this voice carries over and is heard with regard to other matters in the city.

4. *Accountability matters.* Accountability can become an issue. How is accountability handled in the governance structure within the BID and in oversight of the BID? For the most part, we have found that BIDs largely operate under the general public radar: there may be an issue of lack of knowledge of the existence and operations of these entities. It is clear, however, from our observations in the cases we examined, that while BIDs are not generally known by the public, they are certainly known by city leadership: they include city representatives (often appointees) on the boards. City representatives monitor quarterly and annual reports, and city authorities have the final say on granting and renewing authority for the operation of the BIDs. Although little may be known about BIDs among the general public, much is known about their operations within city leadership and city management.

   When asked about their leadership roles in managing BIDs, CEOs' mental models differ. Some see themselves as public administrators, some do not. Some are quite clear that they are operating a not-for-profit agency, that they are serving the interests of the stakeholders, and that they work closely with the board in determining the direction of the BID. These leaders clearly see their roles as serving a limited set of interests within the city, and that their freedom to pursue innovative strategies encourages new capacities of managing (Mitchell, 2001). On the other hand, some see their work as serving the public interest, and those they serve as the citizens in their jurisdiction on the functions that they have agreed upon. In this role, there is a broader interpretation of the role of BID leadership.

5. *Partnership matters.* The BIDs researched for this chapter are each viewed by all parties as providing services complementary to those provided by governments. It is apparent that BID leadership and city leadership share mutual respect for the operational efficiencies of BIDs. This is a critical point for accountability and success of BIDs (Lavery, 1995). Our research indicates that BIDs are improvements over government in providing services of a noncontroversial and specific focus. The clear hallmark of BIDs is that they have the advantages of a specific focus and stabilized funding.

Finally, it is important to point out that BIDs have different meanings for different people. For some, BIDs are a funding tool; for others, a service delivery tool; for others, a common interest tool; and still for others, a development tool. With this many meanings attached to a single instrument, it is a wonder that BIDs can achieve positive outcomes for each of the expectations. To this point, each of the BIDs in our case studies has demonstrated some level of acceptance and staying power—an outcome reflected in the reauthorization votes by both the BID membership and the city councils involved.

Conclusion: Complementary Public Services

The importance of BIDs, and the successes reported here, cannot be underestimated. It seems clear that as BID operations succeed, they will provide added services to targeted areas beyond services that could be provided by urban government (Mallett, 1994). From the interviews we conducted, both governmental officials and BID leadership view BID activities and services as complementary to those provided by government and government operations. Because there is a clear distinction between what services are to be provided by government and what services are to be provided by BIDs, each views the other as complementary to each other's mission and objectives (Pack, 1992). We interpret this finding to mean that citizens can establish and create organized efforts to improve their life in the city, as long as the partnership is established and authority and accountability are clearly understood and carefully monitored (Briffault, 1999). This seems to be the case in the experiences reported in this chapter.

And this success may lead to an evolution of activities or an expansion of services that go beyond the district into other areas of public service. If this evolution takes place, local government service provision may be a very different matter than has been traditionally conceived (Mitchell, 1999).

There are a number of directions that the special district strategy can evolve, some of which will draw the attention of city officials. For example, it is possible that the privatization of service delivery will be expanding only to those who can afford the assessment, thus creating a divide between those who can accomplish added value because of financial capability and those who cannot. One can also conceive of assessment strategies that will bring not only added value, but also a return on investment to only those in the district and not to the general welfare of those surrounding the district. One can also foresee the emergence of multiple special districts that supply narrowly defined services, which would be focused and easy to produce and manage, leaving more complicated, messy, and difficult services to governmental service delivery, which would be viewed as inefficient and ineffective. This outcome may contribute to negative citizen attitudes toward government and its role.

None of the cases we examined exemplified these problems, but it may be useful to speculate on these outcomes should the special district strategy spill over to other services traditionally provided by local governments. In short, future research is needed to examine the secondary impacts of BIDs on the surrounding community (Clark et al., 2001). In addition, comparative examination of BIDs in other geographic regions will allow theoretical interests in BIDs to be expanded, including the assessment of the multiple interpretations of BIDs that range from innovative solutions designed to finance special public needs to obtaining unfair access to the policy process through questionable representation.

References

Assembly Committee on Local Government. 2003. *Committee staff analysis of AB 944 (Steinberg).* http://sen.ca.gov (accessed January 15, 2004).

Briffault, R. 1999. A government for our time? Business improvement districts and urban governance. *Columbia Law Review* 99:365–477.

Bronstad, A. 2002. Downtown BID pays $10,000 to settle suit brought by homeless. *Los Angeles Business Journal*, February 18.

California Streets and Highways Code. The Parking and Business Improvement Area Law (1965). Section 36000. http://www.leginfo.ca.gov/cgi-bin/displaycode?section=shc&group=35001-36000&file=36000-36004 (accessed August 8, 2007).

California Streets and Highways Code. The Parking and Business Improvement Law (1989). Section 36500. http://www.leginfo.ca.gov/cgi-bin/displaycode?section=shc&group=36001-37000&file=36500-36504 (accessed August 8, 2007).

California Streets and Highways Code. The Property and Business Improvement District Law (1994), Section 36600. http://www.leginfo.ca.gov/cgi-bin/displaycode?section=shc&group=36001-37000&file=36600-36604 (accessed August 8, 2007).

California Streets and Highways Code. The Property and Business Improvement District Law (1994), Section 36610. http://www.leginfo.ca.gov/cgi-bin/waisgate?WAISdocID=21912510615+0+0+0&WAISaction=retrieve (accessed August 8, 2007).

California Streets and Highway Code. The Property and Business Improvement District Law (1994), Section 36613. http://www.leginfo.ca.gov/cgi-bin/displaycode?section=shc&group=36001-37000&file=36606-36616 (accessed August 8, 2007).

City of Los Angeles. 2002. *Citywide business improvement district.* Los Angeles City Clerk, Administrative Services Division, Special Assessment Section, Business Improvement Program.

Clark, C., Green, J., and Grenell, K. 2001. Local regimes: Does globalization challenge the "growth machine"? *Policy Studies Review* 18:49–61.

Houstoun, L. O. 2003. *Business improvement districts.* 2nd ed. Washington, DC: Urban Land Institute in cooperation with the International Downtown Association.

Lavery, K. 1995. Privatization by the back door: The rise of private government in the USA. *Public Money and Management* 15:49–53.

Mallett, W. J. 1994. Managing the post-industrial city: Business improvement districts in the United States. *Area* 26:276–287.

Meek, J. W., and Hubler, P. 2006. Business improvement districts in Southern California: Implications for local governance. *International Journal of Public Administration* 29:31–52.

Mitchell, J. 1999. *Business improvement districts and innovative service delivery.* Grant report. The PricewaterhouseCoopers Endowment for the Business of Government.

Mitchell, J. 2001. Business improvement districts and the management of innovation. *American Review of Public Administration* 31:201–217.

Pack, J. R. 1992. BIDs, DIDs, SIDs, SADs: Private governments in urban America. *Brookings Review* 10:18–22.

Wolf, J. F. 2006. Urban governance and business improvement districts: The Washington, DC BIDs. *International Journal of Public Administration* 29:53–67.

Chapter 10

Business Improvement Districts in New York City's Low- and High-Income Neighborhoods*

Jill Simone Gross

Contents

---

* An earlier version of this chapter was published as Gross (2005).

Introduction

Traditional economic development efforts in downtowns across the United States have often been based upon a "field of dreams" approach, which suggested, "if you build it they will come." At its most basic level, these physically oriented tactics were premised on a logic suggesting that if you constructed a physical environment that was visually appealing, generated a feeling of safety, and was accessible, then business and consumers would likely follow (Downs, 1979). The problem with this approach is that after you build it, it must be maintained—in good times and in bad.

Local economic development at its broadest refers to policy designed to create and retain jobs and wealth, with the overarching goal of reducing poverty and promoting economic stability. Stability requires more than simply rebuilding the physical infrastructure, it also requires the creation of an organizational structure that can maintain, promote, and develop an area over time. Business improvement districts (BIDs) have been touted as innovative tools in this regard, in terms of creating wealth and, perhaps more significantly, sustaining a neighborhood during economic downswings (Levy, 2001).

In New York State, BIDs are publicly authorized, legally sanctioned, privately administered institutions that provide services designed to enhance the local business environment (Mitchell, 1999, 2001a, 2001b; Hoyt, 2003; New York State Consolidated Laws, 1981). Though the structure of BIDs (e.g., geographic size, membership, services and functions) and the terms of their financing (e.g., revenue, assessment formulas, and expenditures) will vary by locality, they tend to share a common set of goals—to provide services, deemed by the BID partners to be beneficial to the business environment. The BID partners—the majority of whom are property owners, with representation from businesses, local government, and in certain instances residents—define the agenda of the organization and either directly or via contract provide services (i.e., supplemental sanitation, security, marketing, technical assistance, etc.) within the BID geographic area. Property owners and merchants finance these activities through an agreed-upon self-imposed tax that is collected by the city and returned to the BID to administer. Once the BID is formed, the tax becomes mandatory for all properties within the BID area, and frequently some, if not all, of the tax burden is passed on to merchants renting spaces in those properties.

Across New York State, voting on the BID board of directors is weighted in favor of property owners; thus, their interests tend to dominate. Its members define the BID's geographic boundaries. BID formation requires that a majority of businesses and property owners do not object to its formation. Within the BID area, commercial property owners, merchants, or both pay an additional incremental mandatory tax that is collected by the municipality, but returned to the BID to be spent on geographically specific and locally defined services. The BID therefore is a self-help business service organization (Hoyt, 2003).

The BID strategy, unlike traditional tax abatement strategies in which property owners or businesses are offered tax deductions as an incentive to locate in an area, is a tax augmentation strategy. Here property owners agree to pay additional taxes, which the city collects and returns to a BID management association for application to a wide array of geographically specific, locally defined programs and services, broadly designed to enhance the commercial space in both a physical and psychological sense.

To date the literature on BIDs has focused on the experiences of large BIDs operating in wealthier parts of the central city, such as the Times Square BID in New York City, the Downtown Development District in New Orleans, and the Center City District in Philadelphia (Barr, 1997; Houstoun, 1997; Mac Donald, 1996). Each of these BIDs controls a multi-million-dollar budget, has a large staff (40+), covers a large geographic area (30 blocks or more), and manages a large portfolio of activities (10 or more services provided in a locality). In addition, these large BIDs are often located in stable economic environments (large commercial/retail base, high property values, and ample flows of pedestrian foot traffic). While these large BIDs have certainly enhanced their local areas, the lessons they offer for local economic development professionals with weaker resource bases and situated in poorer neighborhoods are limited. Given that the majority of BIDs in the United States are smaller in size and scope, fulfill a narrower set of functions (Mitchell, 2001a, p. 119), and are often located in weak local economic environments (declining retail/commercial sectors, falling property values, and weak pedestrian traffic flows), it is important to consider the role of these smaller organizations in local development processes. The research question addressed here, therefore, is twofold: What are the differences in the form and function of large and small BIDs? And what are the implications of neighborhood context for development professionals contemplating the formation of a BID in a weak local economic environment? These questions are explored through an analysis of structure, function, and governance in 41 BIDs in New York City.*

My key findings suggest that large and small BIDs fulfill different development functions: the smallest BIDs focus on physical maintenance of an area, mid-sized BIDs tend to concentrate on marketing and promotional activities, and the largest BIDs engage in capital improvement activities, in addition to maintenance and promotion. BID size is associated with differences in revenue, number of businesses, size of businesses, size of the board of directors, number of services provided,

---

* There were 46 BIDs in operation in New York City, with more in the planning stages, in 2003, when I conducted the study reported in this chapter. (As of August 2007, the time of the writing of this chapter, there were 56 BIDs in the city.) I was able to gather data on 41 of New York's 46 BIDs. The other five included four BIDs that had just been formed and one that I was simply unable to get current data on. In addition, because the data was gathered from a variety of sources, and in certain cases there were gaps in the data submitted, it is incomplete. Missing data is indicated in the tables presented in this chapter.

and geographic size of the district. BID behavior tends to vary in relationship to its resource base, type of commercial property represented, the composition and balance of power among key stakeholders, and the wealth of the community in which they are located. For the development professional contemplating forming a BID, this research suggests that understanding these internal and external contextual factors can enable the creation of a BID that is more directly targeted to addressing the specific developmental needs of his or her community.

What follows is a description of the organizational structure and functions of three distinct types of BIDs found in New York City: large corporate, medium-sized Main Street, and small community types (Rogowsky and Gross, 1997, 1998, 2000). Building upon an understanding of these BID types, I then discuss the implications of neighborhood context for BID practice. I conclude by offering insights to development professionals considering the creation of a BID in their community. First, however, I present a brief overview of my research methods.

Research Methods

New York City has a long history with BIDs, dating back to the fiscal crisis of the mid-1970s. At the time, the city sought to ensure more effective management of its investment in physical infrastructure. As one city official commented: "Originally there were assessment districts in Buffalo, Syracuse and four in New York. They were set up to maintain the capital improvements that were carried out using federal and public works money. Part of the deal as regards the initial investment to rebuild was an agreement that these communities would also arrange to maintain the developed areas after that" (interview with Barbara Wolff, assistant commissioner, Department of Business Services, New York City, June 1996).

According to Jerry Mitchell (1999), by the late 1990s New York State had the second largest number of BIDs in the United States, next to California, and 46 of these were based in New York City. Fifty percent were situated in communities with poverty rates that surpassed the national central city residential average (Dalaker and Proctor, 2000).* Thus, not only did the New York City cases offer a wealth of data on BIDs in general, but further, the fact that a large proportion of them are operating in poorer socioeconomic environments provided valuable information pertinent to the more common BID experience nationally.

---

* According to Dalaker and Proctor, on average, some 16.4 percent of central city residents in the United States live below the poverty line. Thus, one half of New York's BIDs are in neighborhoods that by most standards would be considered to have large numbers of poor people. To substantiate the degrees of poverty, we also looked at income levels, median rentals, residential skill bases, and educational attainment. These factors are discussed in detail in the findings section.

The data on the BIDs in New York City came from several sources. The program and financial data on 41 of New York's 46 BIDs came from annual reports and newsletters produced by the BIDs, public audits conducted by the New York City comptroller,* and charity reports from the GuideStar database on charitable organizations.† The measures of BID structure included total revenue, total expenditure, program expenditure, administrative expenditure, staff size, number and types of services provided, geographic scope, and size and composition of the board of directors. With this information, I constructed a database and used it for bivariate descriptive data analyses of the structural and functional features of BIDs.‡

The second part of my research concerned the question of whether BIDs operating in resource-rich neighborhoods functioned differently than those in resource-poor neighborhoods? To be able to answer this question, it was necessary to move beyond the data on the BIDs themselves and begin to consider the environments within which BIDs operated. To compare the experiences of BIDs in wealthy and poor neighborhoods, 2000 Census data on income, poverty, ethnicity, employment, skill base, housing costs, and numbers of immigrants was gathered at the tract level for the 41 BID areas. This data was added to the BID database for analysis. Data on household income, number of individuals in poverty, median rent paid, and the number of individuals in the labor force was used as an indicator of wealth and poverty in the BID neighborhoods. In cases in which the BID area covered more than one census tract, the overall averages across all the census tracts covered by that BID were used. As my interest was in the question of whether BIDs operating in wealthy communities behaved differently from those operating in poor communities, I selected ten BIDs from the poorest and ten from the wealthiest quartiles of the New York City BID sample. The following describes the key features of these two groups:

■ Description of the sample drawn from the poorest quartile: ten cases (five Main Street and five community type BIDs). In these neighborhoods, an average of 52 percent were in the labor force and 33 percent of individuals lived in poverty. The mean annual household income was $23,800, mean rent paid monthly was $561.60, and mean proportion of foreign born was 42 percent.

---

* BIDs are required to submit financial statements to the New York City Comptroller's Audit Committee annually. BIDs with budgets greater than $500,000 are reviewed every two years; those with budgets under $500,000 are reviewed every three years. The comptroller's audit reports offer a wealth of information on finances and operating practices, and many include attitude surveys of property owners and businesses.

† GuideStar is a database that offers public access to financial and program information on nonprofits, based on forms submitted by the nonprofit to the IRS.

‡ Frequency distributions, cross-tabulations, and Chi square were used to analyze the categorical data. In addition to generating basic descriptive statistics on the ordinal and continuous data (i.e., mean, median, mode, and standard deviation), I conducted analyses of variance (ANOVA) and correlation analyses (Pearson and Spearman).

■ Description of the sample drawn from the wealthiest quartile: ten cases (five corporate, four Main Street, and one community type BIDs). In these neighborhoods, an average of 72 percent were in the labor force and 9 percent of individuals lived in poverty. The mean annual household income was $85,235, mean rent paid monthly was $1,513, and mean proportion of foreign born was 27 percent (U.S. Bureau of the Census, 2000).

More detailed case study data on the BID behavior and governance came from primary and secondary sources. The audits generated by the New York City Comptroller's Office between 1999 and 2003 proved to be particularly useful. These audits contained detailed information on operating practices, governance, and financial management of 25 of the city's BIDs (Hevesi, 1997, 2000a, 2000b, 2000c, 2000d, 2000e, 2001a, 2001b, 2001c, 2001d, 2001e, 2001f, 2001g, 2001h, 2001i, 2001j, 2001k, 2001l, 2001m; Thompson, 2002a, 2002b, 2002c, 2002d, 2003a, 2003b, 2003c).

Primary data sources included interviews and participant observation. I conducted 35 semistructured interviews with BID managers, BID board members, BID property owners, policymakers, administrators, and analysts in 1996. Site visits to each of the BIDs selected for case study and five additional interviews with policymakers were conducted between 2000 and 2002.

Structures and Functions of BIDS

Before discussing the various ways in which BIDs were affected by their environments, I begin with a brief overview of the BID model and its role in local community and economic development.

BIDs are self-taxing, self-help organizations. What makes BIDs especially interesting, as a tool of economic development, is that in many regards they fly against traditional economic dependency notions, which suggested that cities were beholden to the demands of business. For example, Peterson (1981) argued that the range of economic development strategies pursued by cities was limited by the mobility of labor and capital. As a result, municipalities were forced to offer large tax incentives to businesses to anchor them in the city. In contrast, the BID phenomenon suggests that under certain circumstances the private sector may be willing to pay more, not less, to continue doing business in an area (Kantor and Savitch, 1998).

BIDs can address the physical needs of an area through the provision of services such as additional sanitation collection, street lighting, capital improvements, and maintenance. In this regard, BIDs fit well with mainstream approaches to economic development, which tend to perceive local markets as the products of choices made by businesses and consumers (Wiewel et al., 1993, p. 81). As one of the municipal public administrators commented: "We are now evolving to the point of realizing that where we have the BID we have the vehicle to make the street what it can be, in response to different markets and different mixes of clientele" (interview with Barbara Wolff, assistant commissioner, Department of Business Services, New York City, June 1996).

Through the provision of various supplementary services (beyond those that the municipality offers), the BID aims to enhance physical conditions, with the goal of influencing the locational choices of businesses and the shopping choices of consumers.

BIDs can add a sense of unity to an area through the creation of uniform signage, capital improvements, and enhancement of public spaces through street planting, holiday lighting, and the maintenance of public seating areas. In this way, BIDs serve important psychological functions for shoppers: BIDs can also generate a feeling of safety through the provision of additional security (guards and cameras, for example) and enhanced street lighting. This generates the perception of a secure environment in which to shop and encourages increased consumer use.

Basically, BIDs are reflections of their members. The impetus for creation comes directly from local stakeholders such as property owners and businesses. In New York, once a BID is created, property owners have the power with regard to decision making and agenda setting on its board of directors.* The voting powers on the boards of directors are weighted in their favor. Thus, BIDs offer these property owners some degree of power over local development activities within the BID area. A BID program manager points out:

> You can go to any BID and find a group of leaders. There may be a dozen, two dozen; however many there are, they can be a really positive force in their neighborhood. And what they really do is manage their neighborhood. The BID gives them a way to manage their neighborhood. Just like a shopping mall, the BID gives these groups a structure. (Interview with Eddy Evy, New York BID program manager, Department of Business Services, August 1996.)

BIDs, therefore, offer services and local political power in exchange for the payment of additional taxes.

BIDs represent a promising community-based economic development tool, providing of course that local property owners are rooted in the community (in many poor communities, property is controlled by absentee landlords). Robert Halpern (1995, p. 125) describes community economic development as "one of the few

---

* New York State law states: "The board of directors of the association shall be composed of representatives of owners and tenants within the district, provided, however, that not less than a majority of its members shall represent owners and provided further that tenants of commercial space and dwelling units within the district shall also be represented on the board. The board shall include, in addition, three members, one member appointed by each of the following: the chief executive officer of the municipality, the chief financial officer of the municipality and the legislative body" (New York State Consolidated Laws, 1981).

[development strategies] that was not imposed on poor neighborhoods but grew out of their own efforts to define their needs, control their fate, and create viable local communities." BIDs are an organizational tool for the management of local development, in which the board members define the agenda. However, the degree to which they can be considered "community economic development entities" needs to be understood in part through the lens of these BID stakeholders. Although BIDs can offer some degree of local control and ownership, much depends on the composition of property owners. As a city program manager comments, "If they own property and operate a retail store, they are more likely to see the advantages of having a BID. But if they only own property, it is harder for them to see" (interview with Joyce Coward, director, Technical Assistance Programs, Department of Business Services, August 1996).

Though the BID offers owners control over their own fate, it is not always the case that the interests of owners are identical to those of either the local merchants or the local residents. Thus, in the minds of some, BIDs can lead to a perversion of the community development concept when owners are not of the community themselves. As one critic comments, BIDs "serve the narrow interests of some groups within the BID at the expense of all the rest" (Adler, 2000, p. 17). Thus, though BIDs do offer power, they do not offer equal power to all interests. Their function in a community, therefore, must in part be understood through an understanding of the stakeholders and their visions.

While BIDs can be parochial, focusing only on the expressed needs of property owners, they can also be responsive to the broader needs of the larger community. In some cases, for example, the BID may serve a less tangible social capital function for the local business community by creating trust among property owners, businesses, and residents. In this way, BIDs can serve as venues for the development of mutually agreed-upon local economic and social development agendas. BIDs offer a forum in which mutual interests can be identified and bridges can be built to local government. A policymaker comments: "The interaction of the business owners and the property owners in the management of this thing is very exciting. These people really work, they come up with new ideas" (interview with Joyce Coward, director, Technical Assistance Programs, Department of Business Services, August 1996). Thus, with effective leadership, BIDs can enhance the capacity of local private sector interests to achieve collective outcomes. This is particularly important for communities in transition:

> Take a BID like Flatbush Avenue in Brooklyn. That's an area that's really changed. I wasn't there, but people tell me that it was a very Jewish business area, and it really changed to an Indian and Caribbean business area. And the cohesion that was there was no longer there. The BID was able to pull these new ethnic groups, and the different kinds of businesses together. (Interview with Eddy Evy, New York BID program manager, Department of Business Services, August 1996.)

BIDs can fulfill a variety of developmental functions. BIDs can function as sustainers of existing development, they can take on a promotional role in which they focus on marketing efforts to consumers, or a developmental role to promote economic growth and lure new business to the area. As it will be illustrated below, some BIDs fulfill all three functions, but most are targeted to a narrower set of activities—shaped by both the organizational features of the BID itself and the environmental context of the neighborhood.

Business improvement districts therefore can help to minimize some of the risk factors associated with doing business in an area. They help to share the burden of physical upkeep and create the perception of security. They create a forum for local business to build common agendas and recognize mutual needs and interests. By creating a partnership among property owners, business, community, and local government, the BID in essence represents a tool through which to enhance the viability of an area as a place to do business. All BIDs aim to enhance business in an area by creating a stable environment in which business is conducted. Although the vision of what a BID can do is promising, the capacity of a BID to function as sustainer, promoter, or developer of an area must be understood within the context of the skills, energy, and vision its members bring to the table and the socioeconomic environment in which the BID is embedded.

In a previous study that I conducted with Edward T. Rogowsky, based on interviews with stakeholders from six BIDs in two neighborhoods, and its follow-ups, we suggested that three types of BIDs could be found in New York: corporate, Main Street, and community (Rogowsky and Gross, 1997, 1998, 2000). BID types differed from one another along structural and functional lines. BIDs with larger budgets and boards of directors tended to provide a wider range of services than smaller BIDs. In this research, we found that large and small BIDs also varied by the functions they performed. Smaller community type BIDs tended to engage primarily in maintenance functions. Main Street BIDs carried out maintenance functions and invested in promotional/marketing activities. Corporate BIDs were involved in capital development projects, in addition to both maintenance and promotion. What follows is a more detailed description of the features of these BID types, followed by a discussion of the statistical validity of the BID typology when applied to a larger New York City sample (n = 41). Tables 10.1 and 10.2 offer a more detailed picture of the structural and functional attributes of each BID type.

As Tables 10.1 and 10.2 illustrate, corporate BIDs were the largest on a variety of organizational or structural measures: they tended to cover larger swathes of land, offered an extensive array of services, and had budgets in excess of $1.5 million. There were 11 corporate BIDs in New York City in 2003. These tended to be the most visible of New York's BIDs—examples included the Times Square BID, the Grand Central Partnership, and the Alliance for Downtown New York.

These BIDs had large boards of directors (30 or more members) with a great deal of professional expertise (lawyers, property developers, financial experts, etc.). Indeed, the boards of many of these organizations were a virtual "who's who" of

Table 10.1 New York BID typology

Structural features	Corporate (N = 11)	Main Street (N = 10)	Community (N = 20)
Revenue range	Greater than $1,000,000	$300,000–$1,000,000	Less than $300,000
Median proportion of revenue spent on BID services	91%	83%	62%
Median proportion of revenue spent on BID administration	9%	17%	38%
Median no. on board of directors	37	24	15
Median geographic scope	31 blocks	10 blocks	14 blocks
Types of property in BID	Corporate office, commercial, retail, government	Retail, commercial, government	Retail
Distribution of property within BID	Large amounts of office and retail space	Moderate amounts of retail and commercial space	Small amounts of retail space
Features of property within BID	Multilevel high-rise, interior shopping arcades and street-level storefront spaces	Street-level storefront and two- to three-story commercial and shopping spaces	Primarily street-level storefronts
Dominant group of property owners in BID	Corporate and commercial	Retail	Retail

Source: GuideStar, 2004; Hevesi, 1997, 2000a, 2000b, 2000c, 2000d, 2000e, 2001a, 2001b, 2001c, 2001d, 2001e, 2001f, 2001g, 2001h, 2001i, 2001k, 2001l, 2001m; New York City Department of Business Services, 1995; Thompson, 2002a, 2002b, 2002c, 2002d, 2003a, 2003b, 2003c.

Table 10.2 Functional features of New York BIDs

	Corporate (N = 11)	Main Street (N = 10)	Community (N = 20)
Median no. of services provided	10	6	4
Featured service provided by BID type[a]	Capital improvements	Area promotion and marketing	Physical upkeep of area
Services provided by BIDs[b]	Security, sanitation, area promotion, holiday promotion, capital improvements, marketing, maintenance, information and social services	Security, sanitation, area promotion, holiday promotion, marketing, graffiti removal maintenance	Sanitation, holiday promotion, graffiti removal
Primary function	Area development and attraction of new businesses to the area	Area promotion and support for development of existing businesses	Area maintenance and retention of existing businesses

Source: GuideStar, 2004: Hevesi, 1997, 2000a, 2000b, 2000c, 2000d, 2000e, 2001a, 2001b, 2001c, 2001d, 2001e, 2001f, 2001g, 2001h, 2001i, 2001k, 2001l, 2001m; New York City Department of Business Services, 1995; Thompson, 2002a, 2002b, 2002c, 2002d, 2003a, 2003b, 2003c.

[a] Over 70% of BIDs in type provide these services.

[b] Over 50% of BIDs in type provide these services.

renowned business experts. For example, on the board of the Alliance for Downtown New York (the largest corporate BID in New York State by all measures) one could find representatives from Standard and Poor's, Goldman Sachs, J. P. Morgan and Chase, the Bank of New York, Cushman and Wakefield, and some 30 other property managers, architects, large retail business owners, and local government officials.

The boards of smaller BIDs were quite different, as one Main Street BID manager commented about her own board of directors: "Most of the property owners here are second generation [immigrants], with limited formal education" (interview with Janet Barkin, director, Jamaica Center Special Assessment District, June 1996). I would suggest that the existence of significant expertise on the boards of corporate BIDs might explain their comparatively low levels of expenditure on administration (15 percent of BID expenditures for this type) vis-à-vis the other BID types.

I found that the corporate BIDs of New York provided a very wide range of services, but one of the services they offered was unique (that is, within the New York sample): capital improvements. For example, the 34th Street Partnership had a capital project staff who oversaw the placement of new street lamps, plantings, and sidewalk enhancements all aimed at generating "a place that people want to be in and to linger…a welcoming destination" (34th Street Partnership, 1995, p. 5).

All of the corporate BIDs of New York provided capital improvement services; in contrast, only two community and four Main Street BIDs provided this type of service. This suggests an important functional distinction for the corporate BID type. Corporate BIDs directly shape commercial growth in ways that few Main Street or community BIDs do—by directly investing in the capital improvements such as widening the sidewalks to accommodate larger pedestrian traffic flows, investments in lighting to allow for 24-hour use, and landscaping to improve the perceived quality of life in an area. It is not surprising to find that corporate BIDs provided these services, given the significant investment required to carry out these large-scale projects. Corporate BIDs, with large revenue streams and boards of directors that commonly include development, legal, and marketing professionals, would appear to be the best suited to conduct these kinds of activities among the three BID types. Interestingly, the Main Street and community type BIDs that did carry out capital improvements were located in high-income neighborhoods, suggesting that even smaller BIDs have the capacity to conduct capital improvements in resource-rich environments.

Main Street BIDs, as Table 10.1 suggests, represented the middling group of BIDs according to all aspects of organizational structure. There were ten Main Street BIDs in the New York City sample. The mean revenue of New York's Main Street BIDs was $572,977. As indicated in Table 10.2, a large proportion of Main Street BIDs were engaged in marketing and promotion activities. This focus appeared to be a reflection of the domination by property owners (commercial/retail interests) on the boards of directors. As one Main Street BID manager commented: "In the BID, the profit motive overshadows any development of community. The property owners here are niche retailers. Their attachment is to the dollar, to profits, not the place. To understand the BID you need to understand the property owners and where they are coming from" (interview with Jill Kelly, director, Fulton Mall Improvement Association, July 1996).

Among the Main Street group of BIDs, 80 percent were involved in area-based promotional activities (as compared with only 50 percent of community BIDs) and 70 percent were involved in marketing activities (as compared with 35 percent of community BIDs), in addition to area maintenance activities. For example, the HUB-Third Avenue BID in the Bronx generated circulars advertising local shops and sponsored special promotions for major shopping days. The BID distributed these free of charge to local merchants and customers. The Lower Eastside BID had a website to advertise its local businesses, produced a shopping guide, and advertised the area in local newspapers and on the radio. The 125th Street BID in Harlem distributed maps and guides that identified some 600 businesses in and around the BID area, as well as identifying banking and other local services that shoppers might need.

The community BID was the smallest BID type by revenue size, board size, and scope of services. There were 20 community type BIDs in New York City. These BIDs, for the most part, focused on basic maintenance with some 85 percent providing sanitation services. As one development professional comments: "I think these [community type] BIDs have been a tremendous help in keeping the area stable and making people feel that this is an okay place to be. I don't think they have taken the next step of positively developing the area. It's more like preventing any deterioration, keeping it clean, keeping it nice" (interview with Helen Levine, Greater Jamaica Development Corporation, July 1996). These BIDs had small budgets; the mean revenue within this group was $176,732. The most common services provided by this group were sanitation and intermittent holiday promotion. For example, the 82nd Street BID in Queens spent the bulk of its revenue on its "sweep team," which provided sanitation services six hours a day, six days per week. The Pitkin Avenue BID in Brooklyn installed decorative lighting and banners in its district during holiday seasons. Many of these BID types also were involved in sporadic marketing efforts, when budgets allowed. Interestingly, in this group many BIDs provided services to quite large areas, despite their small budgets. In fact, the mean number of blocks for these BIDs was 14, though they range in size from 4 to 40 blocks. But these BIDs tended to provide a limited number of services (mean of 4).

It was important also to explore the threefold BID typology statistically to determine if it accurately characterized the New York City BIDs. Analysis of variance (ANOVA) tests were conducted on the three groups (corporate, Main Street, and community) of BIDs to determine whether we could generalize about the structures and function of BIDs in each category. Did most corporate BIDS have similar revenue streams? Did the majority of Main Street BIDs fulfill similar functions in their neighborhoods? Did all community BIDs spend large sums on administration? Or, did BIDs differ significantly from one another? ANOVA tests allowed us to consider how much variation there was between BIDs within each BID type, as well as between BID types. In Table 10.3 I report the results of each ANOVA test according to eight structural measures (size of the board of directors, total revenue, total expenditure, proportion spent on programs, proportion spent on administration, numbers of services provided, and size of geographic area served). In Table 10.4, I report on the five functional measures (business retention, area upkeep and maintenance, physical area development, social development, capital improvements). In each case, the null hypothesis, that no differences exist in the structural or functional attributes of BIDs within corporate, Main Street, and community types, was tested. If the null hypothesis were true, average scores on each measure would be the same across BID types, resulting in F values of no statistical significance.

As Tables 10.3 and 10.4 indicate, statistically significant differences existed for each of the structural and functional attributes of BIDs identified as corporate, Main Street, or community types (p < .05).

BIDs and Neighborhood Context

The final part of the analyses concerned the question of whether contextual differences found in low-income and high-income neighborhoods affected BID practice. Do BID types function differently when situated in resource-rich as compared to resource-poor neighborhoods? Do Main Street and community BIDs located in high-income areas operate differently than those in low-income areas? Because BIDs are geographically rooted, it was speculated that BID structures and functions would also be reflections of the socioeconomic conditions of the residential community in which they were embedded.

Using tract-level census data, the BID sample was divided up by income, median rent, labor force participation, and proportion of foreign born. The BIDs located in the top and bottom quartiles were then separated out for more detailed analyses. From the total group of 41 BIDs, a sample of 20 BIDs was selected: 10 BIDs from wealthy neighborhoods (the top quartile of the larger group) and 10 in poor neighborhoods (selected from the bottom quartile of the larger group).*

---

* The bottom-quartile BID sample included five Main Street BIDs (125th Street BID, HUB-Third Avenue, Washington Heights BID, Lower Eastside BID, and Jamaica Center) and five community BIDs (Pitkin Avenue BID, Graham Avenue BID, Brighton Beach BID, White Plains Road BID, and Grand Street BID). The top-quartile BID sample included five corporate BIDs (Alliance for Downtown, Times Square BID, East Mid-Manhattan, Lincoln Square BID, and Madison Avenue BID), four Main Street BIDs (Bryant Park, 14th Street-Union Square BID, Village Alliance BID, and NOHO NY BID), and one community BID (Columbus Avenue BID).

Table 10.3 Analyses of variance in the structural attributes of BIDs by type

Structural	Source	Sum of squares	df	Mean square	F	Significance
Size of the board of directors	Between groups	1226.737	2	613.368	11.704	.000
	Within groups	1519.732	29	52.405		
	Total	2746.469	31			
Revenue	Between groups	177249606398276	2	88624803199138.20	15.601	.000
	Within groups	215872026936437	38	5680842814116.770		
	Total	393121633334714	40			
Expenditure	Between groups	163625521580742	2	81812760790370.800	17.351	.000
	Within groups	169745360766104	38	4715148910169.560		
	Total	333370882346846	40			
Program expenditure	Between groups	.250	2	.125	3.472	.044
	Within groups	1.043	29	3.598		
	Total	1.293	31			
Administrative expenditure	Between groups	.250	2	.125	3.441	.046
	Within groups	1.052	29	3.626		
	Total	1.301	31			
Total no. of services provided	Between groups	180.130	2	90.065	32.194	.000
	Within groups	106.309	38	2.768		
	Total	286.439	40			
Geographic size of BID	Between groups	23224.122	2	11612.061	3.453	.042
	Within groups	127789.9	38	3262.893		
	Total	151014.0	40			

Source: BID annual reports; interviews; Office of the New York City Comptroller, 1997, 2000, 2001, 2002, 2003; GuideStar, 2004; Hevesi, 1997, 2000a, 2000b, 2000c, 2000d, 2000e, 2001a, 2001b, 2001c, 2001d, 2001e, 2001f, 2001g, 2001h, 2001i, 2001k, 2001l, 2001m; New York City Department of Business Services, 1995; Thompson, 2002a, 2002b, 2002c, 2002d, 2003a, 2003b, 2003c.

Table 10.4 Analyses of variance in BID functions by BID type

BID functions	Source	Sum of squares	df	Mean square	F	Significance
Area upkeep and maintenance	Between groups	26.883	2	13.442	20.988	.000
	Within groups	24.336	38	.640		
	Total	51.220	40			
Area marketing and promotion	Between groups	15.602	2	7.801	7.418	.002
	Within groups	39.959	38	1.052		
	Total	55.561	40			
Area development via capital improvement	Between groups	35.025	2	17.513	26.750	.000
	Within groups	24.877	38	.655		
	Total	59.902	40			

Source: GuideStar, 2004; Hevesi, 1997, 2000a, 2000b, 2000c, 2000d, 2000e, 2001a, 2001b, 2001c, 2001d, 2001e, 2001f, 2001g, 2001h, 2001i, 2001k, 2001l, 2001m; New York City Department of Business Services, 1995; Thompson, 2002a, 2002b, 2002c, 2002d, 2003a, 2003b, 2003c.

Table 10.5   Socioeconomic profile of low- and high-income neighborhoods in BID samples

	New York City as a whole	Low-income group (N = 10)	High-income group (N = 10)
Percentage active in the labor force	58%	52%	72%
Percentage living below poverty level	21%	33%	9%
Median household income	$38,295	$23,800	$85,235
Median household rent	$705	$561	$1,513
Proportion of population who spend 35% or more of their income on rent	34%	40%	31%
Percentage foreign born	35%	38%	24%
Percentage foreign born who entered within the last 10 years	15%	20%	10%
Housing tenure:			
Percentage owners	30%	7%	26%
Percentage renters	70%	93%	74%

Source: U.S. Bureau of the Census, 2000.

Table 10.5 presents a socioeconomic profile of the low-income and high-income BID areas relative to the city as a whole.

Data on New York City as a whole was included here to put this socioeconomic data into the larger context of this global city. When we look at these groups (low and high income) and compare them with the New York City averages, we see that for each of the measures explored, the low-income group in general falls only slightly below the city averages for income measures, and slightly above those averages for poverty, foreign born, etc. The high-income group is significantly different from the citywide averages on all measures. This reveals the increasing gap between the wealthy and poor in New York City. More importantly for my research, it adds weight to the importance of understanding the structure and functions of BIDs operating in resource-poor neighborhoods, because this is in fact closer to the experience for most of New York City's BIDs.

As that table shows, the high- and low-income neighborhoods, in which BIDs were situated, starkly differed from one another. For example, much larger proportions of labor force were employed in the wealthy areas than in the poor neighborhoods, and the household incomes of those living in the high-income neighborhoods were almost four times the level of those found in low-income neighborhoods. I expected that these neighborhood differences would directly affect BID capacity.

For example, local populations would have lower purchasing power and less disposable revenue in the low-income areas than in the high-income areas. Table 10.5 illustrates the differences in income, proportions of income spent on rent, and percentages living below the poverty level. I anticipated that BIDs embedded in these different economic environments would likely have differing revenue streams based in part on the differences in their residential customer bases. BID members pay a locally agreed-upon assessment to maintain the BID. If they charge themselves too much, relative to needed operating costs, the businesses and the BID itself are unlikely to survive. Thus, the socioeconomic factors might affect the BID's capacity to provide economic stability or growth.

The data on foreign born offered an indicator of neighborhood diversity, which might affect a BID's capacity to achieve collective outcomes. The data on the percentage of foreign born within the last ten years offered a proxy measure of neighborhood change. As BIDs are tools for collective action among local businesses and property owners, I expected that BIDs situated in homogenous, stable neighborhoods would function differently than those in diverse, transitional ones. In transitional immigrant communities, BIDs might need to spend more time on building trust between members, on collaboration and agenda setting.

Lastly, as BID membership is weighted in favor of property owners, I expected that communities with larger percentages of renters and lower percentages of owners would have very different membership bases than those at the opposite end of the spectrum. In the low-income group, BID members would not necessarily live in the community, and thus would have less attachment to the broader needs of the community in which the BID was embedded. Self-interest rather than collaboration would motivate BIDs in these neighborhoods, making them less likely to engage in social development activities and more likely to focus on pure economic development.

In the remaining part of this section I discuss the contrasting experiences of community and Main Street BIDs in the low- and high-income neighborhood groups, and the lessons they offer to development professionals contemplating the formation of a BID. This focus is appropriate for two reasons. As mentioned previously, much has already been written about New York's corporate BIDs. The corporate BIDs of New York are only located in high-income communities, thus preventing any meaningful contextual neighborhood comparisons.

Table 10.6 presents an overview of the key differences found in behavior and governance of community and Main Street BIDs in high-income neighborhoods, as compared with those in low-income neighborhoods. Analysis of the data gathered from interviews, audits, and participant observation suggested that three contextual elements were at the center of these differences: local market conditions (property values and consumer base), resource availability within the BID (finance, expertise, and time), and differences in stakeholders (business owners, property owners, and residents). Each of these factors and their implications for BID practice will be discussed below.

Table 10.6 Behavioral differences in Main Street and Community BIDs by neighborhood context

BIDs in low-income neighborhoods	BIDs in high-income neighborhoods
Partner with outside organizations	Rely on internal membership for resources to compensate for low resource base
Diverse set of stakeholders	Uniform set of stakeholders
Low levels of participation by board members	High levels of participation by board members
Redistributive orientation	Distributive orientation
High level of internal conflict among board members over BID agenda	Low level of internal conflict among board members over BID agenda
Lacking in board oversight	Effective board oversight
High propensity for financial management problems	Low propensity for financial management problems

Resource Availability and Market Conditions

Comparisons between BIDs in high- and low-income areas suggested that resources and market conditions have implications for the activities BIDs focus on, the partners they choose to work alongside, and more broadly the distributive orientation of the BID overall. Most importantly, low-income communities tended to have lower property values than wealthy communities. Throughout New York State, BID assessment revenues are based on a formula pegged to the assessed value of real property. As a result, as Table 10.7 illustrates, BIDs in poor communities, for the most part, received less revenue per property for their property tax assessment and covered a smaller geographic area than those in high-income neighborhoods.* Thus, BIDs in low-income neighborhoods had less fiscal and human capital to apply to service provision than those in high-income neighborhoods.

As Table 10.7 indicates, BIDs in low-income neighborhoods had fewer board members, which left them with less human capital to draw upon. One outcome of this, according to audits, was that BIDs in poor communities were more frequently faulted for poor board management of BID activities, and inadequate participation of the board overall. Audits also revealed that the BIDs most often sighted for financial management problems were those in low-income neighborhoods. In contrast, the audits of the BIDs in high-income neighborhoods found

---

* Assessment formulas vary by area. Although all formulas are based on property values, variation comes in terms of whether formulas are based on total square footage of land, total square footage of commercial buildings, or frontal footage on the commercial strip. Formulas are agreed upon by property owners and stated in the district plans. City government set a percentage cap. Any change to the assessment level requires approval by all parties.

Table 10.7 Comparisons of structural features within BID types by high- and low-income groups

	High-income group	Whole BID group	Low-income group
Median assessment revenue			
Main Street	$744,370	$572,977	$479,880
Community	$218,760	$176,732	$132,507
Median no. on the board of directors			
Main Street	22	24	25
Community	18	15	14
Median geographic scope			
Main Street	17	10	5
Community	16	14	9

Source: GuideStar, 2004; Hevesi, 1997, 2000a, 2000b, 2000c, 2000d, 2000e, 2001a, 2001b, 2001c, 2001d, 2001e, 2001f, 2001g, 2001h, 2001i, 2001k, 2001l, 2001m; New York City Department of Business Services, 1995; Thompson, 2002a, 2002b, 2002c, 2002d, 2003a, 2003b, 2003c.

high levels of participation by board members, adequate management and oversight of the BID, and few fiscal management problems.

BIDs were also affected by local market conditions. In low-income communities, residents were the primary consumers of goods provided by the local merchants. With lower income levels, the population had less purchasing power—again generating less revenue for the area as a whole. Not only did area businesses generate less revenue via sales, but they also had far less foot traffic than central shopping districts did. In contrast, BIDs situated in high-income areas not only relied on more revenue due to the higher assessment reaped by higher base property values, but also tended to have multiple consumer bases—residential, worker, and tourist. As David Midler, a market researcher, comments about the market conditions in the 34th Street BID (a corporate BID) area, "Any one of these markets [area residents, office workers, or tourists] is enormous; by itself it would make retailers in other locations quite content." Looking at the office workers, for example, Midler found that the number was equal to the total population of New Haven, Connecticut (34th Street Partnership, 1995, p. 2).

This may explain why, as Table 10.8 illustrates, a larger proportion of BIDs in poor communities allocated resources to area promotion than those in high-income neighborhoods.

A larger proportion of the Main Street BIDs in low-income communities were engaged in area-based promotional activities (100 percent as compared with 75 percent in the high-income Main Street group). This suggests that the high-income areas had a larger consumer base, and thus were able to redirect their focus to other areas of need. For example, 75 percent of the high-income-area BIDs

Table 10.8   Proportion engaged in area promotion

	High-income group	*Low-income group*
Main Street	75%	100%
Community	33%	60%

Source: GuideStar, 2004; Hevesi, 1997, 2000a, 2000b, 2000c, 2000d, 2000e, 2001a, 2001b, 2001c, 2001d, 2001e, 2001f, 2001g, 2001h, 2001i, 2001k, 2001l, 2001m; New York City Department of Business Services, 1995; Thompson, 2002a, 2002b, 2002c, 2002d, 2003a, 2003b, 2003c.

carried out some capital improvement activities (as compared with only 25 percent of the low-income Main Street group).

BIDs in low-income neighborhoods were caught in the difficult situation of having significant problems to cope with but fewer resources to apply. This led some BIDs to provide a very limited range of services that directly addressed only the most visible aspects of decay (i.e., sanitation and sidewalk maintenance). In the area of graffiti removal, a problem often associated with blighted neighborhoods, 100 percent of the community BIDs studied in the low-income neighborhood sample provided this, whereas the community BIDs in the high-income neighborhood did not. This simply suggests that a development professional contemplating the formation of a BID in a low-income community must be prepared to allocate resources to problems specific to the locality, diverting resources from other areas. For resource-poor BIDs this is particularly important; audits suggested that these BIDs were prone to fiscal problems, such as debt, late payments to contracted service providers, and credit problems. Several of the resource-poor BIDs were operating in the red with expenditures that exceeded revenues at the time of my research.

Interestingly, in the interviews I found that this lack of resources in the low-income groups often led these BIDs to engage in outreach to other local partners. As one BID program manager stated:

> So the $3,000,000 BID can say we are concerned about the graffiti, the garbage, or security and go out and buy it, get it done. The BID with $200,000 can't afford to do that much, so they do what they can. But there is still a big gap. That's why the smaller BID needs to reach out to other partners. That's why if it is security, the smaller BID will call the police precinct, while the larger might go out and hire a security force. (Interview with Joyce Coward, director, Technical Assistance Programs, Department of Business Services, August 1996.)

Thus, the smaller BIDs located in low-income neighborhoods may, by necessity, adopt different behaviors to compensate for revenue shortfalls.

Interviews suggested that the low-income group may also have adopted a more community-oriented approach to local area development. As one Main Street BID manager in Jamaica Queens (a low-income immigrant neighborhood) commented,

> In terms of marketing, we work with the other community organizations, the community board, the college, the library, etc. We try to be as visionary as possible, because if you're standing by yourself you're isolated. We are about community, and if you present that, you are going to be successful. We are not like the larger BIDs, like Times Square. We can't take the view that we are omnipotent. (Interview with Janet Barkin, director, Jamaica Center Special Assessment District, June 1996.)

A review of BID activities also indicated that those in poor communities often promoted progressive development activities—the kind of activities that were geared toward the redistribution of economic benefits and sharing the risks of local investment (Reese and Rosenfeld, 2002). For example, the Lower Eastside BID is a Main Street BID, located in an immigrant community in which median household income is $26,000. Audits revealed that this BID was heavily involved in traditional community development activities, such as advocacy, technical assistance, and training for local merchants. Interestingly, it was also found that despite limited resources, some 20 percent of the community BIDs provided social services, while the community BIDs in the wealthy neighborhood did not.

Differences in BID Stakeholders

Comparisons between high- and low-income areas revealed that often there were quite different sets of stakeholders, with implications for the development orientation of the BID (i.e., distributive versus redistributive), but perhaps more significantly these differences appeared to have impacts on internal governance processes (i.e., level of conflict, board management, and board participation).

Interviews suggested that in areas that had experienced decline, commercial property owners tended "to divide up and parcel out" (interview with Jill Kelly, director, Fulton Mall Improvement Association, July 1996) their land for rent, by virtue of the difficulties they found in luring larger merchants to the area. Higher risks associated with doing business in these areas meant that attracting merchants to larger spaces could be a tricky process. Property owners often subdivided their properties into smaller parcels in an effort to garner higher rental rates to compensate for turnover. The result for the BID in such an area was that a highly diverse collection of small businesses tended to dominate. In contrast, in high-income neighborhoods I found stable or growing property values and a population base with higher purchasing power. For local businesses in these neighborhoods, there was often greater competition for space. Here owners tended to rent larger spaces, as the local market would support them. Thus, while the low-income area tended to be dominated by small business, large retail businesses often characterized the high-income area, with smaller businesses being edged out in the competition for space. As one BID manager comments,

> The "mom and pop" shops are concerned with being competitive. They are concerned with the competition brought about by large retail outlets, and they are concerned with escalating rents. In wealthier areas they are not at all concerned about large retail. In fact, if anything, they would like to get more of them. (Interview with Leon Fonfa, senior BID manager, Department of Business Services, August 1996.)

These differences have implications for governance. Small retail business and small lot property holders commonly dominated the BIDs operating in low-income neighborhoods. Not to mention the fact that there were also significant numbers of new immigrant businesses and absentee landlords. Having property owners who were not themselves small business owners, large numbers of very small immigrant businesses, and small numbers of long-standing mom-and-pop shops inevitably made consensus formation and agenda setting that much more difficult, by virtue of the differences in vision. The wealthy neighborhoods had a smaller number of large-lot property holders, many who also operated businesses on their land—resulting in fewer but larger retailers. Though other interests were prominent on the boards of the high-income-area BIDs (i.e., corporate and office users), interviews suggested that this group tended to share common development visions. BIDs in low-income areas were characterized by a highly diverse membership. These BIDs often included many small businesses, whose primary agendas revolved around basic survival, and due to the divergent backgrounds of BID stakeholders (e.g., new immigrant versus long standing), finding common ground and trust among stakeholders was challenging. Thus, the BIDs in low-income neighborhoods often needed to cultivate a wider range of "group process" skills, such as community organizing and group facilitation to compensate for a lack of social capital, than was necessary for the BID located in a wealthy area.

Conclusions: Instrumental Lessons for Economic Development Professionals

Small and large BIDs clearly differed from one another in form and function, and the characteristics of all BIDs were embedded in their neighborhoods. BIDs in low-income communities were faced with a wider range of needs, a wider range of stakeholders, and limited resources (revenue and expertise) to respond. This meant that BIDs in these communities often sought creative solutions to problems through the formation of linkages with local partners. Conversely, BIDs in high-income neighborhoods faced fewer socioeconomic problems, had fewer stakeholders, and greater resources that enabled increased investment in the physical infrastructure of the area.

BIDs can be important development tools in poor and wealthy areas, but development professionals must conduct careful analyses of both the people and the places. What are the lessons for development professionals? Here are a few:

- Know your stakeholders.
- Ensure adequate representation of those stakeholders on the board of directors.
- Identify and prioritize needs according to local context.
- Target resources appropriately. Thus, in the case of low-income communities, advocacy and social capital building may be essential tools for BID success.

Low-income community and Main Street BIDs need to recognize the limitations posed by resource constraints. Audits suggested that small BIDs in low-income communities frequently suffered from financial mismanagement problems and lack of oversight of BID activities. I would suggest that in these neighborhoods BIDs must recognize their resource constraints and perhaps even consider scaling back or prioritizing activities to areas of greatest need. My interviews with key informants and my analysis of city audits suggested that BIDs in low-income neighborhoods were often simply trying to do too much with too little. As a result, they often found themselves in debt, making late payments, or in breach of contract with service providing partners. A BID must recognize the diversity of interests and needs among its property owners (large, small, old, new, immigrant, mom and pop, large retail chains, corporate, etc.). Recognizing these differences is likely to enhance the capacity of the BID to accomplish its goals. So, the lessons for the small BID in a low-income community are perhaps straightforward: recognize resource constraints (fiscal, human, and social capital), reach out to local partners, and target resources to meet the needs of all stakeholders.

References

34th Street Partnership. 1995. *34th Street partnership newsletter for retailers.* New York: 34th Street Partnership.

Adler, M. 2000. Why BIDs are bad business. *New York Times,* February 13, section 14, p. 17.

Barr, H. 1997. More like Disneyland: State action, 42 U.S.C. 1 1983, and business improvement districts. *Columbia Human Rights Law Review* 28:393–412.

Dalaker, J., and Proctor, B. D. 2000. *Poverty in the United States, 1999.* Washington, DC: Government Printing Office.

Downs, A. 1979. Key developments between urban development and neighborhood change. *Journal of the American Planning Association* 45:462–572.

Greater Jamaica Development Corporation. Undated. *Jamaica center: Yesterday, today, tomorrow.* Jamaica, NY: Greater Jamaica Development Corporation.

Gross, J. S. 2005. Business improvement districts in New York City's low-income and high-income neighborhoods. *Economic Development Quarterly* 19:174–189.

GuideStar. 2004. The national database of nonprofit organizations. Williamsburg, VA: Philanthropic Research. http://www.guidestar.org (accessed June 23, 2004).

Halpern, R. 1995. *Rebuilding the inner city: A history of neighborhood initiatives to address poverty in the United States.* New York: Columbia University Press.

Hevesi, A. G. 1997. *Audit report on the internal controls and operating practices of the Grand Central Partnership BID.* Audit MH96-055A. New York: Bureau of Management, Office of the Comptroller.

Hevesi, A. G. 2000a. *Audit report on the internal controls and operating practices of the Washington Heights BID Management Association, Inc.* Audit ME00-134A. New York: Bureau of Management, Office of the Comptroller.

Hevesi, A. G. 2000b. *Audit report on the financial and operating practices of the Steinway Street BID.* Audit MG00-060A. New York: Bureau of Management, Office of the Comptroller.

Hevesi, A. G. 2000c. *Audit report on the financial and operating practices of the Fifth Avenue BID.* Audit MG00-073A0. New York: Bureau of Management, Office of the Comptroller.

Hevesi, A. G. 2000d. *Audit report on the financial and operating practices of the Sunset Park Fifth Avenue BID.* Audit MG00-159A. New York: Bureau of Management, Office of the Comptroller.

Hevesi, A. G. 2000e. *Audit report on the financial and operating practices of the Mosholu-Jerome-East Gun Hill Road BID.* Audit MJ00-083A. New York: Bureau of Management, Office of the Comptroller.

Hevesi, A. G. 2001a. *Audit report on the financial and operating practices of the Bryant Park Management Corp. BID.* Audit MJ01-142A. New York: Bureau of Management, Office of the Comptroller.

Hevesi, A. G. 2001b. *Audit report on the financial and operating practices of the Brighton Beach BID, Inc.* Audit ME01-151A. New York: Bureau of Management, Office of the Comptroller.

Hevesi, A. G. 2001c. *Audit report on the financial and operating practices of the East Brooklyn Industrial Park BID.* Audit MD00-201A. New York: Bureau of Management, Office of the Comptroller.

Hevesi, A. G. 2001d. *Audit report on the internal controls and operating practices of the Flatbush Avenue BID, Inc.* Audit MH01-116A. New York: Bureau of Management, Office of the Comptroller.

Hevesi, A. G. 2001e. *Audit report on the financial and operating practices of the 47th Street BID, Inc.* Audit ME00-199A. New York: Bureau of Management, Office of the Comptroller.

Hevesi, A. G. 2001f. *Audit report on the financial and operating practices of the HUB-Third Avenue BID.* Audit ME01-078A. New York: Bureau of Management, Office of the Comptroller.

Hevesi, A. G. 2001g. *Audit report on the financial and operating practices of the Kings Highway BID*. Audit MG01-080A. New York: Bureau of Management, Office of the Comptroller.

Hevesi, A. G. 2001h. *Audit report on the financial and operating practices of the Lincoln Square BID*. Audit MD00-198A. New York: Bureau of Management, Office of the Comptroller.

Hevesi, A. G. 2001i. *Audit report on the financial and operating practices of the Myrtle Avenue BID*. Audit FL01-082A. New York: Bureau of Management, Office of the Comptroller.

Hevesi, A. G. 2001j. *Audit report on the financial and operating practices of the Madison Avenue District Management Association*. Audit FL01-083A. New York: Bureau of Management, Office of the Comptroller.

Hevesi, A. G. 2001k. *Audit report on the financial and operating practices of the NOHO BID*. Audit FM01-081A. New York: Bureau of Management, Office of the Comptroller.

Hevesi, A. G. 2001l. *Audit report on the financial and operating practices of the Village Alliance BID*. Audit MG00-0189A. New York: Bureau of Management, Office of the Comptroller.

Hevesi, A. G. 2001m. *Audit report on the financial and operating practices of the White Plains Road BID, Inc.* Audit MG01-123A. New York: Bureau of Management, Office of the Comptroller.

Houstoun, L., Jr. 1997. *BIDs: Business improvement districts*. Washington, DC: Urban Land Institute.

Hoyt, L. M. 2003. *The business improvement district: An internationally diffused approach to revitalization*. http://www.UrbanRevitalization.net (accessed July 23, 2003).

Kantor, P., and Savitch, H. 1998. Can politicians bargain with business? A theoretical and comparative perspective on urban development. In *The politics of urban America*, ed. D. Judd and P. Kantor, 228–306. Needham Heights, MA: Allyn and Bacon.

Levy, P. 2001. Paying for the public life. *Economic Development Quarterly* 15:124–131.

Mac Donald, H. 1996. *Why business improvement districts work*. Civic Bulletin 4. New York: Manhattan Institute for Policy Research. http://www.manhattan-institute.org/html/cb_4.htm (accessed 1996).

Mitchell, J. 1999. *Business improvement districts and innovative service delivery*. Grant report. Arlington, VA: The Pricewaterhouse Coopers Endowment for the Business of Government. http:/endowment.pwcglobal.com.

Mitchell, J. 2001a. Business improvement districts and the "new" revitalization of downtown. *Economic Development Quarterly* 15:115–123.

Mitchell, J. 2001b. Business improvement districts and the management of innovation. *American Review of Public Administration* 31:201–217.

New York City Department of Business Services. 1995. *New York City business improvement districts*. New York: Department of Business Services.

New York State Consolidated Laws. 1981. General Municipal, Article 19-A, Business Improvement Districts, Section S 980-M, Section B. Albany, NY: Senate.

Peterson, P. 1981. *City limit*. Chicago: University of Chicago Press.

Reese, L. A., and Rosenfeld, R. A. 2002. *The civic culture of local economic development*. Thousand Oaks, CA: Sage.

Rogowsky, E. T., and Gross, J. S. 1997. To BID or not to BID: Economic development in New York City. *Metropolitics* 1:7–8.

Rogowsky, E. T., and Gross, J. S. 1998. *Managing development in New York City: The case of business improvement districts.* Working Paper 24. New Orleans: National Center for the Revitalization of Central Cities, University of New Orleans, College of Urban and Public Affairs.

Rogowsky, E. T., and Gross, J. S. 2000. Business improvement districts (BIDs) and economic development in New York City. In *Managing capital resources for central city revitalization,* ed. F. Wagner, T. Joder, and A. Mumphrey, Jr., 81–87. New York: Garland Publishing.

Thompson, Jr., W. C. 2002a. *Audit on the financial and operating practices of the Columbus/Amsterdam BID.* Audit MD02-058A. New York: New York City Comptroller's Audit Library.

Thompson, Jr., W. C. 2002b. *Follow-up audit report of the financial and operating practices of the East Brooklyn Industrial Park BID.* Audit MD02-149F. New York: New York City Comptroller's Audit Library.

Thompson, Jr., W. C. 2002c. *Audit report on the financial and operating practices of the Fashion Center BID.* Audit MG01-196A. New York: New York City Comptroller's Audit Library.

Thompson, Jr., W. C. 2002d. *Audit of the internal controls and operating practices of the Lower Eastside BID.* Audit MH02-113A. New York: New York City Comptroller's Audit Library.

Thompson, Jr., W. C. 2003a. *Audit report on the financial and operating practices of the 125th Street BID.* Audit MD03-057A. New York: New York City Comptroller's Audit Library.

Thompson, Jr., W. C. 2003b. *Audit report on the financial and operating practices of the Fulton Mall Special Assessment District.* Audit MG03-062A. New York: New York City Comptroller's Audit Library.

Thompson, Jr., W. C. 2003c. *Audit report on the financial and operating practices of the Times Square BID.* Audit MG03-099A. New York: New York City Comptroller's Audit Library.

U.S. Bureau of the Census. 2000. *Census of population and housing.* Washington, DC: U.S. Bureau of the Census.

Wiewel, W., Teitz, M., and Giloth, R. 1993. The economic development of neighborhoods and localities. In *Theories of local economic development: Perspective across the disciplines,* ed. R. Bingham and R. Mier, 80–99. Newbury Park, CA: Sage.

Chapter 11

Business Improvement Districts and Small Business Advocacy: The Case of San Diego[*]

Robert J. Stokes

Contents

---

[*] This chapter originally appeared as Stokes (2007).

Introduction

The viability of commercial districts has historically been understood in terms of their economic and symbolic importance to the city (Zukin, 1995). However, the virtual disappearance of the retail sector in many urban communities and the concomitant residential decline of these communities have led to the notion that these two processes are linked (Skogan, 1990). One analyst has pointed to the importance of neighborhood commercial districts in enhancing amenities and providing low- to mid-skill-level employment and entrepreneurial opportunities for local residents (Porter, 1997). Another links the provision of an "inward looking" source of economic development, where local dollars circulate among a community's retail trade (Gottlieb, 1997).

Business improvement districts (BIDs) offer an innovation to the problem of urban commercial decline (Briffault, 1999; Levy, 2001a, 2001b; Mitchell, 2001a, 2001b; Pack, 1992). They rely on the legitimacy and coercive power of the political system to mandate the funding of collective action, while offering a range of privately managed services that focus on place promotion as the primary tool for urban revitalization. BIDs represent a continuation of a trend toward the blending of public and private partnerships to affect positive economic outcomes (Mitchell, 2001b; Squires, 1989). BIDs, however, represent a new wrinkle in the tradition of the public–private partnership. Traditionally, the public sector recognizes that private development plays a vital role in the continuation and quality of state functions. This recognition has historically led to the provision of public subsidies related to land acquisition and clearance, collective services, and employment training programs. BIDs, however, afford the creation of public benefits through privately funded services and planning activities (Levy, 2001a, 2001b; Mitchell, 2001b; Pack, 1992).

Although recent scholarship has improved our understanding of the use and effectiveness of BIDs nationally and internationally (Hoyt, 2005; Mallett, 1993; Mitchell, 2001a; Schaller and Modan, 2005; Caruso and Weber, 2006), research has yet to examine the use of BIDs as a citywide program for economic development and small business enhancement. A lion's share of the research and theory about BIDs applied only to larger BIDs located in central business districts (Levy, 2001a, 2001b; Mitchell, 2001a). Indeed, many cities have come to utilize BIDs as a management and funding tool for their largest commercial agglomerations. In many cases, this means that BID use is limited to central business districts or larger entertainment districts. This approach is sensible, as these districts are usually fiscally self-sustaining due to relatively healthy land-based fee assessments. Many cities tend to promote policies that require BIDs to be entirely self-financed, and some recent research has indicated that cities with multiple BIDs may see less capitalized districts as less worthy of BID designations (Gross, 2005; Stokes, 2006; also see Gross's chapter in this volume). The fact that less capitalized districts are typically located in poorer communities that need substantial help in developing a sustainable retail and service environment renders this policy focus unfortunate.

The growing popularity of the BID concept lends some credence to the notion that they are effective agents of small business organization, promotion, and place management—at least to the many retail districts that have originated and sustained the concept over the past decade (Mitchell, 2001a). This work does not offer an individualized evaluation of BID effectiveness but rather an examination of the city of San Diego's novel policy of using BIDs as an integrative tool for neighborhood commercial development. Thus, this work seeks to understand how the city of San Diego has organized its BID program as an agent of citywide economic development for the purposes of a larger small business development strategy. The methods used in this research included an examination of official policy and budget documents, interviews with BID leaders, and city economic development planning officials. Through the use of a case study design, this work seeks to answer several questions:

- How did San Diego come to develop a citywide program for the use of BIDs in light of the issue of district self-sustainability?
- How have BIDs become situated among the city's economic development policy actors?
- How are BIDs in San Diego funded, and what programming do they pursue?
- Does the programmatic or governance structure that defines BIDs make them more or less effective than traditional publicly administered, small business enhancement strategies?
- How should other cities use a citywide BID program to assist in their own community revitalization goals?

Economic Development Planning in San Diego

San Diego has a long history of BID usage, with its first BID chartered in 1970. Also, with 18 BIDs, its program is comparatively large. Although other cities have also used BIDs extensively—most notably New York City, Milwaukee, Chicago, Philadelphia, and Los Angeles—San Diego's program is unique. Described at length below, San Diego's program utilizes a mix of property assessments, merchant fees, public sources of support (city grants), and the entrepreneurial activities of the BIDs themselves to produce revenues and services. Each BID is managed by a nonprofit management corporation and has significant leeway in determining its specific approach to business and community development. The program also benefits from a sizable and growing intermediary nonprofit organization, the BID Council (BIDC), to assist in the formation and administration of program goals. Whereas BIDs themselves are an attempt to collectivize services at a more geographically focused level (the commercial district), the BIDC serves to collectivize small business interests at the city level. Although the BIDC plays a large role in the direction of BID priorities in San Diego, the program itself is directed by the

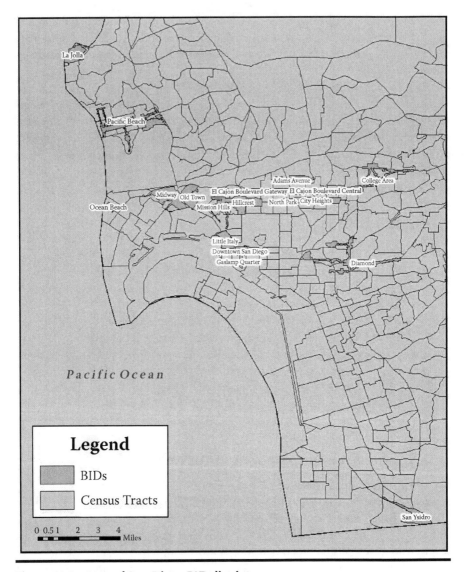

Figure 11.1 Map of San Diego BID districts.

city's Office of Small Business (OSB), and thus gets policy direction and political legitimacy from being a publicly administered program (Morris, 1997).

Recent scholarship on the politics of redevelopment in San Diego applies an urban entrepreneurial framework (Chapin, 2002). Entrepreneurial state-centered development in San Diego takes on many contours and is pursued by myriad federal, state, regional, local, and sublocal governments, authorities, agencies, nonprofit development corporations, and private developers. San Diego's city government possesses three main organizing units for the pursuit of economic development: the

Economic Development Corporation (EDC), the Redevelopment Agency (RA), and the OSB. Operating out of the OSB since 1982 is the city's Small Business Advisory Board. This 11-member board, appointed by the mayor and confirmed by city council, advises the mayor and council on small business enhancement strategies. Typically, this board deals with any law, policy, or procedure that affects the management, operation, or financial stability of small business in the city (San Diego Economic Development Department, 2006).

San Diego contains more than 60,000 registered businesses with fewer than 12 employees, which account for approximately 92 percent of all businesses in the city (San Diego Office of Small Business, 2004). These establishments have accounted for about half of San Diego's job growth since 1991 (San Diego Office of Small Business, 2004). Of the city's workforce, 48 percent work for a concern that employs less than 12 employees. Many of the city's small businesses are located within neighborhood commercial districts; thus, a major focus of the city's community development policy agenda is filtered through these neighborhood commercial districts. Symbolically, neighborhood commercial districts in San Diego are seen as a given neighborhood's "Main Street" (M. Didben-Brown, personal communication, June 10, 2004). The justification for this view is not based on the promotion of economic interests over residential ones but by the disproportionate amount of public, or "social," space that these areas contain.

The OSB, currently the only municipal office of its kind in California, administers several programs for small business development and retention.* The city as a whole invests just over $6 million annually toward small business programs, with most of these funds administered through various OSB programs (San Diego Office of Small Business, 2006). The programs administered by the OSB include the city's BID program; parking meter districts, which turn parking meter revenues back to local commercial areas; a seed capital grant program; and technical assistance coordination. Legally and politically, the OSB also acts as an advocate for small business concerns and coordinates a small business advisory board, a small business troubleshooter, and an infrastructure impact program (San Diego Office of Small Business, 2006).

San Diego has 101 defined neighborhoods that range in population from 10,000 to 50,000, with most having retail areas (San Diego Office of Small Business, 2004). Many of the city's older areas, as in most large cities, have faced growing pains and strong competition from newer communities and large, suburban shopping centers. To combat some of these problems, the city has created a neighborhood revitalization team located within the city's Economic Development and Community Services Department.

---

* New York City's Office of Small Business Services plays a similar role. This office also assists in the formation, management, and planning aspects of BIDs. The importance of BIDs as an engine for small business growth has grown under the administration of Mayor Bloomberg in New York. Unlike San Diego, however, New York does not offer direct funding to its BIDs.

Neighborhood revitalization efforts in San Diego often revolve around the physical environment, especially in relation to social spaces. Thus, revitalization efforts are pursued primarily through a mix of public and private investment in physical improvements to sidewalks, storm drains, retaining walls, landscaped medians, ornamental and safety lighting, public artwork, bus stops, landmark community signage, and electrical facilities for street fairs and events. The city's Office of Neighborhood Revitalization is the organizing unit of government that oversees these physical improvements. This office also coordinates a community-financed program directed at neighborhood beautification and quality-of-life enhancement. To this end, the city pursues place management activities in concert with the OSB and neighborhood groups by relying on two primary approaches: maintenance assessment districts (MADs) and BIDs.

MADs are authorized under California Landscape and Lighting Maintenance District Act of 1972 (California Tax Data, 2007) and the San Diego Maintenance District Procedural Ordinance of 1975 (City of San Diego, 2007). Under the provisions of these laws, the city can assess properties and provide maintenance or improvements to the area based on the amount of benefit the property will receive from the improvements. Currently, more than half of BIDs in San Diego either collect MAD money or deliver MAD services through contracts with the city's Parks and Recreation Administration. Maintenance has also been enhanced by recent efforts to collect property-based assessments.*

BID History and Creation

The process for BID formation in San Diego is similar to that of other cities nationally; that is, 20 percent of merchants in a given district are required to sign a petition in favor of BID creation. If the petition drive meets its goal, city council mails ballots to all district merchants. In order for district formation to fail, those merchants representing 51 percent of the assessed value of the district must formally oppose the district. As a matter of policy, the city counts unreturned ballots as support of the district (or not opposed). This practice led to a lawsuit against the city pursued by a small group of merchants located within the city's Pacific Beach area. In this case, the court held for the city, stating that the process was reasonable and fair (Huard, 1997; Rogers, 1997). Ten of the city's 18 BIDs were created before 1990, and seven were formed in the 1990s. The city's most recent BID, North Bay, was created in 2000. The city has lost one BID, the Moreno BID, which ceased operations in 2002 and was folded into the city's Micro District program.

BID creation in California was complicated with the passing of Proposition 218 in 1996, which resulted in the passage of the Right to Vote on Taxes Act. This law

---

* See the Meek and Hubler chapter in this volume for a typology of the BIDs in California and different assessment methods used in this state.

requires a public vote before the imposition of any new taxes. The first statewide legal test of this law involved BID merchant fees in San Diego. The Howard Jarvis Taxpayers Association (1999) sued over the imposition of BID fees, claiming that the BID enabling law did not require a referendum and was thus illegal under the act. There is language in the act that seeks to define general and special taxes, with special taxes defined as a tax imposed for specific purposes. San Diego city attorneys argued that because BID fees were not based on property values, but on the location of the business and the number of employees, they did not constitute a special tax per se (Rogers, 1997). In 1998, the California State Superior Court held for the city. The court required, however, that merchant fees fund only those services that offered a general benefit to the district, with no specific property owner or merchant benefiting directly from any program or operation (Rogers, 1997). In most San Diego BID budgets, income categories are designated as providing general or specific benefits, with merchant-fee revenues allocated to general benefit programming (see Briffault, 1999, for a legal analysis of BIDs).

Accountability and Public Oversight

The city maintains oversight of BIDs through the OSB. This office administers BID funding and oversees accountability issues. The OSB collects assessment fees on an annual basis, with the assessment included as a separate charge on the business tax bill. The city returns all assessment funds to the BIDs through annual contract agreements. The city implemented this policy to maintain public sector influence and accountability over BID activities. In fiscal years 2003 to 2004, San Diego City Council discontinued BID management contracts for two nonprofit management corporations: Mission Hills and City Heights. Each of these two districts, however, was granted new operating contracts after newly formed nonprofits were constructed by the staff of OSB and BIDC (S. Kessler, personal communication, March 16, 2006). The city can also apply additional levers of influence through a number of public funding mechanisms that are directed toward BIDs. These include Small Business Enhancement Program (SBEP) funds and the federally funded Community Development Block Grant (CDBG) program. SBEP funding is a competitive grant program where BIDs make a case to the BIDC and the OSB for funding to augment small business development programming. In terms of actual programming, most of the activities of BIDs in San Diego qualify for these funds. The OSB also administers the CDBG program. The OSB distributes these funds to eligible BIDs with eligibility based on the demonstration of economic need. A city council member with a BID in his or her district typically initiates CDBG funds. These funds cannot to be used for salaries or business services but must go to physical improvements that benefit the community at large. Thus, in the past, these funds have gone to lighting improvement programs, sidewalk and curb improvements, and landscape improvements (San Diego Office of Small Business, 2004).

BIDC

In 1989, San Diego agreed to incorporate an umbrella organization to assist in the management of the city's growing number of BIDs. The BIDC is similar to other nonprofit umbrella organizations that have arisen in cities around the United States to provide financial and personnel management, research and planning, and advocacy services to CDCs (Stokes, 2006). In essence, these organizations address an ongoing problem of the current decentralized nonprofit model of planning and economic development services, which is that organizations are too small to be effective. Umbrella organizations thus afford some economy of scale to small nonprofits, often working within similar legal and financial operating frameworks.

As a 501(c-6) organization, the BIDC is unique in its scope, budget, and administrative responsibility. Whereas the city of New York manages its BID program through its Office of Small Business Services, which offers BID start-up, planning, and management services, the BIDC adds a direct funding element to its portfolio of services provided to BIDs. The mission statement of the BIDC reads: "to assist in development and dissemination of information, resources, expertise to its member districts, and in supporting them in improving their physical, social and economic environments" (San Diego BID Council, 2004, p. 1). The BIDC was created as an advocacy organization for the small business community in the city and derives its funding through the city's annual business license fee levied on all licensed businesses. As part of a deal with city council, the small business license fee was dropped in 1995 from $125 to $34 per establishment per annum. These funds became the dedicated funding source for the Small Business Enhancement Program (SBEP) administered under city contract by the BIDC. The BIDC receives half of the revenues associated with this fee, despite the fact that only 20 percent of the city's businesses fall within a defined BID district.

The BIDC is charged with nine primary tasks:

1. Communications/public relations
2. Financial management support
3. Maintaining a resource library
4. Assistance in policy and program development for BIDs
5. Tracking and initiation of legislation
6. Contract and reimbursement processing
7. Assistance in BID formation efforts, including public outreach
8. Training of BID staff (including professional training for directors)
9. Development of alternative funding sources (San Diego BID Council, 2001)

The operating budget of the BIDC is just over $1 million for (fiscal year) FY 2006. The vast majority of the BIDC's funding comes from SBEP funds (87 percent) and CDBG reimbursements (10 percent). This level of public support has remained fairly steady through the decade, and the continued level of funding illustrates the political connections contained within the organization. Although city council has tried in the past to level this funding stream and apply a collection fee as well, political friends of the BIDC have managed to maintain this level of funding. A board of directors comprised of BID directors and city officials run the BIDC. In practice, the BIDC acts as a direct liaison between the city's economic development agencies, such as the Office of Small Business, BID officials, and individual BID merchants. The services offered by the BIDC are similar to what would be provided by a city agency charged with organizing BID functions—that is, administrative support for BID members. The BIDC also provides other services, such as the provision of a centralized website and e-mail server for BIDs, a citywide database of businesses, and the creation of a BID foundation that provides seed grants to small businesses.

In 2002, a group of BID directors in San Diego came to the conclusion that the BIDC was not serving its purpose. Scott Kessler, former BID director of the city's Adams Avenue BID, became director of the BIDC and decided to take on larger public policy issues affecting small business. These included the availability of health insurance for the employees of small business in the city. In 2002, the BIDC surveyed small businesses in San Diego and found affordable health care a problem among the city's small businesses. In an attempt to assert scale efficiencies that come from larger collective bargaining leverage, the BIDC then instituted the City Care Benefits program. This program provides health, vision, and dental benefits to the city's small business community. A BIDC-appointed board of trustees runs the program, which has resulted in having more business owners and employees under the care of a health plan due to lower costs associated with group plans (San Diego BID Council, 2006).* The BIDC has also recently embarked on a grant program to assist small businesses in meeting new regulations relating to building retrofitting for seismic disturbances. Here, the BIDC also acts as clearinghouse and coordinator and liaison to link small businesses to structural engineering firms (San Diego BID Council, 2005). Other notable recent accomplishments by the BIDC include:

- Coordinating the city's Main Street program
- Managing and promoting a citywide holiday event (December Nights)
- Developing a business yellow pages with 70,000 business listings
- Successfully advocating for an expansion of a public right-of-way program that allows for less city regulation of outdoor displays and added sidewalk seating for food and beverage establishments
- Providing leadership for the city's proposed planning regulations relating to big-box retailers
- Managing the city-funded tree planting program, which has resulted in the planting of 1,100 trees in BID districts

---

* As of 2004, there were 600 businesses enrolling 1,400 employees in this program (City of San Diego, 2007).

■ Retaining the sole development rights for a proposed urban village located in the San Ysidro BID (San Diego BID Council, 2005)*

Micro Business Districts

In addition to collaborating with the OSB to assist in the ongoing development of the city's BIDs, the BIDC also contracts with the city to help coordinate other business development programs; one such program is the micro business districts program. The micro district program is predicated on the notion that smaller business areas are not as organized as larger business districts, and therefore are not able to take advantage of efforts to collectivize resources and perform revitalization projects (Gross, 2005; Stokes, 2006). Micro business districts provide organized and targeted assistance in areas such as business development and retention, marketing, organization, funding, and special events. Micro districts are designed to serve business districts that have an insufficient number of businesses to form a BID. As the smallest BID in the city contains over 240 licensed businesses, the micro program was created for districts that have 100 to 150 licensed businesses. Micro districts are voluntary and do not require a vote from the business community. Fee structures differ for each district and are voluntary. To date, however, there has yet to be a micro district that has moved toward attaining full BID status. The BIDC also offers program grants to micro districts. In FY 2005, eight such districts have been budgeted a total of $83,000.

BID Activities in San Diego

BIDs in San Diego perform myriad functions. These functions can be organized into three broadly defined groupings: (1) place management of the public environment, (2) production of special events, and (3) planning and political advocacy.†

The first category of functions includes the administration of projects that use funds from the city, MAD funding, and federally sponsored CDBG funds to improve lighting, sidewalks, parks, landscaping, and trees. MAD funding comes

---

* BIDs in the city have long advocated the urban village approach to redevelopment of older commercial areas in San Diego. Currently, three of the villages proposed by the San Diego planning department have significant BID involvement in planning (North Park, El Cajon, and San Ysidro). The San Ysidro village is being developed by the BIDC. This is a 14.5-acre site that will include 1,000 residential units and 170,000 square feet of commercial space (Scott Kessler, BIC director, personal interview, March 2006).

† Services offered by BIDs in San Diego do not stray from BID service findings in national studies (Mitchell, 2001b) and in other locales (Gross, 2005; also see the chapter by Gross in this volume).

from a special assessment on property owners and is dedicated to the planting and maintenance of trees, shrubs, and flower beds in public spaces.

In addition to the management of the physical environment, BIDs in San Diego engage in a wealth of place promotion activities. Indeed, most of the BIDs in the city are decidedly promotional in their service orientation. Thus, the production and promotion of special events, restaurant tours, block parties, weekly farmer's markets, and holiday festivals are added to developing public relations and marketing materials. Nearly one third of BIDs in San Diego produce, coordinate, and promote large-scale street festivals.

Planning and advocacy activities performed by BIDs include the development of site plans and the expression of these plans to city offices for funding consideration. In addition to physical planning, many BIDs develop visual databases for the purposes of commercial promotion and land-use planning activities. Although active in community-oriented programming, only a few of the city's BIDs have endeavored to do economic development programming that does not relate to promotion and special events. These have included providing business training, enhancing community educational facilities, and engaging in transit and land-use planning efforts. BIDs in the city have also advocated the urban village approach to redevelopment of older commercial areas in San Diego. Currently, three of the villages proposed by the San Diego Planning Department have significant BID involvement in planning (North Park, El Cajon, and San Ysidro). The San Ysidro village is being developed by the BIDC. This is a 14.5-acre site that will include 1,000 residential units and 170,000 square feet of commercial space (S. Kessler, personal communication, March 16, 2006). Finally, BID directors formulate, promote, and articulate the interests of the district to local political actors and philanthropic organizations. Much of these efforts are directed toward the development of funding sources for programming and improvements to the district (see Table 11.1).

BID Funding

Fees to merchants are assessed based on the relative benefit reaped from collective improvements and activities. BID leaders determine the formula for the assessment by taking into account the type, size, and location of each business in the district. Fees generally range from $40 to $500 per business each year (San Diego Office of Small Business, 2005). Some newer BIDs have higher fees, typically ranging from $90 to $1,200 per year, with some large anchor businesses paying up to $5,000 annually. BID fees are included as a separate charge on the city-issued business tax bills. The city returns 100 percent of BID assessment funds to BIDs through annual contract agreements; they are not charged for administrative costs associated with collections (San Diego Office of Small Business, 2005).

Table 11.1 Sources of BID income (2005)

Location	Establishments	Fees and assessments	SBEP	CDBG	PBID/MAD	Other	Total
Downtown	900	$85,000	$19,200		$2,911,017	$300,834	$3,316,051
Gaslamp	400	65,000	16,289			255,711	337,000
Hillcrest	1200	86,000	20,943			165,440	272,383
Adams Ave.	548	32,000	16,103	$110,000	52,000	250,143	460,246
El Cajon Gateway	270	26,500	15,546	50,000		112,230	204,276
North Park	250	14,500	15,476	130,000		59,071	219,047
City Heights	430	36,000	16,516	20,000	286,000	112,230	470,746
El Cajon Central	560	60,800	17,260	50,000		112,230	240,290
Mission Hills	370	24,500	16,116			67,713	108,329
Ocean Beach	310	26,000	15,790	50,000	52,000	171,314	315,104
Lo Jolla	1160	187,000	20,734			37,867	245,601
College Area	500	75,000	16,911	235,000	300,000	135,300	762,211
Diamond	340	42,800	15,964	40,000		32,964	131,728
Old Town	440	35,000	16,562			114,032	165,594
Little Italy	430	80,000	16,475	65,000	500,000	242,151	903,626
Pacific Beach	1320	158,000	21,675	261,000		21,490	462,165
San Ysidro	510	141,600	16,675	100,000		26,236	284,511
Midway/North Bay	900	150,000	18,863			25,000	193,863
Total	10,569	1,325,700	313,098	1,111,000	4,101,017	2,241,956	9,092,771
% of total		14.5%	3.4%	12.2%	45%	24%	

Note: Fees and assessments = merchant fees and commercial property assessments; SBEP = small business enhancement program (city of San Diego); CDBG = community development block grant program; MAD = maintenance assessment district; PBID = property assessment district; Other = revenues from events, programming, fees for services.

Due to its merchant-based funding source, San Diego BID assessment levels are nominal compared to comparable organizations around the United States.* Thus, many BIDs in San Diego use merchant fees as leverage for additional funding from a variety of sources. Many BIDs receive additional funding through various city grant programs. These include (1) Small Business Enhancement Program (SBEP), which is a citywide small business grant program; (2) the federally sponsored Community Development Block Grant program (CDBG)†; (3) the transient occupancy tax (TOT), which is a tax on hotel and motel lodging in the city and county; and (4) parking meter revenues.

In total, the city's 18 districts raised more than $9 million in 2005 for services directed to their districts (see Table 11.1). This is up from more than $5 million in 2000. The state legislation passed in 1999 allowed BIDs to collect property-based assessments. In 2001, the city's downtown BID created a property-based assessment district. Just under half of the property assessments for 2005 were related to property-based BIDs (PBIDs) and MAD funds ($4,101,017). The city's downtown BID accounts for $2.9 million of these property-based assessment funds. In 2005, the downtown PBID was reauthorized for 10 more years by a 71 percent vote of property owners. The reauthorization increased the downtown BIDs FY 2006 budget to more than $6 million. Thus, much of the revenue growth for the citywide BID program over the past five years is attributable to property-based assessments. To put this funding level in perspective, the downtown BID in Philadelphia reported a 2005 budget of over $15 million (Center City District, 2005). This wide range of BID resources is reflective of the relative level of market values of downtown property, with Philadelphia having a significant amount of its taxable real property value located in its central business district. The more dispersed economic land use of San Diego reflects a far less built-up downtown.

Despite the overall growth in the citywide BID program revenues, merchant fees in 2005 were down 19 percent ($311,000) from 2001, whereas SBEP funds were down 10 percent over the same period. The respective share of these fund types to the overall level of BID funds dropped from 31 percent for merchant fees in 2001 to 14 percent in 2005, whereas SBEP funds dropped in half from 6.6 percent of overall budgets to 3.3 percent. Despite these drops in merchant fees and city-funded revenues, 12 of the 18 BID budgets rose from 2001 to 2004 despite an overall economic slump. These budget increases are generally attributable to two revenue types: MAD and PBID assessment fees, and the entrepreneurial activities pursued by the BIDs themselves.

---

* The city's downtown BID is a notable exception, with just under $3 million annually collected from property-based assessments. This was raised for fiscal year 2006 by a vote of property owners to above $5 million per annum.

† CDBG funds do not pass through BID organizations in San Diego. That is, the funds are appropriated and dedicated to physical improvements in the district but are managed by city departments (Scott Kessler, personal communication, March 16, 2006).

A majority of San Diego's BIDs derived over half of their income from sources other than assessments or grant funds in both 2001 and 2005. Sources of these funds vary but tended to come from income related to the production of events. Twelve of the 18 BIDs produced 20 events in 2000. These events ranged from all-day music events, arts festivals, and Cinco de Mayo festivals to farmer's markets. In addition to fees from vendors, BIDs were able to profit from the selling of advertising space on banners and signs. In 2004, the number of events produced by San Diego's 18 BIDs grew to 47 (San Diego BID Council, 2005). In a short time, BIDs in San Diego have been able to increase their funding capacity beyond merchant fees and city support through public SBEP funds.

Conclusion and Policy Implications

The widespread development of BIDs in the United States has raised many important questions for policymakers and economic development planning professionals. Not entirely public or private, BIDs offer a hybrid model where the public trades a measure of control for additional resources. BIDs represent a shifting of development responsibilities away from purely public efforts.

Although recent scholarship has tended to focus on the BID concept as a whole (Briffault, 1999), BIDs' use in central business districts (Levy, 2001a; Mitchell, 2001a), or measuring the outcomes attributed to specific BIDs (Caruso and Weber, 2006; Hoyt, 2004, 2005; Stokes, 2002, 2006), there is a growing interest in municipal policies that can assist these localized agents of revitalization while doing a better job in holding them accountable to public values and interests.

Nationally, there is significant variation in the level of public investment into BID operations. The investments most typically made are administrative, whether through the dedication of city staff or resources in the planning and creation of BIDs, the setting up and administration of a fee/assessment collection system, the oversight and auditing of BID operations either annually or periodically, or a combination of any of these.

The city of San Diego has a long history of using BIDs to foster small business development. No other city uses public funds to support BIDs to the extent that San Diego does. What is leveraged by public investment in these organizations is impressive. In 2005, BID revenues dedicated to services totaled $9 million, of which only $1.4 million came from non-fee-based public monies (see Table 11.1). Leveraging private funds to support local public purposes is especially important in California, where there has been a historical political movement at the state level to limit the taxing power of California municipalities. BIDs in San Diego are encouraged to raise capital through entrepreneurial activities to ensure success. City planners interviewed for this research referred to this as a "bottom up" approach to economic development (M. Didben-Brown, personal communication, June 10, 2004).

The future direction of small BIDs in San Diego will be determined by continued support and trust placed in them by the city political structure. Recent fiscal events and political scandals in San Diego have put considerable stress on the city's ability to offer substantial public services related to economic development. This has led to a greater influence of the BIDC as an institutional actor in economic development programming in the city. The BIDC annual report states that planned cuts in staffing for the city's Office of Small Business were forestalled by lobbying efforts by the BIDC (San Diego BID Council, 2005).

The BIDC is indeed a unique organization with regard to small business assistance. Although ostensibly a BID member organization, its role in policymaking and implementation has grown beyond this limited scope. As stated above, only 20 percent of the city's small business operators are located within the boundaries of a BID district. Because the BIDC is granted 50 percent of the city's business license tax, it has expanded its policy reach beyond BIDs. To this end, it has effectively reached out to the city's non-BID-located small business operators through its operation of micro districts, the creation of a group health plan, seismic retrofit programming for small business throughout the city, and its efforts to facilitate the city's village planning concept by acting as a developer in BID areas where these plans are directed.

An examination of BID budgets during the current decade reveals a growing bifurcation in the directions of BIDs in San Diego in terms of funding and services. That is, the more fiscally strong districts are staying on course in the areas of commercial promotion and special event production, whereas less capitalized districts have become more focused on community development in a broader sense. Activities related to this include education and training programming and as an interest in housing and city service provision. Larger districts have tapped into property-based assessment fees that have enabled a broader role in place management activities such as creation and management of streetscapes, security, and sanitation services. This development follows a larger national trend where downtown BIDs have grown in stature in terms of their funding streams, programming, and planning influence (Mitchell, 2001a).

Despite this trend, San Diego continues to afford an institutional capacity for the BIDC and OSB to affect a broader strategy in the area of small business development. Thus, San Diego offers administrative support and policy leadership similar to that offered by New York City and its Department of Small Business Services. It differs from New York in that the BIDC is itself a nonprofit organization and, unlike New York City, provides BIDs with direct public funding for BID programs. Another city with a large and growing BID program is Los Angeles. In Los Angeles, BIDs are managed by the Office of the City Clerk, which lacks a centralized administrative apparatus to assist the development and strategic planning operations of individual BIDs (K. Morrison, personal communication, November 2, 2006). In Philadelphia, an effort of the city's largest BID, the Center City District, to offer technical assistance to developing neighborhood BID districts was short-lived due to grant funding time limitations. Although there is some policy and administrative oversight at the municipal level in these cities, aside from recent efforts in New York City to promote BIDs as an engine for small business development, other cities lack San Diego's concentrated public policy efforts to assist small business enhancement at both the local district level and the municipal level.*

Accountability issues inherent in BID governance schemes have been addressed well by others (Mallett, 1993; Mitchell, 2001a). Suffice it to say that BIDs are special districts, and thus deserve the same accountability critiques these forms of governance have received in the literature (Burns, 1994; Foster, 1997). Caruso and Weber (2006; also in this volume), in constructing a proper evaluative framework for BIDs, rightfully suggest that BIDs receiving public funding should be held to a standard of performance that includes an assessment of their efforts to maintain public values. While the governance structure of BIDs is set up by publicly elected legislative bodies, BIDs' services are usually managed by community-based, nonprofit development corporations. BIDs also engender a critique over the use of private subcontractors in the administration of publicly defined services. The rhetoric of this critique, however, seems directed toward the business orientation of the governors of BID boards, as the same critique more broadly applies to community nonprofit housing or public service providers as well.

Accountability problems faced by BIDs around the country have included instances where BID promoters have failed to properly notify property owners of elections or expansions of service plans (New York City Council, 1997). There have also been isolated instances of abuse of power by BID directors, as well as programming orientations that have been poorly managed (Lansdon and Halpern, 1995). Much of the criticisms (and lawsuits) directed at BID operations have been for their enforcement activities directed toward homeless individuals (Lambert, 1995). In a few cases, BID operators have lost their service contracts with their host cities because of a failure to be effective operators: this has happened to two BIDs in San Diego. In other cases, BIDs have been dissolved over a vote of the property owners in the district. But for the most part, BIDs have come to be embraced by their host cities as providing focused services that facilitate publicly defined benefits to the broader community (Levy, 2001a, 2001b), and in terms of being accountable to internal stakeholders—namely, business owners and commercial property owners—there has been a mere handful of instances in the United States where BID operations have been deauthorized.

In the case of San Diego, BIDs have survived a sustained attack on their right to levy fees and special assessments by antitax organizations. They have also seen individual organizations deauthorized by a vote of local business owners and a

---

* An examination of the minutes for the June 4, 2004, meeting of the city of San Diego Small Business Advisory Board reveals the input of BIDC staff in forestalling planned layoffs of four of the OSB's nine employees (http://www.sandiego.gov/economic-development/pdf/sbminutes040604.pdf, accessed June 9, 2006).

few who have seen their management contracts pulled and replaced with more effective organizations.

The use of BIDs in San Diego and their encouragement to be entrepreneurial organizations has increased the program reach of these organizations, while lessening their need for public subsidy. Although this clearly constitutes a bargain of sorts, the benefits of a citywide BID structure to small business development are clear in San Diego. At the BID level, they enable economies of scale in the areas of marketing and advertising, place management and place making, community and civic engagement, visioning and strategic planning, localized advocacy, and improved city services. At the broader public policy level, the BIDC has endeavored to assist small business by addressing issues that cross over the geographically specific business orientation typically addressed by BIDs. These include improving internal operational efficiencies through employment of networking abilities, collective service efficiencies relating to health care insurance, and regulatory consultations. Finally, as Mitchell (2001a) points out, it is important for business districts to have a centralized office that is responsible for addressing the needs specific to a small business community, as well as the capacity to address larger policy and political advocacy for the collective needs of the small business community citywide. San Diego's policy attitude toward BIDs is that they form an integral part of the city's efforts to maintain viability in its small business sector while at the same time forming an effective organizational apparatus for broader community development efforts.

References

Briffault, R. 1999. A government for our time: Business improvement districts and urban governance. *Columbia Law Review* 99(2) 365–477.

Burns, N. 1994. *The formation of American local governments: Private values in public institutions.* New York: Oxford University Press.

California Tax Data. 2007. *California codes: Streets and highways code.* Section 22500–22509. http://www.californiataxdata.com/A_Free_Resources/legislation/LandLight.asp (accessed February 22, 2007).

Caruso, G., and Weber, R. 2006. Getting the max for the tax: An examination of BID performance measures. *International Journal of Public Administration* 29:187–220.

Center City District. 2005. *Annual report.* Philadelphia: Author.

Chapin, T. 2002. Beyond the entrepreneurial city: Municipal capitalism in San Diego. *Journal of Urban Affairs* 24:565–581.

City of San Diego. 2007. San Diego municipal code. Public improvement and assessment proceedings. www.sandiego.gov/park-and-recreation/pdf/madmunicode.pdf (accessed February 22, 2007).

Foster, K. 1997. *The political economy of special-purpose government.* Washington, DC: Georgetown University Press.

Gottlieb, P. 1997. Neighborhood development in the metropolitan economy. *Journal of Urban Affairs* 19:163–182.

Gross, J. 2005. Business improvement districts in New York City's low-income and high-income neighborhoods. *Economic Development Quarterly* 19:74–189.

Howard Jarvis Taxpayers Association. *Plaintiffs and Appellants v. City of San Diego.* 72 Ca. App. 4th 230 (1999).

Hoyt, L. 2004. Collectivizing private funds for safer public spaces: An empirical examination of the business improvement district concept. *Environment and Planning B.* 31(3) 367–380.

Hoyt, L. 2005. Do business improvement districts make a difference? Crime in and around commercial areas in Philadelphia. *Journal of Planning, Education and Research* 23:185–199.

Huard, R. 1997. Taxpayer group sues San Diego over Prop. 218. *San Diego Union Tribune,* July 4, p. B1.

Lambert, B. 1995. Charges of rousting homeless are made up, group says. *New York Times,* November 8, p. B3.

Lansdon, D., and Halpern S. 1995. When neighborhoods are privatized. *New York Times,* November 30, p. A39.

Levy, P. R. 2001a. Paying for public life. *Economic Development Quarterly* 15:123–131.

Levy, P. R. 2001b. Making downtowns competitive. *Journal of the American Planning Association* 4:16–19.

Mallett, W. J. 1993. Private government formation in the DC metropolitan area. *Growth and Change* 24:385–415.

Mitchell, J. 2001a. Business improvement districts and the "new" revitalization for downtown. *Economic Development Quarterly* 15:115–123.

Mitchell, J. 2001b. Business improvement districts and the management of innovation. *American Review of Public Administration* 31:201–210.

Morris, M. 1997. Small business support systems in San Diego. In *Public investment,* 1–4. Chicago: American Planning Association.

New York City Council. 1997. *Managing the micropolis: Proposals to strengthen BID performance and accountability.* New York: Author.

Pack, J. 1992. BIDs, DIDs, SIDs, SADs: Private government in urban America. *The Brookings Review* 10:18–21.

Porter, M. 1997. New strategies for inner-city economic development. *Economic Development Quarterly* 11:11–27.

Rogers, T. 1997. First court test of Prop. 218 may be here. *San Diego Union Tribune,* June 11, pp. B4–5.

San Diego BID Council. 2001. *Annual report.* http://www.bidcouncil.org (accessed February 15, 2007).

San Diego BID Council. 2004. *Annual report.* http://www.bidcouncil.org (accessed June 15, 2007).

San Diego BID Council. 2005. *Annual report.* http://www.bidcouncil.org (accessed June 15, 2007).

San Diego BID Council. 2006. *Annual report.* http://www.bidcouncil.org (accessed June 15, 2007).

San Diego Economic Development Department. 2006. Small business advisory board. http://www.sandiego.gov/economic-development/business-assistance/small-business/advsbrd.shtml (accessed February 20, 2006).

San Diego Office of Small Business. 2004. *Annual report.* San Diego, CA: Author.

San Diego Office of Small Business. 2005. *Annual report.* San Diego, CA: Author.

San Diego Office of Small Business. 2006. *Annual report.* San Diego, CA: Author.

Schaller, S., and Modan, G. 2005. Contesting public space and citizenship: Implications for neighborhood business improvement districts. *Journal of Planning, Education and Research* 24:394–407.

Skogan, W. 1990. *Disorder and decline: Crime and the spiral of decay in American neighborhoods.* Berkeley: University of California Press.

Squires, G. 1989. *Unequal partnerships.* New Brunswick, NJ: Rutgers University Press.

Stokes, R. 2002. Place management in commercial areas: Customer service representatives in Philadelphia's central business district. *Security Journal* 15:7–19.

Stokes, R. 2006. Business improvement districts and inner city revitalization: The case of Philadelphia's Frankford Special Services District. *International Journal of Public Administration* 29:173–187.

Stokes, R. 2007. Business improvement districts and small business advocacy: The case of San Diego's citywide BID program. *Economic Development Quarterly* 21:278–291.

Zukin, S. 1995. *The cultures of cities.* Oxford: Blackwell.

Chapter 12

Business Improvement Districts' Approaches to Working with Local Governments

James F. Wolf

Contents

Introduction

Business improvement districts (BIDs) have become an important and growing dimension of local and metropolitan governance (Briffault, 1999; Mitchell, 2001; Houstoun, 2003). Briffault argues that BIDs are clearly part of the landscape of public management and governance of cities. Their government-like activities include "the public's use and enjoyment of the streets, parks, squares and other public spaces that are at the heart of urban living,…[they enjoy the]…public power of coercive taxation…[and]…their boundaries, programs, finances and governance structures are shaped by government decisions" (p. 365). As the working relationships between BIDs and local governments grow, understanding those relationships becomes more important. The chapter reports on a survey of 12 BIDs that addressed the strategies and approaches BIDs use to work with local governments. The BIDs that participated in the survey shared the five characteristics identified by Mitchell's (2001) research:

1. They were authorized by states that permit local governments to create BIDs and determine how they can be created, what they can do, and what governing board processes they must observe.
2. They were created through a petition process.
3. Their major source of revenue comes from assessments collected by cities.
4. They are either government agency, nonprofit, or public–private partnerships.
5. The BIDs work for downtown businesses—not for the local governments.

The BIDs represented in this survey can be categorized as large but not the largest. Most of the 12 are drawn from among the ranks of longer-established BIDs in large metropolitan areas, BIDs that have been operating for one or two decades. In most cases, they have steadily expanded their roles and increased their operating budgets. All are downtown BIDs, all have budgets of at least a half million dollars, and all have a full-time staff of at least three persons (with an average of 6.6 persons; see Table 12.1).* In most of the BIDs, these administrative staffs are augmented by an often larger group of street-level workers who may be employees of the BID or employed by a contractor. The BIDs in the survey are located in large metropolitan areas: all but three are located in one of the largest 60 metropolitan areas.

---

* The Washington, D.C., Golden Triangle has only 2 BID employees and administrative staff support on contract with over 40 employees.

Table 12.1   BID Budgets, Staff Size, and Ranking of Metropolitan Areas

Business improvement districts	Annual budget	Administrative staff	Population ranking of metropolitan areas (365 total)
Albany, NY: Central Business Improvement District	$600,000	3	59
Charlotte, NC: Charlotte Center City Partners	3,200,000	13	37
Cincinnati, OH: Downtown Cincinnati	2,264,000	12	24
Fort Worth, TX: Downtown Fort Worth	1,600,000	10	5
Lincoln, NE: Downtown Lincoln Association	1,100,000	4	161
Louisville, KY: Louisville Central Area and Louisville Downtown Management District	1,500,000	6	43
Long Beach, CA: Downtown Long Beach	2,750,000	5	2
Phoenix, AZ: Cooper Square: Downtown Phoenix Partnership	2,300,000	11	14
Portland, ME: Portland Downtown	850,000	4	94
Raleigh, NC: Downtown Raleigh Alliance	850,000	7	54
Roanoke, VA: Downtown Roanoke	500,000	3	153
Washington, DC: Golden Triangle	$3,300,000	2	7
Average	**$1,700,000**	**6.6**	**44**

Source: Annual budgets and size of administrative staffs were collected during interviews of BID executives, July 2005. Annual estimates of the population of combined statistical areas: April 1, 2000, to July 1, 2003, from the U.S. Bureau of the Census web page.

Their operating budgets (average $1.7 million) are also significantly larger than most BIDs. The largest BIDs, such as the Center City BID in Philadelphia and the Downtown DC BID in Washington, D.C., with substantially larger budgets, were not included in the survey.

All the BIDs in the survey were either nonprofit organizations or public–private partnerships.* Most have a menu of program activities that includes advocacy,

---

* Mitchell (2001) reported that while smaller cities tended to have BIDs that were agencies of the local government, the larger ones were usually nonprofits and public–private partnerships.

economic development, safety, street maintenance, and streetscaping. A smaller group includes transportation and social service programs. Beyond these, BIDs vary on the kind of work they perform. Practically all BIDs included in this survey sample were started by and continue to be closely linked to downtown business associations—dues-paying membership organizations that often provide the impetus for establishing the BIDs.* Some BIDs remained closely tied financially and administratively to these associations. Others developed as organizations that were separate from existing downtown business associations. In a few cases, the BID was made up of more than one assessment or improvement district administered by an umbrella organization that was part of a downtown business association. In another, the BID itself created a more broad-based community organization that in turn has become the administrator of the BID.

The survey sample was purposive and nonrandom. The BIDs were selected from the International Downtown Association's member website links. The review of the 12 BIDs included telephone interviews with someone from the executive staff, most often the executive director, as well as extensive review of the BIDs' websites. The results of the interviews were provided to the interviewees for review to ensure that comments were accurately recorded. In addition, remarks by interviewers have been in most cases rendered anonymous and their organization titles vary. They are referred to in this chapter as "BID executives."

The chapter presents a survey of practices and approaches used by BIDs to work with local governments. The focus was not so much on the frequency of a specific approach but rather on the range of practices. Given the small sample size, the survey can only identify different approaches and not make any conclusions about their frequency or effectiveness. This survey is limited to examining the point of view of the BID executives. Clearly, further research that examines the point of view of the local governments would more completely fill out the picture of how BIDs relate to local governments. However, the results of the survey should be helpful for BIDs as they consider alternative approaches for working with their local government. The inventory of approaches may also provide elements useful for further research examining this important area of BIDs' role in local governance.

The chapter begins with a discussion of some overall strategies and approaches that BIDs employ as they work with local governments, and then focuses, in detail, on how BIDs and local governments work on specific kinds of issues. These program areas include safety, exterior cleanliness, streetscape, planning, and economic development. The chapter concludes with a summary of the different approaches and identifies issues that emerged from the analysis that may be useful for future BID research.

---

* One executive director emphasized his assessment that most of the BIDs in the larger areas were in fact just a "tool" for the business association and larger business community to do specific things that enhance the downtown.

BID–City Government Relationships: Conflict or Cooperation?

BIDs create different kinds of working relationships with city governments. To a large extent, the style of the relationships between the two emerged from the specific history of relationships between the downtown business associations and city hall. Most importantly, they vary as to whether the relationship tends to be combative or collaborative. In many cases, the nature of the relationships may also include elements of both approaches within a single BID.

Only 2 of the 12 BID interviewees described their relationship with the city government as being at "arms length." One of these two BIDs has found it necessary to work with other community groups to pressure the city government to adopt policies favored by the downtown business community. This approach limits BIDs' relationship with the city to mostly an aggressive advocacy role. One of the two executive directors noted that he would prefer a more collaborative approach, but that the city is not interested in this kind of relationship at this time.

Five of the BID executives characterized their overall relationship with the city as one that has moved from a combative advocacy role to a more complex one resembling a full partnership. This kind of transition from confrontational to collaborative is captured by the executive director who said that he wanted the BID to work together with the city and be good partners. He thought the current relationship was a clear improvement over the earlier, more difficult one. Now a cooperative atmosphere pervades their relationships. A second BID executive sees a growing level of trust after a long difficult relationship. At one point the downtown business felt the city was pulling back services from the downtown at a level disproportionate with other areas of the city—a violation of the BID legislation. This conflict was difficult to overcome, but both sides worked to improve the relationship. A third BID executive who also experienced this transition from adversarial to cooperative style said that earlier the city government leaders felt that the BID was always going up against the city, and relationships were often contentious. Some members of the city council were even considering giving the contract to someone else. The BID decided that the relationship had to change, and it brought in a new executive director to do this. The board changed its emphasis and began to work at building ongoing working relationships with city departments.

The other five BIDs reported that they have had generally cooperative relationships from the beginning. They believe that a more collaborative relationship allows them to address downtown business issues with the city and at the same time cooperate with the cities to provide specific services to the downtown areas.

Forms of BID–City Government Involvement

Not surprisingly, the extensiveness of involvement of BIDs with city governments varies among BIDs and also within a single BID. At least three models of partnerships emerged in the survey, including ones that were (1) contract based, (2) closely coordinated yet separate collaboration, and (3) integrated and seamless. In some instances, a single BID used a combination of all three.

Contract-Based Relationships

Several BIDs saw their relationship with the city in terms of an explicit contract for service, where the city treats the BID as one of several potential contractors for specific services. The BID enters into the contract with the city, the specifications are clear, there are formal reporting processes, and the contract is reviewed and renewed periodically. With this relationship, the BID acts as a private entity contracting with the city. It represents the business interests, but other community associations could just as well provide the services that the BID offers. An executive that works within this framework described his sense of the situation that the city could just as well go to the chamber of commerce or some other community group if it did not like the service provided by the BID under its contract with the city.

In much the same way, another BID executive believes that the BID acts as an agent of the city and sees the BID as an independent contractor. The contract says what the organization can and cannot do. The contract calls for special governmental services not needed in other parts of the city. There is an annual work plan that is submitted to the city. The BID reports to the city, but usually this is not a problem and the contract does not require the city council's approval. The city initially had a five-year contract, but now there is a one-year renewable contract for up to ten years.

The most common of these kinds of arrangements are those in which the city contracts with the BID to provide an additional level of services in the downtown area. However, the relationship can go in either direction. In some instances, BIDs contract with the city to provide additional services. For example, the Fort Worth BID provides partial support for three mounted police officers. Another BID provides funds for an additional police officer to service the downtown area. The Golden Triangle BID in Washington, D.C., partners with three other DC BIDs, the District of Columbia government, and the Federal Transit Administration for a special downtown bus service. It contracts with the Metropolitan Transit Authority to provide the service.

Closely Coordinated yet Separate Collaboration

The survey found more examples of coordinated yet separate operations between city governments and BIDs than either of the other two models. In this model, the BIDs and city governments have worked out areas of expertise, and have evolved relationships and processes to allow for a great deal of collaboration. This represents a form of cooperative governance with each recognizing the other's competence and areas of operations. A majority of the BIDs in the survey, particularly the larger ones, acknowledged that the most effective relationships were the ones in which both parties saw themselves as in it together but operating collaboratively yet separately. One BID executive captured this kind of relationship when he said that the areas of responsibility are not a clear-cut thing and they have to work it out over time with the city. The overall approach for working with the city is that "we want to make it work." Both sides have their responsibility and both are committed to make it work.

Professional BID staffs play a key role in fostering and maintaining these kinds of relationships. The executive leadership, usually the top two or three officers in the BID, provide the critical political connections with elected and top municipal managers. One BID manager emphasized the kind of trust that has developed between BID and city officials, and this trust allows cooperation, often informal, in a wide range of areas of common interest. Some BIDs have explicitly decided to engage in a strategy that seeks a relationship with the city that builds on trust that allows for active cooperation, and accepts vesting responsibility with either the BID or the city for tasks based on needs and capacities.

Integrated and Seamless—"Joined at the Hip"

One BID executive characterized his relationship with the city as a very close partnership striving to make the downtown area work. This BID has a narrower mission than many others and sees itself primarily as a "clean and green" BID that is "joined at the hip" with the city government. The city decided to outsource these functions to the BID. The city contract is worth almost a third of the BID's budget, and involves trash removal, handicap access facilities, and landscaping. The delivery of these services by the BID is extensively integrated into the operations of the city. The city thought that the BID could do the job more effectively and cost-efficiently than the city itself. Thus, the relationship between BID and city is very close. For example, the BID maintenance director is a former city employee, and he has an excellent working relationship with the city's Department of Public Works, which is in contact with the BID supervisor almost daily.

Another BID's economic development director works very closely with the city's Urban Development Department, which functions as the city redevelopment authority. The BID staff works so closely that the BID's executive director believes that sometimes the BID staff think that the administrator of the city department is a BID employee, and city people think that the BID executive is a city employee. The BID accountant also has to work closely with the city accountant on this BID. There is a lot of trust and good communication between the BID and this department. In this area, the city and the BID make up a seamless team.

Fostering Relationships between BID and City Staff

The importance of establishing working relationships between the BID and the city professional and political leaders was consistently emphasized by the survey respondents. Nearly all the BIDs in the survey rely on establishing extensive working arrangements with all levels of the city professional staffs. Most of the critical interactions occur at the top levels of the BID, particularly with the executive and, in cases where they exist, BID deputy directors. These senior officials are involved in practically all relationships with city personnel. This is in part due to the small sizes of most BID staffs. In one BID, practically all business is dealt with at the staff level on a one-to-one basis with city staff rather than through committees. This includes the BID planning and development director who covers planning and transportation issues with the city, a communications director who works on special projects, and a director for program execution who works closely with the police department's neighborhood policing program.

Stability of these relationships is often the key to effective working processes. Some of the BIDs' executives saw themselves fortunate to have stability at city hall and in the BIDs. One of the BID executives observed that over two decades, his city went through a number of mayors and city managers. Some relationships were very good for some, and others not. He felt that not all mayors and city managers saw the benefit and importance of the downtown. The period of most stable relationship was when the city had one mayor and the BID had one executive director for nearly a decade. He went on to conclude that this stability was good for building effective working relationships because most downtowns depend on the personalities of the top leaders.

While the specific character of these relationships between the BID and city leaders varies, several approaches for working together emerged. Some BID executives have regularly scheduled meetings in addition to as-needed sessions with the city manager and staff. For some, this includes a formal agenda and reports for each of the regularly scheduled meetings. A BID executive may also participate in other meetings as a member or observer, including different task forces and committees. Two other examples more fully capture the nature of these BID executives' working relationships with city leaders. In the first, a more informal approach, the BID executive works with the city manager and key personnel. She also works closely with city council persons, including the BID's district representative as well as three at-large representatives. These relationships with the political leaders are not regularly scheduled; rather, she meets and talks often with elected city officials at different events. A second example illustrates a more formalized model. This executive director works directly with the city manager. He meets with the city manager as needed in addition to regularly scheduled bimonthly sessions. This BID executive prepares detailed reports of how the BID is progressing in its contract with the city and personally delivers a report to the city manager. They go over the report and check on progress and upcoming issues.

In addition, the backgrounds of the city staffs can shape BID–city relationships at the staff level. One BID executive compared her experiences with two different BIDs and felt that a major element in establishing good staff relationships was in large part due to the city's professional administrative staff. In her current city, the city manager and the staff are professionals who understand and do their job well. She believes that they know when it is in the interest of the city to involve the BID in city efforts and when joint projects make sense. She felt that this presence of a professional approach was different from her earlier work in another BID that had a strong mayor and strong council form of government. The relationships with that city's leadership were frequently filtered through the political lens and everything had to make sense politically.

Accountability

State enabling legislation gives cities authority to establish and terminate BIDs, and in addition, some form of sunset provision requires that a BID's charter be periodically reviewed and renewed. This can take the form of annual reviews and periodic BID updates to city council, to more extensive and formal five- or ten-year reviews. Rarely, if ever, has a city failed to renew a BID's charter or contract. However, practically all BIDs must submit to some form of accountability process with the local governments. Although the BIDs in the survey that have more formal contract relationships with city government for specific services were more likely to face closer scrutiny, none of the BIDs reported any extensive or threatening oversight or attempt to control BID activities.

At the same time, most BIDs do take the oversight processes seriously, and often find them useful for maintaining effective working processes with the city governments. For example, one BID that does not have a sunset requirement must have city approval of its budget. The city holds a public hearing during the budget process, and there is also a public hearing following each fiscal year prior to setting the BID assessment rate. The executive director of the BID believes that these reviews provide opportunities for strengthening BID accountability to the community. The Phoenix BID is an example of a more complex accountability process, because there are two different BIDs that the downtown association manages. Each BID comes under the provisions of different state enabling legislation. There are two contracts—one for each of the BIDs. The older one must be reviewed annually and renewed annually. There is no public hearing required, but it must be reviewed. On the other hand, the newer BID has a ten-year sunset provision. While its budget must get city council approval, including an annual hearing, the contract itself is good for ten years.

City membership on BID boards of directors provides yet another way for municipal governments to hold BIDs accountable to either general provisions that established the BIDs or specific service contracts. Practically all of the 12 BIDs include city representatives in one form or another on their governing boards. Some of these city representatives are limited by a nonvoting status, whereas others give city officials full voting status. The Long Beach BID is an example of including city representatives as voting members. There are two city representatives on the board who have voting status, because the city is a property owner and assessment-paying member. One of the voting members is the director of economic development and the second is the chair of the redevelopment agency. There are also two nonvoting members—the two city council representatives from the district in the downtown area. Another BID includes city representation because the city is also a major property owner in the district. This BID's executive believes that as the city develops more land in the downtown, it expects to be able to influence the direction of the BID. He noted that this strong city role in BID governance at times can create confusion in the eyes of other business members who tend to see the BID as the representative of business interests to the city.

How BIDs Work with City Governments: Specific Program Areas

Some program areas involve BIDs more directly with city governments than others. The program areas that consistently require the most coordination with both the BIDs and cities include (1) policy advocacy, (2) safe, clean, and attractive programs, and (3) economic development (including planning, marketing, and special events).

Policy Advocacy

Promoting the interests of the downtown businesses is often a legacy role from the downtown business associations that often spawned the BIDs. In most instances, the BID executive and key board members work with their city government counterparts to seek support for various downtown interests. This advocacy can range from being aggressive and combative to cooperative. Much depends on the history of the relationship between the business community and the city or, more specifically, on the personalities of the city and business leaders.

Two of the BID executives see the advocacy role as the primary role, occupying most of their workday. One of these executives has been in office for ten years and has developed working relationships with key staff and policy leaders of the city. At times, he believes that this role requires confronting ("cage rattling"), and other times, more collaborative approaches. Eight of the 12 BIDs characterized their advocacy role as collegial yet firm, rather than aggressive or combative. At times, however, BID executives experience pressures from local business to take a more aggressive approach in dealings with the city. In spite of this pressure, most BID executives have used more collaborative approaches when they push for support of their agenda with the cities.

Safe, Clean, and Attractive

Most BID programs include activities to enhance the security and attractiveness of the downtown. They are often referred to as "safe and clean" and sometimes "safe, clean, and attractive" programs. The clean and attractive parts of the programs can include sidewalk washing, litter removal, trash collection, maintenance of street signs, and streetscaping. The safety programs usually involve extra security guards, electronic security, and cooperative crime suppression programs with police departments. Street-level workers, often referred to as ambassadors or guides, support both the clean and safe objectives of the BID, as well as serving as hospitality workers for visitors to the downtown.

These programs often consume the largest portion of the BID resources and require extensive day-to-day involvement with city governments. Cities tend to consider these services the most valuable contribution that the BIDs can make to the community. BIDs reported that they often experienced pressure from the city leaders to spend their resources in these programs. Clean and safe programs necessarily require that BIDs coordinate these programs with city police and public works staffs. In smaller BIDs, the executive director serves as the point of contact with these agencies. Those BIDs with larger staffs may employ someone, often with a title of operation director, to manage the overall relationship with the appropriate city agencies. For some BIDs, the relationship is informal and simply involves a person appointed to serve as the contact at the BID and with the city agencies. These managers develop working relationships over time that support frequent, yet continuing informal agreements and working relationships—usually on a case-by-case basis. The larger BIDs may have more formal arrangements, similar to a BID that uses an operation committee. This group meets monthly to discuss police and public works issues and how they relate to BID programs.

Programs to make downtowns safer were included in the portfolio of programs by 11 of the 12 BIDs in the survey. In smaller BIDs, the key part of these efforts is to establish a strong, yet informal, relationship with the police officer assigned to the downtown. In Roanoke, for example, there is a policeman assigned to work with the Downtown Roanoke, Inc., from the police department's downtown district. There are also specific patrols for the district. The policeman usually stops by the Downtown Roanoke, Inc., office every day to discuss issues that may need attention.

Other BIDs also have very formal and extensive relationships with the police. One of these BIDs works closely with the city district-based policing program. There are four sector committees in the city, and the BID facilitates and coordinates these groups. This BID's executive believes that the program works because both the district commander and the BID president attend the district meetings to signal that safe and clean is a priority. These committees provide access and work to solve problems for community groups and individual citizens. In addition to the district meetings, there is an overall safe and clean committee that involves the sector leaders, the head of the downtown association board, the district commander, and the BID executive.

The ambassadors also make up an important component of many BIDs' safety programs. One BID executive commented that the ambassadors enhance the city's public safety work, because of their visibility. They are field employees that provide information, directions, escorts, and other hospitality services to the general public. He also believes that the ambassadors serve as extra eyes and ears for the police department. For example, the police assigned to the downtown area in Portland, Maine, spend time working with the ambassadors. The police e-mail the ambassadors if they think that they may have seen something. The police also alert the ambassadors to watch out for some types of crime that may occur in the area. The point of contact is the district outreach officer, who is assigned to work with the clean and safe staff. The Portland BID works closely with the head of the patrol division of the police department, and the BID executive and staff meet quarterly with him. This group reviews statistics and issues that need attention concerning safety. Finally, this BID participates in a community policing program.

Another BID provides an example of another dimension for collaborating between the BID and the police. In this case, the BID provides a connection with private security agencies working in the downtown area. The BID executive explained that the BID provides behind-the-scenes security services through communications networks with downtown properties and their security representatives. This network addresses crime and emergency response issues. The BID's operations director is the key person that works with this police downtown operations unit and is in close contact with key public safety officials in the city.

BIDs may also support public safety efforts during specific crises. For example, one BID executive related an incident that happened a few weeks earlier when three armed robberies occurred in the downtown area. The BID met with the police and circulated fliers and e-mails. This BID executive also visited the police commander, which led to a commitment by the BID and city to work more closely together. The BID then held a roundtable with the police and local business and property owners, and this event was to be followed by more specialized seminars that the BID will coordinate. Finally, some BIDs have specific contract relationships with city public safety departments. Several of these take the form of paying for enhanced police activity in the downtown areas. For example, the Downtown Fort Worth BID transfers $31,000 to the police budget for security enhancement that provides supplies for a mounted police program.

Sidewalk and street maintenance constitute another major part of most BIDs' work programs. This often involves municipal public works and parks departments. The street-level ambassadors program described above forms an important element of these programs. The extent of BID involvement and working relationships between the BID and city public works agencies varies. One BID executive reported that his BID had full authority to maintain pedestrian right-of-way in downtown, with most of the maintenance work done by the BID staff. This does not involve much interaction with city staff, because the roles and processes have been worked out over time. Another BID, however, reported that it has very close and ongoing relationships with the city, including monthly meetings with the director of public works. The example of perhaps the most intense working relationship is the BID whose director characterized the relationship as one where the BID and the city are "joined at the hip" with the city government. The city decided to outsource the street maintenance functions to the BID, and the contract constitutes nearly a third of the BID's budget. It involves trash removal, handicap access facilities, and landscaping. The BID maintenance director is a former city employee who has an excellent working relationship with the city public works agency. The city public works director is in contact with this BID supervisor almost daily. The city parks agency provides warehouse space for BID equipment and supplies. This integration of BID and city services also includes the city providing the trucks that the BID uses for its street maintenance programs.

In addition to safe and clean programs, many BIDs take on streetscaping activities. In some cases, the BIDs act in place of, with the authority of, or in consort with a city's governing of public spaces. In the Fort Worth BID, there is a design review board for the downtown that establishes design standards and reviews design proposals for downtown projects—big and small. The Golden Triangle BID in Washington, D.C., works closely with the local department of transportation, which has responsibility for public space in the downtown district. The BID has to work with this department of transportation for street sign and sidewalk changes. A third BID has a contract with the city that provides for a sharing of responsibilities for streetscape maintenance.

Planning and Economic Development

Nine of the 12 BIDs in the survey reported that they devote substantial time and resources working with top city leaders and departments in planning and economic development efforts. Only two of the BIDs' executives did not see themselves heavily invested in these areas. One of these BIDs without a strong economic development initiative believes that the city already has a strong economic development unit and there is not a need for a BID role. This BID executive said that when he receives inquiries about potential business relocation to the downtown, he refers them to the city economic development staff. The second BID without an economic development program emphasis indicated that it may reconsider its strategy. Up until now it has primarily been a safe and clean BID. However, the executive director believes that he may have to begin working more closely with local planning agencies, because several significant new publicly funded infrastructure projects are being considered for the downtown area.

Ten of the BIDs have significant ongoing relationships with the city planning and economic development staffs. In one of these cities, the key person for the city's downtown economic development efforts is the BID's director of economic development. Initially, the city paid half of a BID staff person's salary to play an economic development role for the downtown (attract new business and retain existing ones). Eventually, the BID took over the entire role and now pays the entire salary for the BID economic development director. When the city gets an inquiry or news of a possible new business or the possible exit of an existing one, it refers the case to the BID staff person to handle.

Three of the BID executives mentioned that they themselves or their senior economic development staff persons are formally integrated into city economic development activities. This will include regularly scheduled meetings between BID and city top staff. In one city, the BID director meets regularly with the head of the city economic development staff and also schedules as-needed meetings with the city manager and the city manager's office staff. In another city, the BID's chair of the board sits on the board of the local government development corporation.

In addition to setting up formal relationships between individuals from city and BID organizations, some BIDs and cities also establish standing committees. In Cincinnati, for example, the city and BID have set up several committees. One is an office committee that includes a BID staff person and someone from the city business development staff. This committee works to retain and recruit businesses. A second group, the small business committee, is supported by downtown Cincinnati staff and staff from the city's Department of Community Development. This committee is charged with involving more women and minorities in downtown business development. In Raleigh, the Downtown Action Group looks at new business development opportunities as well as longer-term economic development planning opportunities and issues. It includes city department heads, the city manager, and the downtown Raleigh executive director. It meets biweekly and is staffed and managed by the city's Urban Design Center. There is also a staff-level economic development team.

Perhaps the most important roles that a BID can play in its work with a city on economic development efforts are those of facilitator and go-between. One executive director characterized much of his day as sitting down with developers and acting as a go-between for the developer and the city. For example, one of the executives recounted how his BID set up a meeting concerning an architectural firm that was thinking about moving out of the city. This meeting was arranged and facilitated by the BID executive and included the architectural firm representative, the district police commander, and the city economic development director.

Finally, BIDs often take on responsibility for marketing programs. One BID has just completed a branding program and related public relations efforts to create specific identities for downtown that will attract new business and visitors. Another BID has a marketing committee that works closely with the city public affairs director. BIDs offer special events, such as street fairs and musical events, and these activities necessarily involve city agencies involved in permits and parking. In these areas, however, BIDs do not have as tightly linked working relationships with city governments as they do for either the safe and clean or the planning and economic development efforts.

Future Direction of BID–City Government Relationships

The BID executives in the survey were asked to identify ways the BID–city government relationships might develop in the future. Four BID executives felt that the relationships would not change that much. Three from this group emphasized that the relationships over the past few years had already changed from an adversary/advocacy type to more of a cooperative one. For example, one BID executive felt that the BID–city relationship had made a dramatic change already, going from a poor relationship with the city to a great one. The BID has also developed a good deal of legitimacy resulting from developing its operational capacity, and he did not see this cooperative relationship changing.

Several of the other BIDs did foresee some changes, even in instances where the working relationships are already strong. Most involved expanding the range of programs and initiatives that involved BIDs taking over provision of services traditionally carried out by city government. One BID's growing responsibilities for managing a city-owned convention center is an example of taking on a role now performed by the city. Another BID executive, whose relationship with the city has not been particularly strong, felt that the city would like it if the BID took on some additional city functions as its city budget realities become more pronounced. One factor that could slow this expansion of BID roles is the unions. They are strong in the city and have raised concerns in the past about the BID taking over union work.

Another executive director indicated that her board was rethinking the BID's relationship with the city government and was ready to forge a closer, more cooperative approach to solving common issues. Up to now it has primarily been focused on being a business-based clean and safe organization with a small staff. She felt that if the BID wants to get more involved in other areas and become more of a "full service" BID, it would have to be more involved with the city. Two of the BID executives believe that their organizations will likely work more closely with the city in downtown and regional planning. This will likely include financial cosponsorship, staff support, and shared advocacy for strategic planning processes. Finally, one BID is considering making more use of its existing bonding authority to undertake larger projects. Again, this will necessarily require a substantially expanded degree of cooperation with the city planning, finance, public works, and transportation agencies.

Summary

The results of this survey indicate that there is a range of approaches that BIDs and city governments use to work together:

1. Overall, BID–city government relationships form a continuum from adversarial to cooperative, and some BIDs' approaches vary for different issues and programs. Two of the BID executives thought that their organizations tended to be more confrontational than collaborative. Other BIDs reported that, at one time, their relationship was combative but has since become more cooperative. Ten of the 12 BIDs characterized their overall working relationship as currently cooperative.

2. BIDs use at least three different methods in working with city agencies. Again, some BIDs employ combinations of these modes. BIDs may use a variety of forms, depending on the issue and program.

   a. In the first approach, the city contracts with BIDs to provide specific services. The relationship is treated as a contract. Some BIDs also contract with city agencies for services for the downtown.

   b. In the second approach, the BIDs and city agencies coordinate their services but generally work in separate spheres—coordinated yet separate collaboration. The BIDs and cities usually develop ongoing processes for communicating with each other, but both go about doing their own work substantially independent of the other.

   c. A third approach is more integrated and seamless. In these situations, BIDs may share staff or the BID uses city equipment for street cleaning.

3. Staff-to-staff relationships become key vehicles for maintaining effective working processes between city and BID organizations. In several cases, BIDs hire former city personnel to create these stable cooperative relationships. In addition, the extent of professionalization of city personnel can affect the extent of staff collaboration between BIDs and the city agencies. In much the same way, the stability of staff in both the BID and city agencies increases the likelihood of closely integrated or at least flexible working processes.

4. For the most part, BIDs do not face contentious accountability processes. They must participate in hearings and periodic reviews of plans and processes, but such hearings and reviews are more often seen as opportunities to promote communication and advance the BID's priorities than as serious accountability activities.

5. BIDs use various forms of processes to work with city counterparts. These may range from case-by-case contacts with relevant city agencies to more extensive formal working relationships. The formal processes most often involve special committees charged with addressing safety, street maintenance, and planning and economic development activities. The committee structure may

include formal agenda-setting processes, data collection, report production, and regularly scheduled meetings supported by either BID or city agency staff, or both.

6. A special advantage that BIDs contribute to municipal governance is by acting as facilitators for problem solving between the city and downtown businesses.

Issues for Further Exploration

This survey of the 12 BIDs points to the need for further examination of BID–local government working arrangements. Three issues captured the attention of the author: (1) the significance of size for the kinds of BID–city relationships that develop, (2) the extent that a limited number of forms of interaction between BIDs and cities have become institutionalized, and (3) the implications for local governance of the increased intertwining of BID–city government roles.

BID Size and BID–City Government Relationships

One theme that emerged concerned the significance of scale of both the metropolitan area and the BID organization. To what extent do BIDs develop certain approaches for working with municipalities because of size? For example, the smaller BIDs in the survey more than the larger BIDs relied on either highly integrated seamless strategies or a contract-for-service model for working with local governments. The first approach, characterized by one BID executive as "joined at the hip" with the city, may allow smaller BIDs with limited resources to take advantage of the capabilities of local departments of public works and police departments. The one BID that uses the resources of the department of public works—its trucks, garages, and purchasing services—illustrates this approach of close alignment with the city. At the same time, the BIDs from larger metropolitan areas seemed more likely to develop a separate yet cooperative form of relationship model.

These tentative observations suggest several questions for further research concerning scale of the metropolitan area and the BID and the kinds of working relationships that the BIDs develop with the city. As BIDs get larger, do they minimize their role as a business lobby at city hall and move to a more integrated and cooperative model? Do they substantially expand their set of programs, and if so, how does this expansion affect the BID–city relationship? If, in fact, cities are looking to BIDs to take over existing roles that the cities historically have played, the issue of size may be an important element of the change in BID–city relationships. All this seems to point to some BIDs, particularly those in larger downtown areas, taking on the character of a downtown city government.

Institutionalizing BID–City Government Relationships

Clearly, the kinds of relationships BIDs and local governments create are developing and changing. BIDs are now established players in local governance, and as they develop, their relationships with municipalities will also change. At the same time, however, the BIDs in the survey seem to be converging around a model that includes expanding service delivery and planning functions that necessarily require more direct, collaborative, and integrated BID–city government working arrangements. The survey discussed in this chapter appears to support this trend in the institutionalization of BID practices. Wolf (2006) found similar evidence of institutionalization of BID organization forms and practices in a study of the District of Columbia BIDs. In addition, the BID executives participating in the survey were aware of some of the similarities of practices that their BIDs shared with other BIDs. This also suggests that, in some areas, common approaches for working with city governments are occurring.

BID–City Government Relationships and Governance

Finally, practically all the BID executives recognized that their work to one degree or another was intertwined with local government, and hence they were part of the governance processes. These executives emphasized the importance of close and collaborative relationships with local public agencies. The traditional model of the BID as a business association lobbying the city for downtown business interests was consistently less of a priority role than being in active partnership with city agencies. This suggests that while BIDs to some degree still act and think like traditional downtown business associations, they will become even more active as participants in city governance. They have moved a long way from the picture of dues-paying voluntary membership organizations, which resemble local chambers of commerce or boards of trades. Some may find themselves increasingly providing services that could just as easily be provided by the local governments. While only a few could be characterized as "joined at the hip" to any part of the local governments, all 12 have already moved, or see themselves moving, to approaches that more closely resemble local government processes than traditional downtown business associations. As BIDs become more a part of local governance, the importance of understanding of how they work together will increase.

References

Briffault, R. 1999. A government for our time? Business improvement districts and urban governance. *Columbia Law Review* 99:365–477.

Houstoun, L. O. J. 2003. *BIDs: Business improvement districts.* 2nd ed. Washington, DC: The Urban Land Institute in cooperation with the International Downtown Association.

Mitchell, J. 2001. Business improvement districts and the "new" revitalization of downtown. *Economic Development Quarterly* 15:115–123.

Wolf, J. 2006. Urban governance and business improvement districts: The Washington, DC BIDs. *International Journal of Public Administration* 29:53–75.

Chapter 13

Business Improvement Districts in Pennsylvania: Implications for Democratic Metropolitan Governance*

Göktuğ Morçöl and Patricia A. Patrick

Contents

* An earlier version of this chapter was published in Morçöl and Patrick (2006).

Introduction

Business improvement districts (BIDs) have become increasingly popular in the last three decades. They have gained economic and political influence in metropolitan governance, as local governments increasingly relied on them for service delivery. BIDs are not merely tools of service delivery or public policy implementation, however; they are a form of self-governance by property (primarily commercial property) owners. As such, they are participants in public policymaking. This proactive nature of BIDs, combined with their increasing numbers and widening functions, poses challenges to the theory and practice of metropolitan governance.

Pennsylvania's BIDs, the focus of this chapter, are illustrative of these challenges. Pennsylvania is one of the earlier states that legally enabled the creation of BIDs. Pennsylvania also has a wide variation among its BIDs. They have been formed under multiple and evolved laws; thus, they exist in multiple legal forms. The variation of BIDs in the state also ranges from one of the wealthiest and functionally diverse in the nation (Center City District in Philadelphia, with annual revenue of $12.9 million in 2003) to the ones with $3,000 to $5,000 annual revenues (see Tables 13.1 and 13.2). Pennsylvania's BIDs are a good case to study to develop a general understanding of BIDs' roles in metropolitan governance because of their relatively long history and the variations among them.

In this chapter we discuss the results of our empirical research on Pennsylvania's BIDs and their theoretical implications. Multiple theoretical lenses and multiple levels of explanation are needed to understand the BID phenomenon. BIDs may be seen as a form of the privatization of the delivery of public services, or as a policy implementation tool of local governments.* We argue that BIDs are not simply service delivery mechanisms or public policy tools; they are active participants in the network governance processes in metropolitan areas.

Network governance theorists observe that in recent decades the functions of government have been transformed and governance networks emerged. In these networks, government is only one among many actors, and it has become interdependent with the other actors—private and nonprofit organizations (Kickert et al., 1997). Frederickson (1999) point out that because public policies are made and implemented more and more in networks or network constellations in metropolitan areas, the meaning of "public" has broadened, and the distinctions between public and private organizations have blurred. BIDs are among the primary examples of the blurred lines between the public and private; they are often called

---

* See the Justice and Goldsmith chapter in this volume for the BIDs as a policy implementation tool thesis. For the general conceptualization of policy implementation tools, see Salamon (2002).

Table 13.1 Pennsylvania BIDs in the study

BID name	Year started/ terminated (scheduled or actual)	Location	Type of organization	Programmatic priorities (by % of expenditures)	Annual assessments/ annual total revenue (2001–2003)	Sources of total revenues (type of organization)	Board member representation (type of organization)
Allentown Downtown Improvement District Authority	1986/2002	Allentown	Municipal authority	N/A	$450,000 before dissolution	N/A	N/A
Center City District	1990/2015	Philadelphia	Municipal authority	Streetscape 39% Public safety 21% Marketing 13% Planning 5% Administration 20% Neighborhoods 2%	$12.2 million/ $12.9 million	Unknown	Nonprofit 14% For profit 86%
Lancaster Downtown Investment District	1991/2006	Lancaster	Municipal authority	Streetscape 30% Public safety 23% Marketing 11% Administration 36%	$293,000/ $345,000	Public 6% For profit 94%	Public 8% Nonprofit 8% For profit 84%
South Street Headhouse District of Philadelphia	1993/2018	Philadelphia	Municipal authority	Streetscape 35% Public safety 2% Marketing 30% Planning 5% Administration 28%	$341,000/ $497,000	For profit 100%	For profit 78% Residents 22%
Frankford Special Services District	1995/2005	Philadelphia	Municipal authority	Streetscape 35% Public safety 60% Administration 5%	$80,000/ $202,000	For profit 100%	Nonprofit 8% For profit 84% Residents 8%

continued

Table 13.1 (continued) Pennsylvania BIDs in the study

BID name	Year started/ terminated (scheduled or actual)	Location	Type of organization	Programmatic priorities (by % of expenditures)	Annual assessments/ annual total revenue (2001–2003)	Sources of total revenues (type of organization)	Board member representation (type of organization)
Manayunk Special Services District	1997/2007	Philadelphia	Municipal authority	Streetscape 72% Marketing 23% Administration 5%	$150,000/ $150,000	For profit 100%	Nonprofit 14% For profit 86%
City Avenue Special Services District	1997/2022	Philadelphia and Lower Merion Township	Municipal authority	Streetscape 28% Public safety 31% Marketing 2% Administration 40%	$900,000/ $1,000,000	Public 11% For profit 89%	Public 18% Nonprofit 14% For profit 68%
University City District	1997/N/A	Philadelphia	Nonprofit charitable organization	Streetscape 24% Public safety 31% Marketing 7% Planning 17% Administration 14% Neighborhoods 7%	$0.0/ $5.5 million	Charitable contribution 100%	Public 8% Nonprofit 48% For profit 20% Residents 24%
Harrisburg Downtown Improvement District Authority	1999/2004	Harrisburg	Municipal authority	Streetscape 30% Public safety 23% Marketing 14% Planning 4% Administration 26%	$540,000/ $900,000 before dissolution	Public 40% For profit 60%	Public 9% For profit 91%
Harrisburg Downtown Improvement District, Inc.	2004/N/A	Harrisburg	NIDMA (nonprofit)	None	None	None	None

Source: Department of Community and Economic Development records, official documents of BIDs, websites of BIDs, and interviews with BID executive directors.

Note: N/A = not available; NIDMA = Neighborhood Improvement District Management Association.

Table 13.2 Other BIDs in Pennsylvania

BID name	Year started/ terminated (scheduled or actual)	Location	Type of organization	Annual revenue (2001–2003)
Downtown McKeesport Business District Authority	1980/2030	McKeesport	Municipal authority	$5,000
Downtown Monaca Business District Authority	1980/2030	Monaca	Municipal authority	None
West View Borough Business Improvement and Administrative Services Authority	1980/2030 (inactive)	Pittsburgh	Municipal authority	None
Downtown Bradford Business District Authority	1981/2031 (inactive)	Bradford	Municipal authority	None
Clarks Summit Municipal Authority	1982/2032 (inactive)	Clarks Summit	Municipal authority	None
Downtown Clearfield Business District Authority	1982/2032	Clearfield	Municipal authority	None
Mount Pleasant Business District Authority	1983/2033	Mount Pleasant	Municipal authority	$77,000
Beaver Falls Business District Authority	1984/2034	Beaver Falls	Municipal authority	None
Central Business District Authority	1984/2034 (inactive)	Lebanon	Municipal authority	None
City of Butler Renaissance Commission	1985/2035 (inactive)	Butler	Municipal authority	None
Media Business Authority	1985/2035	Media	Municipal authority	$159,000
Ebensburg Business District Authority	1986/2001	Ebensburg	Municipal authority	N/A
New Brighton Business District Authority	1986/2036	New Brighton	Municipal authority	$3,000
Beaver Business District Authority	1987/2037 (inactive)	Beaver	Municipal authority	None
Pottstown Downtown Improvement District Authority	1988/2038	Pottstown	Municipal authority	$54,000
North Fayette Transportation and Business Improvement District	1991/2041	Oakdale	Municipal authority	$703,000
Conshohocken Business Authority	1992/2042	Conshohocken	Municipal authority	$31,000

continued

Table 13.2 (continued)   Other BIDs in Pennsylvania

BID name	Year started/ terminated (scheduled or actual)	Location	Type of organization	Annual revenue (2001–2003)
Ardmore Business District Authority	1993/unknown	Ardmore	Municipal authority	Unknown
Hatboro Business District Improvement Authority	1993/2043 (inactive)	Hatboro	Municipal authority	None
South Abington Township Municipal Authority	1993/2032	Philadelphia	Municipal authority	None
Swarthmore Business District Authority	1993/2043	Swarthmore	Municipal authority	None
Germantown Special Services District of Philadelphia	1995/2025	Philadelphia	Municipal authority	$94,000
Reading Downtown Improvement District Authority	1995/2045	Reading	Municipal authority	$527,000
Pittsburgh Downtown Business Improvement District	1996/N/A	Pittsburgh	Nonprofit charity	$3.0 million
Old City Special Services District of Philadelphia	1997/2022	Philadelphia	Municipal authority	$593,000
North Franklin Township Recreation and Business Improvement District	1998/2048	North Franklin	Municipal authority	$329,000
West Chester Business Improvement District Authority	1998/2048	West Chester	Municipal authority	$218,000
Oakland Business Improvement District	1999/N/A	Pittsburgh	Nonprofit charity	$1.2 million
Washington Business District Authority	1999/2016	Washington	Municipal authority	$110,000
Downtown State College Improvement District	2002/N/A	State College	Nonprofit charity	$453,000
James Street Improvement District	2003/N/A	Lancaster	Nonprofit charity	$1.0 million

Source: Department of Community and Economic Development records, official documents of BIDs, and BID websites.
Note: N/A = not available.

"quasi-governments" (Ross and Levine, 2001), "parallel states" (Mallett, 1993), and "private governments" (Lavery, 1995).

As Morçöl and Zimmermann (Chapter 2 in this volume) point out, this blurring of the line is in fact not new; its roots are in the practices of public governance by private actors in cities in the colonial and revolutionary eras in American history. In his historical analysis of the economy and politics in Philadelphia since the colonial times, Warner (1987) shows that a "privatist" worldview constituted the basis for the proactive involvement of local business leaders in running the city government and delivering public services. Morçöl and Zimmermann argue that the deep roots of privatism have continued to this day and become the enabling ideology for BIDs (i.e., the worldview that socially justified their creation). They also point out that it was not only this enabling ideology, but also the structural changes in metro areas in the 20th century—particularly the economic decline of downtowns, which began in the 1950s, and the fiscal crises of cities, which began in the 1970s—that created the conditions for the emergence of BIDs.

Morçöl and Zimmermann's observations are pertinent to the BIDs in Pennsylvania in particular. To demonstrate this, we trace the evolution of the laws that are pertinent to BIDs in Pennsylvania and discuss the implications of the creation and operations of BIDs for metropolitan governance in the following sections. We focus particularly on the economic and political processes in the creation and continuation or dissolution of BIDs, the proliferation of their functions and powers, and their revenue sources, governance processes, and accountabilities to local governments and general publics. We discuss the implications of our findings for metropolitan governance in the concluding section.

Methods

Ours was part of a larger, nationwide, empirical study on BIDs.* In the nationwide study, we aimed to answer a set of standardized questions about BIDs, which we developed from our readings of the literatures on metropolitan governance and BIDs.† These questions were about the evolution of BID laws; the economic and political processes encountered in the creation of the BIDs, their operation, and the dissolution of the BIDs; the proliferation of the BIDs' functions and powers; the revenue sources and governance processes of the BIDs; and the accountability of BIDs in democratic governance.

We used multiple sources of information to answer the questions. These included BID website documents, public relations documents, and local newspaper articles

---

* For the other research settings, see the Meek and Hubler chapter in this volume, Morçöl and Zimmermann's chapter (Chapter 15 in this volume), and Wolf (2006).

† A full list of the research questions can be found in Morçöl and Patrick (2006). The research design can be obtained from the first author of this chapter.

to gain contextual information; legal documents, such as state laws and BID bylaws, to understand the legal framework and to track the evolution of BIDs in the state; BID financial statements and audit reports to understand their financial strengths and organizational sizes; and interviews with BID directors, board members, local government representatives, state lawmakers, and economic development experts to gain insights about their actual operations and relations with governments. It was necessary to gather information from multiple sources, particularly because the BID phenomenon has multiple aspects and its implications for governance are complex. We attempted to understand the phenomenon from multiple angles and verify our understanding with information from multiple sources.

Some of our interviewees requested confidentiality; therefore, we do not list their names in this chapter. We report summaries of the information we gathered from the interviews, as well as from the legal and other official documents.

The BIDs that existed in Pennsylvania during the period we conducted our empirical study (2003–2004), or those that had existed before and terminated at the time of the writing of this chapter, are listed in Tables 13.1 and 13.2. In our study, we focused particularly on the BIDs listed in Table 13.1. Our geographic focus was the city of Philadelphia, which is one of the cities with the largest numbers of BIDs in the nation. We also included a sample of BIDs in Central Pennsylvania, because of their geographic proximity to us. We also interviewed representatives of the Allentown Downtown Improvement District Authority, because of its unique status (it was one of the earliest functioning BIDs in the state and one of the first that was terminated).

The definitions of BIDs and the names used for them vary from one state to another (see the other chapters in this volume; also see Briffault, 1999; Pack, 1992). In Pennsylvania BIDs have a relatively long and complex history, as we discuss later in the chapter. The complexity and evolution of their legal structures make it somewhat difficult to identify and classify the BIDs in Pennsylvania. We used multiple legal and theoretical criteria in determining which entities to include in Tables 13.1 and 13.2. The BIDs listed in Table 13.1 are quite well known in the state; the ones in Philadelphia are listed at the city's website, and some of them are mentioned in earlier studies (see, for example, Houstoun, 2003).

We obtained the information about the BIDs that are classified as municipal authorities in Table 13.2 from the records of the Department of Community and Economic Development (DCED). These organizations were classified as BIDs in the records of the DCED and their articles of incorporation and audit reports.

We also included in our study a group of organizations that are not officially recognized as business improvement districts. These are the University City District in Table 13.1 and the Pittsburgh Downtown Business Improvement District, Oakland Business Improvement District, Downtown State College Improvement District, and James Street Improvement District in Table 13.2. These are officially classified as charitable nonprofits; as such, they may not be considered "real BIDs," because they are technically not self-assessment districts. We included them in our tables and focused particularly on one of them (the University City District) in our study, because it functioned like other BIDs, as we discuss later in the chapter.

We discuss the different legal statuses of BIDs in the state and their implications in the next section. Our goal was to study various types of BIDs to be able to draw theoretically meaningful conclusions. Philadelphia had the most varied types. We made special efforts to include in our study BIDs operating in different environments in the city (downtown, university campus areas, and minority neighborhoods).

Evolution of the BID Laws in Pennsylvania

The laws that enable the creation of BIDs and govern their operations in Pennsylvania have a long history and are quite complex. This complexity is partly a result of the multiple successive state BID laws. None of these laws have been repealed in their entirety; subsequent laws replaced parts of previous ones. Parts of the successive laws are redundant; these redundancies create confusion and complexity in the legal classifications and day-to-day operations of BIDs. In this section we trace the evolution of Pennsylvania's BID laws and propose a classification of BIDs, based on our interpretation of this evolution.

The first law directly pertaining to BIDs was the Business Improvement Districts Law of 1967. The 1967 act enabled the establishment of BIDs as subunits of local governments and described the procedures for establishing BIDs, which has been the model for the procedures defined in the subsequent laws. The 1967 act applied to Pennsylvania's townships, boroughs, and cities of the second and third class, but not cities of the first class (the city of Philadelphia is Pennsylvania's only first-class city). The Business Improvement Districts Act of 1996, which amended the 1967 act, included Philadelphia as well.

The 1967 act grants the right to the governing bodies of municipalities to designate certain commercial zones in their jurisdictions for special business improvements. Under the 1967 act, these special BIDs are defined as subunits of local jurisdictions. Under the act, the governing authority of the township, borough, or city is authorized to collect extra assessments from commercial properties in the district and provide special services to them. The 1967 act does not prohibit the administration of these special services by an entity separate from the governing body of the municipality, but it does not specifically mention such a possibility either. This ambiguity was resolved later, in 1980, as we discuss below.

Under the 1967 act, to establish a BID, the initiators have to make a plan for improvements and determine a method of assessment. The local government will hold a public hearing to solicit the approval of the plan and the assessment method. The BID has to receive a two-thirds vote among the property owners to be accepted. If it is approved by two-thirds of the property owners, a BID may be created by an ordinance of the governing body of the municipality.

The 1967 act did not specifically enable the creation of BIDs as entities separate from municipalities. The 1980 amendments to the Municipal Authorities Act of 1945 (also known as the Business District Authority Act of 1980) did enable the establishment of BIDs as separate entities. The 1980 act enabled all municipalities in Pennsylvania to establish BIDs as municipal authorities. It states that authorities can be created to "provide business improvements and business administrative services." The 1980 amendments also allow municipalities to create "joint authorities," which would span the territory of two or more municipalities. A large majority of Pennsylvania's BIDs were municipal authorities at the time of the writing of this chapter.

The Municipal Authorities Act of 1945 provides the general framework for the BIDs created under the 1980 amendments. After the Great Depression, Pennsylvania passed the Municipal Authorities Act of 1935 to allow local governments to form separate entities for the purpose of borrowing money outside the constitutional debt limits by issuing revenue bonds. These authorities were part of the state's fiscal recovery plan to improve public works and facilities. They were granted tax-exempt statuses from sales and income taxes and were allowed to issue tax-exempt bonds. The 1935 act was repealed and replaced by the Municipal Authorities Act of 1945, which allowed more flexibility in the creation and operation of municipal authorities. The 1945 act is the current state enabling law that grants municipal authorities (including BIDs) a unique status, which is a blend of public, political, and corporate statuses.*

The establishment of the BIDs as separate entities under the 1980 amendments was a significant change from 1967. For the first time, BID governing bodies were granted autonomy from municipal governments. However, the 1980 amendments granted some power to municipal governments over BID governing bodies as well. Consequently, the 1980 amendments defined a somewhat ambiguous relationship between municipal governments and BID governing bodies.

The 1980 law grants municipal governments limited authority over BIDs, particularly in three areas. First, the creation of a BID must be approved by the governing body of the municipality. The governing body of the municipality has the authority not to approve the creation, even if there is a petition by a majority of property owners in a designated district. The municipality also has the authority to approve the boundaries and business plan of a BID. However, this power would probably not be exercised often, because it would be self-defeating to block the plans of a group of property owners who wish to make business improvements with their own money. Second, BID board members are appointed by the municipal government for five-year terms, and the government is free to appoint only those board members whose activities it likes. Third, the governing body has the authority to unilaterally take over a BID's projects. However, as in the approval of BID plans, this power is probably also not exercised often because it would also be self-defeating.

---

* For an extensive discussion of the history and current status of municipal authorities in Pennsylvania, see Governor's Center for Local Government Services (2002).

The powers of municipal governments over BIDs are further restricted by the general nature of municipal authorities as defined in the 1945 act. The general provisions of the 1945 act separate municipal authorities, including BIDs, from municipal governments. An authority is not considered the creature or agent of the municipality; it is an independent agent of the state: "a public corporation engaged in the administration of civil government" (Governor's Center for Local Government Services, 2002, p. 2). A municipal government cannot limit the powers of a municipal authority, because these powers are designated by law. These powers include the rights to acquire property, exercise eminent domain, borrow money, enter into contracts, make assessments, and appoint police officers (Governor's Center for Local Government Services, 2002). The powers granted to municipal authorities are governmental in nature. As municipal authorities, BIDs may exercise these powers as well.

It is in the logic of creating BIDs that they should be self-assessment districts. This logic is apparent in both the 1967 and 1980 laws. Under both laws, once a BID is established, each benefited property within its boundaries is charged with assessments. The payment of assessments is mandatory and liens can be placed on the properties of owners who refuse to pay. Table 13.1 shows that assessments are indeed the primary sources of revenue for most of the BIDs in Pennsylvania, with the exception of the University City District, which is a charitable nonprofit organization.

One of the important issues for all BIDs across the nation is whether residential properties within these primarily commercial districts should be assessed. Neither the 1967 act nor the 1980 amendments exempted residential property owners from assessments. The 1996 amendments to the 1967 act excluded residents from assessments for "benefit received from administrative services," but it still allowed the assessment of residents based on the benefits they received from the improvements in the district.

The 1996 act attempted to clarify the issues surrounding the assessment of residents, but it was not clear enough. In our interviews we learned that by the late 1990s, BID leaders had become increasingly concerned about the problems created by the "two acts" (the 1996 amendments to the 1967 act and the 1980 amendments to the 1945 act). Under both acts, residents had to be assessed at the same rate as businesses, while not receiving services at the same rates. The representation of residential property owners on the boards of BIDs was an area of concern as well (see our further discussions on this issue in the governance section below). Another problem was that BIDs were not allowed to deliver services beyond their jurisdictions; they could not contract with other entities to deliver sidewalk-cleaning services, for example.*

The Community and Economic Improvement Act of 1998 and the Neighborhood Improvement District Act of 2000 were adopted to address problems such as

---

* Sources of the information in this paragraph are our interview with Jeri Stumpf, who was the executive director of the Urban Affairs Committee of the Pennsylvania House of Representatives during the 1990s and played a major role in drafting the 1998 and 2000 acts, and the following documents: Stumpf (1996, 1998, 2001).

the inequities in residential property assessments, the delivery of services beyond districts, and contracting out. The 1998 act redefined the statuses of BIDs for the "cities of the first class" in Pennsylvania (Philadelphia); the 2000 act expanded the coverage of the 1998 act to the rest of the state. The acts defined a category of neighborhood improvement districts (NIDs) and placed BIDs (improvement districts established in commercial areas for properties used in the business of for-profit activities) in this category. The acts allowed other types of NIDs to be created for other areas—residential, industrial, institutional (i.e., areas populated by nonprofit organizations, such as colleges, universities, schools, museums, theaters, churches, and others), and mixed-use areas. These acts granted the authority to residents to create separate NIDs in residential areas and specific power to BIDs to exempt residential property owners from assessments entirely. The acts also allowed NIDs to deliver services beyond their districts and contract out services. The two main purposes of the 1998 and 2000 acts were to solve some of the ambiguities in the earlier acts and to give BID boards more flexibility.

Under the 1998 and 2000 acts, all the various types of NIDs are to be governed by neighborhood improvement district management associations (NIDMAs), and these are to be incorporated either as municipal authorities (under the 1945 act) or as nonprofit corporations (alternatively, an existing nonprofit development corporation may be designated as the governing body). In either case, the NIDMA boards should be appointed (either according to the provisions of the 1945 act, if an NID is a municipal authority, or according to the pertinent state laws governing nonprofit organizations). The laws also require that the sponsoring municipal government be represented on the NID board by at least one member. All the assessed property owners must also be represented on the board (institutional members may appoint a designee to represent them on the board). Thus, the 1998 and 2000 acts did not replace the status of the BIDs created by the 1980 amendments, but they did add another type of status to it (the nonprofit corporation).

The 1998 and 2000 laws also defined the functions and powers of NIDMA boards more broadly than the 1967 and 1980 laws had done before. Apparently the intent was to give them as much power as they may need or desire. The long list of powers granted include planning and conducting feasibility studies, making capital improvements, owning property, contracting with businesses for the provision of services, advertising, and providing maintenance and security services. We discuss the functions and powers of BIDs in a separate section below.

At the time of the writing of this chapter, all of the laws pertaining to BIDs (the 1967/1996, 1980, and 1998 and 2000 acts) were in effect. Therefore, BIDs could be created in different forms. We identified four possible types of BIDs under the laws in effect in Pennsylvania: BIDs as subunits of local governments (under the 1967 act), BIDs as municipal authorities (under the 1980 amendments), BIDs as nonprofit NIDMAs (under the 1998 and 2000 acts), and BIDs as nonprofit charitable organizations. Although there were no such examples at the time of the writing of this chapter, BIDs may still be created as subunits of municipal governments under the 1967 law. These areas would be governed directly by local governments. We discussed the characteristics of BIDs under the 1980 amendments and the 1998 and 2000 acts earlier in the chapter.

Because there were not many examples of NIDs in Pennsylvania at the time of the writing of this chapter, it is not possible to elaborate in much detail on this type. There was only one NID filing: in 2004, the Harrisburg Downtown District Authority dissolved itself as a municipal authority BID and reincorporated as a nonprofit NIDMA. Our preliminary investigation about this new entity did not yield sufficient information to draw any theoretically meaningful conclusions.

However, it is possible to discuss potential legal implications of the 1998 and 2000 acts. The nonprofit NIDMA status created by these laws is different from the charitable nonprofit organization status of some of the existing BIDs in Pennsylvania (e.g., the University City District). NIDMAs have the power to impose mandatory assessments in their districts, whereas charitable nonprofit organizations do not. The charitable nonprofit BIDs we listed in Tables 13.1 and 13.2 were created by the universities in their respective districts. Although charitable nonprofit organizations technically are not BIDs, they were established for the same reasons as other BIDs (they all share a mission of safety and cleanliness of business areas and neighborhoods), and they operate quite the same way as other BIDs, with the exception of the way their boards are appointed, as we discuss later in the chapter.

The 1998 and 2000 acts give the charitable nonprofit BIDs the option to reincorporate as NIDMAs with the authority to impose mandatory assessments. Although the mandatory assessment authority may be attractive—because it would provide these organizations with a more reliable revenue base than voluntary charitable contributions—the fact that none of these BIDs had switched to the new NIDMA status at the time of the writing of this chapter indicates that their leaders are not enthusiastic about the status change. This lack of enthusiasm is understandable. Large percentages of the revenues of these BIDs come from nonprofit and public organizations, which are tax-exempt. If the BIDs switch to the NIDMA status, they cannot levy taxes on their nonprofit contributors (e.g., universities), which would not serve the purpose of securing reliable or larger amounts of revenues. The mandatory taxation of the private property owners in the districts may not generate significantly larger amounts of revenue either, because, for example, most of the private businesses in the University City District are small (restaurants and small shops). The mandatory taxation may also run the risk of alienating the owners of small properties. It is conceivable that these BIDs will maintain their statuses for a foreseeable future, and thus "charitable nonprofit BIDs" will remain a theoretically valid category for future studies.

Creation of BIDs

The stories of how BIDs were established are important, because these stories help us understand the motivations to create them and provide insights into their operations. Part of the stories can be found in the state enabling laws and local ordinances that actually create them. Also important for our purposes in this chapter are the stories of what actually happened: Who were the leaders? What were the economic and political conditions that enabled, or led to, the creation? To answer these questions, we interpreted the relevant state laws and summarized the stories our interviewees told us.

The legal procedures for establishing and dissolving or renewing BIDs in Pennsylvania are similar to the ones in other states. A state enabling law sets the general parameters. Although the enabling laws in Pennsylvania evolved, the basic procedures of creating a BID have not changed. Local property owners or government leaders may initiate the process. A business improvement plan and an assessment method are presented to the property owners in the designated district for their approval. Public hearings are held to allow property owners to raise their objections. If a certain percentage of property owners do not register their objections in writing, the local government may officially establish the BID; then it appoints the members of its board with an ordinance.* The BID board files its articles of incorporation with the secretary of the state. BIDs are created for limited terms. At the end of its term, the local government may decide to dissolve a BID on its own, or per the request for dissolution by a majority of property owners.†

In Pennsylvania, as in most other states, concerns about increased crime and economic decline lead to the creation of BIDs.‡ The officials of the City Avenue BID cite crime, deteriorating real estate values, and poor public perception as the primary impetuses for the creation of the BID. The University City area, which includes the University of Pennsylvania and Drexel University, was having a crime

---

* In Pennsylvania, the required percentages of property owners to block the establishment of a BID changed over time. The 1967 act stated that to block the establishments of a BID, either more than 50 percent of the persons representing the ownership in the district or owners whose property valuation was assessed for 51 percent or more of the total property valuation in the district had to object. In the 1980 amendments, the required percentage was reduced to 33 percent (at least owners whose property valuation was assessed for 33 percent of the total property valuation in the district). In the 1998 act, it was raised back to the 1967 level (51 percent). In the 2000 act it was reduced to 40 percent.

† The laws in Pennsylvania did not set particular term limits for BIDs. The recent trend seems to be to increase their terms. First BIDs were created for five-year terms; many of them have been extended for longer terms.

‡ See the other chapters in this volume for a comparison of the reasons BIDs are created within other states. Among the states discussed in this volume, Georgia is somewhat different. Georgia's suburban community improvement districts are the products of excessive economic growth, not decline, particularly in suburban shopping areas (see Morçöl and Zimmermann, Chapter 15). Pennsylvania's BIDs seem to represent the nationwide pattern.

problem that was driving away students seeking on-campus housing before the BID was created. Lancaster's business leaders became concerned that the downtown area had a poor public image due to crime. They began to perceive that people feared coming to the downtown area to shop and do business. They made a concerted effort to improve the public image of the downtown business district; the creation of the BID was a product of these efforts. The Frankford neighborhood of Philadelphia was also experiencing a rise in crime, but economic decline was a bigger concern (about 45 percent of businesses had moved away or shut down in a couple of decades) when the BID was created there.

Harrisburg was also experiencing economic decline in its downtown area. Manayunk neighborhood in Philadelphia had never had any crime problems, but the business leaders there wanted to improve the level of cleanliness and economic development in its neighborhoods. Officials from the South Street area in Philadelphia started their BID due to the declining availability of local government and community funds.

All of Pennsylvania's BIDs were established after 1985, despite the fact that the problems of crime and economic decline existed long before the 1980s. The structural changes in urban areas that led to the intensification of these problems began in the 1950s, and cities like Philadelphia began feeling fiscal strains as early as in the 1970s.* Also, as we mentioned earlier, the BID enabling laws existed in Pennsylvania as early as 1967. The time lag between the emergence of these problems and the creation of the first BIDs in Pennsylvania indicates that BIDs are not automatic responses to economic or social problems. It takes the proactive leadership of local business or government leaders and an arduous organizational process to create a BID. Leaders use their informal networks of relationships and organize the property owners in a district, or at least obtain their tacit approval, toward the creation of a BID.

Our interviewees told us that it took them between several months to three years to complete this organizational process. In general, both local government leaders and local business owners collaborated in the creation of Pennsylvania's BIDs, but in some cases one or the other took the initiative. It was government leaders who took the initiative to create the City Avenue BID. It was the opposite for the Manayunk BID, which was initiated by business leaders. Large business owners, real estate developers, or economic development corporations led the formation of the Lancaster, Harrisburg, and Allentown BIDs, but the mayors were actively involved and very supportive. Business leaders initiated the Frankford and South Street BIDs,

---

* See, for example, Mallett (1993, p. 385), who discusses structural changes such as suburbanization and the draining of urban cores of their populations, and thus their tax bases, that took place in the metropolitan areas in the United States in the 20th century. See also Warner (1987, pp. 178–190), who illustrates this process in his case study of Philadelphia. Philadelphia began losing its resident population in the late 19th and early 20th centuries, which was followed by large corporations and other businesses moving their offices to suburbia after World War II.

but the city government was also involved on a limited basis. The University City BID is unique in that the university leaders in the district initiated the BID.* The types of business leaders involved in initiating BIDs varied as much as the types of BIDs. For example, in Lancaster, Manayunk, and Harrisburg, large businesses were more supportive and instrumental than small businesses. But this was not true for all BIDs. At the South Street BID, whose area consists of small business and restaurants, small business owners were very active during the creation process.

A potentially problematic area in the creation of BIDs is interjurisdictional conflicts. Most of Pennsylvania's BIDs are located within the limits of their municipalities, and therefore, they did not face this problem. There is one exception among the BIDs we studied: the City Avenue BID. City Avenue constitutes the geographic boundary between two municipalities—the city of Philadelphia and Lower Merion Township—and the BID spans these two local jurisdictions. In our interviews we learned that the BID was designed this way for the purpose of eradicating public perceptions that the jurisdictions were two separate and unique areas. We also learned that potential problems with forming a BID that spanned two jurisdictions were solved informally, particularly through the good relations between the city council person representing the district in Philadelphia and the township commissioners in Lower Merion. These good relations had their foundations in the cooperation between the two sides that began in the early 1980s in response to the rising crime problem on and around City Avenue. The two municipalities were compelled to collaborate when criminals crossed the line between the jurisdictions after committing their acts. These collaborations led to good relations, which in turn helped solve the difficulties in the creation of the BID in 1997.

Functions and Powers

The functions of Pennsylvania's BIDs, and consequently their power and influence in metropolitan areas, have expanded over time. The expansion of the BID functions can be traced in the successive 1967/1996 acts, 1980 amendments, and 1998 and 2000 acts. The 1967 act, as we mentioned above, defined BIDs as districts that would be managed by the governing bodies of municipalities and authorized the governing bodies to make special improvements in the district. These improvements could be related to sidewalks, retaining walls, street paving, street lighting, parking lots, parking garages, trees and shrubbery purchasing and planting, pedestrian sidewalks, sewers, water lines, and rest areas. The governing bodies could use their powers to remodel or demolish blighted buildings and similar or comparable

---

* The University City District was formed primarily by the three universities in the district (the University of Pennsylvania, Drexel University, and the University of the Sciences), which were joined and actively supported by Amtrak, public hospitals, and the United States Postal Service.

structures. In essence, the 1967 law did not grant any authority to the governing bodies of municipalities that they had not had before, but it authorized them to impose additional taxes on properties in BIDs for improvement purposes. This new authority was significant, because it constituted the basis of the authorities granted in 1980 to the BID boards, which were established as separate entities.

The 1980 amendments to the Municipal Authorities Act of 1945 granted BIDs the authority to make improvements in the same areas as the ones listed in the 1967 act and added to the list "administrative services" for the purposes of providing free or reduced-fee parking for customers, making transportation repayments, designing public relations programs, conducting group advertising, and providing district maintenance and security services.

The 1996 amendments combined the lists of services mentioned in the 1967 act and the 1980 amendments. The 1998 and 2000 acts went further. These two acts authorized NIDMAs to fulfill all the functions listed in the previous acts and authorized them to exercise additional powers, including the rights to prepare planning and feasibility studies for capital improvements, make capital improvements, conduct business retention and recruitment activities, and hire off-duty police officers or private security officers. NIDMAs are also authorized to appropriate and expend funds from the federal, state, and local governments and to contract with and provide services to clients outside their districts.

The gradual expansion of the BID functions and powers in Pennsylvania indicates that they have become important actors in metropolitan governance. This is not only because BIDs do more, but also because the kinds of functions they fulfill and powers they exercise have changed the nature of BIDs. Certainly, not all BIDs are equal in the extent to which they fulfill their legal functions and exercise their legal powers: the more established and wealthier ones do more and are more powerful. However, most BIDs provide some services and exercise some powers; larger BIDs, like the Center City District, exercise more powers.

The programmatic priorities of the BIDs listed in Table 13.1 show that most of the BIDs we studied focus on three key areas: streetscape and maintenance, public safety, and marketing.* BIDs spend approximately 30 percent of their budgets on streetscape and maintenance. These BIDs provide sidewalk cleaning,

---

* We collected this information about programmatic priorities from our interviews with BID executive directors and BIDs' financial statements. Note that the administrative expenses in Table 13.1 may be higher than actual numbers. Possible inaccuracies in our estimates are attributable to the classifications we made, which were not necessarily the same as the ones the BIDs used, and the fact that we did not have access to some of the financial information about the BIDs. Most of the BIDs we interviewed did not allocate payroll and related expenses to programmatic activities, although much of these payroll costs could probably have been allocated to the various programs, had the BIDs utilized a cost allocation system. Given that we did not have the information to make the appropriate allocations, we included total payroll expense and the related fringe benefits in administrative expenses, making the administrative expenses reflected in Table 13.1 higher than they likely are in actuality.

beautification, banners, lighting, signage, trash receptacles, and the like. They spend approximately 25 percent of their budgets on public safety. This includes wages paid to "ambassador" crews (unarmed public safety officers who report incidents to the police and who provide visitors and residents with assistance and directions) and other public safety personnel (off-duty police officers), as well as auxiliary expenses (the expense of providing offices to police officers who work in the district).

BIDs spend another 25 percent of their budgets on marketing and strategic planning. Most BIDs provide marketing services by producing brochures, newsletters, and advertising. BIDs also often arrange festivals and events. Some BIDs even recruit new businesses and help new business owners get settled in the area, and others provide transportation planning and management. A few BIDs started neighborhood initiatives and outreach programs to help low-income children and residents in their areas.

Among the functions and powers of the more established and wealthier BIDs, particularly significant are preparing strategic plans and creating and operating community courts. As we mentioned earlier, the 1998 and 2000 acts authorized BIDs to make strategic plans for their areas.* The authority to conduct strategic planning is significant, because it brings the status of BIDs closer to general-purpose governments. Land-use planning authority in the United States is granted to local governments. Although the planning authority granted to BIDs, particularly in the 1998 and 2000 acts, is not technically land-use planning, when it is done to facilitate "capital improvements," it inevitably affects land-use plans in their respective areas.†

Even more significant is the creation and operation of community courts. Only the Center City District (CCD) in Philadelphia "participates in the operation of" a community court.‡ The role of CCD in the creation and operation of the Philadelphia Community Court is more than mere participation, however. The Center City District Foundation (CCDF), a nonprofit charitable organization formed by the CCD to test and support the initiatives of the CCD, began planning the court in 1997, and the court began operating in 2002. The court's stated purpose is to reduce the number of petty and quality-of-life crimes by requiring offenders to pay for their crimes with community service instead of jail time. There

---

* Arguably, the planning authority was implicit in the 1967 and 1980 acts, because they mention preparation of plans for business improvements. The 1998 and 2000 acts are clearer on the issue. Whether or not clearly mentioned in laws, the planning authority has been inherent in development of BIDs across the United States (see, for example, Houstoun, 2003).

† See Chapter 2 in this volume for a discussion of the implications of the planning authority BIDs have been granted.

‡ The website of Center City District states that the court is operated in partnership with law enforcement and social service agencies. It also states that the court is primarily funded with public sector funds and funds that are raised by the Center City District (http://www.centercityphila.org/ccdprograms.html, accessed May 12, 2004). For other examples of community courts and a discussion of their significance, see Chapter 2 in this volume.

is no explicit authorization in the Pennsylvania laws for a BID to create or operate a community court, but it seems that CCD interpreted the authority in the 1980 amendments to "provide district security services" as their legal basis for the court. The expenses for the community court are listed under public safety expenses in the consolidated statements of the CCD, which includes the CCDF. An examination of these statements reveals that most, if not all, of the community court expenses are borne by the CCDF.*

With their explicit or implicit authorities to plan and operate community courts, BIDs have increasingly become like general-purpose governments. As we mentioned earlier, most of the BIDs in existence at the time of the writing of this chapter had been created as municipal authorities, which were, by definition, special-purpose governments. Special-purpose governments are limited not only in their geographic service areas, but also in their functions (Foster, 1997). Because of their limited foci, they are allowed some exemptions from the requirements for general-purpose governments, such as accountability to general publics and democratic representation in governance. Briffault (1999) argues that as BIDs take on more governmental functions (and more fundamentally governmental ones, like the delivery of justice) and become more like general-purpose governments, the legal procedures they use in the election or selection of their board members should come under scrutiny by the higher courts in the nation.

Revenues

By definition, BIDs are self-assessment districts. Therefore, the main source of their revenues, if not the sole source, should be mandatory assessments. Table 13.1 shows that assessments are indeed the main source of revenue for Pennsylvania's BIDs, but they have other sources of revenue as well. Assessments are 100 percent of some BID's total revenues (Manayunk) and 70 to 95 percent of others'. Most of the BIDs earned about 10 percent of their revenues through fees for service, and a few BIDs received 10 to 20 percent of their revenue through charitable contributions. The only exception in Table 13.1 is the University City District: all of its income was generated through charitable contributions. As mentioned earlier, this is because the University City does not have the right to impose mandatory assessments on property owners.

Other BIDs receive charitable contributions as well. Because nonprofit organizations and governments are exempt from taxes, they often make regular contributions to BIDs at rates they agree on. The figures in Table 13.1 show that public organizations (governments) pay less than 10 percent of BIDs' total revenues,

---

* See Financial Statements and Independent Auditors' Report, Center City District Foundation, 2002–2001; Financial Statements and Independent Auditors' Report, Center City District, 2002–2001.

with the exception of the Harrisburg BID, which is located in the state's capital. In Harrisburg, governments voluntarily contribute almost 40 percent of the BID's revenue.

We should note that although the total revenue figures in Table 13.1 are accurate, the sources of the revenue are only approximations, because the sources of some BID revenues are somewhat difficult to calculate. The table classifies revenue as public if the revenue was given to the BID by a public organization (this category primarily includes government grants, fees for service, and contributions made in lieu of assessments). It classifies the revenue as for profit if the revenue came from a business (this category primarily consists of assessments and fees for service). The table classifies the revenue as charitable contribution if the recipient organization is a charitable nonprofit organization.

The classifications above may seem straightforward, but in fact, it was, at times, difficult to allocate revenue to the various classifications due to the related-party transactions conducted by the BIDs. To ensure competitive bidding, Section 5614(e) of the 1945 act specifically prohibits municipal authorities from entering into contracts that potentially present conflicts of interest. Such contracts include, but are not limited to, agreements with related parties (board members, organizations owned by board members, affiliate organizations, etc.) that result in a liability for the municipal authority. Despite this prohibition, we noted that several of the BIDs routinely engaged in related-party transactions. These transactions were often for management or administrative services, the rental of office space, moving expenses, and more. Although these transactions were disclosed on the financial statements, because generally accepted accounting principles require that they be disclosed, these contractual arrangements with related parties made it difficult for us to determine how the related revenues (and expenditures) should be classified.

Other matters complicated our analyses of revenues and expenditures. BIDs are often affiliated with foundations or economic development corporations with which they share their offices and management teams. The Center City, Manayunk, and Frankford BIDs are examples. Many of these BIDs are barely distinguishable from their respective development corporations or foundations. These BIDs give and receive in-kind contributions and staff support from their respective affiliated organizations, and in some cases, the assessments collected by the BID and grants given to the BIDs by state government are moved directly into the bank accounts of the development corporations or foundations.

The assessment of residential properties has been an issue for Pennsylvania's BIDs. According to the 1967 act, BIDs would be established only in commercial zones. Although this suggests that the lawmakers intended that BIDs would be created on the basis of commercial properties, the law did not make any distinctions among different types of properties. As a result, residential properties were assessed under this law. The 1980 amendments, under which most of today's BIDs were established, did not exempt residential properties or clarify the issue of residential assessments. The 1996 amendments to the 1967 act attempted to bring some clarity, but they did not exempt residential property owners from assessments. They only stated that residents could not be imposed "administrative expenses."

Under the 1967/1996 and 1980 laws, BID boards developed different practices with respect to residential property owners. In our interviews we were told that the founders of many BIDs attempted to gerrymander their districts to exclude residents, but in most cases that was not geographically possible. Some BIDs assessed their residents, others did not, or they assessed residents at rates that were disproportionately lower than those for commercial properties. In our interviews, we found that BID leaders often developed practices to keep residential assessments lower than commercial ones and to provide special services to them.*

One of the reasons the 1998 and 2000 acts were passed was to resolve the issue of residential property assessment, as we mentioned earlier. By creating different types of neighborhood improvement districts (NIDs) for commercial, residential, and institutional properties, these acts aimed to separate residential and nontaxable properties from commercial ones. However, the acts recognized that there would still be residential properties within commercial NIDs and gave their governing bodies the option to exclude them from assessments altogether.

We learned in our interviews that collecting assessments was a challenge for some of Pennsylvania's BIDs, particularly those in lower-income neighborhoods. The collection of assessments is enforceable through property liens and other legal mechanisms. However, BIDs lack the power of coercion to collect assessments, and most BIDs seem to recognize that certain property owners simply do not have the ability to pay because of bad economic conditions. The Allentown BID went out of business when a group of large property owners moved out of its district and others were reluctant to pay their assessments because of the declines in their revenues. The Frankford BID writes off more than a quarter of its assessments to bad debt expense each year.

Pennsylvania's BIDs do not receive large amounts of grant money, but grants are available. Half the BIDs we interviewed did not have any grant money at all, but grants for the remaining BIDs constituted 5 to 25 percent of their revenues. Grants or tax abatements, which are included with government contributions and classified as "public" in the column summarizing sources of revenue in Table 13.1, are available from several state programs, including Home Town Streets, Keystone Improvement Zones, and the Elm Street Project. BIDs can also, at times, get grant money from private partners for economic development, capital improvements, and the like. To some extent, the utilization of grants is dependent upon the executive director's knowledge and ability to seek out and learn about grant opportunities (our interviews revealed disparate knowledge and utilization of grants).

---

* An issue that we could not clarify in our interviews is whether residents were assessed for administrative expenses (the 1996 law requires that they should be exempted from administrative expenses), because in practice it is very difficult to separate administrative expenses from others.

Governance

Some critics of BIDs point out that property owners within districts are not represented proportionately, or equitably, on their boards of directors. In many states, property owners elect board members using weighted voting schemes.* These schemes violate the one person–one vote principle: when votes are weighted according to the values of properties, owners of large properties are given more power in governance (Briffault, 1999). This violation of the principle is not an issue in Pennsylvania, because under the 1980 amendments to the 1945 Municipal Authorities Act, all BID board members are appointed by the local governments that create BIDs. Under the 1998 and 2000 acts, the governing bodies of neighborhood improvement districts (NIDMAs) may be created as municipal authorities or nonprofits. In the former case, board members would be appointed according to the 1945 law. In the latter case, the law only mentions that the board would be appointed according to the bylaws of NIDMA.

Under the 1980 amendments, local governments appoint board members in accordance with the 1945 Municipal Authorities Act, but the law does not mention any specific procedures for the appointments. The 1998 and 2000 acts require that the municipality has at least one representative on the board and the chairperson of the city council (or his or her representative) shall serve on the board. The 1998 and 2000 acts also attempt to ensure a proper representation of property owners (they require that a majority of the NIDMA board be representatives of property owners in the districts), but they are not specific in the procedures of appointing or electing board members. The laws specifically mention the representation of business owners on boards; thus, the laws aim to ensure that tenants of the commercial properties in districts are represented, as well as property owners. Also, the institutions located in the district should be represented.

The bylaws of BIDs are more specific than the laws, and the bylaws of different BIDs define different rules or procedures for the appointments of board members. Most of the bylaws we read attempt to establish equitable representation. For example, because City Avenue spans two municipalities, half of its board members must come from Lower Merion Township and the other half from Philadelphia City. Harrisburg's bylaws give special weight to the representation of city government officials; two city officials must sit on the board—one from the mayor's office and the other from city council.

Because the University City District (UCD) is a charitable nonprofit organization, its board members are not appointed by the city; the existing board elects the new members. Table 13.1 shows that the board members of the UCD are distributed among the four groups of main stakeholders: nonprofits (primarily the three universities that led its creation and contribute the largest percentages of its revenues), public organizations (e.g., the U.S. Postal Service and Amtrak),

---

* For an example of the weighted voting schemes in Georgia, see Chapter 15 in this volume.

private businesses (mainly small businesses), and residents. In our interviews, we learned that larger contributors were given priority when new board members were selected, but special care was taken to ensure the representation of small business owners and residents.

Obviously, laws and bylaws set up the parameters of the representation on boards, but in our interviews we learned that they do not present the full picture. Legally, local governments have the ultimate authority in determining the compositions of boards (they appoint board members), but our interviewees indicated that local business leaders (usually the founders of the BIDs or business leaders with some clout in their communities) usually make the selections and "nominate" new members to the board; the mayor and city council simply rubberstamp the nominations. We did not observe or hear about any conflicts between the local business leaders and the city over the selection of board members during our research.

Our review of actual board members indicates that the nominations by the local business leaders seem to have ensured majority representations of commercial property owners on BID boards. Table 13.1 shows that the boards of the BIDs we included in our study consisted of 68 to 91 percent commercial property owners (for-profit entities). Nonprofits comprised about 14 percent of the boards, and government representatives (public entities) and residential property owners comprised the remaining amount, which was usually less than 18 percent. University City was an exception; because of its special status, the representatives of nonprofit organizations constituted almost half of its board members.

An important issue is the role of residents in governance. Briffault (1999) points out that in most states residents are excluded from BID governance; they may be allowed to speak at public meetings, but they cannot sit on boards or vote for board members. This is not entirely true in Pennsylvania. As we mentioned earlier, under the 1980 amendments, residents are assessed, but some BIDs tried to keep them outside their boundaries. Table 13.1 shows that about half of the BIDs we studied allowed residential property owners to sit on their boards; the other half did not. The BIDs that do allow residential representation usually have more than one such member on the board. For example, the South Street BID has five residential board members. University City and Frankford also have several residents on their boards. Manayunk's BID leaders said that some members of the Manayunk neighborhood council sat on the BID board in the past, but none were doing so at the time of our interviews. Manayunk leaders attributed this to a lack of interest.

Typically BIDs are managed by at least an executive director, and in the case of larger BIDs, such as Center City, by a specialized management team. More important is the fact that some BIDs share their management with their affiliated organizations (development corporations or foundations). Legally, the management of a BID may be contracted out to another organization. In the case of some BIDs, the BID management is indistinguishable from the management of the development corporation or foundation. The Frankford and Manayunk BIDs are examples. These BIDs are managed by their sister community development corporations (the

Frankford Development Corporation and the Manayunk Development Corporation), and the offices of the BIDs are located within the offices of the development corporations. Likewise, the Center City District (CCD), the Center City Foundation (CCF), and the Central Philadelphia Development Corporation (CPDC) work closely together. The CPDC was formed in 1956 as a nonprofit community development corporation; the CCF was formed in 1992 as a charitable organization. The three organizations maintain separate boards but share the same management team and work jointly on many of the same activities (Houstoun, 2003).

Accountability

Accountability is a central problem of public administration, particularly in a democratic system of government. Public officials and organizations that are serving the public should be held accountable for their decisions and activities to the elected representatives of the people, and eventually to the people themselves. It is a legitimate question to ask whether and to what extent the governing bodies of BIDs are held accountable as their influence in metropolitan areas increases and as they become more like general-purpose governments.* In the literature, BIDs are criticized for the lack of accountability to their local governments, to their surrounding communities (cities, counties, and metro areas), and to the property owners in their districts. Although the BID laws set up legal mechanisms of BID accountability to local and state governments, as Briffault (1999) points out, it is not clear if governments actually hold BID governing bodies accountable.

The problem is that the bureaucratic and procedural mechanisms of accountability are not easily applicable to BIDs. To understand the issues in the accountability of BIDs in Pennsylvania, we propose Koppell's (2000) multidimensional conceptualization. He defined accountability in five dimensions:

1. Controllability. Elected officials are expected to control the actions of bureaucrats in implementing their policies.
2. Liability. Officials and bureaucrats are held responsible for their actions; culpability; rewards and punishment.
3. Responsibility. The behaviors of officials and bureaucrats are constrained by rules, norms, and laws.
4. Transparency. Officials and bureaucrats are required to explain their actions in regular public forums, hearings, and periodic reviews.
5. Responsiveness. The actions of officials and bureaucrats are direct expressions of the needs and desires of the people; customer orientation.

---

* The issue of accountability is also discussed in some of the other chapters in this volume.

Among these five dimensions, as Koppell points out, controllability represents the original understanding of accountability in public administration: elected officials should be able to control the actions of bureaucrats who are supposed to implement elected officials' policies. And this is the least relevant form of accountability in the case of BIDs, because BIDs are not the implementation agencies of public policies. The other four are applicable at higher and varying degrees.

As we mentioned earlier, there are four different types of overlapping, but also distinguishable, organizational forms of BIDs in Pennsylvania (subunits of local governments, municipal authorities, charitable nonprofits, and NIDMAs). Each form has different implications for accountability. Because at the time of our research and the writing of this chapter a large majority of BIDs in the state are municipal authorities, we will focus on the accountability of municipal authorities here.

As we mentioned earlier in this chapter, the 1945 act separates municipal authorities, including BIDs, from municipal governments. Local governments are allowed only little control over the operations of BIDs. When a local government creates a BID, it appoints the BID's board members. The local government may also restrict the functions—hence the powers—of BID boards by reviewing and approving their business plans. However, as we said earlier, these appointment and review powers may not be exercised easily against the will of the property owners (or their leaders), because it would be self-defeating to block the plans of a group of property owners who wish to make business improvements with their own money. Thus, once a BID is created, the local government may not limit the BID's powers as a municipal authority (e.g., the rights to acquire property, exercise eminent domain, borrow money, enter into contracts, make assessments, and appoint police officers). Our interviews with BID directors, board members, and government representatives indicate further that local governments do not exercise even their limited ability to control the operations of BIDs. While it is true that local government leaders sit on some BID boards, it seems that local government leaders are happy, even grateful, that BIDs are making improvements in their areas with their own money and, as a result, leave them alone.*

---

* One of the anonymous reviewers of an earlier version of this chapter suggested that local governments may be leaving BIDs alone, because the enabling state laws and the local ordinances that create BIDs have sunset provisions, which can be triggered by a majority vote of the property owners and a BID can be terminated at any time. This mechanism, the reviewer suggested, can be used to hold BID governing boards accountable. The reviewer's point is valid, but termination by vote is only one—and extreme—method of accountability. The Pennsylvania laws do not allow property owners to recall, or not to reelect, particular board members if they are dissatisfied with their performances. In Pennsylvania, local governments can remove board members in the next cycle of appointments, as we mentioned in this chapter. However, more important than the legal provisions are the actual attitudes and behaviors of local government leaders. It was our observation that they prefer a hands-off approach.

BID directors and board members can be held liable in the legal sense of the term. They would be culpable for violating any law, just like any director, manager, or board member of any organization. Therefore, liability is not a distinguishing aspect of the BID leaders' accountability. The same can be said about their accountability in terms of responsibility: they are bound by rules spelled out in the laws, local government ordinances, and their bylaws. However, as we mentioned above, Pennsylvania law grants considerable autonomy to municipal authorities. Therefore, there are not many legal rules to bind BID activities.

Pennsylvania's BIDs are required to be transparent in their activities: they are required to report to the state, they are audited, and their records are open to the public. However, the reporting and auditing of BID activities does not seem to be consequential. Reporting seems to be done pro forma. We are not aware of any substantive reviews of the statements, or legal actions taken as the result of a BID report.

The Pennsylvania BIDs that are formed as municipal authorities are required to submit annual financial statements to the state's Department of Community and Economic Development (DCED). The intention of this requirement is to charge the DCED with an oversight function. We found that all but one of the BIDs in Table 13.1 annually submitted their audited financial statements to the DCED. The BID that did not report to the DCED was the University City District, which is formed as a charitable organization and does not have to submit a report to the DCED. Instead, the University City District is required to annually submit its audited statements to the Bureau of Charitable Organizations of the Department of State, which is the oversight agency for charitable nonprofit organizations.

Among Koppell's five dimensions of accountability, the most meaningful one is responsiveness. The question is, are BIDs responsive to their property owners and general publics in metropolitan areas? Their responsiveness may be assessed on the basis of their performance in reaching their set goals and the satisfaction of their property owners. Some of Pennsylvania's BIDs seem to be making the effort to be responsive to their property owners and larger publics. About half of the BIDs we studied claimed to engage in fairly sophisticated assessments of their own performance. These BIDs measure their own performance by gathering or monitoring information related to occupancy rates, lease rates, employment levels, visitor rates, crime rates, and member satisfaction. They share this information with their property owners and local governments.

The Center City BID has a research staff that produces large amounts of information and disseminates it through its website and annual reports. City Avenue also produces reports and shares them with interested public agencies and property owners. The South Street BID administers member satisfaction surveys and collects information related to the demographics of its district. The University City BID has its own research division, which publishes and shares information with the public, its board, and public agencies.

Conclusions

The results of our study show that in Pennsylvania BIDs have become important actors in the increasingly complex governance processes in metropolitan areas. They were enabled by the state and created by municipal governments in response to problems such as economic decline and increasing crime rates in urban areas, but they are not merely tools to implement governmental policies. They can be more appropriately conceptualized as participants in metropolitan governance.

As we discussed in the preceding sections, the most common legal form for Pennsylvania's BIDs is the autonomous municipal authority. The 1998 and 2000 acts were designed to increase this autonomy, but the exact degree or form of BID autonomy under these acts was not clear at the time of the writing of this chapter. Municipal authorities in Pennsylvania are not tools of local governments, but autonomous agents, by design. In our interviews we found that the limited formal legal authority that local governments have over BIDs is even more limited in its actual operations. Although, legally, BID board members are supposed to be appointed by local governments, they are actually picked by BID leaders and later rubberstamped by local governments. Although there are legal provisions that require BID boards to report to the state and local governments, we found that these reports are pro forma and governments happily leave BID boards alone in their works. The functions of BIDs in Pennsylvania have widened over the years. Particularly important are the authority to conduct strategic planning and the de facto authority the Center City District exercises in operating a community court.

The expansion of BID functions, and particularly the planning and judicial authorities they exercise, brings BIDs closer to local governments. They are increasingly important actors in the network governance in metropolitan areas. As such, they pose challenges to the established notions of accountability in public administration in particular, and to democratic governance in general. The traditional notion of accountability (i.e., controlling the activities of a policy-implementing organization) does not work for BIDs. Local governments have some legal, but very little actual, control over BID boards and directors, but accountability in the sense of responsiveness to property owners' needs and demands and compliance with their own goals is pertinent to BIDs. Some of Pennsylvania's BIDs conduct regular and quite comprehensive evaluations of their activities and property owner satisfaction surveys and share their findings with local governments and general publics, like BIDs in many other states do (Mitchell, 1999).

It may seem that these evaluation studies and surveys are sufficient methods of holding BIDs accountable. However, they do not address all the potential issues. The impacts of BID actions extend beyond their own property owners, and even beyond their geographic boundaries. BID activities impact the use of public spaces in their districts, and thus influence the lives of residents, who may or may not have a voice in the decisions of BIDs, as well as others (people who work in the districts, but do not reside in them, the homeless, and visitors).

Critics like Pack (1992) raise several issues about the possible impacts of BIDs beyond their designated areas. She mentions, for example, that BIDs may affect the taxation abilities of local governments adversely (property owners may think that they can solve their own problems in their small territories and, therefore, may be reluctant to pay taxes—or higher taxes in case of need—to cities); they may redistribute crime in metro areas (because of better security in BIDs, criminals may move to other neighborhoods in metro areas); and they may attract more vigorous businesses, by making their districts more attractive, and leave less vigorous businesses to other neighborhoods.

Pack's (1992) concerns are not far-fetched. For instance, Hughes (2004) promotes precisely what Pack is concerned about—the idea that property owners in Philadelphia do not need the "big city" anymore, and therefore do not need to pay taxes to the city, because they can solve the problems in their own neighborhoods, as BIDs have demonstrated. Hughes argues that the city of Philadelphia needs to be de-consolidated for this reason, and that the BIDs in the city are showing the way to do it. Pack's concern for redistributing crime is also legitimate. In our interviews, some of the BID directors and board members agreed that their BIDs may indeed be redistributing crime, but they did not see anything wrong with ridding their areas of criminals. Pack's concern about depriving other areas of vigorous businesses is also valid: most of our interviewees agreed that their BIDs were attracting more vigorous businesses to their areas, but they saw this as a natural outcome of the competitive economy.

Potential impacts of BIDs on city taxes, redistributing crime, and attracting businesses remind us that assessing their responsiveness to their property owners' needs and demands is not sufficient. An evaluation of their responsiveness to the needs of metropolitan communities would require a broader and contextual understanding. Further complicating the issue of ensuring accountability by way of evaluating BIDs' responsiveness is the fact that they rarely are stand-alone organizations. As we mentioned earlier, the operations, managements, and finances of many BIDs are closely intertwined with development corporations, foundations, and business associations. And most BIDs collaborate closely with local governments in their operations. Their directors and board members are highly influential, if only informally, on the decisions local government leaders make that impact their districts. This intertwining of local government and BID decisions and operations makes it difficult to assess the isolated impacts of the actions of BIDs, as opposed to the impacts of those actions of the local governments.*

Beyond the issue of accountability, there is the issue of democratic representation. The weighted voting schemes used in the elections of BID board members and inequitable representation of residents are criticized in the literature (Briffault, 1999; Pack 1992). In Pennsylvania, technically weighted voting schemes are not

---

* See the Caruso and Weber chapter in this volume for a discussion of the difficulties in separating the effects of BIDs from those of other organizations' metropolitan areas and local governments.

an issue, because board members are not elected. Again, technically residents are represented on some BID boards, and the 1998 and 2000 acts attempted to deal with the problems of residents by allowing BIDs to exclude them from assessments. However, these practices in Pennsylvania do not address the broader issue of the representation of citizens in a democratic governance process. As BIDs become more like general-purpose governments, and as their decisions and actions affect larger segments of metropolitan populations, the representation of affected social groups and individuals in the decision-making mechanisms of BIDs will become more important.

We cannot conclude this chapter by proposing specific solutions to the problems of accountability and representation. Our main goal was to highlight these problems in the context of the BIDs in Pennsylvania. We can offer this broad argument, however: the BID phenomenon, as illustrated in the case of Pennsylvania's BIDs, forces us to rethink accountability and representation in the emerging and complex process of network governance in metropolitan areas. As network governance theorists assert, the classical separation between hierarchies and markets is disappearing and the public and private sectors are becoming interdependent (Teisman and Klijn, 2002). As Frederickson (1999) observes, under the circumstances, the meaning of "public" has broadened, and the distinctions between public and private organizations have become fuzzier. Consequently, public policies are made and implemented more and more in networks or network constellations.

BIDs illustrate the interdependencies between the public and private sectors and the erosion of the distinctions between the public and the private, and they highlight the need to reconceptualize accountability and democratic representation in governance networks.

References

Briffault, R. A. 1999. Government for our time? Business improvement districts and urban governance. *Columbia Law Review* 99:365–477.

Business Improvement Districts Act. 53 Penn. Stat. Ann. §§ 10-1551 (1967).

Business Improvement Districts Act. 53 Penn. Stat. Ann. §§ 54-5401-5406 (1996).

Business Improvement Districts Act. 56 Penn. Stat. Ann. §§ 56-5607-5610 (1980).

Community and Economic Improvement Act. 53 Penn. Stat. Ann. §§ 46-18101-18112 (1998).

Foster, K. A. 1997. *The political economy of special-purpose government.* Washington, DC: Georgetown University Press.

Frederickson, H. G. 1999. The repositioning of American public administration. *PS, Political Science and Politics* 32:701–711.

Governor's Center for Local Government Services. 2002. *Municipal authorities in Pennsylvania.* 9th ed. Harrisburg: Commonwealth of Pennsylvania, Department of Community and Economic Development.

Houstoun, L. O., Jr. 2003. *Business improvement districts.* 2nd ed. Washington, DC: Urban Land Institute and International Downtown Association.

Hughes, M. A. 2004. The surprising lessons of the center city. http//:www.mahughes.org/ showarticles.cfm?artid=25 (accessed June 12, 2004).

Kickert, W. J. M., Klijn, E. H., and Koppenjan, J. F. 1997. *Managing complex networks: Strategies for the public sector.* Thousand Oaks, CA: Sage.

Koppell, J. G. S. 2000. *The politics of quasi-government: Hybrid organizations and the dynamics of bureaucratic control.* Cambridge, UK: Cambridge University Press.

Lavery, K. 1995. Privatization by the back door: The rise of private government in the USA. *Public Money and Management* 15:49–53.

Mallett, W. J. 1993. Private government formation in the D.C. metropolitan area. *Growth and Change* 24:385–416.

Mitchell, J. 1999. *Business improvement districts and innovative service delivery.* Grant report. The PriceWaterhouseCoopers Endowment for the Business of Government.

Morçöl, G., and Patrick, P. 2006. Business improvement districts in Pennsylvania: Implications for democratic metropolitan governance. *International Journal of Public Administration* 29:137–171.

Municipal Authorities Act. 53 Penn. Stat. Ann. §§ 10-1551-1554 (1935).

Municipal Authorities Act. 53 Penn. Stat. Ann. §§ 56-5601-5622 (1945).

Neighborhood Improvement Districts Act. 73 Penn. Stat. Ann. §§ 16D-831-840 (2000).

Pack, J. R. 1992. BIDs, DIDs, SIDs, SADs: Private governments in urban America. *Brookings Review* 10:18–22.

Ross, B. H., and Levine, M. A. 2001. *Urban politics: Power in metropolitan America.* 6th ed. Itasca, IL: F. E. Peacock Publishers.

Salamon, L. M. 2002. The new governance and the tools of public action: An introduction. In *The tools of government: A guide to the new governance,* ed. L. M. Salamon and O. V. Elliott, 1–47. New York: Oxford University Press.

Stumpf, J. 1996. *Eradicating blight and expediting economic development in Pennsylvania in the 21st century: A report to PA general assembly pursuant to House Resolution 91.* Harrisburg, PA: Author.

Stumpf, J. 1998. *House Resolution 91: Legislative solutions for ending blight in Pennsylvania.* Harrisburg, PA: Author.

Stumpf, J. 2001. *Urban revitalization and the eradication of blight.* Harrisburg, PA: Author.

Teisman, G. R., and Klijn, E. 2002. Partnership arrangements: Governmental rhetoric or governance scheme? *Public Administration Review* 62:197–205.

Warner, S. B. 1987. *The private city: Philadelphia in three periods of its growth.* 2nd ed. Philadelphia: University of Pennsylvania Press.

Wolf, J. F. 2006. Urban governance and business improvement districts: The Washington, DC BIDs. *International Journal of Public Administration* 29:53–76.

Chapter 14

Getting the Max for the Tax: An Examination of BID Performance Measures*

Gina Caruso and Rachel Weber

Contents

* An earlier version of this chapter was published as Caruso and Weber (2006).

Introduction

Business improvement districts (BIDs) are financing tools for neighborhood revitalization and are currently used by hundreds of municipalities throughout the United States. BIDs allow a small group of taxpayers to plan, provide, and pay for additional services within their neighborhood. However, the implementation of these programs and the delivery of these services are dependent on the administrative structures set in place to utilize BID funds. Much hinges on the performance of these governance structures; their work must justify the levying of additional taxes on property owners, many of whom are small, locally owned businesses. Moreover, BID improvements are also intended to benefit a broader public. Retail tenants, customers, and city residents are expected to derive some utility from the enhancement of the area and similarly depend on the organization to provide the expected results.

Are BIDs effective means of providing additional services and amenities? How can the effectiveness of a BID be measured? Unfortunately, few BIDs systematically collect information on their organization's performance, and those that do may not be collecting the appropriate data. The lack of appropriate data prevents local property owners from making informed decisions about renewing their BIDs and prevents municipalities from making policy choices about whether to allow public funds to be used for these purposes. As local governments become more stretched fiscally and turn to public–private initiatives for neighborhood revitalization, they need information to help them craft the best solutions and not just ones that fit the circumstances.

This chapter explores the issue of BID performance measures with the goal of enhancing their capacity as diagnostic and prescriptive tools. We examine the different kinds of performance measures in the context of BID designation and evaluation, paying attention to the needs of the varied stakeholders invested in BID performance. We develop a typology of the different kinds of indicators that are most appropriate for the mission and land uses within BIDs and discuss ways to institutionalize the use of these indicators. This research is based on survey data and case studies of the city of Chicago's special service areas (SSAs) as well as an extension of theory in public administration on the appropriate use of performance measurements.*

---

* In Illinois, BIDs are referred to as special service areas (SSAs). Throughout this chapter, the term *BID* will be used to refer to business improvement districts generally, while the term *SSA* will be used to refer specifically to those in Chicago.

The Context and Mechanics of Business Improvement Districts in the United States

BIDs gained popularity in the 1980s and matured into common usage during the 1990s (Mitchell, 2001). Although BID emergence is commonly linked to reduced federal and state aid to cities, these levels of government had invested little in neighborhood redevelopment *before* the declines in funding, choosing instead to focus on larger redevelopment projects (Houstoun, 1997b). Competition with the sanitized environments of suburban malls and high downtown commercial vacancy rates forced many retail districts to rethink the basis for their vitality and decline. They recognized the importance of their collective image in attracting customers and looked to alternative funding and governance structures that would allow them to enhance this image without going through the conventional political channels.

Indeed, part of the appeal of BIDs is their relatively small size and localized responsibilities compared to the larger municipalities in which they are nested. Localism resonates with the notion that lower scales of government are more efficient, innovative, and responsive (Elkins and McKitrick, 1993). If smaller units are only spending local, voluntarily raised sources, the logic goes, they will have incentives to be less profligate. The potential for closer constituency contact also means that services and programs can be better tailored to local needs.

BIDs bring local merchants together to plan for areawide improvements much in the same way that homeowner's associations and their assessments provide the impetus for residents to participate in the decisions that affect their built environments (Alexander, 1989). The dominance of national chains and absentee property owners had worn away at the membership foundation of traditional merchant associations (Levy, 2001). Without a BID, downtown's diverse property owners have few means to act collectively.

The model of voluntary improvement associations that are funded through an involuntary assessment is an attractive middle ground between chambers of commerce (with their associated free-rider problems) and unpopular property tax hikes. BIDs are voluntary in some respects (see the discussion of designation procedures below), and in most cases, they lack the authority of local governments to directly regulate the activities of district property owners, merchants, or residents (Briffault, 1999). At the same time, BIDs benefit from a consistent and potentially larger funding stream than one comprised of membership dues. This allows for the pursuit of long-term and innovative projects not commonly funded by the municipality. Because BIDs mandate the participation of each property owner, they avoid the "Swiss cheese" effect of gaps in service delivery due to volunteer participation or ad hoc funding.

The state enabling legislation and municipal ordinances authorizing BIDs take differing approaches to such basic questions as district designation, responsibilities, finances, and administration (Briffault, 1999). In Illinois, for example, the state statute determines the kinds of real estate that can be taxed, the manner in which it can be taxed, the municipal powers to govern SSAs, the application and public hearing process, and mechanisms for disconnection (i.e., when a property owner chooses to opt out of the assessment) and refunds.* State laws often mandate some form of voting process for property owners in the proposed district to support or oppose BID designation.

Municipal ordinances create the specific districts and authorize the additional tax levy. In 1977, for example, the city of Chicago created its first SSA by passing two ordinances pertaining to all SSAs that followed: a public hearing ordinance and an establishment/levy ordinance. During the 60-day petition period following the public hearing, those who object to the SSA may submit a petition from owners of property in the area and from electors (i.e., residents who are registered to vote but are not property owners). If 51 percent of the property owners and 51 percent of the electors sign the objecting petition, the SSA will not be designated. If an SSA makes it through the petition period, the city's Department of Planning and Development requests that the city council pass an establishment ordinance, which authorizes the SSA name, boundaries, scope of services, term, maximum tax rate differential, and management agreement with a local service provider.

Most BID ordinances across the country provide for property owner- or business-dominated advisory, administrative, or management boards that implement the BID's program and manage its operations (Briffault, 1999). The Chicago establishment ordinance also authorizes the creation of a commission specific to each SSA. The ordinance determines the number of commissioners, qualifications, appointment process, term lengths, and powers. SSA commissioners make recommendations to the city on the districts' annual budget, scope of services, and service provider. The ordinance also authorizes commissions to create bylaws for procedural matters.

In most states and cities, individual districts impose their own tax rate differentials determined by a plan budget. Although BIDs can use various methods to calculate the tax, such as using square or linear footage, Chicago SSAs use an ad valorem tax generated by multiplying the individual SSA tax rate by each property's equalized assessed valuation (EAV). This tax rate is applied to every property that pays taxes within the district's boundaries. Non-tax-paying properties, such as government or nonprofit institutions, may be included within the legal boundaries of the SSA and can choose to pay into a SSA fund. In Chicago the average maximum tax rate (that the annual levy cannot exceed) is 1.2 percent of the SSA's EAV; the lowest tax rate is 0.175 percent and the highest tax rate authorized is 5.0 percent.

In Chicago, as in most other cities, a combined levy-management agreement is created for each SSA on an annual basis. This ordinance authorizes the annual

---

* The 1970 Illinois Constitutional Convention granted municipalities and counties the authority "to levy or impose additional taxes upon areas within their boundaries in the manner provided by law for the provision of special services to those areas and for the payment of debt incurred in order to provide those special services." The process for establishing an SSA is outlined in the Special Service Area Tax Law, 35 Ill. Comp. Stat. § 200-27.

budget, comprised of the funds from the additional levy and any carryover of unspent tax revenue. This ordinance also authorizes the city to contract with a local organization through a management agreement (called a service provider agreement in Chicago) to deliver the BID services. The service provider is commonly a business association or chamber of commerce that sponsors the initial BID development. If a new organization is formed solely to administer the BID, the organization's services typically complement the work of local chambers of commerce and development corporations. For example, while a chamber may focus on business networking, the BID ensures that sidewalks are kept clean.

BIDs typically use their tax levy to fund street cleaning, landscaping, decorative banners, identity markers, and lighting. They develop special events, advertising campaigns, and shopper rebate programs. BIDs also offer façade improvement funding, parking, security, zoning advocacy, and land-use oversight. In Chicago, for example, some SSA service providers operate in-house maintenance programs with employees and own equipment such as tractors, sidewalk-sweeping machines, and snow blowers. BIDs create neighborhood directories, enhance the service providers' websites, and provide seed money for seasonal parades and festivals. Some BIDs provide rebates for storefront improvements, while others institute design guidelines as a means of influencing the built environment in their districts. Still other BIDs provide predevelopment funds for properties in the BID boundaries as well as financing for infrastructure improvements.

BIDs are often mistakenly compared to tax increment financing (TIF) districts and perceived as interchangeable funding tools. TIF districts capture future incremental tax revenue beyond a base over a period of 20-plus years and use it to finance redevelopment projects and pay off municipal loans floated for larger infrastructure projects. Whereas BIDs and TIFs are sublocal fiscal enclaves whose borders affect the scope of services, regulation, and sources of financing, they diverge into their distinct functions as TIFs tend to fund large-scale capital improvement programs and private development costs. In contrast to TIF's capital improvement focus, BIDs do not typically fund private construction projects and, at most, fund predevelopment costs or façade improvements to enhance the general environment. Many BID budgets are small. In New York City, BID annual budgets can run in the millions; in Chicago, they average in the hundreds of thousands (the 2003 average was $256,000 a year).* In recent years, Chicago SSAs have collectively generated a total of about $3.5 million annually. In contrast, the TIF program in Chicago had a fund balance of $157 million in 2004 (Hinz, 2004). Moreover, BIDs are more frequently used in nonblighted communities in need of complementary public services, whereas TIFs are targeted to areas with relatively low property values compared to the rest of the municipality. For these reasons, expectations

---

* Annual SSA budgets in Chicago for 2003 ranged from $65,000 to $665,000. A budget of the average size of approximately $250,000 can typically accommodate a cleaning program, marketing and promotions, and modest economic development initiatives.

(and performance measures) for BIDs must be distinguished from those designed for TIF districts.

How effective have BIDs been? The existing research in this area consists of provocative conjecture and rich case studies. Advocates believe that BIDs increase a municipality's vitality through increased property values, higher sales tax revenues, and a better quality of life for its residents (Feldmann, 1997; Houstoun, 1997b; Levy, 2001; Mitchell, 2001). However, none of these outcomes have been statistically tied to the existence of a BID. Determining the causal effect of BIDs is understandably complicated because of the need to control, by reasonable assumption or appropriate statistical technique, for what would happen without the BID. Although we do not propose a methodology or research design to fill this gap, we would argue that contributing to the lack of evidence of BID's effectiveness is the fact that most BIDs (and the agencies mandated to oversee them) do not attempt to collect data on performance. It is to the issue of performance measurement that we now turn.

Performance Measures

In recent years, scholars and good government advocates have argued strongly for the use of "performance measurements" and "accountability mechanisms" in public programs (Hatry, 1999; Ledebur and Woodward, 1990; Osborne and Gaebler, 1992). Performance measures are a means of regularly measuring the results (i.e., outcomes) of services or programs (Hatry, 1999). The preoccupation with outcomes represents a shift away from monitoring compliance in terms of inputs and process standards and a movement toward measuring program efficiency in terms of the public benefits produced by public funding.

When they are used thoughtfully, performance measures are formulated as part of an overall strategic plan for a program. That is, they are devised ex ante as part of the goals of the program instead of imposed ex post as an afterthought. A good program accounts for both the inputs of the program and the outputs and outcomes. Inputs are the resources used in delivering the various services (direct expenditures, personnel time), outputs are measurable units of services that are delivered within a specified period, and outcomes are the benefits that the stakeholders realize from the services (Hatry, 1999). Organizations use different means of attributing results to program inputs, although few undertake the statistical analysis necessary to demonstrate more robust causality. An analysis of performance may be based on the organization's success in meeting previously articulated service goals (e.g., attractive public way) or efficiency in maximizing the amount of services provided relative to the amount of inputs invested (i.e., the cost per unit of output). Outcomes may include both intermediate program measures and wider societal measures.

Performance measurement may also entail penalties if actual performance does not meet stated expectations. In this manner, measures can be linked to budgeting and resource allocation decisions, where funding levels are adjusted based on results. In theory, defining standards of performance and threatening the use of penalties should induce program administrators to act in ways that promote the stakeholders' welfare.

Performance measures have become more important as local governments have had to do more with less. States and municipalities have been hard hit by the dwindling supply of federal block grants and devolution of administrative responsibility to local governments (Clarke and Gaile, 1998; Fainstein and Fainstein, 1989). Federal aid to states and cities has been declining since its peak in 1978, and the 1994 Congress hastened the process by reducing and terminating some funding and shifting certain responsibilities onto state and local tax bases (Kincaid, 1999). Moreover, statewide property tax revolts resulted in tax cap legislation, such as California's Proposition 13, which limited the revenues available to municipalities for services.

Fiscal austerity has also transformed the geography of public finance by devolving responsibility for many of the costs, risks, and liabilities of economic development to sublocal and quasi-private governance structures such as BIDs and TIFs (Weber, 2002). Increased reliance on these structures reflects a desire to make neighborhood redevelopment a self-financing enterprise and to avoid the redistribution of wealth associated with both the local property tax and higher orders of government regulation. Because BIDs use property taxes generated within the district for infrastructure and services there (i.e., beneficiaries pay for the public services consumed), they are arguably a more efficient means of taxing and spending than the normal budgeting process. However, these districts also operate as quasi-governmental taxing bodies, or "micropoli," without the traditional means of public oversight (Berman, 1997; Pack, 1992). Although in some cases BID decision makers are political appointees, taxpayers and local government often have little control over how BIDs spend mandated tax revenues. For example, even though BIDs hire private security forces with tax dollars, they are often independent of the legal and political structures that serve to constrain the discretion of the police. Indeed, it is their ability to pursue what are essentially *private* agenda with *public* funds that has raised suspicions about BID's lack of accountability.

The simultaneous movement toward smaller governance structures and scarcity of fiscal resources has moved the discussion of performance measures to the forefront of municipal policymaking. Performance measures are one of the few mechanisms available to ensure that these semiautonomous enclaves create actual public benefits, i.e., benefits that are distributed across a wider public than a few merchants and are generally accessible. They can be viewed as a way of reining in the power of these quasi-private structures while also permitting a continued reliance on this more privatized provision of public goods.

BID Performance Measures

To whom and for what should BIDs be evaluated and held accountable? It can be argued that a BID's performance is important to multiple categories of customers or stakeholders: its individual membership of property owners and tenants, its municipality, and the wider citizenry who live, work, or shop in the area.

Beneficiaries may be defined either in terms of monetary contribution or in terms of the impact of the services and programs funded by the BID. Because BIDs generate their revenue from an additional tax on local property owners in the district, these property owners are considered primary among the other potential beneficiaries. BID property owners, and the tenants to whom they pass the additional levy, make the initial sacrifice in expectation of tangible service delivery outcomes.*

Some BID service providers receive other sources of funds for BID-type projects beyond those collected from the property tax levy. For example, a BID managed by a chamber of commerce may combine its BID levy, government grants, membership dues, and sponsorship dollars. Organizations with multiple funding sources use BID funds as a sort of block grant, whereby a regular disbursement is made to the organization for BID-related activities. Co-mingled funds complicate the relationship between fiscal contribution and accountability because property owners become just one of many contributors to the BID, whose policies and programming priorities can be decided by multiple stakeholders. For example, chamber of commerce members may advocate for business networking events while other property owners wish to make streetscape improvements a higher priority.

Because the participation of all the property owners in a BID (which can number in the thousands) is not feasible, several states and cities endorse the creation of commissions of area representatives to oversee BID funds and programming. The commission is authorized to recommend the annual scope of services, budget and levy, and service provider to the city.† As a representative of the property owners, the commission is perhaps the most directly interested and active party in evaluating BID performance.‡

Municipal governments go to great lengths to designate and administer BIDs, and they are also ultimately responsible for the quality of BID expenditures and management. In Chicago, the Department of Planning and Development (DPD) functions as the SSA municipal ombudsman. It processes new SSA applications, oversees budgets and commissioner appointments, and contracts with a service provider to administer the SSA budget and services. Other municipal agencies, such as a city's Department of Transportation, may sign maintenance agreements

---

* Occasionally states or municipalities will have pass-through restrictions on net lease agreements so that tenants do not also pay the BID tax.

† For this reason the management agreement for Chicago SSAs states that those managed by a contractor are prohibited from co-mingling the SSA tax levy with nonlevy funding sources.

‡ In Chicago, commissioners are recommended to the city by the service provider, reviewed by city agencies, appointed by the mayor, and confirmed by city council. Most commissioners are also property owners or lessees of local property owners, and the service providers and the city try to ensure that the commissions reflect land uses, geographic coverage, and demographics of the SSA service area. Commissioner terms typically last two years with renewal possibilities.

with service providers when they implement streetscape improvements. In general, municipalities depend on BIDs to deliver programs and services that aid particular areas within the municipal boundaries. Therefore, although many regard BIDs as "self-policing" and autonomous, BIDs are not immune from the control of city hall and can be seen as accountable to their host municipalities as well as to nonlocal taxpayers that finance general municipal operations.

Indirect stakeholders are those who receive residual benefits from BIDs, such as customers, visitors, local institutions, and residents adjacent to a BID. These parties may be affected by the BID's activities although they may not pay directly for the services (if the tax is not passed on to them in the form of higher prices) or be targeted by the programs and services. Property and business owners adjacent to a BID may realize some spillover benefit from the BID, but more often than not, a BID district edge is distinctive as additional services, such as snow removal and streetscape enhancements, cease abruptly at its boundary. There is concern that residential and business property owners and tenants adjacent to a BID may experience the displacement of problems from the BID, such as panhandling, increased crime, or accumulation of trash. As a result, these property and business owners have a legitimate stake in the outcomes of a BID's activities.

Each of these stakeholders may consider a different measure of performance to be the one that most closely captures what they feel to be the BID's primary obligation. This is because each stakeholder may privilege a different aspect of the organization's mission. For example, while a local government may be more concerned with a BID's ability to increase demand for commercial space and therefore may look to property values to evaluate performance, a merchant may be more concerned that her street is accessible, e.g., well lit and free of snow and ice. Mission statements tend to be generic so that they can accommodate these various objectives and almost always focus on economic and community vitality or revitalization within the BID—often without ever defining these goals. For example, SSA 21 Lincoln Square's mission is a "place based approach to enhance and sustain our commercial area and economic competitiveness" (http://www.lincolnsquare. org/document/bid_ssa.phphttp://).

Identifying the specific missions of BIDs is a first step in avoiding confusion and conflict about performance indicators. A BID that does not seek to enhance security should not be evaluated according to its ability to decrease the number of reported property crimes. This mission statement forms the starting point for identifying specific outcomes to be measured, and therefore the performance indicators needed (Hatry, 1999). As Houstoun (1997a) wisely notes, "Context affects criteria" (p. 14).

In Table 14.1, we organize performance outputs, outcomes, and indicators according to the six principal objectives of BIDs, which together comprise the intangible and often undefined outcome of area revitalization. Previous studies had either confused outputs (programs introduced) with outcomes (effects of the programs) or confused outcomes (customer satisfaction) with means of measuring indicators (surveys, renewal proposals) (see, for example, Mitchell, 2001). We also

Table 14.1 Business improvement district objectives, outputs, potential positive and negative outcomes, and indicators

Objective	Outputs	Potential positive outcomes	Indicators	Potential negative outcomes
Real estate development	Data on local supply, demand, and demographics Relationships with brokers and lenders Participation in lease incentive programs Participation in façade rebate programs Predevelopment grants	Increased demand for district real estate	Increases in property values, occupancy, and lease rates Increase in number of building permits Redevelopment of specific sites and infrastructure according to the needs and mission of BID	Business gentrification and the displacement of desired tenants Undesired change in the character of the neighborhood
Business development	Participation in technical assistance programs (e.g., security, merchandizing, succession planning) Marketing of BID businesses Customer participation in district promotions (e.g., holiday shopping rebate programs) Participation in façade rebate program	Local businesses success, retention, and expansion Commercial mix consistent with district goals	Increase in taxable commercial sales Increase or stability in number of local business establishments Increase in number of jobs Increase in lease terms	Increased automobile congestion, trash, and noise Poaching of businesses from other areas
Convenience	Addition of traffic-calming devices, such as pedestrian crosswalks, and reduction of hazards	Accessibility	Decrease in pedestrian accidents Increase in pedestrian counts Increase in parking facility and metered space occupancy rates	Increase in reported crime and loitering Increase in noise, traffic, and pollution

Convenience (continued)	Improvements to sidewalks Addition of bicycle racks and lanes Addition of bus stops and shelters Institution of appropriate parking restrictions (meters, loading zones, etc.) Addition of wayfinding devices/signage Addition of lighting for autos/pedestrians Existing access routes made ADA compliant		Increase in transit ridership Increase in bicycle rack occupancy rates Increase in accessibility noted by customers in surveys	
Distinctive identity	Completion of branding studies Promotional materials Expenditures on improvements in physical environment (streetscape elements) Administration of design guidelines Festivals and special events Landmark preservation	Sense of place	Percent of survey respondents recognizing the district and its boundaries Percent of survey respondents frequenting the district and the businesses Percent of municipal services/funds spent in district Local and national media recognition Website hits and publication targets Attendance at special events Redemption rates of coupons from BID-sponsored display ads	Loss of choice and diversity in retail mix and public way

continued

Table 14.1 (continued)   Business improvement district objectives, outputs, potential positive and negative outcomes, and indicators

Objective	Outputs	Potential positive outcomes	Indicators	Potential negative outcomes
Aesthetically pleasing environment	Participation in façade rebate program Expenditures on public way maintenance programs (e.g., snow plowing) Addition of streetscape elements Holiday decorations Administration of design guidelines	Clean and attractive public way	Percent of respondents rating attractive appearance Decrease in nuisance complaints (rats, pigeons, dog waste, etc.)	Sanitized space (i.e., loss of original character) Reduction in municipality's essential services Nondistrict areas appear less clean and attractive
Safety	Security patrol Surveillance cameras Increased lighting and tree pruning Panhandling programs Vacant store enhancements Partnerships with police	Sense of security	Decline in number of vacant lots and abandoned buildings Increase in percent of survey respondents feeling safe in area Decline in number of reported crimes	Displacement of crime to non-BID areas Increase in discrimination and profiling

identify potentially undesirable and unintended outcomes that may result from specific BID activities. Ignorance of these may tempt BID administrators to take extreme measures to, for example, increase the perception of safety in the neighborhood because they do not take into account the potentially negative impact that this may have on neighboring communities.

Real Estate Development

One of the main goals of BIDs is to increase the profile of retail real estate within their borders. This involves attracting new developers and tenants as well as retaining successful existing businesses. The effectiveness of a BID as a real estate development tool can be judged by its ability to influence the value of properties inside the district. Achieving the other goals of eliminating development obstacles (such as a lack of available parking) and improving an area's appearance as well as investing in infrastructure and services within BID districts could improve the quality and magnitude of products and services consumed there. If businesses are more profitable or residents feel more secure in the district, demand for property there should increase.

To enhance the local real estate market, BIDs may administer vacancy databases to market space to prospective tenants and promote the area through advertising and trade shows, provide lease incentives, and start façade enhancement rebate programs. BIDs may also track data (household income levels, family sizes, ethnicity, and density) for understanding the demographics of area shoppers to determine the optimal type of commercial uses best suited for the BID district.

If demand increases, the price of land inside the district will be bid up. Therefore, one would expect that an indicator of BID's impact on a district should be detectable over time in an increase in property values. The market response to BID-induced demand will vary with the tightness of the real estate market. The magnitude of its impact will also depend on how BID dollars are actually used within the district and whether property taxes on properties within BIDs are appealed.

The local real estate market's strength can also be evaluated by analyzing the number of filled and vacant properties. Filled storefronts and occupied residential properties are significant indicators of a district's viability. Occupancy rates are the ratio of vacant property or storefronts relative to the total lease-up potential. Lease rates are the cost to rent commercial space and are measured in terms of dollars per square foot. BIDs with active business attraction and retention programs expect to see high lease rates and occupancy rates relative to nearby business commercial centers.

Private investment in real estate—either by existing businesses or through the redevelopment of a new site—may also be considered an indicator of success. A BID may retain a planning consultant to prepare a redevelopment scenario for a site, including building massing, parking ratios, landscaping, and land uses.

A marketing sheet showcasing the plan can be promoted to prospective developers along with requests for proposal (RFPs) for more complex site plans. The desired outcome would be a development that most closely matches the intended plan. Performance indicators other than the completion of the project could include a favorable response to the project at community meetings, support from the municipality, and surveys of customers and area residents indicating their satisfaction with the development. A BID could conduct intercept surveys adjacent to the development as well as contacting representatives from local civic organizations that would have opinions about the project.

Unfortunately, attributing property value, lease rate, and occupancy rate increases and site redevelopment to BIDs is difficult in most instances, for other factors that have nothing to do with a BID may result in the same effect. Municipalities and BID proponents are quick to attribute increases in value to redevelopment policies. An SSA on Chicago's North Side, for example, went from an 86 percent to a 97 percent occupancy rate over a ten-year period—the same period over which the SSA was formed and began programs that targeted vacant storefronts. Advocates point to BID-funded parking garages and public improvements as evidence of the tool's success, but they cannot eliminate other explanations for such increases. In many cases, for example, property values within BIDs were growing at or beyond the municipality's average annual growth rate before they were designated as BIDs.

Despite the complex lines of causality, real estate–based measures are relatively easy to collect. These indicators are often generated from third parties, which makes them more objective. Parcel-level data collected by local associations of realtors as well as tax assessor data can be used to examine real estate values over time. BIDs are discrete taxing districts with specific properties contributing an annual levy, so year-to-year comparisons of tax data are a consistent means of analysis. BID service providers can keep annual records of various types of tax data provided by the county and city comptrollers. Furthermore, an analysis of parcel changes can also provide information that may not be reflected in the aggregate values and tax collections. For example, BIDs with condominium conversions and mixed-use developments creating new identification numbers could suggest a robust real estate market aided by a BID.

Occupancy and lease rates are also easy to collect and can be procured from management companies or by contacting the property owner. A combination of tax bill analysis and field checks helps BID evaluators confirm lease rates and vacancy ratio. Regular checks of the service area for new tenants or vacancies keep the data current and provide a historical view of changes in the real estate market in the defined area.

The primary policy concern with increased demand for real estate in the district is potential business gentrification and displacement of existing tenants. Businesses serving customers of a higher socioeconomic status may move in as may national chains that can afford to pay inflated leases. Initial tenants of the area may be involuntarily displaced if they cannot pay higher property taxes or lease rates. This, in turn, may lead to observable changes in the character of the neighborhood and may threaten its claim to a distinctive identity, one of the other cornerstone goals of area revitalization.

Business Development

The real estate market typically reflects the viability and financial strength of its tenants and owners. Nonetheless, certain objectives and outcomes are more appropriate measures of business success, the benefits of which may or may not spill over into the domain of real estate. In other words, some measures focus on the internal workings of the businesses represented in the district as opposed to the spaces they occupy. Another common BID mission is to enhance the success of existing businesses operating in the district so that they stay in place, thrive, and potentially expand their operations in the area.

BIDs with this mission engage in business visitation programs, becoming familiar with the needs of tenants and property owners. BID representatives may penetrate the "black box" of the businesses, offering technical assistance on topics such as business succession planning, store layout, and merchandizing. BIDs engage in promotional activities such as publishing directories, sponsoring events, and offering holiday rebates. They often offer financial incentives for façade improvements.

Business success is typically measured in terms of sales and employment figures. To that end, the number of new and renewing business licenses in the BID can indicate the number of businesses in the area, and this number can be tracked over time. Taxable retail sales are the cumulative sales of the retailers in the BID, and individual data can be procured through surveys, business visits, or third-party data sets. Sales information, however, may be considered proprietary and therefore not available to BID representatives unless procured by private data companies. In some cases, the municipality itself is a good source of data. For example, new and renewing business licenses and assumed name registrations in a study area are often collected by local agencies.

The outcome of business development programs may be less about increasing the absolute number of businesses in the district and more about achieving an optimal commercial mix. The optimal mix should be defined in a vision statement that ideally came about through a facilitated planning process with property owners. Such a statement may also include a "wish list" of desired commercial users as well as the desired locations for new business development in the district. Cross-referencing report findings to actual BID conditions through regular site reconnaissance and conducting business surveys would help a BID evaluate over time the extent to which this optimal commercial mix is achieved.

Job creation is often viewed as a secondary objective of BIDs who like to distinguish themselves from other more employment-focused economic development programs that fund projects like industrial expansion and workforce development.

Nevertheless, employment and business success are highly interconnected; businesses make hiring decisions based on changes in their product markets, the competence of managers to identify those changes, and the desire and ability to respond to such changes with increased staffing (Penrose, 1959). Filling new orders as demand increases or expanding into new product lines may prompt the application of new resources to personnel, resulting in net job creation. BIDs tend not to focus on the quality of jobs provided (wages and benefits), as that is perceived as the domain of other economic and workforce development organizations. Employment data on the jobs per establishment may come from a survey sampling of businesses in the BID or from other third-party data sets, such Dun and Bradstreet and Info USA. While these data sources provide valuable information, BIDs should be aware of their shortcomings, such as their inability to capture smaller "mom and pop" businesses.

As with the other measures, it is often difficult to attribute sales and employment increases to BID services. Retailers grow because there is an increase in market demand for their products and services. This increase may be spurred by changes in fashion trends or because of increased buoyancy in the economy in general. Only a small fraction of the increased demand may be due to the better façade rebate programs or marketing seminars for which the BID was responsible.

Potential downsides of a thriving business district are negative externalities such as traffic congestion, noise, and trash that make living near or shopping in successful business corridors less desirable. The positive benefit spillovers of the BID's revitalization strategy may be offset by these countervailing externalities—unless the organization takes action to manage these side effects of growth.

Convenience

BIDs often try to influence the movement of automobile, public transit, and pedestrian traffic in their districts to make wayfinding easier for potential customers. Accessibility can draw people to the district, and a perception of the lack of accessibility can repel potential customers who do not wish to navigate the streets and parking lots. A BID's ability to respond to mobility and parking issues can be a significant indicator of the BID's performance. Outputs may include the addition of traffic-calming devices, off- and on-street parking, loading zones, shared car programs, bus lanes, bicycle racks, transit stations, and pedestrian crossing locations. BIDs can devise methods of increasing pedestrian traffic through pedestrian-friendly streetscaping (brighter lighting, wider sidewalks, safer crosswalks, etc.), promoting special events (walking tours, festivals), supporting parking and valet services (subsidized parking fees, parking structures), and supporting public transit (district branding at transit stops, trolley and van service).

Accordingly, positive outcomes would include increased traffic counts for different modes. Pedestrian and automobile counts can be gathered manually at key intersections at certain times of the day, days of the week, and weeks of the year. Pedestrian injury rates should also decrease if the BID is investing in creating a safer, walkable environment. These figures can be compared to similar business districts without BIDs or to the same business district before the BID designation. BIDs can analyze the occupancy rates and revenues from parking facilities within the BID or the numbers of cars valet parked with a BID-sponsored program. Customer intercept surveys can determine the effectiveness of parking wayfinding and signage programs and the extent to which customers make multiple shopping stops.

When retail becomes more convenient, it also becomes accessible to individuals who do not intend to consume the services and products of the local businesses. Loitering and crime may be an unintended consequence of good transit access and friendly streetscapes.

Identity

BIDs attempt to compete with suburban shopping malls and other retail concentrations. They seek to promote a distinctive identity that can justify the additional hassle of getting there or the slightly higher prices of small, locally owned stores. BIDs promote themselves to customers and visitors through special events, advertising campaigns, district directories, websites, and media coverage. Many of the case studies of BIDs from around the country have found that BIDs tend to spend the greatest share of their budgets on promotions and maintenance (Mitchell, 1999; Houstoun, 1997b). BIDs also make improvements in the built environment that are intended to reinforce their identity. Banners, signage, and streetscaping elements are intended to mark the area as unique. On occasion, the enhancement of an existing asset—historic buildings or a marina—becomes a symbol for the entire district.

Outcomes for such promotional programs include enhanced name recognition, which may be proxied by the level of media coverage for a special event or for a destination business in the district BID, distribution numbers of published business directories, and website visit counts. Outcomes in other categories (e.g., business development) measure the success of these activities in attracting people to the district who, in turn, may be spending money in the district and supporting its commercial base. They would include sales increases during a promotional event (compared to sales during a similar time frame that was not as well advertised), redemption rates of coupons from BID-sponsored display ads, and attendance numbers at special events.

A negative and often unintended consequence of identity promotion is the loss of diversity in the retail mix and public way. Marketing is designed to "brand" the district in one particular way, and customers often carry around a singular image of a place. It is possible that this identity—say, for example, as an "antiques district"—may not reflect the nature of all businesses in the area and may crowd out otherwise good tenants (e.g., a computer equipment store) who do not fit the mold. The homogeneity of one marketable image and improvements programs to reinforce that image may also diminish the pleasure of shopping in an area with a diverse business mix and built environment.

Attractiveness

For most BIDs, the most direct goal of the organization is to enhance the public way environment. The public way includes elements in the streetscape such as the sidewalks, light poles, banners, hanging baskets, street furniture (benches, trash receptacles, and kiosks), landscaping, and decorative structures. The public way can also include the streets and landscape medians, malls and plazas, parks, and other spaces open to the public. Because most every adjacent property owner has a stake in the upkeep of the public way, BIDs are an appropriate steward through which improvements to the public realm can be financed and administered.

Typically BIDs have maintenance programs that address such tasks as sidewalk cleaning, snow plowing, sidewalk pressure washing, graffiti removal, and streetscape furniture repair. BIDs commonly purchase street furniture to supplement municipal capital improvements. Beautification programs include historical markers and seasonal decorations. BID service providers commonly subcontract maintenance and beautification services or have an in-house program with employees, equipment, and storage space.

Occasionally BIDs consider individual building façades to be part of the public way as they serve as a streetwall that frames the public way and are visible from the street. Therefore, some BIDs may have individual façade improvement programs that rebate costs of exterior improvements to buildings. Maintaining a building condition's inventory with mapping software can be a valuable diagnostic tool for determining the level of deterioration and preservation of buildings in the BID. Such data complements that on lease/occupancy rates and property values as vacancies tend to be related to the condition of the building.

Performance indicators for the aesthetic quality of the public way are difficult to track because no third-party collects relevant information in a manner similar to a municipality collecting sales taxes or employment figures. Even though the data may be hard to access, the strong focus of most BIDs on this function makes it important to come up with proxies for changes in the environment. Customer and business surveys capture the less tangible qualities of the district. A business survey of attitudes about the BID district and awareness of BID programs can be administered by the municipality or BID via mail, phone, or in-person interviews. The customer attitude survey could be administered at key intersections or randomly selected businesses as well as by written forms left in a deposit box within participating businesses. Respondents are typically asked to rate their level of satisfaction (about the cleanliness or aesthetic appeal of the district) on a scale, prioritize BID programs that they believe are effective, and provide anecdotal evidence about the BID's successes and failures. For municipalities with multiple BIDs, comparing data between BIDs can reveal important trends. Measures other than survey results of a BID's success include a reduction in complaints made to BID and municipal offices about such nuisances as trash, rats, noise, and pigeon debris.

Potentially negative consequences of beautification and maintenance programs include a reduction in municipal expenditures on the area. Although BID services are intended to complement and not substitute for public expenditures, municipal officials may consider BIDs to be a lower priority for city services than other districts without designated stewards because the BID provides a level of service unavailable in non-BID areas. Furthermore, services funded through non-BID revenues such as municipal taxes and bonds may be reduced or eliminated because the city expects the BID to provide longer-term financing. As with identity marketing programs, BIDs take risks of defining "attractive" in a generic way and cleaning the area up in a manner that removes the "grit" that may have attracted some shoppers in the first place. The boundaries between the BID and neighboring areas may seem more distinct (and resented) if street cleaning services drop off abruptly.

Safety

Many BIDs aim to increase the feeling of safety in their district and will often hire private security firms to supplement services provided by the municipal police. Some BIDs install and monitor surveillance cameras in coordination with the municipal police department.

Statistics on crimes committed in BIDs can be kept by the municipal police departments as well as security firms contracted through the BID service provider. The number of reported crimes, arrests, interventions, or assistance provided by security officers could be collected on a regular basis. If possible, data prior to a BID security program should be compared to the period after which the BID security program is in place to see if there is a correlation between crime rates and BID security programs. As vacant lots and abandoned buildings often attract nuisances and make pedestrians feel uncomfortable, an observable decrease in such properties may also be a proxy for increased security. Surveys will also measure how businesses and customers perceive their environment.

BID security programs may unintentionally displace crime and panhandling to adjacent communities because of the increased presence of security personnel on BID streets. Moreover, a concern frequently leveled at private security forces is that they have the ability to engage in profiling and racial discrimination in a manner that the municipal police are forbidden by law. They may feel free to take more drastic steps to protect the neighborhood and their jobs.

A Word about Renewals

Although BID renewals have been treated as a performance indicator by some scholars (Mitchell, 1999; Houstoun, 1997a), we argue that renewals should not be considered formal performance measures. True, local taxpayers pay out-of-pocket for BID programming, and an indicator of their satisfaction with the BID's performance is their willingness to pay the assessment tax once the BID has been operating for several years. In choosing to renew the BID, they are voicing their opinion that the additional tax has been worth it in terms of the benefits received.

In theory, renewals may measure the degree to which informal measures of property owner satisfaction have been met. However, if other performance indicators are not used, BID members may be willing to renew their support because of their *perception* of outcomes as opposed to evidence of actual outcomes. If one believes that property owners are the primary stakeholders, and therefore the best judges of performance, perhaps their perception should carry more weight. But other categories of stakeholders, such as customers or the municipality, may be more insistent on seeing tangible results. If the interests of these stakeholders are not considered, BIDs may continue as governance structures more out of institutional inertia than because they are producing results.

Implementing the Appropriate Performance Measures: The Case of Chicago

Faced with a host of different indicators of performance, which ones should individual BIDs select? This section reports on original research that was conducted in Chicago to determine the extent of performance measurement and to gather information on the appropriateness of specific measures used for tracking performance. Although generalizing from one city's experience may not speak to the diversity of BID organizations and contexts across the country, many of the insights garnered from the in-depth study of Chicago have been confirmed by studies conducted in other cities.

In Illinois, over 200 districts have been created since the enactment of SSA enabling legislation in 1973. The number of Chicago SSAs reached 26 by 2005, and the program generated approximately $3.5 million in 2003. Table 14.2 lists the current Chicago SSAs, and Figure 14.1 maps their distribution throughout the city.

We administered an open-ended questionnaire to project managers of active SSAs in Chicago.* The city's Department of Planning and Development (DPD) provided data and contact information on the SSAs that were active as of June 2003.

---

* The questionnaire was built on those administered by Mitchell (2001) and Houstoun (1997a) and had eight sections: service evaluation, management practices, personal information and characteristics of the service provider/SSA, initial SSA formation, assessment, commissioners, and services.

Table 14.2   Special service areas in the city of Chicago, 2003

SSA	Name	Program activities	Max tax rate	2005 budget
1	State Street	Maintenance and promotional activities	0.405%	$1,310,302
2[a]	Belmont Central	Maintain three-story parking facility	1.50%	$270,293
3[a]	63rd Street Growth Commission	Business recruitment, rehab activities, predevelopment costs, maintenance	1.25%	$578,000
4[a]	95th Street	Business recruitment, maintenance, landscaping	2.00%	$65,000
5[a]	Commercial Avenue Commission	Snow removal, promos, business recruitment, loan packaging, rehab activities	3.00%	$372,540
7	Kedzie Industrial Tract	Maintenance, security	5.00%	$68,600
8[a]	Lake View East	Business recruitment, rehab, promos, technical assistance (T/A) for commercial and economic development	0.41%	$607,000
10[a]	Back of the Yards	Business recruitment, promos, shuttle bus service for seniors, T/A for commercial and economic development	1.90%	$434,558
13[a]	Stock Yards	Security, industrial park landscaping and maintenance	1.90%	$665,186
14[a]	Marquette Park	Residential security program	0.41%	$415,346
16[a]	Greektown	Maintenance of ornamental structures and streetscaping, business retention and promotion	1.00%	$180,906
17[a]	Central Lake View	Security, maintenance and beautification, business promotion and retention, marketing and promos	0.25%	$312,233
18[a]	North Halsted	Maintenance and beautification, business promotion and retention	0.42%	$154,331

continued

Table 14.2 (continued)   Special service areas in the city of Chicago, 2003

SSA	Name	Program activities	Max tax rate	2005 budget
19[a]	Howard Street	Streetscape improvements, security, parking studies, street maintenance	1.00%	$174,449
20[a]	South Western Avenue	Maintenance of streetscape improvements, marketing and promotion of commercial district	1.00%	$135,700
21[a]	Lincoln Square	Maintenance, promotions, and commercial area planning	0.25%	$137,000

[a] Denotes SSAs participating in authors' survey. SSAs listed were actively delivering services for all 12 months of 2003.

Out of 23 SSAs formed by June 2003 in Chicago, there were 16 active entities. Each of the 16 districts was contacted for interviews, with 14 of these 16 responding.

Like Mitchell's (2001) findings, the surveys reveal that half of the SSAs used formal performance measures, while the other half did not. BIDs in other cities, particularly those with larger budgets, may place a higher priority on performance measurement. Interview respondents in Chicago stated that they were not required to do so; in general, commissions did not ask their service providers to conduct detailed analyses to evaluate their programs' performance. The city of Chicago does include a performance measures form when it sends SSA program managers an annual budget packet (that also requires letters of support and an independent financial audit); however, organizations are not penalized if they do not submit the form. The city conducts an internal review of the completed forms, but it is modest at best. Moreover, the form itself is flawed. When listing potential measures, it confuses inputs and outputs with performance indicators. For example, it considers the number of street planters to be a performance outcome, even if the planters themselves are not attractive or are not maintained and potentially detract from the attractiveness of the area. SSAs are allowed to list special events, festivals, and parades as performance measures, yet are not required to estimate if these events attracted customers to district stores. Furthermore, the performance measure responses are not required to relate to the scope of services the organization has proposed to deliver in a given year.

If their commissions were interested in performance, SSA program managers provided this information in commissioner meeting minutes as a verbal report. Typically, the executive director or program manager would articulate the accomplishments of the SSA in an anecdotal fashion—rather than supplying statistics to document the results of the SSA's efforts. Interviews revealed that SSA managers assumed that commissioners were more interested in program outputs than outcomes.

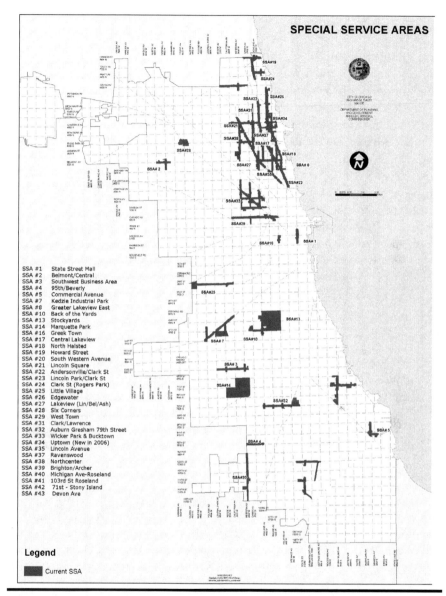

SPECIAL SERVICE AREAS

SSA #1   State Street Mall
SSA #2   Belmont/Central
SSA #3   Southwest Business Area
SSA #4   95th/Beverly
SSA #5   Commercial Avenue
SSA #7   Kedzie Industrial Park
SSA #8   Greater Lakeview East
SSA #10   Back of the Yards
SSA #13   Stockyards
SSA #14   Marquette Park
SSA #16   Greek Town
SSA #17   Central Lakeview
SSA #18   North Halsted
SSA #19   Howard Street
SSA #20   South Western Avenue
SSA #21   Lincoln Square
SSA #22   Andersonville/Clark St
SSA #23   Lincoln Park/Clark St
SSA #24   Clark St (Rogers Park)
SSA #25   Little Village
SSA #26   Edgewater
SSA #27   Lakeview (Lin/Bel/Ash)
SSA #28   Six Corners
SSA #29   West Town
SSA #31   Clark/Lawrence
SSA #32   Auburn Gresham 79th Street
SSA #33   Wicker Park & Bucktown
SSA #34   Uptown (New in 2006)
SSA #35   Lincoln Avenue
SSA #37   Ravenswood
SSA #38   Northcenter
SSA #39   Brighton/Archer
SSA #40   Michigan Ave-Roseland
SSA #41   103rd St Roseland
SSA #42   71st - Stony Island
SSA #43   Devon Ave

Legend

▉ Current SSA

Figure 14.1   Special service areas in the city of Chicago, 2007.

For example, commissioners expressed satisfaction when they saw the SSA cleaning program picking up sidewalk trash and snow, the SSA façade matching program funding storefront improvements, or the parking garage management providing customer parking. Neither commissioners nor SSA managers attempted to make the connection between such outputs and larger outcomes that related to the overall revitalization of the district.

Performance measures among SSAs in Chicago could be described as relational in that they rely on informal accounting and loose parameters of fulfillment (Macneil, 1980). The lack of measured data on SSA performance suggests that subjective and anecdotal data (the impression of cleaner sidewalks, fewer vacancies, more private security personnel) were sufficient for commissioners to feel the SSA was functioning to expected standards.

In most instances, commissions tended to trust the appraisal of the SSA director, who they believed had the most tacit knowledge about the workings of the organization. These directors also, of course, had the most at stake in the assessment and tended to give the SSAs, and indirectly themselves, high ratings. The interviews revealed that, overall, program managers believed their SSA had improved their district and allowed their organization to provide services they otherwise could not afford. SSA funding allowed staff to stay on top of issues, provide relevant services, and monitor service delivery. For example, the manager of the Belmont-Central SSA, which oversees a parking lot, was confident that it offered a much-needed parking facility for shoppers and employees even if it did not collect or analyze parking occupancy data. Although they too were more focused on outputs, program managers suggested that the SSA was responsible for making their districts more attractive, safer, and a pleasure to visit.

The most popular measure used by the surveyed SSAs was the image and appearance of the district followed by a decrease in crime rates and an increase in storefront occupancy rates. Area appearance is one of the most accessible indicators because it takes a simple walk or drive around the district to evaluate the quality of appearance. It is also, however, the most subjective, and few of the SSAs interviewed had conducted any kind of visual preference survey to firm up what were typically individual assessments. Crime data is also relatively easy to acquire, as the police department is required to collect and categorize it according to widely used criteria. For example, Marquette Park SSA, a residential SSA that functions exclusively to provide neighborhood security, relies heavily on crime statistics, phone inquiries, and daily security reports to monitor the effectiveness of its programs. Inventorying storefront vacancies is a relatively easy task for SSA managers, who will frequently tour the district in search of prolonged vacancies. Occupancy data was, on occasion, compared to earlier periods to check the area's progress. In other instances, SSA managers reported that they had a "feel" for when vacancies had reached a critical threshold and interventions were necessary.

Mitchell (2001) discovered a lack of convergence between the mission of BIDs and the performance measures used. That is, a BID that was primarily involved with business retention activities would use appearance-related indicators to measure its performance. Of the six categories of objectives, real estate development, safety, and aesthetically pleasing environment capture the primary missions of the 14 interviewed SSAs. For the most part, these missions were in keeping with what these same organizations expressed as the most appropriate performance measures: the image and appearance of the district followed by a decrease in crime rates and an increase in storefront occupancy rates.

In almost all cases, local property owners had renewed SSA budgets on an annual basis.* However, not all Chicago SSAs formed had continued through the term of their constitutions. Edgewater SSA was too large, and property owners had concerns about the appropriation of program funds. The Downtown Circulator SSA never materialized because the funding and coordination of a large public work project proved too daunting at the time, and the levy was eventually rebated. Lawrence Avenue SSA became mired in a conflict among the service provider, commission, and aldermen over the SSA's program priorities. Hyde Park SSA, despite spending money and resources to pass an establishment ordinance, could not resolve disagreements about the commissioner appointments and service provider and passed an annual $0 budget until the SSA expired.

These cases demonstrate that the dissolution of BIDs does not appear to hinge on their ability to meet performance outcomes but rather on internal politics about budgeting and representation. In other words, the performance of a BID is not always positively correlated with the decision to renew its overlay status. This supports our contention that renewals are not performance indicators in and of themselves, nor can they be considered accurate proxies of such. The longevity of this governance structure and its adherence to its organizational mission are two distinct issues that should not be conflated.

Our appraisal of Chicago SSAs led to several conclusions about selecting the most appropriate performance indicators. First is that mission matters the most. The radically idiosyncratic nature of SSAs in Chicago would confound any attempt to institute one-size-fits-all performance measures. While the SSA ordinances create some similarities among these taxing entities, each one was formed to address unique needs and each has developed according to its own logic in delivering customized programs to its service area. Therefore, meaningful performance measures are those that match the stated objectives of the individual BID (see Table 14.1). A decrease in reported personal crimes may be a useful indicator for a BID, but not the most important one if all of its programmatic expenditures are for business retention.

Related to mission is that the predominant land use within its BID boundaries will affect its mission and scope. For example, commercial district SSAs (the most

---

* In Chicago, SSAs eligible for renewal must go through the same establishment process as new SSAs, except the community outreach to gauge support may not be as extensive. If an SSA establishment ordinance specifies an ending authorization date, the service provider will typically submit a renewal application as this date nears. In the event of a controversial SSA, the city may request that the service provider or commission administer surveys to gauge property owner and elector satisfaction with the SSA. Aldermanic and municipal support will also factor into the renewal decision. Local taxpayers do not vote on the renewal; rather, letters, testimony, and informal petitions reflecting opposition and support are assessed by the city. To address concerns of dissenters or acknowledge changes in district conditions, a renewing SSA may have to make changes to its mission or program goals.

common type in Chicago) are those characterized by a high percentage and concentration of retail and services businesses. Commercial SSA services tend to focus on streetscape elements to define the district's identity, storefront façade programs to improve the area's appearance, safety programs to enhance security, and business promotion activities to assist in the survival and growth of area businesses. Performance measures that are most appropriate for these SSAs include improvements in business and customer assessments of public way quality, occupancy rates, and retail sales trends.

In contrast to commercial district SSAs, Chicago's mixed-use SSAs typically contain a mixture of commercial and residential uses.* First-floor commercial spaces often support apartment or residential condominiums above. All-residential buildings, either rental units or condominiums, as well as single-family homes are interspersed with commercial buildings. Furthermore, there are often light industrial, institutional, and open-space uses within the SSA. SSA managers reported that residential property owners complained that SSAs provided more benefits to commercial tenants and property owners, because they are the uses that generate the trash, attract people to the neighborhood, and benefit directly from area promotions.

Objectives for mixed-use SSAs typically involved business development, appearance, and identity, but safety figured prominently as did managing the potentially negative impact of too much real estate and business development (congestion, property value growth). Managers of these SSAs have to focus on services appealing to both commercial and residential property owners, and whose outcomes have the potential to be mutually supportive (a denser residential base supports commercial uses while an increase in commercial tenants can provide convenient, diverse shopping for residents). Public way enhancements and maintenance tend to be effective in such areas because different land uses can benefit from their stewardship. Mixed-use SSAs in Chicago typically were involved in façade matching programs, senior shuttles, predevelopment financing for senior housing, and a shopper's holiday rebate program.

Third is that expectations of outcomes may vary, and that performance benchmarks need to be set to a reasonable threshold of performance. While sidewalk maintenance may be a common BID program, expectations about the scope of maintenance programs may differ widely among stakeholders. In Chicago, the city agency responsible for SSAs expects local stakeholders to agree on a level of service responsive to their district conditions and with a reasonable cost-benefit ratio. For example, in a dense SSA with significant pedestrian traffic, stakeholders may be

---

* In Chicago, there is one all-residential SSA and two industrial SSAs. Residential SSAs are less common because local residents tend to be larger in number, more diffuse, and harder to organize. Residents are typically unwilling to take on the burden of an additional tax to pay for special services beyond what municipalities already offer them. The two industrial SSAs have focused on transportation access issues, security (prevention of illegal dumping, drag racing), business expansion, and public way maintenance.

willing to pay for a daily, in-house cleaning program to alleviate the trash problem. If there were differing views on the appropriate amount of cleaning, the city might recommend the SSA scale back the program to fewer days per week or to sub-contract the services. These expectations are often articulated in the original SSA establishment ordinance.

Fourth, data for performance measures should be feasible to collect, especially for organizations with small budgets and staffs. It should not be too costly—although the most relevant and important measures often involve the most costly data (e.g., compare the cost of a customer intercept survey to compiling already-available data on crime statistics). Governments should make this process less grueling by provid-ing as much of the raw data as possible and offering assistance in collecting data. In Chicago, for example, a city program called "Retail Chicago" collects commercial data on all of Chicago's neighborhoods, including local spending power, leakage to other commercial districts, and annual business sales.

Reforming the System of BID Performance Measurement

How and when in the process should performance measures be implemented? Performance measures are intended to respond to different stakeholders' demands for accountability. Each stakeholder, therefore, should have a distinct role to play in facilitating the process of measuring BID performance.

A commissioner system, such as the one used in Chicago, lends itself to per-formance measurement. In Chicago, commissioners tend to be city-appointed property owners who oversee the service provider. Appropriate categories of SSA performance indicators can be generated by the commissioners in conjunction with the service providers to support the original and current mission of the district.

These measures can be reviewed and modified by the government agency respon-sible for BID compliance and oversight. Local government takes a broader view on BID accountability than the commission. It can also encourage BIDs to utilize best practices in management and evaluation. City governments may consider either including performance measure collection in the establishment or levy ordinance or building this requirement into a service provider agreement.

Performance assessments could be linked to annual work plans resembling the format in Table 14.1. Submittal of both the work plan and performance assess-ments would be required. In Chicago, SSAs are already required to submit an annual scope of services that tabulates outputs and budgeted inputs. This scope of services could be expanded into a work plan. The service provider and commission could identify proposed outcomes (positive and negative) for each output in the work plan. The service provider, commission, and municipality would determine which sources of data were appropriate for measuring outcomes.

Concurrent with an annual financial audit, the BID could submit a perfor-mance audit based on data collected for the previous year. The municipality could compare the proposed outputs, outcomes, and indicators with the actual ones to determine the performance of the BID that year and to track the organization's progress over time.

Annual BID levies and renewals could be made contingent on demonstrated improvement in the agreed-to performance measures. As we mentioned previously, the lines of causality between BID activity and performance outcomes may be tenuous and difficult to demonstrate without the use of statistical modeling that is beyond the scope of the individual organization or monitoring agency. Nonetheless, it is important that performance data be collected even if it cannot be solely attributed to the BID. The monitoring agency may wish to compare an individual BID's performance to other districts with similar missions and budgets so that it may gauge its success relative to organizations working under similar circumstances. The local government could make recommendations on how the organization's priorities could be reorganized to better meet the agreed-to performance goals and offer nonmonetary incentives (such as awards) for those BIDs that exceeded their performance expectations without creating unintended negative outcomes.

Performance data could be shared with BID stakeholders, such as property owners and tenants, before the renewal application. In Chicago, commissioners annually garner input from the service providers and stakeholders through meetings, surveys, or e-mail before submitting their renewal application. They receive anecdotal feedback on program performance evaluation, cost estimates for new programs, and the political challenges impacting the district. If they shared performance data at this time, it would allow local stakeholders to play an important role in vetting the renewal application. A lack of tangible performance measures has fueled opposition to SSA renewals. Moreover, disclosure of this information would affect the reputation of the organization and would be an incentive for the SSA to take its performance seriously.

One of the desirable qualities of BIDs is their ability to respond to changing conditions in their districts. This is why service providers and commissions should be allowed to adjust indicators based on fluctuations in their mission, programs, and context. For example, the attendance expectations for a street fair may increase over time as the event becomes more popular. Changing performance measures make sense when they support substantive changes in overarching goals; otherwise, annual variation can be perceived as a way of tailoring the measure to meet the performance. Depending on the life span of the BID and the nature of its programming, short-term (annual) and long-term (multiyear) performance measures can be utilized.

Conclusion

Despite the growing popularity of BIDs, property owners, local governments, and business organizations remain cautious about imposing any new tax levies without assurances about specific service delivery outcomes. Implementing a system whereby performance measures are negotiated, evaluated, and required for annual budget renewals is a first step toward the goal of BID accountability. Performance measures are necessary to manage the potentially negative consequences of privatizing the delivery of public services and requiring that these services be self-financed.

BID performance measures, however, must be designed and implemented in ways that allow them to further this goal. Our in-depth analysis of the city of Chicago's SSA program revealed several flaws that could undermine the use of such indicators. First, outputs frequently trumped actual outcomes when SSA commissions and the designated city agency evaluated the performance of the individual organizations. In other words, those in a position to oversee SSA performance confused such things as expenditures on street planters and participation in technical assistance seminars with the larger results that these programs were expected to influence (attractive public way and business development). SSAs and city agencies considered renewal applications to be an accurate proxy of SSA performance despite the fact that SSA dissolution often had nothing to do with the organization's performance. Moreover, the casual manner in which performance information was relayed to decision makers (through meeting minutes or generic forms that were rarely assessed by the city) reflects the loose parameters of expectation fulfillment. Commissioners privileged subjective but firsthand knowledge about outputs (the development of a parking garage) over more objective evidence that their districts had become more convenient shopping destinations as a result of the SSA's interventions.

Unfortunately, by leaving expectations vague, contingent, or unspecified, those in an oversight position weaken their ability to enforce public policy goals. It is likely that Chicago is not alone. In many ways, the politics of local economic development and the difficulties establishing clear lines of causation between public investments and private outcomes in any city make it convenient for all stakeholders involved to avoid the often difficult work of performance measurement. BIDs are tempted to overattribute positive outcomes to their efforts given the difficulty controlling for the other factors that may have had independent influence on these same outcomes.

We have proposed a framework for connecting performance indicators to specific organizational objectives. BIDs need to distinguish and prioritize their missions, and the appropriate performance indicators will flow from these decisions. Municipalities and oversight commissions can then work with the service providers to customize the indicators to benchmarks that make sense for the organization based on the individual organization's goals, budget, and capacity. Even if individual organizations cannot statistically demonstrate that their efforts were solely responsible for the outcomes, their mandated attention to these outcomes may induce more efficient service delivery. The system need not be cumbersome to implement, but may require a change in culture from one based on relationships and impressionistic data to one based on more formalized means of governing these relatively autonomous quasi-public entities.

References

Alexander, G. 1989. Dilemmas of group autonomy: Residential associations and community. *Cornell Law Review* 75:1–74.

Berman, H. E. 1997. *Managing the micropolis: Proposals to strengthen BID performance and accountability.* New York: New York City Council's Committee on Finance.

Briffault, R. A. 1999. Government for Our Time? Business Improvement Districts and Urban Governance. *Columbia Law Review* 99:366–425.

Caruso, G., and Weber, R. 2006. Getting the max for the tax: An examination of BID performance measures. *International Journal of Public Adminstration* 29:187–219.

Clarke, S., and Gaile, G. 1998. *The work of cities.* Minneapolis: University of Minnesota Press.

Elkins, S., and McKitrick, E. 1993. *The age of federalism.* New York: Oxford University Press.

Fainstein, N., and Fainstein, S. 1989. The ambivalent state: Economic development policy in the U.S. federal system under the Reagan administration. *Urban Affairs Review* 25:41–62.

Feldmann, L. 1997. Baltimore's BID for safe streets leads the way. *Christian Science Monitor*, August 21, p. 18.

Hatry, H. 1999. *Performance measurement: Getting results.* Washington, DC: Institute Press.

Hinz, G. 2004. TIF funds bulging with cash. *Crains Chicago*, July 12, p. 1.

Houstoun Jr., L. O. 1997a. Are BIDs working? *Urban Land* 56:32–36.

Houstoun Jr., L. O. 1997b. *Business improvement districts.* Washington, DC: Urban Land Institute.

Kincaid, J. 1999. De facto devolution and urban defunding: The priority of persons over places. *Journal of Urban Affairs* 21:135–167.

Ledebur, L. C., and Woodward, D. 1990. Adding a stick to the carrot: Location incentives with clawbacks, recisions, and recalibrations. *Economic Development Quarterly* 4:221–237.

Levy, P. 2001. Making downtowns competitive. *Planning* 67:16–19.

Lincoln Park Chamber of Commerce. http://www.lincolnsquare.org/document/bid_ssa.php (accessed April 5, 2005).

Macneil, I. 1980. *The new social contract: An inquiry into modern contractual relation.* New Haven, CT: Yale University Press.

Mitchell, J. 1999. *Business improvement districts and innovative service delivery.* Grant report. The PricewaterhouseCoopers Endowment for the Business of Government.

Mitchell, J. 2001. Business improvement districts and the "new" revitalization of downtown. *Economic Development Quarterly* 15:115–123.

Osborne, D., and Gaebler, T. 1992. *Reinventing government.* New York: Addison-Wesley.

Pack, J. R. 1992. BIDs, DIDs, SIDs, and SADs: Private governments in urban America. *Brookings Review* 10:18–21.

Penrose, E. 1959. *The theory of the growth of the firm.* Oxford: Blackwell.

Weber, R. 2002. Extracting value from the city: Neoliberalism and urban redevelopment. *Antipode* 34:519–540.

Chapter 15

Community Improvement Districts in Metropolitan Atlanta*

Göktuğ Morçöl and Ulf Zimmermann

Contents

---

* An earlier version of this chapter was published as Morçöl and Zimmermann (2006).

349

Introduction

In a nation committed to self-help and forming associations, as Tocqueville noted long ago, it is not surprising that when citizens face common problems they will self-organize. This is particularly the case when economic interests are involved, as in the case of homeowners and their associations (McKenzie, 1994) and in the even more economically motivated case of commercial land and business owners. Just like homeowners who have a foremost interest in preserving and enhancing their property values, place-based businesses have an equally foremost interest in promoting their commercial interests and enhancing the profitability of their business locations (Molotch, 1976; Logan and Molotch, 1987). It is in this context that business improvement districts (BIDs) in the United States must be viewed.

America began at a unique confluence of capitalism and democracy, based on a recently emergent concept of private property. As will be discussed below in connection with issues of accountability, the practice of democracy in BIDs is akin to an 18th-century model (or a corporate shareholder model, as will be seen below)—it is limited to property owners, and in this case to exclusively commercial ones. BIDs in general, and the community improvement districts (CIDs) in Georgia in particular, are examples of the long-standing American tradition of self-help and the close affiliation between political rights and property ownership. The emergence of BIDs in the United States was enabled by these American traditions, but particularly the structural changes in metropolitan areas after the Second World War (primarily the economic shifts from city centers to the suburbs) and the sentiments for private action rather than government action that have been growing since the 1970s (as illustrated in the ascendancy of Ronald Reagan and neoconservatism in U.S. politics and that of the public choice paradigm in academia) created the specific conditions under which BIDs emerged (see Chapter 2 in this volume).

The CIDs of Georgia reflect many of the general characteristics of BIDs, but they are also unique in ways that reflect the political culture of the state as well as its changing economic conditions and demographics. Moreover, unlike the BIDs in most other states, Georgia's CIDs are constitutionally established local governments. In the United States, business has always driven government, and business groups influence much government policy through their interest groups. In Georgia these business groups have gone a substantial step further: they have persuaded the state legislature to enable them to charter their own governments—CIDs. This is the privatism issue we discuss in more detail in a separate chapter in this volume.

The main source of revenue for BIDs is self-assessment among commercial property owners; this is, in fact, the reason for their existence. Georgia's CIDs also use self-assessments as a major source of revenue, but what significantly distinguishes them is their ability, as governmental entities, to leverage large amounts of public money from the state and local governments to fund projects in their districts. In the business-friendly political culture of the state, governments are more than willing to partner with CIDs in the form of funding their desired projects. As such, the case of Georgia's CIDs most strongly represents the blurring of the line between the public and the private in public policy.

In general, BIDs are known as urban economic redevelopment organizations. Georgia has urban CIDs with some of these characteristics. But in Georgia CIDs started in the suburbs, and not to reverse economic decline, but to manage the explosive growth and the resulting traffic congestion in and around suburban shopping malls and business centers. As such, they have different priorities and operate somewhat differently from their urban counterparts.

In this chapter, we will discuss the results of our empirical study of the CIDs in Georgia. Our study focused on the unique aspects of Georgia's CIDs as well as their commonalities with their counterparts in other states. Ours was part of a nationwide study on BIDs, and we followed a common research protocol with our colleagues in other states, as we discuss in the next section. In the following sections, we summarize the history of CIDs in the state, discuss their legal foundations and actual operations, and conclude with the theoretical implications.

Method

Our focus in this study was on the CIDs in metropolitan Atlanta. There were eight officially established CIDs at the time of our study (2002–2003). These CIDs are shown in Table 15.1. Others were in the early stages of establishment or discussion.

We aimed to answer a common set of questions we had developed with our colleagues in other states. We used multiple sources of information to answer these questions. We interviewed the executive directors, selected board members (those who had been with the CID for a long time, preferably from the beginning), and selected local government representatives (mainly public officials who worked as liaisons with CID boards or served on them). We also consulted the Georgia constitution; local enabling laws for CIDs; CIDs' bylaws, articles of incorporation, and agreements with local governments; documents at CID websites; and newspaper and local articles about CIDs in Georgia.

A note of justification for our methodological approach is warranted here. Our aim was not to study the CIDs in Georgia to make universal generalizations about business improvement districts; instead, we aimed to develop a contextual understanding of CIDs in Georgia. Together with the studies in other states and countries that are presented in this volume, ours will contribute to a general understanding of the phenomenon. Our study was not designed to produce generalizations by testing hypotheses deductively because our subject matter was not suitable for that kind of a design. The BID phenomenon has only emerged in the last few decades, as this chapter and others in this volume stress. This newness of the phenomenon requires a research design that is suitable for it. The accumulated knowledge on BIDs in the United States and elsewhere is not sufficiently large or articulate to

Table 15.1   CIDs in Metro Atlanta

Name of district	Year established	Annual assessments (2003)	Millage (2003)	Local government jurisdiction	Location type
Cumberland CID	1988	$5.6 million	5	Cobb County	Suburban
Atlanta Downtown ID	1995	$3.0 million	2.5	City of Atlanta	Downtown
Town Center Area CID	1997	$1.9 million	5	Cobb County	Suburban
DeKalb Perimeter CID[a]	1998	$1.2 million	2	DeKalb County	Suburban
Fulton Perimeter CID[a]	2002	$1.4 million	2	Fulton County	Suburban
Buckhead CID	1999	$2.5 million	4	City of Atlanta	In-town
South Fulton CID	1999	$172,000	3	Fulton County	Suburban
Midtown CID	2000	$3.5 million	5	City of Atlanta	In-town

Source: CID websites and interviews with CID directors.

[a] Although they were established separately in two counties of metro Atlanta, DeKalb and Fulton Perimeter CIDs operate in the same business activity center and have a joint management team.

enable researchers to develop specific hypotheses. Also, because of the evolving nature of the BID phenomenon, it is difficult even to specifically categorize BIDs as one type of phenomenon. As can be seen in the other chapters in this volume, what we call BIDs may take on multiple forms and perform a variety of functions, some of which are common to most, but not to all. The emergent and evolving nature of BIDs requires, we think, an exploratory and qualitative research design that employs multiple sources of information to gain a better understanding of their histories, structures, and functions. And this was the methodological approach we took to study Georgia's CIDs.

A Brief History of CIDs in Metro Atlanta

Table 15.1 summarizes some of the key information about the CIDs we studied. The table shows that a majority of the CIDs are located in suburban business centers, and that the Cumberland CID was the first of these in metro Atlanta. This suburban leadership is an important feature of the story of the CIDs in Georgia. There are also urban (downtown and in-town) CIDs in metro Atlanta (Downtown, Midtown, Buckhead). The stories of the suburban and urban CIDs are intertwined and unfolded in response to economic growth and demographic shifts in the greater metropolitan area.

In the United States BIDs arose in response to the problems generated by the mass suburbanization that began in the 1950s and became dominant (demographically and politically) in the late 1980s and 1990s. These problems were twofold and inextricably interrelated. On the one hand, downtowns declined economically as businesses followed inner-city residents into the expanding suburbs; on the other, the economic growth consequently experienced in these new suburban commercial nodes, what Joel Garreau (1991) describes as "edge cities," created problems like suburban sprawl and traffic congestion. While much of the literature on BIDs (see Houstoun, 2003) tends to emphasize ones that were created to revitalize the resulting hollowed-out downtowns, most of Georgia's CIDs originated in the problems caused by what one might call an excess of success in suburban commercial nodes.

The Cumberland CID, Georgia's oldest (established in 1988) and currently the largest, is a case in point. It is located in southernmost Cobb County, just northwest of the city of Atlanta, at the intersection of I-285, Atlanta's loop known as the "Perimeter," and I-75 on its way north to Chattanooga from downtown Atlanta. This is the Cumberland Mall–Galleria area, also known as the "Platinum Triangle," originally founded in 1973 and identified by Garreau (1991, p. 172) as "a classic of the Edge City genre." As Tad Leithead, the Cumberland CID board chair at the time of our study, put it in our interview, paraphrasing Yogi Berra's famous oxymoron, the threat faced by businesses in Cumberland-Galleria was "that place is so crowded nobody goes there anymore." The issue was not, as it is for downtowns, attracting people to the place, but making the place accessible to the numbers of people who wanted to go there. The real estate interests' mantra there was not the usual "location, location, location"; they had that. It was now, as Leithead put it, "access, access, access." People were beginning to go to the new Town Center Mall, 15 miles farther out on I-75, which, about a decade later, would need to form its own CID for the very same reasons. This meant what was needed were transportation improvements that would allow more traffic to flow into the area.

Consequently, one of the most important functions, if not the most important, of the Cumberland CID—and the other suburban CIDs in metro Atlanta—has been transportation improvement. As we will discuss further below, CIDs in Georgia created transportation management associations (TMAs) for their areas and work with them very closely; in many cases, the CID and the TMA are hardly distinguishable. CIDs are also heavily involved in leveraging public monies for transportation improvements projects, primarily for constructing new highway interchanges to increase accessibility to suburban shopping areas (e.g., the Kennedy Interchange recently constructed in the Cumberland-Galleria area) and improving traffic flow at the intersections on urban streets.

The Cumberland CID provided the basic model for the area CIDs, with the exception of the Atlanta Downtown Improvement District (ADID). ADID was formed in 1995 for those typical downtown reasons—an exodus of corporate headquarters and other businesses—though this formation was clearly also motivated by the approach of the next year's centennial Olympic games. A. J. Robinson, a founding board member of ADID, noted in our interview that they looked at the BID models in downtown Philadelphia and other cities, rather than the Cumberland CID, when they formed ADID. He observed the Cumberland CID was "all about building a better transportation system," whereas ADID is typical of other conventional downtown BIDs, with its chief mission being "clean and safe," to make the downtown more hospitable. Accordingly, one of the first initiatives of ADID was the creation of the Ambassadors, a uniformed force distinguished by its white pith helmets, whose members patrol the sidewalks to provide information, assistance, and are, though themselves unarmed, in direct radio contact with the city police. Their efforts are supplemented by a "clean team" that keeps sidewalks vacuumed, power washed, and graffiti-free.

Beginning geographically with ADID, all current CIDs, with the sole exception of the South Fulton CID, are located in the "favored quarter" of the Atlanta metro area, a wedge spreading north from its point in downtown Atlanta. The extraordinary growth the Cumberland-Galleria area faced in the 1980s and the farther-out businesses faced in the 1990s led to the sprawl-related problems (traffic congestion and air pollution) in the favored quarter. The Town Center Area CID was established in 1997; it was followed by Perimeter CID (DeKalb County) in early 1999, Buckhead CID in late 1999, Midtown Improvement District (MID) in 2000, and Perimeter CID (Fulton County) in 2002. The Cumberland CID was the model for the Town Center Area and Perimeter CIDs when they were established because they faced similar problems. The Buckhead and Midtown CIDs are located within the City of Atlanta, thus facing typical urban problems, but they have transportation problems too.

The Town Center Area is located northwest of the Cumberland CID on the same I-75 corridor, and the growth that had been occurring in the Cumberland area exploded in this part of Cobb County as suburbanization grew increasingly dense in the northern and western parts of the county beyond the city of Marietta. The Town Center Area CID's anchor is likewise a shopping mall, as is that of the Perimeter CIDs.* Perimeter Mall is located in a well-to-do suburban area and was already attracting large-scale commercial interests such as office parks with Fortune 500 companies, as Cumberland had done years earlier. But when a new toll road, Georgia 400, was opened right next to it to give more access to the ever-expanding northern suburbs in Fulton County, this area similarly reached the CID-spawning crisis. To fully embrace the scope of this area's expansion, a sister CID was soon created in the adjacent Fulton County portion.

While many large corporations, like Hewlett-Packard, had set up new quarters in the suburban Perimeter CID, many others in the city migrated from downtown to Buckhead. Buckhead was in many ways an early edge city, a fashionable suburb within the city limits, the first area in Atlanta to have built an enclosed suburban mall (Lenox Square) in the 1960s. It is today a high-end entertainment district, and the CID was formed, as in Cumberland-Galleria, to enhance accessibility to and mobility in this now highly dense area.

The Midtown Improvement District is a somewhat different story. As businesses departed downtown during the 1960s and 1970s, they went first to thriving in-town suburbs like Buckhead and then to the expanding farther-out suburbs around Cumberland, Perimeter, and eventually Town Center. Left behind was the area in between, Midtown, which, like many areas on the edge of downtowns, was itself declining. Something of a "hippie haven" in the 1970s, it became more of a criminal hangout in the 1980s, with drugs and prostitution rampant. Midtown began recovering in the second half of the 1990s and quickly became a target for people seeking urban residences in the current "back to the city" trend, and hence a destination of choice for new businesses (primarily restaurants, cafés, and retail shops). Facing a combination of urban and suburban problems, the Midtown Improvement District hired off-duty police officers on an around-the-clock basis to improve safety, while collaborating with the Buckhead CID in the Peachtree Corridor Project to improve the vehicle and pedestrian traffic flow in this main artery they share.

One might wonder—given the problems of downtown, Midtown, and even Buckhead—why these areas had not formed CIDs earlier. This is because there were already organizations in place addressing previously existing needs.

---

* This area is called Perimeter because it is located on or outside the I-285 loop, the "Perimeter," around the City of Atlanta. As a result of the suburban sprawl of the last few decades, I-285 is no longer a boundary of the metro area, but a major "city street" that is used heavily by commuters in their daily commute to work and back home.

Downtown had its Central Atlanta Improvement Association (later known as Central Atlanta Progress [CAP]), a group of downtown's major property owners that established itself separately from the city's chamber in 1941. Also, Midtown had its Midtown Alliance for over 20 years, and Buckhead its numerous business associations (Buckhead Coalition, Buckhead Business Association, Buckhead West Village Merchants Association, etc.) in different periods of time. But these were chamber-like groups (membership organizations) with often much political influence, but ultimately no real authority or taxation power (Stone, 1989). These membership organizations played active roles in the creation of the CIDs and still have very close relations with their CIDs.

How To Form a CID in Georgia

In all states, a few common legal steps are required in the creation of BIDs. An enabling law is passed by the state legislature. The local government is petitioned by a certain percentage of property owners in the proposed district. The local government passes a resolution formally establishing the district and appoints the members of the board. Alternatively, board members may be elected, according to the rules set up by the state legislature. The local government and the BID reach a written cooperation agreement on what specific services the BID will provide.

The process in Georgia follows these general legal steps. The only legally distinguishing aspect of Georgia is that, instead of a single statewide one, an individual enabling law is passed for each local jurisdiction (county or city), even though there are very few differences among these laws. The only noteworthy difference is that the laws for some counties have sunset provisions, while others do not.

The Georgia state constitution has a section on community improvement districts (section VII) in the same article (IX) that defines counties and municipal corporations. It sets two conditions for the creation of a CID: a city or county resolution and the consent of a simple majority of commercial property owners who must also represent at least 75 percent by value of all real property within the district. The district is put into operation by a memorandum of agreement between the governing body of the local government and the leaders of the proposed CID. The local government's governing authority adopts a resolution establishing the district, and a copy of that resolution is filed with the secretary of state and the Department of Community Affairs. Once the district has gotten its board officers together (the board is elected, as we discuss below; the state constitution requires that the governing body of the local government must be represented on the board), it must enter into a cooperation agreement with the county or city.

The state constitution authorizes local governments to approve or reject the creation of CIDs. Although Georgia's political culture makes it unlikely for a local government to reject the petition of 51 percent of business property owners with 75 percent of the property valuation, it can happen. In one of our interviews, we learned that the Fulton County tax assessor's office blocked the creation of a CID in the northern part of the county, citing technical errors in tax records.

In our interviews we aimed to go beyond the constitutionally and legally prescribed procedures to understand the actual political processes of establishing CIDs. Our interviewees explained that, to quickly fulfill the requirements of 75 percent of the property valuation, the organizers of CIDs first persuade the largest property owners in the designated area. With this large amount of property tax already tentatively committed, it is easy to persuade the remaining number of property owners needed to sign on because they will be paying proportionately very little for the prospective improvements in the district. As Leithead, one of the initiators of the Cumberland CID, explained it, they designed the district to include large anchors, such as Home Depot headquarters, and a few large realty firms—Trammell-Crow, the original developers of the Cumberland project, Cousins Properties, Post Properties, etc.—and it only took seven of those to make up the 75 percent of the valuation. In the district they had designed, there were 160 property owners altogether, which meant that they needed to persuade only 74 other owners to have the necessary majority of 81.

Because there usually are property owners who are not willing to participate (typically absentee owners, remote real estate trusts such as pension funds, and big-box stores such as Wal-Mart), leaders seeking to establish CIDs gerrymander the districts in such a fashion as to exclude these. Yet they must make sure that the gerrymandered area complies with the constitutional requirement of contiguity. In the process of establishing the Town Center Area CID, for example, they had to exclude the spot occupied by Wal-Mart, which resulted in a CID map that has a blank spot in the middle and yet satisfies the contiguity requirement.

CID initiators also tend to stay within a single jurisdiction (one city or county). One reason is that if a district were to cover the territories of a county (unincorporated areas) and a city, city property owners would be reluctant to take on the extra expense of CID membership because they are already paying higher property taxes. Another, more important reason from the CID perspective is that CID leaders want to keep the local government interest consonant. The state constitution requires that each local government whose territory the CID occupies should be represented on the board. If the CID occupies the territories of multiple jurisdictions, that will add more local government representatives to their boards and could create conflicts between the local government interests. CID leaders want to avoid conflicts and minimize local government involvement in their governance. The difficulties in dealing with multiple jurisdictions explain the creation of two legally separate CIDs in the Perimeter area—the DeKalb and Fulton Perimeter CIDs—as we mentioned earlier.

Governmental Authorities of BIDs

The governance structures of BIDs may take one of four forms: nonprofit organizations (as in New Jersey and Pennsylvania; see the chapters by Justice and

Goldsmith and by Morçöl and Patrick in this volume), public authorities (as in Pennsylvania; see the chapter by Morçöl and Patrick in this volume), designated areas that are managed directly by the governing authorities of local governments for special purposes (as in the alpha BIDs in California; see the chapter by Meek and Hubler in this volume), and BIDs as another form of local government. Georgia's CIDs are of this fourth type—constitutionally defined local governments. They are not nonprofits, nor are they public authorities that only provide a limited range of services. The wide array of functions they are given makes them virtually general-purpose governments.

Why Georgia went the government rather than the nonprofit route in creating its distinctive CIDs is rooted in local history. When John Williams, the most prominent property owner in the Cumberland-Galleria area, had the vision of what should be done in the area, he took it to the most prominent politician in the county, Joe Mack Wilson, the dean of Cobb County's legislative delegation. While Williams had the vision (as our Cobb County interviewees universally attest) of what some sort of a benefit district could achieve, Wilson had the formal mechanism in hand. Knowing what suburban malls did to downtowns, Wilson had early led the efforts to create the Downtown Marietta Development Authority (Cobb's largest city and county seat), which was approved by voters in 1971 and had the power to tax downtown merchants and landlords for public improvement projects. And this would be the model for the constitutional amendment enabling the creation of CIDs in 1984 and the resulting Cobb County CID legislation drafted by other members of the Cobb delegation in 1985, particularly Republican Johnny Isakson (owner of one of the area's largest real estate firms, Northside Realty, and elected to the U.S. Senate in 2004) and Democrat Roy Barnes (then the state senator, and later governor).

The near-general-purpose government nature of Georgia's CIDs is also illustrated by the range of activities the state constitution empowers them to carry out:

> The purpose of a community improvement district shall be the provision of any one or more of the following governmental services and facilities:
>
> (1) Street and road construction and maintenance, including curbs, sidewalks, street lights, and devices to control the flow of traffic on streets and roads;
> (2) Parks and recreational areas and facilities;
> (3) Storm water and sewage collection and disposal systems;
> (4) Development, storage, treatment, purification, and distribution of water;
> (5) Public transportation;
> (6) Terminal and dock facilities and parking facilities;
> (7) Such other services and facilities as may be provided for by general law (Georgia Constitution, article IX, section VII, paragraph II)

Strategic planning was not listed among the purposes in the constitution, but it was later added as another purpose to the cooperation agreements between local governments and CIDs. For instance, in the 2000 amendments to the cooperation agreements between the CIDs in Cobb County (Cumberland and Town Center) and the county government, "planning, development, and improvement consistent with Cobb County's coordinated and comprehensive planning" is designated as a service of CIDs.

At the time of our study, the website of the Cumberland CID posted announcements about "Blueprint Cumberland," the strategic planning they were undertaking. They announced that they had proposed to the county changes and developments in transportation infrastructure (streets and sidewalks), street-level retailing, and green space in their district. Their plans also included "changes in development and zoning regulations, adoption of urban design standards" (Cumberland CID, 2002). The cooperation agreements of the CIDs in the city of Atlanta—Atlanta Downtown ID, Buckhead CID, and Midtown Improvement District—do not include explicitly stated strategic planning authority for them, but this does not prevent them from engaging in planning, as illustrated in Midtown District's "Blueprint Midtown" project (Midtown Improvement District, 2002).

What is significant about the strategic planning provisions in cooperation agreements is that they essentially grant land-use planning authority to CIDs. Land-use planning authority is generally recognized as the prerogative of local governments. In Georgia at least some CIDs exercise land-use planning authority under the guise of strategic planning. The implications of this are potentially significant, and it deserves further study in the future.

Governing

The governing boards of CIDs have seven or nine members, depending on the representation required by the local government. The state constitution requires that local governments be represented on CID boards, but does not specify a number. The CIDs we studied had six elected members; in Cobb County one other member (the chair) is appointed by the county; in the city of Atlanta there is one appointee each for the mayor, the president of the city council, and the chair of the city's finance committee.

In Cobb County, the enabling law requires that appointed board members are selected from among the property owners in the district (Cobb County Community Improvement Districts Act, 1985). Of the six elected members of a CID board, three are elected by electors (noncontiguous owners of real property within the CID) and three by equity electors (electors who cast votes equal to each $1,000 value of all owned real property within the CID). Electors vote for the first three posts; equity electors vote for the remaining three posts (Amendments to the Cobb County Community Improvement Districts Act, 1988). In other words, each property owner votes once as an elector (one person–one vote) and as many times as warranted by the value of his or her property (one vote for each $1,000 value of his or her property). Thus, it is ensured that the owners of larger properties will have more votes in board elections and, consequently, more representation on boards.

This weighted voting scheme, which is not unique to Georgia CIDs, is criticized by Briffault (1999) for violating the one person–one vote principle. Although Briffault's concern is justified, equal voting rights for all property owners would undermine the creation of BIDs. Without the incentive of having more say in their operations, owners of large properties would not be willing to join BIDs, much less to put in the great effort to establish them.

Another controversial principle regarding the election and composition of BID boards is the exclusion of residents (Briffault, 1999). The Georgia state constitution exempts CID residents from assessments, and hence from voting for CID board members. The CID directors and board members are keenly aware that resident representation is an issue. Although we know of no incident involving residents' conflicts with CIDs, the CID leaders are aware of the incidents involving the older BIDs in New York City. To preempt potential resident discontent in their districts and to curry their favor, CIDs have increasingly made efforts to invite residents to their meetings and to get them involved in community planning, as attested in our interviews.

CID Revenues and Leveraging

By definition, the fundamental source of CID revenues is self-assessments. The assessments are add-ons to the existing property tax. In Georgia the maximum permitted is 5 mill (see Table 15.1 for CIDs' specific millage rates). What is significant about Georgia's CIDs is their reliance on other sources of revenue. In general, the other sources of BID revenues include voluntary tax-exempt donations by businesses, proceeds of bonds, and federal and state grants. Overall, less than 10 percent of BID funds come from government sources, according to Briffault (1999). Georgia seems to be an exceptional case: CIDs leverage substantial amounts of money from governments (grants, direct investments, services, etc.).

The leveraging ratios vary considerably among the CIDs, and there is no uniform method of calculating exact ratios. We will limit ourselves to a couple of illustrations. It is reported that CIDs in Georgia attract public dollars at the rates of 1/6 or 1/10 (Stephens, 2001; Reese, 2001). In a recent major transportation improvement project (the Kennedy Interchange on Interstate 75), the Cumberland CID is cited to have had a 1/10 ratio: the CID spent $7 million developing the plans, with total costs (to the state and the CID) ultimately amounting to $77 million (Hardin, 2000). The Town Center Area CID similarly has collected about $10 million and gotten $100 million in improvements (Stephens, 2001). The Perimeter CIDs meanwhile make even higher claims (DeKalb and Fulton Perimeter CIDs, 2002). In the project of constructing a loop around the I-75/I-285 overpass/intersection, which was completed in late 2003, Cumberland CID contributed $1.1 million to the total of $81.1 million, the rest of which came from state and federal funds (Burns, 2003).

The ratios for the in-town CIDs have been somewhat lower, between 1/6 and 1/4, but that is not for lack of ability or clout; it is mainly because capital improvements in the city are made on already existing infrastructure and hence less costly, whereas the vast new infrastructure expansions in the suburbs require such huge sums (Monti, 1999). An example is the contribution by the Buckhead CID to the Peachtree Corridor Project. In 2001 the CID had committed $1.98 million to the project to which federal, state, and city governments had committed $6 million (Buckhead CID, 2003), a ratio of 1/3.

We should note here once again that there is no reliable or uniform method of calculating the ratios cited by CID leaders or those cited in local papers and business publications. It is certainly possible that some of these ratios, like the projections by Perimeter CIDs, are exaggerated by CID leaders seeking to create a positive image with their property owners and prospective investors in their districts. The Perimeter CIDs' ratios are based on the projections of large-scale transportation investments by the state government (particularly constructions of a rail line along the Interstate 285 corridor), which are far from certain. But no matter how exaggerated or unrealistic these ratios may be, they shed some light on the way Georgia's CIDs operate—and they expand the issue of accountability because these expenditures are public funds.

As our interviewees explained to us, the typical mode of operation for CIDs in Georgia is that they invest their own monies for feasibility studies for transportation-related capital improvement projects to get ahead in the competition for state money. During the feasibility study phase of a project, state and local government representatives (e.g., engineers) collaborate closely with the CID. Once the feasibility study is done, the CID's project holds significant advantage over others that are competing for state transportation money because this saves the county or state money conducting its own feasibility studies. This is why CIDs' project ideas are readily accepted by the state and local departments of transportation (DOTs). Also, because the engineers are already familiar with the project, they can more easily implement it. And because the CID has already had close contacts with the engineers and other officials in the DOT, it can influence the implementation of the project.

The CID's leaders see their investments in feasibility studies as entrepreneurial risks. Sometimes they lose. The Cumberland and Town Center Area CIDs together spent about $3.4–3.8 million (sources differ on the exact amount) on a feasibility study for a light-rail project reaching from Town Center over Cumberland into Midtown, and the then governor Roy Barnes, who favored mass transit projects, pledged $2.8 billion in construction funds (Reese, 2001, p. 56; Grillo, 2002), but when Barnes was ousted in 2002 by an antimetropolitan gubernatorial candidate, that money went to rural interests. Politically no county or city government could take the same risk. Even when they lose in their gambles, CIDs gain politically for taking risks on behalf of the community. By investing in feasibility studies and attracting state and federal dollars to their areas, CIDs gain the political support of the county commissioners and the county's delegation in the legislature, not to mention their member of Congress. There is little or no public burden perceived, and hence no political risk to local politicians, in such studies, because the district's residents are not taxed, and any public money that subsequently does come in comes from what seem to be outside sources, the state and federal governments, and thus seems free.

It must be noted that the discovery of the magic of leveraging was somewhat serendipitous. The original idea of CIDs was, as noted, to tax themselves for improving their areas. But when the new Cumberland CID looked at its assessments (it would get about $3 million from its members in its first year) and the needs of infrastructure construction (which were projected to require $500 million in the long term), board members realized that they would never be able to build them. It was here that historical contingency and political connections came in: Tom Moreland had retired after 30 years as Georgia's DOT commissioner and now had his own engineering consulting firm. CID members consulted with him and his firm came up with a comprehensive plan that the CID could then shop around to state and federal funding sources, with all the local political support behind them—and this worked for the reasons we explained above. It was the success of this in the 1990s that then led the other business associations—from the newest and outermost Town Center to the oldest and innermost Midtown—to adopt this magical mechanism, which would leverage these vast sums.

Intergovernmental Relations

There are two sets of intergovernmental relations that need to be addressed. The first is that of the CID with its county (or city) and the state, and the second is that of relations among CIDs in the metropolitan area. We should note here that we consider relations among CIDs as intergovernmental relations because, as we mentioned earlier, CIDs are constitutionally sanctioned local governments. However, we use the term *local government* only for counties and cities, in keeping with the traditional usage of the term, and to prevent potential confusion. We should also note that the intergovernmental relations we describe in this section are based mainly on our interviews and on some local reporting; our aim is to go beyond the legal framework and describe the actual politics involved.

The nature of the CID–state/local government (county or city) relations appears to vary. Particularly noteworthy are the differences between Cobb County and the others (DeKalb and Fulton counties and the city of Atlanta). In the ethnically and economically more homogeneous (and wealthier) Cobb County, the relations are described unanimously as "a great partnership." In the more densely urbanized and diverse Fulton and DeKalb counties, relations are described in our interviews as "cooperative but political." There is also some commonality among the three counties: all the CID directors and other top professionals constantly work at their relations with their local governments. They routinely demonstrate to county officials the great benefits the CIDs are providing for the counties by regular reports and constant interaction, and by giving county officials and politicians the credit for the improvements the CIDs have leveraged (i.e., the state and federal money they attracted to their districts). As Cumberland's Leithead put it during our interview, the CID "brings the funds, political will, and the full weight of the business community to bear on a project to allow the commissioners to implement a project they need for their district and which is also good for us. It's a win-win at the end of the day....When we do the ribbon cutting, the person who gives the speech, it's the chairman of the county commission. We give 100 percent of the credit [to him or her]." He characterized the occasion of the annual report they give to the county as "a love-in."

In the city of Atlanta the relations are somewhat conflictual. Scotty Greene, executive director of the Buckhead CID, observed: "The conflicts come down to the sort of rich-poor, black-white politics of the city of Atlanta. Even though we are doing the designing and engineering and coming up with the local match to federal dollars, we still have to overcome rich-poor, black-white politics." Another of our sources, who did not want to be identified, observed that there is a large difference between the CID–local government relations in Cobb County and the city of Atlanta. In Cobb County, if the CID offers a plan, the county says "go for it" and follows through (for example, getting the construction project under way). In the city of Atlanta, it often takes a year simply to get a contract agreed upon—and then the CID still has to make its own arrangements to implement improvements.

The relations among the CIDs in the metro area are both competitive and collaborative. CIDs are in competition for state and federal dollars, but they understand that they are also in competition with other potential metro/state recipients. This is one reason area CIDs have increasingly sought to work together so that, for example, they can share grants to create transportation networks between them. As several of the CID leaders stressed, they clearly understand that there is strength in numbers and that they can get more support from the legislature if they present plans for cooperative ventures that will benefit broader portions of the metropolitan area.

This cooperative spirit is demonstrated in several ongoing transportation-related projects. For instance, though the plans for rail projects in the metro area fell through for lack of gubernatorial support, as we mentioned, the Cumberland and Perimeter CIDs have been working on a joint plan to address transportation issues in the I-285 corridor that connects them, which seems to have received state support (Atlanta Regional Commission, 2004). There are also smaller-scale projects under way, such as a joint new signage system between downtown and Midtown, a part of the larger Peachtree Corridor Project, which would provide trolley type transportation from downtown to Midtown and Buckhead (Saporta, 2004).

Accountability

BIDs have been criticized for lack of accountability to their local governments, to their surrounding communities (cities, counties, and metro areas), and to the residential property owners in their districts. As we mentioned earlier, BIDs are enabled by state laws and created by local government resolutions. The state enabling laws and local government resolutions require varying degrees of accountability to local and state governments. But as Briffault (1999) points out, it is not clear if governments actually hold BID boards accountable, or if they ignore their legal obligations and let BIDs operate virtually independently.

In Georgia CIDs have no more obligations to report to the state government than cities and counties do, because, as noted, they are, for all intents and purposes, autonomous local governments. And, as close kin of special districts, CIDs are exempt from the one person–one vote requirement of general-purpose governments in any case, as per the 1973 Supreme Court decision in *Sayler Land Co. v. Tulare Lake Basin Water Storage District* (Burns, 1994, p. 12). The only obligation CID boards have is to file their articles of incorporation and bylaws with the Department of Community Affairs and sign service agreements with local governments. It can be argued that CIDs are accountable to the state eventually, because the state has the authority to allow their creation and dissolution. Indeed, but such is the case with all local governments within the state; according to Dillon's rule, counties and cities are creatures of the state, and the state technically has the authority to create and dissolve all local governments.

Neither counties nor cities have legal authority to hold CIDs accountable. As mentioned before, their only legal authority over CIDs is in their creation: for a CID to be created, it should be approved by the county or city in which it will be located. However, cities or counties do not have the authority to dissolve CIDs, if, for example, they disapprove of their acts. CIDs have their own terms, which vary across jurisdictions according to the individual local enabling legislature (for reasons we were not able to determine); in Cobb County, for example, CIDs are scheduled for termination after six years, though the practice has in fact been for constituents to renew them by a majority vote of the property owners.

It can be argued that counties and cities may hold CIDs accountable by exercising their oversight authority through their representatives on CID boards. That is possible, but in our interviews we found that local government representatives are mostly unaware of the details of the operations of CIDs. There is no indication that local government representatives see a need to learn about their operations. The local government representation on CID boards is mostly pro forma. In Cobb County the local government representatives on CID boards are property owners or business leaders in the district, as we mentioned; they are no different from the other board members in that sense. In the city of Atlanta, there is some tension in the city-CID relations, and the city representatives on the boards are "outsiders." But, we were told, the city representatives are too busy with their own affairs to be seriously involved in the details of the operations of CIDs. For all practical purposes, the CID boards in both Cobb County and the city are left alone by their respective local governments. Thus, like full-fledged cities, CIDs are accountable only to their constituents—though, of course, this does not include district residents, only the unevenly represented business and property owners, as discussed above. It may be that, to the extent that CIDs expand their activities (especially on the residential front, as is happening now in Cumberland and Town Center), residents' demands for representation and accountability will increase. This issue is likely to come before the courts in years to come.

As we noted, CID boards voluntarily share information about their operations (mostly their successes) with local government representatives. Our interviewees told us that they do so to maintain good relations with local governments. They are keenly aware that they need the financial and organizational support of local governments for their projects.

Effectiveness of CIDs

Perhaps the best real measure of CIDs' accountability is provided, as it is with other local governments, by the effectiveness perceived by their constituents, the shareholders. In our interviews we asked about the effectiveness and efficiency of CID operations. We asked if CID management teams had evaluated the effectiveness of their operations. We also asked directors, board members, and local government representatives about their own opinions of the effectiveness of CID operations.*

The interviews with the executive directors of CIDs indicate that they did conduct evaluations of their performances, but not systematically. What specific aspects of their performance they evaluated and the evaluation methods they used varied; the differences are primarily between the suburban and city CIDs. The primary problems for the suburban CIDs—in fact, the reasons for their existence—are transportation related. Accordingly, they study traffic patterns, the numbers of visitors who pass through their districts, and the occupancy rates for office parks and shopping centers. The CIDs in the city of Atlanta are concerned more about the perceptions of their areas not only among the residents and businesses in their districts, but also among tourists, business (convention) visitors, and suburbanites whom they try to attract to the districts for entertainment. They conduct surveys particularly about the perceptions of cleanliness and safety (typical urban BID issues).

In our interviews the directors and board members said that they perceive the operations of their CIDs as very effective, stating this is partly because CIDs are "nonbureaucratic and more like business" and partly because they only need to look

---

* For a broader view of BID effectiveness and methods of assessing it, see the chapter by Caruso and Weber in this volume.

out for themselves and for their specific interests, which are homogeneous, and not the rest of the county or city and its more diverse interests. The local government representatives generally agreed that CIDs are effective and similarly attributed that to the fact that they focus on narrowly defined issues in small geographic areas. Perimeter CIDs' president Yvonne Williams corroborated this specific focus with the example of Hewlett-Packard, which, as one of the very large employers in the Perimeter CIDs, had an immediate concern with the quality of the infrastructure in the area. The Perimeter CIDs were able to focus on that immediately, whereas the county had many other pressing issues and was usually thinking in broader, more countywide terms.

One measure of CIDs' effectiveness might be property values, and although some say they have definitely increased in their districts, many acknowledge that too many other variables influence property values simply to credit CIDs (see Caruso and Weber in this volume). In the case of Midtown, for example, the work of its Alliance in the 20 years preceding the creation of the CID (Midtown Improvement District [MID]) certainly did a lot to clean up this former red-light district and opened the way for residential gentrification, which in turn attracted businesses. The new vitality of Midtown called for substantial further improvements. MID, which is a creation of the Alliance and whose governance structure is closely intertwined with it, conceivably has played its part in such further improvements.*

CID directors and board members generally believe they have made a difference in attracting more businesses, because, they say, prospective businesses and residents see the CID as something like a guarantee of quality of life in the area. Michael Hughes, Cobb County economic development director and CID liaison, says that when he talks to prospects they will frequently cite CIDs as an asset. CID directors and board members do not feel that any businesses have left their districts because of the additional taxation for their CIDs.

Another measure of CIDs' effectiveness in metro Atlanta is traffic and transportation; there it is clear that the suburban ones (Cumberland, Perimeter, Town Center Area) have indeed improved both, building capacity to not only handle more traffic going in and out of the areas, but also to traverse the districts themselves, with shuttle services and more pedestrian-friendly alternatives. They have also, through the transportation management associations (TMAs) associated with them, instituted various vanpool and other carpooling programs, which have had at least a modest degree of success, especially if there are individual large employers that promote them and, even more especially, offer the essential incentive—the "guaranteed ride home." These factors do not apply equally to the in-town CIDs generally, but they, too, have worked on making their neighborhoods more pedestrian-friendly and

---

* The close relations between the Midtown Alliance and MID can also be seen at their joint website. The website of MID is under "About Us" at the website of the Alliance (accessed June 27, 2007, from http://www.midtownalliance.org/MID_overview.html).

negotiable; for example, the Buckhead CID has established a shuttle service to facilitate getting around within its area.

It is also clear that their constituents (property owners and local governments) view CIDs as effective; the CIDs that have reached their sunset terms have been renewed for another term, and there do not appear to have been any defectors or detractors. In that sense they have met the only legal accountability requirement they need to—they have spent their stakeholders' money prudently and have been rewarded with a new term.*

Discussion

As we noted, Georgia's CIDs reflect some of the general characteristics of BIDs, but they also differ in important ways. Most of the CIDs in metro Atlanta, even some of the CIDs in the city of Atlanta, have suburban characteristics. They were not created in response to urban decline, but to deal with the problems of fast economic growth. Among the eight CIDs that existed at the time of our empirical study, six were operating either in the fast-growing business centers in the northern suburbs (Cumberland, Town Center Area, and the DeKalb and Fulton Perimeter CIDs) or in the economically vibrant in-town areas of the city (Buckhead and Midtown), all of them in the favored quarter, whose tip is the north side of downtown (in which ADID is holding its own).

The programmatic priorities of the CIDs reflect the varying problems they were created to solve. While the top priorities of the Atlanta Downtown ID are typical of other downtown BIDs (safety and cleanliness), the northern metro CIDs (both the suburban and in-town ones) cite transportation improvements and capital investments in their areas as their top priorities. (Midtown represents an intermediate case; it has both suburban and urban priorities.) These northern suburban and in-town areas are the "victims" of their economic successes, and their CIDs were created mainly to facilitate access to funding to solve the traffic congestion problem.

To better understand the significance of the traffic congestion problem in these areas, one needs to remember that metro Atlanta has consistently been ranked among America's most congested metro areas. This congestion problem arose as a result of the explosive population growth in recent decades, particularly in the northern suburbs, and the lack of adequate public transit in the metro area. For decades, the state government pursued the policy of absorbing this growth by building more and more highways and secondary roads. Consequently, in the late 1990s metro Atlanta was declared the sprawl capital of the United States (Lacayo, 1999; Pedersen et al., 1999; Bullard et al., 2000).

---

* Caruso and Weber (in this volume) differ on this issue in that they do not see the renewal of a BID's term as an indicator of its effectiveness.

As we noted earlier, the CIDs in the metro area collaborate among themselves and with local and state governments to solve these transportation problems. The closeness of the collaborations between CIDs on the one hand and local and state governments on the other, the leveraging power CIDs exercise, and the governmental authority granted to them in Georgia raise important theoretical issues. Arguably, BIDs are becoming increasingly powerful actors in the governance of metropolitan areas (see our theoretical chapter in this volume). With their governmental status and intergovernmental networks, Georgia's CIDs are among the most powerful BIDs in the United States, and they illustrate sharply the potential challenges BIDs will pose to the theory and practice of metropolitan governance.

To better understand these challenges, we need to look into the history of cities in the United States and the political economy of urban life.* Urban scholars such as Warner (1987), Monti (1999), and Hall (1998) remind us that in the colonial period American cities were founded as commercial enterprises and that business interests played large roles in their governance. Hall observes that trade was one of the most basic raisons d'être of most great cities, not only in America but also in all other continents and throughout human history. What is significant in the case of American cities is that from early times on there has been an established tradition of private governance, often with public resources—what we would call public–private partnerships today (Hall, 1998, p. 612).

As Hall (1998) points out, from the very beginning cities had to solve problems of order and human organization. This requires collective action, but not necessarily public action in the sense we use the term *public* as "governmental" today. He stresses that collective action may consist of private agents. Such was the case in American cities: private agents engaged in collective action from the beginning (p. 6). As is well known, the excesses in the intermingling of the interests of private agents with collective interests and the ensuing corruption led to the rise of Progressivism and the increasing public assumption of urban services in the early 20th century. Hall points out that during the 20th century our cities seem to have swung full circle from private to public and back to private agency again. The deregulation movement in the 1970s, privatization and decentralization/devolution in the 1980s (Thatcher, Reagan), and ascendancy of "public choice" in the second half of the 20th century as the theoretical umbrella and justification for these movements represent the latest swing.

The BID phenomenon of the late 20th and early 21st centuries is part of the swing toward governance by private agents, particularly by commercial property owners. Ross and Levine (2001) call BIDs and similar entities "quasi-governments," Mallett (1993) calls them "parallel states," and Lavery (1995) "private governments." Georgia's CIDs, with their constitutionally sanctioned governmental powers and

---

* For an extensive discussion of the political economy and history of the cities in the United States, see Chapter 2 in this volume ("Metropolitan Governance and Business Improvement Districts").

their pro-business operational environment, are prime examples of governance by private (business) agencies.

What is the motivation for the agents of business interests to play active roles in the governance of their locations (e.g., direct governance as in the case of BIDs)? Molotch's "growth machine" theory is most helpful in explaining the rise of BIDs in general, and Georgia's CIDs in particular (Molotch, 1976; Logan and Molotch, 1987). Because the economic essence of cities is growth, local political elites and governmental institutions forge coalitions—growth machines—to promote it. The fuel of this machine is the actual and potential profitability of urban land. To the degree that "competing land-interest groups collude to achieve a common land-enhancement scheme, there is a community" (Molotch, 1976, p. 311). Particularly those who have the most to gain or lose from land-use decisions in the locality (local businessmen, locally oriented financial institutions, lawyers, syndicators, realtors) join the growth machine coalition. Molotch calls these groups of businesses "place-based" businesses. Growth machines use governments to gain resources that will enhance the growth potential of the area in question.

In our study, we found that leading players in the CID creation and operation were indeed place-based business owners, "place entrepreneurs" in the language of Logan and Molotch (1987). These are not necessarily local firms, but firms that have large investments, and hence large stakes, in the attractiveness and economic development of these particular localities, chiefly large commercial real estate firms and banks, whose primary business is real estate. The organizations represented on the CID boards show that place-based businesses, with few exceptions, dominate CID boards. The predominance of commercial real estate firms on the boards is followed only by banks. The only exceptions are Coca-Cola and Georgia-Pacific Downtown, but these two have close historical associations with the city; BellSouth in Midtown, also a long-term Atlanta tenant; Hewlett-Packard, Cox, and UPS in Perimeter; and Heidelberg and Carl Black in Town Center.

Logan and Molotch (1987) point out, "Whether the geographical unit of their interest is as small as a neighborhood shopping district or as large as a national region, place entrepreneurs attempt, through collective action and often in alliance with other business people, to create conditions that will intensify future land use in an area" (p. 32). While Logan and Molotch stress that capital is mobile, more so than labor, and can choose which city or urban area to make into a growth machine, the capital investors in CIDs have not only their initial investment to preserve but increasing sunk costs that commit them to these specific places—they do, after all, have to be in some place. And to be successful, they also need to be able to attract and retain labor, which is certainly one reason (besides attracting other investors and, often, customers) they have also invested in transportation improvements and various forms of commuter programs (e.g., TMAs) and districtwide transit programs (e.g., the Buckhead shuttle).

What are the implications of CIDs for public administration theory and practice? First, the results of our study demonstrate that BIDs in general should be taken seriously by public administration theorists and practitioners because they have become important actors in metropolitan governance. Particularly Georgia's CIDs are important because of their governmental powers and powers to influence, even make, public policies. BIDs have become part of the new and expanded "public administration problem," to use Salamon's conceptualization (2002). It has become generally accepted in recent years that public agencies form "partnerships" with private and nonprofit organizations for the delivery of public services. Our study sheds some light on the nature of the partnerships between the governments and CIDs in Georgia. There are indications that CIDs are more than partners; their directors and boards are de facto local policymakers and public administrators. Their decisions on issues such as traffic patterns and capital investments for transportation improvements amount to major policy decisions for metropolitan areas. CID leaders do not make policy decisions or carry out policies by themselves—they have to rely on local and state governments for money, expertise, and enforcement power in many policy areas—but our findings suggest that their influence in the policy process considerably transcends their legal structures. They are increasingly powerful actors in the metropolitan governance process. As such, their roles in governance processes need to be studied more in depth and systematically in the future.

Second, the case of CIDs indicates that public administration theorists should take political economy and history seriously. Urban scholars help us locate the roots of BIDs in the American urban tradition of collective action by private actors. Molotch underscores not only the significance of the motivation for economic growth in metropolitan areas, but also how local politicians and business leaders forge coalitions to promote growth. Public administrators are witting or unwitting participants in these coalitions. Without making a judgment on the normative desirability of this participation, we can argue that it is better to be aware of it.

References

Amendments to the Cobb County Community Improvement Districts Act. 1988. *Georgia Legislative Documents* 2, 3887. http://neptune3.galib.uga.edu/ssp/cgi-bin (accessed May 1, 2002).

Atlanta Regional Commission. 2004. *State of the region report*. Atlanta, GA: Atlanta Regional Commission.

Briffault, R. 1999. A government for our time? Business improvement districts and urban governance. *Columbia Law Review* 99:365–477.

Buckhead CID. 2003. Financial statements of Buckhead CID. www.buckheadcid.org/financial01.htm (accessed September 15, 2003).

Bullard, R. D., Johnson, G. S., and Torres, A. O. 2000. *Sprawl city: Race, politics, and planning in Atlanta*. Washington, DC: Island Press.

Burns, M. 2003. Cumberland-area parkway opens. *Marietta Daily Journal*, November 20, pp. B1/B4.

Burns, N. 1994. *The formation of American local government: Private values in public institutions*. New York: Oxford University Press.

Cobb County Community Improvement Districts Act. 1985. *Georgia Legislative Documents*, 2, 4009. http://neptune3.galib.uga.edu/ssp/cgi-bin (accessed May 1, 2002).

Cumberland CID. 2002. Blueprint Cumberland. http://www.commuterclub.com/blueprint.htm (accessed December 18, 2002).

DeKalb and Fulton Perimeter CIDs. 2002, November 20. *DeKalb and Fulton Perimeter CIDs' strategic implementation plan, 2003–2007: Focus on the future.*

Garreau, J. 1991. *Edge city: Life on the new frontier.* New York: Doubleday.

Grillo, J. 2002. Doing it themselves: Atlanta's CIDs have their own plans for solving traffic woes. *Georgia Trend* 18:85–90.

Hall, P. 1998. *Cities in civilization.* London: Weidenfeld and Nicolson.

Hardin, M. 2000. Red-hot CIDs get a grip on gridlock. *Georgia Trend* 16:56–57.

Houstoun, L. O., Jr. 2003. *BIDs: Business improvement districts.* 2nd ed. Washington, DC: Urban Land Institute.

Lacayo, R. 1999. The brawl over sprawl. *Newsweek*, March 22, pp. 44–48.

Lavery, K. 1995. Privatization by the backdoor: The rise of private government in the USA. *Public Money and Management* 15:49–53.

Logan, J. R., and Molotch, H. L. 1987. *Urban fortunes: The political economy of place.* Berkeley: University of California Press.

Mallett, W. J. 1993. Private government formation in the D.C. metropolitan area. *Growth and Change* 24:385–416.

McKenzie, E. 1994. *Privatopia: Homeowner associations and the rise of residential private government.* New Haven, CT: Yale University Press.

Midtown CID. 2002. Blueprint Midtown. www.midtownalliance.org/aboutus/programs.htm (accessed December 24, 2002).

Molotch, H. L. 1976. The city as a growth machine: Toward a political economy of place. *American Journal of Sociology* 82:309–331.

Monti, D. J. 1999. *The American city: A social and cultural history.* Malden, MA: Blackwell.

Morçöl, G., and Zimmermann, U. 2006. Community improvement districts in metropolitan Atlanta. *International Journal of Public Administration* 29:77–99.

Pedersen, D., Smith, V. E., and Adler, J. 1999. Sprawling, sprawling... *Newsweek*, July 19, pp. 22–27.

Reese, K. 2001. Dollars-and-sense solutions. *Georgia Trend* 17:55–59.

Ross, B. H. and Levine, M. A. 2001. *Urban politics: Power in metropolitan America.* 6th ed. Itasca, IL: F. E. Peacock Publishers.

Salamon, L. M. 2002. The new governance and the tools of public action: An introduction. In *The tools of government: A guide to the new governance*, ed. L. M. Salamon and O. V. Elliott, 1–47. New York: Oxford University Press.

Saporta, M. 2004. Midtown, downtown become one town. *Atlanta Journal-Constitution*, November 8, p. F3.

Stephens, E. 2001. CID businesses self-tax to fund improvements. *Atlanta Business Chronicle*, September 7, p. 3C.

Stone, C. N. 1989. *Regime politics: Governing Atlanta, 1946–1988.* Lawrence: University Press of Kansas.

Warner, S. B., Jr. 1987. *The private city: Philadelphia in three periods of its growth.* 2nd ed. Philadelphia: University of Pennsylvania Press.

Chapter 16

Contesting Public Space and Citizenship: Implications for Neighborhood Business Improvement Districts*

Susanna Schaller and Gabriella Modan

Contents

---

* An earlier version of this chapter was published as Schaller and Modan (2005).

Introduction

Business improvement districts (BIDs) are proliferating across the United States, hailed as an effective economic development and revitalization strategy not only for downtowns but also for residential city neighborhoods. As they transform urban landscapes and reconfigure the meaning and uses of public space, BIDs frequently spawn struggles over what it means to act like a "good citizen" and use public space "appropriately." However, the very struggles that BIDs often bring to the surface in neighborhood interactions are often obscured in the institutional processes of developing and implementing neighborhood revitalization projects.

This chapter examines conflicting views about public space and citizenship* in Mount Pleasant, a multiethnic, multiclass, quickly gentrifying neighborhood in Washington, D.C., where the local Business Association and Community Development Corporation was considering instituting a neighborhood business improvement district (NBID) on the neighborhood's main commercial corridor. Much research on BIDs has noted that BIDs place constraints on the negotiation of public space and notions of citizenship (Christopherson, 1994; Mallett, 1994). In Washington, D.C., as elsewhere, innovations associated with BIDs—such as increased trash pickup, storefront standardization, and renovations on one hand, and stricter loitering ordinances and architectural innovations discouraging socializing in public space on the other hand—go hand in hand with restrictions on freedom of association and rising rents and property values (Mallett, 1994). Taking a social production approach, we argue that NBIDs exacerbate tensions over space. This is especially the case in economically and ethnically mixed neighborhoods in which multiple constituents, with differing levels of access to the public decision-making process, hold divergent conceptions of what constitutes acceptable use of streets, parks, and building stoops. In such neighborhoods, it is very often the case that the

---

* We define citizenship rights here not only as the recognition of formal citizenship and the right to vote, but also as a concept rooted in political, social, and cultural investment in rights to education, housing, livelihood, and the use of public spaces. In the case of Washington, D.C., many of the neighborhood residents are undocumented immigrants who have constructed a strong sense of community identity and are actively struggling over these latter rights.

constituents who are marginalized from the public decision-making process are the same people who are most vulnerable to changes in the housing market. As rents and property taxes increase, the residents who were ostensibly to benefit from such innovations may be displaced from the neighborhood, and the democratic spaces of interaction where social networks are created and maintained may disappear.

Although BID scholarship has laid out how BIDs can limit the democratic nature of the public sphere and exclude various views of citizenship and public space, little of this research has focused on the micropolitics of NBIDs, and few researchers have examined the specific notions of citizenship and public space that actual community members hold. Therefore, we have little ethnographic insight into the specific kinds of conceptions of space that BIDs exclude and into whose visions of the neighborhood get picked up and privileged in discourses promoting BIDs. In this chapter, we take an ethnographic and discourse-based approach to examining conceptions of Mount Pleasant that are held by a variety of neighborhood constituents, and we focus on groups that are often excluded from the public decision-making process. We analyze two sets of data: (1) a community mapping project in which community members encode multiple conceptions of neighborhood space in maps they draw of the neighborhood and discussions about those maps, and (2) exchanges about quality-of-life issues on the neighborhood's e-mail list.

Through this approach, we contextualize theories of public choice and of class and ethnic relations in revitalization projects within the situated interaction of specific community constituents. The NBID plan in Mount Pleasant reproduced representations of space that correspond to urban economic development policy prescriptions informed by public choice theory. These dominant representations of space (Lefebvre, 1991) inherent to the BID model and conceived by policymakers, we argue, advance class and ethnically inflected representations of space (Smith, 2002). We contrast the NBID representation of space with representations put forth by community members who are marginalized from the local public decision-making process. This methodology gets at the way that urban planning theories play out on the ground and in the lives of real people. Furthermore, it opens a "space" for negotiation between the spatial representations of urban theorists, planners, and practitioners on the one hand and community members on the other hand.

Our findings illustrate that notions of appropriate uses of public space, neighborhood revitalization, and citizenship are conditioned by class and ethnic relations. Characteristics such as immigration status, property ownership, class and cultural alignments, and tenure of neighborhood residency influence the ways that individuals want to and are able to assert their claim over neighborhood space (Katznelson, 1981; Lowenstein, 1989). Our approach highlights how important it is for city officials, planners, and community development practitioners to integrate community members' views at every stage of the planning process and to critically assess the impact a BID structure may have on the particular contours of individual communities, before joining the trend to apply the BID model to urban neighborhoods.

The Social Production of Space

Lefebvre (1991) argues that social spaces are shaped through the interaction of the built environment with *spatial practices* (actions that occur in or in regard to a given geographical space), *representations of space* (society's dominant systems of knowledge and evaluation that underlie hegemonic physical and symbolic production of spaces), and *spaces of representation* (spaces as experienced and imagined on the ground by inhabitants). Through the triadic model of spatial practices, representations of space, and spaces of representation, Lefebvre sets in relation to one another (1) the spaces constructed by planners in maps and surveys; (2) the spaces that arise as a result of the practices of political alliances, investment patterns, zoning ordinances, technological innovations, and patterns of class and ethnic social and power relations; and (3) lived spaces, which can give birth to alternative, nonhegemonic cultural, political, and economic practices (Lefebvre, 1991, pp. 38–39).

From this perspective, urbanization is simultaneously an economic, political, social, imaginative, and spatial process (Soja, 1989; Harvey, 1990). Urban landscapes are constitutive of and constituted by localized social, cultural, and economic relations that are embedded in larger economic processes. Therefore, to understand the impact that an NBID may have on a given neighborhood, we need to examine how the spatial practices and spatial representations of community members, planners, theorists, and practitioners are likely to affect neighborhood spaces (cf. Low, 1996; Mitchell, 2001; Rodman, 1993).

BIDs and Public Choice Theory

What BIDs Are

BIDs are institutionalized as nonprofit organizations, but they hold the power to secure a funding stream by levying fees on local commercial properties. Administered by a voluntary board of directors, BIDs take on a range of activities; most commonly, they supplement public services such as street cleaning, security, infrastructure rehabilitation, and urban design (Mallett, 1994; Houstoun, 1997; Mitchell, 1999). They may purchase specialized trash cans, lampposts, and signage, among other capital renovations. Moreover, they frequently provide a security force—often labeled "good-will ambassadors"—who patrol the streets (Mitchell, 1999).

In an era when central cities are struggling to survive economically, BIDs provide an excellent mechanism to package, market, sell, and thus restructure urban space as a cultural commodity (Zukin, 1995; Mitchell, 2003).* BIDs have thus emerged as a creative response to city fiscal stress and abandonment. However,

---

* Diversity itself can become a commodity. As one neighborhood merchant noted, comparing Mount Pleasant to a commercial corridor in suburban Maryland, "When you take this international concept but put it on a silver platter with public safety, you have a huge money maker."

the model also has drawbacks. Ordinarily, commercial tenants and residents have very little voice in the establishment and management of BIDs. Once established through a petition of property owners, business owners, or both, the BID board of directors becomes insulated from public accountability, for board members cannot be voted out of office. In addition, voting power and decision-making power on the board is often weighted toward property owners (Christopherson, 1994). This, Mallett (1994) notes, represents a constriction of contemporary citizenship rights within the urban arena.* In this manner, BIDs are deliberately removed from public democratic channels of accountability, and their decision-making processes consequently are removed from public deliberation or challenge. BIDs, then, are structured as a means of managing space rather than as democratic models of governance, and they are legitimized by the concept of improved efficiency (Davies, 1997; Briffault, 1999; Stokes, 2002).

Public Choice Theory

The BID concept developed largely out of planning perspectives that are rooted in public choice theory. Public choice theory defines both the notion of citizenship and the role of government within economic parameters. The persuasive power of public choice theory resides in its espousal of individual freedom and choice and its framing of citizenship in terms of individual consumer choice and preferences. Aggregate choices made by self-interested, rational individuals within a sufficiently competitive arena are considered to produce efficient and optimal social outcomes in the provision of public services and goods (Tiebout, 1956; Webster, 1998; Savas, 2000). Thus, the same principle applies to purchasing a car using monetary currency as to "purchasing" a community using the currency of mobility to buy the optimal ratio of tax burdens to services (Tiebout, 1956; Savas, 2000). Public choice theorists individualize citizenship rights and reduce individuals to their functions as simple consumers of both privately and publicly provided goods and services. At the same time, they assume that individual citizens possess equal purchasing power and equal ability to move (Starr, 1987). The positive potential of this argument resides in the idea that the central city can proactively compete with suburban districts to attract businesses and consumers by offering an optimal set of tax burden, services, and atmosphere (Houstoun, 1997; Briffault, 1999).

Scholars critical of public choice theory and privatization point out that the mobility as well as the purchasing power of both individual consumers and business owners are historically conditioned (Starr, 1987; Lowery, 1998). People's opportunities to exercise their preferences in shaping the public spaces they inherit

---

* "In complex interdependent urban environments...in urban special districts, property qualifications for voting have been abolished as a result of judicial scrutiny. Business improvement districts reverse this trend in urban areas by reinstating property based voting systems in the election of BID officials" (Mallett, 1994, p. 282).

and inhabit are aided or impeded by historical cultural, social, and political modes of inclusion and exclusion (Lowery, 1998; Banerjee, 2001).* The spatial practices both promoted and constrained by BIDs create a representation of public space that serves to restructure public space to attract a specific class of consumers and residents, particularly well-to-do ones who have retreated to the suburbs and malls (Houstoun, 1997; Briffault, 1999).

Through private–public partnerships, BIDs reconfigure neighborhood space into specialized, mass-marketable, consumer-friendly environments. To reinvigorate the urban economy, they self-consciously market the strengths of the city retail experience—particularly in contrast to suburban mall environments—emphasizing amenities such as pedestrian-friendly sidewalks, heterogeneous architectural environments, and bustling streets with easy access to public transportation. In doing so, however, BIDs also reinvent the urban landscape as a sanitized economic space—in other words, an urban mall (Sorkin, 1992; Mitchell, 2003). By catering to middle-class and upper-class mass-market sensibilities, in effect, they mediate consumer preferences and choices (Sorkin, 1992; Zukin, 1995). However, subjecting the function of formerly public neighborhood spaces to an exclusively economic market logic to appeal to citizens whose primary role as social actors is reduced to that of consumers narrows the domain of interaction with the environment and with fellow citizens; there is little room for social contestation where citizens of diverse interests and backgrounds negotiate their daily political, economic, and social interactions through public space.

Thus, BIDs—particularly neighborhood BIDs—become problematic entities: they avail themselves of the public power to levy self-imposed taxes or fees and to reinvest these exclusively in narrowly identified community endeavors for aims that benefit a narrow constituency and serve a primarily commercial function.

Decentering Public Choice Theory: The Micropolitics of an NBID

Mount Pleasant, Washington, D.C.

A visitor to Washington, D.C., who ventures off the mall soon realizes that the city is divided into Washington, the federal city, and the District of Columbia (D.C.), a mosaic of neighborhoods, many if not most of which are racially/ethnically segregated. Mount Pleasant, located in the northwest quadrant just west of 16th Street NW,† is

---

* These include, for example, restrictive covenants, redlining, and exclusionary zoning (Goldsmith and Blakely, 1992; Massey and Denton, 1993; Pendall, 2000).

† Numbered streets start at 1 around the center point between the east and west quadrants and increase in number to both the west and east (e.g., 51st Street NW, 2nd Street NW, 1st Street NE, 2nd Street NE).

notable for its multiethnic character. It is home to Latinos/as, African Americans, Euro-Americans, and Vietnamese, to name the most prominent (but by no means the only) ethnic groups in the neighborhood. Mount Pleasant has also been home to groups like Washington, D.C.'s hard-core music scene and the D.C. Mennonite community. Economically, residents' incomes vary from the six-figure range to below the poverty line. This span in income is reflected in the variety of housing stock in the neighborhood, which includes apartment buildings, ranging from fancy condos to overcrowded and unsafe tenements; stately detached houses on the National Historic Register; and rowhouses set up as single-family dwellings, split into apartments, or used as shared group houses.

Mount Pleasant Street, the neighborhood's main commercial thorough-fare, is host to most of the neighborhood's public social activity. The street is a five-block-long corridor of low-lying brick buildings with about 60 businesses, including small grocery stores, beauty shops and barbers, restaurants/bars, dry cleaners, a pharmacy, a video store, a bakery, a jewelry store, a bank, used-furniture stores, a real estate agent, two dentists, laundromats, check cashing and money wiring services, and many variety stores. At the end of the street is a small park. Adding to the retail mix are street vendors selling various products from produce to pocketbooks to Spanish language music. In 1999, at least 70 percent of the businesses were minority owned, in most cases by Latinos/as or Koreans. Only 27 percent of the businesses owned their premises (Latino Economic Development Corporation, 1998; Gibson, 1999).

There are a number of large apartment buildings on the street, some of which are rental buildings and some of which are co-ops or condominiums. Although a few are economically mixed, most house working-class or poor residents. Latino/as predominate, but most buildings are ethnically mixed, with some combination of African Americans, Vietnamese, and to a lesser extent Euro-Americans, as well as a few more recent refugee immigrants such as Somalis, Kurds, and Bosnians. For many residents of Mount Pleasant Street and other neighborhood streets, Mount Pleasant Street represents a site for grocery shopping, running errands, socializing, and keeping up social networks. By and large, Euro-Americans, who tend to live west of Mount Pleasant Street, often in the neighborhood's more expensive single-family houses, do not socialize on Mount Pleasant Street.

Demographic changes in Mount Pleasant have been and continue to be accompanied by struggles over the physical and social reconstruction of the neighborhood at large and the commercial corridor specifically. Throughout the 1990s, these struggles were conditioned by unequal access to capital as well as to civic and political sites of power, as can be seen from the 2000 U.S. census figures. In the two census tracts that make up Mount Pleasant, whites constituted 30 and 37 percent of the neighborhood population; 43 and 53 percent, respectively, owned property, and as a group, they earned a per capita income of $34,670 and $35,044. African Americans made up 29 and 18 percent of the neighborhood population; 22 and 40 percent were homeowners, and as a group, at $21,098 and $25,017, they earned a per capita income significantly lower than whites. Latinos/as, who constituted 28 and 34 percent of the population, earned a per capita income of $12,202 and $11,961 and were predominantly renters, demonstrating an extremely low homeownership rate at 12 percent in both census tracts. Asians constituted 7 and 6 percent of the neighborhood population; 13 and 19 percent owned property, and the median income was $18,680 and $21,427. (However, the Vietnamese immigrants in the group designated as "Asian" have significantly lower incomes and rates of homeownership.) It is worth noting that the category "other races" earned the lowest income in the neighborhood—$10,252 and $7,948 in the two census tracts (U.S. Census Bureau, 2003).

Many Euro-American civic organization members disdain the look and feel of Mount Pleasant Street. In the mid-1980s and 1990s, Euro-American homeowners were at the forefront of civic organization activities that promoted the formation of a historic district and "quality of life" or street beautification projects. These residents are deeply community minded and care a great deal about the neighborhood. However, by and large, the projects that they undertake have had little input from Latino/a and Vietnamese constituents and particularly from lower-income residents. Low-income Latino/a, Vietnamese, and African American residents exhibit patterns of low participation in neighborhood-based civic associations. This may reflect a more immediate preoccupation with livelihood needs, insecure homeownership status, and marginalization due to language exclusion and documentation status. Furthermore, although many civic groups voice a desire to be inclusive of the diverse voices of the neighborhood, they do little grassroots outreach to welcome and encourage Latino/a, Vietnamese, and African American residents to attend, and those who do attend frequently remark that one must have significant prior knowledge of the topics being discussed, understanding of the meeting structure, and an acquaintance with the others present to fully participate. These factors constrain formal political power and participation in public decision-making forums, and consequently threaten to silence specific concerns that excluded neighbors have regarding community life and economic development. As a consequence of these dynamics, the projects that locally focused civic groups conduct end up being projects aimed at making neighborhood spaces such as Mount Pleasant Street and the park align with their own aesthetics and attitudes about what kinds of activities and physical environments correspond to their feelings of comfort and security.

Washington, D.C.'s "Revitalization" Projects and the Mount Pleasant NBID

Recent revitalization in Washington, D.C., as evidenced by the Department of Housing and Community Development's programmatic focus on homeownership programs and commercial corridor revitalization projects, has prioritized strengthening the city's tax base (District of Columbia Department of Housing and Community Development [DHCD], 2002). As neighborhoods like Mount Pleasant become recast as "in need of revitalization," the city's institutional aims often dovetail with and reinforce funding mechanisms that promote discourses of quality of life advanced by higher-income, often Euro-American residents, many of whom have only recently moved into the area. In mixed-income neighborhoods such as Mount Pleasant, with inadequate institutionalized safety nets such as rent control to secure the tenure of low-income residents and small businesses, revitalization is a political process wherein unequal access to economic, political, and social capital determines the ability to stay.* The Mount Pleasant NBID emerged within this context.

The NBID plan grew out of a somewhat rocky collaboration between two local business associations (one from Mount Pleasant and one from neighboring Adams Morgan) and a local community development corporation (CDC) promoting the BID model as a means of neighborhood revitalization. In some ways, the business associations were already functioning as voluntary NBIDs, in that they organized supplemental street cleaning, beautification projects such as flower planting, and community festivals. The CDC's proposal to formalize an NBID rested on the argument that it would distribute the financial and time burden of these voluntary efforts more evenly across all businesses.† Besides innovative financing, the NBID proposal coincided with the fairly traditional BID schema. Washington, D.C. law at the time required the approval of 51 percent of property owners and 51 percent of business owners, and a majority of the members on the BID board had to be property owners. Furthermore, voting could be structured to reflect the proportion of funds property owners contributed to the organization.‡ In such an incarnation, BIDs have the potential to create a jurisdictional district in which property owners gain disproportionate decision-making power. The design of the Mount Pleasant NBID did not challenge this schema. On the contrary, the NBID was developed in

---

* The city council recently passed a revised rent control law, the Rent Control Reform Amendment Act of 2006, which has instituted rent caps on residential properties of owners who own more than four units built before 1975. The law restricts rent increases for the elderly and disabled even further. Exemptions for improvements, rehabilitation, and landlord hardship have been included; these would allow further rent increases.

† In the current analysis, we discuss the NBID only in terms of how it proceeded in Mount Pleasant; Adams Morgan, which was also part of the original NBID plan, took a different course. Adams Morgan is an adjacent neighborhood where the main commercial corridor, which has become a regional as well as nationally recognized entertainment district, ultimately established a BID in 2006. Interests, conditioned by neighborhood power relations and their linkages to citywide BID advocates and political actors, aligned to provide the momentum needed to create the Adams Morgan Partnership BID, although it has and continues to be controversial. Additionally, community stakeholders had different views of both the NBID and their neighborhood (see Schaller, 2007).

‡ See the section of the D.C. code that deals with business improvement districts (Business Improvement District Enabling Legislation of 1996).

negotiations with only the business associations and commercial property owners (as opposed to all the business owners on the corridor); final approval would entail a petition process of the business owners, with no input from residents or other community actors.

Although the NBID was designed with consumer income in mind, residents who live in the numerous apartment buildings along the commercial corridor and who constitute a significant consumer base for local businesses were not conceived of as stakeholders in the project. Moreover, NBID promotional materials reveal that the activities of the NBID were internally predefined by the CDC. These materials propose supplemental street cleaning, security, streetscape improvement, marketing services, and cultural events. Notably, more than 50 percent of the proposed budget was apportioned to security.

Examining Ideologies of Space

Data and Methodology

In Mount Pleasant, the dominant representations of space on which the BID model rests are reflected in both the document promoting the NBID and Euro-American civic group perspectives about rights to neighborhood space. To get at perspectives about neighborhood belonging and uses of public space that are at odds with the NBID proposal and largely absent from public decision-making meetings, we examine disputes on the Mount Pleasant Forum e-mail list, as well as conflicting perspectives that emerged from the mapping project.

Mapping

The mapping project was conducted in the spring and summer of 2000 as the first stage of a large-scale neighborhood visioning project run by a Latino/a CDC where we both worked at the time (the same CDC that was spearheading the NBID). The project was funded by a grant to strengthen neighborhood assets and resources by promoting collaboration between neighborhood constituents—both institutions and individuals—with no prior history of working together. The visioning project included a three-phase mapping project, an oral history project with the first successful housing cooperative in the neighborhood, and the creation of a neighborhood resource center at the local public library, to include English as a second language, General Equivalency Diploma, and citizenship resources, as well as information on community organizations and research on the neighborhood.

In the first phase of the mapping project, the CDC partnered with a Vietnamese youth center, the local public library, and a predominantly Euro-American neighborhood civic organization; in addition, members of a predominantly Latino/a housing cooperative located on the commercial corridor took part in the mapping project as participants in the CDC's housing initiatives. The second phase of the project was to add a multiethnic housing cooperative association (whose membership included Latinos/as of multiple national backgrounds, African Americans, Euro-Americans, and Afro-Caribbeans) and a multiethnic, locally based youth research group.

Because Mount Pleasant community members are often suspicious of or hesitant to participate in research, we took a social networks approach (cf. Milroy, 1987) to the mapping project and worked through already established social networks so that people would feel more at ease and to generate more discussion than might have been possible in groups of strangers. The first round of the mapping project was conducted with members of the collaborating organizations. We started with six groups of community members who knew each other, representing four constituent groups: (1) the predominantly Euro-American civic organization, (2) Latino/a residents of a low-income housing cooperative, (3) housing organizers from the Latino/a community development corporation (these were employees who were community members and who were not involved in the design and planning of the mapping or visioning project and who were not involved in the NBID initiative), and (4) three groups of teenagers in the Vietnamese youth center's summer program. The mapping workshop facilitators for each group were visioning project staff who had social ties with the group in question.

Facilitators asked participants to draw maps of the neighborhood that showed "how [they saw] this part of town," and stated that "maps should show the important things that would make someone from somewhere else understand what the neighborhood is like, and what life here is like." After the map drawing part of the workshop, each person explained his or her map to the group. To compensate for varied levels of literacy skills, we paid considerable attention to the presentation and discussion portion of the workshops, as participants contributed equally to the conversation regardless of literacy skills.*

Facilitators encouraged participants to ask questions or make comments on each other's maps. The data generated in the workshops consists of both the maps themselves and the conversations about the maps. The purpose of the first round of mapping workshops was to gather baseline data of multiple ways that community members construct neighborhood space and to identify community members who (along with the youth and housing groups who would participate in the second phase of the project) were interested in becoming facilitators to conduct mapping workshops within their own social networks in various locales, for example, at beauty shops, bars, churches, laundromats, and among neighbors and friendship groups.

---

* A skilled note taker was present at each workshop to record the discourse. Such workshops could also be audio- or video recorded; we did not do so in this study because workshop participants were extremely uncomfortable about being recorded.

In addition to broadening the demographic base of the mapping data, the second phase of the mapping project was to be used to identify community members to participate in larger-scale community development visioning projects. The third phase of the project was to work across, rather than within, social networks, to bring together participants from different mapping workshops to work on setting agendas for community development, and to strengthen relationships across ethnic, socioeconomic, and age groups.

Because of institutional reorganizations and staff changes at the CDC leading the mapping project, the second and third phases of the project were never completed. This means that there are some limitations to the data available for the present study. First, there was only one African American participant in the mapping workshops—a member of the civic group—and he was present only for the post-map-drawing discussion part of the workshop. Thus, the present analysis gives little insight into the views of African American community members. The lack of African American participants may reflect the declining African American population in Mount Pleasant and the consequent change in the local political power structure; had this study been done even five years prior, there would have been more African Americans in the locally elected civic group and more African American tenants in the housing cooperative building. The perspective that this African American participant voiced in the discussion largely corresponded with those expressed by the Euro-American civic group members, which points to the possibility that socioeconomic/occupational class or level of education may play a greater role in divergent representations of space than race and ethnicity per se. Second, it is difficult to know to what extent age plays a role because in the data, age and ethnicity are conflated. However, given that the perspectives of the Vietnamese teenagers are in many ways convergent with those of the Latino/a adults, age does not seem to be as determining a factor as ethnicity or class. Further research is therefore needed to investigate the interaction of ethnicity, class, and age, as well as of gender, in the representation and experience of urban space.

Electronic Constructions of Space: The Mount Pleasant Forum

The Mount Pleasant Forum is a neighborhood e-mail list that announces local events and items or services people are offering or looking for, and where Mount Pleasant residents, community workers, and merchants discuss community issues and controversies. At the time of data collection (1999–2000), the list had around 1,000 members. The list presents a diversity of opinions and enables heated debates about community life. Despite the large number of list participants, however, the forum reaches only a limited segment of the community because it is accessible only to those who have the technical and (English) literacy skills, material resources, and free time needed to access and participate in Internet-based discussion. In addition to people who subscribe to the list, some other community members have it forwarded to their e-mail, and still others read hard copies printed out by their housemates or partners or posted on apartment building bulletin boards and at the public library. The forum plays an important role in the community, and debates on the list often resurface as agenda items in civic group meetings where community development policies and projects are determined.

Borders, Leisure, and Using Public Space

Public choice theory is built partially on the assumptions of free choice and mobility. However, in practice, choice is often constrained and mobility coerced through displacement due to local real estate markets. In mixed-income neighborhoods contemplating NBID innovations, it is critical to take into account the impact of an NBID model on the discursive, political, social, and physical displacement of community members because the NBID jurisdiction may circumscribe the definition of who constitutes the local community. Because NBIDs have the potential to form a local quasi-government institution with the power to collect revenues and to reallocate these resources within their geographical jurisdiction, the micropolitics of how neighborhood boundaries are constructed and institutionalized should be integral to a discussion surrounding the establishment of an NBID.

Furthermore, neighborhood boundaries onto which NBIDs may be grafted are socially constructed and often embedded in historical conflicts. The 1920s' move of Mount Pleasant's eastern boundary from 14th to 16th Street, for example, became a fixed jurisdictional boundary that came to segregate African Americans from Euro-Americans (Gale, 1987).* Constructions of the neighborhood's eastern border as an ethnic border and consequent tensions over this border thus have a long history and are often reiterated in contemporary discourses.

A comparison of the maps from the mapping project reveals a disparity between the various mapping groups' portrayals of neighborhood boundaries and public space usage (see Figures 16.1 and 16.2). Comparing local conceptions of neighborhood space to conceptions promoted in formal revitalization project proposals is key to gaining an understanding of whose perspectives on neighborhood life get privileged and institutionalized. The sharpest differences between the mapping groups emerge in delineations of Mount Pleasant's contours, uses of public space, and attitudes toward safety, danger, and what constitutes appropriate public behavior. In the mapping project, the civic group members talked about the neighborhood in ways that were consistent with the NBID's commercialized vision of space. Furthermore, this group's maps conform most closely to the perceptions of neighborhood borders promoted by the city and represented in the NBID, the majority of civic organizations and many CBOs, and by many of the professional class.

---

* For a discussion of the role of race and ethnicity in shifting neighborhood boundaries, see Lendt (1960) and Katznelson (1981) on their descriptions of Washington Heights in New York City.

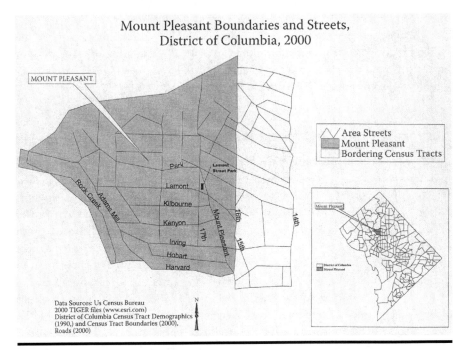

Figure 16.1   Mount Pleasant official boundaries and streets, District of Columbia, 2000.

In the civic group's descriptions of their maps, participants naturalized the neighborhood boundaries, portraying them predominantly as static geographical features that are "just there" rather than as social borders that have been created by government agencies or the spatial practices of some community members.

These participants focused on the physical—the topography of the neighborhood— explaining that the parkland and hilly terrain to the north, west, and south enclose the neighborhood and make it self-contained. These mapmakers all drew 16th Street as the neighborhood's eastern border. Although 16th Street is a boundary that would seem to be part of a built rather than "natural" environment, this street emerges in civic group participants' drawings and descriptions as an equally static and strong, thick geographical boundary that contributes to isolating Mount Pleasant from other neighborhoods. This group also saw 16th Street as separating racial groups, and separating relative crime from relative safety. One participant remarked,

> 16th Street is a demarcation line. What goes on over there is usually kept over there. There are different kinds of activities. More recently, the criminal element has been brought down because of the metro station.

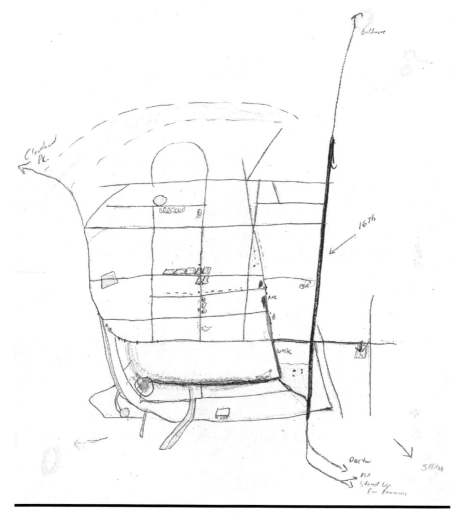

Figure 16.2   Mount Pleasant: Civic group boundaries.

Another participant added:

> Before the metro came in, I didn't have occasion to go over there [the other side of 16th Street] very much, now I'm going over there every day. It feels safer, looks safer. [But] it's a little peninsula, 'cause [the metro's] the only place to go, you or me have no other reason to go there.

Such demarcations did not hold true for the other mapping groups (see Figures 16.3 and 16.4). On the maps of the Latino/a community development organization, the Latino/a tenants, and the Vietnamese youth center teenagers, the

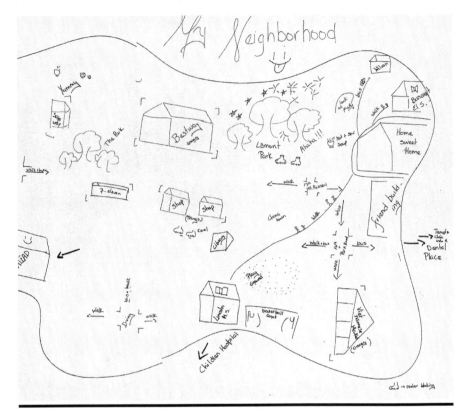

Figure 16.3   Mount Pleasant: Vietnamese youth group map.

borders of the neighborhood were drawn further to the east and the south and generally did not extend into the more expensive and more Euro-American western part of the neighborhood. On the Vietnamese youth group map in Figure 16.3, for example, the rough borders are Mount Pleasant Street to the west and 14th Street to the east.

Whereas the civic group's borders were primarily based on the static neighborhood topography and jurisdictional boundaries, the other groups' borders were strongly tied to uses of space. Rather than being organized (solely) by geographical layout, these maps were organized around embodied experience. In other words, they were strongly based on activities in which map drawers participate on a frequent basis and places where such activities occur. (Embodied experience did play some role in civic group maps—for example, in regard to the metro and their fear of crossing over 16th Street into the adjacent neighborhood—but to a much more limited extent.)

The Vietnamese and Latino/a mapmakers also defined the contours of Mount Pleasant through structures of feeling (Williams, 1985); although most of their maps excluded the wealthier, predominantly single-family dwelling areas west of

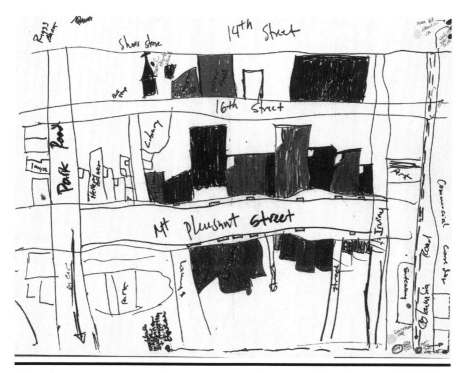

Figure 16.4   Mount Pleasant: Latino/a community development corporation (CDC) map.

Mount Pleasant Street, they included Columbia Road, a commercial corridor located southwest of the official Mount Pleasant borders. These mapmakers remarked that they put Columbia Road on their maps because "it feels like Mount Pleasant Street." Latino/a participants also noted businesses on Columbia Road that play important roles in the Latino/a community. (See right side of Figure 16.4.) For example, one participant exclaimed that "Zodiac was the only place in 1985 that you could get Spanish music." Such comments show the prominence of the view among many Latinos/as that Mount Pleasant is predominantly a Latino/a place.*

Similarly, Vietnamese participants used markers of embodied experience to construct Mount Pleasant as a Vietnamese place. For example, in contrast to civic group members' geographically isolated maps, in which Mount Pleasant was drawn as an island in a sea of emptiness, many of the teenagers' maps show the neighborhood as connected to other Vietnamese places. Often, 16th Street and Park Road—the street with the highest concentration of Vietnamese residents in the neighborhood— are drawn as the main axes around which the neighborhood is organized. This can be seen in Figure 16.5, where 16th Street is portrayed not as a

---

* With the intense gentrification that has gone on in the neighborhood since this data was collected, this view may have changed.

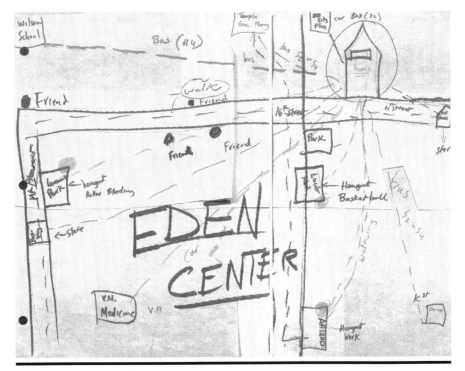

Figure 16.5   Eden Center Mount Pleasant Vietnamese youth group map.

barrier but as a thoroughfare that links Mount Pleasant to Vietnamese institutions and establishments in Maryland and Virginia. It is this neighborhood map's spatialization of Vietnamese identity that enables the Vietnamese strip mall Eden Center, which is in the outer Northern Virginia suburbs, to appear in the map's center.

The various mapping groups conceived ways to use neighborhood spaces—particularly the commercial corridor—quite differently. Whereas the low-income resident groups did not define spending money as an integral component of socializing in neighborhood space, for members of the civic group and one member of the community development group, a considerable amount of such socializing was discussed as connected to consumption, particularly food and drink.

The Vietnamese and Latino/a mapmakers' socializing in public space leads to a different perception about what public space is for. Those who frequently use neighborhood spaces such as sidewalks, building stoops, and the park talked about these sites as places to "hang out" and "meet friends"; on the contrary, those who do not tend to socialize in such spaces tended to link appropriate use of public space to whether people have a legitimate goal. For example, one member of the Euro-American civic group remarked that on Mount Pleasant Street, "people are just hanging out idly; you get the sense that they're up to no good. It's depressing that people don't have any other things to do with their time."

This view relies on a deficit model, a model that also undergirds BID-type renovation projects. People socializing in public space, from this perspective, simply do not have the resources to engage in other activities (Modan, 2002, 2007). Yet this conception of public space as a venue primarily suited for market-based interactions contrasts starkly with the other groups' narrations, which describe the pleasures of running into friends, talking on the street, rollerblading on the basketball court, and listening to mariachi musicians in the park. The civic group's view that such uses of public space are inappropriate leads to a common but inaccurate conflation of hanging out in public space with disadvantage, drunkenness, and suspicious or illegal activities: civic group members describe "people entering stores, people buying things, having a purpose" as "more comforting." It is exactly these sentiments that have been incorporated in the NBID's emphasis on an increased security force and more stringent loitering statutes.

The Vietnamese and Latino/a maps and their concurrent explanations reveal a Mount Pleasant that is markedly different from the one proposed by the NBID. These mapmakers generally do not consider the wealthier, more Euro-American part of official Mount Pleasant (the western part of the neighborhood) to be part of their neighborhood. In their view, the neighborhood is defined through use of public space rather than through static government-sanctioned borders. The implication of this is that people who use public space in the neighborhood are important stakeholders in the neighborhood. The NBID proposal, however, ignores this experience-based view of the neighborhood and defines its jurisdictional boundaries in accordance with official borders, borders also promoted by civic group participants.

Because civic groups and civic group meetings are also the vehicles for public decision making, civic group members are consequently able to exploit (whether intentionally or not) the similarity between their borders and the government-defined borders and to add legitimacy and authority to their views of who is included in or excluded from Mount Pleasant and whose vision of the neighborhood prevails. Notably, the people who view the boundaries of the neighborhood as fixed and as geographically determined are also the people who have the most means to stay in the neighborhood—homeowners not affected by increasing rents or renters who do not have financial difficulties in paying rent increases. On the other hand, the borders of the other mapping groups are social and flexible and can be stretched to include people who move east, where rents up until very recently have been lower.* This kind of construction of borders allows people who move east to remain community members. They can still be considered to have a legitimate stake in what happens in the neighborhood and a legitimate right to a neighborhood voice. With the rigid boundaries, which are also proposed as the NBID boundaries, someone who moves across them is no longer defined as a community member. In other words, both the civic group perspective and the NBID boundaries deny

---

* With massive market-oriented redevelopment around the metro station on 14th Street, rents east of 16th Street have been steadily rising in the last few years.

community members moving east a voice in neighborhood decision making despite the fact that their social networks, schools, shopping, and patronage of other institutions still center on the neighborhood.

Danger, Culture, and Restructuring Public Space

Although the civic group's characterizations of public space in the mapping project are quite anomalous in comparison with the other mapmakers, in the context of local public discourse about Mount Pleasant Street we see that the civic group's ideas about appropriate and inappropriate behavior are consistent with the views of Mount Pleasant's more wealthy and well-connected residents. An analysis of e-mails on the local listserv about safety, cleanliness, and orderly conduct on and around Mount Pleasant Street further exposes the ethnic and class tensions surrounding competing claims made on public space. In discussions of community controversies in public sites such as the e-mail forum, Mount Pleasant residents frequently cite socializing on the street without consuming as problematic and threatening behavior. Furthermore, their proposed interventions to get rid of such behavior often entail the restructuring of public space in ways that are removed from an inclusive public accountability. In this manner, the attitudes and actions of members of the professional class reinforce policy approaches that focus primarily on creating a sense of safety and orderliness on the commercial corridor. These actions and attitudes and the resultant places are conditioned by class and cultural standpoints.

A prime example of this phenomenon is a discussion about an annual fund-raising event planned by another civic organization, a gala catered dinner with a $50 ticket in the park at the end of Mount Pleasant Street. This event caused quite a bit of controversy in the neighborhood and heated exchanges on the listserv. Whereas one commonly promoted perspective on the listerv highlighted the displacement and structural (economic) exclusion of the usual users of the park, another prevalent view focused on the "reclaiming" of public space by people who did not usually patronize the park, from people using it for "inappropriate" and criminal purposes. But the reclaimers' view of the park—in the words of one list participant, it is a place "usually used to drink, sleep, spit, and perform illicit business transactions"— contrasts starkly with perspectives of this same park held by the low-income Vietnamese teenagers and Latino/a tenants, as well as the medium-income Latino/a community development workers of the mapping project.

These mapping participants identified the park and the neighborhood streets as places of leisure where they meet friends, take their children to play, hang out, and go to find community. Like their higher-income neighbors, some of these residents also discussed the parks and streets as threatening places where one might encounter violence, but they generally considered danger more likely to be present at night. Some asserted that the neighborhood was not dangerous if one was not alone.

Whereas more quality-of-life community members like the e-mail writer saw people spending time in public space—irrespective of the activities they were conducting—as generally threatening and "up to no good," many of the Latino/a and Vietnamese mapping workshop participants remarked that people on the street made them feel more comfortable. These participants, for example, commented, "On Mount Pleasant Street, I always feel safe; it doesn't matter what time of day or night" or "I don't feel safe on the side streets 'cause it's not a lot of people."

Local discourses of public space are also often embedded in racialized constructions of danger. This was present in observations made by both mapping workshop participants and forum posters. As one Vietnamese teenager remarked, "After 9 P.M., I cannot go outside because some black people hate me; they hate some Asians, some Vietnamese people got mugged." In ascribing the danger to hate, this speaker acknowledges racial tensions in the neighborhood, and thus links danger to larger sociopolitical issues.

On the forum, we see similar constructions. However, whereas the low-income and youth mapping participants' descriptions tend to focus on actual criminal activities and underlying racial tensions, on the forum, many racialized stories of threat focus on hanging out in and of itself as a problem. As one forum writer remarks,

> About the groups of men who hang all day on the fence on Frazier Street…they like to stare threateningly at white males who walk by, and of course, they make disgusting comments to any woman who walks by.* I imagine most women reading this would feel way safer on any Georgetown street than on Mount Pleasant Street. In Georgetown, they (meaning residents and businesses) do not tolerate drunken loiterers harassing pedestrians. This is not a racist or cultural attack but a discussion about making our street safe for us and our children.

The speaker, a self-described homeowner who "recently moved into the neighborhood," shows his discomfort with different people and distinct modes of using public space by constructing young Latino men† as threatening potential criminals. By gendering the discourse and inserting the disclaimer that "this is not a racist or cultural attack" (thereby, contrary to his claim, bringing race and culture into the

---

* Although the writer constructs these men as anonymous and a menacing and threatening presence in the neighborhood, in point of fact, the young men who hung out at this fence in 1999–2000 were the same group of friends who met daily to socialize, generally did not drink, and were often quite polite to women, making comments such as "Hola señora, que le vaya bien" ("Hello ma'am, have a nice day"), using the formal grammar form. Whereas there are certainly men on the street who are drunk or who make more vulgar remarks, these particular men cannot be counted in that group.

† The inference that the men in question are Latino derives from the reference to "a racist or cultural attack" as well as the fact that the majority of men who socialize on Mount Pleasant Street and on the particular street corner mentioned are Latino.

discussion and highlighting them as potentially relevant lenses through which to read his comment), he frames his commentary in terms of the public welfare while reinforcing commonly held cultural stereotypes.

The writer continues that "there is little the police can do unless there is an assault or something" (as the behavior of these men is not actually criminal), and he poses several public and collective solutions. What is crucial to understanding his suggestions is that like the NBID proposal, they are suggestions that would reconfigure the physical space on this contested street corner by means that are removed from public accountability. One such strategy that the writer offers is "to remove the fence," offering to "do the work for free," thus situating himself as a good neighbor.* He goes on to suggest that the installation of "bright lights would probably disperse them a bit," presumably by increasing public surveillance. Finally, he 'jokingly' remarks that he has "seriously considered getting several of my male friends to 'occupy' the fence for an afternoon."

In setting up a comparison between Mount Pleasant and Georgetown—a wealthy, predominantly Euro-American neighborhood—the writer reveals his aspirations for the neighborhood; at the same time, he asserts the right to lay a physical claim to neighborhood space, even though the fence is the private property belonging to the Latino/a market on the corner.

A large portion of the NBID's proposed budget is allocated toward security or "goodwill ambassadors." Given the tensions on Mount Pleasant Street, however, many community organizers and community-based organization professionals view the institutionalization of privatized security as serving the interests of a few residents and predict that people assembled in small groups will be harassed for "loitering" and asked to move on. Thus, NBID security measures threaten to disrupt current street life, which is characterized as much by public drinking as it is by widespread public enjoyment of leisure activities such as listening to music; catching up with friends; attaining work; arguing about local, national, and international politics; and renewing and strengthening social networks and support systems.

Conclusions

Although an NBID may regulate public life on the street in Mount Pleasant, increase the perception of safety for certain constituents, and restructure the business environment to suit its preferences, it also threatens to suppress the varied expression of human interaction, constrain the capacity of small businesses to stay afloat, and inflame already existing tensions. In Mount Pleasant, surveillance of public space and the narrowing of citizenship into consumership cause intense neighborhood conflict. The increased surveillance of street life under an NBID has

---

* Recently, this fence has been replaced with a wrought-iron one that is impossible to sit on. Rather than causing dispersion, however, the new fence just gets leaned on.

the potential of deepening the current social and ethnic cleavages and reinscribing onto the urban geography historical class, ethnic, and racial prejudices.

BIDs concentrate power in a narrow set of actors, primarily property owners and secondarily business owners. The NBID framework, modeled on public choice theory, threatens to reinforce political constellations that further exclude traditionally marginalized low-income residents and small businesses. Consequently, it is crucial that critiques levied against BIDs, particularly NBIDs, focus on questions of neighborhood power relations. Although NBIDs pose similar problems as BIDs, these problems are exacerbated at the neighborhood level because they threaten residential-based social networks that aid residents in attaining health care, child care, educational resources, job leads, legal advice, and so on.

Neighborhood power relations, as we have illustrated, are embedded in normative discourses on public space, discourses that should form part and parcel of an analysis of public accountability and citizen participation. It was an analysis of these very relations that caused the Mount Pleasant Business Association to opt out of the BID project. Too many business owners in Mount Pleasant saw the BID project as another step in a gentrification process that was driving longtime residents from the neighborhood, and a means to privatize services that they considered to be part of the public good, and thus the responsibility of the city to which they pay some of the highest taxes in the country.

Public neighborhood spaces have the unique capacity to function as places where citizens can confront one another and engage conflict directly. Mount Pleasant has a number of spaces in which community members do just that. For example, a group of activist residents formed a street theater group and put together a performance in the local park that focused on issues of gentrification. Through drama, they confronted and engaged the multiple forms of racism, sexism, and classism that they observed in the daily practice of local residents, politicians, and businesses as well as in the discussions on the neighborhood e-mail forum. Through parody, biting humor, and channeled expression of anger, they created moments of intense discomfort and hysterical relief. At the same time, their work also engaged people on the plaza in open debate about these issues. Processes of community building that simultaneously elicit discomfort and debate support the construction of an inclusive notion of citizenship because they unmask our fallibility as a society and make salient our own complicity in reproducing a system of economic, social, and political inequity. Revitalization strategies such as NBIDs, on the other hand, respond to and, through selective resource allocation, institutionalize the vision, needs, and desires of groups of constituents and stakeholders who already command greater access to economic and political capital.

As planning practitioners, whether working at community-based organizations, in government offices, or as political activists, one of our responsibilities should remain the deliberate reclaiming of public spaces as truly public forums in which citizen engagement can be expanded through community processes that highlight and empower alternative voices to interrogate whom "possessive" and consumptive individualism really benefits (cf. Zukin, 1995). The dynamic recasting of the urbanization process through the lens of social production of space should be of particular interest to planners who, whether unwittingly or designedly, have participated in the development of an instrumental, rationalized conception of urban space that masks or distorts the power relations undergirding its restructuring (Sandercock, 1998).

The case study of Mount Pleasant illustrates how the dominant representation of the neighborhood corresponds with the allocation of local political and economic power, and that the convergence of these has privileged institutional and elite boundaries, functions, and meanings attributed to neighborhood spaces. At the same time, our discussion of the neighborhood micropolitics demonstrates that diverse neighborhood constituents have created a particularly local dynamic through their everyday practices, creating alternative spaces of representation that can counteract the dominant spatial practices that threaten many constituents' claims to the neighborhood. A qualitative analysis of neighborhood public discourse and participatory planning activities such as the mapping workshop is useful in understanding the urban situations that (N)BIDs are imposed on. Such an analysis highlights the class and ethnic conflicts over claims to and interpretations of public space that BIDs mask.

References

Banerjee, T. 2001. The future of public space: Beyond invented streets and reinvented places. *APA Journal* 67:9–24.

Briffault, R. 1999. Government of our time: Business improvement districts and urban governance. *Columbia Law Review* 99:365–477.

Business Improvement District Enabling Legislation of 1996. District of Columbia Official Code. 2006 edition. Division I, Government of District. Title 2, Government Administration. Chapter 12, Business and Economic Development. Subchapter VIII, Business Improvement Districts. http://government.westlaw.com/linkedslice/default. asp?SP=DCC-1000 (accessed July 20, 2007).

Christopherson, S. 1994. The fortress city, privatized spaces, consumer citizenship. In *Post-Fordism: A reader*, ed. A. Amin, 409–427. Cambridge, MA: Blackwell.

Davies, M. 1997. Business improvement districts. *Washington University Journal of Urban and Contemporary Law* 52:187–224.

District of Columbia Department of Housing and Community Development (DHCD). 2002. *Consolidated plan for the District of Columbia fiscal year 2000 action plan.* Washington, DC: Author.

Gale, D. 1987. *Washington, DC: Inner city revitalization and minority suburbanization.* Philadelphia: Temple University Press.

Gibson, J. 1999. *Neighborhood business improvement district (BID) development.* Washington, DC: Latino Economic Development Corporation.

Goldsmith, W., and Blakely, E. 1992. *Separate societies: Poverty and inequalities in U.S. cities.* Philadelphia: Temple University Press.

Harvey, D. 1990. *Condition of postmodernity: An enquiry into the origins of cultural change.* Cambridge, MA: Blackwell.

Houstoun, L. 1997. *BIDs: Business improvement districts.* Washington, DC: Urban Land Institute and International Downtown Association.

Katznelson, I. 1981. *City trenches: Urban politics and the patterning of class in the United States.* New York: Pantheon.

Latino Economic Development Corporation. 1998. *The "I Love Mount Pleasant" business directory.* Washington, DC: Author and Mount Pleasant Business Association.

Lefebvre, H. 1991. *The production of space,* trans. D. Nicholson-Smith. Cambridge, MA: Blackwell.

Lendt, L. 1960. A social history of Washington Heights, New York City. Unpublished manuscript. New York: Columbia-Washington Heights Community Mental Health Project.

Low, S. 1996. Spatializing culture: The social production and social construction of public space in Costa Rica. *American Ethnologist* 23:861–879.

Lowenstein, S. 1989. *Frankfurt on the Hudson: The German-Jewish community of Washington Heights 1933–1983, its structure and culture.* Detroit, MI: Wayne State University Press.

Lowery, D. 1998. Consumer sovereignty and quasi-market failure. *Journal of Public Administration Research and Theory* 8:137–172.

Mallett, W. 1994. Managing the postindustrial city: Business improvement districts in the United States. *Area* 26:276–287.

Massey, D., and Denton, N. 1993. *American apartheid: Segregation and the making of the underclass.* Cambridge, MA: Harvard University Press.

Milroy, L. 1987. *Language and social networks.* New York: Blackwell.

Mitchell, D. 2001. *Cultural geography: A critical introduction.* Malden, MA: Blackwell.

Mitchell, D. 2003. *The right to the city: Social justice and the fight for public space.* New York: Gilford.

Mitchell, J. 1999. Business improvement districts and innovative service delivery. Grant report for the Pricewaterhouse Coopers Endowment for Government. http://www.businessofgovernment.org/pdfs/Mitchell.pdf (accessed September 2001).

Modan, G. 2002. "Public toilets for a diverse neighborhood": Spatial purification practices in community development discourse. *Journal of Sociolinguistics* 6:487–513.

Modan, G. 2007. *Turf wars: Discourse, diversity, and the politics of place.* Malden, MA: Blackwell.

Pendall, R. 2000. Local land use planning: Regulation and the chain of exclusion. *Journal of American Planning Association* 66:125–142.

Rent Control Reform Amendment Act of 2006. District of Columbia Code 2006 Edition. Division VII, Property. Title 42, Real Property. Chapter 35, subchapters 1 and 2. http://www.dcra.dc.gov/dcra/frames.asp?doc=/dcra/lib/dcra/information/rental_house/rent_control_pamphlet_8.04.06.pdf (accessed July 19, 2007).

Rodman, M. 1993. Beyond built form and culture in the anthropological study of residential community spaces. In *The cultural meaning of urban space,* ed. R. Rotenberg and G. McDonogh, 123–138. London: Bergin and Garvey.

Sandercock, L., ed. 1998. *Making the invisible visible: A multicultural planning history.* Berkeley: University of California Press.

Savas, E. S. 2000. *Privatization and public private partnerships.* New York: Chatham.

Schaller, S. 2007. Bidding on urbanity with business improvement districts: Re-making urban places in Washington, DC. Unpublished Ph.D. dissertation, Cornell University.

Schaller, S., and Modan, G. 2005. Contesting public space and citizenship: Implications for neighborhood business improvement districts. *Journal of Planning Education and Research* 24:394–407.

Smith, N. 2002. New globalism, new urbanism: Gentrification as global urban strategy. *Antipode* 34:427–450.

Soja, E. W. 1989. *Postmodern geographies: The reassertion of space in critical social theory.* London: Verso.

Sorkin, M. 1992. *Variation on a theme park: The new American city and the end of public space.* New York: Hill and Wang.

Starr, P. 1987. *The limits of privatization.* Washington, DC: Economic Policy Institute.

Stokes, R. J. 2002. Business improvement districts: Their political, economic and quality of life impacts. Unpublished Ph.D. dissertation, Rutgers University.

Tiebout, C. M. 1956. The pure theory of local expenditures. *Journal of Political Economy* 64:416–424.

U.S. Census Bureau. 2003. Census tracts 27.1 and 27.2. Census 2000 Summary File 1 (SF 1), 100-Percent Data Files H11A–I. Census 2000 Summary File 3 (SF 3), Sample Data, Detailed Tables Files P157A–I. http://www.census.gov (accessed July 22, 2003).

Webster, C. 1998. Public choice, Pigouvian and Coasian planning theory. *Urban Studies* 31:53–75.

Williams, R. 1985. *Marxism and literature.* New York: Oxford University Press.

Zukin, S. 1995. *The culture of cities.* Cambridge, MA: Blackwell.

BIDS IN CANADA, BRITAIN, AND IRELAND

Chapter 17

The Strategic Evolution of the BID Model in Canada*

Tony Hernandez and Ken Jones

Contents

Introduction

Downtowns have traditionally been the economic hub for larger market areas or regions providing a major source of employment (e.g., corporate head offices and

---

* This chapter first appeared as Hernandez and Jones (2005) and is reproduced with minor changes by permission of the publisher.

401

government functions/services) and the location of a mix of business types (e.g., finance, retail, personal and business services) providing access to a broad range of goods and services. The downtowns have also served a range of social and cultural functions (Yeates, 1998). They are often the center for tourism and heritage and house services and cultural amenities such as hospitals, courthouses, churches, museums, theaters, and universities. These areas are home to a diverse resident population, typically living within relatively high-density housing. Downtowns are central places where people work, live, and spend their leisure time. As Lea et al. (2003, p. 1) note, a city is often judged by the economic, social, and cultural vitality of its downtown. The downtown shopping area has historically played an important role in defining the image of a city. For example, New York City is associated with the perceived health and vibrancy of 5th Avenue, Chicago by State Street and Michigan Avenue, Paris by Les Champs Elysées, London by Oxford Street, Montréal by Ste. Catherine Street, and Toronto by Yonge Street and Bloor-Yorkville.

For Canadians, downtowns have traditionally been regarded as safe, healthy, and vibrant places, especially when compared to their U.S. counterparts. However, multiple pressures from the suburbanization of population and commercial structure (facilitated by car-based transport infrastructure expansion), the general aging of the downtown, and the demise of the downtown department stores have resulted in the signs of decline in many of Canada's downtowns. The long-term health of the downtown is associated with a variety of factors that include continued investments in public transit to serve the core, the ease of access and availability of parking, lack of crime, the existence of residential population, a significant downtown workforce, a mix of high-quality retail and services, a well-established and -funded cultural infrastructure, a strong tourism base, and a clean environment (Lea et al., 2003). Maintaining, promoting, and investing in the multiple functions of these areas remain essential to avoid the cycle of decline that leads to the hollowing out of the downtown, as has been witnessed across many urban areas in the United States, for example, Detroit and Cleveland. Evidence of the downtown decline in Canada has led to an increased interest in downtown revitalization (see, for example, Feehan and Feit, 2006; Filion et al., 2004; Mason, 2003; Canadian Institute for Planners, 2002; Holle and Owens, 2002; Canadian Urban Institute, 2001; Levy, 2001; Robertson, 1999).

This chapter details the changing nature of retail and service activity in Canada's downtowns and examines the role and effectiveness of business improvement districts (BIDs) in promoting downtown vitality.* The chapter is divided into four sections. In the first section, the Canadian urban retail context is established with data on population and retail sales trends over time. This temporal perspective highlights the significant structural shifts in urban retailing in Canada and

---

* In Canada business improvement districts (BIDs) are officially known as business improvement areas (BIAs). In this chapter I will use the more generally known term *business improvement districts*.

provides a framework within which downtown BIDs can be assessed. The second section tracks the development, structure, and function of BIDs in the Province of Ontario; examples of typical activities undertaken by BIDs are provided. The third section presents a case study that details the development and activities of the Downtown Yonge BID and outlines a range of metrics that can be used to measure BID performance. The chapter concludes by discussing the role of strategic planning within downtown revitalization.

Urban Change in Canada

In Canada, similar to many developed nations, the shift from rural to urban population has taken place at a rapid rate over the last half century (McCann and Smith, 1991). In 1931, 54 percent of Canada's population was classified as urban; by 2001 this had increased to 80 percent (Statistics Canada, 2003). The nine major metropolitan areas in Canada with a resident population of over 500,000 (in descending order: Toronto, Montréal, Vancouver, Ottawa-Gatineau, Calgary, Edmonton, Québec, Winnipeg, and Hamilton) were home to 16 million people in 2001, more than half of Canada's total population. However, 45 percent of the 140 urban areas (so defined by Statistics Canada) lost population between 1996 and 2001. Among those cities with less than 250,000 population, the ratio is 64 of 124 (52 percent). Urban growth has largely been confined to the major metropolitan areas (Simmons, 2003); for example, from 1996 to 2001, Calgary's population grew by 15.8 percent, Toronto's by 9.8 percent, Edmonton's by 8.7 percent, and Vancouver's by 8.5 percent. The increasing concentration of population in major metropolitan centers has been fueled by the preference among new immigrants (the driving force of population growth in Canada) to reside in the largest cities. Despite the 4 percent growth rate in total population across Canada from 1996 to 2001—notably the slowest rate of population growth in Canada since the depression in the 1930s—a large number of urban areas has experienced declines in population. This is a signal to those businesses located in small to mid-sized urban areas that their markets are decreasing in absolute size. These changes are significantly altering the economic, social, and cultural structure of urban Canada (Bunting and Filion, 2000).

The rural–urban shift and concentration of population in major urban centers has taken place in parallel with the widespread suburbanization of population. An analysis of the downtown municipalities (downtown/inner urban) and outer municipalities (suburbs) in the top 27 metropolitan areas reveals the differential growth rates between the urban core and suburbs (Statistics Canada, 2002). While the population of the core municipalities increased 4.3 percent between 1996 and 2001, the surrounding suburbs grew at 8.5 percent. The growth in the suburban municipalities has been driven by migration (national and international) and natural increase (young families choose to live and raise children in the suburbs). Of the top 25 fastest-growing municipalities in Canada in 2001, 17 were those that surrounded the downtown municipality of a major metropolitan area (Statistics Canada, 2002). The significance of this suburbanization is in the resulting impact that such movement and growth of population has on the commercial structure. The Canadian population is increasingly locating in sprawling suburbs—mirroring the trends in the United States.

As a result, many areas have witnessed a steady suburbanization of commercial activity. The major structural shift in retail activity was seen in a wave of development of large suburban regional and super-regional shopping centers in the late 1970s and 1980s (Jones and Simmons, 1990) and, more recently, in the significant growth in large-format retailing and associated power center expansion (see Hernandez et al., 2006; Simmons and Hernandez, 2004a, 2004b). These out-of-center or edge-of-center commercial venues attract consumers for a range of reasons, including ease of access, free parking, a strong mix of tenants, depth and breadth of the retail offered, and perceived price-level differentiation. Such retail developments have taken place in tandem with extensive new subdivision residential expansions. The out-of-town retail development in Canada has not been subject to the same level of planning and control as in the U.K. (Webber et al., 2005; Department of the Environment, 1996). In Canada it is not uncommon for retail development companies to "land-bank" in the urban–rural fringe, purchasing land and simply waiting for residential developments to occur—securing the prime retail locations in the process. In combination, these trends in population settlement, retail structure, and planning policy are placing increasing competitive pressures on businesses located in downtowns.

Downtown Retailing in Canada

The origins of downtown retailing in Canada can be traced as far back as the Hudson Bay Trading Company operating trading posts and general stores in the 1700s (Hudson Bay Company, Inc., 2004; Bryce, 1902), through to the rise of the T. Eaton Company and the opening of its first department store in 1869 in downtown Toronto (Santink, 1990; Nasmith, 1923; T. Eaton Company, 1919), to the widespread growth of department stores across Canada and the investment in major downtown malls in the 1970s and 1980s (Doucet, 2001). Retailing has always played an important role in the functioning of the Canadian downtown. As Lea et al. (2003) note, "downtowns, historically, are the highest order, unplanned retail node in the urban economy" (p. 1). The demise in 1999 of the Canadian retail icon the T. Eaton Company, a company that maintained its downtown focus, provided a signal as to the fragile state of the health of downtown retailing in Canada. Eaton's bankruptcy brought to the forefront the structural transformation of the Canadian retail landscape. The dominance of downtown in the retail hierarchy has been steadily eroded by more than three decades of retail suburbanization. The traditional downtown department store, once the pinnacle of Canadian retailing, has been superseded by a wave of large-format discount department stores and general merchandisers that have located primarily in the suburbs (Fyfe et al., 2004; Hernandez, 2004; Hernandez et al., 2004; Simmons, 2001; Simmons and Graff, 1998).

Since the early 1990s large-format retailing has been the driver of new retail development across metropolitan Canada. The majority of the growth has been driven by U.S. cross-border retailers, such as Wal-Mart, the Home Depot, Costco, and Best Buy (Boyle, 2003; Daniel and Hernandez, 2006; Hernandez et al., 2003). These retailers have favored the low-cost operating environment of the suburbs and clustered in increasingly large numbers within a range of power retail configurations (Simmons and Hernandez, 2004a). The first major power center opened in the northern suburbs of Toronto in 1990. By 2005, the Centre for the Study of Commercial Activity (CSCA) at Ryerson University identified 340 power centers (defined as locations with at least 3 large-format retailers in operation), including almost 7,000 stores, of which 2,500 were large format. The total floor area in power centers was 115 million square feet—roughly equivalent to 25 percent of the floor area of all conventional shopping centers. Power centers are now a significant component of the national commercial structure. It was estimated that the large-format retailers located in power centers accounted for approaching 20 percent of total retail sales in Canada in 2005.

The impact of this growth of the retail vitality in the downtowns is evident in retail sales trends. Statistics Canada compiles the Small Area Trade Retail Estimates (SARTRE) database, which provides information on retail sales and the number of retail locations by sector at the forward sortation area (FSA) level—a small postal geography (Statistics Canada, 1999). SARTRE combines data from survey and taxation sources to give a picture of all incorporated retailers in Canada. The data is disseminated on an annual basis albeit with a three-year delay in release (e.g., 2003 data was made available in 2006). Based on this data it is possible to estimate sales trends across Canada (Pearce et al., 1999) and to compare the performance of downtown FSAs across the major metropolitan markets.

Tables 17.1 and 17.2 provide comparisons of constant dollar retail sales for the nine largest metropolitan areas for the 1989–1998 and 1999–2003 periods. It should be noted that Statistics Canada changed the way in which it classifies retail activity in 1999, migrating from the Standard Industrial Classification (SIC) to the North American Industrial Classification (NAIC) system. As a result, a longitudinal comparison between 1989 and 2003 is not possible; instead, the data is divided into two reporting periods in the tables. In addition, the downtown areas were defined by FSA and are a "best approximation" of the downtown core based on information on retail structure, land use, and population densities (e.g., the FSA postal geography boundaries may not perfectly match with the idealized definition of the downtown area).

Canada's major metropolitan downtown areas experienced, in total, a –15.7 percent decline in their retail sales levels between 1989 and 1998 (see Table 17.1). Of the nine major metropolitan areas listed in the table, only Calgary posted a

Table 17.1 Retail sales by major metropolitan downtown area: 1989–1998 and 1999–2003 (excluding automotive sales, parts, and service, constant $CDN)

Downtown[a]	1989[b]	1998	Change 1989–1998	%Change 1989–1998	1999[c]	2003	Change 1999–2003	% Change 1999–2003
Toronto	2,403,172	2,086,693	−316,479	−13.2	2,850,543	3,106,346	255,804	9.0
Montréal	1,101,538	962,744	−138,794	−12.6	1,366,634	1,515,098	148,465	10.0
Vancouver	901,959	879,581	−22,377	−2.5	1,347,852	1,426,731	78,880	5.9
Ottawa	153,172	88,898	−64,275	−42.0	141,735	121,549	−20,185	−14.2
Calgary	394,483	440,681	46,198	11.7	649,552	749,744	100,192	15.4
Edmonton	429,320	222,575	−206,744	−48.2	469,920	348,505	−121,416	−25.8
Québec	302,243	294,270	−7,973	−2.6	309,001	405,815	96,814	31.3
Winnipeg	465,748	271,980	−193,768	−41.6	575,752	406,094	−169,658	−29.5
Hamilton	329,281	219,116	−110,165	−33.5	316,817	368,809	51,991	16.4
Total	6,480,915	5,466,536	−1,014,378	−15.7	8,027,806	8,448,693	420,887	5.2
Canada	146,408,000	149,417,940	3,009,940	2.1	179,883,100	198,502,057	18,618,957	10.4

Source: Statistics Canada (2006).
[a] Downtown area defined according to forward sortation areas (FSAs).
[b] 1989 constant dollars based on Standard Industrial Classification (SIC) retail codes.
[c] 1999 constant dollars based on North American Industrial Classification (NAIC) retail codes.

Table 17.2   Retail sales contribution* of the downtown by major metropolitan area: 1989–1998 and 1999–2003 (excluding automotive sales, parts, and service)

Downtown[a]	1989[b] %	1998 %	Change 1989–1998	1999[c] %	2003 %	Change 1999–2003
Toronto	12.2	10.8	−1.4	7.7	9.2	1.5
Montréal	7.6	6.8	−0.9	5.5	6.5	1.0
Vancouver	12.1	9.9	−2.1	9.2	9.0	−0.2
Ottawa	4.4	2.2	−2.2	2.0	1.8	−0.2
Calgary	10.2	9.2	−1.0	8.5	8.8	0.3
Edmonton	10.4	4.9	−5.5	6.0	4.2	−1.8
Québec	11.0	10.0	−1.0	6.7	7.8	1.1
Winnipeg	15.9	9.4	−6.5	11.3	7.9	−3.4
Hamilton	12.4	8.8	−3.6	7.1	7.3	0.2
Average	10.1	8.2	−1.9	6.8	7.6	0.8

Source: Statistics Canada (2006).
* Percentage of sales generated in the downtown by total retail sales for the metropolitan area (e.g., in 1989, 12.2% of the total sales in the Toronto metropolitan area were generated in the downtown; this declined to 10.8% in 1998).
[a] Downtown versus non-downtown area defined according to forward sortation areas (FSAs) and census metropolitan areas (CMAs).
[b] 1989 based on Standard Industrial Classification (SIC) retail codes.
[c] 1999 based on North American Industrial Classification (NAIC) retail codes.

constant dollar sales gain between 1989 and 1998. Calgary's growth has been attributed to the expansion of the Prairies oil and gas industry and associated head office functions. A number of the major downtowns experienced significant losses; for example, Edmonton's downtown retail sales declined by almost 50 percent, Winnipeg and Ottawa witnessed losses of more than 40 percent, and Hamilton's downtown retail sales were reduced by one-third between 1989 and 1998. These declines can be compared against an overall increase of 2.1 percent retail sales (in constant dollars) across Canada. The 1999 to 2003 data provide evidence of a slight recovery with an overall sales growth of 5.2 percent in the major metropolitan downtowns. However, the total sales growth in these downtowns was still less than half the national average and subject to substantial variability: Calgary's downtown continued to grow, Québec posted a tourism-fueled recovery, Winnipeg and Edmonton experienced significant declines, and the other downtowns posted modest gains or losses. Whereas most of the major downtowns experienced decline, the major markets witnessed substantial growth in the suburbs. For example, between 1991 and 2003, retail sales in Toronto grew by 52.2 percent, in Montréal by 30.4 percent, and in Vancouver by 34.9 percent (Statistics Canada, 2004).

Table 17.2 shows the retail sales contribution of the downtown areas by major metropolitan areas. In 1989, 12.2 percent of the total retail sales in the Toronto metropolitan area were generated within the downtown core; by 1998 this declined to 10.8 percent. Even in the boomtown of Calgary, the relative growth of the suburbs has resulted in the downtown contributing less and less in retail sales between 1989 and 1998. The data for 1999 to 2003 show some modest increases in downtown contributions in Toronto, Montréal, Calgary, Québec, and Hamilton and continued decline in Winnipeg and Edmonton.

These retail trends in the major metropolitan markets also impact the downtowns of smaller urban areas. Businesses located in "small-town" Canada have the added difficulties of competing with surrounding larger urban areas that siphon consumer expenditures from the local economy, a situation further impacted by the movement of large-format retailers to these small-town markets (Hernandez et al., 2005). Indeed, conventional wisdom suggests that the local downtown economies of many of Canada's small towns are susceptible to the success of a few relatively large off-center retail developments. In some cases, the perceived threats of large-scale retail development to existing local businesses in smaller communities have resulted in anticorporate activism and increased hostility to major retail corporations (Marquard, 2006; Norman, 2004; Quinn, 2000; Mitchell, 2000).

Business Improvement Districts in Ontario

The BID approach started in Canada in 1970 when businesses in Toronto's Bloor West Village expressed a need to prevent a further loss of local business to new shopping centers located in the suburbs.* The BID approach is centered on the concept of collective action and defined as an association of businesses and property owners within a designated geographical area who work together to promote and improve local business. The primary aim of businesses is to attract more consumers (i.e., tourists, residents, employees, etc.) into the area for shopping, business, and entertainment purposes. This can be achieved through street beautification, tax incentives, place marketing, and the promotion and hosting of local events (e.g., wine festivals, street theater, music concerts). BIDs exist in many different forms and can vary in size from less than 50 to more than 2,000 members. The boundary of a BID is usually defined along a main arterial road or several streets or city blocks. Today, there are over 300 BIDs across Canada, of which more than 200 are in Ontario, with 60 in the Greater Toronto Area (GTA).

Provisions for creating and operating a BID are contained in section 220 of the Municipal Act of 2001 (Ministry for Municipal Affairs and Housing [MMAH], 2001). The creation of a BID requires the approval of the local council and support

---

* For a detailed account of the creation of the first BID in Canada, see the Hoyt chapter in this volume.

of at least two-thirds of the member businesses. Once a BID is designated, any business within its area is subject to pay BID levies. This differentiates BIDs from other urban revitalization schemes, such as town center management (TCM) in the U.K., in which businesses participate voluntarily. TCMs are based on major stakeholder support: a small number of major retail chains within a town center fund streetscape improvements and security schemes (Medway et al., 1999, 2000, Paddison, 2003; Pal and Sanders, 1997; Warnaby et al., 1998, 2004, 2005; Whyatt, 2004). In BIDs funding comes largely from the BID members in the form of an annual levy, which is calculated as a proportion of property tax valuation, with collection and distribution of funds administered by the local council. The BID's budget and expenditures are subject to the approval of the local council and the BID management board, which is comprised of BID members and council officials. In addition, municipalities may have separate programs to assist existing BID activities through grants. The pooling of resources among members is the cornerstone of the BID approach. The mandate of a BID, as set out in the Municipal Act, is twofold: (1) to improve, beautify, and maintain public lands and buildings within its area, and (2) to promote the area as a business and shopping area.

Canadian BIDs typically undertake activities in five broad areas (MMAH, 2001):

1. *Marketing*: Understanding who area customers are and creating effective promotions to retain and expand the customer base.
2. *Business recruitment*: Working with property owners to ensure that available space is occupied, and that an optimum business and service mix is achieved and maintained.
3. *Streetscape improvement and other amenities*: Providing for more customer-friendly lighting, signage, street furniture, planters, banners, and sidewalk treatment.
4. *Seasonal decorations*: Creating a unique and pleasant environment for customers and staff of all businesses, retail and nonretail, through the use of decorations that are appropriate to the season and holiday.
5. *Special events*: Organizing and partnering in special events that highlight the unique attributes of the area and increase customer visits.

Many BIDs also partner with local police agencies to reduce crime, property damage, and other forms of antisocial behavior. Downtowns choose to implement BIDs because BIDs typically allow businesses to undertake projects that they could otherwise not do alone, develop new approaches, take needed risks, and adapt quickly to capitalize on new opportunities. Most recently, downtowns are using BIDs as a means to improve their competitiveness within the markets they serve. To this end, BIDs help businesses present a united front by encouraging cooperation in the business community and an integrated secured source of funding. For example, the Bloor West Village BID celebrated its 35th anniversary in 2005, with BID advocates noting that since the BID was created, the area has seen an increase of over 125 businesses to 400 today. As the Ministry of Municipal Affairs and

Housing reported, Toronto's Bloor West Village, an area once rundown, unkempt, with high vacancy rates and low retail sales, has been transformed into one of Toronto's busiest retail strips (City of Toronto Council Economic Development Department, 2002, 2003; Ministry for Municipal Affairs and Housing, 2001).

In general, BIDs are seen as a mechanism to increase sales revenues by enticing more consumers to use local businesses. BIDs have been credited with increasing property values (Ellen et al., 2007), halting the deterioration of downtowns, reducing crime (Hoyt, 2005a; Brooks, 2006), increasing sales and profits, improving the tax base, and decreasing retail vacancy—in sum, encouraging the development of a vibrant local economy. Over the last decade there have been an increasing number of studies measuring the impacts of BIDs in areas such as crime or property valuation (see, for example, Ashworth, 2003; Briffault, 1999). It should be noted that the BID concept has also been in use for a number of years in the United States, New Zealand, and South Africa (Hoyt, 2005b), and has more recently been implemented in the U.K. (Office of the Deputy Prime Minister, 2004; Hogg et al., 2003; http://www.ukbids.org).

Case Study: Downtown Yonge BID

The Downtown Yonge BID is the largest BID in the Province of Ontario, with more than 2000 members, comprising a mix of businesses and property owners. The BID was established in July 2001, replacing the former Yonge Street Business and Residents Association. The geographical boundary is centered on Yonge Street and Dundas Street, covering an area approximately 1 mile north to south and half a mile east to west (see Figure 17.1). The BID is home to a combination of residents, businesses, and cultural institutions: a resident population of approximately 5,500 persons, Toronto's major downtown mall (the Eaton Center, whose area covers 1.6 million square feet and includes two department stores: Sears and the Hudson Bay flagship), the Atrium on the Bay and College Park office/retail centers, two major chain hotels (the Delta Chelsea and Marriott), major employers with 8.2 million square feet of office space and approximately 26,500 office workers (Toronto police headquarters, Ryerson University, and Old City Hall), the Maple Leaf Gardens (the former hockey arena of the Toronto Maple Leafs), theaters (the Canon Theatre, Massey Hall, and the Elgin Winter Gardens), and one of the oldest retail strips in Ontario (Yonge Street).

In 2003, the redeveloped Dundas Square, a European-styled downtown square with water fountains (Figure 17.2), was opened to the public. The square acts as the focal point for the Yonge-Dundas revitalization plan, providing public open space in the heart of the downtown that can be used for community activities and corporate events (http://www.ydsquare.ca). Dundas Square is surrounded by new development projects for retail and entertainment uses, such as the Olympic Spirit (a $34 million four-story sports entertainment venue), the development of

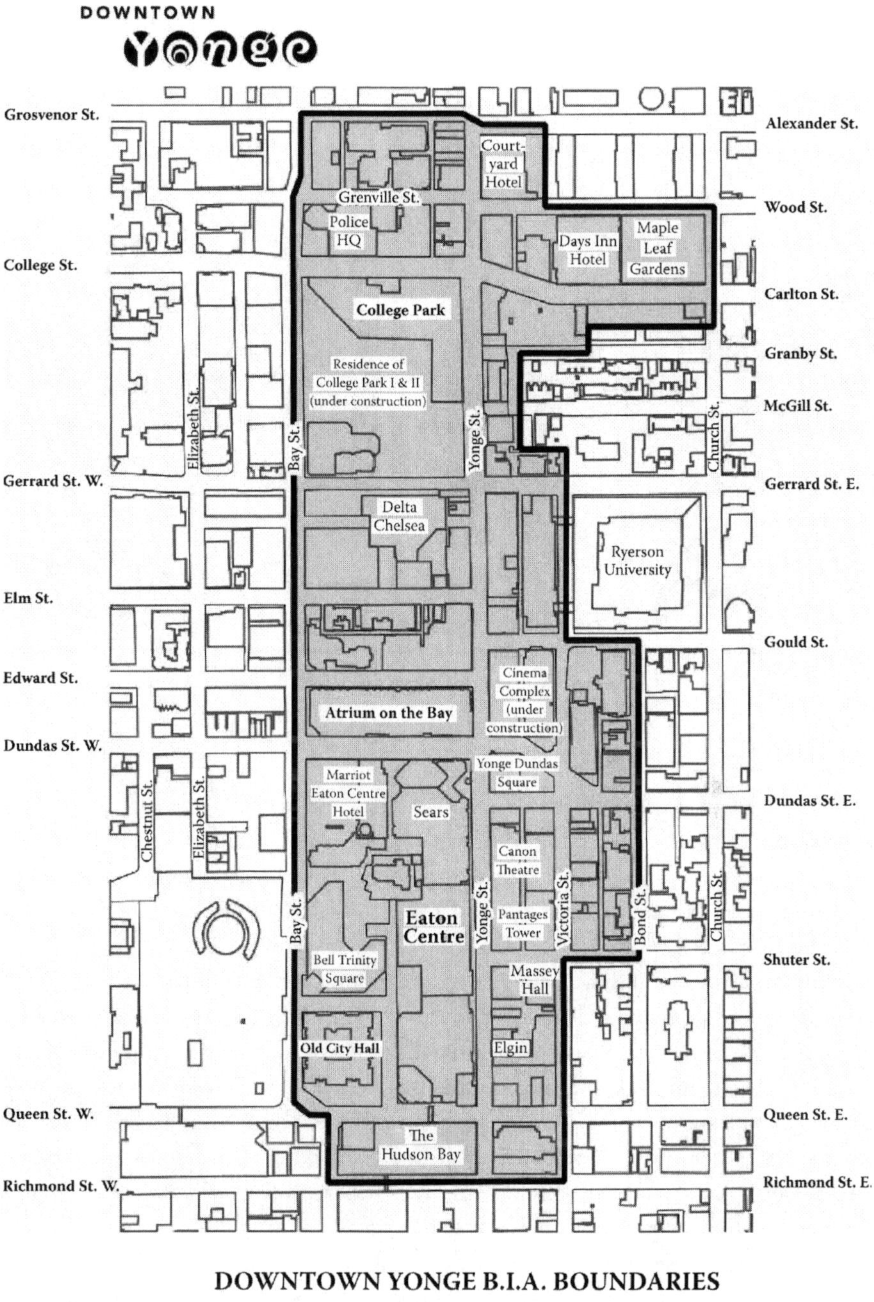

DOWNTOWN YONGE B.I.A. BOUNDARIES

Figure 17.1   Geographic Boundary of the Downtown Yonge BID.

Figure 17.2 View of Dundas Square (at intersection of Yonge St. and Dundas St.).

a $160 million major entertainment and retail complex, and the recent addition of two major fashion retailers facing Dundas Square (the Gap and H&M). This southern area of the Downtown Yonge BID has also recently benefited from the renovation of the Eaton Center and the Hard Rock Café building. The resident population in the area will increase with new residential condominium developments at the Residences of College Park I and II (52- and 45-story buildings) and the Pantages Tower (45-story building) in the theater area.

The BID has invested in a wide range of community improvements: the addition of new sidewalks; increased policing to reduce crime, drugs, and illegal vending; the operation of property cleanup campaigns to encourage (and require) owners to address deficiencies in their buildings; hiring a full-time maintenance crew to keep the streets clean and remove graffiti and illegal posters; promoting façade improvements; and working with the Harbourfront Community Center to add artistic murals in the area. The BID has also secured the right for retailers within the BID to open on statuary holidays.

The northern section of the Yonge retail strip houses a number of adult-entertainment retail stores and services, along with a mix of fast-food stores, an array of discount mixed retailers, and an urban youth center (see Figure 17.3).

Figure 17.3 View looking north on Yonge St. (at intersection of Yonge St. and College St.).

Although the BID has been successful in reducing crime rates in the area, the perception among many Torontonians of drug-related crime within this particular area remains high.

Currently the BID is in the process of rolling out a strategic plan and implementing "place branding" initiatives in the Downtown Yonge area, including the development of a comprehensive website (http://www.downtownyonge.com) and promoting streetscape branding and seasonal decoration, as has been witnessed in other areas of Toronto (e.g., Little Italy, Cabbagetown, Chinatown). In fall 2004, the BID installed 35-foot traffic poles with Downtown Yonge BID logo banners at the major intersections to demarcate the boundaries of the BID, along with the recent addition of branded street signage.

The strategic objectives for the BID include: (1) to bring more consumers downtown, (2) to continue to keep the area clean and safe, (3) to engage the association's members and leverage their talents and resources to improve the BID, (4) to make the area alluring—with lights and seasonal décor, notably at Christmas—and give it a clear identity, and (5) to get the word out that Yonge Street has changed. Their mission statement summarizes these objectives:

The Downtown Yonge BID serves its members who want a vibrant, accessible, safe commercial, shopping and entertainment climate in Downtown Yonge, with a wide variety of offerings. It supports the members and their customers by improving the area, and helping to create a reason to come there. (Downtown Yonge BID, 2004, p. 1.)

The Downtown Yonge BID achieved a number of goals in its first three years of operation, focusing primarily on safety and cleanliness of the environment. As the BID evolves into more strategic planning activities, it starts to focus on the long-term vitality of the downtown area. The need to develop evaluation metrics becomes more critical for benchmarking the performance of the BID and setting priorities and future targets (Atkinson and Archer, 2006). There is a number of basic metrics that can be used to assess the level of business improvement within the BID.* Table 17.3 provides examples of such metrics within economic, cultural, and environmental categories as an alternative perspective to the standard socioeconomic "quality of life" measures (see Federation of Canadian Municipalities, 2004).

Table 17.4 provides an illustration of the use of some of the metrics: tracking retail change and vacancy for the Downtown Yonge BID. The table shows the increase in services in the BID and the decrease in fashion and general merchandise retail stores. The vacancy rate has also decreased in the BID, while increasing in the city of Toronto in general. The availability of such data in geographically referenced format allows the BID to focus on areas within the BID, for example, comparing the retail strips within the BID with the three enclosed malls (Eaton Center, College Park, and the Atrium). It also provides a mechanism to track the externalities of retail activity, for example, the impact of redevelopment at the Eaton Center on nearby retail strips. This type of comparative analysis is particularly useful for BID management, especially during critical review periods, such as annual board member meetings and city council approval of budgets. In partnership with the Ministry of Municipal Affairs and Housing and eight Ontario-based BIDs, the CSCA has been developing a pilot project geodata warehouse to provide BIDs with performance metrics through a Web-enabled interface. The geodata warehouse seeks to assist BIDs in assessing their market potential and competitive environment, facilitating communication between BIDs, and encouraging the development of shared strategies between BIDs in similar circumstances. The project has integrated summary demographic data, BID survey data, and the CSCA's existing commercial structure databases into an online geodata warehouse.

---

* See the Caruso and Weber chapter in this volume for an extensive discussion of BID assessment criteria.

Table 17.3 Selected economic, cultural, and environmental BID performance metrics

Economic	Percentage retail sales growth
	Business confidence (e.g., surveys of BID members)
	Percentage of vacant properties
	Ratio of business openings to closures
	Number of years in business
	Percentage of major retail/service chains
	Shopping quality index
	Pedestrian counts
	Change in business property/leasing values
	Employment by industry/occupation type
	Level of new job creation
	Unemployment rate
	Change in residential property values
	Change in rental housing (availability and rental values)
	Change in market income (resident households)
	Number of new residential properties
Culture and tourism	Number of tourists (provincial, national, international)
	Hotel occupancy rates/average room rates
	Average length of stay
	Tourist expenditures
	Number of cultural/arts events
	Percentage of resident population in the "creative class"
Environment	Number of reported crimes by type
	Perception of crime
	Level of policing
	Garbage collections per week
	Investment in street cleaning initiatives
	Perception of cleanliness/graffiti
	Investment in streetscape improvement
	Number of façade improvements
	Number of streetscape enforcements

Table 17.4 Change in retail mix of Downtown Yonge BID

Business Type (No.)	1996	1998	2001	2003	Change	% Change 1996–2003	
						Within Downtown Yonge BID	Within city of Toronto
Automotive	0	0	0	1	1	n.a.	1.0
Food Services	146	145	147	150	4	2.7	16.2
Services (business and personal)	90	98	92	103	13	14.4	29.6
Manufacturing/distribution services	5	7	6	10	5	100.0	142.9
Food retail	38	40	37	42	4	10.5	0.0
Fashion retail	159	163	155	154	–5	–3.1	0.5
General merchandise retail	11	9	9	6	–5	–45.5	–9.4
Household and appliance retail	27	28	23	28	1	3.7	25.2
Other	153	155	170	163	10	6.5	11.1
Number of vacant properties	79	90	98	75	–4	–5.1	19.0
Total	708	735	737	732	24	3.4	15.6
Vacancy rate (%)	*1996*	*1998*	*2001*	*2003*	*Change*		
Downtown Yonge BID							
Retail strip	12.2	8.1	9.9	8.9	–3.3		
Shopping mall	10.6	14.4	14.9	10.9	0.3		
Total	11.2	12.2	13.3	10.2	–1.0		
City of Toronto							
Retail strip	9.6	9.7	10.5	10.5	0.9		
Shopping mall	10.8	12.0	9.0	8.3	–2.5		
Total	9.8	10.1	10.2	10.1	0.3		

Emerging Strategies

The BID concept has evolved and must continue to evolve. According to the Ministry of Municipal Affairs and Housing (2001), the main function of BIDs has been "to improve, beautify, and maintain public lands and buildings within the BID, beyond that which is provided by the municipality at large" (p. 2). However, once the initial attraction is successful and the area sees an improvement in traffic, the BID often takes on a different, more focused role. This may mean increasing market research, adopting more focused target marketing, acting as an advocacy organization for policy changes, operating as a communication vehicle between business and various levels of government, and working with property owners to provide advice on the mix of tenants. As BIDs' objectives evolve from basic operational and tactical tasks to more strategic tasks, the need for more improved data relating to BID performance becomes critical. Strategy is about making choices, and because BIDs operate within strict budgetary constraints, cost-effective decision support is critical for effective long-term BID planning.

The BID model is based on partnership between the BID and the local council, property owners and tenants (including local employers), the local community, and other BIDs. The "sphere of influence" of a BID, however, is both local and limited. Yet, increasingly, many of the forces of change that the BID has to deal with are beyond its control and relate to broader issues. These can include downturns in the regional or local economies, systemic shifts in commercial structures, new forms of competition, alterations in the transport system, changes in tourist behaviors, and fundamental demographic shifts. For example, retailing in the downtown area of Toronto was negatively impacted by a number of external shocks in the 2001–2003 period. These events include the aftereffects of 9/11 and the SARS outbreak (with 33 deaths attributed to SARS [SARs deaths in Toronto, 2003]) in Toronto that resulted in significant losses of U.S. and international tourists and conventions. It was widely reported anecdotally that as a result of these uncontrollable events, many retailers in the downtown experienced a 15 to 20 percent reduction in their annual retail sales.

One constant reality that BIDs in particular and policymakers in general must respond to is the fact that the retail economy is constantly undergoing change. To be successful in a dynamic environment requires the adoption and commitment to holistic planning approaches. In the case of BIDs, these strategic initiatives need to be developed, supported, and coordinated at the city, regional, provincial, and national levels to formulate "city building" policies that promote downtowns as places to work, live, and spend leisure time. These broader urban planning strategies are highly politicized, subject to dramatic changes, and extend well beyond the scope of individual BIDs.

As we have demonstrated in this chapter, downtowns are complex environments that have experienced decline across Canada in recent years. As a potential remedy for deteriorating downtowns, BIDs provide numerous advantages. They allow local, often independent, businesses to operate as a unified and more influential entity. BIDs also provide downtown areas with combined resources and an entrepreneurial perspective that the community otherwise could not access. Through this collective approach, BIDs can contribute to the revitalization of downtown areas by improving their competitiveness in the urban markets in which they are located. BIDs, however, are impacted by many factors that are beyond their direct control, and the typical sphere of influence for most BIDs is fairly limited. As James Robinson, executive director of the Downtown Yonge BID highlights, "Strategy is about choice. Downtown Yonge cannot do everything it might like to accomplish. It must choose its strategic options wisely" (J. Robinson, personal communication, April 3, 2006). Therefore, as more BIDs look to develop strategic plans and create their vision of the downtown, the need to partner with other urban planning organizations, commercial and residential developers, government agencies, and the community will become increasingly important. This form of partnership is both healthy and essential. Successful and vibrant downtown retail areas are an essential element of healthy downtowns. The challenge is to develop a holistic and strategic planning approach that integrates all the key constituencies. If we do not act judiciously, healthy downtowns, a fundamental element of Canadian urban life, will slip away.

References

Ashworth, S. 2003. Business improvement districts: The impact of their introduction on retailers and leisure operators. *Journal of Retail and Leisure Property* 3:150–157.

Atkinson, M., and Archer, J. 2006. Retail revitalization and recruitment. In *Making business districts work*, ed. D. Feehan and M. D. Feit, 293–310. New York: The Haworth Press.

Boyle, R. J. 2003. US retailers expanding into Canada: Will it ever end? *International Council of Shopping Centers Research Quarterly* 10:1–3.

Briffault, R. 1999. A government for our time? Business districts and urban government. *Columbia Law Review* 99(2):365–477.

Brooks, L. 2006. Volunteering to be taxed: Business improvement districts and the extragovernmental provision of public safety. Unpublished manuscript.

Bryce, G. 1902. *Remarkable history of the Hudson's Bay Company.* 2nd ed. London: Sampson, Low, Marston and Co.

Bunting, T., and Filion, P. 2000. *Canadian cities in transition.* 2nd ed. Toronto, Canada: Oxford University Press.

Canadian Institute for Planners. 2002. *Towards a Canadian urban strategy.* Ottawa, Canada: Author.

Canadian Urban Institute. 2001. *Smart growth in Canada.* Toronto, Canada: Author.

Centre for the Study of Commercial Activity (CSCA). 2004. *Retail sales database.* Data file. Toronto, Canada: Ryerson University.

City of Toronto Council Economic Development Department. 2002. *Business improvement areas: Strengthening local neighbourhoods.* Toronto, Canada: Author.

City of Toronto Council Economic Development Department. 2003. *Business improvement area operating handbook*. Toronto, Canada: Author.

Daniel, C., and Hernandez, T. 2006. *Canada's leading retailers*. CSCA Research Report 2006-09. Toronto, Canada: Ryerson University, CSCA.

Department of the Environment, HMSO. 1996. *Planning policy guidance: Town centres and retail developments*. Ottawa, Canada: Author.

Doucet, M. 2001. *The department store shuffle: Rationalization and change in the Greater Toronto Area*. CSCA Research Report 2001-05. Toronto, Canada: Ryerson University, CSCA.

Downtown Yonge BID. 2004. *Downtown Yonge strategic plan 2004–2007*. Toronto, Canada: Author.

Ellen, I., Schwartz, A., and Voicu, I. 2007. The impact of business improvement districts on property values: Evidence from New York City. Brookings-Wharton Papers on Urban Affairs. 1:1–31.

Federation of Canadian Municipalities. 2004. *Quality of life reporting system*. Ottawa, Canada: Author.

Feehan, D., and Feit, M. D., eds. 2006. *Making business districts work*. New York: The Haworth Press.

Filion, P., Hoernig, H, Bunting, T., and Sands, G. 2004. The successful few: Healthy downtowns of small metropolitan regions. *Journal of the American Planning Association* 70:328–343.

Fyfe, N., Jones, K., Lea, T., and Lussier, R. 2004. *General merchandisers in Canada*. Research Report 2004-02. Toronto, Canada: Ryerson University, CSCA.

Hernandez, T. 2004. *Emerging trends in general merchandise retailing*. Research Report 2004-10. Toronto, Canada: Ryerson University, CSCA.

Hernandez, T., Erguden K., and Bermingham, P. 2005. *Market thresholds: Major retail chains in Canada, 2004*. Research Letter 2005-07. Toronto, Canada: Ryerson University, CSCA.

Hernandez, T., Erguden K., and Bermingham, P. 2006. *Power retail: Growth in Canada and the GTA*. Research Letter 2006-05. Toronto, Canada: Ryerson University, CSCA.

Hernandez, T., and Jones, K. 2005. Downtowns in transition: Emerging BIA strategies. *International Journal of Retail and Distribution Management* 33:789–805.

Hernandez, T., Jones, K., and Maze, A. 2003. *US retail chains in Canada*. Research Letter 2003-10. Toronto, Canada: Ryerson University, CSCA.

Hernandez, T., Lea, T., Spagnolo, A., and Maze, A. 2004. Shopping centers, power retailing and evolving retail environments: A comparison of the retail markets of Dallas-Fort Worth and Toronto. *Journal of Shopping Center Research* 11:55–112.

Hogg, S., Medway, D., and Warnaby, G. 2003. Business improvement districts: An opportunity for SME retailing. *International Journal of Retail and Distribution Management* 31:466–469.

Holle, P., and Owens, D. 2002. *Fixing Winnipeg's downtown: Big picture policy changes to revitalize the inner city*. Policy Series 14. Winnipeg, Manitoba: Frontier Center for Public Policy.

Hoyt, L. M. 2005a. Do business improvement district organizations make a difference? Crime in and around commercial areas in Philadelphia. *Journal of Planning Education and Research* 25:185–199.

Hoyt, L. M. 2005b. *The business improvement district: An internationally diffused approach to revitalization.* Washington, DC: International Downtown Association.

Hudson Bay Company, Inc. 2004. The Hudson Bay Company retail stores. http://www.hbc.com/hbc/e_hi/stores/original6.htm (accessed May 5, 2006).

Jones, K., and Simmons, J. 1990. *Location, location, location.* Toronto, Canada: Nelson Publishing.

Lea, T., Jones, K., and Bylov, G. 2003. *Retail trends in downtown Canada.* Research Letter 2003-03. Toronto, Canada: Ryerson University, CSCA.

Levy, P. R. 2001. Making downtowns competitive. *Planning,* April, pp. 16–19.

Marquard, W. H. 2006. *Wal-Smart: What it takes to really profit in a Wal-Mart world.* New York: McGraw-Hill.

Mason, M. 2003. Urban regeneration rationalities and quality of life: Comparative notes from Toronto, Montreal and Vancouver. *British Journal of Canadian Studies* 16:348–362.

McCann, L. D., and Smith, P. J. 1991. Canada becomes urban: Cities and urbanization in historical perspective. In *Canadian cities in transition,* ed. T. Bunting and P. Fillion, 69–99. Toronto, Canada: Oxford University Press.

Medway, D., Alexander, A., Bennison, D., and Warnaby, G. 1999. Retailers' financial support for town centre management. *International Journal of Retail and Distribution Management* 27:246–255.

Medway, D., Warnaby, G., Bennison, D., and Alexander, A. 2000. Reasons for retailers' involvement in town centre management. *International Journal of Retail and Distribution Management* 28:368–378.

Ministry of Municipal Affairs and Housing, Government of Ontario. 2001. *An introduction to business improvement areas.* Toronto, Canada: Author.

Mitchell, S. (2000). *The home-town advantage.* Maine: Institute for Local Self-Reliance.

Nasmith, G. 1923. *Timothy Eaton.* Toronto, Canada: McClelland and Stewart.

Norman, A. 2004. *The case against Wal-Mart.* St. Johnsbury, VT: Raphel Marketing.

Office of the Deputy Prime Minister, HMSO. 2004. *The business improvements districts regulations: 2004.* Ottawa, Canada: Author.

Paddison, A. 2003. Town centre management (TCM): A case study of Achmore. *International Journal of Retail and Distribution Management* 31:618–627.

Pal, J., and Sanders, E. 1997. Measuring the effectiveness of town centre management schemes: An exploratory framework. *International Journal of Retail and Distribution Management* 25:70–77.

Pearce, M., Jones, K., and McNally, B. 1999. SARTRE: New insights. *Ivey Business Journal,* May/June, pp. 53–56.

Quinn, B. 2000. *How Wal-Mart is destroying the world and what you can do about it.* Berkeley, CA: Ten Speed Press.

Robertson, K. A. 1999. Can small-city downtowns remain viable? *Journal of the American Planning Association* 65:270–283.

Santink, J. 1990. *Timothy Eaton and the rise of his department store.* Toronto, Canada: University of Toronto Press.

SARS deaths in Toronto. 2003. http://news.bbc.co.uk/1/hi/world/americas/2973984.stm (accessed May 5, 2006).

Simmons, J. 2001. *The economic impact of Wal-Mart stores.* Research Letter 2001-12. Toronto, Canada: Ryerson University, CSCA.

Simmons, J. 2003. *Cities in decline: The future of urban Canada.* Research Letter 2003-07. Toronto, Canada: Ryerson University, CSCA.

Simmons, J., and Graff, T. 1998. *Wal-Mart comes to Canada.* Research Report 1998-09. Toronto, Canada: Ryerson University, CSCA.

Simmons, J., and Hernandez, T. 2004a. *Power retailing: Close to saturation.* Research Report 2004-08. Toronto, Canada: Ryerson University, CSCA.

Simmons, J., and Hernandez, T. 2004b. *Power retailing in Canada major urban markets.* Research Report 2004-09. Toronto, Canada: Ryerson University, CSCA.

Statistics Canada. 1999. *SARTRE: Not just another existential database.* Ottawa, Canada: Government of Canada.

Statistics Canada. 2002. *A profile of the Canadian population: Where we live, 2001 census.* Ottawa, Canada: Government of Canada.

Statistics Canada. 2003. *Canada at a glance: 2003.* Ottawa, Canada: Government of Canada.

Statistics Canada. 2004. *Retail monthly sales data.* Ottawa, Canada: Government of Canada.

Statistics Canada, 2006. *Small area retail trade estimates.* Ottawa, Canada: Government of Canada.

T. Eaton Company. 1919. *Golden jubilee: 1869–1919.* Toronto, Canada: Author.

Warnaby, G., Alexander, A., and Medway, D. 1998. Town centre management in the UK: A review, synthesis and research agenda. *International Review of Retail, Distribution and Consumer Research* 8:15–31.

Warnaby, G., Bennison, D., and Davies, B. J. 2005. Marketing town centres: Retailing and town centre management. *Local Economy* 20:183–204.

Warnaby, G., Bennison, D., Davies, B. J., and Hughes, H. 2004. People and partnerships: Marketing urban retailing. *International Journal of Retail and Distribution Management* 32:545–556.

Webber, S., Hernandez, T., and Jones, K. 2005. *Planning policy and power retail development.* Research Report 2005-02. Toronto, Canada: Ryerson University, CSCA.

Whyatt, G. 2004. Town centre management: How theory informs a strategic approach. *International Journal of Retail and Distribution Management* 32:346–353.

Yeates, M. 1998. *The North American city.* 5th ed. New York: Longman.

Chapter 18

British Town Center Management: Setting the Stage for the BID Model in Europe[*]

Alan Reeve

Contents

---

[*] This chapter first appeared as Reeve (2004) and is reproduced with minor changes by kind permission of the editors of the journal in which it appeared.

Introduction

This chapter presents an overview of literature and research in the area of town center management (TCM), based on work in progress. It must be noted at the outset that although TCM is a potentially rich subject area for academic writing and research, very little of substance has actually been published or undertaken to date. This paucity is acknowledged by a number of other commentators in the 1990s (see Warnaby et al., 1998; Medway, 1998; Pal and Sanders, 1997), and little appears to have changed since then in this respect.

The chapter is in two parts. The first part begins with a brief history of TCM in the British context and describes the current practice situation. The second part briefly reviews recent academic research interest in the area, particularly as far as this relates to the built environment disciplines. It identifies a number of themes that deserve research attention, but which to date have been somewhat underexplored. The final section offers some conclusions regarding the role of academic research in relation to this emerging profession.

Background to TCM in the U.K.

The Culture and History of TCM

To understand the current context of TCM as a putative professional practice, as well as the conditions in which research and writing have been carried on, it is useful to say a little about the history and changing rationale of town center management in the U.K. Of course, town center management—albeit by other names, in other places—has been undertaken as an aspect of local urban management in other countries in recent years. The Mainstreet and Downtown programs in the United States, beginning in the mid-1980s, indeed prefigured some aspects of TCM in Britain (see Page and Hardyman, 1996; Houghton, 1997). TCM has also been practiced for some years now in Holland and other European countries (see Ennen and Ashworth, 1998; ATCM and Leeds Metropolitan University, 1999; Hogg et al., 2000). But TCM in the U.K. has always had a uniquely British quality. This is arguably because of the greater separation of the two cultures of the private and public sectors compared with the United States, say, as well as for more mundane legal and financial reasons. While acknowledging the importance of the international dimensions of TCM, this chapter focuses primarily on the U.K. experience.

The practice of TCM is some 20 years of age in Britain. Its emergence can be closely identified with a number of more general changes in the values and practices of business, government, and planning over this time. For example, the notion of the privatization of public services has been at the heart of the TCM movement. This is clearly paralleled elsewhere in health, policing, education, and prisons. But the idea of public and private partnership is a defining characteristic of TCM, not a late addition, as it has been in these other areas. This style or attitude of thought is reflected in the fact that most town center managers tend to think of town center users as *customers*. This clearly implies an instrumental attitude to users, which is central to many aspects of TCM practice.

The function and remit of town center managers and their initiatives today are extremely diverse. Originally management focused largely on maintaining the day-to-day upkeep of the main shopping streets: street cleaning, the removal of graffiti, and reporting vandalism to the appropriate authorities. This is the so-called janitorial* level of activity that continues to underpin many TCM schemes today. Some early initiatives, in the late 1980s, such as those in Reading and Redbridge in the south of England, also aimed to market their centers, and to provide a forum for dialogue between the retail community and the local authority. Today, many schemes are concerned with more strategic-level initiatives. These often involve high-cost improvements to the physical fabric of the town center, such as pedestrianization, or the installation of CCTV systems. Equally, they may be concerned with the repositioning of the town center in relation to its local or regional competitors through extensive promotional campaigns. All of these require access to substantial funding, often beyond what has traditionally been available from local authority sources. As a consequence, managers are increasingly involved in making complex bids for major grants under, for instance, EU or Single Regeneration

---

* The term *janitorial* is commonly used to refer to one level of activity associated with TCM, denoting such activities as street cleaning, the maintenance of the physical fabric of the town center, and reporting problems to the local authority and police. Although it implies a low-level response to what are often merely symptoms of a deeper malaise, it is not intended to be read pejoratively. It might be argued that any concerted effort to improve the physical environment of the town center must be positive.

Budget (SRB) programs (see ATCM and Leeds Metropolitan University, 1999). In fact, one characteristic of TCM in many places is that it is becoming a new model of urban regeneration (see Reeve and Otsuka, 2004).

It is worth stressing that the contemporary picture of TCM practice is a mixed one. The trends indicated above do not apply everywhere. This is to a large measure because a number of local authorities have been cautious about encouraging the growth of a new form of urban management. There are concerns that TCM is driven by commercial values and is acquiring powers that are not as democratically accountable as those traditionally held by local authorities. For instance, anecdotal evidence would suggest that there is often a conflict of values and priorities between town center managers as de facto local authority officers and appointed officers (see Evans, 1997).

Why TCM in the Late 1980s?

It has been commonly argued (see, for example, Baldock, 1989; Evans, 1997; Stansbury, 1995; Oc and Tiesdell, 1998; Wells, 1991) that town center management somehow emerged in the late 1980s as a rational response to the economic decline of traditional town centers. In particular this has been seen as a reaction to the unchecked growth of purpose-built shopping malls and the direct threat they represented to the traditional high street as a retail location. Indeed, some commentators believe that TCM directly copied the practices of shopping center management to compete on a more equal footing: "Borrowing the model of shopping centre management, leading retailers called for TCM to improve the upkeep of the town centre" (ATCM, 1994, p. 2).

In some senses this is clearly true. TCM schemes have always been interested in creating pleasant shopping environments. But there was something else at work at the end of the Thatcher period in the early 1990s. The private business sector was pressing to create what it saw as a more coherent urban management approach, and one more responsive to its interests. This was at the same time as the rapid spread of "quality" shopping environments posed direct competition for the custom of U.K. multiples, such as Boots the Chemist and Marks and Spencers, prime sponsors of TCM schemes, and prime movers in the early days of the TCM as a whole in the U.K. context. Even by the mid-1980s shopping malls had clear attractions to shoppers over the traditional high street. They were often cleaner, warmer, drier, safer, and more predictable and accessible. As the decade came to a close, these obvious attractions were combined with the offer of a crude form of hyperreal escapism in the first of the out-of-town mega-malls—the Metro Center, Gateshead, in the northeast of England. To the media-saturated consumer they were becoming aesthetically rich environments as well (Reeve, 1995). They were also convenient for parking and provided easy access to those who could afford private transport. This fact alone continues to make such places broadly exclusive, and therefore attractive to their natural constituency, compared with the relatively democratic space of most town centers.

The reason that TCM emerged when it did is probably much more complex than this, however, and more interesting from the perspective of policy and urban management. Competitive pressures from out-of-town retail competition are an inadequate explanation for the growth of a radically new form of urban management. The fact that retail and property have largely driven TCM interests is of course true. Shopping is usually the main activity and provision in U.K. town centers (see as an illustration Lockwood, 1997, 1999), but town centers are not just shopping centers without a roof and doors. The way in which TCM took off as an idea, and as a "movement"* to use Chris Hollins's term (quoted in Reeve, 1995), needs to be explained by more than simply a threat sensed by vested money interests, and by more than the claims of such interests to be acting in the public good. For TCM to develop required the recognition of a need for such an approach by the public sector as well. Evans (1997), for example, argues that the growth of TCM must be understood in a context of the disempowering of local government, both administratively and fiscally, in the Thatcher years. The convergence of private and public sector interests in TCM was not a deliberately constructed and imposed form of the privatization of the public services, but something voluntarily, if reluctantly, entered into by both local authorities and the private sector. TCM arose, arguably, in the partial vacuum created by the Right's fear of local autonomy, and in a state in which many local authorities were desperate to find at least the mechanisms to act strategically. As Evans (1997) puts it:

> While local government expenditure cuts continued and competitive bidding for supplementary urban funding supplanted distribution according to need, there was noticeably increasing private sector frustration at the lack of strategic planning of public infrastructure. (p. 126)

Partnership, Government Policy, and the Values of TCM

By default, TCM held out an opportunity to help resolve a crisis for town centers implicit in all of this. The fact that TCM remains a largely voluntary activity can be seen as either an indictment of central government's abrogation of duty to local needs, particularly in the 1980s and 1990s, or a healthy response by the forces of a free market. TCM's principal modus operandi has acquired certain respectability because of the general acceptance in other areas of public life of the partnership

---

* This term is highly suggestive of a managerial philosophy that underpins much of TCM, one that is closely allied to a commercial perspective that in its worst expression sidesteps questions of accountability or doubt.

ethos. At heart this means that the value of a project can often only be underwritten by the willingness of the private sector to support it.*

The management of town centers in TCM is an activity discrete from both the local authority's traditional role as overseer of public space provision and servicing, and the private sector's role as market-driven provider of amenities based on consumer demand. In this guise it has also received favor from central government, and more broadly among built environment professionals. The 1994 Select Committee on the Environment acknowledged its potential for urban regeneration (see British Property Federation [BPF], 1995), while the revised *Planning Policy Guidance* (PPG)† *Note 6*, June 1996, *Town Centres and Retail Development*, Annex C: *Town Centre Management* (Department of the Environment, 1996) noted that:

> Effective management and promotion of town centres will help to enhance their vitality and viability. Many factors affecting the quality of a town centre lie outside the planning system. In partnership with the private sector and the local community, local authorities should develop a town centre management initiative, which may lead to appointing a town centre manager to improve links between public and private sector initiatives.

The catch-all term *vital and viable* town centers, popularized though not coined by the Urban and Economic Development Group Ltd. (URBED) (Department of the Environment and URBED, 1994), has also inextricably linked the idea of town center success at a societal and cultural level (which is at the heart of the term *vitality*) with the need for commercial viability.

So, for a number of reasons, TCM had and has found its time. These reasons sketched out above can be summarized as:

1. Changing political values with regard to the relationship between the public and private sectors
2. Commercial and economic pressures associated with the growth of new retail forms and environments
3. The inability of local authorities to respond to such pressures in a way that would convince property and commercial interests

---

* Here there is clearly the risk of a dangerous elision of cost and value; in other words, only those activities and functions that can be costed, financially, are valued and seen as important in terms of what a town center should be about.

† PPGs and subsequently planning policy statements are the main policy articulations in the U.K. that drive public sector and government planning practice.

The Attitude of Professional Institutions to TCM

As TCM was beginning to take off in the early 1990s, so a number of professional institutions concerned with town center issues began producing notes for their members on it, both to inform and inculcate their own perspective on its potential for themselves.* For example, the British Property Federation's pamphlet on TCM saw it as a good thing, but stressed that property owners thinking of contributing to local schemes should "expect private sector disciplines to apply to TCM schemes generally, and more particularly, to any direct financial contribution it may make" (BPF, 1995, p. 2).

Likewise, the Royal Institute of Chartered Surveyors (RICS) produced a guidance note in 1994 on TCM for its members. While welcoming what town center management represents, this was again cautious, arguing that any funding from the private sector should only be forthcoming if the local authority were "fully committed" and "already carrying out its statutory responsibilities" (RICS, 1994, p. 10). In the case of both these institutions, then, there is a clear recognition of the potential value of TCM to property interests in town centers, along with a quite explicitly negative perception of public sector values and conduct.

The English Tourist Board has also felt it appropriate to produce a note, as part of the "Insights" series about TCM, aimed at those working in local tourism offices. Again we can see an attempt to define town center management from the perspective of a particular industry and, in this case, to highlight the synergy between tourism and TCM:

> There is a vital role for visitor management plans, tourism and economic development strategies and local (land use and transport) plans to complement and work with TCM to ensure that the full benefits of tourism are achieved with a minimum negative impact on the immediate environment and local communities. TCM will often provide the enabling mechanism to meet, in part, the objectives of these other structures by implementing practical projects. (English Tourist Board, 1995, p. A-24.)

Defining Town Center Management

But what is town center management? According to Wells (1991), Peter Spiddell of Marks and Spencers coined the term in 1980 at a retail conference entitled "Town Centres of the Future." The concept was then elaborated by Jonathan Baldock in 1989 and refined by Wells in his seminal study:

---

* See Warnaby et al. (1998) for a useful analysis of the different perspectives placed on this emerging activity by the various professional and institutional bodies.

> Town centre management is a comprehensive response to competitive pressures, which involves development, management and promotion of both public and private areas within the town centre. (Wells, 1991, p. 24.)

In this pamphlet, Wells goes on to stress that TCM is about managing the town center for all users and for all parts of the town center, not just retail streets. The definition offered is of what Wells presumably felt TCM ought to be, and possibly was at the time. But it really only defines a set of aspirations, not the practice as it is everywhere in Britain today. As we will see, the reality is that retail interest has tended to dominate many schemes, and the conflict of cultures between public and private remains in many cases unresolved. It is also the case that TCM schemes have very clear, if often unstated, spatial boundaries, which are retail activity and property related. It tends to concentrate effort and resources on the central business districts (CBDs) of a town where commercial activity happens to be. This is underpinned by the fact that, as Wells's work identified, the three main functions of TCM are *management, development,* and *marketing.*

This view of the main activities of TCM is shared by others working in the field (see also Stansbury, 1995; RICS, 1994) and continues to characterize the practice. These make up a hierarchy in which the most developed schemes take on board promotion and marketing, while the newest schemes focus almost exclusively on day-to-day management, at a "janitorial" level, of the physical environment of the town center. (See below for a fuller discussion of TCM's roles.)

Guy (1993) offered a slightly broader definition when he claimed that

> [TCM] incorporates many of the hitherto usually separate concerns of town planning, leisure, public health and publicity departments. Secondly, it implies a co-operative rather than confrontational relationship with the private sector. (p. 36)

Again, this description needs to be compared carefully with the actuality where very few TCM initiatives effectively bring together all of the local authority departmental interests implied here, even for the purposes of setting objectives.

A further refinement has been added by Warnaby et al. (1998) to defining TCM. They claim that the accepted definitions are too narrow for academic purposes, and offer instead the following:

> Town centre management is the search for competitive advantage through the maintenance and/or strategic development of both private areas and interests within town centres, initiated and undertaken by stakeholders drawn from a combination of public, private and voluntary sectors. (p. 18)

This clearly develops earlier notions by acknowledging the role of the voluntary sector for the first time. It also usefully implies that TCM needs to be defined in terms of its ambitions rather than simply its specific structures or contingent tasks. However, it also wrongly places stress on the goal of "competitive advantage." The best TCM schemes take full stock of the potential of their town center and, consequently, sometimes aim at managing decline rather than unrealistic growth. Its use of the term *stakeholder* also begs a number of questions, for example: What are stakeholders in this context? What is their accountability? How do they fit with the existing democratic structures of local government?

The Spread and Organizational Characteristics of TCM Schemes

TCMs have had a reasonably rapid growth, at least in terms of the number of managers and management schemes that have come into being over the last 12 years. The two initiatives in the mid-1980s (York and Redbridge) were closely followed by Nottingham and Falkirk. In 1994 there were 60 TCMs; there are now well over 300. These TCM initiatives are extremely varied in terms of support and structure. The majority are part local authority and part private sector funded; some are purely public sector. Two are run as limited companies, although their income is derived in part from public sector sources; these are based in Coventry and Bristol. TCMs vary, also, in terms of their responsibilities and remit, as indicated earlier, from the janitorial to the quasi-strategic. But in reality, none have statutory authority or an elected legitimacy that would give them direct access to the decision-making apparatus of a town such that they can claim to have a truly strategic dimension. All they can do is to articulate a set of broad aims or aspirations for a town center and attempt to persuade the key interests to subscribe to these. Their position outside of the administrative setup of local authorities can be seen as an advantage in this. To use the jargon of retail that is often applied in practice, one role of a TCM is to get all "stakeholders" to "sign up" to a "shared vision." The terms are placed in quotation marks because this is the particular language of management.

The success of a TCM initiative depends on two factors. The first of these is how it is structured, and therefore how it is related to the local authority. The second is how it is funded and the level of this funding. The structure or organization of TCM schemes generally takes one of several models. The Association of Town Center Management (ATCM) has identified nine, but these can be simplified to about four types (for a more detailed description, see ATCM with Boots, 1997; ATCM and DoE, 1997).

The simplest of these models is represented by those initiatives that do not always have a named or appointed manager as such, but which consist of a "forum." This is a meeting held once or twice a year to discuss and define broad TCM strategies. These are then actioned by a steering group and subsidiary working groups with responsibilities for particular areas of activity—access, security, marketing, and so on. According to the ATCM, the ideal model of an initiative at this level is one that is participated in by all interests in a town center, from the local authority to the chamber of commerce, police, voluntary organizations, retailers, and the community. As in all the other models of TCM structures, the degree to which such a broad and seemingly democratic participation actually exists is open to question. The reality undoubtedly varies from one scheme to another.

A second general type is what the ATCM calls the town center manager. Here a steering group directs an individual, paid for by contributions from private and public sectors. The manager is a coordinating figure whose role is largely to network between different interests in a town, and to ensure that the aims and objectives for the initiative as defined by the steering group are implemented. The third type allows for essentially the same role for an initiative as that above. But in this case the manager is appointed either exclusively by the local authority—and may actually be a local authority officer—or by the private sector, usually the chamber of commerce, who will liaise directly with a local authority officer within, say, the planning department.

The fourth type is that of the City Center Company, defined by the ATCM as "companies established to take over the management responsibility of specific geographic area, employing staff and raising revenue" (ATCM with Boots the Chemist, 1997, p. 17). This is an unusual form of TCM initiative, modeled to a degree on the business improvement district (BID) experience in the United States (see Travers and Weimar, 1996; Houghton, 1997; and the chapters on BIDs in this volume). Coventry and Bristol have City Center Companies whose role is to run some of the janitorial services of the local authority. In the case of Coventry, this has been possible because of the tenure of the local authority over the town center as the principal property owners (see Oc and Tiesdell, 1997).

The above is a fairly crude characterization of TCM structures, and each of the approximately 300 initiatives in operation to date is probably unique in one respect or another. This is because of particular local circumstances, the apathy or enthusiasm of different interests, and variations in funding regimes and mechanisms. Indeed, this variety has been seen as a virtue by the ATCM (1994): "An effective TCM must be based in the community,* and be able to innovate and evolve according to the local communities needs" (p. 35).

Nonetheless, a number of general factors apply in all schemes and all models, both in terms of what might be described as their life cycle and in terms of the circumstances that have a specific effect on their power and objectives. Most TCM initiatives begin from the forum model. Here a number of interested parties who believe there is a need for a more coordinated approach to town center issues come together. Usually the local authority is the initiator. Less commonly it is the private

---

* The difficult questions of whether communities are real entities and whether all constituent elements are capable of being represented within a TCM initiative need to be asked here.

sector in the form of the chamber of commerce, or one of the main funding retailers (see below). Having established a basis for discussion between different interests, and an agenda for action, the forum will evolve over possibly two or three years into the next stage. This is a fully formed TCM initiative, where funding has been secured to appoint a manager or management team. Subsequent development will primarily center around the type of tasks taken on under the initiative, involving an increasingly broader range of actors and interests, and setting increasingly strategic objectives. At the mature stage, TCM will not only be concerned with the quality of the physical environment at a day-to-day level, but will also be interested in long-term investment to ensure the improvement in such quality, and the marketing and promotion of the town center. It will also be concerned with identifying larger sources of funding for more ambitious projects. Some schemes remain at the janitorial level, and this may be appropriate depending on the responsibilities and ability of the local authority to take the strategic view (see ATCM with Donaldsons, Healey, and Baker, 1994; Pal and Sanders, 1997; Medway, 1998).

Warnaby et al. (1998) have implied a further and subtler categorization of schemes based on a conceptual framework in which types might be identified. They argue that it is important to understand the relationship between three elements (p. 24):

1. The structure or organization
2. The extent to which resourcing is provided by the public or private sectors
3. The activities engaged in

As they acknowledge, the problem is that the type of model that they propose requires refinement and testing by example if it is to be useful in explaining why schemes function in the way they do, or in predicting outcomes from initiatives.

TCM Funding

A cynic might say that TCM is an attempt to do planning on the cheap. This is only partly true. The role of most TCM initiatives is *in addition* to the statutory responsibilities of local authorities: providing extra street cleaning, public events, and fund-raising for CCTV, and so on. However, the expectations placed on managers often go far beyond what they are actually capable of delivering, mainly because of the shortage of finance, combined with unrealistic expectations and lack of adequate training (see Reeve, 1995, 1997). But of these, the issue of funding is always the most pressing for managers, and it is worth saying a little about this in setting the context for a research agenda.

Some research has been carried out into where funds come from for TCM schemes, although much more could be done. Medway (1998) has looked at the role of retailers in the sponsorship of TCMs and has produced some interesting findings. He discovered that there is a great reluctance for local traders to contribute any direct financial support to schemes. The majority of funding continues to come from five large retailers: Boots the Chemist, Marks and Spencers, Burton Group, Sainsbury's, and Sears. They concluded that only 5 percent of multiple sponsor schemes, and 1 percent of independents. This is quite damning in light of the new role in town centers for TCM identified by the Urban Task Force (1999, pp. 120–121). Retail or private sector funding was also preferred in the form of free-standing payments as opposed to ring-fenced money given for individual projects such as the installation of CCTV or pedestrianization work. Where this money was given, they also found a clear bias from retailers toward schemes run in partnership between private and public sectors, or those few with sole private backing, and toward giving money to predominantly public-sector-based initiatives. They accounted for this by suggesting that local authorities in many cases would actually prefer to forego funding unless it was exclusively in their control.

Aside from the actual cost to themselves, the reluctance of the independent retailing sector in supporting initiatives can be explained in two ways (see Stansbury, 1995; Guy, 1993; Forsberg et al., 1999; Hogg et al., 2000). The first reason is the lack of direct and measurable evidence of the return for moneys spent. It is extremely difficult to demonstrate that a particular contribution will lead to increased turnover or profit. The second is that there is a strong perception of free riding. Thus, retailers are reluctant to support schemes financially when the benefits will accrue equally to those businesses that are not contributing.* Many local retailers and other businesses also take the not surprising view that they are already being taxed through the existing local rating system, and that some of this should be directly ring-fenced for the local TCM initiative, so that contributions would be equitable (see Evans, 1997). With respect to the first argument here, early research (ATCM, 1994) was inconclusive and sometimes contradictory with regard to TCMs and their effects on the commercial successes of towns. However, more recent research (Lockwood, 1997, 1999) clearly indicates that TCMs have a positive commercial effect, at least with the narrow indicators of footfall and turnover derived from an analysis of the performance of the multiples.

Private sector funding is usually given to cover the costs of the manager, in space, salary, and for other administrative needs. Often, although this is increasingly not the case, managers are seconded from the large multiples such as Marks and Spencers, and Boots the Chemist in particular. Given the problem of funding, it is hardly surprising that in many instances managers spend a great deal of their time looking for money for potential projects, including the continuation of their own posts. These are usually limited by contract to two or three years at the most.

---

* Forsberg et al. (1999) provide a fascinating account of three schemes in Denmark, theorizing the issue of contributing and noncontributing stakeholders using the notion of "the tragedy of the commons." As Forsberg et al. (1999) neatly summarize: "What is common to the greatest number has the least care bestowed upon it" (p. 316).

TCM as a Profession: The Manager and the Association of Town Center Management (ATCM)

Finally, in filling in some of the background issues necessary to provide an adequate context for thinking through where research needs to be developed, there is the issue of the managers, their status, and their suitability for the tasks given to them. This also touches on the broader institutional structures of TCM as a putative profession and the role of the Association of Town Center Management.

Two pieces of research have examined the role and competencies of managers. Oxford Brookes University conducted a study into the competencies of managers (Oxford Brookes University, 1994). Then, in 1997, the ATCM commissioned a study into the training needs of managers (Reeve, 1997). These studies found that approximately a third of practicing managers at those times came from a retail background, under a fifth from local authorities, and the rest were made up of individuals trained in a variety of areas, mostly in business, design, and the professions. Many were not educated to graduate level, and some were from security and shopping center management areas.

The selection of people for the job varies according to a number of factors. These are principally the perception of a local authority or other employer of the needs of the job, and the level of salary available. A review of TCM job advertisements in 2002 suggested a range of £18,000 to, in one exceptional case, £50,000. Most posts are salaried at between £22,000 and £35,000. This implies middle management level, or, in the public sector, mid-career professional level. The motivation of managers themselves has hardly been researched. It is a matter at this stage of speculation what sort of person is attracted to a job that has great expectations placed upon it, but that offers a relatively low income and little long-term job security. Added to this, many managers are in mid-career, but opting for posts in which as yet there is no clear career structure in Britain. The upshot of all of this is that what often determines the success of managers is their instinctive ability to network, their charisma, and their skills in self-promotion. At this stage, there is no profession as such of TCM, although the ATCM is de facto the professional body representing managers. Managers do not have to be members of ATCM, because they are not part of a profession and are not in that sense licensed to practice.

The ATCM was set up in 1991 with a broad remit, and as a voluntary body, supported by fees from members combined with money and staff time from some of the large retailers. At that stage no public money was committed to the organization, although the Department of the Environment, Transport and the Regions has in the last year or two provided some limited funding to allow the association to develop. According to its own publicity material, the ATCM exists to promote the idea of TCM, to organize conferences and seminars as a means of developing good practice, to provide information about various aspects of town center management, to develop practical research in the field, and to provide appropriate skills training for the job.

Recent discussions on the part of the author with the ATCM imply that they are reluctant for it to become a profession—presumably because this would allow it to be confined to a specific institutional and legal role, much in the same way as planner or chartered surveyor. It is uncertain whether managers themselves take this liberal view that TCM should not become limited in definition through becoming a legally constituted profession. Aside from seminars and workshops run by the ATCM, which have in part a training function, there are very few courses specifically designed to address the training needs of managers. The educational policy of the ATCM seems to have changed in the last two years. It has moved toward the view of practical, short-term training in what managers believe they need, rather than something at producing the "reflective practitioner" (Oxford Brookes University, 1998, p. 3). In terms of a formally recognized and independently accredited qualification, the ATCM is interested in adopting the National Vocational Qualification (NVQ) structure for managers.

This overview of the history of TCM and key issues in the U.K. context allows us to now consider the implications of the topic for research. The second section of this chapter focuses on this.

Research Potential and a Research Agenda

Overview

The initial comments have already indicated the richness of the field, and its potential for academics and researchers in a number of areas. These are probably planning, urban design, urban management, urban regeneration, retailing, crime and security, policy studies, local government studies, tourism and marketing, and business management. Less obviously, it might include cultural geography and cultural studies, social anthropology, heritage, and conservation. However, the literature and the research from which it mostly comes is extremely uneven in both quality and scope (see Medway, 1998; Warnaby et al., 1998). As Page and Hardyman (1996) assert, "There has been a paucity of serious research on the rationale, significance and role of TCM schemes" (p. 154). This view is supported by Evans (1997), who argued even as recently as three years ago that despite its modishness, the impact of TCM on the viability of town centers has been little investigated. Although that situation is changing, research by the author of this chapter into the literature suggests that this is happening only very slowly.

Perhaps one reason for this lack of serious research activity is that no single host discipline can legitimately claim TCM as its own, although tentative efforts have been made by university schools of architecture and planning, as well as urban management, business, and retail. The reason for this is, presumably, the fact that TCM does not fit comfortably in any of the traditional academic subject areas, just as it is often the cause of friction between a number of professional interests.

Another reason for the lack of academic interest is that, as noted earlier, there are fewer than a handful of courses in the U.K. that take any interest in the subject. The need to research the topic as a means of informing teaching hardly exists at this point. There is little evidence that this is changing.

It is also clearly the case that the venue for the practice of TCM—cities and towns—has the capacity in itself to sustain the interest and research probing of an enormous range of subjects. In this sense it is a suitable candidate for testing the paradigmatic shift in academic work away from tightly bounded subject areas to interests that, by traditional standards, are multidisciplinary, requiring the application of a wide range of methods and research techniques.

The focus of the rest of this chapter, however, is on the potential for research into TCM that has direct relevance to the built environment disciplines, including design, planning, and urban management. The discussion is roughly divided between topics to do with TCM as an activity in its own right, and as a putative profession, and topics to do with the effects and role of TCM in town centers. This is a slightly arbitrary move, but hopefully helpful in focusing questions of appropriate methods for research.

Research in Town Center Management as an Activity

Town center management as an activity has received little attention in the academic world, as we have seen—except as a by-product of broader changes in the management, financing, and administration of cities (see Evans, 1997; Ennen and Ashworth, 1998). Where attention has been spent it has largely been to do with the problem of funding and, to a lesser degree, the accountability of TCM within existing democratic structures of local government. But these concerns have usually, again, been seen as side issues to what TCM is aiming to do. But it can be argued that TCM should be understood and researched as an activity in its own right to grasp some of the fundamental changes occurring in the decision-making culture of town and city centers. This is because it represents potentially at least one expression of a radical shift in the way that the traditional separation of legal and institutional responsibilities is being thought about, functionally and fiscally. The cultures of decision making and power at the local level might be one focus of TCM research. The literature already suggests areas of discord, disjunction, and conflict arising when local authorities feel threatened by the charisma of the private sector in TCM initiatives, perceiving this as a "buying in" to certain business opportunities (ATCM, 1994; BPF, 1995). The private sector has rarely had a reciprocal problem with the idea that there might be a relationship between financial investment and the right to make decisions.

Similarly, research into the experience of managers from different backgrounds and the bearing that their different "initial cultures" has on the way they perform would throw light on this aspect of TCM. The investigation of how conflicts of value generated by professional and situational contexts are resolved would require the development of new research methods. But these could provide great insight into the operation of urban management and decision making beyond TCM. This would be useful not only from a sociological perspective, but also because it could highlight the difference in goal setting and values of the two sectors in relation to town centers. Warnaby et al. (1998) hint at this and suggest that a clear understanding of the differences in attitude, performance, values, motivation, and organization between private and public sector bodies could usefully be applied to the study of the operation and culture of TCM schemes. Moreover, they suggest that the explicit and implicit *political* values of different stakeholders need to be studied. This at least resonates with the author's own work (Reeve, 1995) where the (false) idea that TCM should be an "apolitical" activity was identified as a common perspective from private sector interests involved in TCM.

Closely bound up with the question of the values of the two cultures is the issue of how success is measured. More of this in the second part of the discussion, but it is worth flagging at this point because what indicators are deemed appropriate as measures must have something to do with the culture and values of those applying them.

Aside from the two studies referred to earlier (Reeve, 1997; Oxford Brookes University, 1994), the changing professional status and skills identified by employers as suited for the job have been much neglected. This stems from two perspectives: first of expectations placed on individual managers, and second of tracking the emergence of a new profession or proto-profession. TCM is unlike any previous professional body whose role has at least in part been taking a form of responsibility for the health of the built environment. Architecture, planning, and chartered surveying, for example, developed as professions based on discrete tasks and roles. The boundaries of the powers, responsibilities, and functions of these have been susceptible to legal definition and institutional expression. Not so with TCM. The relationship of any professional body—such as the ATCM—in this respect to the other professional institutions might provide yet another focus for research.

Researching the Impacts and Effectiveness of TCM

The outcome of different types of TCM initiatives (forum, private limited company, mixed public and private sector TCM, etc.) has been little researched. The pamphlet *The Effectiveness of Town Centre Management* (ATCM with Donaldsons, Healey, and Baker, 1994) touched on the topic, as have a few other studies, most notably Pal and Sanders (1997), which looked at the relationship between inputs and outputs of TCM schemes, including TCM organization as an input.

An important dimension of the issue of structure is that of funding for TCM initiatives. More research needs to be carried out here to determine the cost effectiveness of different types of investment from different sorts of funders and funding

Table 18.1 Framework for analyzing TCM impacts

Customer impact	Users	Brokers	Fixers
Physical environment			
Social environment			
Economic environment			

Source: Pal and Sanders (1997).

structures. The work of Warnaby et al. (1998) might be developed in this regard. Likewise, Pal and Sanders (1997) provide a strong framework for this prospective research. They propose a complex model for analyzing cost effectiveness in TCM. This uses a matrix to relate customers to environmental impacts (see Table 18.1).

This framework is then further developed into a set of indicators that are justified in terms of their meaning for different customers, and their capacity to measure impact on the different types of environment that they define (see below). The framework is clearly capable of being taken further into a highly sophisticated tool for understanding TCM in the context of larger issues.

Falk (1998) has articulated a number of criticisms of the current system of business rates in town centers, concluding that these act as a serious disincentive to continued investment and vitality: "As the larger organisations increasingly invest out of town, the small businesses that remain shoulder the burden of contributing towards national taxes without seeing any return in terms of improvements to the area in which they operate" (p. 12). The part solution that he advocates includes the institution of town improvement zones (TIZs) loosely modeled on the North American BIDS experience, because these will "enable partnerships to formalise their structures and secure contributions from the main beneficiaries" (p. 14).

TIZs are also an approach to funding TCM advocated by the Department of the Environment, Transport and the Regions (DETR) and Urban Task Force (1999, pp. 120–121). Acknowledging the problem of free riding under a voluntary system, the task force makes the following recommendation: "Place Town Improvement Zones on a statutory footing, enabling local authorities to work with local businesses to establish jointly funded management arrangements for town centres and other commercial districts" (p. 121).

The Urban Task Force's conclusions regarding the application of TIZs build on earlier exploratory work by the ATCM with Leeds Metropolitan University (date uncertain, but around 1999). Based on a close review of current funding strategies for TCM, and a number of case studies, ATCM and Leeds Metropolitan University concluded that this was their preferred model for the mature stages of a TCM initiative. They set out a "prospectus" for TIZs that is clearly driven by business thinking and sees the town center as a predominantly commercial environment.

Curiously, the eight possible income streams for TIZs that this study identifies do not seem to include local authority sponsorship (p. 25).

TIZs and BIDs raise the question of the intellectual legitimacy of the TCM approach if it seeks to place largely arbitrary limits to its geographical territory. This is because they are dependent on being able to define with absolute precision the spatial limits of a town center, or quarter in which investment will be made. Two further areas for research are suggested here. The first might be concerned with how the limits of TCM, spatially, are currently set. How are town centers defined by the practice of TCM in the way they are, and what might this tell us about its goals and objectives? Such research could well develop thinking by the DETR (1998), already alluded to, that has attempted to construct a clear basis for the definition of town centers in terms of their spatial or geographical extent or boundaries. The second might be concerned with the difference between TCM as a form of urban regeneration and other regeneration strategies and programs, and indeed, their connections. A Ph.D. student has recently completed her dissertation working on this issue at the Joint Center for Urban Design at Oxford Brookes University (Otsuka, 2005).

There is thus a substantial and ongoing debate regarding the most effective means of funding TCMs and their operations. Unfortunately, research into the practical application and relative effectiveness of different funding mechanisms is limited by the difficulty of conducting experimental work in this area. Research is limited to drawing inferences from practices elsewhere, where circumstances and cultures may be so different that such comparisons can only be speculative in their conclusions.

Partnership* as an aspect of funding, and with the questions relating to organization that it implies, has been the focus again of some research interest over the last few years, most notably the ATCM-sponsored work (ATCM and URBED, 1997): a survey of 47 schemes. This concluded that for private funding to be made available there was a need for schemes to generate clear data relating to commercial performance (see also Hogg et al., 2000). The inference for research that might be drawn from this is that the issue of partnerships would be an appropriate starting point for examining values in TCM.

The issue of partnership has research implications beyond the policy and value level, and clearly touches on questions of implementation and project management, or *action planning*, as the preferred TCM term. Little detailed investigation using a case study approach has been conducted examining the degree to which the town center manager becomes involved at critical stages of capital projects such as pedestrianization, or the installation and operation of CCTV. It might be argued that if his or her role is confined to that of marketing, network, and fund-raising, and severed from the detailed decision making that constitutes project management,

---

* Warnaby et al. (1998) point out that *partnership* is a term used indiscriminately, and that understanding how public–private cooperation actually works requires close empirical, case study–based research.

then he or she has very little real power to effect change. Coventry and Bristol as examples of semiautonomous, limited companies would be good test cases here.

Measuring Impacts and the Use of Indicators

The issue of funding and outputs is clearly directly related to the question of measures of success. Here TCM research overlaps significantly with other fields, such as urban design and, say, transport planning, and we begin to shift from specifically TCM topics to those more indirectly related to the activity. The measures or, more fashionably, the indicators available to other disciplines might be more systematically applied in the work of research to assess the success of TCM schemes. There is increasing pressure on managers to show that the projects that they have argued for have performed well, but they often lack the resources and time to make meaningful measurements, except at a very crude and often anecdotal level. URBED's seminal work (DoE and URBED, 1994) shows the problem. Although it sketches out some useful indicators—footfall, turnover, quality of life in various senses—it almost treats them as if they were all to be valued equally. This is also true of the indicators recommended in *Planning Policy Guidance Note 6* (DoE, 1996, figure 1):

Diversity of uses
Retailer representation and intentions to change representation
Shopping rents
Proportion of vacant street-level vacancy
Commercial yields on nondomestic property
Pedestrian flows
Accessibility
Customer views and behavior
Perception of safety and occurrence of crime
State of town center environmental quality

Tomalin (1997) provides a detailed critique of PPG6 and discusses the relative benefits of different approaches to the implementation of indicators. These range from the largely subjective use of health checks, based on the attitudes and impressions of managers themselves, to fully integrated data collection and evaluation techniques employing a range of methods. Using the work of Kent County Council in this area, she also argues that what is needed is a properly thought through approach to the definition of core and specific indicators—i.e., those that apply across all towns and those that are derived from the particular needs and ambitions of individual centers. She claims that data is lacking to allow a comparison between town centers in terms of their economic and other types of performance. However, she acknowledges that "the process of developing a reliable and robust town centre database is not a simple one. Government policy has changed with every successive

PPG6 since 1993, and it is difficult for any authority to follow the guidance with confidence" (p. 390).

Hogg et al. (2000) have recently undertaken a major piece of research examining the application of key performance indicators (KPIs) in a sample of town center management initiatives in the U.K. Their work again calls for a nationwide approach, and one that is grounded through benchmarking so that any data generated by the application of KPI surveys can be compared spatially and across time. The indicators that they are concerned with in terms of their usage are listed below (Hogg et al., 2000, p. 12):*

Car park usage
Town center footfall figures
Vacant property rate
Town center theft
Shoplifting
Town center user surveys
Retail sales
Town center violence
Zone A property rents
Retail investment
Public transport usage
Capital investment
Yield (as defined by PPG6)
Trade diversion
New job creation
Nonretail floorspace
Other

The premise on which their research is based, that sponsors and investors in TCM schemes need hard evidence of the benefits of the approach to convince them to continue investing, implies a serious limitation in the work. This is a criticism that might also be leveled at Tomalin's discussion. The problem is that the underlying values in both are primarily commercial ones as far as they are underpinned by seeing the town center as first and foremost a place for retail and commerce. The measure of a town's success is taken as its success in relation to users as *customers*. The indicator approach is also limited by the nature of the data that it is able or willing to countenance as having a value. It has to be capable of being quantified. It might be argued that qualitative approaches can be equally useful for evaluating success, in terms of user perception of quality, or streetscape changes over time. A great deal of work needs to be done to develop a sound theoretical basis for a

---

* For a comparison, see the Caruso and Weber chapter in this volume on the indicators of the performances of BIDs.

more inclusive approach to the notion of performance and measuring success than methods based on the exclusive use of quantifiable indicators allow (Shipley et al., 2000). If the only indicators used are based on commercial values, then the risk is that commercial values will become the only measures of success for town centers.

What is also needed is an approach that combines methods for understanding change and performance against clear criteria, with methods for weighting performance against the particular values and democratically decided needs of a town. Not all towns aspire to the same thing. For instance, as Pal and Sanders ask, is gentrification always a positive indicator? The Placecheck* initiative sponsored by the Urban Design Alliance (UDAL) may provide clues to this (see Cowan, 2002).

Of course, the continuation of TCM as an approach in itself requires that its benefits be demonstrated to all those responsible for its funding. In this sense it is not surprising, in the U.K. context at least, that the indicators employed are to a degree governed by their relevance to sponsors' interests. This touches on another area of debate that could be developed into a piece of empirical work: examining the motivation of contributing and noncontributing interests in town centers in the U.K. Using the work of Forsberg et al. (1999) would be a possible starting point.

Case Study Approaches

Perhaps the most interesting and rigorous research has been that which sees TCM as one factor among several in explaining a particular urban issue. That is, research is needed that regards TCM not as the solution of first choice—albeit one that needs to be given the right tools—but as one approach within a whole range of approaches to urban management, for example, Oc and Tiesdell's (1997, 1998) discussion of safety and security in Coventry and Nottingham. Their work provides an excellent model for close, case-study-based research, intelligently reviewing the similarities and differences between the two places in terms of their complete urban, political, and historical situations.

The case study approach is one that has much to commend it in this field, particularly longitudinally where proper controls can be constructed. That is, there is potentially great value in research that compares towns over time, and across time, using baseline information. Asking what good is TCM requires research capable of capturing long-term achievements and trends and comparing places with one another to help reveal actual causes and the impact of real variables, such as the presence or absence of a TCM initiative. Of course, TCM is in its relative infancy, and thus there are both an opportunity and a problem in carrying out longitudinal research on it. Aside from Oc and Tiesdell's study, the ATCM have undertaken

---

* Placecheck is an ongoing initiative that was launched in the U.K. in 1998. The core Placecheck method was written by Rob Cowan and developed under a funding program managed by Dan Bone, on behalf of the Urban Design Alliance with funding from the then Department of Transport Local government and the Regions and English Partnerships.

a number of minor case studies (ATCM with DoE, 1997; ATCM, 1998a, 1999), as has Lockwood (1997, 1999). But these are somewhat flawed in that either their focus has been very narrow or too superficial. The ATCM material also suffers because it is concerned with good *practice*, and is therefore proselytizing rather than objectively distanced.

The excellent works by Lockwood (1997, 1999) illuminate the problem. Both of the Lockwood surveys are the products of a major research undertaking examining a wide range of data across a great number of places. However, valuable as this work is, the qualitative indicators that part of the work draws on are necessarily undeveloped and crude. The ATCM's published case studies (ATCM, 1998a, 1998b; ATCM and DoE, 1997) provide more of a snapshot than an in-depth, scientifically conducted analysis. This compares unfavorably with a number of programs in the United States. Here, because of the direct relationship between levels of funding and turnover, initiatives are very closely monitored in terms of at least the commercial impacts and performance of schemes themselves. This, incidentally, points to a major and unsurprising problem with much of the consultancy and research work sponsored by the ATCM, with the best intentions, no doubt. The conclusion that TCM might be a redundant, not to say destructive, activity cannot be entertained in its work. The starting point is that it always has potential to be a good thing; it is simply a matter of designing schemes properly and funding them adequately. They cannot ask what is unaskable to them.

The Town Center Environment: Other Research Issues

Oc and Tiesdell's (1997) study of safety and security is not only significant for its methods, but the topic in itself has received a great deal of attention over the last few years. It has been examined from a wide range of perspectives: from the perspective of policing (Fyfe, 1995) to that of electronic surveillance (CCTV) and its application in town centers (Reeve, 1995, 1996). CCTV has attracted much funding within TCM schemes (see Medway, 1998), but support for its use is often based on anecdote, and the view that if other towns have it, it must be a good thing. Whether it actually creates the benefits popularly suspected for it is as yet largely undetermined. Again, this issue deserves closer attention because it has a direct impact on the democratic nature of public space within British cities, and the role of TCM in affecting that.

Another potential area of research is into attitudes of users of town centers to TCM. Helen Wooley's study with the ATCM (ATCM and Sheffield University, 1997), although limited in scope, at least provides a starting point for understanding what users want from town centers, and such work is vital in informing the sorts of decisions town center managers make as part of their role.

One area close to my own interests in TCM in the U.K. and abroad is that of the commodification and potential privatization of public space, with its implications of both social control and aesthetic homogenization (see Reeve, 1996). This constitutes a debate that has ramifications far beyond the tactics of TCM in public space. The issue of commodification has been examined as a general social phenomenon by writers and urban critics from Sennett (1993) to Sorkin (1992) and Zukin (1995) (see also Fyfe, 1995; Hannigan, 1998; Hayward and McGlynn, 1995; Punter, 1990). More particularly, the relationships among *investment agencies,* or sponsors of TCM schemes, *organizational structures* of TCM, and the *values applied in practice* with regard to acceptable and unacceptable forms of behavior deserve further attention. This is not a matter that might be significant simply because it happens to trouble liberal academics. Banning orders imposed on individuals for antisocial behavior, for instance, excluding them from town centers, can have very material consequences. A magistrate in Romsey, in southeast England in 2000, condemned one such order as a serious infringement of human rights. The effect on the individual concerned was to make it impossible for him to claim the social security benefits to which he was entitled because the Department of Social Security office was in the town center from which he had been excluded, and it was here that he was required to sign on every two weeks to claim his benefits.

Planning, Urban Design, Architecture, and the Role of TCM in Setting Agendas

Another major area for research and thinking is that of the relationship between TCM and the other practices that affect the environment of town centers, and in particular urban design, planning, and architecture. The general question that needs to be asked is, to what degree is there a reciprocal engagement between TCM and these other activities? Is TCM beginning to have an effect on thinking about physical planning, or place making?

To start answering these questions it is worth reflecting on a comment by Evans (1997) regarding the power of government policy to set the agenda for town centers, and hence to prescribe to a degree what planners, architects and urban designers can do:

> Whatever the relationship between cause and effect, the treatment of town centres has hardly been a success story in policy-making terms. Each policy phase has generated as many problems as it has solved, either through excessive zeal and insensitivity or inertia and neglect. (p. 132)

British planning seems to be shifting its attention to the question of urban regeneration and urban "renaissance," with all the attendant dangers implied by that. The Urban Task Force report (1999) is an advocate of TCMs under the TIZ model and argues that,

For the retail businesses situated in the town centre, commercial health is inextricably linked to the quality of the urban environment. If people are not attracted to use the town centre then footfall declines, sales fall and profit vanishes.

Likewise, as I mentioned earlier in this chapter, the revised PPG6 sets out a broad agenda for the role of TCMs in the regeneration of town center environments. The U.K. government White Paper on urban matters (DETR, 2000) has something to say about the direction planning practitioners should take when developing local plans and strategic instruments for town centers. However, the DETR publication (2000), which provides guidance on the application of urban design in planning, says nothing about the link between physical design and urban management, or TCMs. This calls into question claims of "joined up thinking" in government policy.

What the previous paragraph points to is the need for research into exactly how the practices of TCMs, particularly the types of projects they develop and implement, are being coordinated with the other functions of local government and private sector development. There may be a role for managers in helping to articulate together sustainable approaches to the planning and design or the refitting of town centers, but the degree to which and in what ways this may already be happening is unclear. At an extreme, TCM may come to represent a new form of urban governance, with powers to direct investment and the management of public space. The question of whether this will be a good or bad thing needs to be asked before this specter of TCM as a form of governance becomes an actuality.

The International Context

Finally, the international perspective can give insight into the strengths and limitations of practice in the U.K., and some work has been conducted with this in mind. Ennen and Ashworth (1998) have looked, albeit briefly, at the difference between the Dutch experience of city center management and that in the U.K. Their conclusions are somewhat broad—principally that TCMs in the U.K. are too narrowly focused on the day-to-day running of town centers, compared with Holland, where city center management is able to take a more strategic role. They argue that this is largely because TCM in Holland is controlled almost entirely within the public sector.

Also, some empirical work has been carried out in Denmark. Forsberg et al. (1999) focused on the question of free riders and analyzed the reasons of stakeholders in three towns for supporting or not supporting local TCM initiatives. They came to the conclusion that a TCM's success depends very much on the way in which it is funded, along with the perceived benefits and costs of contributing to it by stakeholders. While Forsberg et al.'s work provides some insight into the practices of TCMs outside of the U.K., its real concern is with the broader topic of "cooperative behavior" in the commercial context, and particularly the relationship between public and private sector values rather than those practices.

Travers and Weimar (1996) have examined the business improvement districts (BIDs) in the United States, where funding of projects operates more in the form of a local tax than it can in the U.K., where there are no mechanisms for raising taxes locally. Nonetheless, the sort of model they have described has also been seen as possible for the U.K. by Nicholas Falk in his advocacy of "town trusts" (ATCM and URBED, 1997), and by the ATCM in its theoretical experimentation with TIZs, as I mentioned earlier in this chapter. Indeed, the ATCM was experimenting with a series of pilot BID projects to test the efficacy of this model of funding at the time of the writing of this chapter (see Reilly, 2004). But the North American practice of central business district and main street management calls for a type of research that is concerned with issues beyond that of funding mechanisms. There is a whole raft of questions to be asked here about the nature of the relationship between business and the public sector, the role of the mayor and that of local stakeholders, as well as how the limits spatially and functionally are defined around BIDs as against public authority activities.*

Conclusions

The practice of town center management has at best received only patchily limited research attention, in particular from the perspective of the disciplines under the built environment heading. This is both understandable and so far a missed opportunity. It is not often that an entirely new mode of operation, profession, or set of practices in a particular field comes into being, and arguably this is what the TCMs in the U.K. represent. The fundamental questions are still there to be asked. They might be set out as follows, but in no particular order:

1. What status, among the built environment professions, does TCM have, and is it likely to have?
2. What are the powers of TCM in terms of local governance, and how have these been achieved and legitimated?
3. If it is an activity that contributes a net gain to town centers, how should it be supported and controlled?
4. What can individual cases tell us about values and potentials of TCMs and the methods they use?
5. Does the TCM model have a future?
6. What can be learned from the international experience of city center management?

---

* These issues and others are discussed in the chapters on BIDs in this volume.

7. In what, if any, ways are towns with TCM initiatives different as a consequence of having TCMs, compared with those without this form of management?
8. What is the relationship between TCM as a new form of urban governance (if this is indeed the part it aspires to be) and traditional forms of local government?
9. What are the central values within TCM, and do these represent a shift in perspective on the purpose and role of town centers from spaces of "civitas" to spaces of "societas,"* and what is lost in that shift?
10. In relation to any of the above, who is best placed to ask such questions—with respect to both technique and knowledge, and value—academics, TCM practitioners, political theorists, economists, and so on?

These are at least some of the obvious and more general concerns that academics working in the built environment disciplines might have. There are undoubtedly many more. The fact is, given the paucity of work in this area, the field has much potential for anyone with the time and interest to examine it.

References

ATCM. 1998a. *Handbook of managers.* London: Association of Town Center Management.

ATCM. 1998b. *A guide to good practice.* London: Association of Town Center Management.

ATCM and DoE. 1997. *Managing urban spaces in town centres.* London: Association of Town Center Management with Chesterton, HMSO.

ATCM and Leeds Metropolitan University. Undated (probably 1999). *Step change: The case for town improvement zones.* London: Association of Town Center Management.

ATCM and Sheffield University Department of Landscape. 1997. *Young people and town centres.* London: Association of Town Center Management.

ATCM and URBED. 1997. *Town centre partnerships.* London: Association of Town Center Management.

ATCM with Boots the Chemist. 1997. *Developing structures to deliver town centre management.* London: Association of Town Center Management.

ATCM with Donaldsons, Healey, and Baker. 1994. *The effectiveness of town centre management.* London: Association of Town Center Management.

Baldock, J. 1989. Town centre management: Its importance and nature. In *Creating the living town centre,* ed. W. Le-Las, M. Bradshaw, and P. Robshaw, 50–58. Conference Proceedings of the Civic Trust. London: Civic Trust.

BPF. 1995. *Town centre management, a policy initiative.* London: British Property Federation.

Comedia. 1991. *Out of ours: A study of economic, social and cultural life in twelve town centres in the UK.* London: Comedia and the Gulbenkian Foundation.

---

* "Societas" implies a public realm in which people behave in ways that are determined by self-interest, even though this may be satisfied through collective action; "civitas" implies a public realm in which there is a sense of collective responsibility, and that self-interest is secondary to this.

Cowan, R. 2002. *Placecheck: An introduction.* http://www.placecheck.info (accessed December 8, 2002).

DETR. 1998. *Town centres: Defining boundaries for statistical monitoring.* London: The Stationery Office.

DETR. 2000. *Our towns and cities: The future—Delivering an urban renaissance.* The Urban White Paper.

DETR and the Urban Task Force. 1999. *Towards an urban renaissance.* London: DETR Publications.

DoE. 1996. *Planning policy guidance note 6: Revised, town centres and retail development.* London: Department of the Environment.

DoE and URBED. 1994. *Vital and viable town centres: Meeting the challenge.* London: HMSO.

English Tourist Board. 1995. Town centre management. *Insights* 7:A21–A25.

Ennen, E., and Ashworth, G. 1998. City centre management: Dutch and British experience of a new form of planning. *European Spatial Research and Policy* 5:5–15.

Evans, R. 1997. *Regenerating town centres.* Manchester, UK: Manchester University Press.

Falk, N. 1998. Resourcing the revival of town and city centres. *Built Environment* 24:6–15.

Forsberg, H., Medway D., and Warnaby, G. 1999. Town centre management by co-operation, evidence from Sweden. *Cities* 16(5):315–322.

Fyfe, N. 1995. Policing the city. *Urban Studies* 32:759–778.

Guy, C., ed. 1993. *Town centres: Investment and management.* Papers in Planning and Research 143. Cardiff, Wales: Department of City and Regional Planning, University of Wales, College of Cardiff.

Hannigan, J. 1998. *Fantasy city: Pleasure and profit in the post-modern metropolis.* London: Routledge.

Hayward, R., and McGlynn, S. 1995. Town centres we deserve? *Town Planning Review* 66:321–328.

Hogg, S., Harvey, J., and Medway, D. 2000. Measuring the effectiveness of town centre management. *Town and Country Planning*, April, pp. 117–119.

Houghton, L. 1997. *Business improvement districts.* New York: Downtown Association, Inc.

Lockwood, J. I. 1997. *The Lockwood survey.* Nottingham: Urban Management Initiatives.

Lockwood, J. I. 1999. *The Lockwood survey.* Nottingham: Urban Management Initiatives.

Medway, D. 1998. Retailer funding of town centre management schemes in the UK. In *Proceedings of the Marketing and Managing Urban Centres Conference.* Manchester, UK: Manchester Metropolitan University.

Oc, T., and Tiesdell, S., eds. 1997. *Safer city centres, reviving the public realm.* London: Chapman.

Oc, T., and Tiesdell, S. 1998. City centre management and safer city centres: Approaches in Coventry and Nottingham. *Cities* 15:85–103.

Otsuka, N. 2005. Town centre management and urban regeneration: Defining the boundaries. Unpublished Ph.D. thesis, Oxford Brookes University, Joint Centre for Urban Design.

Oxford Brookes University, Schools of Architecture and Business. 1994. *Competencies of town centre managers.* Oxford: Oxford Brookes University Press.

Oxford Brookes University. 1998. *Course handbook to the Cert/Dip TCM course.* Oxford: Oxford Brookes University Press.

Page, S., and Hardyman, R. 1996. Place marketing and town centre management: A new tool for urban revitalization. *Cities* 13:153–164.

Pal, J., and Sanders, E. 1997. Measuring the effectiveness of town centre management schemes, an exploratory framework. *International Journal of Retail and Distribution Management* 25:70–77.

Punter, J. 1990. The privatisation of the public realm. *Planning Practice and Research* 5:9–16.

Reeve, A. 1995. Urban design and places of spectacle. Unpublished Ph.D. thesis, Oxford Brookes University, Joint Center for Urban Design.

Reeve, A. 1996. The private realm of the managed town centre. *Urban Design International* 1:61–68.

Reeve, A. 1997. *Town centre management, training needs assessment: A report.* Oxford: Oxford Brookes University, School of Architecture Publications.

Reeve, A. 2004. Town centre management: Developing a research agenda in an emerging field. *Urban Design International* 9:133–150.

Reeve, A., and Otsuka, N. 2004. Town centre management as regeneration: Defining the boundaries. *Urban Design Quarterly* 91:17–20.

Reilly, J. 2004. Business improvement districts: Funding the future of town centres. *Urban Design Quarterly* 91:20–23.

RICS. 1994. *Town centre management, guidance note.* London: Royal Institute of Chartered Surveyors.

Sennett, R. 1993. *The fall of public man.* London: Faber and Faber.

Shipley, R., Reeve, A. R., and Grover, P. 2000. Manual of research methods for conservation impact assessment. Unpublished, Oxford Brookes University.

Sorkin, M., ed. 1992. *Variations on a theme park: The new American city and the end of public space.* New York: Noonday.

Stansbury, M. 1995. Town centre management: The story so far. In *Town centres: Investment and management*, ed. C. Guy. Papers in Planning and Research 143. Cardiff, Wales: Department of City and Regional Planning, University of Wales, College of Cardiff.

Tomalin, C. 1997. Town centre health checks. *Planning Practice and Research* 12:383–392.

Travers, T., and Weimar, J. 1996. *Business improvement districts, New York and London.* London: The Greater London Group, the London School of Economics, with the Corporation of London.

Urban Task Force. 1999. *Towards an urban renaissance.* London: Urban Task Force.

Warnaby, G., Alexander, A., and Medway, D. 1998. Town centre management in the UK: A review, synthesis and research agenda. *International Review of Retail, Distribution and Consumer Research* 8:15–31.

Wells, I. 1991. *Town centre management: A future for the high street?* Geographical Papers 109. Reading University Department of Geography.

Zukin, S. 1995. *The cultures of cities.* Oxford: Blackwell.

Chapter 19

Business Improvement Districts in England: The UK Government's Proposals, Enactment, and Guidance

---

Martin Blackwell

Contents

Introduction

The government of the United Kingdom exercises jurisdiction over the area commonly referred to as the British Isles, but it is also possible for the U.K. government to make regulations that apply only to England, and this is what has occurred in respect to business improvement districts (BIDs). This chapter discusses a legislative position that is applicable only in England and not to other parts of the United Kingdom.

The North American origin and evolution of BIDs is discussed by Levy (2001). The introduction of BIDs to England has been prompted by the apparent success of the BID models in the United States (Mitchell, 1999). The framework created for the introduction of BIDs in England is notably different from the American model. The English proposal is based on the supplementary taxation of the majority of business occupiers (rather than property owners) after a BID proposal has been voted in. The taxation is based on the rating system that applies to nondomestic properties. There are circumstances in which property owners may be taxed, although these are secondary to the tax on occupiers.

This chapter considers the voting mechanism for creating a BID in England and how the supplementary levy is applied. In England the payment of the levy is compulsory once a BID has been established. The supplementary levy and its amount are based on the English rating system. The rating system ascribes a rental value to each property, which is then taxed; the supplementary levy is a further tax. This is akin to property tax assessment serving as the base upon which the levy is then charged. The method of introduction in England gives rise to a number of issues for the success of a BID. The mechanism behind BID proposals is explored in detail. The chapter also considers the creation of BIDs to date and those initial proposals that have been unsuccessful.

The Legislative Framework for BIDs in England

The mechanism by which BIDs are created in England is under the Business Improvement Districts (England) Regulations 2004, Statutory Instrument 2004 No. 2443. Statutory Instruments are secondary legislation in English law created out of primary enabling legislation, in this case the Local Government Act (2003). The act confers upon the secretary of state the power to make the regulations approved by both Houses of Parliament. These regulations came into force on September 17, 2004.

Under the Local Government Finance Act (1988) a rateable value is set for each hereditament. A hereditament is a unit of occupation. It may be one freehold title or a combination of more than one title; similarly, it may be the same as the area of one lease or several leases combined. There is a range of reasons why a rate payer may want a hereditament split or merged; these relate to the tax paid or how the property is valued. A hereditament may not be straightforward to determine, and a number have been determined by the courts. Moorings and fishing rights may well have a rateable value based on that particular hereditament; they are a right connected with land and by law can have a rateable value. In general terms, all rights in or connected with land are heritable—hence the origin of hereditament. A chattel is not itself rateable unless used, enjoyed with, and enhancing the value of the land (Cinderella Rockerfellas Ltd v. Rudd, Potter LJ at paragraph 14). The rateable value for the hereditament is based on the rental value of the property subject to certain statutory assumptions (Local Government Finance Act, 1988; Rating [Valuation] Act, 1999).

Key to understanding the operation of BIDs in England is an appreciation of the concept of the hereditament. Hereditament is defined in the Statutory Instrument as meaning

> Anything which is or is treated as being a hereditament by virtue of the provisions of or any provisions made under section 64 of the 1988 Act [the Local Government Finance Act 1988] including any hereditament to which regulation 6 of the Non-Domestic Rating (Miscellaneous Provisions) Regulations (1989) applies but otherwise excluding any hereditament to which regulations made under section 64(3)(b) of the 1988 Act apply.

A hereditament is of fundamental importance as it is the unit of property that is subject to nondomestic rating. It is this unit to which the supplementary levy of the BID will apply and around which the voting mechanisms for establishing a BID are focused. The Statutory Instrument makes reference to section 64 of the 1988 Local Government Finance Act. Section 64(1) of this act contains the definition of hereditament, phrased as: "A hereditament is anything which, by virtue of the definition of hereditament in section 115(1) of the [General Rate Act 1967], would have been a hereditament for the purposes of that Act had this Act not been passed."

We therefore have a situation in which the Business Improvement District Regulations in England, which came into force in 2004, use as a basis a definition contained in an act of 1988. This act in turn applies a definition of a hereditament from an earlier piece of legislation dating from 1967. Section 115(1) of the General Rate Act (1967) provides a definition of hereditament to be applied, although this definition in itself requires explanation and interpretation. Section 115(1) of the General Rate Act (1967) states: "Hereditament means property which is or may become liable to a rate, being a unit of such property which is, or would fall to be, shown as a separate item in the valuation list."

A unit of property shown on a valuation list is therefore at the heart of the BID process in England for two key reasons. The first is that to create a BID there has to be a voting process, discussed below, which is based on the local rating list. It is those hereditaments on the local rating list to which votes are attached. The second point is that if a BID is established, the supplementary levy to the local rate is applied to hereditaments within the BID area. The levy is not optional if a BID has been approved and created; the charge has to be paid and can be recovered via statutory provisions.

The Importance and Relevance of the 1988 Local Government Finance Act

In response to the U.K. government's proposal and subsequent enactment of BID legislation, Blackwell (2005) wrote of problems that may result from these proposals. In particular, the levy still taxes occupiers and not owners. The concerns remain, as the enacted legislation in respect to points raised does not differ materially from the consultation document underlying the proposal [Consultation Paper on Draft Business Improvement Districts (England) Regulations 2004]. Where the enacted legislation differs from the consultation document is in providing for a simple majority vote by rateable value, rather than requiring a 75 percent by rateable value vote in favor.

Rates in England are a tax on property occupation (not ownership per se, although owners may be taxed for certain empty property). There is a split between residential property and commercial property; commercial property is in fact more accurately defined as nondomestic. The definition of nondomestic is deliberately wide to include things like moorings, advertising hoardings, public conveniences, canals, and railways; essentially, as the name implies, nondomestic is taken to cover everything that is not residential. Exemptions in respect to charging and different treatment of different property based on use or occupation have been created, but these fail to be considered after deciding whether a hereditament is nondomestic. It is these exemptions and differing treatments that in part add to the transparency difficulties with BIDs in England.

The Statutory Instrument excludes "any hereditament to which regulations made under section 64(3)(b) of the 1988 Act apply." The effect of this is to exclude all those hereditaments on the central rating list. For a BID-proposing body in England to claim that all nondomestic rate payers will pay is misleading; the levy will apply only to those hereditaments on the local list.

The fact that there are two rating lists in England is not widely appreciated. Shown on the local list will be hereditaments that fall within the administrative area of a particular local authority, or those substantially in one authority's area. The central rating list includes such hereditaments as railway lines, canals, pipelines, telecommunications, and other infrastructure. The central list contains, among others, those hereditaments that cross many authority boundaries or fall within a number of authority areas. It also includes hereditaments like power stations and railway stations, which are treated as part of a network, although these can be defined locally.

Prior to the Local Government Act (1988), rating was essentially a local tax, a position that this act fundamentally altered: "The revolutionary change made by the 1988 Act was to convert non-domestic rates from a local tax into a central tax," quoting Lord Hoffman in *Edison* (2003). There are wide-ranging implications resulting from this, to the success and transparency of BIDs in England. There is a central rating list and a local rating list. Only those hereditaments on the local list are entitled to vote, and only local list hereditaments are taxed. Not all property has the vote or is taxed. Yet it is possible, as was the case in *Edison First Power Limited v. Central Valuation Officer* (2003), for a hereditament to move from the central list to a local list. Therefore, it is possible for a hereditament to be moved from the central list to a local list within a BID area, in theory, therefore, from a position in which the supplementary levy is not paid to one where it is.

Would this mean apparent taxation without representation, the former central list hereditament not taking part in the BID voting but now being subjected to the levy? Regulation 17 of the Statutory Instrument would seem to suggest that an alteration ballot of all those subject to the BID levy would be necessary, because 17(1) states, "Where there is a proposal to alter," and at (c), "the BID levy in such a way that would," and at (c)(i), "cause any person to be liable to pay the BID levy who was not previously liable to pay," an alteration ballot would be required.

Regulation 16 of the Statutory Instrument does make provision for a BID body to make alterations to the BID arrangements without an alteration ballot, provided this is stated in the original BID arrangements, but such a provision does not override regulation 16(2). This provides that the geographical area of the BID and the BID levy, by either increase or person liable to pay, cannot be altered without a further ballot.

In view of the cost and procedure necessary for organizing a ballot, those proposing a BID in England may wish to reduce the likelihood of central list hereditaments transferred to the BID area. This may influence the original BID area proposed.

Although it is theoretically possible for a hereditament to move from the central list to a local list and be within a BID area, there are relatively few BID areas to date (May 2006), and there are few movements of hereditaments from the central list to a local list. The BID areas that do exist are listed in Appendix A. However, there are many reliefs, exemptions, and variations in charging that do present severe distortions to the rating system that is being used as the basis for BID voting and charging.

Many of the changes result from the Local Government Finance Act (1988), which has fundamentally altered the nature of rating, as noted by Lord Hoffman in *Edison* (2003). It appears that the authors of the Statutory Instrument have attempted to graft local proposals for BIDs onto legislation that on further inspection is not ideally suited to the purpose.

Voting for a BID

The regulations provide that in order for a BID to be created, a majority of rate payers by hereditament must vote in favor; there also must be a majority by rateable value. The original consultation proposed a 75 percent majority by rateable value, but this has been reduced in the enacted instrument to a simple majority.*

Regulation 8 of the Statutory Instrument contains the definition of persons entitled to vote. Those persons are those nondomestic rate payers that would be liable for the BID levy at the date of publication of the notice of the ballot. Those persons who become relevant nondomestic rate payers between the date of the notice and the date of the ballot will not be entitled to vote.

The regulation uses the expression "to be liable for the BID levy"—those liable will be those shown on the local rating list. The local rating list is subject to many alterations, additions, and deletions that arise in themselves from an appeal process. The process can take time, which means that at any point a particular local rating list will almost certainly be subject to an appeal to alter it. There may therefore be a strict liability, as the appeals can be backdated, but that has yet to appear on a particular local rating list. Given the number of appeals and nature of the appeals system, to alter a local rating list, the mechanism does not lend itself to identifying, in a timely fashion, those liable for a levy that is forward looking. It is only capable of identifying those that would have been responsible at some point in the past.

Between the original enactment of the BID legislation and May 2006 there had been 34 BID ballots, 28 successful and 6 unsuccessful, with one unsuccessful vote being successful at a reballot. Most positive support by both number of

---

* The original proposal resembles the rule used in the state of Georgia in the United States. The state constitution requires that to form a BID, the owners of those properties whose total market value constitutes at least 75 percent of the total value of all the properties in the proposed district must support its formation (see Chapter 15 in this volume).

rate payers (92 percent) and percentage of rateable value (97 percent) occurred in the Birmingham Broad Street BID on May 26, 2005. This has also seen the highest turnout at 65 percent of any positive BID vote. Of the six BID votes that were unsuccessful, the Industrial Estate of Altham (February 25, 2005), saw the highest total turnout of 79 percent, with 52 percent positive by rateable value and 49 percent positive by number of rate payers. This vote illustrates how close BID ballots can be under the regulations. But of some additional concern must be the turnout rates, which average below 50 percent.

Appendix B lists those BID ballots taking place prior to May 2006 that have resulted in a negative vote either by number or by rateable value. Appendix A lists those ballots that have been successful over the same period.

The Purpose of English BIDs

Each BID proposal is to be accompanied by a proposals document outlining the purpose of the BID and the exact nature of the levy. The BID purpose is subject to consultation, although anecdotally there is a need for further research into how effective this is. Those promoting the BID have the opportunity to frame the ballot question (i.e., the BID purpose), and it is clear that different occupier interest groups wish to see different things.

The Birmingham Broad Street BID is the most successful to date in terms of those voting in favor. This BID proposal actually provided for different levies on the rateable value for different categories of users. Licensed premises in the core area pay a levy of 2 percent of the rateable value, other businesses in the core area 1 percent, and those in the outer area 0.5 percent. This structure recognized the concerns of many businesses that the demands placed upon the BID in large part arose from the "nighttime economy": it was therefore considered desirable to levy those benefiting the most (licensed premises) at a different rate. Appendix A provides further detail about the levies and the threshold for payment (i.e., the minimum applicable rateable value) within BID areas that have been voted for.

The majority of BID proposals do not have a stepped levy structure; however, there is one levy paid by those that qualify regardless of perceived or actual benefit arising from the BID. For example, the Reading BID, which was approved, has a flat 1 percent levy on those businesses with a rateable value of more than £10,000 within the BID area. The Reading BID proposal is divided into three objective areas: to provide a cleaner and better maintained city center, to provide a safer city center, and to provide a better promoted city center. Each of these areas has allocated tasks and an associated budget. The tasks are (1) regular street washing, graffiti/fly poster removal, and repainting street furniture; (2) a team of police community support officers, CCTV signage, business security agreement, and child safety scheme training; and (3) Christmas lighting, additional hanging baskets, marketing campaigns, and shopping and leisure guides.

Other administrative areas have police community support officers provided through funds that are not recovered from a BID. In order for English BIDs to receive renewal mandates, there must be added value. There is a concern that BID funding is being used to pay for activities that should be occurring in any event out of general taxation. The belief that the proposed activity "should be occurring anyway" appears to be the general reason behind those initial votes that have been negative. Each BID proposal document will contain a service level agreement that should state the existing level of service and the benefits to flow from a successful BID. Careful preparation and management of the ongoing service delivery will be crucial components to BIDs that are established for a fixed period, receiving a renewal mandate.

It is also necessary to make sure all in the BID area receive benefit from the proposals. Forty-eight percent of occupiers within the Reading BID area are retailers, and the thrust of the BID objectives can be seen to favor them. For the 13 percent of occupiers that are pure office users there is less apparent value added (figures taken from the Reading BID proposal document). BIDs are a place marketing scheme, and those that benefit more from the place have more to gain. As Symes and Steel (2003) observe, "Despite the high minded claims of many BID managers, BIDs are in essence simply localised attempts at 'place marketing'" (p. 304). Certain BIDs have addressed benefit concerns by excluding those who may appear to derive little benefit from a BID that is aimed at place marketing, for example, office occupiers, which are excluded from charging in Great Yarmouth and Plymouth.

The Reading BID relates to those premises within the BID area having a rateable value of more than £10,000. Some of the distortions caused by small business and other reliefs discussed later will be avoided at this level, but certainly not all. This £10,000 threshold for the levy is not mandatory; it is a figure arrived at by the BID proposer. For example, the Keswick (a smaller town in the Lake District National Park) BID, more marginally successful by number of votes cast at 55.4 percent, applies the levy to those with rateable values of £2,900 or more. The Bedford BID levy is at 2 percent of rateable value but only applies to those with a rateable value of £7,000 or above; the highest threshold is £250,000 in London's West End. The West Bromwich Industrial area BID has a cap that results in a maximum sum paid by means of the levy at £4,000 per annum.

The differences in rateable value application do enable a BID body to tailor the levy to the circumstances of the local area, but there is a need to be clear about the point at which charging occurs. That applicable in one area is clearly not necessarily the same as that in another area.

Appendix A illustrates the wide range adopted for charging: from levies of 0.5 to 4 percent (the maximum permitted by the regulations is 5 percent), from areas where no exemption is made on the grounds of rateable value (Kingston), to the New West End Company, which only levies hereditaments in excess of rateable value £250,000.

There is a further fundamental difficulty with these thresholds. Rateable values are not fixed and may be altered by improvements to premises, and there is also a revaluation every five years at which figures may rise or fall. While the category of occupier (say, those with rateable values over £7,000) may remain the same, there may be a large number of new occupiers brought within the scope of the levy who did not originally have the opportunity to vote for it.

The Complexity of Business Rates, Reliefs, and Exemptions

The BID levy is attached as a percentage increase to the rateable value. The levy may be one figure for all, or a different sum for different categories of occupier, as with the Birmingham Broad Street BID. Rates in England are a tax on occupation and are normally paid by the occupier. What if the property is vacant? If a lease exists and the liability is with a tenant, although not in occupation, that tenant will be liable for empty rates. If there is no tenant and the property is in the control of the owner, then that party will be liable for empty property rates.

The amount of empty property rates paid will depend on a number of factors. First, the property could be exempt entirely from empty property rates, as is the case with listed buildings and those properties described as industrial. Second, the former occupier could be a registered charity. Such organizations benefit from favorable treatment under rating, when in occupation they receive a mandatory 80 percent relief from rates paid, and can claim discretionary relief for the remaining 20 percent. When empty, charity premises attract a mandatory 90 percent relief and the remaining 10 percent is subject to discretionary relief.

The extent of reliefs under rating is again believed not to be widely understood. There is quite clearly an issue in democracy if each rate payer is being given a vote, and a hereditament has a vote by rateable value, yet the impact on different categories of occupier and hereditament differs.

A number of property types are exempt from rating altogether. These are listed in schedules to the Local Government Finance Act 1988 and include premises used for the purposes of religious worship and certain Crown property. If located in a BID area, these properties will benefit from its advantages without incurring the levy.

The size of the hereditament, and whether it is the occupier's only business premises, can also make a difference to the rates paid prior to any levy. The basic rate paid is calculated by multiplying the rateable value of the hereditament by the uniform business rate. Apart from that, the uniform business rate is not uniform: for larger hereditaments it is 43.3p in the current year (06/07), and for smaller hereditaments it is 42.6p (06/07). Larger and smaller hereditaments and the fact that they have different definitions inside and outside of London are discussed under the "Small Business Rate Relief" section below.

The above illustrates the base calculation for arriving at rates paid, which is then often distorted significantly. One common potential distortion is transitional relief; the rateable value has been recalculated every five years since 1988. There have been both sharp increases and decreases in rateable value, which is based on a rental value in accordance with statute, and these increases and decreases led to sharp changes in rates paid. For political reasons it was decided to smooth both increases and decreases by limiting and capping the same. The mechanism by which this is achieved is transitional relief. As a supplementary distortion, existing and new occupiers are not necessarily treated in the same manner when it comes to transitional relief.

The uniform business rate paid by smaller occupiers differs from that of larger occupiers, empty property is treated differently dependent upon type and whether it is a listed building, and charities are treated differently, yet all have the same voting rights. The extent of reliefs and variance in treatment continues, as a brief survey will demonstrate. These types of reliefs and treatments are small business rate relief, empty and unused property, charities and charity shops, nonprofit organizations that are not registered charities, rural villages of population under 3,000, nonagricultural businesses on agricultural land, and nonmandatory reliefs.

Small Business Rate Relief

Small business rate relief came into effect on April 1, 2005. Those eligible businesses having rateable values below £5,000 will obtain a 50 percent rate relief on liability. This relief then decreases on a sliding scale for rateable values over £5,000 up to £10,000. To qualify for this relief rate payers must only have one property or one main and other properties, provided none of the other properties have a rateable value greater than £2,200 and the combined rateable value is under £15,000 (£21,500 in London). The small business multiplier previously discussed is used for these hereditaments as opposed to the standard multiplier. Eligible businesses with rateable values of between £10,000 and £14,999 (£10,000 to £21,499 in London) will not see a relief as such, but have the small business multiplier used rather than the standard multiplier. Rate payers must apply for these reliefs each year, and there is a mandatory timetable for receipt of applications.

Several distortions are caused by the process, if, for example, we focus on the Keswick BID previously mentioned. This BID levies all those with rateable values of £2,900 or more. Yet this threshold figure is not the same as any figure used elsewhere to determine taxation boundaries, for example, the empty property figure of £2,200 discussed below, or the small business rateable value threshold of £10,000, or the multiplier threshold of £14,999. It would be more logical to align the threshold charging figure with the £2,200 level. Although the Reading BID applying to rateable values of £10,000 or more sits more logically with the small business relief threshold, there is still a distortion caused by the potential application of the small business multiplier up to a rateable value £14,999. The result is that those with a rateable value of more than £14,999 will pay in percentage terms more overall than those with rateable values above £10,000 but below £14,999.

Empty and Unused Property Relief

The special treatment of industrial and listed buildings has already been commented upon. The provisions that apply to all property are that for the first three months of being empty no rates are paid. After this initial three-month period industrial property and listed buildings continue to be exempt. The Finance Act of 2007 (to follow the budget of the chancellor of the exchequer delivered in March 2007) makes further changes to empty rate provisions; these are to become less attractive. A further existing exemption, regardless of type of property, applies when the rateable value is below £2,200; then the property will be classed as small and attract empty property relief. Interestingly, that which is a small property here is the same for those buildings inside London as it is for those outside. For those properties that do not attract full empty property relief, the charge after the first three months will be based on 50 percent of the full figure.

BID levies will need to be clear about their treatment of empty property; an empty property still has a rateable value and therefore could be levied. The Kingston BID, for example, is specific in stating that no reliefs or exemptions will apply and that empty property will be levied. This clear statement must be regarded as good practice in the interests of transparency.

Relief for Charities and Charity Shops

If a property is used wholly or mainly for charitable purposes or the administration of a charitable trust for charitable purposes only, there is an automatic 80 percent reduction in the rates bill when the property is occupied. The reduction is 90 percent when the property is empty. In the case of both occupied and empty premises the charity may apply to the local authority for discretionary relief for the remaining sum. These reliefs also apply to charity shops, a feature of many English high streets, although strictly applying the regulations, the shop must be for the sale of goods wholly or mainly donated and the money raised applied to charitable purposes.

A charity in effect has increased voting rights due to the rateable value, which does not compare in terms of rates paid with those of noncharities. The BID treatment of charities does differ, for example, they are exempted from the charge in Great Yarmouth or, alternatively, elsewhere subjected to a reduced or full charge.

Relief for Nonprofit Organizations That Are Not Registered Charities

These have no automatic entitlement to relief, although there is discretion available to the local billing authority to grant relief or exemption from payment. The occupying organization must be non-profit-making and use the property for certain charitable, philanthropic, religious, or recreational purposes.

Different local billing authorities have applied reliefs and exemptions without consistency, leading in December 2002 to the Office of the Deputy Prime Minster to issue detailed guidance on the provision of such reliefs (Rate Reliefs, 2002).

The fact that parties may benefit from various mandatory or discretionary reliefs or exemptions is unlikely to be widely known at the time of a BID vote, leading to possible resentment afterward if the vote is close or the purpose of the BID promotes various constituencies above others.

Relief for Rural Village of Population under 3,000

While most business improvement districts will relate to urban centers, certain rural pilot areas have been discussed as subjects, and for completeness in commenting on reliefs and exemptions, those under this heading are discussed.

Relief for Nonagricultural Business on Agricultural Land

A scheme of relief of between 50 percent (mandatory) and 100 percent (discretionary) was offered until August 16, 2006, on qualifying buildings previously used for at least 183 days during the year ended August 14, 2001, for agricultural purposes, provided that the property was on the rating list prior to April 1, 2005, and that the rateable value was below £7,000. The ending of this fixed-period relief provides a reminder that such reliefs can be taken away as well as introduced. The position in respect to rating reliefs and charging is actually very fluid.

Nonmandatory Reliefs

The headings above provide for local authority discretion to grant certain reliefs or exemptions from rates paid often in addition to a basic mandatory relief. There is a further discretion given to local authorities to grant severe hardship relief of up to 100 percent to businesses that are regarded as particularly important to the local community. If this happens, local council tax (residential) payers will pay part of the cost of the relief.

If part of the property is not being used and unoccupied for a short period, it is possible for the local authority to grant relief with respect to the empty part, provided it is clearly unoccupied and beyond use for a short period. Practically, an occupier considering this relief would be advised to contact a specialist chartered surveyor about grounds for splitting the hereditament into two (or more). If it is possible to split the hereditament, this may be more beneficial.

Those in a BID area may well ask of a local authority its policy with respect to nonmandatory relief.

How Problematic Are Exemptions and the Various Relief Mechanisms in Practice?

The problems presented by certain relief schemes could be more onerous on the success of a BID proposal than appears to be the case. Many rate payers are unaware of the various reliefs and exemptions that exist. If rate payers are aware of them, many of the distortions that can be caused may not be readily apparent or in financial terms may appear marginal. The use of thresholds for charging the levy may reduce certain distortions, although, of course, one is created in that those below the threshold do not pay the levy at all. The different multipliers for small and large rateable value hereditaments create a distortion that remains if the threshold for the levy is below the ceiling for the small business multiplier. This later point can be illustrated by reference to the Reading BID. There, only those with a rateable value over £10,000 vote in the ballot, and only those above this rateable value threshold pay the levy. There is a slight distortion for those benefiting from the small business rate multiplier; they will in effect pay fractionally more as a percentage of the base rateable value by voting for the levy than those larger businesses. A £12,000 rateable value is cushioned; ignoring the BID, by the potential application of the small business multiplier, a rateable value of £16,000 (outside London) would not be cushioned, as the standard multiplier is used. If a levy is set at, say, 1 percent, above a figure of £10,000, then the £12,000 property is not cushioned against the increase when compared to a rateable value of £16,000.

Where thresholds for voting and charging have been set that fall within various reliefs or exemptions, the potential for an adverse reaction increases. A party having a rateable value of £3,000 will have the same voting rights (although not rateable value weighting) as a party with a rateable value of £20,000. The rates paid by the former will be cushioned considerably by various means, to the extent that the percentage actually paid under this form of taxation is much less than that paid by the larger occupier. Those proposing BID documents should therefore give careful thought to linking thresholds with the various exemptions and reliefs that are in place. The degree of consistency that would result from voting weight and liability in terms of actual payment, being in equal proportion, would aid transparency.

Voting weight and liability in terms of actual payment will not be equal in all cases and for all occupiers. Charities, for example, will have a voting weight related to a rateable value that is not used as the mechanism for the basis of payment as it is with other occupiers, charities having a mandatory relief of 80 percent. Different BID areas have adopted a different approach to the treatment of the levy on charities.

The Crown and various other property types that are exempt from rates paid will still benefit from expenditure within the BID area.

The accuracy of the rating lists used as the basis for the voting mechanism and the time taken to address any changes via appeal will certainly present challenges to BID democracy in those areas where the rating list is subject to frequent alteration.

Empty property will also present difficulties, due to the range of applicable charges and the fact that these charges may be met by the owner. Empty industrial property is exempted from a basic rates charge at present; therefore, to levy on empty industrial property within a BID will attract a charge not otherwise present. This fact was recognized by the West Bromwich Industrial area's BID team, which decided to exempt empty property from the levy. This creates a consistency of treatment that again has much to commend it.

Poorly thought out procedures and administration have been identified as causing problems with a number of American BIDs, for example, the Madison Avenue and NOHO BIDs in New York. The NOHO BID saw the city of New York administration notify owners of the voting, but not occupiers; property owners could pass the costs of the BID on to the tenants and had no reason to vote against it. The first those tenants knew of the BID success was when they received notification, after the ballot. One key problem identified by considering the NOHO BID exists in England—that of the tax being levied on occupiers while owners benefit from increased property values. The problem with implementation in such circumstances is explored by Berman (1997). Those seeking to promote BIDs in England would be encouraged to learn from these previous problems.

BID Benefits to Property Owners

There is a paradox with BIDs that tenants will need to come to terms with: the usual mechanism by which rents are reviewed in England is "open market rental value." Increase the attractiveness of a location, and demand for property of a particular type within that location can be expected to increase. If demand for property increases, then the rental cost of that space will also increase. A long lease is not a barrier to rental increases; these are normally reserved within the lease on an open-market basis. Tenants paying into a BID to improve an area, or the services and provision within it, may be contributing to an increase in attractiveness that will in turn lead to an increase in the rent they pay.

Property owners can be seen to welcome their occupiers contributing to an increase in attractiveness and consequently demand and in-turn value. In the longer term, tenant occupiers may question the English BID model that centers on taxing them rather than property owners.

One difference (and weakness) of the English model as compared to the North American original is the emphasis on taxing occupiers, when in the long run property owners will benefit to a larger extent if the BID is successful (or if it is unsuccessful, have the costs of trying the approach met by occupiers).

Some BID areas have secured voluntary contributions from property owners, for example, the New West End, while others, for example, Rugby, will reduce the BID levy if the discounted sum is met by the owner. The extent of owner contributions over time is the subject of ongoing research, as is the influence of owner (as distinct from tenant) representatives on BID boards.

Findings

Different BID bodies have adopted different approaches to the distortions caused by the rating system upon which the levy is based. The treatment of charities and empty property will benefit from a clear statement of liability; no such clear statement exists at present. No BID body is believed to have addressed specifically empty listed buildings; clarity here would be recommended. The Finance Act of 2007 introduces changes to reliefs that make them less generous; the complexities caused with the interrelationship with BIDs should be reduced, although not removed entirely.

More fundamentally, only those local rating lists have the right to vote and are taxed; this is not the same as saying all business occupiers have the right to vote and pay the levy. The problem identified by consideration of the NOHO BID—that of occupiers paying and owners gaining—has not been taken on board by the English regulations, which tax occupiers for the ultimate benefit of owners. A point recognized recently as the All Party Urban Development Group's "Business Matters Report," released July 19, 2007, recommends a compulsion on landlords in BID areas to pay a levy.

Conclusions and Recommendations

Those BIDs with the greatest sector focus and appropriateness of levy to place marketing appear from the results in Appendix A to attract the strongest support. Retailers and others may well benefit by having office occupiers in the central business district and should be cautious about creating a tax incentive for them to locate out of town. The short-term gain to retail occupiers of an attractive place marketing scheme may outweigh concerns regarding the ultimate benefit belonging to owners. Those BID proposals with a less specific focus and less reliance on the need for place marketing prove to be less attractive to voters.

The most successful BIDs will be those with the clearest focus and opportunities for benefit. Care should be taken to ensure that existing service delivery is in fact supplemented by the BID levy and that the levy is not used as a general source of funding to plug gaps elsewhere. Many of the generic headings for BID expenditure arise from top-down government policy initiatives rather than locally driven needs. More local accountability and true separation from central government policy will foster more engaging BIDs at a local level.

The fundamental problem remains in England that occupiers within successful BID areas will ultimately be voting for an increase in their own rent.

The regulations should be amended to ensure that there is a balance between tax and benefit to both owners and occupiers. At present this does not exist. There should also be clarity within each BID proposal about how the various distortions caused by basing the BID levy on rateable values are to be addressed. Those schemes that are the most successful to date are those with a greater retail focus centered on place marketing that benefits from visitor presence. There is less evidence that wider BID schemes are as popular; here the greater disadvantages to those not in need of place (office usually occupies) may be outweighing the benefits to others (usually those in the retail or leisure sector).

References

All Party Urban Development Group. 2007. Business Matters Report. http://www.allpartyurbandevelopment.org.uk/reports.html (accessed July 22, 2007).

Berman, H. 1997. *Managing the micropolis: Proposals to strengthen business improvement district performance and accountability.* New York: Council of the City of New York.

Blackwell, M. 2005. A consideration of the UK government's proposals for business improvement districts in England: Issues and uncertainties. *Journal of Property Management* 23:194–203.

Business Improvement Districts (Wales) Regulations 2006.

Cinderella Rockerfellas Ltd v. Rudd. EWCA Civ 529 (2003).

Consultation Paper on Draft Business Improvement Districts (England) Regulations 2004.

Edison First Power Limited v. Central Valuation Officer. UKHL 20 (2003).

General Rate Act 1967. http://www.parliament.uk/parliamentary_publications_and_archives/parliamentary_archives.cfm (accessed May 10, 2006).

Levy, P. R. 2001. Paying for the public life. *Economic Development Quarterly* 15:124–131.

Local Government Finance Act 1988. http://www.official-documents.gov.uk (accessed May 6, 2006).

Mitchell, J. 1999. *Business improvement districts and innovative service delivery.* Grant report. New York: PricewaterhouseCoopers.

Rate reliefs for charities and other non-profit-making organisations. 2002. London: Office of the Deputy Prime Minister.

Rating (Valuation) Act 1999. http://www.official-documents.gov.uk (accessed April 24, 2006).

Symes, M., and Steel, M. 2003. Lessons from America: The role of business improvement districts as an agent of urban regeneration. *Town Planning Review* 74:301–313.

Appendix A:
Positive BID Ballot
Results (until May 2006)

Location	% voting for	Number voting for	% RV for	Actual RV for	Turnout %	Vote date	Amount of levy as %	RV threshold (charging)
Kingston (London Borough)	66	218	66	20,853,300	37	Oct./Nov. 2004	1	No reductions or exemptions
Heart of London	70.73	87	73.19	29,480,275	62	Dec. 2004	1	50,000
Bankside London	75	115	66	12,006,805	48	Jan. 2005	2	10,000
Holborn London	82	189	77	34,901,050	50	Jan./Feb. 2005	1	10,000
Coventry	78.3	206	75.1	10,197,750	38.3	Feb. 2005	0.9	3,000
Plymouth	77	235	66	11,745,810	58	Feb./March 2005	1	None; not charged to offices and certain others
Paddington London	87	165	88	10,319,250	50.79	Feb./March 2005	1.5 hotels 2 others	5,000
New West End London	60.56	86	69.24	100,983,350	52.77	March 2005	1	250,000
Bedford	77	150	81		37	March 2005	2	7,000
Lincoln	79	257	83	13,283,470	44	March/April 2005	1	5,000
Birmingham Broad St.	92	158	97	29,153,200	65	May 2005	2.1 or 0.5	
Bristol Broadmead	60		56		59	June 2005	1.5 0.75 (see note)	12,000
Blackpool	89	Center 291	74	7,709,135	40	July/Aug. 2005	Seafront 1.5 Center 1	

							Bands 2001–5000 RV pay £140; bands 400,001–500,000 RV pay £17,000	
Rugby	65.6	196	58.1	5,098,575	46.8	Sept. 2005		2,000
Keswick	55.4	128	67	2,814,250	50.4	Sept. 2005	1	2,900
Liverpool City	62	160	51	17,014,000	56	Sept. 2005	1.2	10,000
London Bridge	71	113	78	31,077,500	50	Oct./Nov. 2005	1.25	10,000 are exempt from the levy and ballot; ceiling 50,000
Winsford (Cheshire)	89		71		64	Oct./Nov. 2005		Fixed annual levy within RV bands; no charity relief; RV 5,000 or less levy 199; RV 400,000+ levy 1,750
Reading	68	90	60	8,715,000	38	Oct./Nov. 2005	1	10,000
Bolton Ind. Estates	71.5	88	84	3,912,800	46	Nov./Dec. 2005		
Camden London	84		83		50	Feb./March 2006	1	40,000
Waterloo London	73.77	90	91.85	8,324,100	49.79	Feb./March 2006	21 for charities	5,000

continued

Location	% voting for	Number voting for	% RV for	Actual RV for	Turnout %	Vote date	Amount of levy as %	RV threshold (charging)
Hainault Bus Park (Urban Essex)	85		93		52	March 2006		
Great Yarmouth	82		88		44	March 2006	1.5 / 0.5 west of haven bridge	8,000 No charge for charities and certain others
Ealing (London Borough)	65.5		63.9		51	March 2006	1 (See note)	10,000
Hammersmith (London Borough)	56.6	99	69.7	23,295,000	48.7	March 2006	1	30,000
West Bromwich Ind.	79	30	85	1,174,510	48	March/April 2006	4	No base; capped at 4,000 (actual) max charge
Swansea	74	238	65	13,868,750	44.4	April/May 2006	1	5,000

Notes: Swansea is included in the table although it is in Wales, not in England. This ballot was under the Business Improvement Districts (Wales) Regulations 2006. The amount of the levy is at the time of voting. For example, Hammersmith has an annual fixed increase of 3 percent, so in the second year the multiplier will be 1.03 percent. Some BIDs are based on the 2000 rating list, others on the 2005, or in the case of Plymouth, with reference to both. Bristol Broadmead—The 0.75 percent applies within the mall galleries where a service charge exists and the balance is met by the center owners. Rugby—A pro-rata discount can be obtained if the owner pays the balance. Ealing—30 percent discount for those in the Ealing Broadway Center, 50 percent discount for those in the Arcadia center. In addition to exemptions mentioned, a number of BIDs do not levy car parks, advertising hoardings, and telecommunications masts. Postscript: At the end of May 2006, Brighton had a successful BID ballot, while a further successful ballot took place in Ipswich in July 2006.

Appendix B: Negative BID Ballot Results (until May 2006)

Location	% voting for	% voting against	% RV for	% RV against	Turnout %	Vote date
Maidstone	49	51	60	40	33	Feb. 2005
Altham Ind. Estate	49	51	52	48	79	Feb. 2005
Runnymede	40	60	47	53	58	Feb./March 2005
Liverpool City	51	49	47	53	37	Feb./March 2005
Southport	52	48	48	52	59	Oct./Nov. 2005
Malton and Norton	43	57	57	43	50	March/April 2006

Note: Liverpool City subsequently held a positive reballot. Maidstone and Runnymede voted twice against the establishment of the BID.

Chapter 20

The Adoption of the BID Model in Ireland: Context and Considerations*

John Ratcliffe and Brenda Ryan

Contents

---

* This chapter first appeared as Hernandez and Jones (2005) and is reproduced with minor changes by permission of the publisher.

Introduction: A New Era of Urban Revitalization

Managing urban regeneration in Ireland's towns and cities is only a relatively recent endeavor in comparison with most other European countries. Since the enactment of the Urban Renewal Act in 1986, urban regeneration, specifically in Dublin, has been property led, owing to a series of tax incentive schemes introduced under the act. Such initiatives have been successful to the extent that they stimulated major physical renewal. However, success has proven limited in terms of integrating local communities, with a failure to link property-led regeneration with social renewal. The funding framework for urban regeneration in Ireland has mostly relied on a system of grant-based programs, again of limited success and value. Furthermore, the role of gap funding by grant subsidies in regeneration projects is now being severely downsized, due to the interpretation of new EU state aid. This, aligned with the fact that the government is increasingly unable to fund significant spending on public services, points to the need to find alternative ways of financing urban regeneration. Additionally, Ireland is currently experiencing a growth in population, which is focused in urban areas. This is resulting in an ever-greater demand on the services provided by the local authority. Dwindling national budgets and increasing public expectations have created frustration in many Irish towns and cities, and fueled the recognition for the need for a new innovative mechanism for urban rejuvenation. The adoption of the business improvement district (BID) model in Ireland is expected to deliver a new era of urban revitalization to our towns and cities.

The introduction of the BID model to Ireland has been pioneered by the business community. Through a background of increased competition and insufficient public spending for supplemental services, the private sector realized it needed to take control and ownership of the city. Tom Coffey, chief executive of the Dublin City Business Association (DCBA), a professional association for retailers, is the leading advocate for BIDs in Ireland. He maintains that BIDs will transform the management of the city's streets by providing a framework for the business community and local authority to work together to raise the standards of the areas in which the BID model is applied. Coffey explains, "BIDs will help Irish towns and cities compete at an international level with cities such as New York, Paris and Milan" (Coffey, cited in Dublin City Business Association, 2006e, para. 3). The national government supports the BID model and recognizes the opportunity it presents to harness business innovation for the benefit of the urban environment and the public. According to public record, "BIDs will provide a whole new impetus for businesses to work with local authorities and local residents around the country to help improve the areas in which they trade. We welcome the foresight of the business community in pursuing BIDs. Collectively we will distinguish our towns and cities in this increasingly competitive global environment" (House of the Oireachtas, 2006b).* With consensus on the need to manage the city in a changing world, the private and public sectors have worked toward the establishment of enabling BID legislation in 2006, and the DCBA has established the Dublin City Center BID Company with a target date for full operation of January 1, 2008.

This chapter outlines the progress of the BID model in Ireland as of the time of its writing and addresses some of the issues and controversies surrounding its adoption. In particular, the chapter focuses on the introduction and application of the BID model for Dublin, Ireland's national capital. This is achieved through analysis of existing BID-like entities operating in the city and the plans and vision for the proposed Dublin City Center BID. The following questions will be addressed. How is the BID model likely to transfer to an Irish context? What are the likely benefits of the BID in Ireland? And does it have the ability to instigate a new era of revitalization for Irish towns and cities?

The Road to BIDs in Ireland: Planning and Legislative Phase

Ireland's leading BID proponent, Tom Coffey, chief executive of the Dublin City Business Association (DCBA), initiated the journey of BIDs to Ireland in 1999. The planning phase lasted about five years and involved extensive networking and dialogue. Information sharing and promotion of the BID model in Ireland was facilitated through conferences and seminars instigated by the business community and attended by world leaders in the BID industry. A site visit was also made by leading members of business and government to inspect the workings and success of the BID model in New York City. The legislative phase, however, has been a slow and procrastinated process. Irish BID legislation was expected to be passed by the Irish Parliament in 2003, but due to national elections, was delayed. The Irish BID

---

* House of the Oireachtas is the name of Irish Parliament.

legislation, under the Local Government (Business Improvement Districts) Act, was passed in December 2006.

Meanwhile the DCBA is in the process of developing a business plan and seeking business consensus for Ireland's first BID: the Dublin City Center BID. In anticipation of this, the Dublin City Center BID Company has been formed and, as mentioned above, is expected to initiate operations in January 2008. Table 20.1 outlines the road to BIDs in Ireland.

Review of Proposed Irish Legislation

The Local Government (Business Improvement Districts) Act will authorize BIDs under national statute. In summary, it provides for "the establishment of Business Improvement Districts, within the functional areas of rating authorities, to enable schemes under which projects, services and works are carried out for the benefit of those districts, to finance the schemes by providing for the imposition and collection of a levy on rateable properties situated in those districts" (House of the Oireachtas, 2006b, p. 3). The following section outlines details of the proposed Irish BIDs' legislation and reviews the associated issues.

Stakeholders

The Irish BID system is based on the occupiers (rate payers) being the principal decision makers and stakeholders. It is the occupier/rate payer of the relevant property, not the property owner, who is liable to pay the levy in the established BID.* This is interpreted by some as a fundamental flaw in the legislation and operation of a BID, as the long-term interest in the economic well-being of an area is believed to reside with the property owner (Ratcliffe and Flanagan, 2004). The DCBA was keen to bring the property owners on board to share the costs with the occupiers; however, due to the heavy presence of absentee landlords and consortium ownership, it was not possible to establish ownership of many properties (McLoughlin, 2003). As a compromise, the DCBA invited property owners to participate as members of the BID board of directors and provide consultation throughout the process of establishing the proposed Dublin City Center BID.

Financing

The form of sustainable funding for the BID model in Ireland is via a surcharge on the business rate, and those liable to pay the BID contribution include any occupier

---

* See the Meek and Hubler chapter in this volume for a similar example in California: merchant-based BIDs, where business owners, not necessarily property owners, are levied.

Table 20.1   Timeline: Road to BIDs in Ireland

1999	Tom Coffey, CEO of the Dublin City Business Association and member of Strategic Policy Committee (SPC) on Finance in Dublin City Council, recommends to various public and private sector agencies and organizations the BID model for Ireland.
March 1999	The Dublin Institute of Technology, Faculty of the Built Environment, commissions a study on BIDs entitled "Managing and Financing Urban Regeneration: A Preliminary Study of the Prospective Use of Business Improvement Districts in Ireland" (Ratcliffe et al., 1999).
2000	BIDs conference, organized by the DCBA and the Dublin Institute of Technology (DIT), in Dublin Castle
May 2001	Senior executives of the DCBA, Dublin City Council, and representatives from the Dublin Civic Trust visit New York to inspect firsthand the work of BIDs and speak with senior officials.
2001	The BID model receives 100% support in a vote by the Dublin City Council. The Strategic Policy Committee (SPC) launches an active promotion of BIDs, bringing BIDs presentations to five area committees in Dublin. Each endorses the BID model. The BID model gains support from the trade unions, IBEC (Irish Business and Employers Confederation), Dublin Chamber of Commerce as well as other Chambers in the country, and the Department of the Environment and Local Government (DoELG).
November 2001	Draft legislation is drawn up by the DoELG and amended by the SPC.
January 2002	A conference for private sector advocates and government officials, organized by the DIT BID model: the Dublin City Center BID and the DCBA report considerable enthusiasm for the establishment of BIDs.
2003	BID legislation is expected to be introduced, but a national election delays the anticipated action.
January 2006	The Dublin City Center BID Company is established to coordinate the introduction of the BID.
February 2006	A BID workshop is hosted by the DCBA and Dublin City Council. The conference is attended by 110 delegates, which include representatives from the chambers of commerce, local authorities, government departments, Garda Síochána (police), and other organizations of interest. After the BID conference, Coffey states, "For the first time I believe there is a real appreciation among the membership and the civil service of the positive difference and contribution that BIDs will make once they are finally established in this country" (Dublin City Business Association, 2006c).

Table 20.1 (continued)   Timeline: Road to BIDs in Ireland

June 2006	Irish BID legislation is approved by the Seanad (Ireland's Senate) and goes to the Dáil (Ireland's House of Representatives) for the summer recess.
December 2006	Irish BID legislation is passed and becomes national law, via the Local Government (Business Improvement Districts) Act of 2006.
2007	The DCBA prepares a BID proposal for a Dublin City Council referendum on the Dublin City Center BID. Consultation to secure key business support is mainly driven by Tom Coffey of the DCBA.
October 2007	The Dublin City Council pass the referendum approving the implementation of the Dublin BID. The ratepayers in the BID area voted to establish the BID by a majority of 77%.
January 2008	The first BID services will be introduced from January 2008.

of relevant property or owner of vacant property. The BID contribution levy is to be calculated annually based on the rateable valuation of property, and the annual BID multiplier is to be determined by the BID company's board. The BID multiplier will depend on the size of the BID and the level of services and improvements to be carried out in the BID, the designation of which is left to the discretion of the proponent putting the scheme forward for approval. This allows for the BID levy to be set at a level specific to the BID in question, facilitating the adaptability of the BID mechanism to varying Irish contexts.

The total income from the annual BID contribution cannot exceed the annual estimated expenditure for the BID scheme minus any other form of income other than the BID levy. Other sources of income may include voluntary donations or sponsorship. However, revenue from voluntary contributors is not foreseen as being a highly significant addition to the overall BID budget, unlike the U.K. model, which receives large revenues from government and the private sector.

Adoption Procedures

After the BID proponent delivers the rating authority (i.e., the local governing authority in which the BID resides) with a copy of the BID proposal, the BID plan is to be made available for public inspection. The rating authority invites submissions from the public on the proposal, and if the authority is satisfied that the scheme does not conflict with the interests of the local community, the BID scheme may be approved. The rating authority then holds a plebiscite (regulations for which are now being drafted by government) to ascertain the level of support for the proposal among rate payers of rateable property within the proposed BID. All occupiers of relevant property and owners of vacant property have the right to vote, with each rateable property in the proposed BID afforded one vote in the plebiscite. A minimum of 50 percent of those who vote must be in favor to carry the process further. If passed, the rating authority then votes on the proposed BID. One-third of the total number of members of the authority concerned must vote in favor of the resolution for it to be passed. Once the BID has been approved, the final notice must be published in a newspaper and all occupiers within the boundary of the BID must be notified.

The implementation of the petition/plebiscite system can perhaps be interpreted as an unnecessary costly and cumbersome addition to the Irish BID approval process. From studies that examine BIDs in the United States, it is noted that BIDs in states with easy-to-use BID laws (such as states allowing the adoption of BIDs via the objection system or a simple decision by local government) have proved at least as effective in doing their job as BIDs in states with costly petition systems in place. In addition, the Irish system has an absence of weighted voting. This contrasts with the UK BID approval system, which requires affirmative votes by more than half of the qualified business voters and more than half of the value of the businesses. This is also somewhat akin to state laws in the United States that require petitions by half of properties by value.* The Irish system is considered beneficial to smaller business, and represents a more equitable power structure, as the BID cannot be dominated by a small number of highly valued properties (McLoughlin, 2003).

Governance

A BID must be established as a company limited by guarantee, and representative of local businesses and the local authority. It is empowered to carry out the range of services and improvements set out in the business plan. The local authority, as partner, uses its revenue collection powers to accumulate the special contribution on behalf of the businesses and provides the funds collected, net of its costs, to the company to pay for the services and improvements to be carried out. In this manner, there is a tight working partnership between the BID and the local authority.

Each BID company must have a board of directors consisting of no less than six members, who elect a chairman. A BID board can be made up of property owners, tenants, residents, and the local authority. The invitation of non-levy-paying members to the board, such as the property owners and residents, ensures a greater form of democratic representation. However, at least two-thirds of the directors should be rate payers of rateable property in the BID. The rating authority is so entitled that if the board consists of less than 13 members, 1 of those members shall be selected by the chairman and 1 shall be selected by the manager. If the board of directors consists of 13 or more members, 2 of those members shall be selected by the chairman and 2 shall be selected by the manager. In reaction to the legislation

---

* See the Morçöl and Zimmermann chapter (Chapter 15) in this volume for an example in Georgia.

being passed by the Irish Senate, the Irish Chamber of Commerce welcomed the indication that the BID company chairman would not be a member or official of a rating authority and the provision that at least two-thirds of the BID board would be representatives of rate payers or persons nominated by the rate payers. These measures are perceived by the chamber of commerce as being core to the success of BIDs by ensuring that businesses have an opportunity for direct input into the quality of services in the BID (Chambers Ireland, 2006).

Term Limits

The BID board is authorized for five years. The BID may be dissolved, provided there is no debt, by a petition of 70 percent of relevant property occupiers. The Irish Chamber of Commerce welcomes this, maintaining that it is critical that BIDs have limited terms, thus ensuring that the services and associated funds do not become subsumed into general local authority funding. According to Chambers Ireland (2006), "Five years is adequate for achieving an agreed target. If further work, outside the remit of the original BID scheme is proposed, it can then be recommended to the ratepayers who have the opportunity to ratify another BID scheme" (para. 5). The reauthorization process also ensures the vitality of the BID, with the ability to change board members and affect change in leadership.

Supplemental Service Clause

A service agreement with the local authority is a requirement in Irish legislation. The draft legislation provides a local authority "baseline" services agreement, as follows: "A local authority shall not eliminate or reduce the level of any correspond-ing services customarily provided to a BID which is the subject of a BID initiative, unless a reduction in that service is a pro-rata reduction necessitated by fiscal con-siderations or budgetary priorities within the whole of the administrative area of the local authority" (House of the Oireachtas, 2006a, p. 8). This measure ensures that all investment made through BIDs will be both additional and complementary and is a significant factor in whether businesses choose to accept and support the BID model. According to Chambers Ireland (2006), "the private sector already contributes significantly to local authorities' current and capital expenditure giving upwards of one billion in commercial rates alone in 2005. To avoid the possible perception of this as another form of taxation, all of the activities carried out by a BID must be wholly additional or supplementary to existing services carried out by the relevant local authority. In short, there must be no erosion of existing local authority services once a BID has been established" (para. 4). The existence of the baseline services agreement is fundamental in addressing the expressed concerns of the private sector.

The Vision for Business Improvement Districts in Dublin

The city center of Dublin is a microeconomy with an annual turnover estimated at €1.5 billion. There are 145,000 people living and working within the area and an average daily footfall of 660,000. With over 4,000 shops and 10 department stores and shopping centers, Dublin City Center has the largest concentration of shops in the country. The Dublin region now has a population of almost 2 million people, with over 250 million visits to the city center recorded a year.

The Dublin City Business Association

Members of the DCBA are the chief BID advocates in Ireland, and they assume many BID-like functions in the Dublin region. The DCBA is a professional association representing the interests of all who do business in the city center, including the retailers, property owners, and transport organizations. They have a voluntary business membership, which collectively employs over 25,000 people in Dublin City Center, who pay in excess of €78 million in rates each year to Dublin City Council (the municipal authority). Established in 1970, the DCBA operates on behalf of its members, with local and national governments, to ensure that the city is accessible and has an attractive and sophisticated retail and leisure environment for visitors and customers. Its members invest in redevelopment and improvements of their own stores and work together in initiatives to improve the city center offering as a whole. This is facilitated through an annual voluntary membership fee, ranging from €800 to €5,000, depending on the number of high-street outlets in operation. The DCBA (2006c) believes that local area-based management is an essential tool in sustaining progress in the city environment, especially in an increasingly competitive market.

DCBA Activities and Achievements

The DCBA resembles a BID in its functions and activities. In addition to representing the interests of its members with local and national governments, the DCBA focuses efforts on marketing, security, access, and addressing environmental and planning issues. At any given time, the organization is working on a number of initiatives. Current and historical projects, along with an evaluation of their performance, are described as follows.

Dublin City Council and the DCBA work cooperatively to undertake advertising and public relations campaigns to highlight and promote the city center. The campaigns include television, radio, and poster advertising, to highlight the travel options, shopping, and leisure experience that the city center has to offer. One of the most recent marketing exercises has been the development and promotion of the new city brand: "Make the City Yours." In 2003, the DCBA marketing committee, in partnership with Dublin City Council, developed the logo for Dublin City Center to convey a new brand identity for the capital city. The logo incorporates the spire monument as the new symbol of Dublin and is devised to embody and promote Dublin city as a center for culture, leisure, extensive shopping choice, a thriving city atmosphere, and area of historic interest (Dublin City Business Association, 2003b). Recent surveys carried out by the Irish market research company Behaviour and Attitudes on behalf of DCBA reveal that the Spire of Dublin is now seen as the new icon for the city (Dublin City Business Association, 2006d). The marketing campaign was perceived as a success and all of the DCBA members and the Dublin City Council have committed to a further three-year program at a cost of approximately €1.5 million.

The DCBA also researched and organized late-night shopping and Sunday shopping through the street and area committees. In the late 1960s, shops closed at lunchtime on Saturdays and the pace of business was rather slower than it is today. Over time, the city opened for shoppers to reflect the new society emerging in Dublin. Now shops are open seven days a week; Sunday is the third busiest day of the week. Late-night shopping on Thursdays was led by DCBA members, and currently the shopping day is extending as shops remain open later.

In addition, the DCBA prints and circulates 1 million free copies of the Dublin Visitor Map annually. It is freely available to all residents and tourists visiting the city center and is now the leading tourist information product on the market (Dublin City Business Association, 2003a). The DCBA is a knowledge resource, providing members with access to market research information on relevant business issues such as integrated area action plans, land-use and transportation legislation, street cleaning, traffic management, footfall counts, consumer attitude profiles, and long-term strategic policy. The DCBA operates a comprehensive system of electronic CCTV* footfall counting, allowing the DCBA to monitor consumer trends, which in turn provides a useful management tool for businesses.

With respect to access, the DCBA established the Fly Dublin Direct Committee, which triggered a more open-skies policy to Dublin. It instigated the Dublin Transport Initiative (DTI) and a €5 billion investment in transport infrastructure, and promoted the development and use of 20 city center car parks for shoppers.

Security is also an important component of the plan. In the late-night and early-morning hours the city center is perceived as menacing and uninviting as a result of alcohol-related violence. The DCBA works with the police and Dublin City Council to raise awareness and combat the causes of the public disorder issue. In the 1980s, the DCBA initiated and co-funded (along with the Department of Justice and the Gardaí) the CCTV system on streets in the city center. This, combined with the extensive CCTV systems in shops and offices, has made a substantial contribution in keeping Dublin safe for customers, staff, and visitors,

---

* Closed-circuit television (CCTV) often used for surveillance in areas that need security.

with the city now considered one of the safest in the world (Dublin City Business Association, 2003a).

The plan also calls for city planning and environmental improvements. In 1980, the DCBA, with the Department of Environment, initiated the pedestrianization of key retail streets in Dublin City Center (among them, Henry Street and Grafton Street). The introduction by the DCBA of electronic CCTV footfall counting has confirmed the success of the city center as a walking and people-friendly city, with a footfall increase of over 300 percent in the last 20 years. According to the DCBA, "Many people, including overseas visitors, remark on how nice our pedestrian streets are. Overseas town centre managers are astonished at the bustling crowds on our city streets" (Dublin City Business Association, 2005, para. 2). Moreover, DCBA members have been involved in sponsoring and installing street art in public places—notably the statues of James Joyce, the ladies with the shopping bags, the girl swinging from a lamppost, and the Molly Malone. All of these statues were a significant departure away from revolutionary, political, and religious images to reflect a more people-friendly, peaceful democracy. A large number of temporary art pieces, such as the moving bird on O'Connell Street and the world-famous Cow Parade, have also been displayed. The Spire of Dublin is perhaps the most recent public art project. As illustrated in Figure 20.1, through comprehensive marketing campaigns and dedication to innovative street art, the DCBA has helped create a rejuvenated Dublin City Center.

Overall, despite the perceived threat of out-of-town shopping centers and decreased public spending available for city center improvements, DCBA footfall figures confirm that people are returning to the city center in large numbers. The average footfall in the city center is now over 4 million a week; this is attributed most significantly to the improved transport infrastructure, improved consumer confidence, and completion of redevelopment works in the city. According to Coffey, "This success justifies the investment made by the retailers and the City Council in infrastructure and development in the capital over the last few years" (T. Coffey, personal interview, June 23, 2006).

Why BIDs for Dublin?

The DCBA has been campaigning, since 1999, for the introduction of the BID model to Ireland—a movement spawned by both challenges and opportunities existing in the Dublin and Irish national context. There are four key forces that explain why the BID model is an acceptable alternative in Ireland at this juncture: increased competition from suburban shopping malls; increased public expectations, especially with regard to cleanliness and safety; diminished public resources; and the opportunity to build on the momentum that exists around revitalizing downtown Dublin.

"Make the City Yours!"

"A visit to our Capital City is an experience like no other. Over 660,000 people walk the city's high streets every day, creating a buzz and atmosphere that cannot be replicated. People spend hours in 'town' leisurely sipping cappuccinos on the new Liffey Boardwalk with friends, watching the world go by in St. Stephen's Green, viewing the art on Merrion Square or taking a stroll down Grafton Street to soak up the unique ambience created by buskers, street performers, string quartets and the laughter and chatter of the passing crowd"(DCBA, 2006).

Dublin's Spire, is the world's tallest monument. Erected by DCBA members for the new Millenium, it reflects a modern Ireland that points to the future, and at the same time is a local focal point and reflects passing Dubliners. The Spire is now a new icon for the city, providing a new and vibrant identity for Ireland's capital city.

Figure 20.1 Place making.

The late 1990s saw the implementation of several plans for suburban shopping developments. Such developments as Liffey Valley and Blanchardstown shopping centers on the edge of the city resulted in falling rates of footfall in the city center. The opening of Dundrum shopping center in 2005 led to increased concern over city center business. Competition from suburban and regional shopping malls coupled with a reputation for public disorder and unkempt streets have damaged the image of the city and drawn customers and tenants elsewhere. The Irish public is becoming increasingly concerned and disenchanted with low standards of cleanliness and general environmental quality on the streets (T. Coffey, personal interview, June 23, 2006).

With an increasingly mobile and affluent population, the public is demanding high standards similar to those seen in other countries. The challenge that Irish towns and cities confront today is the ability to provide customers with an experience similar to that provided by other international capital cities: streets that are clean, safe, and aesthetically pleasing. Moreover, the city is currently experiencing a growth in population and an ever-greater demand on the services provided by the local authority. The forecast of additional people living in Dublin's City Center by 2010 is 60,000 (Dublin BIDs, 2006). As a result, Dublin City Council resources are being stretched thin in an effort to provide the requisite management services required. Though Dublin City Center has benefited from physical regeneration policies and initiatives during the 1990s, secondary sites and other areas are not fully benefiting or reaching their potential. The introduction of the BID model to Ireland is expected to impact secondary streets, which will become the incubation ground for the next generation of high-street businesses (T. Coffey, personal interview, June 23, 2006).

Equally important is the fact that Dublin City Center and its environs are undergoing a significant capital investment period that includes the LUAS (light rail), Port Tunnel, Smithfield Square, James Joyce Bridge, Macken Street Bridge, and O'Connell Street Plaza. These projects have increased access to the city center and —together with the success of the DCBA marketing brand, "Make the City Yours"—have enhanced the city's destination quality. According to Tom Coffey, "Dublin City Center has changed so much in recent years; it looks better than it ever has and we want to remind people about its unique atmosphere and character and to encourage them to rediscover the city as it is today" (personal interview, June 23, 2006). Central to that mission is that those who live, work, and visit the city find it a safe, clean, and enjoyable place to be (Dublin City Business Association, 2006c). The DCBA promotes the BID model to achieve these aims.

What a BID Has To Offer

Although the DCBA already supports a range of BID-like functions, members claim that the BID model can deliver a more strategic and comprehensive system of city management. According to Coffey, "BID brings business community structures into an efficient business model, rather than a voluntary model, and will create a new form of civic leadership for the city" (personal interview, June 23, 2006). He believes that the BID model offers the following elements:

- *Clarity*: The BID model provides a clear business community structure due to its legal status and organizational properties.
- *Certainty*: The BID model, due to the certainty of a multiyear revenue and its five-year mandate, gives stakeholders a foundation upon which to develop comprehensive and future-orientated plans.
- *Equity*: The BID model adequately deals with the problem of free riders because it ensures that all who benefit from the investments in the designated district contribute by means of a compulsory payment.
- *Efficiency*: The BID model supports paid staff, thus eliminating the issues associated with voluntary-member-based organizations. While voluntary members dedicate much of their time to fund-raising efforts, paid staff can focus attention to the efficient and effective management of the district.

Dublin City Center BID

The DCBA is promoting one large BID for Dublin City Center (the Dublin City Center BID) and is currently facilitating the delivery of this vision through a sustained two-year consultation process with local businesses in an effort to achieve consensus on the plan. The Dublin City Center BID Company, a separate organization with its own board and priorities, has been established and will operate and promote the BID in 2008. Currently, the geographic boundaries of the City Center BID are being negotiated, as of the time of the writing of this chapter, yet it is clear that the key high streets (Grafton Street, Henry/Mary Street and O'Connell Street) will constitute the core. While the BID is expected to include the area south of Parnell Street extending to St. Stephens Green, the Temple Bar area is omitted. The BID may extend east as far as Connolly station and is expected to extend westward to Capel Street. These core and periphery streets are those contained within the red line in Figure 20.2. There are approximately 4,200 rate payers in the proposed BID area, the majority of which are retail establishments. The daytime economy, consisting of fashion, footwear, and some office functions, currently pays 75 percent of rates to Dublin City Council, compared to 4 percent from the pub sector, or nighttime economy.

A levy of between 1 and 2 percent of the business rate is being planned for the BID. According to business plan proposals, this is a sufficent rate to implement the aforementioned services. It is anticipated that the City Center BID will supplement its annual budget with voluntary payments from the properties and institutions that are rate-exempt. Budget projections are not yet available; however, the

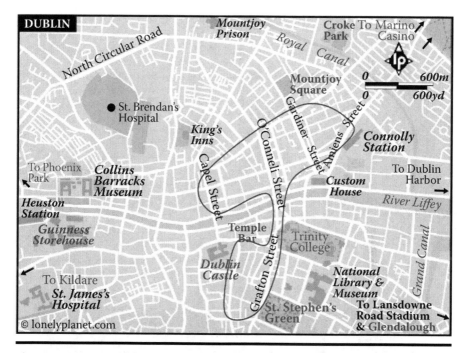

Figure 20.2   Map of Dublin City Center and proposed BID boundary.

expected membership base is between 1,000 and 4,000 rate payers, which means that the BID can expect an annual budget of several million Euros.

Dublin City Center BID Activities

Dublin City Center BID activities are planned to focus primarily on the following areas:

- *Environmental management*: Activities include the removal of litter and chewing gum, street washing and graffitti removal, and the greening of the streets through the installation of shrubs and flower plantings.
- *Economic development*: Activities include the deployment of hospitality officers, local area marketing and public relations, the installation of banners, the scheduling of special events, and attracting and retaining businesses.
- *Capital improvements*: Activities involve local transport access initiatives for shoppers, the installation of street furniture and signage for businesses, shop-front design and public art, and new parking solutions.
- *Social inclusion*: Activities include local initiatives enabling businesses to get involved directly with communities in the BID area as well as helping to integrate multiethnic residents into the Irish economy and civic society.

Imagine!

"Dublin is a cosmopolitan and sophisticated city. It is a city we can be proud of with its new Luas, Liffey Boardwalk and rejuvenated O'Connell Street it looks better than ever. Now imagine a Dublin city with landscaped streets, without chewing gum, without graffiti, with no overflowing rubbish bins, with no broken paths, with no drunken revellers on our streets, no dilapidated buildings, a city with a welcoming and embracing environment, with hospitality wardens helping people, family friendly facilities, special community care and amenity projects......Business Improvement Districts will transform our Capital City to reach its full potential. BIDs will provide a framework for local businesses to achieve a new look and feel for our Capital City." (Dublin BIDs, 2006)

Figure 20.3 Vision for the Dublin City Center BID.

The vision for Dublin City Center BID, as outlined in Figure 20.3, is planned for realization through a number of initiatives. During the first five-year term, BID services will focus on street environmental enhancement and landscaping, and subsequently progress to promotional and capital investment activities, including marketing, street security, shop-front design, local community initiatives and introduction of amenities. BID ambassadors are expected to be introduced by year 2. The BID also intends to collaborate with the city council and the Irish legal system by envisioning a system of temporary job provision for homeless individuals. Tom Coffey of the DCBA also anticipates eventual implementation of a Community Courts Initiative, similar to that operating in Manhattan and Philadelphia at present.* This is aimed at helping to solve the city's problem of misdemeanor crime such as alcohol-related public disorder, vandalism, graffiti, and drug offenses. It is anticipated that this would be up and running two years into the BID (Dublin City Business Association, 2006b). Crucial to the functioning of the BID is the development of modern communication and information technology services. For

---

* Please see the Morçöl and Patrick chapter in this volume for a discussion of the community court in Philadelphia. For a more general discussion of community courts that are operated by BIDs, see the Morçöl and Zimmermann chapter (Chapter 15) in this volume.

example, a comprehensive information technology system will be set up, whereby all rate payers will be connected via e-mail. An electronic newsletter system will assist close communications and coordinated marketing strategies. A working group has been established with the Dublin City Council to progress a new system of structures management in the city via CCTV and global positioning system (GPS) that will provide rate payers with critical data for strategic and up-to-the-minute data for managing their district (T. Coffey, personal interview, June 23, 2006). The Dublin City Center BID proposal is in the process of being drafted, and it is clear the BID board is dedicated to key BID priorities, with a mandate of continual ambitious improvements throughout the initial BID term.

Transferability Issues

Through the rates database, the DCBA has been assessing and actively lobbying the 4,200 rate payers within the proposed Dublin BID. Through a comprehensive and well-argued two-year campaign, the DCBA is leaving little up to chance. It maintains that there is "dynamic support" for the project and is confident that the proposal will get a majority vote. The work of Tom Coffey of DBCA in championing the BID concept has been key to building this process of business consensus, and progressing a popular mandate for BIDs in the city. However, a 4,000-strong petition vote will prove very costly and laborious.

There are a host of issues that are involved in the transferral to BIDs in Dublin. One of the foremost issues is how businesses will react to having to "switch from free to fee." However, a smooth transition to a BID is anticipated for Dublin City Center. Due to the activities of the Dublin City Business Association in the city center for the last 30 years, there is a strong history of civic spirit and self-help. There is strong business consensus and willingness to work together voluntarily and support joint initiatives to aid the city as a whole. This is displayed in the provision of the Christmas lights on city center high streets, for example, with 80 percent of businesses in those streets paying for the lights. The BID is being welcomed as a mechanism to build on this partnership and, crucially, to involve the whole of the business community in participating and contributing toward such projects.

Another argument regarding the introduction of the BID model is the financial burden placed on business due to the payment of the BID levy, and the national attitude toward taxation. Regarding the specification of the BID multiplier, the priority was to decide on a charge that would facilitate real and measurable improvements, rather than a rate that would be satisfactory to local business (T. Coffey, personal interview, June 23, 2006). The 1 to 2 percent BID levy anticipated by the DCBA is seen as an acceptable level of contribution by business. Second, the BID proponents do not consider the BID as a mechanism to introduce a mandatory tax. They argue that a tax is decided by government and originates from government, whereas a levy originates from the citizen rate payer. The rate payers decide whether to instigate an added payment; therefore, it is a voluntary process. However, the introduction of a BID levy is interpreted as facilitating the moderation of existing city council rates. With the introduction of a new levy on business, the council will not need to increase taxes.

The Irish BID model proposes strong interaction with the local authority. Such partnership with the local authority may not be seen as favorable to the private sector. However, as the DCBA notes, businesses in the proposed BID area already have a history of joint action with the local authority, through actions with the DCBA and via the payment of business rates. The DCBA considers the significant involvement of the local authority as vital, as they hold the "democratic mandate" for the city.

On the issue of accountability and maintaining vitality within the BID company, the Dublin City Center BID board has not been fully formed yet, but it anticipates the inclusion of non-rate-payers such as residents and property owners. In particular, the DCBA is anxious to get the property owners on board and have involved them in the initial consultation process of the BID. Outside stimulation and information sharing is also vital in ensuring greater accountability and dynamics within the BID. The proposed BID plans to use third-level institutions as an important "intellectual resource." The Dublin Institute of Technology has already been active in promoting and researching the BID concept by providing academic reseach and analysis for the emerging BID concept in Ireland. Further opportunities for professional enrichment and interaction have been developed through conferences and seminars carried out throughout the BID planning and legislative process in Ireland.

BID-Like Entity: Traders in the Area Supporting the Cultural Quarter

Traders in the Area Supporting the Cultural Quarter (TASCQ) is a BID-like entity operating in the Dublin City Center region and will be bordering the Dublin City Center BID when it is established in 2008. TASCQ is chosen as a case study for this chapter, as it is the closest representation to a functioning BID in Ireland and can provide us with an understanding of how a BID may function in Ireland in the future, as well as possible problems it may encounter. Of interest is the fact that TASCQ has not chosen to go down the route of becoming a BID. The reasons for its decision may offer additional insights.

TASCQ describe themselves as "responsible traders working together to promote, maintain, enhance and develop Temple Bar through co-operative marketing initiatives and the provision of additional environmental services" (Traders in the Area Supporting the Cultural Quarter, 2006, para. 1). Temple Bar is a cultural, historic, and small business neighbourhood in the heart of Dublin City

Center (see Figure 20.2). The area is a mixed-use city center location. It is home to almost 3,000 residents, a base for over 400 businesses, and attracts an average of 60,000 people every day (Temple Bar Properties, 2006).

In the beginning of the 1990s, a plan to turn the disadvantaged, yet culturally significant, Temple Bar area into a bus depot was defeated and the government launched the Temple Bar initiative as a flagship project to mark Dublin's year as European City of Culture 1991. Three separate agencies—Temple Bar Properties Ltd. (TBP), Temple Bar Renewal, and Dublin City Council—were charged with the management and regeneration of Temple Bar. By 1998, the physical development was completed and the area was marketed as a cultural quarter. However, by that time, Temple Bar had developed a reputation as a binge-drinking location and was suffering from ongoing negative publicity. Despite its strong internationally known brand and abundance of cultural organizations, it was considered that the area was "oversold" as a cultural quarter (M. Harte, general manager, TASCQ, personal interview, May 23, 2006). Drinking was prominent and the area was generally considered unclean, unsafe, and devoid of family-friendly activities.

As a result, Partnership TASCQ was organized in the late 1990s as a development company to address the image of the cultural quarter. The partnership incorporated Dublin City Council, Temple Bar Properties, and about 20 publicans* in the area. A separate fund was established for the operations of this new partnership. Businesses voluntarily paid into this fund, which was managed by Temple Bar Properties, the development company in the area. The combined fund allowed for additional street cleaning by Dublin City Council and the provision of free tourist information. By 2000, the informal partnership began to deteriorate, losing key members. The businesses felt they needed more independence from Temple Bar Properties and the council and—with a general lack of structure, direction, and control—there was little room for further innovation and development within the partnership (M. Harte, personal interview, May 23, 2006). The involvement of Temple Bar Properties also excluded a large amount of businesses from joining the partnership due to past issues with the businesses and the development company.

Although cleanliness levels in Temple Bar had improved, the area continued to suffer from perceptions that it was exclusively a destination for binge drinkers. Temple Bar also had to respond to factors that were affecting the city as a whole, namely, increased competition and limited public spending. According to Harte, Temple Bar and Dublin City "are in direct competition with other major destinations like Paris, London and increasingly cities in the former Eastern Block countries, such as Prague. However, the capital's tourism sector is affected by reduced Government funding, making it difficult for Dublin to challenge its competitors. Therefore, it's up to the private sector to make the investment and assist in marketing the City effectively" (Harte, cited in TASCQ Press, 2004). Against

---

* Those owning or operating a public house (bar).

these driving forces, the stalled partnership realized it was necessary to restructure its organization to deliver a more dedicated approach.

Restructuring occurred parallel with the introduction of the BID concept to Ireland. Members of Temple Bar Properties visited New York in 2001 along with a contingent from the Dublin Chamber of Commerce, the Dublin City Business Association, and Dublin City Council to observe how BIDs operate. The Temple Bar group considered the introduction of the BID model to Temple Bar, but decided to set up their own BID-like company.

In 2003, the independent company TASCQ was formed as a professional association representing traders in Temple Bar. It consists of the existing base of business members of Partnership TASCQ as well as some key members from Temple Bar Properties, but it is now under a more formal structure and new set of proposals and programs. TASCQ sponsors action to ensure a clean, safe, dynamic, and fun environment, but relies on a system of annual voluntary donations and operates without the direct involvement of local government.

Members of the restructuring Partnership TASCQ for Temple Bar perceived that the BID model would not be fully transferable to the Temple Bar context for three reasons. The most important reason related to financing. Draft Irish legislation in 2003 was proposing a maximum of 10 percent returned business rates per premises to the BID. According to financial projections, the returned rate was considered too low. By applying the rates database for the Temple Bar area and a figure of 15 percent returned business rates, it was calculated that if a BID was established it would generate €1 million annually and incorporate 400 businesses. This was compared to the annual budget of €300,000, which was supported by a membership base of 30 businesses. The introduction of a BID in Temple Bar would therefore increase membership tenfold, yet only triple the annual budget. Overall, the system of voluntary donations was considered more appropriate to Temple Bar because it produced higher yields per premise. Second, it was contemplated that 30 businesses were a lot easier to satisfy than 400; an imposition of a compulsory levy on 400 businesses would be a burdensome endeavor. In the proposed Irish BID legislation, the Dublin City Council, many believed, would have too significant a role in the operations by collecting and redistributing the levy and holding seats on the board. TASCQ wanted to maintain its independent status and ownership to ensure that local businesses would have a significant role and not be subservient to the council (M. Harte, personal interview, May 23, 2006).

TASCQ Structure

Voluntary associations like the TASCQ and a BID differ mainly in their principal sources of revenue. Table 20.2 compares the TASCQ with the BID model.

TASCQ is a membership-based company where traders apply annual membership fees to the cost of improving the physical environment in the area. The cost of

Table 20.2 Comparison between proposed Irish BID and TASCQ

	Proposed Irish BID law	TASCQ
Financing mechanism	Self-taxation, via a mandatory levy on the annual business rate	Voluntary membership fee
Participants	100% of rate payers in designated district	Voluntary business participation
Funds collected by	Local authority	TASCQ
Government represented on board	Yes	No
Authorization	Publicly sanctioned	Private company

Table 20.3 TASCQ board and revenue structure

Membership category	Revenue	Board seats
Temple Bar Properties		Automatic seat
Alpha category (mainly publicans/hotels)	Members who pay an annual subscription in excess of €10,000	4
Beta category (smaller pubs/restaurants)	Members who pay an annual subscription of €3,000–€10,000	3
Gamma category (mainly retail/services)	Members who pay an annual subscription of €500–€2,999	2
Total	€250,000/year from membership fees	10

membership is calculated on a case-by-case basis, taking the type and size of the business into consideration, and current subscriptions range from €500 to €45,000 per annum. The company is set up in such a way as to ensure that larger businesses heavily subsidize the smaller members, yet all members receive the same level of service. TASCQ is governed by a board of ten directors, who are democratically elected by the members. They meet on a quarterly basis. TASCQ's annual income is approximately €400,000. Allocation of seats on the board and breakdown of revenue structure are outlined in Table 20.3. TASCQ's membership profile is outlined in Figure 20.4.

TASCQ Activities and Achievements

TASCQ's key priority is marketing and promoting Temple Bar. These activities include providing additional environmental services, specific marketing of the area, and improving security services. Cleaning alone accounts for greater than a third of TASCQ's overall budget, spending over €150,000 per annum on additional cleaning services. Administration and staff account for about 40 percent, with TASCQ

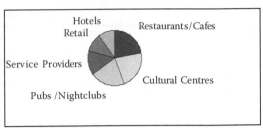

Participating businesses display a TASCQ member plaque outside their premises. Visitors to Temple Bar are informed that by supporting these 'responsible traders', their money will be invested back into the local environment and community, to support a clean and attractive space.

Figure 20.4   TASCQ membership profile.

employing five full-time and one part-time staff. Marketing and security services account for the remainder of the budget.

Future for TASCQ

TASCQ will soon be operating alongside the proposed Dublin City Center BID. TASCQ has developed within the same context as the emerging Dublin City BID, both with similar aims, yet each has decided to respond differently to the driving forces and needs of a changing city.

TASCQ remains dedicated to its voluntary system of donations and has no plans to transfer to compulsory areawide payments. Its does not interpret the presence of "freeloaders" as a significant issue. TASCQ is expanding each year and is increasingly gaining the interest and support of big business operators in the area. With annual growth rates of between 40 and 50 percent, it is moving toward its vision of becoming one of the biggest traders in the city and developing into a powerful lobby group (M. Harte, personal interview, May 23, 2006). In TASCQ's own words,

TASCQ will continue to maintain, upgrade and enhance the Temple Bar area to the benefit of its members and all who live, work or visit the district. It will promote the arts, tourism, trade and commerce in Dublin's cultural quarter, and prove that voluntary co-operation and commitment can make a real difference to business performance and the quality of community and urban life. (Traders in the Area Supporting the Cultural Quarter, 2006, para. 8.)

Conclusion: BIDs for Ireland

As highlighted earlier, Ireland faces some critical challenges over the next few years. Local officials and civic leaders believe that, to compete with other global cities, Dublin must become cleaner, greener, and safer. Services must be of the best quality and function as keystones of the economy (Ratcliffe, 2002). According to Tom Coffey of the DCBA, BIDs will bring tangible and immediate benefits to the towns and cities across Ireland where local businesses have chosen to introduce them (Dublin City Business Association, 2006a). The BID-like models and entities discussed in this chapter confirm the effectiveness of such mechanisms in an Irish context. Both models, the DCBA and TASCQ, have used performance evaluation criteria (such as footfall counting, cleanliness checks, crime statistics, customer surveys, etc.) within their operations to quantify the effectiveness of their activities. This practice is planned in the emerging Irish BID models, which will benchmark their activities and facilitate a goal-driven scheme. The DCBA and TASCQ are clear embodiments of the spirit of BIDs to engage the creativity of the private sector in managing and improving the local business environment. They illustrate the potential creativity that can be employed in Irish BIDs in the future, and confirm that private sector responsibility works for our towns and cities. BIDs, which operate on the assumption that "government should be less involved with direct service provision" (Ratcliffe et al., 1999), reflect the growing "self-help culture" that has taken hold in Ireland since the birth of the "Celtic Tiger" Irish economy. They also illustrate the growing cooperation by a variety of parties in the state and private sectors, many of whom are competitors (Dublin City Business Association, 2003a).

Irish BID candidates include the cities and towns of Cork, Galway, Waterford, Carlow, Kilkenny, and some suburban Dublin communities. The cities of Galway and Cork already have BID-like structures in place and may transition more smoothly to the BID model. However, there is a number of issues that these potential emerging Irish BIDs might face and a number of ways in which the BID model may transfer. The Irish Chamber of Commerce has welcomed the publication of the Local Government (Business Improvement Districts Bill) in 2006 and has publicly stated that its member chambers will take an active role in high-quality BID proposals. According to Chambers Ireland (2006), "Chambers, which are essentially local networks of businesses, provide a natural foundation to build upon in establishing a BID. Indeed some chambers have developed expertise in establishing and running similar urban renewal initiatives which should prove valuable in the development of BIDs" (para. 7).

Priorities for emerging Irish BIDs are likely to center on issues of marketing, maintenance, environmental improvements, and security. However, in contrast to the Dublin case studies outlined in this chapter, BIDs in other towns and cities are likely to be smaller, and may therefore concentrate their activities on marketing efforts. This is particularly relevant in a climate of decreasing long-stay tourists, which often results in increased competition between Ireland's towns and cities. Cleanliness is also a significant Irish urban management issue and is likely to be one of the initial points addressed by emerging BIDs in Ireland. Safety issues may play a lesser role, but emphasis would be placed, in particular, on public disorder issues associated with the nighttime economy. Fortunately, flexible legislation allows for the adaption of the BID to suit individual Irish circumstances. The Dublin City Center BID's business plan, for example, illustrates the flexibility of national legislation in allowing the evolution of project goals throughout the five-year BID scheme. This permits the BID to innovate, which is essential because Ireland's ability to learn from international practice is limited. There are two additional points worthy of mention. First, Irish BID legislation does not dictate the composition of the BID board, leaving the designation to the discretion of the BID. And the BID multiplier is also left to the discretion of the BID, allowing an adaptable framework in the future designation of the BID.

In closing, Ireland—in its thriving modern Celtic Tiger economy—is moving beyond jaded urban renewal policies to something bigger, better, and brighter for its towns and cities. According to the minister for community, rural and Gaeltacht affairs (O'Cuiv, 2004):

> The Government promoted BIDs in the belief that it has the potential to further regenerate Dublin City Centre. However, I believe that BIDs could have an even more wide-ranging impact and could be implemented across the country in both urban and rural settings. This bill will fulfill yet another commitment in the Programme for Government, which was "to support initiatives to expand corporate social responsibility" while building an inclusive society. (p. 2)

In the end, the success of BIDs in Ireland lies in the energy, vitality, and vision driving the BID process. We have been engaged in a six-year process of international learning and local preparation to bring the BID concept to Ireland. We have the vision and the vitality. All we need now is the vehicle.

References

Chambers Ireland. 2006. Chambers welcome publication of BIDs. Chambers of Commerce Ireland, Press Office. http://www.chambers.ie/article.php?newsid=401 (accessed July 2006).

Dublin BIDs. 2006. *Dublin BIDs: Making things better for business.* http://www.dublinbids. com (accessed June 2006).

Dublin City Business Association. 2003a, April 2. Fifth addition of Dublin visitor map and guide 2003. DCBA press release. http://www.dcba.ie (accessed June 2006).

Dublin City Business Association. 2003b, November 4. Launch of new Dublin city logo: New identity and new advertising campaign for Dublin city. Press release. http:// www.dcba.ie (accessed June 2006).

Dublin City Business Association. 2005, January 7. Half a million footfall on city centre streets. Press release. http://www.dcba.ie (accessed June 2006).

Dublin City Business Association. 2006a. DCBA: The voice of city merchants. http://www. dcba.ie (accessed June 2006).

Dublin City Business Association. 2006b, March 28. DCBA chairman calls for the establishment of a community court pilot project for the city centre. Press release. http:// www.dcba.ie (accessed June 2006).

Dublin City Business Association. 2006c, March 28. DCBA chairman looks forward to the Introduction of BIDs. Press release. http://www.dcba.ie (accessed June 2006).

Dublin City Business Association. 2006d. Dublin city business association launches three year marketing campaign. Press release. http://www.dcba.ie (accessed June 19, 2006).

Dublin City Business Association. 2006e. Dublin city business association welcomes publication of business improvement district legislation. Press release. http://www. dcba.ie/index.cfm/search/BIDs/loc/2-4-1/articleId/109E6DCA-9BF7-3096-95B5C837EC2F77A6.htm (accessed June 16, 2006).

Dublin City Council. 2005. Retail, Dublin City Development Plan 2005–2011, chap. 8. Dublin, IR: Dublin City Council.

House of the Oireachtas. 2006a. Draft local government (business improvement districts) bill number 38 of 2006. Explanatory memorandum. Dublin, IR: Seanad Eireann, House of the Oireachtas.

House of the Oireachtas. 2006b. Local government (business improvement districts) act. Dublin: Seanad Eireann, House of the Oireachtas. http://www.oireachtas.ie/ Viewprnt.asp?UserLang=EN&fn=/documents/bills28/acts/2006/a4206.pdf (accessed July 2006).

McLoughlin, L. (2003). *Business improvement districts: Volunteering to be taxed.* Unpublished degree thesis, Dublin Institute of Technology, Bolton Street, Dublin, Ireland.

O'Cuiv, E. 2004, November. Corporate social responsibility and business improvement districts. Speech by the Minister for Community, Rural and Gaeltacht Affairs to the Chamber of Commerce, Clontarf Castle, Dublin.

Ratcliffe, J. 2002. Enhancing urban vitality and viability. *Business Ireland Magazine*, April, pp. 32–35.

Ratcliffe, J., Branagh, S., and Williams, B. 1999. *Fiscal incentives and urban regeneration: A preliminary study of the prospective use of business improvement districts and tax increment finance districts in Ireland.* Dublin: Bolton Street, Dublin Institute of Technology.

Ratcliffe, J., and Flanagan, S. 2004. Enhancing the vitality and viability of town and city centres: The concept of the business improvement district in the context of tourism enterprise. *Property Management* 22:377–395.

TASCQ Press. 2004. TASCQ help bridge the "information gap" in Temple Bar. *TASCQ Press Room*, April. http://www.visit-templebar.com (accessed June 2006).

Temple Bar Properties. 2006. *Dublin's cultural quarter.* http://www.temple-bar.ie (accessed June 2006).

Traders in the Area Supporting the Cultural Quarter. 2006. *TASCQ: Visit Temple Bar.* http://www.visit-templebar.com/sh759y.html (accessed June, 2006).

Index

499

O

P